CPA LIABILITY

CPA LIABILITY

MEETING THE CHALLENGE

RICHARD L. MILLER, JR.
GERALD P. BRADY

A Ronald Press Publication
JOHN WILEY & SONS
New York • Chichester • Brisbane • Toronto • Singapore

Library of Congress Cataloging in Publication Data:

Miller, Richard L. (Richard Leo), 1948–
  CPA liability.

  "A Ronald Press publication."
  Includes index.
  1. Accountants—Malpractice—United States.
I. Brady, Gerald P. II. Title.

KF2920.3.M55 1986   346.7303'3   85-12334
ISBN 0-471-88751-X   347.30633

Printed in the United States of America

10 9 8 7 6 5 4 3 2 1

PREFACE

"Those were the days, my friend, we thought they'd never end . . . ," or so accountants might have believed in 1931 when Chief Judge Cardozo wrote the landmark decision in the *Ultramares* case. Any jubilation by the accounting profession was short-lived, for in 1933 and 1934 Congress passed the Securities Act and Securities Exchange Act, both of which exposed accountants to new vistas of liability. The trend toward increased professional liability has accelerated in the intervening decades since *Ultramares* was decided. In July 1985 accountants' exposure to liability may possibly have reached its apex.

First, on July 1, 1985, the United States Supreme Court rendered its opinion in *Sedima vs. Imrex*, a critical and anxiously awaited civil RICO case. The Court laid to rest the accountants' (and businesses') hopes for a narrow construction of the statute whereby civil RICO would be held not to apply in the absence of criminal convictions against the defendant. (For a detailed analysis of the importance and application of civil RICO to accountants, see Chapter 10.)

Next, on July 19, 1985, an $11 million judgment was assessed by a federal jury in Washington, D.C., against a major CPA firm for breach of contract, negligence, and fraud (to a large extent the heart of this book). *Ironically the firm had rendered a qualified opinion for the years in question*. Naturally, the firm will appeal. However, assuming the worst, let us not forget basic partnership law, which imposes *individual liability* against the partners in the event partnership assets are insufficient to meet partnership liabilities.

Bad news sometimes seems to come in bunches, for on July 25, 1985, the Florida State Board of Accountancy, for the first time in its history, suspended the tenth largest CPA firm in the United States from obtaining new audit clients for 60 days. The Board of Accountancy's action may be a precursor to an impending period of regulatory activism on the part of federal and state regulators. Against this backdrop of escalating liability and regulatory activity there are many within the accounting profession who claim that the profession has been victimized by a "crisis in credibility."

The authors believe that these "worst of times" may become the "best of times" for accountants. To be sure, these are challenging times for the accounting profession. Adversity, however, is not without opportunity for those who are willing and able to

229358

meet the challenge. The current times have heightened accounting practitioners' awareness of their legal responsibilities and have encouraged accountants to firmly resolve that steps be undertaken to improve professional practices and minimize the risk of legal liability.

For over a half century accountants in the United States have been perceived by the public as professionals who possess and exercise the highest competence and integrity. The profession has worked hard at earning public respect. Current events reflect that the profession must intensify its efforts to maintain the public trust. Credibility with the public is the bedrock on which the accounting profession is grounded.

Our thanks to Dean John "Sandy" Burton of the Graduate School of Business, Columbia University, for reviewing parts of the manuscript in the early stages of the book. We also thank Maude Brady, who provided us with a layperson's editorial proofreading of the manuscript and typed the various drafts of this manuscript.

Finally, we would be remiss if we did not express our greatest gratitude to Dee, Tim, Wendy, and Ali Miller, and to Maude, Joe, and Pete Brady. Their enduring patience has made this possible.

RICHARD L. MILLER, JR.
GERALD P. BRADY

Chicago, Illinois
New York, New York
March 1986

CONTENTS

Chapter 8   Tax Practice—Responsibility and Liability   339

Chapter 9   State, Federal, and Professional Regulation of Accountants   379

CPA LIABILITY

CHAPTER 1

INTRODUCTION

¶ 1.01 Motivation—Build a Fire! The Accountant's Clear and Present Need for an Understanding of the Subject of Accountant's Liability

Most law schools recognize the importance of accounting for lawyers, since it directly relates to corporate law and taxation. At many schools, the Accounting for Lawyers course is either mandatory for all or a prerequisite for other courses. However, the more sophisticated or wiser law students jokingly recognize that in reality *there is no accounting for lawyers*. They are a unique breed, *sui generis* (peculiar) in many respects, or some might even say just plain unintelligible. Often they even seem to speak another language. However, their mentors do recognize the necessity of understanding certain fundamentals of accounting as it applies to various areas of law. Similarly, accountants are obligated to have at least a minimal understanding, or in some cases, a very high degree of understanding, of law. Consider the judge's admonition in the excerpt from the *Herzfeld v. Laventhol* case[1]:

> The November 22 and 26 contracts came to Laventhol's attention on or about December 1st through its partners, Chazen and Lipkin, and Schwabb, the audit manager. Schwabb sought Lipkin's advice about the proper way to report the transactions in the audit. Lipkin sought to gather the pertinent information by meeting with Scott, a FGL vice president, and Firestone. Scott told him that FGL was busy acquiring the necessary documentation. Firestone said that the agreements were legitimate and described Continental's principal, Max Ruderian, as an experienced real estate operator and a wealthy individual. Laventhol learned that Continental had a net worth of $100,000 and that its assets consisted of "miniature golf courses plus other assets." Ruderian's business practice was to "buy and resell prior to final payment on his sales contracts."
>
> Lipkin also examined the sales contracts. He was an attorney but had only practiced one year. He concluded that the contracts were legally enforceable. He consulted another Laventhol partner who assured him that there need be no concern about Ruderian. Ruderian's references concurred in the appraisal.
>
> Lipkin also consulted over the telephone with a Los Angeles attorney. The attorney did not see the contracts, nor were the contracts in their entirety read to him, despite the fact

---

[1] 516 F.2d 811 (2d Cir. 1976).

that his offices were only one-half hour away by cab. Nevertheless, the attorney gave a telephone opinion that they were valid and enforceable.

The first tangible results of Laventhol's accounting efforts appear in its audit enclosed in its letter to FGL, dated December 6, 1969. In the consolidated balance sheet as of November 30, 1969, the amount of $1,795,500 was recorded "as unrealized gross profit." The same characterization was given to this assumed profit in the income statement with a reference to an explanatory Note 4. This Note only explained the $1,795,500 by stating that "Because of the circumstances and nature of the transactions, $1,795,500 of the gross profit thereon will be considered realized when the January 30, 1970, payment is received."

From the very outset of the audit, the danger signals were flashing.

1.   Even if Laventhol accepted the agreements as not "phony," on the face of the Monterey agreement there were two conditions to be performed, i.e., approval by FGL of a title search and a leaseback. There was no proof that they were performed or that Laventhol made any effort to verify these facts.

2.   Normally on transactions of such magnitude and vital importance, corporate minutes, resolutions and other corporate papers authenticating the transaction would be examined. No proof of such examination was presented.

3.   Laventhol demonstrated an awareness that the legality of the agreement with Continental might be important. However, a telephone call to an attorney who did not even see or read the agreement and who only heard such excerpts as Laventhol's partner chose to read to him, scarcely qualifies as a legal opinion as to enforceability.

4.   As for Continental, Laventhol knew that it had contractually committed itself to pay $15,300,000 to FGL and that Continental had assets of only some $100,000, consisting mostly of miniature golf courses. Laventhol was aware that Max Ruderian was a well-known, successful, and wealthy real estate operator and had signed the Continental agreement but there is no document which evidences that Ruderian's wealth was in any way committed to the Continental purchase.

This excerpt indicates that the CPA should have some understanding of at least the following areas of law: contracts, real property, suretyship, and corporations. It further admonishes the accountant to seek a legal opinion where there is doubt about the law in question. Finally, the court indicates that halfhearted attempts will undoubtedly be to no avail. The point is that the CPA must have sufficient knowledge of various areas of law in order to perform the audit. Adequate understanding is necessary both to recognize the legal problem and to realize that some help is probably needed.

The degree of understanding, whether high or low, depends on a multitude of factors, including among others: the area of law involved, the accountant's type of practice, and the existing relationship between the accounting and legal professions, particularly in the area of taxation. Unquestionably, the modern-day accountant must have an understanding of law, particularly accountant's legal liability, the area of law that governs the practice of accounting. This conclusion is forcibly stated in *Horizons of a Profession*,[2] which explores the common body of knowledge for CPAs: "Since CPAs, because they are professionals, are responsible for their professional acts, it is our urgent recommendation

---

[2] Roy and MacNeill, *Horizons of a Profession*, p. 243 (1967). [The book was the result of a study sponsored by the Carnegie Foundation and the AICPA.]

that the beginning CPA have extensive knowledge of the law pertaining to his rights and duties." It is obvious that this conclusion applies with equal if not greater force to all CPAs, beginning or otherwise.

[1]   Goals

Our goals are clear:

To present the law of accountant's liability in an intelligible manner and at a level that is understandable by CPAs. In seeking to attain this goal, we have related the law to the practice of the profession wherever feasible.

To present the development and current state of the law applicable to the CPA. Particularly the most recent developments (e.g., see ¶10.01).

To provide a provocative and lively presentation of the subject matter (e.g., the use of hypothetical trial and liability situations throughout).

To suggest precautions and procedures to be followed in order to minimize exposure to liability and to provide a thorough analysis of the various defenses available to the accountant in the event of a lawsuit.

To provide a useful and teachable text for use in course work or discussions of the subject matter.

[2]   Introductory Comments

Let us begin our journey into the world of accountant's liability with the landmark case of *Ultramares v. Touche*, which was, at the time it was decided, a rich and rewarding case for CPAs. The case was decided by the New York Court of Appeals in 1931, with Chief Judge Benjamin Cardozo writing the now classic opinion. *Ultramares* is an excellent starting point since it is not only the most famous accountant's liability case, but also may well mark a turning point in the modern-day law of accountant's liability. At the time of the decision, the law of accountant's liability was almost exclusively judge-made, and thus, it was a pure, state common law area. There was no federal law on the subject and state statutory enactments were virtually nonexistent. The area today largely retains its common law flavor, although the inroads that have been made as a result of the Securities Act of 1933 and the Securities Exchange Act of 1934 are considerable. *Ultramares* is concerned with the four major concepts that are a recurring theme throughout this work—*negligence*, *privity*, and *fraud*, and *their interrelationship*.

This was the same Judge Cardozo who later became a Justice of the Supreme Court of the United States and who had written the definitive opinion imposing liability upon manufacturers of negligently produced goods that cause harm to the ultimate consumer. Privity was conclusively rejected as a bar to third-party lawsuits brought by consumers against the remote manufacturer. Would this rule be followed and applied to accountants? The *Ultramares* case came to the New York Court of Appeals on appeal by both parties. Plaintiff proceeded in the trial court on two theories: the first, negligent misrepresentation;

the second, fraudulent misrepresentation. The jury in the trial court found for the plaintiffs based upon negligence, but this was overruled by the judge and the suit dismissed. The Appellate Division of the Supreme Court reversed the trial court's judgment for the defendant on the negligence part of the judgment and directed the jury verdict to be reinstated. It also affirmed dismissal of the second cause of action based upon fraud. Both parties disagreed with that part of the decision that adversely affected them and appealed to the New York Court of Appeals, New York State's highest court.

Although the court is primarily concerned with *privity*, the key concepts of *negligence* and *fraud* mentioned previously are also an integral part of the decision. The case was one of first instance, never having been presented to the court previously, and like no other case, presents not only the clash of these concepts but also gives the underlying policy considerations used to justify the retention of privity at least as applicable to the facts of the case. It is the most famous and oft-cited case in the entire area of accountant's liability. We will be examining this landmark opinion in subsequent chapters, particularly the fraud chapter (see Chapter 4).

[3]   *Ultramares Corp. v. Touche:* A Landmark Decision

Ultramares Corp. v. Touche
255 N.Y. 170, 174 N.E. 441
(N.Y. 1931)

CARDOZO, Chief Judge.

The action is in tort for damages suffered through the misrepresentations of accountants, the first cause of action being for misrepresentations that were merely negligent and the second for misrepresentations charged to have been fraudulent.

In January, 1924, the defendants, a firm of public accountants, were employed by Fred Stern & Co., Inc., to prepare and certify a balance sheet exhibiting the condition of its business as of December 31, 1923. They had been employed at the end of each of the three years preceding to render a like service. Fred Stern & Co., Inc., which was in substance Stern himself, was engaged in the importation and sale of rubber. To finance its operations, it required extensive credit and borrowed large sums of money from banks and other lenders. All this was known to the defendants. The defendants knew also that in the usual course of business the balance sheet when certified would be exhibited by the Stern company to banks, creditors, stockholders, purchasers or sellers, according to the needs of the occasion, as the basis

of financial dealings. Accordingly, when the balance sheet was made up, the defendants supplied the Stern company with thirty-two copies certified with serial numbers as counterpart originals. Nothing was said as to the persons to whom these counterparts would be shown or the extent or number of the transactions in which they would be used. In particular there was no mention of the plaintiff, a corporation doing business chiefly as a factor, which till then had never made advances to the Stern company, though it had sold merchandise in small amounts. The range of the transactions in which a certificate of audit might be expected to play a part was as indefinite and wide as the possibilities of the business that was mirrored in the summary.

By February 26, 1924, the audit was finished and the balance sheet made up. It stated assets in the sum of $2,550,671.88 and liabilities other than capital and surplus in the sum of $1,479,956.62, thus showing a net worth of $1,070,715.26. Attached to the balance sheet was a certificate as follows:

Touche, Niven & Co.
Public Accountants
Eight Maiden Lane
New York
February 26, 1924.

Certificate of Auditors

We have examined the accounts of Fred Stern & Co., Inc., for the year ending December 31, 1923, and hereby certify that the annexed balance sheet is in accordance therewith and with the information and explanations given us. We further certify that, subject to provision for federal taxes on income, the said statement, in our opinion, presents a true and correct view of the financial condition of Fred Stern & Co., Inc., as at December 31, 1923.

Touche, Niven & Co.
Public Accountants.

Capital and surplus were intact if the balance sheet was accurate. In reality both had been wiped out, and the corporation was insolvent. The books had been falsified by those in charge of the business so as to set forth accounts receivable and other assets which turned out to be fictitious. The plaintiff maintains that the certificate of audit was erroneous in both its branches. The first branch, the asserted correspondence between the accounts and the balance sheet, is one purporting to be made as of the knowledge of the auditors. The second branch, which certifies to a belief that the condition reflected in the balance sheet presents a true and correct picture of the resources of the business, is stated as a matter of opinion. In the view of the plaintiff, both branches of the certificate are either fraudulent or negligent. As to one class of assets, the item of accounts receivable, if not also as to others, there was no real correspondence, we are told, between balance sheet and books, or so the triers of the facts might find. If correspondence, however, be assumed, a closer examination of supporting invoices and records, or a fuller inquiry directed to the persons appearing on the books as creditors or debtors, would have exhibited the truth.

This action, brought against the accountants in November, 1926, to recover the loss suffered by the plaintiff in reliance upon the audit, was in its inception one for negligence.

On the trial there was added a second cause of action asserting fraud also. The trial judge dismissed the second cause of action without submitting it to the jury. As to the first cause of action, he reserved his decision on the defendants' motion to dismiss and took the jury's verdict. They were told that the defendants might be held liable if with knowledge that the results of the audit would be communicated to creditors they did the work negligently, and that negligence was the omission to use reasonable and ordinary care. The verdict was in favor of the plaintiff for $187,576.32. On the coming in of the verdict, the judge granted the reserved motion. The Appellate Division affirmed the dismissal of the cause of action for fraud, but reversed the dismissal of the cause of action for negligence, and reinstated the verdict. The case is here on cross-appeals.

The two causes of action will be considered in succession, first the one for negligence and second that for fraud.

1. We think the evidence supports a finding that the audit was negligently made, though in so saying we put aside for the moment the question whether negligence, even if it existed, was a wrong to the plaintiff.

If the defendants owed a duty to the plaintiff to act with the same care that would have been due under a contract of employment [with the plaintiff] a jury was at liberty to find a verdict of negligence upon a showing of a scrutiny so imperfect and perfunctory.

We are brought to the question of duty, its origin and measure.

The defendants owed to their employer a duty imposed by law to make their certificate without fraud, and a duty growing out of contract to make it with the care and caution proper to their calling. Fraud includes the pretense of knowledge when knowledge there is none. To creditors and investors to whom the employer exhibited the certificate, the defendants owed a like duty to make it without fraud, since there was notice in the circumstances of its making that the employer did not intend to keep it to himself. A different question develops when we ask whether they owed a duty to these to make it without negligence. If liability for negligence exists, a thoughtless slip or blunder, the failure to detect a theft or forgery beneath the cover of deceptive entries may expose accountants to a liability in an indeterminate amount for an indeterminate time to an indeterminate class. The hazards of a business conducted on these terms are so extreme as to enkindle doubt whether a flaw may not exist in the implication of a duty that exposes to these consequences. We put aside for the moment any statement in the certificate which involves the representation of a fact as true to the knowledge of the auditors. If such a statement was made, whether believed to be true or not, the defendants are liable for deceit in the event that it was false. The plaintiff does not need the invention of novel doctrine to help it out in such conditions. The case was submitted to the jury and the verdict was returned upon the theory that even in the absence of a misstatement of a fact there is a liability also for erroneous opinion. The expression of an opinion is to be subject to a warranty implied by law. What, then, is the warranty, as yet unformulated, to be? Is it merely that the opinion is honestly conceived and that the preliminary inquiry has been honestly pursued, that a halt has not been made without a genuine belief that the search has been reasonably adequate to bring disclosure of the truth? Or does it go farther and involve the assumption of a liability for any blunder or inattention that could fairly be spoken of as negligence if the controversy were one between accountant and employer for breach of a contract to render services for pay?

The assault upon the citadel of privity is proceeding in these days apace. . . . In the field of the law of torts a manufacturer who is negligent in the manufacture of a chattel in circumstances pointing to an unreasonable risk of serious bodily harm to those using it thereafter may be liable for negligence though privity is lacking between manufacturer and user (*MacPherson v. Buick Motor Co.*, 217 N.Y. 382.

[However] what is released or set in motion is a physical force. We are now asked to say that a like liability attaches to the circulation of a thought or a release of the explosive power resident in words. Nothing in our previous decisions commits us to a holding of liability for negligence in the circumstances of the case at hand, and that such liability, if recognized, will be an extension of the principle of those decisions to different conditions, even if more or less analogous. The question then is whether such an extension shall be made.

The extension, if made, will so expand the field of liability for negligent speech as to make it nearly, if not quite, coterminous with that of liability for fraud. Again and again, in decisions of this court, the bounds of this latter liability have been set up, with futility the fate of every endeavor to dislodge them. Scienter has been declared to be an indispensable element except where the representation has been put forward as true of one's own knowledge or in circumstances where the expression of opinion was a dishonorable pretense. Even an opinion, especially an opinion by an expert, may be found to be fraudulent if the grounds supporting it are so flimsy as to lead to the conclusion that there was no genuine belief back of it. Further than that this court has never gone.

. . .

This has not meant, to be sure, that negligence may not be evidence from which a trier of the facts may draw an inference of fraud, but merely that if that inference is rejected, or, in the light of all the circumstances, is found to be unreasonable, negligence alone is not a substitute for fraud. Many also are the cases in the courts of equity that have distinguished between the willful or reckless representation essential to the maintenance at law of an action for deceit, and [one of negligent] misrepresentation.

Our holding does not emancipate accountants from the consequences of fraud. It does not relieve them if their audit has been so negligent as to justify a finding that they had no genuine belief in its adequacy, for this again is fraud. It does no more than say that if less than this is proved, if there has been neither reckless misstatement nor insincere profession of an opinion, but only honest blunder, the ensuing liability for negligence is one that is bounded by the contract, and is to be enforced between the parties by whom the contract has been made. We doubt whether the average business man receiving a certificate without paying for it and receiving it merely as one among a multitude of possible investors, would look for anything more.

2.   The second cause of action is yet to be considered.

The defendants certified as a fact, true to their own knowledge, that the balance sheet was in accordance with the books of account. If their statement was false, they are not to be exonerated because they believed it to be true. We think the triers of the facts might hold it to be false.

In this connection we are to bear in mind the principle already stated in the course of this opinion that negligence or blindness, even when not equivalent to fraud, is none the less evidence to sustain an inference of fraud. At least this is so if the negligence is gross.

The defendants were put on their guard by the circumstances touching the December accounts receivable to scrutinize with special care. A jury might find that with suspicions thus awakened, they closed their eyes to the obvious, and blindly gave assent.

We conclude, to sum up the situation, that in certifying to the correspondence between balance sheet and accounts the defendants made a statement as true to their own knowledge, when they had, as a jury might find, no knowledge on the subject. If that is so, they may also be found to have acted without information leading to a sincere or genuine belief when they certified to an opinion that the balance sheet faithfully reflected the condition of the business.

Whatever wrong was committed by the defendants was not their personal act or omission, but that of their subordinates. This does not relieve them, however, of liability to answer in damages for the consequences of the wrong, if wrong there shall be found to be. . . . The question is merely this, whether the defendants, having delegated the performance of this work to agents of their own selection, are responsible for the manner in which the business of the agency was done. As to that the answer is not doubtful.

[The court reversed the Appellate Division's judgment that an action for negligence could be properly maintained without privity being established and remanded the case for trial based upon the theory of deceit (fraud). The case was never subsequently brought to trial.]

[a]   **Comments on _Ultramares v. Touche_.**   Note that Chief Judge Cardozo provides several methods of satisfying the _scienter_ requirement for stating a cause of action based upon deceit (fraud) other than a showing that the defendant lied and knew it. "Fraud includes the pretense of knowledge when knowledge there is none." Furthermore, he indicated:

> Even an opinion, especially an opinion by an expert, may be found to be fraudulent if the grounds supporting it are so flimsy as to lead to the conclusion that there was no genuine belief back of it. Further than that this court has never gone. This has not meant, to be sure, that negligence may not be evidence from which a trier of the facts may draw an inference of fraud (_Derry v. Peek_), but merely that if that inference is rejected, or, in the light of all the circumstances, is found to be unreasonable, negligence alone is not a substitute for fraud.

From a practical standpoint, the attorney will plead both causes of action. If the negligence cause of action is barred by privity, then the fraud theory is the alternate avenue of approach, and if there is enough evidence to go to a jury, there is still a fair chance of recovery since juries in such cases are said to be pro-plaintiff. In fact, forget for a moment what Chief Judge Cardozo _said_, let's look at what he _did_. He dismissed the negligence cause of action for lack of privity but sent the case back to the trial court for a trial based upon fraudulent misrepresentation. For a further discussion of the fraud aspects of the case, see *infra* ¶4.05.

¶ 1.02   Overview: The Attorney-CPA's Speech

At the annual meeting of the Society for the Prevention of Imposition of Additional Liability upon Accountants, the guest speaker was J. Filmore Takeover, Esq., Senior Partner of the law firm of Takeover, Dazzel, and Wynn, counsel to the Society. Takeover is a CPA in addition to being a lawyer. Takeover delivered his annual review of legal developments affecting accountants in a paper entitled, "The Demise of Privity: A Limitation We Have Known and Loved." He indicated that this was another turbulent year for the profession on all fronts, both civil and criminal. As he saw it, one of the accountant's dilemmas during the year was the ever-diminishing utility of privity as a bar to third-party actions. In one way or another, third-party liability has been expanded to a point where privity is all but obsolete. He noted that the widespread expansion of the right to maintain class actions had exacerbated the problem. He then proceeded as follows:

Fellow Accountants, you and I are all aware of the fact that the liability we face from our clients has historically not been as frightening or overwhelming as the potential liability to third parties. It can be partially controlled or limited by the contractual undertaking with the client and to which we agree. Furthermore, even if something does go wrong, and if it is decided that we were negligent, the amount of liability is usually not catastrophic. In fact, in most instances the problem can be resolved by a settlement with the client which will neither impose a large amount of liability nor result in unfavorable notoriety to individual practitioners or firms, nor will it bring disrepute upon the profession. It is true that under some circumstances, large amounts of liability can be imposed as a result of failure to perform a proper audit or due to the rendering of advisory services. A negligently performed audit for the client can be costly. However, such events are infrequent. As I have stated to you on previous occasions and I think you will agree, although none of us wants to engage in negligent behavior, all of us do so on occasion. When this occurs, some liability may be imposed upon us. But this is not the major danger we face, for there is only one party who can sue us, the extent of the liability is usually well determined, and the fee can be adjusted accordingly in order to reflect the possible potential liability appropriate under the circumstances. For example, it is obvious that if a defalcation audit is to be undertaken (this being beyond the scope of the normal audit that we perform), we must charge an additional fee in order to compensate for the additional time and in order to reflect the additional risk assumed as a result of this special type of audit.

If all we had to worry about was the direct liability to the party or parties that we contract with, then we could rest much more easily at night. Furthermore, the sky-high cost of malpractice insurance that we purchase to protect ourselves in the event of some liability arising out of the performance of our professional undertakings would be much less. Thus, our most important problem is not that of liability to our clients, but instead potential liability to those who make use of the report but who are not our clients, paid us nothing, and are not in privity of contract with us, but who are nevertheless recognized as proper parties to sue and recover damages from us for mere negligence.

But let's look at an important recent Supreme Court of the United States case, *Touche Ross & Co. v. Reddington.*[3] [Takeover summarized the case as follows:]

> Petitioner accounting firm was retained by a securities brokerage firm (Weis) registered with the Securities and Exchange Commission (SEC) and a member of the New York Stock Exchange (Exchange), and in this capacity audited Weis' books and records and prepared for filing with the SEC the annual reports of financial condition required by § 17(a) of the Securities Exchange Act of 1934 (1934 Act) and implementing regulations. Subsequently, because of Weis' precarious financial condition, respondent Reddington was appointed as trustee in the liquidation of Weis' business pursuant to the Securities Investor Protection Act (SIPA). During the liquidation, Weis' cash and securities on hand, as well as a sum of money advanced by respondent Securities Investor Protection Corporation (SIPC) to the trustee under the SIPA, proved to be insufficient to make whole those customers who had left assets or deposits with Weis. The SIPC and the trustee then filed an action for damages against petitioner in District Court, seeking to impose liability upon petitioner by reason of its allegedly improper audit of Weis' financial statements and alleging that because of such improper conduct petitioner breached duties owed to the SIPC, the trustee, and others under the common law, § 17(a), and the regulations, and that this misconduct prevented Weis' true financial condition from becoming known until it was too late to forestall liquidation or to lessen the adverse financial consequences to Weis' customers. The District Court dismissed the complaint, holding that no claim for relief was stated because no private cause of action could be implied from § 17(a). The Court of Appeals reversed, holding that § 17(a) imposes a duty on accountants, that a breach of this duty gives rise to an implied private right of action for damages in favor of a broker-dealer's customers, and that the SIPC and the trustee could assert this implied cause of action on behalf of Weis' customers.
>
> Held: There is no implied private cause of action for damages under § 17(a).
>
> (a)   In terms, § 17(a) simply requires broker-dealers to keep such records and file such reports as the SEC may prescribe, and does not purport to create a private cause of action in favor of anyone. The section's intent, evident from its face, is to provide the SEC, the Exchange, and other authorities with a sufficiently early warning to enable them to take appropriate action to protect investors before a broker-dealer's financial collapse, and not by any stretch of its language does the section purport to confer private damages, rights or any remedy in the event the regulatory authorities are unsuccessful in achieving their objectives and the broker-dealer becomes insolvent before corrective steps can be taken.
>
> (b)   The conclusion that no private right of action is implicit in § 17(a) is reinforced by the fact that the 1934 Act's legislative history is entirely silent on whether or not such a right of action should be available. This conclusion is also supported by the statutory scheme under which other sections of the Act explicitly grant private causes of action. More particularly, a cause of action in § 17(a) should not be implied that is significantly broader than the one granted in § 18(a), which provides the principal express civil remedy for misstatements in reports but limits it to purchasers and sellers of securities.
>
> (c)   The inquiry in a case such as this ends when it is determined on the basis of the statutory language and the legislative history that Congress did not intend to create, either expressly or by implication, a private cause of action. Further inquiries as to the "necessity" of implying

---

[3] 442 U.S. 560 (1979), Syllabus.

a private remedy and the proper forum for enforcement of the asserted rights have little relevance to the decision of the case.

(d)   Section 27 and the remedial purposes of the 1934 Act do not furnish a sufficient ground for holding that the federal courts should provide a damages remedy for petitioner's alleged breach of its duties under § 17(a). Section 27 merely grants jurisdiction to federal district courts over violations of the Act and suits to enforce any liability or duty thereunder and provides for venue and service of process and creates no cause of action of its own force and effect and imposes no liabilities. And generalized references to the "remedial purposes" of the Act do not justify reading a provision "more broadly than its language and the statutory scheme reasonably permit."

One might conclude that *Touche v. Reddington* merely involved the standing of the parties to sue under Section 17 of the 1934 Act, based upon an implied right of action. Having decided the case on this basis, the court said little about the underlying privity issue. But I assure you, it was there. Note the plaintiffs were not eligible to use Section 18 of the 1934 Act since they were not buyers or sellers of securities as required by that section.

You are undoubtedly aware of the result previously reached by the U.S. Supreme Court in the *Hochfelder* case, which attempted to convert Section 10(b) and Rule 10b-5 into a vehicle for recovery by third parties against the accountant for negligence, despite the fact that the section was phrased in terms of fraud. Had Hochfelder won, then third parties would be able to prevail based upon a showing of mere negligence. Reddington, on the other hand, attempted an end run. The tactic was to rely upon a previously untried section of the Act, namely Section 17(a), which at the time pertinent to the case read:

Every national securities exchange, every member thereof . . . and every broker or dealer registered pursuant to . . . this title, shall make, keep and preserve for such periods, such accounts, correspondence . . . and other records, and make such reports, as the Commission by its rules and regulations may prescribe as necessary or appropriate in the public interest or for the protection of investors.

Rules required by the SEC state that the reporting parties accompany their reports with audited financial statements. The plaintiffs argued that Section 17 gave an aggrieved private party an implied right to recover damages in the event that the accountants (Touche Ross) *negligently* performed their part of the Section 17 obligation. If the plaintiffs were able to prevail, they would avoid the usual pitfalls facing plaintiffs suing accountants. First, the privity requirement is nonapplicable under the 1934 Act, and second, proving fraud with its requirement of establishing *scienter* would have been avoided.

Thus, the door to Pandora's box might be further opened. The question before the Supreme Court in *Reddington* was not whether Touche Ross was negligent (we'll never know), but whether the plaintiff had the standing or implied right to sue at all under Section 17. However, if Reddington had won privity would not be a bar to Section 17 actions based upon negligence under the 1934 Act. Thank God he lost!

That's the good news. Unfortunately, there is more bad news than good. Starting with *Ultramares*, which was subsequently followed in virtually all jurisdictions and which represents the high water mark for privity as a limitation upon the rights of third parties to sue a negligent accountant, the path of the law has been largely downhill except for a few states that have reiterated the *Ultramares* privity limitation. First, Cardozo indicated that an action for fraud was not subject to the privity limitation. In addition, he indicated that actual fraud was not the exclusive basis for satisfying the scienter requirement; constructive fraud or gross negligence can be enough. The broader these theories are expanded, the weaker privity becomes as a defense. Next came the Federal Securities Acts of 1933 and 1934, which rejected privity as a defense under federal securities law. Finally, the preponderance of states that have recently considered the privity defense have no longer followed *Ultramares*. (See Chapter 3, ¶3.04.)

[1]   Questions from the Floor

MRS. WALSH: In your presentation, you emphasized liability for negligence and the rights and limitations of third parties to prevail under this theory; why isn't fraud a viable alternative for the plaintiff?

MR. TAKEOVER: The trouble with the remedy of fraud (deceit) from the standpoint of recovery by a plaintiff, in addition to the fact that it is not present in most cases, is that it is exceptionally hard to prove. Your question is a good one but could almost be the subject of a separate lecture. However, as you will recall, the plaintiff invariably has the burden of proof and this is the case insofar as a claim based upon fraud is concerned. But, you may ask, why is the proof of fraud so onerous? The answer is contained in the definition of fraud or in the elements that must be proven in order to obtain relief. The key stumbling block or element is the requirement that plaintiff show that the defendant made the materially false statement with "a knowledge of falsity," or scienter as it also is called. Pause for a moment and reflect upon this requirement and several significant problems arise. First, it is a highly subjective test, is is not? That is, it turns on the requisite knowledge of the party being sued, the defendant. Next, how does one establish the requisite knowledge of falsity in a court of law? The answer is, you ask the defendant, since he or she is the one, to the virtual exclusion of all others, who knows whether or not *he* or *she* knew. Unfortunately, not all litigants tell the truth, or more charitably stated, they have confused recollections which emerge as a denial of knowledge. Were this the only way of sustaining the burden of proof, the situation would appear to be nearly hopeless unless another witness or witnesses could be produced to whom the defendant had professed his or her guilty knowledge. How likely is this to occur? True, if it is possible to get the case to the trier of fact (the jury or the judge), the trier may find for the plaintiff based solely upon the conflicting testimony of the parties. Plaintiff says: "Yes, defendant knew he was lying," while defendant staunchly denies this. Now where are we? Well, plaintiff has the burden of proving his or her allegations by establishing that the defendant did, more probably than not, know. Thus, under these circumstances, if we assume the evidence to be exactly balanced, the plaintiff loses. However, there is always the hope and possibility that the trier of fact will not believe the testimony of the defendant even though it is made under oath. But it is probably not a good percentage bet. Now you can see the plaintiff's dilemma more clearly. Were this the entire story, fraud would be relegated to the theoretical, but impractical, category.

Fortunately, for plaintiffs, this is not the end of the story. The courts were well aware of the quandary that would result if scienter began and ended with the requirement of showing *subjective knowledge* of falsity. Thus, a most important gloss was added to the scienter requirement early on, and it was articulated in terms of "a reckless disregard for the truth." In doing so, we have moved away from the absolute requirement of knowledge and have injected some objectivity into the picture. The plaintiff's chances have been improved and fraud appears to be a more viable cause of action. Thus, if the defendant had no valid basis in fact for making the statements he made, the plaintiff may prevail even though the defendant actually believed what he said was true or at least professes he so believed them to be true. Nevertheless, scienter remains the key stumbling block to recovery from the standpoint of proof.

Judges are masters of the art of distinguishing away cases, making exceptions without doing violence to *stare decisis* and, let's face it, making law where this is deemed appropriate. Perhaps as a result of judicial disfavor with the narrowness and ineffectiveness of the tort of fraud, the judges have added some additional means for the plaintiff to recover. These are gross negligence and constructive fraud. Neither are well defined and could be examples of the old adage that "hard cases make bad law." Gross negligence on the defendant's part, at a minimum, would be evidence of a reckless disregard for the truth. This undoubtedly is a correct use of the concept if we can only figure out when conduct becomes grossly negligent. A more controversial use of gross negligence in respect to the scienter requirement occurs when gross negligence is deemed to satisfy the scienter requirement as a matter of law. We've come a long way from our major premise when this occurs. Constructive fraud is analogous to *quasi* contract. Neither fraud nor the contract actually exist, but "almost" is enough. Now we have to struggle with determining what constitutes "almost."

Despite the fact that the approach has been to consider the expansion of the term *scienter* in relation to the plaintiff's problem in satisfying the burden of proof, it is clear, is it not, that an expansion of the possibility or actuality of recovery for fraud has an important impact on privity. This is the case since fraud is not subject to the privity limitation imposed upon a plaintiff who is seeking to recover against the accountant for negligence. The route may be circular, but the end result is the same.

MRS. SHARP: I'm still not clear on what if anything your previous answer has to do with privity?

MR. TAKEOVER: I'll be happy to clarify this. Fortunately, the answer is fairly straightforward up to a point. To the extent that privity is clearly a bar to recovery, resort to fraud with its expanded version of scienter would be the sensible tactic. Plaintiff would plead either constructive fraud or gross negligence as a way to avoid dismissal of the case. Where the law is unclear is how much more is factually required to sustain the constructive fraud or gross negligence theories, as contrasted with a claim based upon negligence.

MR. DUBIOUS: I overheard a couple of attorneys discussing something called RICO, the first letter standing for "racketeer," and how it posed not only a civil liability threat to accountants but permitted the recovery of treble damages to boot. I don't know where those attorneys practice law, but I hope it's Zanzibar!

MR. TAKEOVER: RICO stands for "Racketeer Influenced and Corrupt Organizations" and is a comparatively new "kid on the block" insofar as accountant's liability is concerned. It has been held to apply to accountants in the Seventh Circuit U.S. Court of Appeals, although the case has not been completed. It was remanded by the appeals court for trial after that court sustained RICO's applicability to accountants. It's a shocker and provides for treble damages. (For a more comprehensive discussion of Civil RICO, see Chapter 10.)

MR. FEARFUL: I came across a similar experience relating to criminal fraud as it applies to accountants. The attorney indicated that criminal fraud and civil fraud, which I am familiar with, are virtually identical. Not only that, he indicated that an accountant could be found guilty of criminal fraud even though he was not being paid off or had not actively aided or advised the perpetrator on how to accomplish the foul deed.

MR. TAKEOVER: Once again, what you heard is essentially correct. The danger is there. (For a detailed analysis of this aspect of liability, see ¶5.02).

The question period lasted late into the night. Among the questions raised by the audience were questions relating to privileged communication, SEC administrative proceedings, tax practitioner liability, and others. [All of these questions will be discussed in the chapters that follow.] The session finally ended, and afterwards the parties adjourned to the bar. The concluding remark by one of the participants was: "Well, at least being forewarned hopefully means being forearmed."

¶ 1.03   Glossary of Legal Terms

The following legal terms are found in cases contained in this book. Most of them are from the law of procedure, as contrasted with substantive law, such as the law of torts and contracts, with which this book is fundamentally concerned. An understanding of these terms will often help you in focusing upon the precise issue or issues facing the court and the ultimate conclusion the court reached. Certainly, the *Ultramares v. Touche* case is a good illustration of this point. This initial familiarization with the terminology will also enable you to read the cases without being puzzled or confused by these terms and will undoubtedly prove beneficial to your understanding of the book. Note that, where possible, cross-references have been given to other parts of the book where you can observe the term used in an accounting context.

ACTUAL CAUSATION.   This term is used in negligence as a requirement for recovery. If, despite the defendant's negligence, the accident would have occurred in any event, then the negligence did not cause the accident and recovery will be denied. The courts frequently use a "but for" test in resolving the issue. The test is phrased in terms of: "But for" defendant's negligent conduct, would the accident have occurred? If the answer is no, then defendant's conduct was causal. In other words, the negligent conduct of the defendant must have contributed in whole or in part to the plaintiff's injury. If the accident would have occurred in any event, even if the defendant had not been negligent, then the actual cause requirement is not met. For example, if the negligent act was the negligent failure to signal for a turn, but the plaintiff was not looking, we have an accident that was not caused by the defendant's negligence. Of course, in the case of fraud, reliance must be established as the basis for recovery.

ANSWER (in pleading).   The pleading of a party in response to allegations that have been made in the original complaint or in subsequent counterclaims.

AMICUS CURIAE.   Latin for "friend of the court." An amicus curiae is not a party to the litigation but nonetheless submits a brief to the court either pursuant to a statute or on the invitation of a party or of the court. The AICPA frequently submits such a brief; it did so in respect to *Sedima v. Imrex*, the landmark civil RICO case which was recently decided by the U.S. Supreme Court.

BENCH TRIAL.   A case in which the parties waive the right to trial by a jury which results in the trial judge deciding both the facts and the law. It is not uncommon that the parties in complicated cases would prefer to have a single judge decide the outcome rather than put the questions of fact and the verdict to a jury for its determination.

BURDEN(S) OF PROOF.   The plaintiff has the burden of proving the facts or claims that are made in the complaint. Generally in civil litigation, this burden may be met by persuading the trier of fact (judge or jury), by the preponderance of evidence, that it is *more probable than not* that the facts or claims asserted are true. Thus, a feather on evenly balanced scales of justice is enough to sustain the burden. However, in civil fraud cases a substantial number of states and the federal courts have adopted a more difficult burden of proof, namely, the fraud must be established by clear and convincing evidence. In criminal cases the burden is phrased in terms of *beyond a reasonable doubt*. It can be readily seen that this is a substantially heavier burden of proof than in the trial of an issue of fact in a civil case. There is a saying in the law that he who has the burden of proof loses more often than not.

COLLATERAL ESTOPPEL.   This term has the effect of preventing (estopping) a party, invariably the defendant, from denying a fact that has been proved against him, in a prior case. Thus, it resembles *res judicata, infra*, but with one significant difference, it is one-sided. Only the plaintiff may establish proof of the fact by this route. The reason for this is that the defendant in case number one had his day in court, that is, had the opportunity to prove the falseness of the fact or claim asserted by another or different plaintiff. Therefore, the defendant is prevented from doing so a second time. But in case number two, we have a different plaintiff than in case number one, and one who has not had a day in court. Therefore, the plaintiff in the second case is not estopped by any adverse finding of fact by the court in the prior case. See ¶ 9.01[2][a].

COMMON LAW.   The general description of the legal systems that have their origins in the law of England. Common law systems prevail in the United States, Canada, England, and most of the former lands of the British Empire. They are characterized by jury trials, the heavy weight given to judicial precedents, and the adversarial nature of litigation. Furthermore, it is the body of law that has been created by the courts in the absence of statutory law. Common law also consists of case law created by the courts in the course of construing existing statutory laws.

COMPLAINT.   In civil practice, it is the first formal pleading by the plaintiff of the allegations against the defendant. It also typically states in a conclusionary manner the legal theory or theories upon which liability is predicated and the relief sought.

COUNTERCLAIM.   A claim by a party (usually the defendant) that, if proven, would either defeat a claim made by the other party or establish the basis for recovery by the defendant under a distinct cause of action.

COMPARATIVE NEGLIGENCE.   A recent but nevertheless major and widely adopted change in the law of negligence. Under prior common law, the plaintiff was barred from recovering against the negligent defendant if it was established that the plaintiff was also at fault (negligent). Dissatisfaction arose where the contributorily negligent plaintiff was only slightly negligent but was nevertheless precluded from recovery. The shift to the comparative negligence rule results in the trier of fact determining the percentage of negligence of each party and permitting recovery by the plaintiff, but only to the extent of the defendant's percentage of negligence times plaintiff's damages. Some states have adopted pure comparative negligence, whereas others use a modified form. Pure comparative negligence applies no matter what the percentage of plaintiff's negligence may be. Hence, a plaintiff who is found to be 80 percent negligent will still recover 20 percent of his or her damages. Modified comparative negligence requires the plaintiff to be less negligent than the defendant, that is, he must not be found to have been more than 50 percent negligent. See ¶ 7.08.

CONFLICT OF LAWS.   That body of law dealing with the determination of which jurisdiction's or state's law should be applied to the facts of a particular case or controversy to be decided. Since substantive law may vary from jurisdiction to jurisdiction (e.g., the privity rule), it may be of major importance to have the court select the "right" state's law which is to be applied to your case when the laws of more than one jurisdiction could be applied. There is no federal common law of torts, contracts, or other common law areas. Thus, a federal district court will resort to the conflict of law rules in the state in which it is sitting in order to determine which jurisidiction's law applies. Where two or more states have a contact with the parties or the transaction such that it would not be unreasonable for the forum (the court hearing the case) to use either of the state's laws, the conflict rules determine. If the conflicts question is not raised, the forum will use its own substantive law.

DIRECTED VERDICT.   The entry of a decision by the judge in favor of one party to a case when the evidence introduced by the other party is so lacking in probative force that no reasonable jury could believe that it proves a cause of action.

CUSTOM OF THE INDUSTRY.   A standard or test used in deciding whether the defendant was negligent in a given case. If the defendant followed the custom of the industry, this will at least be helpful in ascertaining whether he was at fault. It is clear, however, that following the custom of the industry will not be conclusive. Failure to follow the custom of the industry will normally be fatal. For some cases where GAAP and GAAS were not determinative of the question of fault, see ¶ 3.01[2].

DICTUM.   Latin for "that which is said." The dictum of a reported decision are the statements by the judge that are not essential for reaching the conclusion and that, are not binding precedent in future judicial determinations. It is an indication of how the court might decide such a question if it arose in a future case. The holding by the court in the particular case is limited to the facts in the dispute presented to the court.

DISCLAIMER OR EXCULPATION CLAUSE.   This consists of an express statement, usually in writing, to which the now aggrieved party (the plaintiff) has previously contractually agreed not to assert certain claims or liabilities that would otherwise be available. In an accounting context, such a disclaimer would typically be used in connection with an engagement that is to be rendered without an audit. For example, see ¶ 7.04.

DIVERSITY OF CITIZENSHIP.   Diversity exists when a party of one state litigates against a party of another state or country. Diversity of citizenship, plus alleged damages of $10,000 or more, is the most common manner in which federal courts have jurisdiction of a controversy that does not involve federal law. Of course, federal courts have jurisdiction over cases that involve federal law (e.g., Securities Act violations).

INSTRUCTIONS OF LAW.   In a jury trial the trial judge instructs the jury on the applicable law. It is the jury's obligation to apply the instructed law to the facts as determined by the jury. Theoretically the jury may not disregard the judge's instructions on the law.

JUDGMENT NOTWITHSTANDING THE VERDICT.   J.N.O.V. is the abbreviation for "judgment non obstante verdicto." The phrase is Latin for "notwithstanding the verdict." A judgment n.o.v. is a judgment granted by the judge after the jury has entered a contrary verdict.

JURISDICTION.   Those areas of the law in which a court has the constitutional authority to decide cases or controversies. Also, the physical territory from which cases may be brought to a particular court for legal determination.

JURY TRIAL.   A case in which the jury determines the facts and reaches a verdict based on the facts and the court's instructions of law.

MOTION TO DISMISS (demurrer).   A most-useful preliminary device which takes exception to the sufficiency in point of law of a pleading based on the facts alleged. The motion is made upon receipt of the plaintiff's pleading and in effect says, "so what, even if you prove all you allege, the law does not recognize this to be a sufficient basis for granting relief." If granted the defendant wins the case at this point, barring an appeal. The motion avoids needless expense and delay.

NONSUIT.   A judgment by the judge, sitting without a jury, which is granted on motion by the defendant when the plaintiff is unable or unwilling to prove the facts originally alleged.

PLAINTIFF IN ERROR.   In some states this name designates the party who is appealing the judgment of a lower court. This appellation applies regardless of whether the party was a plaintiff or defendant in the lower court. This reversal often causes confusion in the mind of the reader. It is best to think in terms of the role the parties took as plaintiff or defendant at the trial level or simply to think in terms of the plaintiff being the client or third party and the defendant being the accountant.

PRECEDENT.   Any previous judicial decision that has not been specifically overruled or negated by legislative action. Theoretically, the court should always apply the precedent to the facts of the case at bar, but it is often able to avoid doing this by distinguishing away the prior case on the facts. However, in certain instances, the court may directly and expressly overrule an existing precedent. In an accounting context, some states have overruled their prior position on privity which was based upon *Ultramares v. Touche* (see ¶¶ 1.01[3] and 3.04).

PRIVILEGED COMMUNICATION.   As used in the law of evidence, it is a communication, oral or written, made, for example, to an attorney in professional confidence and which may not be divulged and entered into evidence against a party properly asserting the privilege. It has very little application to communications made by a client to the accountant except in a limited number of jurisdictions, which have created such a privilege by statute.

PROCEDURAL LAW.   Those laws and rules that relate to the methods of administering justice and conducting trials. Procedural law does not directly relate to the basic rights of citizens, but it has a major impact on how these rights are enforced.

PROXIMATE CAUSE.   This is also referred to as "legal cause." It is one of the elements necessary to state a cause of action for negligence. In general the law of negligence requires that there be a reasonably close causal connection between the conduct and the resulting injury. The proximate cause may be the first act in a long chain of events. It is also clear that, because of convenience, public policy, and a rough sense of justice, the law may arbitrarily decline to follow the events beyond a certain point and it does so by resort to "proximate cause" as the justification.

RES JUDICATA. Latin for "a decided matter." As a general rule, when the courts have answered a particular question of law, it becomes res judicata and a court in a subsequent case will not permit either of the parties in the original or first case to relitigate the same question. See also *collateral estoppel, supra.*

RESPONDEAT SUPERIOR. "Let the master answer." This is a basic agency rule that imposes liability on the master or principal for the acts of a servant-agent, whether or not the acts were wrongful or against the orders of the principal, if the servant-agent is one over whom the principal exercises control or has the power to do so. The principal is liable for torts or other acts of such agents committed within the scope of the employment. This is a form of vicarious or strict liability since it matters not whether the principal is in any way at fault. As to nonservant-agents, a somewhat less onerous standard applies, that is, the principal will have liability for a nonservant-agent's acts if committed within the scope of his authority. The application of this rule to accountants is obvious. The principal (the CPA firm engaging another to work for it) will have such liability imposed upon it. The same rule applies to individual accountants who employ others.

RESTATEMENTS OF LAW. A synthesis and tabulation of the state law as it is found in the 50 states of the Unites States at a given time. It is not law in the sense that it has been adopted by any jurisdiction by statute or that it is judge-made law. However, it is highly influential, since it does represent what the majority of states are doing, and uniformity has some social value. It was prepared by the leading scholars, judges, professors, and professionals in the individual area of law. There are restatements of numerous areas of law, including contract, torts, and agency—the most important areas for the accountant. Many are now in a second edition. Perhaps the most important restatement rule for accountants is contained in the *Restatement of Torts,* 2nd, *Section 552,* which represents the restatement's position on the privity question (see ¶ 3.04).

STARE DECISIS. Latin for "to stand decided." Stare decisis is the legal doctrine that the principles of previously decided cases should not be abandoned. The judiciary should overturn long-standing precedents only in the rarest of circumstances. Instead, such changes should be left to the legislature. See also *precedent.*

STATUTORY LAW. Statutes promulgated by state or federal legislatures that impose legal responsibilities and/or create legal rights and duties. Statutory laws are created independent of common law which is judge-made law.

SUBSTANTIVE LAW. Those laws that regulate daily human activity: rights, commerce, duties, property ownership, and the like. Substantive law contrasts with procedural law, which determines how the laws regulating human conduct are to be administered.

SUMMARY JUDGMENT, MOTION FOR.   A request or plea to the court whereby a party to an action moves to have the court grant a judgment in his or her favor based upon the assertion that there are no real triable issues of fact. Such a motion is based upon the pleadings, documentary evidence, and affidavits establishing the facts submitted in support of the motion. If the motion is granted the need for a trial is obviated. The granting of the motion to either party is a final judgment unless an appeal is taken. It in effect converts the dispute to a question of law which the judge decides. It is exceptionally useful in cases wherein the opposing party's pleading is a sham, but unless factually attacked will continue to subsequent stages of litigation thereby causing delay and expense. It is frequently used in cases involving accountant's liability, for example, see ¶ 4.04[2][b].

TRIER OF FACT.   In a bench trial the judge is the trier of the fact. In a jury trial the jury determines what facts have been proven. In deciding what the facts are, the trier of fact is entitled to judge what weight is to be attached to any evidence and what credibility should be accorded to a witness's testimony.

CHAPTER 2

AN ACCOUNTANT'S RESPONSIBILITIES TO CLIENTS AND THE PUBLIC

¶ 2.01 Unique Nature of Accountant's Public Responsibility and Liability

There can be no doubt that it is the word *public* in Certified Public Accountant that gives rise to the unique and troublesome liability climate in which the accountant must practice. The three excerpts that follow provide an excellent view of the policy factors that affect the accountant's legal status. Each takes a different vantage point and each provides valuable insight into the liability problem. The excerpts from the U.S. Supreme Court (¶ 2.01[2]) and the Supreme Court of New Jersey (¶ 2.01[3]) are illustrative of the former court's application of *public* policy to the accountant's attempt to assert a privilege for communication with the client involving the tax accrual file, and the latter court's use of *public* policy in deciding whether to allow privity to bar third-party lawsuits against accountants. In both instances the policy factor was instrumental in the court's reaching a decision contra the profession.

[1] View of the Profession

The following excerpt is taken from John Carey's book, *Professional Ethics of Public Accounting* (New York: AICPA, 1946), pp. 13–14. At the time this was written, he was the executive director of the AICPA, where he served with distinction for many years. The following excerpt has been frequently cited with favor by both the federal and state courts:

> Whenever he certifies a financial statement the certified public accountant is potentially, at least, rendering a service to two or more parties whose interests may come into conflict—management and stockholder, borrower and lender, purchaser and seller. He may, and often does, serve simultaneously competitors in the same line of business, without fear on the part of either client that he will favor the one or the other. It is the peculiar obligation of the

21

certified public accountant, which no other profession has to impose on its members, to maintain a wholly objective and impartial attitude toward the affairs of the client whose financial statements he certifies. The certified public accountant acknowledges a moral responsibility (and under the Securities Act this is made a legal and financial responsibility) to be as mindful of the interests of strangers who may rely on his opinion as of the interests of the client who pays his fee. This is at the same time a heavy burden and a proud distinction. It marks the certified public accountant as an individual of the highest integrity; a tough-minded technician whose judgment cannot be unbalanced by the strongest pressures, who stakes a hard-earned professional reputation on his ability to express a fair and just opinion on which all concerned may rely; in the broad sense, a highly useful servant to society as a whole.

The certified public accountant, therefore, in providing accounting statements which all concerned may accept as disinterested expressions, based on technically sound procedures and experienced judgment, may serve as a kind of arbiter, interpreter, and umpire among all the varied interests. Thereby he can eliminate the necessity for costly separate investigations by each party at interest, as well as endless doubts, delays, misunderstandings, and controversies which are so much sand in the economic machine.

[2]   U.S. Supreme Court's Most Recent View of the Accountant's Public Responsibility

The following language is taken from the 1984 case of *United States v. Arthur Young & Co.* (see ¶ 8.03[3][b] for the decision):

Nor do we find persuasive the argument that a work-product immunity for accountants' tax accrual workpapers is a fitting analogue to the attorney work-product doctrine established in *Hickman v. Taylor, supra.* The *Hickman* work-product doctrine was founded upon the private attorney's role as the client's confidential advisor and advocate, a loyal representative whose duty it is to present the client's case in the most favorable possible light. An independent certified public accountant performs a different role. By certifying the public reports that collectively depict a corporation's financial status, the independent auditor assumes a public responsibility transcending any employment relationship with the client. The independent public accountant performing this special function owes ultimate allegiance to the corporation's creditors and stockholders, as well as to the investing public. This "public watchdog" function demands that the accountant maintain total independence from the client at all times and requires complete fidelity to the public trust. To insulate from disclosure a certified public accountant's interpretations of the client's financial statements would be to ignore the significance of the accountant's role as a disinterested analyst charged with public obligations.

[3]   View of the Supreme Court of New Jersey

In 1983 the Supreme Court of New Jersey in *Rosenblum v. Adler* (see ¶ 3.04) made the following observations about the public aspects of an accountant's duties and to whom these duties are owed. The issue before the court was the applicability of privity as a defense by accountants to bar third-party suits:

At one time the audit was made primarily to inform management of irregularities and inefficiencies in the business. . . . That function remains one of the principal reasons for the audit. Gradually a need for independent audits was generated by public ownership of business enterprises and by requirements of the stock exchanges and the Securities and Exchange Commission (SEC). Institutional investors, investment specialists, stockholders, and lenders demanded more and reliable information. It is now well recognized that the audited statements are made for the use of third parties who have no contractual relationship with the auditor. Moreover, it is common knowledge that companies use audits for many proper business purposes, such as submission to banks and other lending institutions that might advance funds and to suppliers of services and goods that might advance credit. The SEC twenty-five years ago stated: "The responsibility of a public accountant is not only to the client who pays his fee, but also to investors, creditors and others who may rely on the financial statements which he certifies." *In re Touche, Niven, Bailey & Smart*, 37 S.E.C. 629, 670 (1957). These uses as well as governmental requirements make financial statements reviewed by independent qualified accountants indispensable. . . .

¶ 2.02   Where Do the Legal Duties of an Accountant Arise?

[1]   Contract and Applicable Contract Law

The most important thing you should know about contract law as it relates to your potential liability as an accountant is that the contract or engagement letter, as it is called, will be the first thing the courts will examine in determining liability. Was the work to be audited or unaudited? Was it to include a search for defalcations? For what purpose is it to be used and by whom? Was there a disclaimer? Were any specific exceptions taken?

Invariably the accountant drafts the engagement letter. If one does not exist, it certainly should. The Statute of Frauds, which requires that certain contracts be in writing to be enforceable, rarely applies to the usual contracts that accountants make with their clients. However, despite the inapplicability of the statute, the old adage of "getting it in writing" certainly does pertain. As a general proposition, courts construe faulty draftsmanship or ambiguity contained in a contract against the party responsible for it. Unquestionably this maxim applies even more in the case of an accountant, who as a professional should be able to state the undertaking and its terms precisely and carefully. A carefully drafted contract that indicates explicitly what is to be done and what is not a part of the commitment will be helpful in settling disputes if the occasion arises. The one thing that the cases indicate is that this will be a likely cause of litigation. This is particularly so and often critical in the case of compilation and review and other nonaudit engagements. Hopefully, the contract will be so clear that it will prevent the dispute from coming up. Of course, this is what a good contract should do and is an integral part of contract law.

Contract law applicable to a CPA or accountant's contract for services does not vary greatly from general contract law applicable to any contract for services. A "contract" is commonly defined as: a promise or a set of promises for the breach of which the law gives a remedy, or the performance of which the law in some way recognizes as a duty.

The types of promises that a court will enforce must meet four requirements and possibly a fifth, if the Statute of Frauds applies. The offer and acceptance requirement must be satisfied and the promise must be supported by a legal consideration. Legal capacity to contract by the parties must also be present but is not a commercially significant problem and certainly is *de minimus*, or insignificant, in relation to contracts for accounting services. The legality requirement could have greater significance particularly as a result of recent developments regarding price fixing which are discussed below. Finally, the Statute of Frauds is generally inapplicable to the accountant's contract since it is not one "which from the time of the making thereof cannot be performed within one year." However, the desirability of having a written contract even though such is not required has been discussed previously.

The typical contract between an accountant and client is an *express bilateral* contract, which can be written or oral. Express in this context simply means that the agreement is created by the use of language. Where such language is missing, the law would customarily find that the parties had nevertheless entered into a contract implied in fact as a result of their actions, that is, performance of services by the accountant with the implied understanding that they are to be paid for.

The contract is bilateral in that both parties are making promises. The legal consideration requirement is satisfied by the mutual promises to perform. In concluding this brief discussion, it should be recognized that the major legal concepts applicable to accountants' contracts were drawn from basic contract law. When an accountant's legal responsibility arising as the result of a contract is not defined in this book, the general rules of contract law would apply. This is also true of negligence, agency, fraud, and partnership law.

Related to the legality aspect of contract law is antitrust law. The terms and conditions under which an accountant agrees to enter a contract for professional services are governed to a certain extent by antitrust law considerations. Thus, legal duties may arise because of the inter-working of contract and antitrust law. In an early landmark antitrust opinion by the U.S. Supreme Court, Justice Stone declared price-fixing among competitors to be *per se* illegal, that is, without legal justification.[1] The mere fact that the defendants engaged in the activity, no matter what their alleged justification, was without further proof a violation of the Sherman Act. Section 1 of the act provides: "Every contract, combination or conspiracy in restraint of trade is hereby declared illegal." The defendants were members of a plumbing fixtures manufacturers trade association and taken collectively, dominated the market. They attempted to justify their price-fixing arrangement under "the rule of reason." Subsequent decisions have almost unanimously reaffirmed and expanded this application of *per se* illegality to any parties engaging in or conspiring to fix prices. The pervasive application of the price-fixing *per se* illegality approach is summed up in Justice Douglas's famous footnote 59 to the Supreme Court's opinion in *Socony-Vacuum* (1940)[2]:

> Under this indictment proof that prices in the Midwestern area were raised as a result of the activities of the combination was essential, since sales of gasoline by respondents at the increased prices in that area were necessary in order to establish jurisdiction in the Western District of Wisconsin. Hence we have necessarily treated the case as one where exertion of the power to fix prices (i.e., the actual fixing of prices) was an ingredient of the offense. But that does not mean that both a purpose and a power to fix prices are necessary for the

---

[1] *United States v. Trenton Potteries Co.*, 273 U.S. 392 (1927).

[2] *United States v. Socony-Vacuum Co.*, 310 U.S. 150 (1940).

establishment of a conspiracy under § 1 of the Sherman Act. That would be true if power or ability to commit an offense was necessary in order to convict a person of conspiring to commit it. But it is well established that a person "may be guilty of conspiring although incapable of committing the objective offense." And it is likewise well settled that conspiracies under the Sherman Act are not dependent on any overt act other than the act of conspiring. It is the "contract, combination . . . or conspiracy in restraint of trade or commerce" which § 1 of the Act strikes down, whether the concerted activity be wholly nascent or abortive on the one hand, or successful on the other. And the amount of interstate or foreign trade involved is not material since § 1 of the Act brands as illegal the character of the restraint not the amount of commerce affected. In view of these considerations a conspiracy to fix prices violates § 1 of the Act though no overt act is shown, though it is not established that the conspirators had the means available for accomplishment of their objective, and though the conspiracy embraced but a part of the interstate or foreign commerce in the commodity. Whatever may have been the status of price-fixing agreements at common law the Sherman Act has a broader application to them than the common law prohibitions or sanctions. Price-fixing agreements may or may not be aimed at complete elimination of price competition. The group making those agreements may or may not have power to control the market. But the fact that the group cannot control the market prices does not necessarily mean that the agreement as to prices has no utility to the members of the combination. The effectiveness of price-fixing agreements is dependent on many factors, such as competitive tactics, position in the industry, the formula underlying price policies. Whatever economic justification particular price-fixing agreements may be thought to have, the law does not permit an inquiry into their reasonableness. They are all banned because of their actual or potential threat to the central nervous system of the economy.

The existence or exertion of power to accomplish the desired objective becomes important only in cases where the offense charged is the actual monopolizing of any part of trade or commerce in violation of § 2 of the Act.

Per se illegality was extended further in Keifer-Stewart Co. v. Joseph E. Seagram & Sons, 340 U.S. 211 (1951), when the Supreme Court refused to distinguish between agreements designed to raise prices and agreements intended to effect a price reduction.

But what does this have to do with accountant's liability, you may justifiably ask? Well, there never has been a case charging accountants with price-fixing. Perhaps there never will be. However, there never had been such a case brought against the Virginia State Bar for price-fixing until the *Goldfarb* case, which is summarized below. Obviously, the Virginia State Bar and the lawyers who were its members did not seem to be worried about the application of Section 1 of the Sherman Act to them. The analogy of the *Goldfarb* situation to the accounting profession is obvious:

Goldfarb v. Virginia State Bar, 421 U.S. 773 (1975). When the Goldfarbs sought a title examination in connection with financing the purchase of a home in Fairfax County, Virginia, they consulted numerous Virginia lawyers, the only persons permitted by law to perform such a function. All of the lawyers who were contacted quoted a fee at or above the minimum fee schedule published by the Fairfax County Bar Association. The County Bar Association had no enforcement authority, but the Virginia State Bar Association, to which all Virginia lawyers must belong, had published reports condoning minimum fee schedules and indicating that, in some cases at least, it would be unethical for lawyers to ignore such schedules. However, no formal proceedings had been instituted by the State Bar Association to punish deviations from minimum fee schedules. The Goldfarbs, after having the title to their home examined by a lawyer charging the minimum fee, brought a class action against the State

Bar and County Bar Associations alleging that the operation of the minimum fee schedule violated Section 1 of the Sherman Act. The Supreme Court sustained their claim.

The County Bar argued that the fee schedule was merely advisory and that its promulgation and enforcement did not constitute price fixing. The Court indicated that a "purely advisory fee schedule" might raise different issues, but here "a fixed, rigid price floor arose from [the bar associations'] activities: every lawyer who responded to [the Goldfarbs'] inquiries adhered to the fee schedule, and no lawyer asked for additional information in order to set an individualized fee. The price information disseminated did not concern past standards, . . . but rather minimum fees to be charged in future transactions, and those minimum rates were increased over time. The fee schedule was enforced through the prospect of professional discipline from the State Bar, and the desire of attorneys to comply with announced professional norms . . . ; the motivation to conform was reinforced by the assurance that other lawyers would not compete by underbidding. This is not merely a case of an agreement that may be inferred from an exchange of price information, . . . for here a naked agreement was clearly shown and the effect on prices is plain. . . ."

The County Bar further argued that the learned professions, including the practice of law, did not come within the terms "trade or commerce" in Section 1 of the Sherman Act, because competition was inconsistent with the professional obligation to provide service to the community. The Supreme Court disagreed, unable to find any basis for such a "sweeping exclusion." Neither the nature of the occupation nor its public-service aspect was found to be sufficient to provide "sanctuary from the Sherman Act." "Congress intended to strike as broadly as it could in § 1 of the Sherman Act," and "it cannot be denied that the activities of lawyers play an important part in commercial intercourse, and that anti-competitive activities by lawyers may exert a restraint on commerce." The Court indicated, however, that in other contexts "[t]he public service aspect, and other features of the professions, may require that a particular practice, which could properly be viewed as a violation of the Sherman Act in another context, be treated differently."

The Court also rejected arguments: (a) that the transactions in issue did not have sufficient impact on interstate commerce; and (b) that the involvement of the State Bar was specifically sanctioned by state law and was thereby immunized against antitrust attack.

Although there has never been a case charging price-fixing by accountants, the American Institute of Certified Public Accountants (AICPA) was forced to repeal its prohibition against competitive bidding for a professional engagement by CPAs. The United States proceeded against the Institute under Section 1 of the Sherman Act alleging that the prohibition of competitive bidding was anticompetitive, a form of price-fixing, and illegal *per se*. The Institute agreed to a consent decree which withdrew its competitive bidding rule which had indicated that such a practice was unethical.[3]

In addition, there is one federal case, *United States v. Texas State Bd. of Pub. Accountancy*,[4] which declared a state board's prohibition against competitive bidding to be an illegal price-fixing conspiracy. The attempt to insulate the state's action as a valid action under state law was rejected as it was in *Goldfarb, supra*.

In conclusion, the scope of the prohibition against price-fixing is so broad that it behooves individual accountants or groups to scrupulously avoid conduct that could amount to an illegal price-fixing engagement.

---

[3] *United States v. AICPA*, Accountancy L. Rep. (CCH) ¶ 64,082 (D.D.C. 1972).
[4] 592 F.2d 919 (5th Cir. 1979), *cert. denied*.

Another anticompetitive agreement that is often resorted to by industry, lawyers, and accountants is the covenant not to compete or other types of restraints on the practice of the profession incidental to the sale of a firm or the withdrawal of a partner or staff member. Fortunately, the states have held that such restrictions protect legitimate needs of the promisee and hence are valid under state law if they are *reasonable*. Reasonableness is tested in terms of the scope of the restriction on the promisor's engaging in the practice of accounting, in relation to the geographic area and duration necessary to protect the promisee.

[2]   Tort Law

Long before there were accountants, there existed a body of law distilled from the early English cases known as torts. The word *tort* is virtually undefinable for any meaningful purpose. The most we can say is that the duties that arise from tort law are neither contractual nor consensual. They are imposed upon us by the government, either by the judiciary or the legislature. There are three different categories of tort law—negligence, intentional tort, and strict liability. Looking at tort law in its broadest sense, one can see that it is a highly dynamic, rapidly changing area of law; that the imposition of greater liability is apparent; and that strict liability, that is, liability without fault, is on the ascent.

Negligence is the most commonplace tort. It is also the dominant theory upon which an accountant's liability is predicated. Chapter 3 of this book is devoted to an analysis of the application of negligence to the accounting profession. It is also clear that to the extent that the citadel of privity is dismantled, negligence becomes an even more likely basis for accountant's liability. By permitting third parties to sue on this theory, tort liability is being immeasurably increased. Fraud is the next most important threat to the accountant. It has probably borne a heavier load in the accountant's liability area because third parties previously precluded from recovery based on negligence naturally turned to fraud and its progeny as a means of avoiding privity and of recovering from the accountant. Fraud is one of the many intentional torts that govern our behavior and create liability when we engage in them. Fraud is intentional in the sense that the party misrepresenting the facts has knowledge of the falsity of the representations that were made (scienter). To put it bluntly, the frauddoer is lying and knows it. As mentioned earlier and as we shall see in detail, this knowledge aspect of fraud has been substantially expanded at least in part to avoid the inherent subjectivity in establishing that the defendant lied. One final point about fraud and the intentional torts in general is the possible assessment of punitive damages against the wrongdoer in addition to the usual damages that may be recoverable. Except in rare cases, the damages recoverable for negligence do not include punitive damages.

One final intentional tort that should be mentioned is the intentional interference with a contractual relationship. Luring away a valued employee of another with knowledge that an enforceable contractual relationship exists can and does impose liability on the party engaging in such conduct. However, if the employment contract is terminable at will by the parties, there is no enforceable contract, hence no intentional interference with a contractual relationship.

Increased application of strict liability appears to be the destiny of tort law as it applies to society in general. Massive changes have occurred in the recent past. First, no-fault auto insurance has been adopted by the preponderance of jurisdictions as a result of legislative enactment. In addition, the judiciary in virtually every state has followed Judge Traynor's opinion, by a unanimous Supreme Court of California in *Greenman v. Yuba Power Products, Inc.*,[5] which imposed strict liability on the manufacturers of defective products. To the extent strict liability is adopted, the resort to negligence as the basis of recovery is diminished. Strict liability does not currently apply to the accountant, although liability for the tortious conduct of an accountant's servant-agent (employee) is a form of strict liability that does apply to accountants. That is, an accountant acting for the firm and acting within the scope of his employment will impose liability on the accounting firm for torts committed. This is so despite the fact that the firm itself was in no way at fault in hiring, educating, or otherwise dealing with its employee. The same rule applies to the acts of partners pursuant to the Uniform Partnership Act.

[3]   Federal and State Statutes

Serious imposition of liability both civil and criminal by federal and state statutory enactment can be realistically said to have begun with the Securities Act of 1933 and the Securities Exchange Act of 1934. This basis of liability will be explored in detail throughout the book. Again, as was seen in the tort area, liability is on the ascent. The Foreign Corrupt Practices Act of 1977, the Racketeer Influenced and Corrupt Organizations Act of 1972, and the 1976 Tax Reform Act are clear evidence of the expanding statutory liability at the federal level. In that the states have a tendency to mirror federal legislation and regulation, the overall impact of statutory liability is becoming increasingly onerous. In no small part, these changes have been in response to the great sophistication and complexity evident in the world of finance and the fact that financial disaster, particularly of a large corporation, affects not only creditors and investors but also employees and even the overall economy of our nation. Political philosophy notwithstanding, it is fair to say that federal and state statutory regulation of the accountant has increased significantly in a short period of time, and it will undoubtedly continue to do so in the future.

¶ 2.03   Legal Implications of Failure to Perform These Duties

The previously described sources of an accountant's legal duties are accompanied by a corresponding right in the party or parties to whom the duty is owed. The breach of the duty may result from the acts of the defendant-accountant or from the omission to perform acts that the law requires. A common example of the use of this approach, and its widespread applicability, may be taken from federal securities law, which talks in terms of "false statements and omissions."

---

[5] 59 Cal.2d 57 (1962).

[1]   Breach of Contract

The state's judge-made common law is the source of this type of liability. Failure of an accountant to perform at all an agreed-to undertaking, delegation of the accountant's duty to perform to another which results in a material variance of the performance, and the negligent performance of the undertaking are all common examples of an accountant's breach of the contract. There is an obvious overlap between contract law and the tort of negligence. A negligent performance of the contractual obligation constitutes a breach of contract and is actionable under contract law in a lawsuit brought by the accountant's client. There is an implied promise that the engagement will be performed in a non-negligent manner. At the same time, the negligent conduct gives rise to a separate cause of action based upon negligence which may be asserted by the client. Under modern pleading statutes both would be alleged. Of course, there will be only one recovery. Sometimes one theory applies and not the other. For example, the total failure to perform would constitute a breach of contract, but would probably not be actionable under tort law. In addition, there may be a substantive or procedural difference that makes one theory the only theory available. This would be the case where the statute of limitations bars recovery in tort but still permits the case to proceed based upon the longer statute applicable to causes of action for breach of contract. From a practical standpoint, the overlap is nearly total and the end result for the victorious plaintiff, the amount of damages, will be the same. Thus, the distinction is largely a matter of form rather than substance. However, the negligence theory is clearly the favorite basis for recovery. One plausible explanation is that it places the defendant-accountant in a less favorable position in the eyes of the trier of fact, particularly with the jury since the theory is based upon fault. This book is a testament to the favored position that negligence has attained in the minds of plaintiffs *and their attorneys*. You will soon see how many cases are negligence cases as contrasted with breach of contract.

[2]   Negligence and Fraud

It is these two bases of accountant's liability that are the primary source of the accountant's legal problems. Both common law and statutory law use negligence and fraud as the primary devices to police the accountant's performance. This is also the case whether state or federal law is applicable. Furthermore, as you will see, the substantive law applicable to civil fraud and criminal fraud are basically the same. Failure to meet the negligence standard of care or engaging in fraud will result in a breach of the duty owed to the client, and in all probability to non-client third parties as well. As the privity defense diminishes, third-party liability expands. The first step in solving the liability problem is an awareness of it and of its dimensions. The second is the study of the liability phenomenon and the third is the acquisition of sufficient knowledge to at least blunt its impact. This book is devoted to those ends.

[3]   Strict Liability

It is readily apparent that such a basis of liability places the defendant in the position of a guarantor of his conduct or performance. If things go wrong, the defendant will invariably be called upon to respond in damages. The imposition of such liability upon accountants is frightening to contemplate. However, no court has held or even suggested that strict liability is applicable to accountants. In *Rosenbaum v. Adler* (see ¶ 3.04, *infra*) the Supreme Court of New Jersey summarizes the discussion of the possible application of strict liability to doctors and dentists, quoting from another New Jersey case. The court stated that:

> [D]octors and dentists should not be held to a duty of strict liability because they furnish services essential to society that are so necessarily and intimately related to public health that their obligation ought to be expressed in a duty to exercise reasonable competence and care to their patients; that the importance of these services "outweighs in the (policy) scale any need for imposition . . . of the rules of strict liability in tort."

CHAPTER 3

LIABILITY FOR NEGLIGENCE

¶ 3.01 Negligence in General

We, including accountants, are all tortfeasors. Every time we fail to live up to the standard of "the reasonably prudent person" and as a result harm another person or his or her property or cause economic loss, we have engaged in tortious conduct, that is, negligence. Negligence is one branch of the overall law of torts. The other branches are intentional torts, such as deceit or fraud, and strict liability. *Tort law* is a difficult concept to define, and many legal scholars suggest that a meaningful definition of the term is impossible. One attempt would involve us in a negative definition: tort law deals with the imposition of civil sanctions in situations that are not covered by the law of contracts. Another attempt would stress that tort law determines whether or not a loss suffered by one member of society should be borne by that person or placed on someone else. There is nothing consensual about tort liability; frequently the two persons involved may never have seen or heard of one another before the loss occurred.

The basic question that the law of negligence is intended to answer is: Who should bear the loss caused by an unintentional injury, one that the defendant neither intended nor desired to have happen? In answering this question, the tort of negligence uses "fault" as the basis for allocating the loss between the injured party and the defendant. It follows that if the defendant can establish that he was *not legally at fault*, then he was not negligent and therefore will not be liable for the damages that that person's conduct caused. In ascertaining whether the defendant is at fault, the courts measure the defendant's conduct against what a reasonably prudent person would have done under the circumstances. But, just as there is no Santa Claus, there is no real "reasonably prudent person," or reasonably prudent accountant for that matter. Since there is no such person, but merely a hypothetical "reasonably prudent person," application of this yardstick to the facts of the particular case and deciding what conduct is negligent is often a difficult task, as we shall see. The reasonably prudent person's characteristics in general include his personal physical attributes, normal intelligence and mental capacity, normal perception and memory, and a minimum of experience and information common to the community. In addition, Dean Prosser, the leading commentator on torts, adds a final attribute, namely: "such superior skill and knowledge as the actor has, or holds himself out as having, when he undertakes to act."

This last attribute can clearly be recognized as being critical to the subject at hand, since it applies to the lack of due professional care, skill, and competence by the CPA. Notice also that although "fault" is the basis for liability, negligence is not judged in the personal terms of the specific defendant but instead in terms of the reasonable person. The "reasonable person" standard is a simple and practical one. Although subjective determination of fault would be more in keeping with the ethical basis of the doctrine, it is impractical to investigate the strengths, weaknesses, and idiosyncrasies of each and every defendant. Although potentially unfair to those defendants who do not measure up to the standard of the reasonable person, the objective approach has the merit of uniformity and ease of application.

There are two practical factors that substantially reduce the chances of liability being imposed for negligence, even if someone is harmed as a result of one's negligent conduct. The first is that in Anglo-American jurisprudence, the plaintiff invariably has the burden of proof. (Although, as we shall see shortly, there is a major departure from this basic proposition as it applies to accountants under the Securities Act of 1933.) The burden of proof in a civil case that must be met by the plaintiff, simply stated, is that he or she must persuade the trier of fact that the allegations "are more probably true than not true." Add to this basic problem of proof the fact that the plaintiff must bear the cost of litigation, and you can see there are some significant hurdles to overcome, even assuming negligence.

On the other hand, juries are said to be pro-plaintiff, at least in negligence cases, and it is often asserted that juries give the benefit of doubt to the plaintiff if there is a wealthy defendant, such as a major corporation or a prestigious accounting firm, or if insurance protection is suspected by the jury. Juries are also known to be generous to plaintiffs, especially with other people's money. Although jury behavior is not law, its practical importance from a judicial-process standpoint is obvious. In this connection, consider the following judicial observations regarding jury behavior:

Escola v. Coca Cola Bottling Co. of Fresno
24 Cal.2d 453, 150 P.2d 436 (1944)

TRAYNOR, Judge.

I concur in the judgment, but I believe the manufacturer's negligence should no longer be singled out as the basis of a plaintiff's right to recover in cases like the present one. In my opinion, it should now be recognized that a manufacturer incurs an absolute liability when an article that he has placed on the market, knowing that it is to be used without inspection, proves to have a defect that causes injury to human beings. . . .

In leaving it to the jury to decide whether the inference [of negligence raised by *res* *ipsa loquitur*, the thing or event speaks for itself without the necessity of further proof] has been dispelled, regardless of the evidence against it, the negligence rule approaches the rule of strict liability. It is needlessly circuitous to make negligence the basis of recovery and impose what is in reality liability without negligence. If public policy demands that a manufacturer of goods be responsible for their quality regardless of negligence there is no reason not to fix that responsibility openly.

Ahbrandi v. Helmsley
63 Misc.2d 997, 314 N.Y.S.2d 95 (1970)

YOUNGER, Judge.

Plaintiff's injuries were not trivial. I am as confident as one can be about these matters that, had the case been tried to a jury, the jury would have determined the sum of plaintiff's damages in a substantial amount, deducted a portion equivalent to the degree of his negligence, and returned a verdict for the difference. In short, as every trial lawyer knows, the jury would likely have ignored its instructions on contributory negligence and applied a standard of comparative negligence.

It would be comfortable for me simply to guess what the jury's verdict would have been and then file a one-sentence decision holding defendants liable in that amount. Comfortable but false. My duty is to apply the law as I understand it, and I do not understand that, no matter what a jury might do, a judge may pretend to make a decision on the basis of contributory negligence while actually deciding on comparative negligence.

Seffert v. Los Angeles Transit Lines
California Supreme Court (1961)
56 Cal.2d 498, 394 P.2d 337, 15 Cal.
Rptr. 161

PETERS, Judge.

Defendants appeal from a judgment for plaintiff for $187,903.75 entered on a jury verdict. Their motion for a new trial for errors of law and excessiveness of damages was denied.

. . .

The judgment appealed from is affirmed.
GIBSON, Circuit Judge, WHITE, Judge, and DOOLING, Judge, concurred.

TRAYNOR, Judge.—I dissent.

[I]t is my opinion that the award of $134,000 for pain and suffering is so excessive as to indicate that it was prompted by passion, prejudice, whim, or caprice.

Before the accident plaintiff was employed as a file clerk at a salary of $375 a month. At the time of the trial she had returned to her job at the same salary and her foot had healed sufficiently for her to walk.

Finally, an attorney will usually be available on a contingent-fee basis, thereby eliminating the major cost of a lawsuit in the event the plaintiff loses. This is also true in the case of a class action where the fee is shared by parties participating in the suit or paid by the losing party-defendant if the plaintiff wins. All of this is neither new nor particularly startling. There is some belief among accountants that they are being singled out for increased liability. Such would not appear to be a justifiable conclusion. Certainly manufacturers of products that have been defectively manufactured and that cause bodily harm have much more severe liability problems. They are strictly liable for defectively manufactured products, that is, they are liable without fault. Other professionals, such as lawyers and doctors in particular, are also facing expanded liability.[1] No court has applied the strict liability standard to such professionals, including accountants.

---

[1] As indicated previously strict liability has not been applied to doctors or dentists. However, liability for malpractices applicable to other professionals has at least kept abreast with accountants.

[1]   Elements of a Cause of Action

In order for a plaintiff to win a case based upon the tort of negligence, he must plead and prove the elements or requirements necessary to state a cause of action. Dean Prosser provides an excellent summation[2]:

> Negligence, as we shall see, is simply one kind of conduct. But a cause of action founded upon negligence, from which liability will follow, requires more than conduct. The traditional formula for the elements necessary to such a cause of action may be stated briefly as follows:
>
> 1.   A duty, or obligation, recognized by the law, requiring the actor to conform to a certain standard of conduct, for the protection of others against unreasonable risks.
>
> 2.   A failure on his part to conform to the standard required. These two elements go to make up what the courts usually have called negligence; but the term quite frequently is applied to the second alone. Thus it may be said that the defendant was negligent, but is not liable because he was under no duty to the plaintiff not to be.
>
> 3.   A reasonable close causal connection between the conduct and the resulting injury. This is what is commonly known as "legal cause," or "proximate cause."
>
> 4.   Actual loss or damage resulting to the interests of another.

[2]   Standard of Care

No matter what the standard of care that a person in general, or an accountant in particular, is obligated to attain in order to avoid negligent conduct, it is articulated in a highly generalized and imprecise manner. As previously discussed, the requisite test to be applied to the defendant's conduct is phrased in terms of the care that a "reasonably prudent person" would exercise under the circumstances. It is sometimes frustrating for the orderly and conscientious accounting student or practitioner who seeks certainty in the law to deal with this imprecise standard. The only consolation is that it is not your lack of intelligence, but rather the "nature of the beast" that causes the difficulty. But could the standard be drafted in any other way and still be applicable to the myriad of activities and conduct we collectively engage in? Undoubtedly, it was with this problem in mind that Judge Learned Hand attempted to place the elusive concept of negligence in better perspective with the now classic language of the *Carroll Towing* case. Obviously, the formula is not a panacea; it does not purport to answer any question; rather, it is mainly useful in framing the questions.

United States v. Carroll Towing Co.
159 F.2d 169 (2d Cir. 1947)

[Plaintiff's barge was cast adrift from its moorings through the negligence of defendant corporation's servants, for whose acts it is legally responsible. The barge ultimately sank but the trial judge refused to award the plaintiff full damages for the sinking on the ground that the plaintiff had been negligent in not having on board the barge at all times a

---

[2] Prosser, *Torts* (St. Paul, MN: West Publishing, 4th Ed., 1971), p. 143.

custodian who would have been able to minimize the damage after the barge was cut loose.]

LEARNED HAND, Judge.

. . . It appears from the foregoing review that there is no general rule to determine when the absence of a bargee or other attendant will make the owner of the barge liable for injuries to other vessels if she breaks away from her moorings. However, in any cases where he would be so liable for injuries to others, obviously he must reduce his damages proportionately, if the injury is to his own barge. It becomes apparent why there can be no such general rule, when we consider the grounds for such a liability. Since there are occasions when every vessel will break from her moorings, and, since, if she does, she becomes a menace to those about her, the owner's duty, as in other similar situations, to provide against resulting injuries is a function of three variables: (1) the probability that she will break away; (2) the gravity of the resulting injury, if she does; (3) the burden of adequate precautions. Possibly it serves to bring this notion into relief to state it in algebraic terms: if the probability be called P; the injury L; and the burden B; liability depends upon whether B is less than L multiplied by P; *i.e.*, whether B [is less than] PL. Applied to the situation at bar, the likelihood that a barge will break from her fasts, and the damage she will do, vary with the place and time; for example, if a storm threatens, the danger is greater; so it is, if she is in a crowded harbor where moored barges are constantly being shifted about. On the other hand, the barge must not be the bargee's prison, even though he lives aboard; he must go ashore at times. . . . We hold that it is not in all cases a sufficient answer to a bargee's absence without excuse, during working hours, that he has properly made fast his barge to a pier, when he leaves her. In the case at bar the bargee left at five o'clock on the afternoon of January 3rd, and the flotilla broke away at about two o'clock in the afternoon of the following day, twenty-one hours afterwards. The bargee had been away all the time, and we hold that his fabricated story was affirmative evidence that he had no excuse for his absence. At the locus in quo— especially during the short January days and in the full tide of war activity—barges were being constantly "drilled" in and out. Certainly it was not beyond reasonable expectation that, with the inevitable haste and bustle, the work might not be done with adequate care. In such circumstances we hold—and that is all that we do hold—that it was a fair requirement that the Conners Company should have a bargee aboard (unless he had some excuse for his absence), during the working hours of daylight.

[Affirmed as to reduce damage award to plaintiff, based on a unique admiralty damage rule that closely resembles the comparative negligence doctrine which is discussed *infra*.]

Nevertheless, these are some types of conduct or activities to which a more precise definition may be applicable. *The T.J. Hooper* case that follows, also by Judge Hand, is concerned with an attempt by the defendant to define negligence in terms of "the custom of the industry."

The T.J. Hooper
60 F.2d 737 (2d Cir. 1932)

[Suit by cargo owners for loss of cargo being carried on barges being towed by the tugs Hooper and Montrose on a trip from Norfolk, Virginia, to New York. The weather was fair without ominous symptoms as the tows passed the Delaware breakwater. Serious trouble did not arise until the tugs were some 60–70 miles to the north, when the winds freshened and rose to a gale. A few hours later a barge on the Hooper's tow was out of hand and leaking. Leaks were soon discovered on another barge. Both eventually sank. The trial court found that had the tug masters received the weather forecasts of an approaching storm by radio while still along the Virginia shore they would not have set out to sea. The trial court held for the cargo owners.

After stating the facts above, Judge LEARNED HAND continued:]

They did not [receive weather reports], because their private radio receiving sets, which were on board, were not in working order. These belonged to them personally, and were partly a toy, partly a part of the equipment, but neither furnished by the owner, nor supervised by it. It is not fair to say that there was a general custom among the coastwise carriers to so equip their tugs. One line alone did it: as for the rest, they relied upon their crews, so far as they can be said to have relied at all. An adequate receiving set suitable for a coastwise tug can now be got at small cost and is reasonably reliable if kept up; obviously it is a source of great protection to their tows. Twice every day they can receive these predictions, based upon the widest possible information, available to every vessel within two or three hundred miles and more. Such a set is the ears of the tug to catch the spoken word, just as the master's binoculars are her eyes to see a storm signal ashore. Whatever may be said as to other vessels, tugs towing heavy coal laden barges, strung out for half a mile, have little power to manoeuvre, and do not, as this case proves, expose themselves to weather which would not turn back stauncher craft. They can have at hand protection against dangers of which they can learn in no other way.

Is it then a final answer that the business had not yet generally adopted receiving sets? There are, no doubt, cases where courts seem to make the general practice of the calling the standard of proper diligence; we have indeed given some currency to the notion ourselves. Indeed in most cases reasonable prudence is in fact common prudence; but strictly it is never its measure; a whole calling may have unduly lagged in the adoption of new and available devices. It never may set its own tests, however persuasive be its usages. Courts must in the end say what is required; there are precautions so imperative that even their universal disregard will not excuse their omission. But here there was no custom at all as to receiving sets; some had them, some did not; the most that can be urged is that they had not yet become general. Certainly in such a case we need not pause; when some have thought a device necessary, at least we may say that they were right, and the others too slack.

[Decree affirmed.]

Why did the defendant fail in its reliance on the legal defense that it had complied with the custom of the industry? Suppose you fail to meet the threshold level of the industry, are you negligent? Is not the custom of the industry at least of some evidentiary weight in deciding whether a given defendant is negligent? Why should the custom of the industry not be determinative in all cases? It surely would provide greater certainty.

The analogy to the custom of the industry in the world of professional accounting is found in such pronouncements as generally accepted accounting principles (GAAP) and generally accepted auditing standards (GAAS). But just as the custom of the industry is not always determinative of the care that a member of a given industry must exercise, so also the standards set by the accounting profession may be deemed inadequate. You have all heard of the famous McKesson and Robbins management fraud case of 1933, which involved $19 million of fictitious inventory and receivables out of $87 million of total assets. At the time of the fraud, auditing standards did not require observation of inventories or confirmation of receivables. In fact, almost on the eve of the revelation in the McKesson and Robbins case, the New York Society of CPAs adopted a resolution giving the auditor the right to rely upon management representations as to physical quantities and valuation of inventories. This being the case, you can readily appreciate that the custom of the industry cannot be taken as conclusive in determining reasonableness. Also consider the following excerpt from *R.I. Hospital Trust v. Swartz*[3]:

> Our conclusions with respect to the report and disclosure are reinforced by reference to industry standards of what should have been done in these circumstances. While industry standards may not always be the maximum test of liability, certainly they should be deemed the minimum standard by which liability should be determined. Brief references to American Institute of Certified Public Accountants, Statements on Auditing Procedure No. 33 (1963) are sufficient to prove the point.

And as stated by the Seventh Circuit Court in the *Hochfelder* case[4]:

> We come then to the fundamental issue in this lawsuit: Whether the uncontroverted evidence reveals that Ernst & Ernst conducted its audits with all due care and in accordance with generally accepted auditing standards. Plaintiffs contend that Ernst & Ernst negligently failed to detect and report an alleged lack of adequate internal accounting controls of First Securities which resulted from Nay's "mail rule" and that Ernst & Ernst thereby failed to meet generally accepted auditing standards. [See Chapter 4, for the facts and a more complete version of the opinion.]
>
> It is clear that as part of Ernst & Ernst's duty to conduct its audit in accordance with generally accepted auditing standards it was incumbent on it to investigate First Securities' system of internal accounting controls.

Standards of Field Work

> There is to be a proper study and evaluation of the existing internal control as a basis for reliance thereon and for the determination of the resultant extent of the tests to which auditing procedures are to be restricted.

> [The court subsequently considered another alleged duty of Ernst & Ernst, namely to investigate whether First Securities was in compliance with N.A.S.D. rules. In finding that this duty was not required, the court made the following observations:]

> And, although the defendant correctly states that generally accepted auditing standards do not ordinarily require such investigation, we do not find that entirely compelling. The teaching of The T.J. Hooper, 60 F.2d 737 (2d Cir. 1932), is not lost to us for we recognize that we are not constrained to accept faulty standards of practice otherwise generally accepted in an industry or profession. Moreover, the potential for imposition of liability on a broker or dealer for noncompliance with N.A.S.D. rules would seem to undermine the auditor's ability to represent that the financial statements fairly reflect the financial position of the broker or dealer unless some sort of inquiry were made into compliance with those rules.
>
> To countenance the duty of inquiry advocated by plaintiffs, however, would in our judgment be inappropriate. To direct full examination for compliance with the various rules of all the self-regulatory organizations to which a broker or dealer might belong would be to impose a burden of inquiry—otherwise not demanded by contract, statutory law, or professional practices—of indefinable proportions which arguably could never effectively and completely be implemented. We cannot subscribe to a situation whereby the accountant has the burden of an investigation which is unascertainable and everchanging.

---

[3] 455 F.2d 847, 852 (4th Cir. 1972).
[4] *Hochfelder v. Ernst & Ernst*, 503 F.2d 1100, 1109, 1113 (7th Cir. 1974).

Perhaps in no other case besides *United States v. Simon*[5] is the custom of the industry standard considered and found by the court to be not enough to exonerate the defendants, here Simon and the members of his staff. Although it is a criminal fraud case, it is obvious that the defendants' following of GAAP and GAAS should logically afford them with a highly persuasive or nearly conclusive argument in favor of a finding that their conduct was not criminal. However, the court did not do so; instead it stated:

> Defendants asked for two instructions which, in substance, would have told the jury that a defendant could be found guilty only if, according to generally accepted accounting principles, the financial statements as a whole did not fairly present the financial condition of Continental at September 30, 1962, and then only if his departure from accepted standards was due to willful disregard of those standards with knowledge of the falsity of the statements and an intent to deceive. The judge declined to give these instructions. Dealing with the subject in the course of his charge, he said that the "critical test" was whether the financial statements as a whole "fairly presented the financial position of Continental as of September 30, 1962, and whether it accurately reported the operations for fiscal 1962." If they did not, the basic issue became whether defendants acted in good faith. Proof of compliance with generally accepted standards was "evidence which may be very persuasive but not necessarily conclusive that he acted in good faith, and that the facts as certified were not materially false or misleading."
>
> Generally accepted accounting principles instruct an accountant what to do in the usual case where he has no reason to doubt that the affairs of the corporation are being honestly conducted. Once he has reason to believe that this basic assumption is false, an entirely different situation confronts him. Then, as the Lybrand firm stated in its letter accepting the Continental engagement, he must "extend his procedures to determine whether or not such suspicions are justified." If as a result of such an extension or, as here, without it, he finds his suspicions to be confirmed, full disclosure must be the rule, unless he had made sure the wrong has been righted and procedures to avoid a repetition have been established. At least this must be true when the dishonesty he has discovered is not some minor peccadillo but a diversion so large as to imperil if not destroy the very solvency of the enterprise.

¶ 3.02   Federal Securities Regulation: Statutory Gloss

[1]   Historical Setting

To quote Oliver Wendell Holmes on the subject of understanding law, "A page of history is worth a pound of logic." Let us start with a page of 18th-century English history:

> The mania for speculation broke loose. Stock soared in three months from 128 to 300, and within a few months more to 500. Amid the resounding cries of jobbers and speculators a multitude of companies, some genuine and some bogus, was hatched. By June 1721 the South Sea stock stood at 1050. Robert Walpole himself had the luck to make a handsome

---

[5] *United States v. Simon*, 425 F.2d 796 (2d Cir. 1969), *cert. denied*, 397 U.S. 1006. (1970).

profit on his quiet investments. At every coffeehouse in London men and women were investing their savings in any enterprise that would take their money. There was no limit to the credulity of the public. One promoter floated a company to manufacture an invention known as Puckle's Machine Gun, "which was to discharge round and square cannon-balls and bullets and make a total revolution in the art of war," the round missiles being intended for use against Christians and the square against the Turk. Other promoters invited subscriptions for making salt water fresh, for constructing a wheel of perpetual motion, for importing large jackasses from Spain to improve the breed of English mules, and the boldest of all was the advertisement for "a company for carrying on an undertaking of Great Advantage, but no one to know what it is." This amiable swindler set up a shop in Cornhill to receive subscriptions. His office was besieged by eager investors, and after collecting £2,000 in cash he prudently absconded.[6]

It's fascinating reading, isn't it? It shows in light of subsequent events how history often repeats itself. It tells us something about human nature and the credulity of human beings. Finally, it reveals that society may sometimes need protection from its own foibles as well as from the ever-present predatory elements of society.

Coming now to the 20th century and the Great Depression of 1929, the congressional hearings on the stock market collapse of 1929 revealed once again flagrant instances of misrepresentation in the initial sale of securities. They also revealed widespread subsequent price manipulation, the existence of financial marketplaces that could often best be described as "dens of thieves," and flagrant misuse of office by certain officers and directors. The situation in 1929 was probably as bad as that described by Churchill. Congress reacted forcefully. It initially enacted two landmark pieces of legislation—the Securities Act of 1933 (1933 Act) and the Securities Exchange Act of 1934 (1934 Act). These Acts were followed by subsequent enactments and amendments, but they were of a less pervasive nature. The 1934 Act created the Securities and Exchange Commission (SEC), which was to administer these laws. In this connection, the SEC was granted broad power to promulgate various implementing rules, of which Rule 10b-5 is the most famous. This legislation replaced to a major extent the then modest and ineffective state judicial and legislative efforts to protect the public in securities dealings.

Congress's efforts in meeting this challenge of restoring at least a semblance of order and confidence in the securities and financial markets have proven to be successful. Serious damage had taken place and accountants were found to have contributed to the debacle. Nevertheless Congress chose to continue to rely in no small part upon the accounting profession to help solve the dilemma. Audited financial statements are crucial to compliance with the 1933 and 1934 Acts. However, in that the profession had been found wanting in many respects prior to the crash of 1929, and in that something more drastic was believed necessary in order to provide protection for the investor, Congress therefore made major changes regarding accountants' liability under the federal Securities Acts. Chief among these changes are those contained in the 1933 Act.

---

[6] Winston S. Churchill, *A History of the English Speaking Peoples*, Vol. III (New York: Dodd Mead, 1956), pp. 110–111.

[2]   Principal Negligence Provisions of the Securities Act of 1933 Applicable to Accountants

Prohibitions Relating to Interstate Commerce and the Mails

SECTION 5. **(a)** Unless a registration statement is in effect as to a security, it shall be unlawful for any person, directly or indirectly—

(1) to make use of any means or instruments of transportation or communication in interstate commerce or of the mails to sell such security through the use or medium of any prospectus or otherwise; or

(2) to carry or cause to be carried through the mails or in interstate commerce, by any means or instruments of transportation, any such security for the purpose of sale or for delivery after sale.

(b) It shall be unlawful for any person, directly or indirectly—

(1) to make use of any means or instruments of transportation or communication in interstate commerce or of the mails to carry or transmit any prospectus relating to any security with respect to which a registration statement has been filed under this title, unless such prospectus meets the requirements of section 10; or

(2) to carry or cause to be carried through the mails or in interstate commerce any such security for the purpose of sale or for delivery after sale, unless accompanied or preceded by a prospectus that meets the requirements of subsection (a) of section 10.

(c) It shall be unlawful for any person, directly or indirectly, to make use of any means or instruments of transportation or communication in interstate commerce or of the mails to offer to sell or offer to buy through the use or medium of any prospectus or otherwise any security, unless a registration statement has been filed as to such security, or while the registration statement is the subject of a refusal order or stop order or (prior to the effective date of the registration statement) any public proceeding or examination under section 8.

Information Required in Registration Statement

SECTION 7. The registration statement, when relating to a security other than a security issued by a foreign government, or political subdivision thereof, shall contain the information, and be accompanied by the documents, specified in Schedule A. [Schedule A requires audited financial statements.]

Civil Liabilities on Account of False Registration Statement

SECTION 11. **(a)** In case any part of the registration statement, when such part became effective, contained an untrue statement of a material fact or omitted to state a material fact required to be stated therein or necessary to make the statements therein not misleading, any person acquiring such security (unless it is proved that at the time of such acquisition he knew of such untruth or omission) may, either at law or in equity, in any court of competent jurisdiction, sue—

(1) every person who signed the registration statement;

(2) every person who was a director of (or person performing similar functions) or partner in, the issuer at the time of the filing of the part of the registration statement with respect to which his liability is asserted;

(3) every person who, with his consent is named in the registration statement as being or about to become a director, person performing similar functions, or partner;

(4) every accountant, engineer, or appraiser, or any person whose profession gives authority to a statement made by him, who has with his consent been named as having prepared or certified any part of the registration statement, or as having prepared or certified any report or valuation which is used in connection with the registration statement, with respect to the statement in such registration statement, report, or valuation,

which purports to have been prepared or certified by him;

(5) every underwriter with respect to such security.

If such person acquired the security after the issuer has made generally available to its security holders an earning statement covering a period of at least twelve months beginning after the effective date of the registration statement, then the right of recovery under this subsection shall be conditioned on proof that such person acquired the security relying upon such untrue statement in the registration statement or relying upon the registration statement and not knowing of such omission, *but such reliance may be established without proof of the reading of the registration statement by such person* [emphasis added].

(b) Notwithstanding the provisions of subsection (a) no person, other than the issuer, shall be liable as provided therein who shall sustain the burden of proof—

(3) that . . .

(B) As regards any part of the registration statement purporting to be made upon his authority as an expert . . . (i) he had, after reasonable investigation, reasonable ground to believe and did believe, at the time such part of the registration statement became effective, that the statements therein were true and that there was no omission to state a material fact required to be stated therein or necessary to make the statements therein not misleading, or (ii) such part of the reg-

istration statement did not fairly represent his statement as an expert.

(c) In determining, for the purpose of paragraph (3) of subsection (b) of this section, what constitutes reasonable investigation and reasonable ground for belief, the standard of reasonableness shall be that required of a prudent man in the management of his own property.

(e) The suit authorized under subsection (a) may be to recover such damages as shall represent the difference between the amount paid for the security (not exceeding the price at which the security was offered to the public) and (1) the value thereof as of the time such suit was brought, or (2) the price at which such security shall have been disposed of in the market before suit, or (3) the price at which such security shall have been disposed of after suit but before judgment if such damages shall be less than the damages representing the difference between the amount paid for the security (not exceeding the price at which the security was offered to the public) and the value thereof as of the time such suit was brought: Provided, that if the defendant proves that any portion or all of such damages represents other than the depreciation in value of such security resulting from such part of the registration statement, with respect to which his liability is asserted, not being true or omitting to state a material fact required to be stated therein or necessary to make the statements not misleading, such portion or all such damages shall not be recoverable.

[3]   Comment and Discussion on the Securities Act of 1933

[a]   Privity.   Any person acquiring securities described in a registration statement may sue for faud *or negligence* an accountant who attaches an auditor's certificate to financial statements that contain a false statement or omission, even though he is neither the accountant's client nor known as the intended beneficiary of the accountant's engagement. Thus the 1933 Act substantially broadens the accountant's liability to third parties for negligence. It is obvious that this statutory abolition of privity in respect to public offerings of securities covers a vast number of persons who were, as third parties, precluded from having the standing to sue accountants for negligence as a result of the *Ultramares v. Touche* decision. As you will recall from Chapter 1, a fundamental policy factor supporting the decision in *Ultramares* was the fear or reluctance by the court to "expose accountants to a liability in an indeterminate amount for an indeterminate time to an *indeterminate class*" (emphasis added). Congress clearly rejected this rationale. Thus a substantial class of people previously excluded by privity from suing the accountant for negligence are now able to do so without question if the 1933 Act applies.

[b]   Burden of Proof.   The 1933 Act places upon the accountant-defendant the burden of establishing freedom from negligence (i.e., the exercise of due diligence) in connection with an alleged false statement or misleading omission in financial statements submitted in connection with the registration of securities. This runs contra to the fundamental proposition prevailing in Anglo-American law that the plaintiff has the burden of proving his or her case in order to obtain relief. From a practical viewpoint, this shifting of the burden of proof is a most significant change. Establishing by the preponderance of evidence that one has not engaged in tortious conduct is a lot tougher to achieve than is the requirement merely to rebut a claim by the plaintiff after plaintiff has attempted to meet this burden of proof. To reiterate, there is an old saying in the law that "he who has the burden of proof loses more often than not."

[c]   Materiality.   This aspect of the 1933 Act is discussed in the *Escott v. BarChris* case § 3.03 *infra*. Materiality is a difficult concept to pin down and much will depend on the particular facts and circumstances of the case. However, the court does provide us with the following test:

> Early in the history of the Act, a definition of materiality was given in Matter of Charles A. Howard, 1 S.E.C. 6, 8 (1934), which is still valid today. A material fact was there defined as:
>
> > "a fact which if it had been correctly stated or disclosed would have deterred or tended to deter the average prudent investor from purchasing the securities in question."
>
> •   •   •
>
> The average prudent investor is not concerned with minor inaccuracies or with errors as to matters which are of no interest to him. The facts which tend to deter him from purchasing a security are facts which have an important bearing upon the nature or condition of the issuing corporation or its business.

[d]   Reliance.   Although ignorance is typically *not* bliss in the eye of the law, there are some notable exceptions (e.g., the good faith requirement for holding in due course a negotiable instrument). The 1933 Act has also adopted the "ignorance is bliss" approach for the question of investor reliance. The question is not whether the investor did in fact rely upon the audited financial statements or omissions at the time of the purchase of the registered stock. Instead, to defeat an investor's claim it must be shown that he had knowledge of the falsity or omission. Thus, if the investor never received a copy of the prospectus or if, having received it, immediately threw it in the wastebasket, the investor's reliance is unimpeachable. Since this is what typically happens, the use of the reliance requirement defensively is effectively eliminated except in the rare case where it can be proved that the plaintiff actually was aware of the alleged falsity or omission in the prospectus.

The changes contained in the 1933 Act's requirements, taken as a whole, certainly represent a drastic departure from common law negligence. Liability for negligence under the 1933 Act as a practical matter borders on strict liability. Apparently the only viable approach for the defendant-accountant to avoid liability is to establish that the defendant exercised due diligence in all phases of the undertaking, from the inception to the effective date.

[e] Post Certification Date Duty to Review Under the Securities Act of 1933—S-1 Review. The 1933 Act also imposed upon the accountant an extension of the duty to investigate by extending responsibility for material developments affecting the audited financials beyond the traditional date as of the certification. Instead the 1933 Act requires that the audited financials be substantially unchanged as of the effective date of the offering of the securities. In effect this requirement, which is contained in Section 8 of the Act, mandates additional surveillance of the audited company and takes the form of an S-1 Review. Not only may liability be predicated on the fact that the audit itself was negligently performed, but also the performance of the subsequent review of events which occurred up to the effective date and the release of the securities to the public may result in liability for negligence. Simply put, the audited financials must remain meaningful as of the time of the offering. Thus the accountant must review on the eve of the offering. This aspect of the 1933 Act is discussed extensively in *Escott v. BarChris Construction Corp.*, which follows. In effect, this provides plaintiffs with an additional basis upon which to predicate liability against the accountant.

¶ 3.03   *Escott v. BarChris*

The *Escott v. BarChris* case which follows is not only the leading case in liability for negligence under the 1933 Act, but also is a remarkable case in many respects. First, as you will see (and also in many of the privity cases that follow), many of the issues litigated were being considered in 1968 for the first time, some 35 years after adoption of the 1933 Act. In addition, the opinion contains an almost text-like treatment of the applicable accounting and law. The full opinion is in excess of 55 pages and cutting it to manageable size was most difficult since the facts of the case were largely applicable to all of the parties, including Peat, Marwick & Mitchell. The case contains a discussion of the question of materiality, the due diligence defense, causality, the S-1 Review, and other possible defenses. Even as edited, it is a long case; however, it is "the" case and there is much to be learned from it.

[1] Seminal Case

Escott v. BarChris Construction Corp.
United States District Court
283 F. Supp. 613
SDNY (1968)

MCLEAN, District Judge.

This is an action by purchasers of 5½ per cent convertible subordinated fifteen year debentures of BarChris Construction Corporation (BarChris). Plaintiffs purport to sue on their own behalf and "on behalf of all other and present and former holders" of the debentures. When the action was begun on October 25, 1962, there were nine plaintiffs. Others were subsequently permitted to intervene. At the time of the trial, there were over sixty.

The action is brought under Section 11 of the Securities Act of 1933 (15 U.S.C. § 77k). Plaintiffs allege that the registration statement with respect to these debentures filed with the Securities and Exchange Commission, which became effective on May 16, 1961, contained material false statements and material omissions.

Defendants fall into three categories: (1) the persons who signed the registration statement; (2) the underwriters, consisting of eight investment banking firms, led by Drexel & Co. (Drexel); and (3) BarChris's auditors, Peat, Marwick, Mitchell & Co. (Peat, Marwick).

• • •

Defendants, in addition to denying that the registration statement was false, have pleaded the defenses open to them under Section 11 of the Act, plus certain additional defenses, including the statute of limitations.

• • •

On the main issue of liability, the questions to be decided are (1) did the registration statement contain false statements of fact, or did it omit to state facts which should have been stated in order to prevent it from being misleading; (2) if so, were the facts which were falsely stated or omitted "material" within the meaning of the Act; (3) if so, have de-

fendants established their affirmative defenses?

Before discussing these questions, some background facts should be mentioned. At the time relevant here, BarChris was engaged primarily in the construction of bowling alleys, somewhat euphemistically referred to as "bowling centers." These were rather elaborate affairs. They contained not only a number of alleys or "lanes," but also, in most cases, bar and restaurant facilities.

• • •

The introduction of automatic pin setting machines in 1952 gave a marked stimulus to bowling. It rapidly became a popular sport, with the result that "bowling centers" began to appear throughout the country in rapidly increasing numbers. BarChris benefited from this increased interest in bowling. Its construction operations expanded rapidly. It is estimated that in 1960 BarChris installed approximately three per cent of all lanes built in the United States. It was thus a significant factor in the industry, although two large established companies, American Machine & Foundry Company and Brunswick, were much larger factors. These two companies manufactured bowling equipment, which BarChris did not. They also built most of the bowling alleys, 97 per cent of the total, according to some of the testimony.

BarChris's sales increased dramatically from 1956 to 1960. According to the prospectus, net sales, in round figures, in 1956 were some $800,000, in 1957 $1,300,000, in 1958 $1,700,000. In 1959 they increased to over $3,300,000, and by 1960 they had leaped to over $9,165,000.[1]

---

[1] Plaintiffs attack the accuracy of this figure. Their claim in this respect will be considered hereinafter.

For some years the business had exceeded the managerial capacity of its founders [Vitolo and Pugliese]. . . . Neither was equipped to handle financial matters.

Rather early in their career they enlisted the aid of Russo, who was trained as an accountant. He first joined them in the days of the partnership, left for a time, and returned as an officer and director of B & C Bowling Alley Builders, Inc. in 1958. He eventually became executive vice president of BarChris. In that capacity he handled many of the transactions which figure in this case.

In 1959 BarChris hired Kircher, a certified public accountant who had been employed by Peat, Marwick. He started as controller and became treasurer in 1960. In October of that year, another ex-Peat, Marwick employee, Trilling, succeeded Kircher as controller. At approximately the same time Birnbaum, a young attorney, was hired as house counsel. He became secretary on April 17, 1961.

In general, BarChris's method of operation was to enter into a contract with a customer, receive from him at that time a comparatively small down payment on the purchase price, and proceed to construct and equip the bowling alley. When the work was finished and the building delivered, the customer paid the balance of the contract price in notes, payable in installments over a period of years. BarChris discounted these notes with a factor and received part of their face amount in cash. The factor held back part as a reserve.

In 1960 BarChris began a practice which has been referred to throughout this case as the "alternative method of financing." In substance this was a sale and leaseback arrangement. It involved a distinction between the "interior" of a building and the building itself, i.e., the outer shell. In instances in which this method applied, BarChris would build and install what it referred to as the "interior package." Actually this amounted to constructing and installing the equipment in a building. When it was completed, it would sell the interior to a factor, James Talcott Inc. (Talcott), who would pay BarChris the full contract price therefor. The factor then proceeded to lease the interior either directly to BarChris's customer or back to a subsidiary of BarChris. In the latter case, the subsidiary in turn would lease it to the customer.

Under either financing method, BarChris was compelled to expend considerable sums in defraying the cost of construction before it received reimbursement. As a consequence, BarChris was in constant need of cash to finance its operations, a need which grew more pressing as operations expanded.

In December 1959, BarChris sold 560,000 shares of common stock to the public at $3.00 per share. This issue was underwritten by Peter Morgan & Company, one of the present defendants.

By early 1961, BarChris needed additional working capital. The proceeds of the sale of the debentures involved in this action were to be devoted, in part at least, to fill that need.

The registration statement of the debentures, in preliminary form, was filed with the Securities and Exchange Commission on March 30, 1961. A first amendment was filed on May 11 and a second on May 16. The registration statement became effective on May 16. The closing of the financing took place on May 24. On that day BarChris received the net proceeds of the financing.

By that time BarChris was experiencing difficulties in collecting amounts due from some of its customers. Some of them were in arrears in payments due to factors on their discounted notes. As time went on those difficulties increased. Although BarChris continued to build alleys in 1961 and 1962, it became increasingly apparent that the industry was overbuilt. Operators of alleys, often inadequately financed, began to fail. Precisely when the tide turned is a matter of dispute, but at any rate, it was painfully apparent in 1962.

In May of that year BarChris made an abortive attempt to raise more money by the sale of common stock. It filed with the Securities and Exchange Commission a registration statement for the stock issue which it later withdrew. In October 1962 BarChris came to the end of the road. On October 29, 1962, it filed in this court a petition for an arrangement under Chapter XI of the Bankruptcy Act. BarChris defaulted in the payment of the interest due on November 1, 1962 on the debentures.

The Debenture Registration Statement

In preparing the registration statement for the debentures, Grant acted for BarChris. He had previously represented BarChris in preparing the registration statement for the common stock issue. In connection with the sale of common stock, BarChris had issued purchase warrants. In January 1961 a second registration statement was filed in order to update the information pertaining to these warrants. Grant had prepared that statement as well.

Some of the basic information needed for the debenture registration statement was contained in the registration statements previously filed with respect to the common stock and warrants. Grant used these old registration statements as a model in preparing the new one, making the changes which he considered necessary in order to meet the new situation.

The underwriters were represented by the Philadelphia law firm of Drinker, Biddle & Reath. John A. Ballard, a member of that firm, was in charge of that work, assisted by a young associate named Stanton.

Peat, Marwick, BarChris's auditors, who had previously audited BarChris's annual balance sheet and earnings figures for 1958 and 1959, did the same for 1960. These figures were set forth in the registration statement. In addition, Peat, Marwick undertook a so-called "S-1 review," the proper scope of which is one of the matters debated here.

The registration statement in its final form contained a prospectus as well as other information. Plaintiffs' claims of falsities and omissions pertain solely to the prospectus, not to the additional data.

The prospectus contained, among other things, a description of BarChris's business, a description of its real property, some material pertaining to certain of its subsidiaries, and remarks about various other aspects of its affairs. It also contained financial information. It included a consolidated balance sheet as of December 31, 1960, with elaborate explanatory notes. These figures had been audited by Peat, Marwick. It also contained unaudited figures as to net sales, gross profit and net earnings for the first quarter ended March 31, 1961, as compared with

the similar quarter for 1960. In addition, it set forth figures as to the company's backlog of unfilled orders as of March 31, 1961, as compared with March 31, 1960, and figures as to BarChris's contingent liability, as of April 30, 1961, on customers' notes discounted and its contingent liability under the so-called alternative method of financing.

Plaintiffs challenge the accuracy of a number of these figures. They also charge that the text of the prospectus, apart from the figures, was false in a number of respects, and that material information was omitted. Each of these contentions, after eliminating duplications, will be separately considered.[2]

1960 Net Sales, Net Operating Income and Earnings per Share

The earnings figure set forth at page 4 of the prospectus shows net sales for the calendar year 1960 of $9,165,320. Plaintiffs claim that this figure was overstated by $2,525,350. They assert that it necessarily follows that the figure of $1,742,801 shown in the prospectus as net operating income for 1960, and the figure of earnings per share of $.75, were also incorrect.

The net sales figure included amounts actually billed by BarChris for alleys completed by it in 1960 and amounts considered billable, although not in fact billed, for alleys not completed but still in process at the end of the year. The latter amounts were computed by using the percentage of completion method. The fact that this method was employed was disclosed in a footnote to the earnings table on page 4 of the prospectus.

---

[2] The testimony on many subjects in this case is confused. It is scattered over some 6,500 pages of stenographic minutes without any coherent explanation all in one place. To some extent this was inevitable, in view of the number of defendants, each of whom cross-examined the witnesses, plus the fact that plaintiffs, for the most part, were compelled to prove their case out of the mouths of hostile witnesses. I have examined this material, but there is no need to recount it in great detail in this opinion. On each issue I shall state plaintiffs' contention and my findings of fact with respect to it, which are based upon all the evidence related to that issue.

Alleys in Process on December 31, 1960

[1] The greater part of the alleged overstatement of net sales is attributable to the use of the percentage of completion method. It accounts for $2,002,250 out of the total alleged overstatement of $2,525,350. Plaintiffs contend that the percentage of completion method should not have been used at all, i.e., that nothing should have been included in sales for alleys on which construction was still in progress on December 31, 1960. They say further that in any event this method was not properly applied, so that the amount included for such transactions was incorrect, even assuming that it was appropriate to include something for them.

By and large, I do not accept these contentions. The evidence shows that generally accepted accounting principles sanction the inclusion in sales for one year of part of the consideration ultimately to be received for work in progress which spreads over more than one year. Otherwise the figures would be distorted by reflecting the entire consideration in the sales for the year in which the work was finally completed. The same principle had been followed by BarChris, with Peat, Marwick's knowledge and approval, in 1959. I find that it was proper to employ it also for 1960.

I also find that, except for two specific instances hereinafter noted, this principle was correctly applied in determining the amount to be included in 1960 sales for these uncompleted jobs.

• • •

Consequently, I do not accept plaintiffs' contention in this respect.

I turn now to plaintiffs' other criticisms of the 1960 net sales figure. [The court proceeded to analyze the sales figures for five bowling alleys.]

Capitol Lanes

Capitol was also known as Heavenly Lanes. The premises were located in East Haven, Connecticut.

Heavenly Lanes was listed in the 1960 computations as a completed contract. The contract price of $330,000 was included in 1960 sales.

BarChris originally had a contract to construct Heavenly Lanes for an outside customer. Despite all the testimony on this subject, the date of the contract and the name of the customer never emerged. In any event, it is clear that that customer did not go through with the contract.

On July 29, 1960, BarChris entered into a contract with its wholly-owned subsidiary, BarChris Leasing Corporation, described in the contract as the purchaser, to build this alley. BarChris went ahead and constructed the alley and completed it before December 31, 1960. It never sold it to any outside interest. Purely as a financing mechanism, it sold the alley to Talcott, a factor, who leased it back to Capitol Lanes, Inc., a new corporation organized by BarChris in December 1960, the stock of which was owned by Sanpark Realty Corp., itself a wholly owned subsidiary of BarChris.

Capitol Lanes, Inc. operated the alley beginning in December 1960. BarChris's minutes show that BarChris contemplated its operation as early as November 22, 1960. There is no doubt that nothing should have been included in the 1960 sales figure for this alley. Consequently, the sales figure was inflated by $330,000.

• • •

Summary

[2] To recapitulate, I find that the 1960 sales figure of $9,165,320, as stated in page 4 of the prospectus, was inaccurate in that it included the following amounts which should not have been included:

Worcester	$101,200
Atlas-Bedford	47,700
Burke	25,000
Capitol	330,000
Howard Lane Annex	150,000
Total	$653,900

The total figure, instead of $9,165,320, should have been $8,511,420.

It necessarily follows that the figure for net operating income for 1960 appearing on page 4 of the prospectus was also incorrect.

The extent to which it was incorrect depends upon the extent to which the incorrect sales figure for the five alleys in question was carried into profits.

In the case of Capitol, an alley completed in 1960, the difference between its contract price and its cost was reflected in profits. This difference was $89,773. Since the alley was not sold, no profit should have been taken on it. Hence, as to this alley, profits were inflated by $89,773.

The same is true of Howard Lanes Annex. Here the sum incorrectly included in profits was $72,846.

• • •

It follows that profit, and consequently net operating income, was overstated in the following amounts:

Capitol	$ 89,773
Howard Lanes Annex	72,846
Burke	25,000
Worcester	36,280
Atlas-Bedford	22,706
Total	$246,605

The net operating income, instead of $1,742,801, should have been $1,496,196.

Since the net operating income figure was incorrect, it necessarily follows that the ultimate result of the entire table, i.e., the earnings per share figure, was incorrect. The evidence does not permit precise determination of the amount of this error. Since the net operating income figure as restated is approximately 14 per cent less than the figure stated in the prospectus, it would seem to be true, speaking roughly, that the earnings per share figure should be reduced by approximately the same percentage. To do so would produce an earnings per share figure of approximately 65¢ per share rather than 75¢.

1960 Balance Sheet

The prospectus contained a balance sheet as of December 31, 1960 of BarChris and consolidated subsidiaries. This was audited by Peat, Marwick. Plaintiffs attack its accuracy on a variety of grounds.

Current Assets

They charge that current assets were grossly overstated because several items were incorrectly classified as current. These are discussed below.

Cash

[3] Cash on hand as of December 31, 1960, as per the balance sheet, amounted to $285,482. This amount actually was on hand on that day. But plaintiffs contend, and I believe correctly, that certain rather peculiar circumstances relating to this cash balance should have been disclosed.

The evidence is that Talcott held certain reserves in the sum of $147,466.80 as security with respect to customers' notes discounted with Talcott by BarChris Financial Corporation, a wholly owned subsidiary of BarChris. The accounts of BarChris Financial Corporation were not consolidated with those of BarChris in the balance sheet, as the accounts of the other subsidiaries were. BarChris Financial Corporation was covered only by a blind reference to "Investments In (At Equity) And Advances to Non-Consolidated Subsidiary."

On December 22, 1960, at Russo's request, Talcott released the $147,466.80 to BarChris Financial Corporation temporarily, on the latter's agreement to redeposit it with Talcott not later than January 16, 1961, so that Talcott could continue to hold it as security. BarChris Financial Corporation then paid $145,000 of this sum to BarChris, which put it into one of BarChris's bank accounts. It was thus reflected in the cash balance as of December 31, 1960.[3]

---

[3] In his memorandum of December 23, 1960 explaining this transaction, Russo stated that "James Talcott may misfile this letter and, therefore, the return of this money to them may not be required." The evidence shows that Talcott did not overlook it. The evidence indicates, although not very clearly, that BarChris restored to Talcott all but $50,000 of this $147,466.80. Whether it did so by January 16, 1961, in accordance with its agreement, does not appear. As late as April and May 1961, Talcott was still demanding that BarChris restore the remaining $50,000 and Russo was apparently putting Talcott off. It does not clearly appear whether BarChris ultimately paid this $50,000 to Talcott.

Plaintiffs claim that this transaction was arranged by Russo in order to increase BarChris's cash temporarily, so that its financial condition would look better on December 31, 1960. No other explanation was offered by defendants and I can see none.

As far as the accuracy of the balance sheet is concerned, the $145,000 undoubtedly was an asset of BarChris Financial Corporation, subject only to Talcott's lien. It would seem that under the circumstances it would have been more accurate to include this amount, not in cash, but in "investment in non-consolidated subsidiary." The latter item is not a current asset, hence to put it there would have reduced current assets by $145,000. In any event, to treat it as cash on hand without some explanation of the temporary character of the deposit was misleading. The incident is important for the light that it sheds upon BarChris's business practices. This has a bearing upon the credibility of some of BarChris's officers and the weight to be given to their testimony in other respects.

Trade Accounts Receivable

[4] The balance sheet includes in current assets trade accounts receivable in the sum of $1,722,643. Plaintiffs assert that $1,157,973 of this total was improperly classified as current. This is the sum of amounts due from purchasers of seven different alleys. None of these amounts had been due for more than ninety days. The contracts provided that the customers would pay by delivering notes payable over a period of years. Plaintiffs say that only that portion of the receivable which would be represented by notes payable within one year should have been treated as a current asset.

But it is clear that BarChris's practice was to discount such notes, as soon as it received them, with a factor. Upon discounting them, BarChris would receive at once in cash the full amount of the notes, less such reserve as the factor might retain as security. This practice was disclosed in a footnote to the balance sheet. In view of this fact, I find that these receivables were properly classified as a current asset.

Federal Lanes

[5] Plaintiffs also complain about a receivable due from Federal Lanes representing a down payment under its contract for the purchase of an alley. The amount was $125,000. It had been overdue since July 31, 1960. As it turned out, BarChris never did collect this $125,000. Federal eventually went into bankruptcy. Plaintiffs say that the uncollectibility of this debt was so obvious on December 31, 1960 that a full reserve should have been set up against it, thereby reducing current assets accordingly.

Russo seems to have believed that $100,000 of this $125,000 had been paid by the delivery by Federal and the acceptance by BarChris of 36,400 shares of Federal stock in lieu of cash. Of course, if this were true, $100,000 was not a receivable at all, and the stock should have been shown as an asset of BarChris. This was not done.

The agreement between Federal and BarChris on this subject was not lucidly expressed. However, it is clear that, Russo notwithstanding, BarChris's accounting department did not treat the receipt of this stock as part payment. Instead, they treated it on BarChris's books as security for an account receivable still unpaid in the amount of $125,000. It was because of the existence of this security, which on December 31, 1960 had some value, plus the existence of additional security in the form of a mortgage, that it was decided to treat this $125,000 as fully collectible.

There are other facts, in addition to the age of this receivable, which cast doubt on the wisdom of this decision. Federal had also delivered notes to BarChris in payment of the balance of the purchase price over and above the down payment. These notes were discounted with Talcott. On December 31, 1960 they were in arrears to the extent of $24,366.66. This was substantially more than the arrearages of any other customer on notes discounted with Talcott as of that date. This was a clear indication, if any were needed, that all was not right with Federal.

I am well aware that this question of adequate reserves must be determined in the light of the facts as they existed at the time, not as they later developed. Nevertheless, I believe that the prospects for Federal were so bad, even on December 31, 1960, that some reserve should have been set up against the probability that this $125,000 would never be collected. In view of the security in the form of the stock and the mortgage, a reserve of the full $125,000 would not appear to have been necessary. I find that a reserve of at least $50,000 should have been created, and that the current assets should have been reduced in that amount.

Howard Lanes Annex

[6] Trade accounts receivable included $150,000 for Howard Lanes Annex. As previously found, this alley was not sold to an outside buyer. At best, this was a receivable due from a consolidated subsidiary of BarChris. It should not have been included in the balance sheet, which purported to eliminate intercompany transactions.

Factor's Reserves

[7] Among current assets was an item labeled "Financial Institutions on Notes Discounted" $2644,689. This was the amount of the reserves withheld by factors on customers' notes discounted with them by BarChris and consolidated subsidiaries. As the notes were paid by the customer to the factors, the reserves were released proportionately by the factors to BarChris. This was explained in a footnote to the balance sheet.

There is no doubt that this money was an asset of BarChris. There is no attack upon the accuracy of the figure. The claim is that it was not a current asset and should not have been so classified because (1) part of the reserve, in the normal course of events, would not have been released within one year; and (2) some of it might not be released at all, for some of the customers' notes held by the factors were already in arrears. It seems to be true that it could not reasonably be anticipated that all the reserves would be released within one year, as the notes were payable over several years. I believe, therefore, that plaintiffs are correct in their first contention and that this item, in part, at least,

should not have been classified as a current asset.

Work in Progress

[8] Next we come to an item under current assets labeled "Charges to customers on contracts in progress (note 2) * * * $1,671,945." Note 2 explained that:

"Charges to customers on contracts in progress represent the approximate sales value of work completed for the year ended December 31, 1960 determined by applying the estimated percentages of completed work to the total contract values."

Plaintiffs repeat their contention that the percentage of completion method should not have been employed at all and that nothing should have been included for work in progress. I have already ruled against plaintiffs on this point in discussing the 1960 sales figure.

In addition, plaintiffs say that in any case this was not a current asset. This contention is answered by what I have already said with respect to the $1,157,973 included in trade accounts receivable. The approximate sales value of the jobs in progress on December 31, 1960 was properly classified as a current asset because it could reasonably be expected that within a year this value would be represented by customers' notes which BarChris could discount and thereby obtain immediate cash.

Summary

[9] Plaintiffs have not established their claim that the BarChris current assets were grossly overstated in the balance sheet. What it boils down to is (1) $145,000 included in cash would more properly have been included in "Investment in Non-consolidated Subsidiary"; (2) current assets should have been reduced by a $50,000 reserve on Federal Lanes; (3) trade accounts receivable were overstated by $150,000 by including Howard Lanes Annex; (4) "Financial institutions on notes discounted $264,689" should have been treated, at least in part, as a noncurrent asset.

At most, net current assets should have been reduced by the total of these items, $609,689, which would have made them $3,914,332, instead of $4,524,021.

Contingent Liabilities as of December 31, 1960

• • •

[11,12] I turn now to the alternative method of financing with Talcott. This is complicated by the fact that these sale and leaseback arrangements with Talcott took two forms. BarChris's contingent liability was not the same in each.

The first form (referred to for convenience as Type A) involved the sale of the "interior" of an alley by BarChris to Talcott and the leasing of the interior by Talcott directly to BarChris's customer. The second (Type B) involved the sale of the interior by BarChris to Talcott, the leasing back of the interior by Talcott to a BarChris subsidiary, BarChris Leasing Corporation, and the lease of the interior by BarChris Leasing Corporation to the customer.

As to each Type A arrangement, BarChris signed and delivered to Talcott a written guaranty of the customer's, i.e., the lessee's, performance under the lease from Talcott. In each instance, this guaranty contained a limitation of BarChris's liability thereunder to a specified dollar amount. Although the guaranties did not expressly so state, in fact this dollar amount, in each instance, was 25 per cent of the customer's total obligation under the lease.

In Type B arrangements, BarChris executed and delivered to Talcott a written guaranty of the performance of BarChris Leasing Corporation under its lease from Talcott. The obligation of BarChris under its guaranty was not limited in any way. Thus, BarChris was contingently liable to the extent of 100 per cent for the performance by BarChris Leasing Corporation of its obligation under its lease.

Footnote 9 to the balance sheet, in stating that BarChris's contingent liability as of December 31, 1960 under the alternative method of financing was approximately $750,000, failed to take account of this difference. The

$750,000 figure was computed on the basis of 25 per cent of the lessee's obligation under the lease, regardless of whether the lessee was a customer or was BarChris Leasing Corporation.

There were three Type B leases included in this computation, those involving Asbury Lanes, Yankee Lanes (Torrington), and Capitol (Heavenly). The obligation of Torrington was $320,627.50 and of Asbury $288,766.68, a total of $609,394.18. This was the amount of BarChris's contingent liability on these two leases, not 25 per cent thereof, or $152,348.54. BarChris's contingent liability was thus understated as to these two leases by $457,045.64.

The situation as to Capitol (Heavenly) is different and worse. The amount of its lease obligation was $325,000. Capitol was not leased by BarChris Leasing Corporation to an outside customer. It was leased to a BarChris subsidiary. This was an inter-company transaction. Consequently, in this instance BarChris, on a consolidated basis, was directly, not contingently, liable. Hence, instead of including 25 per cent of this $325,000 in contingent liabilities in a footnote, the full $325,000 should have been reflected in the balance sheet as a direct liability of BarChris.

Apart from the figures, the statement in footnote 9 reading, "This contingent liability will decline during the term of the leases which expire in seven years," was not wholly accurate. As to Type A transactions, inasmuch as BarChris's contingent liability on its guaranty of the customers' leases was expressed in terms of a fixed dollar maximum, there would be no decline in that liability until the customer's obligation was reduced by payments to a sum less than that maximum.

For convenience, I will refer at this point to two remarks in the text of the prospectus which relate to this subject.

In describing the alternative method of financing, the prospectus states on page 6:

> "[W]hen the financial institution leases directly to the operator, the Company's contingent liability to the financial institution is limited to 25% of the operator's rental payments for the unexpired period of the lease."

This statement is literally correct, but it is only part of the story. It describes only BarChris's contingent liability on Type A transactions. There is no mention of the fact that on Type B transactions BarChris's contingent liability is 100 per cent. The omission of this additional explanation makes the prospectus to some extent misleading.

[13] Also on page 6 the prospectus states:

> "As of December 31, 1960, the Company had completed and sold ten building interiors for an aggregate price of $2,271,000 under this alternative method of financing."

This statement also was not wholly accurate. As of December 31, 1960, BarChris had sold nine building interiors, not ten. Also, one of them, Torrington, was not yet finished as of that date, so that it was not "completed and sold." By May 16, 1961, however, BarChris had sold ten building interiors. In fact, the total was then eleven, if two Cromwell jobs are counted separately. Also by May 16, Torrington had been completed. The inaccuracy in the statement as of December 31, 1960 is *de minimis*.

Summary

The net result is as follows:

Add to contingent liabilities:	
3/4ths of liability on	
Asbury and Torrington	$457,045
Deduct Capitol:	81,250
Net understatement of	
contingent liability	$375,795

Hence, instead of $750,000, the contingent liability figure under the alternative method of financing should have been $1,125,795. Capitol should have been shown as a direct liability in the amount of $325,000.

Reserves

[14] Plaintiffs also criticize the reserves, or lack of them, in the balance sheet. First, they claim that the reserve for doubtful accounts receivable in the amount of $54,481 was inadequate.

"Accounts receivable" in this context means indebtedness of customers which had not as yet been paid by delivery by the customer to BarChris of notes which BarChris could discount with a factor. The $54,481 covered such accounts which were more than ninety days past due on December 31, 1960. Up to that time BarChris's experience had been good, on the whole, in converting accounts receivable into discountable notes.

The amount of such reserve is a matter of accounting judgment. The evidence does not convince me that the accountant's judgment here was so clearly wrong that the balance sheet can be found to be false or misleading for lack of a higher reserve.

[15] Plaintiffs also claim that BarChris should have set up a reserve against its contingent liability on customers' notes discounted with factors and on customers' leases guaranteed. Some of these notes were in default on December 31, 1960. The factors however, had not demanded that BarChris repurchase any of them. Talcott contented itself with sending notices to BarChris periodically advising it that certain accounts were in arrears and asking BarChris's "assistance" to "bring these accounts up to date."

According to Talcott's records, on December 31, 1960 there were eleven customers out of forty who were behind in paying their notes. For the most part, the amounts involved were small. Five were under $5,000. Only three were over $10,000. Of these, only one, Federal, was over $20,000. None of the lessees was behind in his rent.

Another factor, Henry W. T. Mali & Co., Inc. (Mali), with whom the notes of four customers had been discounted by BarChris Financial, reported that of the four, one, Northford Lanes, was in arrears. BarChris apparently had paid these arrears to Mali for Northford's account.

I have already discussed Federal, which is a special case. The question is whether, apart from Federal, it was misleading to omit any reserve for all the other contingencies.

The executive committee minutes show that as early as November 3, 1960, Russo had expressed the opinion that BarChris "would be in the business of operating bowling alleys sometime in the future because of defaults by some of our customers." This remark provoked a discussion which led the executive committee to conclude that if BarChris were forced to take over the operation of a customer's alley, "the least which can be expected is that the notes to BarChris would be met from the operation." In other words, BarChris's officers in November 1960 believed that recapture of an alley would not cause a loss to BarChris. They believed that BarChris would be able to meet its obligations to Talcott with respect to such a repossessed alley.

As events ultimately turned out, BarChris was forced to respossess a number of alleys, and the optimism of its officers in November 1960 as to the effect on BarChris did not prove to be justified. In the light of the subsequent events, it is easy to say that prudence would have dictated the establishment of some reserve as of December 31, 1960. But these matters are always more clearly discerned in retrospect than they are at the time. In my opinion, BarChris's officers were sincere in their belief at the end of 1960 that BarChris was in no real danger of loss from customers' defaults. Apart from Federal, I conclude that their belief, viewed as of that time, was reasonable. The evidence does not establish that the balance sheet as of December 31, 1960 was false or misleading for lack of a reserve against contingent liabilities.

The 1961 Figures

The prospectus sets forth on page 4 the amount of BarChris's net sales, gross profits and net earnings for the three months ended March 31, 1961, in the amounts of $2,138,455, $483,121, and $125,699, respectively. These figures were unaudited, as the prospectus stated. On page 6 the prospectus set forth $5,101,351 as the amount of BarChris's contingent liability as of April 30, 1961 on customers' notes discounted, and "approximately $825,000" as its contingent liability under the alternative method of financing. Plaintiffs challenge the accuracy of these figures.

Contingent Liabilities as of April 30, 1961

The issue here is essentially the same as that previously discussed with regard to the contingent liability figures as of December 31, 1960. The April 30, 1961 figures were

prepared by Trilling. The figure for contingent liability on notes discounted was correctly computed on the basis of 50 per cent of the unpaid balance of notes discounted with Talcott.

As to the alternative method of financing, the full amount of the lessee's obligation, rather than 25 percent thereof, should have been included.

The net result is as follows:

Add:	Asbury	$207,612.51
	Torrington	234,182.64
	Olympia	255,600.00
	Total	$697,395.15
Deduct:	Capitol	$78,541.67
Net Understatement of Contingent Liability on Type B Transactions		$618,853.48

Instead of $825,000, the contingent liability on the alternative method of financing was at least $1,443,853. Moreover, the liability of $314,166 on Capitol was a direct liability, not a contingent one.

Net Sales, Gross Profit and Net Earnings

[16] Plaintiffs correctly contend that the net sales of $2,138,455 for the three months ended March 31, 1961 were overstated.

This figure included $269,810 for Bridge Lanes. I have previously noted that the stock of the original customer for this alley, Biel Land & Development Company, was acquired by BarChris in the spring of 1961. The date of acquisition was March 24, 1961. Subsequently, BarChris operated this alley through a subsidiary. Once it began to operate it, it did not sell it at any time thereafter, as far as appears. There is no doubt that by March 31, 1961, this transaction had become an intercompany one. It should not have been included in first quarter 1961 sales.

Yonkers Lanes is in the same category. The amount included in sales for this alley was $250,000. On May 4, 1961, BarChris organized a subsidiary, Yonkers Lanes, Inc., which eventually operated this alley. Whether BarChris originally had intended to operate it, or whether at the outset it had a customer for it, is not clear from the testimony. However, the minutes of a meeting of BarChris's executive committee held on March 18, 1961 show that as of that date BarChris had no contract with a customer for this alley. It seems clear that by March 31, 1961 this was an intercompany transaction and should not have been included in first quarter sales.

• • •

[18] I also find that plaintiffs have not proved that the amounts included in first quarter sales, on the percentage of completion method, for Torrington Lanes and Newington Lanes were improperly computed. Although there is some evidence to the effect that the costs of these jobs eventually turned out to be higher than expected, the evidence is too scanty to prove that this should have been anticipated and allowed for in computing the first quarter figures.

The net result is that the March 31, 1961 net sales figure was overstated as follows:

Bridge Lanes	$269,810
Yonkers Lanes	250,000
Total	$519,810

The net sales figure, therefore, should have been $1,618,645, not $2,138,455.

It necessarily follows that the gross profit figure of $483,121 was wrong to the extent of the gross profit included for Bridge Lanes and Yonkers Lanes. These amounts were:

Bridge Lanes	$125,755
Yonkers	105,000
Total	$230,755

The gross profit therefore should have been $252,366, instead of $486,121. Net earnings would necessarily be reduced proportionately. The evidence does not permit calculation of the exact amount of the reduction.

"Backlog" as of March 31, 1961

The prospectus stated on page 5:

"The Company as of March 31, 1960, had $2,875,000 in unfilled orders on its books. As of March 31, 1961, the comparable amount was approximately

$6,905,000. Substantially all of the latter orders are scheduled and are expected to be completed in 1961."

Plaintiffs contend that the figure of $6,905,000 was erroneous. There is no doubt that it was, to a substantial extent. It is impossible to determine, however, precisely what the figure should have been.

The difficulty results from the fact that BarChris's books did not contain a record of unfilled orders as of March 31, 1961. Russo testified that he prepared a list of them which was the basis for the figure in the prospectus. The list was never produced. Its absence gave rise to controversy as to what alleys were on the list and what were not. Despite all the testimony and argument on this subject, the matter was never completely settled.

Out of all this testimony, however, some things clearly emerge. Although it is not possible to specify each and every alley which was included in the total of $6,905,000, there is no dispute about the fact that certain alleys were included. And it is clear that alleys were included for which BarChris, as of March 31, 1961, held no valid enforceable contracts.

T-Bowl

I shall first consider the group of six alleys referred to as the "T-Bowl" group. The principal figure in these transactions was August E. Tumminello. In December 1960 or January 1961, he, at the urging of Vitolo, signed six undated documents on BarChris's printed form of purchase contract. The name of the purchaser at the head of the respective documents was stated as "T-Bowl, Groton," "T-Bowl Milford," "T-Bowl, No. Attleboro," "T-Bowl Baltimore," "T-Bowl Saverna Park," and "T-Bowl Odenton." On five of the six documents the same name appeared after the word "Purchaser" at the bottom, followed by the signature, "August E. Tumminello Pres." On the sixth, that pertaining to North Attleboro, nothing appeared at the bottom after the word "Purchaser" except Tumminello's signature as "Pres."

In fact, there were no corporations entitled T-Bowl Groton, T-Bowl Milford, etc. These names were merely designations of the geographical area of the proposed alley.

Each of these "purchase contracts" purported to be for the "interior" of an alley. Each stated that the "purchaser" agreed to purchase "the equipment set forth below." Nothing was set forth below. Each document stated that "specifications are attached." No specifications were attached. Each recited that a specific part of the purchase price had been paid upon the signing of the contract. Nothing was paid at that time.

Birnbaum, BarChris's secretary and house counsel, advised his fellow officers that these documents were not legally enforceable contracts. The minutes of BarChris's executive committee meeting of March 18, 1961 included each of these alleys in a list of "jobs which are presently being constructed, or will soon be commenced, and on which no contracts with customers have been written."

On May 2, 1961, a corporation known as T-Bowl International Inc. was organized. Tumminello was its president. Russo was a director. This corporation sold common stock to the public in September 1961. The issue was underwritten by Peter Morgan & Company, one of the underwriting group in the BarChris debenture issue involved here. The T-Bowl prospectus stated:

> "At June 30, 1961, T-Bowl had consolidated negative working capital of $229,058.79 * * *."

This financing appears to have succeeded. Out of its proceeds T-Bowl International Inc. finally made the down payments to BarChris with respect to the six T-Bowl jobs. Birnbaum caused a line to be drawn through the name of the purchaser on each of the six documents, i.e., T-Bowl Groton, etc., and the words "T-Bowl International Inc." to be written in in ink. The documents were not executed.

Five of the six alleys were eventually built by BarChris, long after May 16, 1961. One, Severna Park, was never built because its site was condemned for a highway.

[19, 20] It is undisputed that the total contract price of these six alleys, $2,205,000, was included in the backlog figure. I find that it was inaccurate and misleading to include it.

I have made due allowance for the fact that BarChris's contract draftsmanship was frequently inartistic. Consequently, I do not regard as determinative the fact that the T-Bowl documents were carelessly drawn and executed. But the difficulty here goes beyond such defects in form. The evidence shows, and I so find, that Tumminello's agreement made in late 1960 or early 1961 to purchase the interior equipment of the six alleys was contingent upon the future organization and successful financing of the corporation which turned out to be T-Bowl International Inc. Whether or not this could ultimately be accomplished was by no means certain on March 31, 1961. Indeed, one may wonder how purchasers were found in September 1961 for the stock of a new corporation starting out in life with a "negative working capital of $229,058.79."

Doubtless BarChris's officers in the spring of 1961 hoped that this could be accomplished. But the prospectus did not purport to set forth hopes. "Unfilled orders on its books" which are "scheduled" means firm enforceable contracts with purchasers who have made their down payments and who can reasonably be expected to perform their commitments. The six T-Bowl orders did not meet that test. The fact that, as it eventually turned out, five of the six transactions were consummated, does not alter the conclusion that they could not fairly be treated as scheduled orders on BarChris's books as of March 31, 1961.

Bowl-a-Way

[21] It is undisputed that $1,400,000 was included in the backlog figure for this alley. The contract for its construction was not signed until August 9, 1961, BarChris never finished building it.

As of March 31, 1961, there was no firm commitment with respect to this transaction. There had been negotiations, but agreement had not been reached on financing terms. A BarChris memorandum dated April 24, 1961 and the BarChris executive committee minutes of the same date so indicate. It was inaccurate and misleading to treat this transaction as a scheduled unfilled order on the books as of March 31, 1961.

• • •

Summary

For convenience, the various falsities and omissions which I have discussed in the preceding pages are recapitulated here. They were as follows:

1. 1960 Earnings
   (a) Sales
As per prospectus	$9,165,320
Correct figure	8,511,420
Overstatement	$ 653,900
   (b) Net Operating Income
As per prospectus	$1,742,801
Correct figure	1,496,196
Overstatement	$ 246,605
   (c) Earnings per Share
As per prospectus	$ .75
Correct figure	$ .65
Overstatement	$ .10
2. 1960 Balance Sheet Current Assets
As per prospectus	$4,524,021
Correct figure	3,914,332
Overstatement	$ 609,689
3. Contingent Liabilities as of December 31, 1960 on Alternative Method of Financing
As per prospectus	$ 750,000
Correct figure	1,125,795
Understatement	$ 375,795
Capitol Lanes should have been shown as a direct liability	$ 325,000
4. Contingent Liabilities as of April 30, 1961
As per prospectus	$ 825,000
Correct figure	1,443,853
Understatement	$ 618,853
Capitol Lanes should have been shown as a direct liability	$ 314,166
5. Earnings Figures for Quarter ending March 31, 1961
   (a) Sales
As per prospectus	$2,138,455
Correct figure	1,618,645
Overstatement	$ 519,810
   (b) Gross Profit
As per prospectus	$ 483,121
Correct figure	252,366
Overstatement	$ 230,755

6. Backlog as of March 31, 1961
As per prospectus	$6,905,000
Correct figure	2,415,000
Overstatement	$4,490,000
7. Failure to Disclose Officers' Loans Outstanding and Unpaid on May 16, 1961 — $ 386,615
8. Failure to Disclose Use of Proceeds in Manner not Revealed in Prospectus
   Approximately $1,160,000
9. Failure to Disclose Customers' Delinquencies in May 1961 and BarChris's Potential Liability with Respect Thereto
   Over $1,350,000
10. Failure to Disclose the Fact that BarChris Was Already Engaged, and Was about to Be More Heavily Engaged, in the Operation of Bowling Alleys

Materiality

[30, 31] It is a prerequisite to liability under Section 11 of the Act that the fact which is falsely stated in a registration statement, or the fact that is omitted when it should have been stated to avoid misleading, be "material." The regulations of the Securities and Exchange Commission pertaining to the registration of securities define the word as follows (17 C.F.R. § 230.405 (*l*)):

> "The term 'material', when used to qualify a requirement for the furnishing of information as to any subject, limits the information required to those matters as to which an average prudent investor ought reasonably to be informed before purchasing the security registered."

What are "matters as to which an average prudent investor ought reasonably to be informed"? It seems obvious that they are matters which such an investor needs to know before he can make an intelligent, informed decision whether or not to buy the security.

[32] Early in the history of the Act, a definition of materiality was given in Matter of Charles A. Howard, 1 S.E.C. 6, 8 (1934), which is still valid today. A material fact was there defined as:

> "* * * a fact which if it had been correctly stated or disclosed would have deterred or tended to deter the average prudent investor from purchasing the securities in question."

[33] The average prudent investor is not concerned with minor inaccuracies or with errors as to matters which are of no interest to him. The facts which tend to deter him from purchasing a security are facts which have an important bearing upon the nature or condition of the issuing corporation or its business.

Judged by this test, there is no doubt that many of the misstatements and omissions in this prospectus were material. This is true of all of them which relate to the state of affairs in 1961, i.e., the overstatement of sales and gross profit for the first quarter, the understatement of contingent liabilities as of April 30, the overstatement of orders on hand and the failure to disclose the true facts with respect to officers' loans, customers' delinquencies, application of proceeds and the prospective operation of several alleys.

The misstatements and omissions pertaining to BarChris's status as of December 31, 1960, however, present a much closer question. The 1960 earnings figures, the 1960 balance sheet and the contingent liabilities as of December 31, 1960 were not nearly as erroneous as plaintiffs have claimed. But they were wrong to some extent, as we have seen. Would it have deterred the average prudent investor from purchasing these debentures if he had been informed that the 1960 sales were $8,511,420 rather than $9,165,320, that the net operating income was $1,496,196 rather than $1,742,801 and that the earnings per share in 1960 were approximately 65¢ rather than 75¢? According to the unchallenged figures, sales in 1959 were $3,320,121, net operating income was $441,103, and earnings per share were 33¢. Would it have made a difference to an average prudent investor if he had known that in 1960 sales were only 256 per cent of 1959 sales, not 276 per cent; that net operating

income was up by only $1,055,093, not by $1,301,698, and the earnings per share, while still approximately twice those of 1959, were not something more than twice?

These debentures were rated "B" by the investment rating services. They were thus characterized as speculative, as any prudent investor must have realized. It would seem that anyone interested in buying these convertible debentures would have been attracted primarily by the conversion feature, by the growth potential of the stock. The growth which the company enjoyed in 1960 over prior years was striking, even on the correct figures. It is hard to see how a prospective purchaser of this type of investment would have been deterred from buying if he had been advised of those comparatively minor errors in reporting 1960 sales and earnings.

[34] Since no one knows what moves or does not move the mythical "average prudent investor," it comes down to a question of judgment, to be exercised by the trier of the fact as best he can in the light of all the circumstances. It is my best judgment that the average prudent investor would not have cared about these errors in the 1960 sales and earnings figures, regrettable though they may be. I therefore find that they were not material within the meaning of Section 11.

The same is true of the understatement of contingent liabilities in footnote 9 by approximately $375,000. As disclosed in that footnote, BarChris's contingent liability as of December 31, 1960 on notes discounted was $3,969,835 and, according to the footnote, on the alternative method of financing was $750,000, a total of $4,719,835. This was a huge amount for a company with total assets, as per balance sheet, of $6,101,085. Purchasers were necessarily made aware of this by the figures actually disclosed. If they were willing to buy the debentures in the face of this information, as they obviously were, I doubt that they would have been deterred if they had been told that the contingent liabilities were actually $375,000 higher.

This leaves for consideration the errors in the 1960 balance sheet figures which have previously been discussed in detail. Current assets were overstated by approximately

$600,000.[4] Liabilities were understated by approximately $325,000 by the failure to treat the liability on Capitol Lanes as a direct liability of BarChris on a consolidated basis. Of this $325,000 approximately $65,000, the amount payable on Capitol within one year, should have been treated as a current liability.

As per balance sheet, cash was $285,482. In fact, $145,000 of this had been borrowed temporarily from Talcott and was to be returned by January 16, 1961 so that realistically, cash was only $140,482. Trade accounts receivable were overstated by $150,000 by including Howard Lanes Annex, an alley which was not sold to an outside buyer.

As per balance sheet, total current assets were $4,524,021, and total current liabilities were $2,413,867, a ratio of approximately 1.9 to 1. This was bad enough, but on the true facts, the ratio was worse. As corrected, current assets, as near as one can tell, were approximately $3,924,000, and current liabilities approximately $2,478,000, a ratio of approximately 1.6 to 1.

Would it have made any difference if a prospective purchaser of these debentures had been advised of these facts? There must be some point at which errors in disclosing a company's balance sheet position become material, even to a growth-oriented investor. On all the evidence I find that these balance sheet errors were material within the meaning of Section 11.

Since there was an abundance of material misstatements pertaining to 1961 affairs, whether or not the errors in the 1960 figures were material does not affect the outcome of this case except to the extent that it bears upon the liability of Peat, Marwick. That subject will be discussed hereinafter.

The "Due Diligence" Defenses

Section 11 (b) of the Act provides that:

---

[4] This figure assumes that the entire $264,680 of factors' reserves was noncurrent. Some part of it probably was current on the theory that part would be released by the factors within one year, but this amount cannot be determined on the evidence and, in any case, it would seem to have been small.

"* * * no person, other than the issuer, shall be liable * * * who shall sustain the burden of proof—

• • •

(3) that (A) as regards any part of the registration statement not purporting to be made on the authority of an expert * * * he had, after reasonable investigation, reasonable ground to believe and did believe, at the time such part of the registration statement became effective, that the statements therein were true and that there was no omission to state a material fact required to be stated therein or necessary to make the statements therein not misleading; * * * and (C) as regards any part of the registration statement purporting to be made on the authority of an expert (other than himself) * * * he had no reasonable ground to believe and did not believe, at the time such part of the registration statement became effective, that the statements therein were untrue or that there was an omission to state a material fact required to be stated therein or necessary to make the statements therein not misleading`* * *.''

Section 11(c) defines "reasonable investigation" as follows:

"In determining, for the purpose of paragraph (3) of subsection (b) of this section, what constitutes reasonable investigation and reasonable ground for belief, the standard of reasonableness shall be that required of a prudent man in the management of his own property."

[35] Every defendant, except BarChris itself, to whom, as the issuer, these defenses are not available, and except Peat, Marwick, whose position rests on a different statutory provision,[5] has pleaded these affirmative defenses.

• • •

As to each defendant, the question is whether he has sustained the burden of proving these defenses. Surprising enough, there is little or no judicial authority on this question. No decisions directly in point under Section 11 have been found.

---

[5] This statutory provision will be quoted in discussing Peat, Marwick's liability *infra*.

[36] Before considering the evidence, a preliminary matter should be disposed of. The defendants do not agree among themselves as to who the "experts" were or as to the parts of the registration statement which were expertised. Some defendants say that Peat, Marwick was the expert, others say that BarChris's attorneys, Perkins, Daniels, McCormack & Collins, and the underwriters' attorneys, Drinker, Biddle & Reath, were also the experts. On the first view, only those portions of the registration statement purporting to be made on Peat, Marwick's authority were expertised portions. On the other view, everything in the registration statement was within this category, because the two law firms were responsible for the entire document.

The first view is the correct one. To say that the entire registration statement is expertised because some lawyer prepared it would be an unreasonable construction of the statute. Neither the lawyer for the company nor the lawyer for the underwriters is an expert within the meaning of Section 11. The only expert, in the statutory sense, was Peat, Marwick, and the only parts of the registration statement which purported to be made upon the authority of an expert were the portions which purported to be made on Peat, Marwick's authority.

[37] The parties also disagree as to what those portions were. Some defendants say that it was only the 1960 figures (and the figures for prior years, which are not in controversy here). Others say in substance that it was every figure in the prospectus. The plaintiffs take a somewhat intermediate view. They do not claim that Peat, Marwick expertised every figure, but they do maintain that Peat, Marwick is responsible for a portion of the text of the prospectus, i.e., that pertaining to "Methods of Operation," because a reference to it was made in footnote 9 to the balance sheet.

Here again, the more narrow view is the correct one. The registration statement contains a report of Peat, Marwick as independent public accountants dated February 23, 1961. This relates only to the consolidated balance sheet of BarChris and consolidated subsidiaries as of December 31, 1960, and the related statement of earnings and retained earnings for the five years then ended. This is all that Peat, Marwick purported to certify. It is perfectly clear that it did not purport to certify the 1961 figures, some of which are expressly stated in the prospectus to have been unaudited.

Moreover, plaintiffs' intermediate view is also incorrect. The cross reference in footnote 9 to the "Methods of Operation" passage in the prospectus was inserted merely for the convenience of the reader. It is not a fair construction to say that it thereby imported into the balance sheet everything in that portion of the text, much of which had nothing to do with the figures in the balance sheet.

I turn now to the question of whether defendants have proved their due diligence defenses. The position of each defendant will be separately considered.

•   •   •

[48] The purpose of Section 11 is to protect investors. To that end the underwriters are made responsible for the truth of the prospectus. If they may escape that responsibility by taking at face value representations made to them by the company's management, then the inclusion of underwriters among those liable under Section 11 affords the investors no additional protection. To effectuate the statute's purpose, the phrase "reasonable investigation" must be construed to require more effort on the part of the underwriters than the mere accurate reporting in the prospectus of "data presented" to them by the company. It should make no difference that this data is elicited by questions addressed to the company officers by the underwriters, or that the underwriters at the time believe that the company's officers are truthful and reliable. In order to make the underwriters' participation in this enterprise of any value to the investors, the underwriters must make some reasonable attempt to verify the data submitted to them. They may not rely solely on the company's officers or on the company's counsel. A prudent man in the management of his own property would not rely on them.

[49] It is impossible to lay down a rigid rule suitable for every case defining the extent to which such verification must go. It is a question of degree, a matter of judgment in

each case. In the present case, the underwriters' counsel made almost no attempt to verify management's representations. I hold that that was insufficient.

[50, 51] On the evidence in this case, I find that the underwriters' counsel did not make a reasonable investigation of the truth of those portions of the prospectus which were not made on the authority of Peat, Marwick as an expert. Drexel is bound by their failure. It is not a matter of relying upon counsel for legal advice. Here the attorneys were dealing with matters of fact. Drexel delegated to them, as its agent, the business of examining the corporate minutes and contracts. It must bear the consequences of their failure to make an adequate examination.

[52] The other underwriters, who did nothing and relied solely on Drexel and on the lawyers, are also bound by it. It follows that although Drexel and the other underwriters believed that those portions of the prospectus were true, they had no reasonable ground for that belief within the meaning of the statute. Hence, they have not established their due diligence defense, except as to the 1960 audited figures.[6]

• • •

Peat, Marwick

Section 11(b) provides:

"Notwithstanding the provisions of subsection (a) no person * * * shall be liable as provided therein who shall sustain the burden of proof—

• • •

"(3) that * * * (B) as regards any part of the registration statement purporting to be made upon his authority as an expert * * * (i) he had, after reasonable investigation, reasonable ground to believe and did believe, at the time such part of the registration statement became effective, that the statements therein were true and that there was no omission to state a material fact

required to be stated therein or necessary to make the statements therein not misleading * * *."

This defines the due diligence defense for an expert. Peat, Marwick has pleaded it.

The part of the registration statement purporting to be made upon the authority of Peat, Marwick as an expert was, as we have seen, the 1960 figures. But because the statute requires the court to determine Peat, Marwick's belief, and the grounds thereof, "at the time such part of the registration statement became effective," for the purposes of this affirmative defense, the matter must be viewed as of May 16, 1961, and the question is whether at that time Peat, Marwick, after reasonable investigation, had reasonable ground to believe and did believe that the 1960 figures were true and that no material fact had been omitted from the registration statement which should have been included in order to make the 1960 figures not misleading. In deciding this issue, the court must consider not only what Peat, Marwick did in its 1960 audit, but also what it did in its subsequent "S-1 review." The proper scope of that review must also be determined.

It may be noted that we are concerned at this point only with the question of Peat, Marwick's liability to plaintiffs. At the closing on May 24, 1961, Peat, Marwick delivered a so-called "comfort letter" to the underwriters. This letter stated:

"It is understood that this letter is for the information of the underwriters and is not to be quoted or referred to, in whole or in part, in the Registration Statement or Prospectus or in any literature used in connection with the sale of securities."

Plaintiffs may not take advantage of any undertakings or representations in this letter. If they exceeded the normal scope of an S-1 review (a question which I do not now decide) that is a matter which relates only to the crossclaims which defendants have asserted against each other and which I have postponed for determination at a later date.

The 1960 Audit

Peat, Marwick's work was in general charge of a member of the firm, Cummings, and

---

[6] In view of this conclusion, it becomes unnecessary to decide whether the underwriters other than Drexel would have been protected if Drexel has established that as lead underwriter, it made a reasonable investigation.

more immediately in charge of Peat, Marwick's manager, Logan. Most of the actual work was performed by a senior accountant, Berardi, who had junior assistants, one of whom was Kennedy.

Berardi was then about thirty years old. He was not yet a C.P.A. He had had no previous experience with the bowling industry. This was his first job as a senior accountant. He could hardly have been given a more difficult assignment.

After obtaining a little background information on BarChris by talking to Logan and reviewing Peat, Marwick's work papers on its 1959 audit, Berardi examined the results of test checks of BarChris's accounting procedures which one of the junior accountants had made, and he prepared an "internal control questionnaire" and an "audit program." Thereafter, for a few days subsequent to December 30, 1960, he inspected BarChris's inventories and examined certain alley construction. Finally, on January 13, 1961, he began his auditing work which he carried on substantially continuously until it was completed on February 24, 1961. Toward the close of the work, Logan reviewed it and made various comments and suggestions to Berardi.

It is unnecessary to recount everything that Berardi did in the course of the audit. We are concerned only with the evidence relating to what Berardi did or did not do with respect to those items which I have found to have been incorrectly reported in the 1960 figures in the prospectus. More narrowly, we are directly concerned only with such of those items as I have found to be material.

Capitol Lanes

First and foremost is Berardi's failure to discover that Capitol Lanes had not been sold. This error affected both the sales figure and the liability side of the balance sheet. Fundamentally, the error stemmed from the fact that Berardi never realized that Heavenly Lanes and Capitol were two different names for the same alley. In the course of his audit, Berardi was shown BarChris's contract file. He examined the contracts in the file and made a list of them. The file must have included a contract with an outside purchaser for Heavenly Lanes, although no such contract was ever produced at the trial, for Berardi included Heavenly on his list. Apparently there was no contract in the file for a lane named Capitol because that name did not appear on Berardi's list.

Kircher also made a list of jobs. Heavenly was on his list. Capitol was not. Berardi compared the two lists and satisfied himself that he had the proper jobs to be taken into account. Berardi assumed that Heavenly was to be treated like any other completed job. He included it in all his computations.

The evidence is conflicting as to whether BarChris's officers expressly informed Berardi that Heavenly and Capitol were the same thing and that BarChris was operating Capitol and had not sold it. I find that they did not so inform him.

Berardi did become aware that there were references here and there in BarChris's records to something called Capitol Lanes. He also knew that there were indications that at some time BarChris might operate an alley of that name. He read the minutes of the board of directors' meeting of November 22, 1960 which recited that:

> "* * * the Chairman recommended that the Corporation operate Capitol Lanes, 271 Main Street, East Haven, Connecticut, through a corporation which would be a subsidiary of Sanpark Realty Corp."

The minutes further recorded that:

> "* * * it was unanimously agreed that the officers of the Corporation exercise their discretion as to operating Capitol Lanes through the aforesaid subsidiary on an experimental basis."

The junior accountant, Kennedy, read the minute book of Capitol Lanes, Inc., a Connecticut corporation organized in December 1960. The book contained a certificate of incorporation which empowered the corporation, among many other things, to own and manage bowling alleys. There was no minute in the book, however, that indicated that the corporation actually did own or manage one.

Berardi knew from various BarChris records that Capitol Lanes, Inc. was paying rentals to Talcott. Also, a Peat, Marwick work paper bearing Kennedy's initials recorded that Capitol Lanes, Inc. held certain insurance policies, including a fire insurance policy on "contents," a workmen's compensation and a public liability policy. Another Peat, Marwick work paper also bearing Kennedy's initials recorded that Capitol Lanes, Inc. had $1,000 in a fund in Connecticut. A note on this paper read:

> "Traced to disbursements book—advanced for operation of alley—not expensed at 12/31/60."

Logan's written comments upon the audit contained an entry reading as follows:

> "When talking to Ted Kircher in latter part of '60 he indicated one subsidiary is leasing an alley built by BarChris—the profit on this job should be eliminated as its ownership is within the affiliated group."

Opposite this note is an entry by Berardi reading as follows:

> "Properties sold to others by affiliates. Capitol Lanes is paying currently lease rentals which amount to a lease purchase plan."

This note is somewhat ambiguous. If by "others" Berardi meant outside buyers, then it would seem that he should have accounted in some way for this sale, which he did not do. Presumably, by "others" he meant "other affiliates." Hence, he regarded the transaction, whatever he thought it to have been, as an intercompany one. Apparently Logan so understood Berardi's explanation.

Berardi testified that he inquired of Russo about Capitol Lanes, and that Russo told him that Capitol Lanes, Inc. was going to operate an alley some day but as yet it had no alley. Berardi testified that he understood that the alley had not been built and that he believed that the rental payments were on vacant land.

I am not satisfied with this testimony. If Berardi did hold this belief, he should not have held it. The entries as to insurance and as to "operation of alley" should have alerted him to the fact that an alley existed. He should have made further inquiry on the subject. It is apparent that Berardi did not understand this transaction.

In any case, he never identified this mysterious Capitol with the Heavenly Lanes which he had included in his sales and profit figures. The vital question is whether he failed to make a reasonable investigation which, if he had made it, would have revealed the truth.

Certain accounting records of BarChris, which Berardi testified he did not see, would have put him on inquiry. One was a job cost ledger card for job no. 6036, the job number which Berardi put on his own work sheet for Heavenly lanes. The card read "Capital Theatre (Heavenly)." In addition, two accounts receivable cards each showed both names on the same card, Capitol and Heavenly. Berardi testified that he looked at the accounts receivable records but that he did not see these particular cards. He testified that he did not look on the job cost ledger cards because he took the costs from another record, the costs register.

[54, 55] The burden of proof on this issue is on Peat, Marwick. Although the question is a rather close one, I find that Peat, Marwick has not sustained that burden. Peat, Marwick has not proved that Berardi made a reasonable investigation as far as Capitol Lanes was concerned and that his ignorance of the true facts was justified.

Howard Lanes Annex

Berardi also failed to discover that this alley was not sold. Here the evidence is much scantier. Berardi saw a contract for this alley in the contract file. No one told him that it was to be leased rather than sold. There is no evidence to indicate that any record existed which would have put him on notice. I find that his investigation was reasonable as to this item.

• • •

This disposes of the inaccuracies in the 1960 sales figures. I turn now to the errors in the current assets which involve four items: cash, reserve for Federal Lanes, factors' reserves and Howard Lanes Annex, which latter I have already covered.

As to cash, Berardi properly obtained a confirmation from the bank as to BarChris's cash balance on December 31, 1960. He did not know that part of this balance had been temporarily increased by the deposit of reserves returned by Talcott to BarChris conditionally for a limited time. I do not believe that Berardi reasonably should have known this. Although Peat, Marwick's work papers record the fact that these reserves were returned, there was nothing to indicate that the payment was conditional. Russo obviously did not reveal this fact. It would not be reasonable to require Berardi to examine all of BarChris's correspondence files when he had no reason to suspect any irregularity.

As to the reserve on Federal Lanes, there is little to add to the earlier discussion of this subject in this opinion. I appreciate that in that instance the court has substituted its judgment for that of Russo and Berardi. For the reasons previously mentioned, I believe that their judgment was clearly wrong.

As to factors' reserves, it is hard to understand how Berardi could have treated this item as entirely a current asset when it was obvious that most of the reserves would not be released within one year. If Berardi was unaware of that fact, he should have been aware of it.

The net result, as far as current assets are concerned, is that Peat, Marwick is responsible for the errors as to reserves but not for those involving the cash item and the receivable from Howard Lanes Annex.

Contingent Liabilities

Berardi erred in computing the contingent liability on Type B leaseback transactions at 25 per cent. He testified that he was shown an agreement with Talcott which fixed the contingent liability at that amount. In this testimony he was mistaken. No such document is contained in Peat, Marwick's work papers. The evidence indicates that it never existed. Berardi did not examine the documents which are in evidence which establish that BarChris's contingent liability on this type of transaction was in fact 100 per cent. Berardi did not make a reasonable investigation in this instance. Although I have found that the error in understating contingent liabilities as of December 31, 1960 would not have deterred a prospective purchaser, the error is nevertheless of some importance because it apparently led Trilling into making a larger error in computing the contingent liability figure as of April 30, 1961.

The S-1 Review

The purpose of reviewing events subsequent to the date of a certified balance sheet (referred to as an S-1 review when made with reference to a registration statement) is to ascertain whether any material change has occurred in the company's financial position which should be disclosed in order to prevent the balance sheet figures from being misleading. The scope of such a review, under generally accepted auditing standards, is limited. It does not amount to a complete audit.

Peat, Marwick prepared a written program for such a review. I find that this program conformed to generally accepted auditing standards. Among other things, it required the following:

"1. Review minutes of stockholders, directors and committees. * * *

"2. Review latest interim financial statements and compare with corresponding statements of preceding year. Inquire regarding significant variations and changes.

• • •

"4. Review the more important financial records and inquire regarding material transactions not in the ordinary course of business and any other significant items.

• • •

"6. Inquire as to changes in material contracts. * * *

• • •

"10. Inquire as to any significant bad debts or accounts in dispute for which provision has not been made.

• • •

"14. Inquire as to * * * newly discovered liabilities, direct or contingent * * *."

Berardi made the S-1 review in May 1961. He devoted a little over two days to it, a total of 20½ hours. He did not discover any of the errors or omissions pertaining to the state of affairs in 1961 which I have previously discussed at length, all of which were material. The question is whether, despite his failure to find out anything, his investigation was reasonable within the meaning of the statute.

What Berardi did was to look at a consolidating trial balance as of March 31, 1961 which had been prepared by BarChris, compare it with the audited December 31, 1960 figures, discuss with Trilling certain unfavorable developments which the comparison disclosed, and read certain minutes. He did not examine any "important financial records" other than the trial balance. As to minutes, he read only what minutes Birnbaum gave him, which consisted only of the board of directors' minutes of BarChris. He did not read such minutes as there were of the executive committee. He did not know that there was an executive committee, hence he did not discover that Kircher had notes of executive committee minutes which had not been written up. He did not read the minutes of any subsidiary.

In substance, what Berardi did is similar to what Grant and Ballard did. He asked questions, he got answers which he considered satisfactory, and he did nothing to verify them. For example, he obtained from Trilling a list of contracts. The list included Yonkers and Bridge. Since Berardi did not read the minutes of subsidiaries, he did not learn that Yonkers and Bridge were intercompany sales. The list also included Woonsocket and the six T-Bowl jobs, Moravia Road, Milford, Groton, North Attleboro, Odenton and Severna Park. Since Berardi did not look at any contract documents, and since he was unaware of the executive committee minutes of March 18, 1961 (at that time embodied only in Kircher's notes), he did not learn that BarChris had no contracts for these jobs. Trilling's list did not set forth contract prices for them, although it did for Yonkers, Bridge and certain others. This did not arouse Berardi's suspicion.

Berardi noticed that there had been an increase in notes payable by BarChris. Trilling admitted to him that BarChris was "a bit slow" in paying its bills. Berardi recorded in his notes of his review that BarChris was in a "tight cash position." Trilling's explanation was that BarChris was experiencing "some temporary difficulty."

Berardi had no conception of how tight the cash position was. He did not discover that BarChris was holding up checks in substantial amounts because there was no money in the bank to cover them.[7] He did not know of the loan from Manufacturers Trust Company or of the officers' loans. Since he never read the prospectus, he was not even aware that there had ever been any problem about loans from officers.

During the 1960 audit Berardi had obtained some information from factors, not sufficiently detailed even then, as to delinquent notes. He made no inquiry of factors about this in his S-1 review. Since he knew nothing about Kircher's notes of the executive committee meetings, he did not learn that the delinquency situation had grown worse. He was content with Trilling's assurance that no liability theretofore contingent had become direct.

Apparently the only BarChris officer with whom Berardi communicated was Trilling. He could not recall making any inquiries of Russo, Vitolo or Pugliese. As to Kircher, Berardi's testimony was self-contradictory. At one point he said that he had inquired of Kircher and at another he said that he could not recall making any such inquiry.

There had been a material change for the worse in BarChris's financial position. That change was sufficiently serious so that the failure to disclose it made the 1960 figures misleading. Berardi did not discover it. As far as results were concerned, his S-1 review was useless.

[56, 57] Accountants should not be held to a standard higher than that recognized in their profession. I do not do so here. Berardi's review did not come up to that standard. He did not take some of the steps which Peat, Marwick's written program prescribed. He did not spend an adequate amount of time on a task of this magnitude. Most important of all,

---

[7] One of these checks was a check to the order of Peat, Marwick in the amount of $3,000. It was dated April 4, 1961. It was deposited by Peat, Marwick on May 29, 1961.

he was too easily satisfied with glib answers to his inquiries.

This is not to say that he should have made a complete audit. But there were enough danger signals in the materials which he did examine to require some further investigation on his part. Generally accepted accounting standards required such further investigation under these circumstances. It is not always sufficient merely to ask questions.

[58] Here again, the burden of proof is on Peat, Marwick. I find that that burden has not been satisfied. I conclude that Peat, Marwick has not established its due diligence defense.

The Causation Defense

[59] Section 11(a) provides that when a registration statement contains an untrue statement of a material fact or omits to state a material fact, "any person acquiring such security * * * may * * * sue." Section 11(e) provides that:

> "The suit authorized under subsection (a) may be to recover such damages as shall represent the difference between the amount paid for the security (not exceeding the price at which the security was offered to the public) and (1) the value thereof as of the time such suit was brought, or (2) the price at which such security shall have been disposed of in the market before suit, or (3) the price at which such security shall have been disposed of after suit but before judgment if such damages shall be less than the damages representing the difference between the amount paid for the security (not exceeding the price at which the security was offered to the public) and the value thereof as of the time such suit was brought * * *."

Section 11(c) then sets forth a proviso reading as follows:

> "Provided, that if the defendant proves that any portion or all of such damages represents other than the depreciation in value of such security resulting from such part of the registration statement, with respect to which his liability is asserted, not being true or omitting to state a material fact required to be stated therein or nec-

essary to make the statements therein not misleading, such portion of or all such damages shall not be recoverable."

Each defendant in one form or another has relied upon this proviso as a complete defense. Each maintains that the entire damage suffered by each and every plaintiff was caused by factors other than the material falsities and omissions of the registration statement. These factors, in brief, were the decline in the bowling industry which came about because of the fact that the industry was overbuilt and because popular enthusiasm for bowling diminished.

These adverse conditions had begun before these debentures were issued, as evidenced by the growing defaults in customers' notes discounted with Talcott. Talcott did not discount any new notes for BarChris after April 1961. BarChris's financial position, as we have seen, was materially worse in May 1961 than it had been on December 31, 1960.

As time went on, conditions grew worse, both for BarChris and the industry. The receipts of alley operators diminished. New construction of alleys fell off. By 1962 it had almost ceased.

There is a wide disparity in the factual pattern of purchases and sales of BarChris debentures by the plaintiffs in this action. Some plaintiffs bought theirs when the debentures were first issued on May 16, 1961. Others bought theirs later in 1961. Still others purchased theirs at various dates in 1962, some even as late as September 1962, shortly before BarChris went into Chapter XI. In at least one instance, a plaintiff purchased debentures after BarChris was in Chapter XI.

There is a similar disparity as to sales. Some plaintiffs sold their debentures in 1961. Others sold theirs in 1962. Others never sold them.

The position taken by defendants in their affirmative defenses is an extreme one which cannot be sustained. I cannot say that the entire damage suffered by every plaintiff was caused by factors other than the errors and omissions of the registration statement for which these defendants are responsible. As to some plaintiffs, or as to part of the damage sustained by others, that may be true. The only practicable course is to defer decision of this issue until the claim of each individual plaintiff is separately considered. As stated at the outset, this opinion is devoted only to matters common to all plaintiffs.

Other Defenses

Defendants have pleaded additional defenses of estoppel, waiver, release and the statute of limitations. The first three apply, if at all, only to certain plaintiffs, not to every one. These issues, therefore, are also deferred.

I will treat the defense of the statute of limitations in the same way. This may depend to some extent upon the knowledge of individual plaintiffs. Therefore, the question can more readily be determined when the evidence with respect to each separate plaintiff is reviewed.

· · ·

Defendants' motions to dismiss this action, upon which decision was reserved at the trial, are denied. Motions made at various times during the trial to strike certain testimony are also denied, except in so far as such motions pertain to evidence relating to the issues still undecided.

Pursuant to Rule 52(a), this opinion constitutes the court's findings of fact and conclusions of law with respect to the issues determined herein.

So ordered.

[2]   Comments on *Escott v. BarChris*

Notice the court's emphasis on the unhealthy state of the industry and of BarChris. Couple this with the fact that Berardi, a relatively inexperienced senior accountant, performed most of the work. The court observed that:

> Berardi was then about thirty years old. He was not yet a CPA. He had had no previous experience with the bowling industry. This was his first job as a senior accountant. He could hardly have been given a more difficult assignment.

> After obtaining a little background information on BarChris by talking to Logan and reviewing Peat, Marwick's work papers on its 1959 audit, Berardi examined the results of test checks of BarChris's accounting procedures which one of the junior accountants had made, and he prepared an "internal control questionnaire" and an "audit program."

With hindsight, the choice of Berardi to perform the audit was obviously unwise. However, even with foresight, in view of the situation it would seem that Peat, Marwick was almost inviting trouble.

The question of causation is essentially one of fact, and the court indicates that this may vary with the particular plaintiff's case and thus be subsequently determined on an individual basis. The common defense to all the defendants was, of course, the adverse conditions of the bowling industry, which had been publicized prior to the issuance of the debentures. It would seem appropriate to note that the U.S. Supreme Court has never decided a case involving an accountant's liability under Section 11 of the 1933 Act. It would appear that the *Escott v. BarChris* case was destined to be that case. However, *BarChris* was subsequently settled by the parties. In addition, despite Section 11's unfavorable changes in the burden of proof, reliance and privity regarding a defendant's liability under the 1933 Act, litigation has been sparse. One conclusion that might be drawn from these facts is that accountants have risen to the challenge and by the use of greater care, time, and effort have performed admirably when performing this type of an engagement.

[3]   Negligence and the Securities Exchange Act of 1934

Section 18 of the 1934 Act also provides a civil remedy for false or misleading statements in respect to a material fact, typically contained in the annual report (the 10-K Report). However, the similarity to Section 11 of the 1933 Act ends there. Both buyers and *sellers* of securities may sue, but they must prove *actual reliance and causation*. In addition under Section 18 the accountant may avoid liability if it can be established that "he acted in good faith and had no knowledge that the statement was false." Small wonder that litigation under the 1934 Act has almost invariably been based upon Section 10(b) and Rule 10b-5, which does not impose as onerous a burden of proving reliance as does Section 18.

¶ 3.04   Lack of Privity as a Defense

Just what does this not-so-common English noun mean? *Webster's Dictionary*[7] defines *privity* as used in law as "a connection or bond of union between parties, as to some particular transaction." The most common privity and the one we will primarily be concerned with is privity of contract, which simply stated means the relationship between the parties to a contract. Typically, at early common law, the parties were the promisor and the promisee exclusively.

Let's look at a little history first and then look at the state of privity in other common types of transactions before we consider privity as it applies to the accountant-defendant. Early common law rigidly adhered to the privity requirement. It applied the rule almost with a passion. Either you were a party to the contract or you were not, and if not, then you had no rights under it. Thus, for example, if you had *not* purchased a product from the manufacturer, you could not sue the manufacturer but instead could sue the retailer exclusively. Consequently, if you were a mere third party who was named in the contract or was affected by it, rather than being a party to it, you did not have the proper standing to sue on the contract. The procedural device used to bar the plaintiff from proceeding is the demurrer or motion to dismiss, and this is used early in the proceeding. Privity has nothing to do with the factual issue raised, for example, the defendant's alleged negligence, and is decided by the judge as a matter of law. It was and still is, in a limited number of states, a highly effective legal device in the accountant's liability area that knocks the plaintiff right out of court or, better still, causes the plaintiff not to sue because the result is a foregone conclusion.

Volumes have been written on the privity defense and its demise in the product liability area and its past and current status in relation to the accountants' liability problem. However, for fundamental reasons, it no longer merits extensive treatment in this book. The first reason for this statement is that the CPA can do almost nothing in respect to benefiting from this defense unless he is willing to move to one of the few jurisdictions which retain the *Ultramares* rule regarding privity. Next, it is going to be hard to find

---

[7] *Webster's New Intercollegiate Dictionary*, G. & C. Merriam Co., Springfield, MA, 1981.

such a jurisdiction. The clear trend in virtually all jurisdictions today, which have considered the question recently, is to reject it or to substantially narrow its application in respect to CPAs. Finally, as the chart which follows indicates, there are numerous theories, for example, third party beneficiary and fraud, as well as the federal securities acts, which bypass or eliminate the privity defense. Therefore, we are presenting a brief treatment of this dying defense which consists of the *Rosenblum v. Adler* case, which synthesizes the common law approaches, and a summary chart [Figure 3.1] which we hope may be worth a thousand words. To put it another way, privity, like "The old grey mare, she ain't what she used to be," or, if you prefer, "lack of privity is a swiss cheese defense."

[1]   Three Varying Rules

Rosenblum v. Adler
261 A.2d 138
New Jersey Supreme Court (1983)

The opinion of the Court was delivered by

SCHREIBER, Judge.

This case focuses upon the issue of whether accountants should be responsible for their negligence in auditing financial statements. If so, we must decide whether a duty is owed to those with whom the auditor is in privity, to third persons known and intended by the auditor to be the recipients of the audit, and to those who foreseeably might rely on the audit. Subsumed within these questions is a more fundamental one: to what extent does public policy justify imposition of a duty to any of these classes?

I

The issues herein arose on defendants' motion for partial summary judgment. The facts that follow were, therefore, adduced from the record in a light most favorable to the plaintiffs. The plaintiffs Harry and Barry Rosenblum brought this action against Touche Ross & Co. (Touche), a partnership, and the individual partners. Touche, a prominent accounting firm, had audited the financial statements of Giant Stores Corporation (Giant). These plaintiffs, allegedly relying on the correctness of the audits, acquired Giant common stock in conjunction with the sale of their business to Giant. That stock subsequently proved to be worthless, after the financial statements were found to be fraudulent. Plaintiffs claim that Touche negligently conducted the audits and that Touche's negligence was a proximate cause of their loss.

Giant, a Massachusetts corporation, operated discount department stores, retail catalog showrooms and art and gift shops. Its common stock was publicly traded, its initial public offering having been made pursuant to a registration statement filed with the Securities and Exchange Commission (SEC) in 1969. Giant was required to file audited financial statements with the SEC as part of its annual report to stockholders and Touche conducted those audit examinations during the fiscal years 1969 through 1972. Giant's fiscal year was the twelve months ending January 30.

In November 1971 Giant commenced negotiations with the plaintiffs for the acquisition of their businesses in New Jersey (H. Rosenblum, Inc. and Summit Promotions, Inc.). These enterprises had retail catalog showrooms in Summit and Wayne. The merger negotiations culminated in an agreement executed on March 9, 1972. During the discussions two significant events occurred. First, on December 14, 1971, Giant made a public offering of 360,000 shares of its common stock. The financial statements included in the prospectus of that offering contained statements of annual earnings for four years ending January 30, 1971, as well as balance sheets as of January 30 for each of those years, which had been audited by Touche. Touche's opinion affixed to those financials stated that it had examined the statements of earnings and balance sheets "in accordance with generally accepted auditing standards" and that the financial statements "present[ed] fairly" Giant's financial position. Similar data had been incorporated in Giant's annual report for the year ending January 30, 1971. Second, Touche began its audit of Giant's financials for the year ending January 29, 1972. The attached Touche opinion bore the same language affixed to the 1971 statements.

One of the Touche partners, Armin Frankel, was present at some of the merger discussions. It does not appear that he participated in the negotiations, though the plaintiffs assert that they received the January 1971 audited statements during a meeting at which Frankel was present. Although he denies making the projection, Frankel is also alleged to have stated during one meeting that the preliminary figures of the 1972 audit then under way indicated it was going to be "a very strong year for Giant Stores, it is probably going to be the best in history. . . ."

The merger agreement provided that the Rosenblums would receive an amount of Giant stock, up to a maximum of 86,075 shares, depending upon the net income of their enterprises for their fiscal year ending December 31, 1971. The closing was to be scheduled between May 15 and May 31, 1972. Giant agreed that as of the closing it would represent and warrant that there had "been no material adverse change in the business, properties or assets of Giant and its Subsidiaries since July 31, 1971." The plaintiffs claim they relied upon the 1972 audited statements before closing the transaction on June 12, 1972. The Rosenblums received Giant common stock, which had been listed on the American Stock Exchange in February 1972 and was being traded on that Exchange when the merger was effected. After the Rosenblum closing, Giant made another public offering of common stock in August 1972. Touche furnished for this Giant registration statement the audited financial statements for each of the five fiscal years

ending January 29, 1972, to which was affixed Touche's unqualified opinion.

Giant had manipulated its books by falsely recording assets that it did not own and omitting substantial amounts of accounts payable so that the financial information that Touche had certified in the 1971 and 1972 statements was incorrect.[1] The fraud was uncovered in the early months of 1973. Trading in Giant stock on the American Stock Exchange was suspended in April 1973 and never resumed. On May 22, 1973, Touche withdrew its audit for the year ending January 29, 1972. Giant filed a bankruptcy petition in September 1973. The Giant stock received by the plaintiffs in the merger had become worthless.

The plaintiffs' four count complaint, predicated on the audited financials for the years ending January 30, 1971 and January 29, 1972, charged fraudulent misrepresentation, gross negligence, negligence and breach of warranty. Touche moved for partial summary judgment. It sought to have the court dismiss the claims based on alleged negligence in making the audit for the year ending January 30, 1971 and on alleged negligence, gross negligence and fraud in making the audit for the year ending January 29, 1972. The trial court granted the motion with respect to the 1971 financials and denied it as to the 1972 financials. Thus taking into account the decisions of the trial court and the Appellate Division the propriety of the trial court's disposition of Touche's entire motion for partial summary judgment is now before us.

II

An independent auditor is engaged to review and examine a company's financial statements and then to issue an opinion with respect to the fairness of that presentation. That report is customarily attached to the financial statements and then distributed by

---

[1] The SEC found that Touche's audit for the 1972 statements did not meet the requirements of the accounting profession. The SEC entered a consent order of censure against Touche. *In re Touche Ross & Co.*, Securities Exchange Act Release No. 15978, *Fed. Sec. L. Rep.* (CCH) ¶ 72, 175A (1979).

the company for various purposes. Recipients may be stockholders, potential investors, creditors and potential creditors. When these parties rely upon a negligently prepared auditor's report and suffer damages as a result, the question arises whether they may look to the auditor for compensation. In other words, to whom does the auditor owe a duty? The traditional rule is that the auditor's duty is owed only to those with whom he is in privity or to those who are known beneficiaries at the time of the auditor's undertaking. This rule is commonly attributed to an opinion of Chief Judge Cardozo in *Ultramares v. Touche*, 255 N.Y. 170, 174 N.E. 441 (1931). A second rule has been expressed in Section 552 of the *Restatement (Second) of Torts*. Under the *Restatement*, liability is extended to a known and intended class of beneficiaries. For example, if the auditor knows that the report is to be prepared for bank borrowing, then his duty would run to the bank to whom the company delivered the opinion. A third rule is that the auditor's duty is owed to those whom the auditor should reasonably foresee as recipients from the company of the financial statements for authorized business purposes. See *JEB Fasteners v. Marks*, Bloom & Co. [1981] 3 All E.R. 289, 296.

A claim against the auditor is realistically one predicated upon his representations. Though the theory advanced here by the plaintiffs is directed to the service performed by accountants and thus is in the nature of malpractice, their claim can be viewed as grounded in negligent misrepresentation. In the complaint the plaintiffs seek recompense for economic loss from a negligent supplier of a service with whom the claimants are not in privity. It has generally been held with respect to accountants that imposition of liability requires a privity or privity-like relationship between the claimant and the negligent actor. We must examine a number of issues in order to determine whether we should so limit such actions in New Jersey.

First, we shall consider whether, in the absence of privity, an action for negligent misrepresentation may be maintained for economic loss against the provider of a service. This involves (1) a negligent misrepresentation, (2) in furnishing a service, (3) that results in economic loss, (4) to a person not in privity with the declarant.

Second, we shall determine what duty the auditor should bear to best serve the public interest in light of the role of the auditor in today's economy.

III

[1] Negligent misrepresentation is a legally sound concept. An incorrect statement, negligently made and justifiably relied upon, may be the basis for recovery of damages for economic loss or injury sustained as a consequence of that reliance. *Pabon v. Hackensack Auto Sales, Inc.*, 63 N.J. Super. 476, 164 A.2d 773 (App. Div. 1960), presents an example of a valid physical damage claim predicated upon misrepresentation. The driver of an automobile sued the automobile dealer and manufacturer for damages sustained when his steering wheel locked and the automobile went out of control and struck a pole. A judgment of involuntary dismissal at the close of the plaintiff's case was reversed. One theory advanced by the plaintiff was based on the negligent representation made by the dealer that the steering characteristic plaintiff had encountered prior to the accident was not the result of any deficiency, but rather was normal. The Appellate Division observed that negligence might be inferred from the falsity of the representation. It commented:

> A false statement negligently made, and on which justifiable reliance is placed, may be the basis for the recovery of damages for injury sustained as a consequence of such reliance. . . . The statement need not be a factual report, but may consist of an expert opinion. Justification for the imposition of a duty of care upon the speaker is found in the respective positions of the one making the representation and the relying party, the former purporting to exercise the skill and competency compatible with his profession or calling, the latter openly placing his faith on such reputed skill. There must be knowledge, or reason to know, on the part of the speaker that the information is desired for a serious purpose, that the seeker of the information intends to rely upon it, and that if the information or opinion is false or erroneous, the relying party will be injured in person or property.

[2] Recovery of economic loss, due to negligent misrepresentation by one furnishing a service, has long been permitted when there existed a direct contractual relationship between the parties or when the injured third party was a known beneficiary of the defendant's undertaking. Thus, for example, in *Economy B. & L. Ass'n v. West Jersey Title Co.*, 64 N.J.L. 27, 44 A. 854 (Sup. Ct. 1899), the plaintiff agreed to loan $3,000 to one Moore secured by a first mortgage on Moore's property, title to which was to be certified by a title insurance company. Moore advised the defendant title insurance company of his agreement and retained the defendant to make the search and certificate. Moore delivered the certificate to and obtained the loan from the plaintiff. The plaintiff was held to have a good cause of action against the certifying title company when it was discovered that the carelessly made title search had not disclosed a prior recorded mortgage.

Our case law, however, has been split on whether privity or a similar relationship is necessary in a suit against the supplier of a service for negligent misrepresentation causing economic loss.

• • •

We have never passed upon the problem of an accountant's liability to third persons who have relied on negligently audited statements to their economic detriment. Many other jurisdictions have limited an accountant's liability to those with whom the accountant is in privity. The earliest decision in the United States our research has uncovered is *Landell v. Lybrand*, 264 Pa. 406, 107 A. 783 (1919), holding that an accountant was not liable for misstatements in a company's financial statements to a third person who had relied upon the financials and had purchased the company's stock. The leading opinion is that of Chief Judge Cardozo in *Ultramares v. Touche*, 255 N.Y. 170, 174 N.E. 441 (1931). In rejecting a claim against an accounting firm for a negligent audit relied upon by a third person who advanced credit to the firm's client, he wrote:

> If liability for negligence exists, a thoughtless slip or blunder, the failure to detect a theft

or forgery beneath the cover of deceptive entries, may expose accountants to a liability in an indeterminate amount for an indeterminate time to an indeterminate class. The hazards of a business conducted on these terms are so extreme as to enkindle doubt whether a flaw may not exist in the implication of a duty that exposes to these consequences. [255 N.Y. at 179–80, 174 N.E. at 444]

Chief Judge Cardozo, like Chief Justice Beasley in *Kahl*, believed that imposition of this type of exposure would be an undue burden upon the declarants, when balanced against the functions they performed. In *Glanzer v. Shepard*, 233 N.Y. 236, 135 N.E. 275 (1922), Judge Cardozo had held liability did exist in favor of a third party when it was shown that the certification was made for the use of that third person. There a bean seller contracted with the defendant, a professional weigher, to weigh and certify a shipment of beans being sold to the plaintiff. The plaintiff's suit against the professional weigher was upheld because the weigher knew the certification was to be used by the plaintiff. *Ultramares* and *Glanzer* acknowledge the existence of a duty only in favor of the person for whose "primary benefit" the statements were intended.

Many commentators have questioned the wisdom of *Ultramares and Glanzer*. Criticism of the primary benefit rule led in part to the adoption of Section 552 of the *Restatement (Second) of Torts*, which limited liability for negligent misrepresentation to the loss:

> suffered (a) by the person or one of a limited group of persons for whose benefit and guidance he intends to supply the information or knows that the recipient intends to supply it; and (b) through reliance upon it in a transaction that he [the auditor] intends the information to influence or knows that the recipient so intends or in a substantially similar transaction.

When applied to an auditor, the *Restatement* limits the persons to whom he owes a duty to his client, to intended identifiable beneficiaries and to any unidentified member of the intended class of beneficiaries. The only extension in the *Restatement* beyond *Ultra-*

mares and Glanzer appears to be that the auditor need not know the identity of the beneficiaries if they belong to an identifiable group for whom the information was intended to be furnished. There is a substantial split of authority among the courts, some following *Ultramares* and others adopting the *Restatement*. See Annot., "Liability of public accountant to third parties," 46 A.L.R.3d 979, 989 (1972).

[3] Both *Ultramares* and the *Restatement* demand a relationship between the relying third party and the auditor. Unless some policy considerations warrant otherwise, privity should not be, and is not, a salutary predicate to prevent recovery. Generally, within the outer limits fixed by the court as a matter of law, the reasonably foreseeable consequences of the negligent act define the duty and should be actionable.

[4, 5] We long ago discarded the requirement of privity in a products liability case based on negligence. It is interesting to compare his language in *MacPherson* with his position in *Ultramares*. In *MacPherson* Cardozo wrote:

> The contractor who builds a scaffold invites the owner's workmen to use it. The manufacturer who sells the automobile to the retail dealer invites the dealer's customers to use it. The invitation is addressed in the one case to determinate persons and in the other to an indeterminate class, but in each case it is equally plain, and in each case its consequences must be the same [liability for negligence, regardless of the lack of privity].
>
> There is nothing anomalous in a rule which imposes upon A., who has contracted with B., a duty to C. and D. and others according as he knows or does not know that the subject-matter of the contract is intended for their use. [111 N.E. at 1054]

It is clear that an action for negligence with respect to an injury arising out of a defective product may be maintained without privity. The negligence involved may be that ascribable to negligent misrepresentation.

[6] The cases demonstrate that negligent misrepresentations referring to products may be the basis of liability irrespective of privity. Damages for products liability have not been limited to physical injury. Recovery for eco-

nomic loss has also been permitted. In *Santor v. A & M Karagheusian, Inc.*, 44 N.J. 52, 60, 207 A.2d 305 (1965), Justice Francis observed that

> [f]rom the standpoint of principle, we perceive no sound reason why the implication of reasonable fitness should be attached to the transaction and be actionable against the manufacturer where the defectively-made product has caused personal injury, and not actionable when inadequate manufacture has put a worthless article in the hands of an innocent purchaser who has paid the required price for it.[2]

Why should a claim of negligent misrepresentation be barred in the absence of privity when no such limit is imposed where the plaintiff's claim also sounds in tort, but is based on liability for defects in products arising out of a negligent misrepresentation? If recovery for defective products may include economic loss, why should such loss not be compensable if caused by negligent misrepresentation? The maker of the product and the person making a written representation with intent that it be relied upon are, respectively, impliedly holding out that the product is reasonably fit, suitable and safe and that the representation is reasonably sufficient, suitable and accurate. The fundamental issue is whether there should be any duty to respond in damages for economic loss owed to a foreseeable user neither in privity with the declarant nor intended by the declarant to be the user of the statement or opinion.

IV

There remains to be considered whether the public interest will be served by a proposition holding an auditor responsible for negligence to those persons who the auditor should rea-

---

[2] A number of jurisdictions have adopted the approach set forth in *Santor*, but permitting recovery in tort for economic loss in such cases is not as yet the majority rule. See cases cited in *Pennsylvania Glass Sand v. Caterpillar Tractor Co.*, 652 F.2d 1165, 1171 n. 17 (3d Cir. 1981) (applying Pennsylvania law). The leading case holding that economic loss is not recoverable is *Seely v. White Motor Co.*, 63 Cal.2d 9, 45 *Cal. Rptr.* 17, 403 P.2d 145 (1965).

sonably foresee will be given the audit to rely upon and do in fact place such reliance on the audit to their detriment. Should there be such a duty imposed? Chief Justice Weintraub in *Goldberg v. Housing Auth. of Newark*, 38 N.J. 578, 583, 186 A.2d 291 (1962), explained the judicial analysis that must be made:

Whether a duty exists is ultimately a question of fairness. The inquiry involves a weighing of the relationship of the parties, the nature of the risk, and the public interest in the proposed solution.

See also Suter v. San Angelo Foundry & Machine Co., 81 N.J. 150, 172–73, 406 A.2d 140 (1979); *Newmark v. Gimbel's Inc.*, 54 N.J. 585, 596–97, 258 A.2d 697 (1969) (stating that doctors and dentists should not be held to duty of strict liability because they furnish services essential to society that are so necessarily and intimately related to public health that their obligation ought to be expressed in a duty to exercise reasonable competence and care to their patients; that the importance of these services "outweighs in the [policy] scale any need for imposition . . . of the rules of strict liability in tort"); *Caputzal v. The Lindsay Co.*, 48 N.J. 69, 75–76, 222 A.2d 513 (1966); 2 Harper & James, *Law of Torts* § 18.6, at 1052 (1956) (suggesting policy considerations involve balancing of several factors: " the burden [that the suggested duty] would put on defendant's activity; the extent to which the risk is one normally incident to that activity; the risk and the burden to plaintiff; the respective availability and cost of insurance to the two parties; the prevalence of insurance in fact; the desirability and effectiveness of putting the pressure to insure on one rather than the other, and the like").

The fairness of the imposition of a duty on accountants cannot be appraised without an understanding of the independent accountant's auditing function. It is particularly important to be aware of the independent auditor's role in order to assess the propriety of imposing any duty to those who may rely on the audit.

Accounting is the act of identifying, measuring, recording, and communicating financial information about an economic unit. In

W. Pyle & J. White, *Fundamental Accounting Principles* 1 (1972). It has been said that

accountability has clearly been the social and organizational backbone of accounting for centuries. Modern society and organizations depend upon intricate networks of accountability which are based on the recording and reporting of these activities. This process of accounting is essential to the proper functioning of society and organizations. Accounting, therefore, starts with the recording and reporting of activities and their consequences, and ends with the discharging of accountability. This basically describes accounting, at least if we attempt to interpret the existing practice rationally. We may, therefore, say that *accountability is what distinguishes accounting* from other information systems in an organization or in a society. [Y. Ijiri, "Theory of Accounting Measurement," Studies in Accounting Research No. 10 (American Accounting Association) 32 (1975) (emphasis added)]

The company prepares the financial statements in the first instance. The independent auditor's role in the accountability process is to scrutinize management's accountability reports. Commission on Auditors' Responsibilities, American Institute of Certified Public Accountants, *Report, Conclusions and Recommendations* 1 (1978). The auditor must make such an examination so as to enable him to express an opinion on the fairness of the financial presentation in the statements. The professional standards of the American Institute of Certified Public Accountants express the auditor's function as follows:

The objective of the ordinary examination of financial statements by the independent auditor is the expression of an opinion on the fairness with which they present financial position, results of operations, and changes in financial position in conformity with generally accepted accounting principles. [Statements on Auditing Standards, 1 AICPA, Professional Standards, § 110.01 (1972)][3]

---

[3] Similarly, the Securities and Exchange Commission requires that the auditor's examination be made in accordance with generally accepted auditing standards. As amended in Release No. AS-195, Reg. § 210.2-02, 41 Fed.Reg. 35479 (1976).

The auditor is concerned with generally accepted accounting principles, that is, acceptable assumptions, procedures and techniques for the preparation of financial statements. Dawson, "Auditor's Third Party Liability," 46 *Wash.L.Rev.* 675, 691 (1971). Auditing standards have been developed by the American Institute of Certified Public Accountants governing examination of statements and reporting as to whether generally accepted principles and practices have been followed. Statements on Auditing Standards, 1 AICPA, Professional Standards, § 110.01 (1972).

To perform these functions the auditor must, among other things, familiarize himself with the business, its operation and reporting methods and industry-wide conditions. It is necessary to understand the financial and accounting characteristics and practices of the enterprise. In short, the auditor must be so knowledgeable that he can render an "informed opinion."

There are certain limitations within the accounting framework. The proper accounting treatment of some matters may not be settled. For example, research and development might be written off immediately as an expense or capitalized and disposed of over a period of time. Similarly, there is considerable debate over the proper method for depreciating intangible assets. An auditor's review is subject to similar constraints because the financial statements cannot be more reliable than the underlying accounting methodology. The auditor must critically evaluate the accounting principles selected to measure performance, but some of the basic data upon which the auditor relies are not as a practical matter verifiable. The auditor is neither required to investigate every supporting document, nor deemed to have the training or skills of a lawyer or criminal investigator. Commission on Auditor's Responsibilities, American Institute of Certified Public Accountants, *Report, Conclusions and Recommendations* 45 (1978).

[7–9] Nonetheless, the independent auditor should be expected to detect illegal or improper acts that would be uncovered in the exercise of normal professional skill and care. The auditor should exercise reasonable care in verifying the underlying data and examining the methodology employed in preparing the financial statements. The accountant must determine whether there are suspicious circumstances and, even in the absence of suspicious circumstances, make a reasonable sampling or apply some testing technique. Hawkins, "Professional Negligence Liability of Public Accountants," 12 *Vand.L.Rev.* 797, 805 (1959). This does not mean the auditor will always be able to discover material fraud. Yet the audit, particularly when it uncovers fraud, dishonesty, or some other illegal act, serves an undeniably beneficial public purpose.

At one time the audit was made primarily to inform management of irregularities and inefficiencies in the business. See Hallett & Collins, "Auditors' Responsibility for Misrepresentation: Inadequate Protections for Users of Financial Statements," 44 *Wash.L.Rev.* 139, 178 (1968); Comment, "Accountant's Liability for Negligence," 48 *Fordham L.Rev.* 401, 405 (1979). That function remains one of the principal reasons for the audit. Gradually a need for independent audits was generated by public ownership of business enterprises and by requirements of the stock exchanges[4] and the Securities and Exchange Commission (SEC).[5] Institutional investors, investment specialists, stockholders, and lenders demanded more and reliable information. It is now well recognized that the audited statements are made for the use of third parties who have no contractual relationship with the auditor. Moreover, it is common knowledge that companies

---

[4] *New York Stock Exchange Co. Manual*, § A67–78, 24.13, 24.24.

[5] The Securities Act of 1933 requires that the prospectuses filed with respect to public offerings of securities include certified financial statements 15 *U.S.C.A.* §§ 77g, aa (1981). Many companies must file an annual report, Form 10-K, containing certified financial statements within 90 or 120 days of the end of each fiscal year. The Securities Exchange Act of 1934 requires that independent certified financial statements be included in annual reports, which must be filed by almost all companies having assets of at least $1,000,000 and 500 holders of a class of equity securities. 15 *U.S.C.A.* § 781 (g)(1) (1981).

use audits for many proper business purposes, such as submission to banks and other lending institutions that might advance funds and to suppliers of services and goods that might advance credit. The SEC twenty-five years ago stated: "The responsibility of a public accountant is not only to the client who pays his fee, but also to investors, creditors and others who may rely on the financial statements which he certifies." *In re Touche, Niven, Bailey & Smart*, 37 *S.E.C.* 629, 670 (1957). These uses as well as governmental requirements make financial statements reviewed by independent qualified accountants indispensable. Government has increasingly utilized accounting as a means to control business activities. Some examples of such use are public utility rate regulation and regulation of banks and insurance companies. The SEC has emphasized accountability through disclosure, accomplished in part by examinations and reports of independent auditors under the Securities Act of 1933 and the Securities Exchange Act of 1934.

In *In re Kerlin*, SEC Accounting Release 105 (1966), the Securities and Exchange Commission observed:

> A public accountant's examination is intended to be an independent check upon management's accounting of its stewardship. Thus he ha[s] a direct and unavoidable responsibility of his own, particularly where his engagement relates to a company which makes filings with the Commission or in which there is substantial public interest.

The auditor's function has expanded from that of a watchdog for management to an independent evaluator of the adequacy and fairness of financial statements issued by management to stockholders, creditors, and others. Broad, "The Progress of Auditing," 100 *J. Accountancy* 38, 38–39 (1955); Hallett & Collins, "Auditors' Responsibility for Misrepresentation," 44 *Wash.L.Rev.* 139, 178 (1968).

The changing function of an independent public accountant has been described as follows by J. Carey, one-time executive director of the American Institute of Accountants, in *Professional Ethics of Public Accounting* (1946) at 13–14:

Whenever he certifies a financial statement the certified public accountant is potentially, at least, rendering a service to two or more parties whose interests may come into conflict—management and stockholder, borrower and lender, purchaser and seller. He may, and often does, serve simultaneously competitors in the same line of business, without fear on the part of either client that he will favor the one or the other. It is the peculiar obligation of the certified public accountant, which no other profession has to impose on its members, to maintain a wholly objective and impartial attitude toward the affairs of the client whose financial statements he certifies. The certified public accountant acknowledges a moral responsibility (and under the Securities Act this is made a legal and financial responsibility) to be as mindful of the interests of strangers who may rely on his opinion as of the interests of the client who pays his fee. This is at the same time a heavy burden and a proud distinction. It marks the certified public accountant as an individual of the highest integrity; a tough-minded technician whose judgment cannot be unbalanced by the strongest pressures, who stakes a hard-earned professional reputation on his ability to express a fair and just opinion on which all concerned may rely; in the broad sense, a highly useful servant to society as a whole.

. . . The certified public accountant, therefore, in providing accounting statements which all concerned may accept as disinterested expressions, based on technically sound procedures and experienced judgment, may serve as a kind of arbiter, interpreter, and umpire among all the varied interests. Thereby he can eliminate the necessity for costly separate investigations by each party at interest, as well as endless doubts, delays, misunderstandings, and controversies which are so much sand in the economic machine. [Quoted in *In re Touche, Niven, Bailey & Smart*, 37 *S.E.C.* 629, 671 (1957)]

The two most important qualities of the auditor are the expertise that he brings to the project and the independence with which he performs his task. See Wixon & Kell, *Accountants' Handbook* 28.1 (4th ed. 1956). The auditor is not only labeled as independent, but also is expected to be independent in fact. The public accountant must report fairly on the facts whether favorable or unfavorable to the client. See 82 *J. Accountancy* 449, 453 (1946). It is generally in management's interest that the financial statements reflect performance in the most favorable light. There is an inherent divergence of interests between management and third persons who will rely upon these statements. Without the auditor's oversight, management might be tempted to tilt certain items in its favor or to commit outright misrepresentation.

The Legislature has expressed its concern for the competence of accountants by enacting the Public Accounting Act of 1977, which requires that public accountants be certified or registered upon fulfilling certain standards. *N.J.S.A.* 45:2B–1 to –37. The declared legislative purpose of the Act is

> to promote the dependability of information which is used for guidance in financial transactions or for accounting for or assessing the status or performance of commercial and noncommercial enterprises, whether public or private. The public interest requires that persons attesting, as experts in accounting, to the reliability or the fairness of presentation, of such information be qualified in fact to do so; that a public authority competent to prescribe and assess the qualifications of public accountants be established; and that the attestation of financial information by persons professing expertise in accounting be reserved to persons who demonstrate their ability and fitness to observe and apply the standards of the accounting profession. [*N.J.S.A.* 45:2B–2]

The objection to imposing a duty on accountants to third persons to whom the statements have been given by the company for proper business purposes is the spectre of financial catastrophe. It is feared that the unknown costs will be so severe that accounting firms will not be able to absorb the losses that will be visited upon them, particularly because in all likelihood the audited clients will be judgment proof or unable to satisfy their share of the indebtedness due. The reasonableness of this concern is questionable.

[10,11] Many who would benefit from the rule that an auditor owes a duty of reasonable care to those to whom the company may foreseeably deliver the audit are now protected. Accounting firms are presently liable to purchasers of securities in public offerings when they have misstated a material fact in the financial statements. Securities Act of 1933, 15 *U.S.C.A.* § 77k (1981). It is interesting to compare the elements constituting liability under the Securities Act of 1933 with the traditional negligence (non-privity) standard. Accountants' liability under Section 11 is often available where an action for ordinary negligence would not succeed. Under section 11 the plaintiff need not prove scienter, negligence, or proximate cause; the burden of proof is on the accountants to establish freedom from negligence or "due diligence." *See generally Herman & MacLean v. Huddleston,—U.S.—, —,* 103 *S.Ct.* 683, 687, 74 *L.Ed.*2d 548, 555 (1983). Section 18 of the Securities Exchange Act of 1934 creates a civil liability for any person who causes a misleading statement to be made in any report filed with the SEC under the 1934 Act. 15 *U.S.C.A.* 78r. The plaintiff must prove reliance and the defendant is not responsible if "he acted in good faith and had no knowledge that such statement was false or misleading." Under those statutes privity is not a defense and accountants may have substantial liabilities to third persons. *Escott v. BarChris Construction Corp.,* 283 *F.Supp.* 643 (S.D.N.Y. 1968) (auditor liability under Section 11 of Securities Act of 1933); *Fischer v. Kletz,* 266 *F.Supp.* 180 (S.D.N.Y.1967) (auditor liability under Section 18 of the Securities Exchange Act); *see generally, Ernst & Ernst v. Hochfelder,* 425 *U.S.* 185, 207–211, 96 *S.Ct.* 1375, 1387–1389, 47 *L.Ed.*2d 668 (1976).[6] Even under the rule of *Ultramares* accounting firms are liable, irrespective of privity, to all third persons for fraud and gross

---

[6] Proof of intent to deceive or defraud is also the primary element necessary for liability under section 10(b) of the Securities Exchange Act of 1934, 15 *U.S.C.A.* 78(b). *See Herman & MacLean v. Huddleston,* —— *U.S.* at ——, 103 *S.Ct.* at 688, 74 *L.Ed.*2d at 556. An accountant can be held liable for the same conduct under section 10(b) and under section 11 of the 1933 Act. *ID* —— *U.S.* at ——, 103 *S.CT.* at 690, 74 *L.Ed.*2d at 559.

negligence that raises an inference of fraud. *Ultramares*, 174 *N.E.* at 448–49; see also *Merit Ins. Co. v. Colao*, 603 F.2d 654, 657–58 (7th Cir. 1979) (applying Illinois law), cert. denied, 445 *U.S.* 929, 100 *S.Ct.* 1318, 63 *L.Ed.*2d 763 (1980); *State Street Trust Co. v. Ernst*, 278 *N.Y.* 104, 112, 15 *N.E.*2d 416, 418–19 (1938); *Duro Sportswear v. Cogen*, 131 *N.Y.S.*2d 20 (1954), aff'd, 285 *App.Div.* 867, 137 *N.Y.S.*2d 829 (1955).

Independent auditors have apparently been able to obtain liability insurance covering these risks or otherwise to satisfy their financial obligations. We have no reason to believe that they may not purchase malpractice insurance policies that cover their negligent acts leading to misstatements relied upon by persons who receive the audit from the company pursuant to a proper business purpose.[7]

_____

[7] Accountants have been able to obtain insurance covering their liability under the securities laws. While such liability is imposed under different circumstances, it is often easier to establish and can be similar in amount to that imposed here.

In 1976, a survey taken by the Practicing Law Institute indicated that accounting firms had little difficulty in obtaining insurance at a reasonable cost. One insurance plan is "sponsored monthly by the American Home Insurance Company and the Federal Insurance Company, the American Home writing the initial coverage, with the Federal taking the excess coverage." Practicing Law Institute, Tax Law and Practice. Transcript Series, No. 4, Accountants' Liability (J. McCord, ed., 1969). Moreover, a new insurance program sponsored by AICPA covers all claims against the insured including defense costs, except those involving intentional fraud. See Levine & Marks, *Accountants' Liability Insurance— Perils and Pitfalls*, J. Accountancy, Oct. 1976, at 59, 60. The accountant is insured for liabilities up to five million dollars, and the plan is designed for firms with staffs of less than 250 people. Rollins Burdick Hunter, AICPA Professional Liability Insurance Plan (1979) (on file with *Fordham Law Review*). Like all insurance policies, these liability policies offer the accounting profession the advantage of risk-spreading. [48 *Fordham L.Rev.* at 415, n. 81]

The imposition of a duty to foreseeable users may cause accounting firms to engage in more thorough reviews. This might entail setting up stricter standards and applying closer supervision, which should tend to reduce the number of instances in which liability would ensue. Much of the additional costs incurred either because of more thorough auditing review or increased insurance premiums would be borne by the business entity and its stockholders or its customers.

[12,13] The extent of financial exposure has certain built-in limits. The plaintiffs would have to establish that they received the audited statements from the company pursuant to a proper company purpose, that they, in accordance with that purpose, relied on the statements and that the misstatements therein were due to the auditor's negligence and were a proximate cause of the plaintiff's damage.[8] The injured party would be limited to recovery of actual losses due to reliance on the misstatement.[9] Negligence of the injured party could bar or limit the amount of recovery under the Comparative Negligence Act. *N.J.S.A.* 2A:15–5.1. The accounting firm could seek indemnification or contribution from the company and those blameworthy officers or employees. The auditors could in

_____

See also 5 *Nat'l L.J.* 1 (1983).

At oral argument defendants contended that the cost of insurance to cover the claims of all foreseeable users of audits would be catastrophic. Suffice it to say that defendants have not alerted us to data either within or outside the record to support this position.

[8] In *Toromont Industrial Holdings Ltd v. Thorne, Gunn, Helliwell & Christenson* [1976] 62 *D.L.R.*(3d) 225, [1976] 73 *D.L.R.*(3d) 122, the Ontario High Court found that the negligent audit was not the cause of the plaintiffs' takeover bid, that is, that the plaintiffs would have made the purchase anyway. The Ontario Court of Appeals found that the negligent audit had damaged the plaintiffs to the extent that they were forced to incur the cost of preparing a new audit.

[9] It is the actual loss suffered, not the benefit of the bargain, that the plaintiff may gain as recovery. *See Scott Group Ltd. v. McFarlane* [1978] 1 *N.Z.L.R.* 553 (opinion of Cooke, J.) [New Zealand] *West Coast Finance Ltd. v. Gunderson, Stokes, Walton & Co.* [1974] 44 *D.L.R.*(3d) 232 [1975] 56 *D.L.R.*(3d) 460 [Canada].

some circumstances, such as when auditing a privately owned company, expressly limit in their certificates the persons or class of persons who would be entitled to rely upon the audit. Some commentators recognize that a "factor which may limit the foresight of reasonable reliance is the presence of a disclaimer of responsibility attached to the information." Stanton & Dugdale, "Recent Developments in Professional Negligence—II: Accountant's Liability to Third Parties," 132 *New L.J.* 5 (1982). *See also Hedley Byrne & Co. v. Heller Partners* [1964] AC 54, [1963] 2 *All E.R.* 575 (holding disclaimer was effective). In the final analysis the injured party should recover damages due to an independent auditor's negligence from that auditor. This would shift the loss from the innocent creditor or investor to the one responsible for the loss. Accountants will also be encouraged to exercise greater care leading to greater diligence in conducting audits. See 44 *Wash.L.Rev.* at 177 (stating that "[a]lthough courts may be the poorest forum in which to formulate standards, civil liability is probably the most effective means . . . of providing a sufficient incentive for the profession to undertake further self-regulation").

Similar thoughts were expressed in *Rusch Factors, Inc. v. Levin:*

> Why should an innocent reliant party be forced to carry the weighty burden of an accountant's professional malpractice? Isn't the risk of loss more easily distributed and fairly spread by imposing it on the accounting profession, which can pass the cost of insuring against the risk onto its customers, who can in turn pass the cost onto the entire consuming public? Finally, wouldn't a rule of foreseeability elevate the cautionary techniques of the accounting profession? For these reasons it appears to this Court that the decision in *Ultramares* constitutes an unwarranted inroad upon the principle that "[t]he risk reasonably to be perceived defines the duty to be obeyed." *Palsgraf v. Long Island R.R.*, 248 *N.Y.* 339, 344, 162 *N.E.* 99, 100, 59 *A.L.R.* 1253. [284 *F.Supp.* 85, 91 (D.R.I.1968) (applying Rhode Island law) (dictum)]

Recently Justice Wiener, in his article "Common Law Liability of the Certified Public Accountant for Negligent Misrepresentation," concluded:

> The time has come to absolve the negligent accountant of this anachronistic protection. Accountant liability based on foreseeable injury would serve the dual functions of compensation for injury and deterrence of negligent conduct. Moreover, it is just and rational judicial policy that the same criteria govern the imposition of negligence liability, regardless of the context in which it arises. The accountant, the investor and the general public will in the long run benefit when the liability of the certified public accountant for negligent misrepresentation is measured by the foreseeability standard. [20 *San Diego L.Rev.* 233, 260 (1983)]

[14] When the independent auditor furnishes an opinion with no limitation in the certificate as to whom the company may disseminate the financial statements, he has a duty to all those whom that auditor should reasonably foresee as recipients from the company of the statements for its proper business purposes, provided that the recipients rely on the statements pursuant to those business purposes.[10] The principle that we have adopted applies by its terms only to those foreseeable users who receive the audited statements from the business entity for a proper business purpose to influence a business decision of the user, the audit having been made for that business entity. Thus, for example, an institutional investor or portfolio manager who does not obtain audited statements from the company would not come within the stated principle. Nor would stock-

---

[10] A similar thought was expressed by Judge Woolf in *JEB Fasteners Ltd. v. Marks, Bloom & Co.* [1981] 3 All E.R. 289, 296 [Queen's Bench, England], who endorsed the view that auditors should be liable to those who foreseeably and reasonably rely on their representations of the financial position of the audited entity.

Judge Woolf agreed with another jurist who found it "paradoxical that no duty of care should be owed to those who can be foreseen likely to sustain damage if carelessness existed, but that a duty of care should be owed to those, their clients, in respect of whom there is no foreseeable risk of damage" when the defalcation is due in the first instance to the client. *Id.* at 296.

holders who purchased the stock after a negligent audit be covered in the absence of demonstrating the necessary conditions precedent. Those and similar cases beyond the stated rule are not before us and we express no opinion with respect to such situations.

Certified financial statements have become the benchmark for various reasonably foreseeable business purposes and accountants have been engaged to satisfy those ends. In those circumstances accounting firms should no longer be permitted to hide within the citadel of privity and avoid liability for their malpractice. The public interest will be served by the rule we promulgate this day.

V

A. The 1971 Audit

Both the trial court and the Appellate Division ruled that the plaintiffs' claim based on negligent preparation of the 1971 audit could not be sustained because the accountants were not aware at the time the audit was prepared of the existence of the plaintiffs or of a limited class of which the plaintiffs were members. The defendant's audit had been completed on April 16, 1971 and Giant's merger discussions with the plaintiff did not begin until the following September.[11] Therefore the defendants had no knowledge of the Rosenblums or the prospective merger at the time of the preparation of the audit and there could be no liability under *Ultramares* or the *Restatement*.

It may be contended under one view of the evidence that the defendants knowingly permitted and authorized plaintiffs' use of the 1971 audit. In doing so, they were aware that the plaintiffs would rely on that audit. Under these circumstances, the defendants implicitly represented to the plaintiffs, as they had represented in their certificate to Giant, that defendants had examined the 1971 statements of earnings and balance sheet

"in accordance with generally accepted auditing standards" and that the financial statements "present[ed] fairly" Giant's financial position. There is evidence that the plaintiffs relied on these financial statements. It was also reasonably inferable that the audit had been made carelessly and negligently, resulting in false statements and in the plaintiffs' loss.

Defendants' presence and participation in the merger proceedings were not gratuitous. Any representations were made by defendants on behalf of their client Giant. Liability would be sustainable under the traditional rationale of *Glanzer v. Shepard, supra*, and *Economy B. & L. Ass'n v. West Jersey Title Co., supra*.

However, the facts supporting this position are somewhat attenuated. We are not unmindful that *R.* 4:46–2 provides that summary judgment shall be entered when "there is no genuine issue as to any material fact challenged." Implicated is the policy consideration that "protection is to be afforded against groundless claims" to save the expenses of protracted litigation and "reserve judicial manpower and facilities." *Robbins v. Jersey City*, 23 N.J. 229, 241, 128 A.2d 673 (1957); *see also United Rental Equip. Co. v. Aetna Life & Cas. Ins. Co.*, 74 N.J. 92, 99, 376 A.2d 1183 (1977). We therefore deem it appropriate to apply the somewhat broader principle enunciated above because the trial court may be faced with this issue at the trial. In adopting that position we are aware of the observation of Chief Justice Weintraub in *Busik v. Levine*, 63 N.J. 351, 363, 307 A.2d 571, appeal dismissed for want of substantial federal question, 414 U.S. 1106, 94 S.Ct. 831, 38 L.Ed.2d 733 (1973), that "[w]hether an issue will be dealt with narrowly or expansively calls for a judge's evaluation of many things, including the need for guidance for the bar or agencies of government or the general public." *See also Rova Farms Resort v. Investors Ins. Co.*, 65 N.J. 474, 502, 323 A.2d 495 (1974).

When the defendants prepared the Giant audit, they knew or should have known that Giant would probably use the audited figures for many proper business purposes. They knew that it was to be incorporated in Giant's annual report, a report that would be trans-

---

[11] The same audit report was used in the prospectus and registration statement covering 360,000 shares of Giant common stock offered on December 14, 1971.

mitted to each Giant stockholder, and would be filed with the SEC in conjunction with Giant's proxy solicitation material for its annual stockholder meeting.[12] The defendants also knew or should have known that the audited financial statements would be available and useful for other proper business purposes, such as public offerings of securities, credit, and corporate acquisitions. These were clearly foreseeable potential uses of the audited financials at the time of their preparation. Giant and the defendant auditors knew that these financial statements would be used at least until the next financial statements had been audited and released.

Defendants became aware of plaintiffs' existence and their intended use of these statements before the plaintiffs relied on the accuracy of these financials. The defendants knew that the merger agreement included a representation that the prospectus used for the public offering in December 1971 contained no untrue statement of a material fact and did not omit to state any material fact. The defendants knew that this prospectus included their opinion that the financials had been prepared in accordance with generally accepted accounting principles and fairly presented Giant's financial condition. The defendants' representations were of a continuing nature and their obligation was a continuing one. See Fischer v. Kletz, 266 F.Supp. 180 (S.D.N.Y.1967), (accountants discovering inaccuracy after audit was released held under duty to disclose after-acquired information).

[15] Defendants' ignorance of the precise use to which the statements would be put does not eliminate their obligation. Applying the principle previously stated, we find first that it is necessary only that Giant, the entity for whom the audit was being made, used it for a proper business purpose. There was no limitation in the accountants' opinion. They could reasonably expect that their client would distribute the statements in furtherance of matters relating to its business. Having inserted the audit in that economic stream, the defendants should be responsible for their careless misrepresentations to parties who justifiably relied upon their expert opinions.

[16] On the motion for summary judgment the facts viewed favorably from the plaintiffs' perspective are that the defendants negligently prepared their audit of Giant's financial statements reflecting Giant's operations for the twelve months ending January 30, 1971 and its financial status on that date. These statements were subsequently delivered by Giant, in furtherance of its business, to the plaintiffs for their consideration in determining whether to sell their enterprises to Giant, whether to accept Giant stock and how much stock to seek. Indeed, the defendants became aware of the fact that these financials had been delivered to the plaintiffs in connection with the proposed merger. The plaintiffs, allegedly relying upon the defendants' express representations, entered into the merger agreement which was subsequently consummated. As a result, plaintiffs claim to have suffered damages. Under these circumstances, the courts below erred in striking the cause of action predicated on the negligent auditing of the financial data for the year ending January 30, 1971.

B. The 1972 Audit

[17] The trial court denied defendants' motion to dismiss the plaintiffs' claims of fraud and negligence ascribable to the 1972 audit. The defendants contend that the plaintiffs had already signed and were bound by the merger contract executed on March 9, 1972 at the time the audit was issued in April 1972. Therefore, the defendants argue that there could be no causal relationship between defendants' alleged fraud and negligence and the plaintiff's damage. However, the merger agreement contained a Giant representation and warranty that there would be no material adverse change in its business, property or assets at the time of the closing. We cannot say on this record that disclosures of the true Giant situation exposed by a non-negligent audit would not have justified the plaintiffs' refusal to consummate the deal. There is a factual dispute over whether the plaintiffs re-

---

[12] The audit was necessary in conjunction with the SEC Form 10-K. This had to be filed within 90 or 120 days after the end of Giant's fiscal year on January 30, 1971.

lied on the 1972 audit. We do note that there is evidence in the depositions that the plaintiffs expected to receive the 1972 audited figures before the closing and would have refused to consummate the transaction if these data had reflected a material adverse change in Giant's business. Moreover, adequate disclosures might have exposed a fraud on the part of Giant that would have justified rescission of the contract. A contractual obligation alone does not require one to close a financially disastrous transaction when valid grounds exist to disavow the contract.

Irrespective of whether the defendants had actual knowledge of Giant's proposed use of the 1972 audit in connection with the merger, it was reasonably foreseeable that Giant would use the audited statement in connection with the merger and its consummation. This is particularly so since the de-fendants were familiar with the merger agreement and had been engaged by Giant to audit the books and records of the plaintiffs' enterprises for the purpose of the merger. The trial court properly denied defendants' motion.

The judgment granting defendants' motion for partial summary judgment with respect to the 1971 financial statements is reversed and that denying defendants' motion for partial summary judgment with respect to the 1972 financial statements is affirmed. The cause is remanded to the trial court for further proceedings consistent with this opinion.

For reversal and remandment—Chief Justice WILENTZ and Justices CLIFFORD, SCHREIBER, HANDLER, POLLOCK, O'HERN and GARIBALDI—7.

For affirmance—None.

[2]   Recent Developments in Other States

As the *Rosenblum v. Adler* case indicates, in respect to accountants the general privity rule currently applicable in the United States is being considered *de novo* or is being reconsidered by the courts of many jurisdictions. Currently three divergent approaches have emerged.

First, an ever-diminishing number of jurisdictions have retained the traditional favorable privity limitation stated in *Ultramares v. Touche* (*supra*, ¶ 1.01 [2]). However, to the extent there has been no recent reaffirmation by a given state's supreme court, the "pure" privity limitation must be considered to be of doubtful validity.

The middle ground position as discussed in the *Rosenblum* case is contained in the Restatement Rule 552 set forth below in its entirety. At present, this would appear to be the rule adopted by the majority of courts which have recently reconsidered the privity rule. Thus, the once powerful *Ultramares* privity limitation which was created by New York State has been substantially eroded.

The third approach, the one adopted by the New Jersey court in *Rosenblum*, is a resort to the general rule of common law negligence which was articulated in the most famous and one of the most controversial tort cases ever decided—*Palsgraf v. Long Island R.R. Company*.[13] The narrow limitation placed upon a plaintiff's right to recover by that case is phrased in terms of "reasonably foreseeable harm" to the plaintiff or the class of people to which the plaintiff belongs. Obviously, such a rule offers virtually no hope for accountants seeking to avoid lawsuits by third parties. This "reasonably foreseeable" rule has also been adopted in 1983 by the Wisconsin Supreme Court in *Citizens Bank v. Timm, Schmidt & Co.*[14] This approach also prevails in the United Kingdom.

---

[13] 248 N.Y. 339, 162 N.E. 99 (1928).

[14] 113 Wisc. 376 (1983).

The overall picture of the role privity now plays in respect to defendant-accountants can be readily grasped from the synthesizing table presented below. Privity even at its best appears to be a "swiss cheese" rule—and at its worst, non-existent.

Restatement Rule: NEGLIGENT MISREPRESENTATION
SECTION 552
Information Negligently Supplied for the Guidance of Others

1. One who, in the course of his business, profession or employment, or in any other transaction in which he has a pecuniary interest, supplies false information for the guidance of others in their business transactions, is subject to liability for pecuniary loss caused to them by their justifiable reliance upon the information, if he fails to exercise reasonable care or competence in obtaining or communicating the information.

2. Except as stated in Subsection (3), the liability stated in Subsection (1) is limited to loss suffered

    a. By the person or one of a limited group of persons for whose benefit and guidance he intends to supply the information or knows that the recipient intends to supply it; and

    b. Through reliance upon it in a transaction that he intends the information to influence or knows that the recipient so intends or in a substantially similar transaction.

3. The liability of one who is under a public duty to give the information extends to loss suffered by any of the class of persons for whose benefit the duty is created, in any of the transactions in which it is intended to protect them.

Figure 3.1 shows the decline of the accountant's privity defense.

Accountant's Privity Defense

1. Third Party Beneficiary Status
2. Actual Fraud
3. Constructive Fraud
4. Gross Negligence
5. The Federal Securities Acts
6. The Restatement Rule
7. Judicial Overrule and Rejection

Figure 3.1.   The decline of the citadel of privity.

[3]   Postscript: The Fourth Rule

During the final production stage of this book, i.e., just prior to the return of page proofs, the New York State Court of Appeals added a fourth rule regarding the privity defense. This new rule will undoubtedly be referred to as the "linkage-conduct" or "direct nexus" rule. On the above chart (Figure 3.1) this revised New York rule would be placed between the Restatement rule and that of the *Ultramares* case. However, it certainly is closer to

Ultramares than to the Restatement rule, which is specifically rejected. This rule was stated in two cases jointly decided by the New York State Court of Appeals, to wit: *Credit Alliance Corp. et al. v. Arthur Andersen & Co.* and *European American Bank and Trust Company v. Strauhs and Kaye et al.*[15] The court stated the rule as follows:

> Before accountants may be held liable in negligence to noncontractual parties who rely to their detriment on inaccurate financial reports, certain prerequisites must be satisfied; (1) the accountants must have been aware that the financial reports were to be used for a particular purpose or purposes; (2) in the furtherance of which a known party or parties was intended to rely; and (3) there must have been some conduct on the part of the accountants linking them to that party or parties, which evinces the accountant's understanding of that party or parties' reliance.

The impact this decision (by the court which gave us *Ultramares*) will have in other jurisdictions is problematical. However, it should be noted that the court's rationale provided little or nothing in the way of analysis of the policy factors which led it to apply the privity limitation to the creditor in *Credit Alliance*. Furthermore, in the *European American Bank* part of the decision, which was decided in favor of the noncontractual creditor, the court provides a clear guide to creditors on how to satisfy the "linkage-conduct" or "direct nexus" test stated in (3) above.

[4]   Some Other Limitations and Defenses

There are several general limitations placed upon the plaintiff's demand for recovery against an admittedly negligent defendant. The first limitation is that the negligence must actually have caused or contributed to the plaintiff's injury. Put another way, it must be found that "but for" the defendant's negligence, the plaintiff would not have been injured. If this be the case, then the defendant's negligent conduct is causal. Further, if the plaintiff would have been injured anyway, that is, regardless of the defendant's negligence, the plaintiff may not recover. For example, assume a defalcation audit was negligently performed but after all the thefts had occurred. If it is established that the thefts would not have been prevented even if the audit was done in a non-negligent manner, then the auditor's negligence is not causal. It is clear that the fact that the audit was negligently performed cannot be said to have any causal connection to the defalcations which have occurred prior to the undertaking.

In general, the most frequently resorted to defense in a common law negligence action is the negligence of the plaintiff. Contributory negligence as a defense is explored fully in Chapter 7. But contributory negligence as a total bar to plaintiff's recovery is rapidly vanishing in negligence law. Instead, approximately three-quarters of the states have abandoned contributory negligence in favor of comparative negligence. Under a comparative negligence standard, the parties are allowed to recover damages not attributable to their own fault. Of those jurisdictions adopting comparative negligence, the majority

---

[15] 65 N.Y. 2d 636 (1985).

have chosen the "modified" approach. Under this approach, the plaintiff's negligence must not amount to more than 50 percent if a recovery is to be obtained. The "pure" form of comparative negligence permits apportionment of damages according to the relative fault of the parties, whatever percentage this may be. Of course, in the final analysis this is a task left to the trier of fact, and this will be the jury if the plaintiff is entitled to a jury trial.

CHAPTER 4

LIABILITY FOR FRAUD

¶ 4.01   Definition of Fraud

An accountant's exposure to liability for fraud involves risks of significant economic and social penalties. From an economic standpoint a finding of fraud can literally subject an accountant to liability in "an indeterminate amount to an indeterminate class" of persons. A party found liable for fraud may also be assessed punitive damages which have no causal connection to the actual economic injury incurred. Punitive damages are intended to deter and punish fraudulent wrongdoing. It is an "add on" and is determined by the trier of fact, usually the jury.

Aside from the grave economic consequences which may be visited by a fraud action, the taint of being branded as a professional who engaged in a fraud may irreparably injure an accountant's ability to render services in the future for other clients. The impairment of professional reputation and credibility may bring about significant long-term injury to a professional accountant quite apart from the payment of money damages. Given the significant risks involved, it is important that an accountant avoid conduct which could enmesh him in a lawsuit for fraud. An essential starting point for avoiding fraud is a clear understanding of what type of conduct constitutes fraud.

Fraud may be defined as:

1. Conduct by a person or entity involving a false representation;

2. The false representation relates to a material fact;

3. The representation is made by the person or entity with knowledge or "inferable knowledge" of its falsity;

4. The representation is justifiably relied upon by another person or entity;

5. The person or entity who relies on the misrepresentation suffers economic damages as a proximate cause of that reliance.

The foregoing elements of fraud may be further refined as follows.

[1]   Conduct Involving a False Representation

Fraud involves a false representation of some type. Mere nondisclosure is not enough unless one of the following circumstances are present:

1. A party engages in active or affirmative conduct designed to prevent the discovery of the truth;
2. A party makes an incomplete disclosure of the facts, omitting to disclose other material facts necessary for a complete understanding of the full truth;
3. A party occupies some special relationship of trust or fiduciary responsibility to another party which imposes a duty to disclose the truth;
4. A party knows that the conduct of a second party involves a fraud, and with that knowledge the party substantially assists the second party's fraud.

[2]   False Representation of a Material Fact

Misrepresentation of an immaterial fact will not support a lawsuit for fraud. The basic test of materiality is whether a reasonable person would attach importance to the fact misrepresented in determing his or her choice of action in the transaction or event in question.

[3]   Knowledge or "Inferable Knowledge" of the False Representation

Fraud occurs where a person or entity makes a representation that the party actually knows is false. Fraud also exists where a party's knowledge of the falsity of the representation can be inferred from the party's conduct.

Conduct by a party that involves (1) reckless disregard for the truth, or (2) gross negligence may be sufficient to support an inference of fraud.

[4]   Justifiable Reliance

To the extent a party's reliance on a misrepresentation is unforeseeable or unwarranted, the party's recovery may be barred. A party charged with fraud, however, may not defend based on the relying party's contributory negligence.

[5]   Economic Injury Proximately Caused

Economic injury caused by a party's reliance on a fraudulent representation is recoverable. If the economic injury was occasioned by factors other than a party's reliance on a false representation, there can be no recovery in fraud.

¶ 4.02   A Practical Explanation of Fraud: Attorney's Speech

For a practicing accountant, mastering the textbook definition of fraud is simple. The more difficult task is obtaining an understanding of the concept of fraud as it relates to the risks and demands of professional practice.

To facilitate further anaylsis of fraud, let us take a seat at the monthly dinner meeting of the local chapter of CPAs, where the famous civil defense lawyer, I.M. Tuff, defender of accountants, is about to address questions from the audience:

MR. LEDGER: Mr. Tuff, I'm confused as to what the differences are between a fraud lawsuit and a negligence lawsuit. They seem almost the same, but that can't be right. Can it?

TUFF: The elements of a lawsuit for fraud are identical in most respects to the legal elements required to prove negligence with one critical exception—the "state of mind" of the defendant is a significant element in a fraud action. The plaintiff must prove in any fraud case that the defendant made a materially false statement with "knowledge of its falsity," or *scienter* as it is also called.

MR. LEDGER: *Scienter*! What's that, some type of social disease?

TUFF: It may be a social disease for the unwary accounting practitioner. *Scienter* is a fancy Latin word which loosely translated means "to know." Proof of *scienter* is of course a more exacting requirement than merely proving that a defendant failed to exercise due professional care, skill, and competence under the circumstances. It is more exacting because an accountant's duty to refrain from making fraudulent representations runs to all who might foreseeably rely on the representation and could, in Judge Cardozo's words, expose the accountant "to a liability in an indeterminate amount for an indeterminate time to an indeterminate class." This includes, in a common law action for deceit, the possible imposition of punitive or exemplary damages that far exceed a plaintiff's actual damages and that are designed to deter and punish conduct deemed socially unacceptable.

MR. ACCOUNT: I can't imagine any circumstances in which a decent, law-abiding accountant would become involved in a fraud. What the heck, under your definition, Mr. Tuff, all I have to do to avoid fraud is simply avoid making representations that I know are false! Right?

TUFF: Wrong! It's not that easy. To begin with the fact that an accountant is a "decent" person is irrelevant. Indeed, there are cases that clearly state that to prove fraud, a plaintiff need not prove that a defendant was an "evil" or "wicked" person who has "designs on someone's purse."

MR. ACCOUNT: Wait a minute . . . are you telling us that to prove a fraud a plaintiff doesn't have to prove that I had a motive to defraud?

TUFF: That's right.

MR. ACCOUNT: Doesn't a plaintiff have to prove that I actually intended to defraud him?

TUFF: Evidence that a person actually intended to defraud another is the highest order of fraud. This is sometimes referred to as "actual fraud."

MR. ACCOUNT: I'm confused, what other type of fraud can there be other than actual fraud?

TUFF: Constructive fraud.

MR. ACCOUNT: What is that?

TUFF: Constructive fraud is conduct that falls short of proving an actual intent to defraud but involves something more than negligence.

Constructive fraud consists of conduct that lies between making a false representation solely because of a failure to exercise due care and intentionally making a representation that is actually known to be false.

MR. LEDGER: Mr. Tuff, your explanation of fraud to Mr. Account has completely confused me. How does one commit constructive fraud?

TUFF: If an accounting practitioner engages in conduct where he or she makes a false representation (1) without a belief in its truth; or (2) with a reckless disregard for its truth or falsity; or (3) in some instances, by engaging in conduct that involves gross negligence; the accountant may have perpetrated a fraud.

MR. LEDGER: Why is it called "constructive fraud?" It sounds destructive to me.

TUFF: It is constructive because the defendant's knowledge of the false representation is not proven directly from the evidence but is inferred from the circumstances.

It is the rare case where a defendant's subjective intent can be proven. There is no way we can peer into a defendant's mind and prove that he actually intended to defraud. Usually, people do not engage in discussions where they make explicit, damaging admissions that they actually intended to defraud another.

In the absence of such testimony, a party proving a fraud must look at what the defendant said and did or failed to say or do. If a defendant acted so recklessly in disregarding the truth, it may be that he knew that things weren't aboveboard and honest.

MR. LEDGER: Tuff, this constructive fraud doctrine sounds like a way for a plaintiff to make a mountain out of a molehill. I mean, couldn't a plaintiff make a fraud case out of simple negligence?

TUFF: Something more than an isolated act of negligence is necessary. It is possible, however, that several acts of negligence may in combination

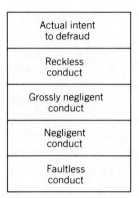

Figure 4.1.   Evidence measuring cup.

reflect a pattern of gross negligence, which could give rise to an inference of fraud. It depends on the evidence of the case.

Perhaps I can explain by diagraming for you what I'll call an "evidence measuring cup." Assume you have a cup into which the plaintiff must place "scoops" of evidence. The measuring cup has various layers or levels for measuring culpability.

At the very bottom is a level for conduct that is faultless. If the plaintiff's scoops do not exceed this level, there is no liability. The next level is for negligent conduct. Above this is the level for grossly negligent conduct. Higher on the cup you find a level for reckless conduct, and at the highest level we find the measuring line for a knowing or actual intent to defraud. (See Figure 4.1.)

Using our measuring cup example, it may be that an isolated act does not exceed the level of faultless conduct. It also is possible that one act or a "single scoop" of evidence may be so substantial that it fills the entire measuring cup. It is possible that a single "scoop" of evidence rises no higher than negligence but that it is accompanied by several similar "scoops" of evidence of wrongdoing. In combination these acts may cumulatively rise to the level of gross negligence, or indeed, recklessness.

MR. ACCOUNT: Tuff, it sounds like you are a baker not a trial lawyer. Tell me, what's the bottom line on protecting myself—what's my duty?

TUFF: To avoid negligence, you must satisfy your duty of due care. To avoid fraud, you must successfully discharge your duty of honesty. Good faith is a defense to a fraud case. Good faith is often defined as possessing a "white heart and an empty head."

MR. ACCOUNT: You mean if you are an absolute blockhead, you may be able to defend against a fraud action.

TUFF: That's correct, but I know very few professional blockheads—and they are lawyers, not accountants!

¶ 4.03   A Courtroom Application of Proving Fraud

Abstract definitions of fraud are merely a starting point in understanding how fraud may exist in circumstances where a professional accountant has rendered services. A fuller understanding of fraud may occur by analyzing a particular factual situation and determining whether an accountant has discharged the duty of honesty.

Imagine that you are a juror in an accountant's liability case. The plaintiff is a shareholder of a bankrupt corporation, Defunct Company, which was victimized by a $10 million management fraud. The defendant accounting firm, Fearful Company, is charged by the plaintiff with negligence and fraud for issuing a "clean opinion," when in fact the audited financial statements were materially misleading.

We will join the trial at two critical junctures. First, the "moment of truth," namely, cross-examination by plaintiff's attorney of defendant's partner-in-charge of the audit examination, Mr. Fearful. Second, the closing argument to the jury by the plaintiff's attorney.

The critical issue in the trial is whether the auditing firm breached its duties of due care and honesty by failing to disclose the fraud that management perpetrated by creating fictitious accounts receivable.

[1]   Cross-Examination of Mr. Fearful by Plaintiff's Attorney

Q: Mr. Fearful, it was your responsibility, was it not, to review the audit work performed on Defunct Company's accounts receivable?

A: Yes it was.

Q: And am I correct in understanding that all of the audit work performed by your firm is reflected in the audit work papers, which were introduced into evidence as Plaintiff's Exhibit 10?

A: That's correct.

Q: And you reviewed those work papers prior to approving your firm's issuance of a clean opinion?

A: Yes, sir.

Q: And I gather from the fact that you issued a clean opinion that it was your opinion at the time you issued your Audit Report that the $16 million shown in Defunct's financials as accounts receivable were fairly presented in conformity with generally accepted accounting principles?

A: Yes, that was my opinion at that time.

Q: In fact accounts receivables were overstated by approximately $10 million of fictitious contracts, correct?

A: I believe the overstatement was $9,227,600—but we didn't know it at the time we issued our report.

Q: Well, we'll get into the question of your knowledge, Mr. Fearful, but before we do that I want to ask you some questions regarding your firm's customary audit procedures for accounts receivable.

A: Yes.

Q: Your audit program for the Defunct audit indicates, does it not, that receivable confirmations should be sent to an audit sample of contracts that represents 75 percent of the total dollar amount of outstanding contracts?

A: Yes, but . . .

Q: And yet your firm only sent out confirmations to an audit sample that represented 40 percent of the total dollar amounts of outstanding contracts receivable?

A: Yes.

Q: Why did you depart from your own audit program?

A: There were two factors. First, we were pressed for time because of unusual circumstances that we encountered in auditing inventory—and our client said that it was important that we finish our report because of a merger that the client was contemplating entering into. Second, we felt that the reduction of the audit sample by 35 percent was justifiable because we were able to check other documentation that the client provided to verify the validity of the accounts receivable.

Q: This "other documentation" was provided to you by Defunct's management?

A: Yes.

Q: And, in fact, the documentation was fictitious, was it not?

A: Well yes, but we had no reason to believe that it was fictitious. It looked good to us.

Q: Mr. Fearful, of those confirmations which you sent out, you received first responses from only 50 percent?

A: That's true.

Q: So, you had to send second confirmations to 50 percent?

A: Correct.

Q: And that did not strike you as unusual?

A: Not really.

Q: Well, when was the last audit that you engaged in where you had only a 50 percent response?

A: For Defunct?

Q: For any audit client?

A: Well, I'm sure I had one before, but I can't recall offhand.

Q: The audit supervisor, Mr. Bright, thought the 50 percent response was poor, did he not?

A: Well, I'm not sure of that.

Q: Mr. Fearful, I show you Plaintiff's Exhibit 6, the audit supervisor's review comments, and ask if that refreshes your recollection as to whether Mr. Bright concluded that further audit inquiry was necessary?

A: Well, that was his conclusion, but he didn't have the total picture of things, the client's need for the audit report, and, of course, he really was not that experienced in these types of matters.

Q: You mean, he was inexperienced in facilitating frauds?
Defense Attorney: Objection, your Honor, that's argumentative.
Cross-examination by Plaintiff's Attorney Continues:

Q: Mr. Fearful, you knew, did you not, that 85 percent of those first confirmations that you did receive back were addressed to the debtors in care of post office boxes?

A: Yes, I knew that.

Q: It didn't strike you as unusual that these confirmations were transmitted to various post office boxes and not directly to the corporations to which they were intended?

A: Not really.

Q: And you assumed that the post office boxes were rented by the various corporations to whom they were addressed?

A: Yes, we did.

Q: Now you say "we did," and yet the junior auditor on this engagement, Mr. Skeptical, raised the question with you as to whether it was possible that all of these post office boxes were rented by Defunct's management?

A: He did, but at the time I looked at that as just the wild imagination of a very young and inexperienced auditor—I mean, it's just not good practice to go around suspecting your clients of fraud.

Q: Mr. Fearful, I would like to show you what's marked as Plaintiff's Exhibits 30 through 50. You recognize those documents don't you?

A: Yes, they are the confirmation forms which our accounting firm used on the Defunct audit.

Q: In each of these 20 confirmations the customer claimed that their outstanding balance was $1,000 less than listed, correct?

A: Yes.

Q: Although there was a discrepancy, your firm did not follow up at all on the reason for the discrepancy, did you?

A: No. It was not necessary to follow up on these accounts receivable because the discrepancy was too small to warrant additional examination.

Q: Mr. Fearful, you also failed "to follow up," to use your words, on the fact that you received absolutely no response on 50 percent of the second confirmations?

A: (Silence.)

Q: Did you hear my question?

A: Yes. It wasn't necessary to look further at these accounts; they weren't material under our guidelines.

Q: Well now, did you look at the evidence that Mr. Skeptical brought to you which indicated that Defunct's $100,000 contract with the Wizard Company was false?

A: I talked to Defunct's Vice President for Sales, who told me that Wizard had reneged on the $100,000 contract after agreeing to it but before Defunct sent Wizard any product.

Q: And you didn't bother to check with Wizard to verify the truth of what Defunct's V.P. was telling you?

A: No. All that was needed at that point was a simple reversing entry.

Q: That simple, huh?

A: Yeah.

Q: It was also pretty simple to ignore the fact that one of your other audit clients did not owe Defunct $210,000 on an account carried on Defunct's books?

A: I'm not sure I follow you.

Q: You knew, did you not, that Tip-off Corporation was listed as a Defunct account receivable of $210,000?

A: Yes.

Q: At the same time you were auditing Defunct your firm was also auditing Tip-off, and you were in charge of that examination, correct?

A: Correct.

Q: In the course of auditing Tip-off you discovered, did you not, that Tip-off did not list any account payable to Defunct?

A: Well, I guess I knew—I mean, yes, I knew that.

Q: And it did not occur to you that there was an irreconcilable factual difference between these two corporations?

A: No.

Q: And you didn't think to ask anyone at Tip-off regarding that difference?

A: No.

Q: And you didn't think to look at the confirmation in your work papers, which fictitiously confirmed that Tip-off owed $210,000 to Defunct?

A: No.

Q: You didn't think much at all, did you Mr. Fearful, regarding this transaction?

A: Well, I guess I just didn't put the pieces together from the separate audits, but we are not detectives, you know, that's not my responsibility.

Q: It's not your responsibility to see the obvious—that a $10 million fraud was being pulled off right before your own eyes?

   Defense Attorney: Objection, Your Honor, to counsel's argument.

   Court: Sustained.

[2] Closing Argument by Plaintiff's Attorney

PLAINTIFF'S ATTORNEY: Ladies and gentlemen of the jury, as you review the evidence in this case, you cannot avoid the conclusion that the Fearful Company accounting firm engaged in auditing procedures that were a departure from professional practices in the accounting profession. Indeed, the practices involved here represented a departure from Fearful Company's own audit procedures.

As you analyze the evidence it is clear that Fearful Company did not conduct the Defunct audit with due professional care, skill, and competence. But the evidence reflects more than mere negligence. The evidence goes much further and leads to only one conclusion. Fearful Company conducted this audit with such a reckless disregard for the truth that one cannot help but conclude that Fearful knew the truth and wanted to either ignore it or bury it or hope that it just went away.

The evidence reflects that Fearful Company cut corners on this audit. You will recall my cross-examination of Mr. Fearful, who admitted that they did not abide by their own firm's audit program. Instead of confirming 75 percent of the total dollar value of accounts, they did only 40 percent.

And what was their reason for this? Mr. Fearful would have you believe that they cut this corner to expedite their audit, and that they were justified in doing so because they relied on management's self-serving, *fictitious* documentation!

Clearly, a professional auditor acting with due care, competence, and professional skill would not take an audit "shortcut" of this magnitude and involving such an important item as Defunct's accounts receivable.

I respectfully submit, ladies and gentlemen, that if we based our analysis of fault on this evidence alone—the evidence reflects negligence. But as you know, the additional evidence of wrongdoing by Mr. Fearful continues much further.

It is evidence that leads us to the allegations of Count Two of the complaint, which charges Fearful Company with fraud. Count Two specifically charges Fearful with "knowingly" misrepresenting Defunct's financial position by overstating accounts receivable by $10 million.

Before addressing the facts that prove Mr. Fearful's fraud, I would like to discuss certain instructions of law which I believe Judge Justice will give to you.

First, Judge Justice will instruct that "you are to consider only the evidence received in this case." He will further instruct that "you should consider this evidence in the light of your own observations and experiences in life. You may draw such reasonable inferences as you believe to be justified from proven facts."

Ladies and gentlemen, as the trier-of-fact it is up to you to determine what inferences you will draw from this evidence. In making your conclusions you may rely on your experiences—that is, you do not leave life's experiences at the doorway of this courtroom; you bring those experiences with you during your deliberations.

You will also be instructed as to the types of evidence that the plaintiff may use to prove its case, namely, direct and circumstantial. Judge Justice will instruct you that:

Direct evidence is the testimony of a person who claims to have personal knowledge of the commission of the wrongdoing which has been charged, such as an eyewitness. Circumstantial evidence is the proof of a chain of facts and circumstances which tend to show whether the defendant is guilty or not guilty. The law makes no distinction between the weight to be given either direct or circumstantial evidence. Therefore, all of the evidence in the case, including the circumstantial evidence, should be considered by you in arriving at your verdict.

A significant instruction in your deliberations will be the definition of *knowingly*. Fearful Company has been charged with knowingly misrepresenting the truth. Judge Justice will instruct you that:

When the word "knowingly" is used in these instructions it means that the defendant realized what he was doing and was aware of the nature of his conduct, and did not act through ignorance, mistake or accident. Knowledge may be proven by defendant's conduct, and by all the facts and circumstances surrounding the case. No person can intentionally avoid knowledge by closing his eyes to facts.

In reviewing all the evidence in this case ask yourself this question: Did Mr. Fearful act through "ignorance, mistake, or accident"? Or was Mr. Fearful's conduct so reckless, so grossly negligent that at best they "intentionally avoided knowledge by closing their eyes to facts" that they surely saw.

The evidence reflects, ladies and gentlemen, that Mr. Fearful ordered a cutback on the scope of the customary firm audit procedures for accounts receivable. Was this a result of a "mistake or accident" on Mr. Fearful's part? Or was this done to avoid the truth, to avoid discovering more than what Mr. Fearful already knew?

Of those confirmations sent out, Fearful Company received an unusually poor response. You will recall that the audit supervisor, Mr. Bright, approached Mr. Fearful but was brushed off—no further follow-up. You heard Mr. Fearful testify that Mr. Bright was "inexperienced"; Mr. Bright did not have the "total picture of things." Consequently, Mr. Fearful refused to order further audit inquiry on the nonresponding confirmations. Did Mr. Fearful decline to do further investigation because of a "mistake" or "accident" on his part? Had he done more he surely would have discovered that the nonresponding confirmations were part of the $10 million of fictitious accounts.

Ignorance? accident? mistake? Or did Mr. Fearful close his eyes to the truth?

There is more. Mr. Skeptical, a junior auditor at the time, discovered that many of the confirmations were addressed to post office boxes. Mr. Skeptical raised the questions: Is it possible that these boxes were merely phony fronts for the confirmations? Is it possible that Defunct's management controls the boxes and therefore the confirmations?

As young and inexperienced as he was, Mr. Skeptical could see the truth and did not want to avoid it. What was Mr. Fearful's response to all of this? He did absolutely nothing. Did Mr. Fearful make a "mistake," was he "ignorant," or did he fail to act because of "bad faith" on his part?

Perhaps the most compelling evidence of Mr. Fearful's lack of good faith is his failure to investigate the circumstances relating to the $100,000 contract with Wizard Company and the $210,000 contract with Tip-off Corporation. Both contracts were on Defunct's books and both were fictitious. Mr. Fearful admitted that he knew of these contracts, and he further admitted that he knew there was a serious question as to whether they were properly reflected on the books.

Indeed, Mr. Fearful could not avoid admitting that he knew of these questionable circumstances. In the face of this evidence of fraud what did Mr. Fearful do? He did nothing other than willingly accept lame excuses offered by management of Defunct.

I ask you, ladies and gentlemen, did Mr. Fearful fail to follow up on these contracts because of a "mistake" on his part? Did he fail to act because of ignorance? Does Mr. Fearful, who has a college degree, is a certified public accountant under the laws of this state, and has had many years of auditing experience—does Mr. Fearful strike you as a fool who knew nothing of what was going on?

I respectfully submit, ladies and gentlemen, that Mr. Fearful is not a fool, he was not an unwitting dupe of this fraud. Mr. Fearful's conduct was not merely grossly negligent, it was recklessly indifferent to the truth. The bottom line in this case is that Mr. Fearful knew the truth and wanted to avoid it. Perhaps he hoped that the problem would cure itself or would simply go away without involving him.

Perhaps Mr. Fearful was afraid that confronting the truth would only implicate him. Perhaps he acted simply for the sake of making his audit fees.

We will never know what motivated Mr. Fearful to participate in this fraud. That's not important. It's enough that we know that Mr. Fearful participated.

¶ 4.04   Fraud: Common Law and Statutory Sources

Like negligence, the sources of an accountant's civil liability for fraud are principally found in certain provisions of the federal securities laws, the so-called antifraud provisions, the chief of which is referred to as Rule 10b-5, and in the common law cause of action for fraudulent representation, also known as an action for deceit.

[1]   Common Law

Common law or judge-made law is a source of liability for fraud. Under the common law an accountant's duty of honesty extends to all persons or entities who foreseeably rely on the accountant's professional service.

Thus, for example, an accountant's duty of honesty runs to all persons or entities who might foreseeably rely on audited financials. At the same time the accountant's duty of due care may only extend to a limited class of financial statement users whose reliance was actually foreseen or known by the accountant.

In an action for fraud or deceit a plaintiff may seek punitive or exemplary damages. As the names suggest, these are damages that are designed solely to deter or punish fraud. An award of punitive damages is totally separate from awarding a party actual or compensatory damages.

To illustrate, assume that an accountant recklessly issues an audit report that causes a bank to loan $150,000. The loan goes bad, and despite efforts to liquidate collateral, the bank is still out of pocket $25,000. There may be little or no cost justification for the bank to sue the accountant for $25,000. However, if the accountant's recklessness gives rise to a claim for fraud, the bank may properly seek punitive damages in an amount far in excess of its actual loss, for example, an amount equal to 25 percent of the accountant's gross yearly billings for all firm clients.

[2]   Statutory Law

The principal statutory source that gives rise to lawsuits against accountants is the federal securities laws. The primary antifraud provision of the federal securities laws is called Rule 10b-5.

[a]   Rule 10b-5.   Rule 10b-5 is, as its name signifies, a rule which was promulgated by the SEC pursuant to the Commission's power to promulgate rules that facilitate the enforcement of the Securities Exchange Act of 1934.

Rule 10b-5 is derived from Section 10 (b) of the 1934 Act. Section 10 (b) makes it "unlawful for any person, directly or indirectly, by the use of any means or instrumentality of interstate commerce or the mails, . . . to use or employ, in connection with the purchase or sale of any security . . . any manipulative or deceptive device or contrivance in contravention of [the Commission's] rules and regulations. . . . "

Rule 10b-5 provides:

Employment of manipulative and deceptive devices.
It shall be unlawful for any person, directly or indirectly, by the use of any means or instrumentalities of interstate commerce, or of the mails . . .

(a) To employ any device, scheme, or artifice to defraud,

(b) To make any untrue statement of a material fact or to omit to state a material fact necessary in order to make the statements made, in the light of the circumstances under which they were made, not misleading, or

(c) To engage in any act, practice, or course of business which operates or would operate as a fraud or deceit upon any person,

in connection with the purchase or sale of any security.

Rule 10b-5 prohibits conduct that would also be prohibited under the common law in an action for fraud. In certain respects, however, Rule 10b-5 is not as expansive as the common law:

(1)   Punitive damages are not recoverable under Rule 10b-5.

(2)   If the fraud causes a person *not* to purchase or *not* to sell a security to his economic detriment, there is no cause of action under Rule 10b-5.

(3)   If the fraud occurs without using in any way an interstate instrumentality such as the telephone lines or mail, there is no jurisdictional basis to assert a 10b-5 lawsuit.

(4)   The fraud must be in connection with the purchase or sale of a *security*. Thus, for example, fraud in connection with a $10 million bank loan will not give rise to a 10b-5 action, while fraud in connection with the sale of 25% of the stock of "Mom and Pop" grocery for $1000 could give rise to a 10b-5 lawsuit.

Rule 10b-5 is a means by which a plaintiff may bring a lawsuit in federal court. Although it is often stated that there are procedural advantages to suing in federal court, the quality of justice between state and federal court is not different. The substantive advantages of one judicial forum over another are virtually nonexistent.

[b]   *Ernst & Ernst v. Hochfelder*.   With respect to accountants, there once was a substantive advantage that Rule 10b-5 afforded plaintiffs that was not available in state court. Prior to the U.S. Supreme Court's decision in *Ernst & Ernst v. Hochfelder*, certain federal courts had decided that a Rule 10b-5 action could be grounded on negligent conduct by an accountant. Under this approach, a plaintiff could avoid the privity limitations placed on common law negligence lawsuits brought against accountants. In effect, plaintiffs could accomplish under Rule 10b-5 that which *Ultramares* prohibited. In 1976 the U.S. Supreme Court eliminated this advantage with its decision in *Ernst & Ernst v. Hochfelder*.

The issue in *Hochfelder* was whether mere negligence was enough to violate Rule 10b-5, or if conduct amounting to scienter was required. *Hochfelder* was a unique case in that the plaintiffs admitted that they "did not accuse Ernst & Ernst of deliberate, intentional fraud, merely with inexcusable negligence."

Ernst & Ernst v. Hochfelder
425 U.S. 185 (1976)

Mr. Justice POWELL delivered the opinion of the Court.

The issue in this case is whether an action for civil damages may lie under § 10 (b) of the Securities Exchange Act of 1934 (1934 Act) ... and Securities and Exchange Commission Rule 10b-5, in the absence of an allegation of intent to deceive, manipulate, or defraud on the part of the defendant.

I

Petitioner, Ernst & Ernst, is an accounting firm. From 1946 through 1967 it was retained by First Securities Company of Chicago (First Securities), a small brokerage firm and member of the Midwest Stock Exchange and of the National Association of Securities Dealers, to perform periodic audits of the firm's books and records. In connection with these audits Ernst & Ernst prepared for filing with the Securities and Exchange Commission (Commission) the annual reports required of First Securities under § 17 (a) of the 1934 Act, . . . It also prepared for First Securities responses to the financial questionnaires of the Midwest Stock Exchange (Exchange).

Respondents were customers of First Securities who invested in a fraudulent securities scheme perpetrated by Leston B. Nay, president of the firm and owner of 92% of its stock. Nay induced the respondents to invest funds in "escrow" accounts that he represented would yield a high rate of return. Respondents did so from 1942 through 1966, with the majority of the transactions occurring in the 1950's. In fact, there were no escrow accounts as Nay converted respondents' funds to his own use immediately upon receipt. These transactions were not in the customary form of dealings between First Securities and its customers. The respondents drew their personal checks payable to Nay or a designated bank for his account. No such escrow accounts were reflected on the books and records of First Securities, and none was shown on its periodic accounting to respondents in connection with their other investments. Nor were they included in First Securities' filings with the Commission or the Exchange.

This fraud came to light in 1968 when Nay committed suicide, leaving a note that described First Securities as bankrupt and the escrow accounts as "spurious." Respondents subsequently filed this action for damages against Ernst & Ernst in the United States District Court for the Northern District of Illinois under § 10 (b) of the 1934 Act. The complaint charged that Nay's escrow scheme violated § 10 (b) and Commission Rule 10b-5, and that Ernst & Ernst had "aided and abetted"

Nay's violations by its "failure" to conduct proper audits of First Securities. As revealed through discovery, respondents' cause of action rested on a theory of negligent nonfeasance.

After extensive discovery the District Court granted Ernst & Ernst's motion for summary judgment and dismissed the action.

The Court of Appeals for the Seventh Circuit reversed and remanded, holding that one who breaches a duty of inquiry and disclosure owed another is liable in damages for aiding and abetting a third party's violation of Rule 10b-5 if the fraud would have been discovered or prevented but for the breach.

• • •

We granted certiorari to resolve the question whether a private cause of action for damages will lie under § 10 (b) and Rule 10b-5 in the absence of any allegation of "scienter"—intent to deceive, manipulate, or defraud. . . . We conclude that it will not and therefore we reverse.

Federal regulation of transactions in securities emerged as part of the aftermath of the market crash in 1929. The Securities Act of 1933 . . . was designed to provide investors with full disclosure of material information concerning public offerings of securities in commerce, to protect investors against fraud and, through the imposition of specified civil liabilities, to promote ethical standards of honesty and fair dealing. . . . The 1934 Act was intended principally to protect investors against manipulation of stock prices through regulation of transactions upon securities exchanges and in over-the-counter markets, and to impose regular reporting requirements on companies whose stock is listed on national securities exchanges. . . . Although the Acts contain numerous carefully drawn express civil remedies and criminal penalties, Congress recognized that efficient regulation of securities trading could not be accomplished under a rigid statutory program. As part of the 1934 Act Congress created the Commission, which is provided with an arsenal of flexible enforcement powers.

Section 10 of the 1934 Act makes it "unlawful for any person . . . (b) [t]o use or employ, in connection with the purchase or sale of any security . . . any manipulative or deceptive device or contrivance in contravention of such rules and regulations as the Commission may prescribe as necessary or appropriate in the public interest or for the protection of investors." . . . In 1942, acting pursuant to the power conferred by § 10 (b), the Commission promulgated Rule 10b-5. . . .

* * *

During the 30-year period since a private cause of action was first implied under § 10 (b) and Rule 10b-5, a substantial body of case law and commentary has developed as to its elements. Courts and commentators long have differed with regard to whether scienter is a necessary element of such a cause of action, or whether negligent conduct alone is sufficient. In addressing this question, we turn first to the language of § 10 (b), for "[t]he starting point in every case involving construction of a statute is the language itself." Section 10 (b) makes unlawful the use or employment of "any manipulative or deceptive device or contrivance" in contravention of Commission rules. The words "manipulative or deceptive" used in conjunction with "device or contrivance" strongly suggest that § 10 (b) was intended to proscribe knowing or intentional misconduct.

In its *amicus curiae* brief, however, the Commission contends that nothing in the language "manipulative or deceptive device or contrivance" limits its operation to knowing or intentional practices. In support of its view, the Commission cites the overall congressional purpose in the 1933 and 1934 Acts to protect investors against false and deceptive practices that might injure them. The Commission then reasons that since the "effect" upon investors of given conduct is the same regardless of whether the conduct is negligent or intentional, Congress must have intended to bar all such practices and not just those done knowingly or intentionally. The logic of this effect-oriented approach would impose liability for wholly faultless conduct where such conduct results in harm to investors, a result the Commission would

be unlikely to support. But apart from where its logic might lead, the Commission would add a gloss to the operative language of the statute quite different from its commonly accepted meaning. . . . The argument simply ignores the use of the words "manipulative," "device," and "contrivance"—terms that make unmistakable a congressional intent to proscribe a type of conduct quite different from negligence. Use of the word "manipulative" is especially significant. It is and was virtually a term of art when used in connection with securites markets. It connotes intentional or willful conduct designed to deceive or defraud investors by controlling or artificially affecting the price of securities.

Although the extensive legislative history of the 1934 Act is bereft of any explicit explanation of Congress' intent, we think the relevant portions of that history support our conclusion that § 10 (b) was addressed to practices that involve some element of scienter and cannot be read to impose liability for negligent conduct alone.

* * *

The [Congressional] Report therefore reveals with respect to the specified practices, an overall congressional intent to prevent "manipulative and deceptive practices which . . . fulfill no useful function" and to create private actions for damages stemming from "illicit practices," where the defendant has not acted in good faith. The views expressed in the House Report are consistent with this interpretation. . . . There is no indication that Congress intended anyone to be made liable for such practices unless he acted other than in good faith. The catchall provision of § 10 (b) should be interpreted no more broadly.

* * *

When a statute speaks so specifically in terms of manipulation and deception, and of implementing devices and contrivances—the commonly understood terminology of intentional wrongdoing—and when its history reflects no more expansive intent, we are quite unwilling to extend the scope of the statute to negligent conduct.

(c)   Comments on *Hochfelder*.   The U.S. Supreme Court reached its decision in *Hochfelder* solely on the basis of statutory construction, including review of the legislative history underlying Section 10 (b) and the securities laws in general. The Court thus declined to render its decision based on "policy" considerations, although the Court was not above noting that "hazards" may be engendered through the imposition of a negligence standard, observing:

> As we find the language and history of § 10 (b) dispositive of the appropriate standard of liability, there is no occasion to examine the additional considerations of "policy," set forth by the parties, that may have influenced the lawmakers in their formulation of the statute. We do note that the standard urged by respondents would significantly broaden the class of plaintiffs who may seek to impose liability upon accountants and other experts who perform services or express opinions with respect to matters under the Acts. Last term, in *Blue Chip Stamps*, 421 U.S., at 747–748, the Court pertinently observed:
>
>> While much of the development of the law of deceit has been the elimination of artificial barriers to recovery on just claims, we are not the first court to express concern that the inexorable broadening of the class of plaintiff who may sue in this area of the law will ultimately result in more harm than good. In *Ultramares Corp. v. Touche*, 225 N.Y. 170, 174 N.E. 411 (1931), Chief Judge Cardozo observed with respect to a liability in an indeterminate amount for an indeterminate time to an indeterminate class:
>>
>>> The hazards of a business conducted on these terms are so extreme as to enkindle doubt whether a flaw may not exist in the implication of a duty that exposes to these consequences. *Id.* at 179–180, 174 N.E., at 444.
>
> This case, on its facts, illustrates the extreme reach of the standard urged by respondents. As investors in transactions initiated by Nay, not First Securities, they were not foreseeable users of the financial statements or Ernst & Ernst's certificates of opinion. See n.9, supra. The class of persons eligible to benefit from such a standard, though small in this case, could be numbered in the thousands in other cases. Acceptance of respondents' view would extend to new frontiers the "hazards" of rendering expert advice under the Acts, raising serious policy questions not yet addressed by Congress.

In *Hochfelder* the U.S. Supreme Court defined *scienter* as "a mental state embracing intent to deceive, manipulate or defraud."

With respect to recklessness as an element of *scienter*, the Court states in footnote 12 of its opinion:

> In certain areas of the law, recklessness is considered to be a form of intentional conduct for purposes of imposing liability for some act. We need not address here the questions whether in some circumstances reckless behavior is sufficient for civil liability under Section 10 (b) and Rule 10b-5.

Although the U.S. Supreme Court left open the question of whether reckless behavior may be sufficient for liability under Rule 10b-5, subsequent federal court decisions have ruled that the *Hochfelder* decision did not intend to exclude the common law's constructive fraud doctrine of recklessness from Rule 10b-5's prohibitions.

¶ 4.05   Constructive Fraud: Middle Ground

Given the devastating liability exposure that potentially attends a claim of fraud, proving fraud requires more than merely showing that the defendant failed to do what a reasonable person would do. Conduct that falls short of proving that a defendant actually knew a representation was false may nevertheless be a sufficient basis upon which to bring an action for fraud. Simply stated, an action for fraud may exist for something more than negligence and yet less than an actual intent to defraud.

The conduct that lies between making a false representation solely because of a failure to exercise due care, and making a representation known to be false, consists of making a false representation (1) without belief in its truth or (2) with a reckless or grossly negligent disregard for its truth or falsity. To illustrate the common law's treatment of this "middle ground" or "constructive fraud" doctrine, there is no better case than Judge Cardozo's decision in *Ultramares v. Touche*.

[1]   *Ultramares Corp. v. Touche*
174 N.E. 441 (N.Y. 1931)

[The court's decision is printed at ¶ 1.01[3].]

CARDOZO, Circuit Judge.

The action is in tort for damages suffered through the misrepresentation of accountants, the first cause of action being for misrepresentations that were merely negligent, and the second for misrepresentations charged to have been fraudulent.

* * *

Capital and surplus were intact if the balance sheet was accurate. In reality both had been wiped out, and the corporation was insolvent. The books had been falsified by those in charge of the business so as to set forth accounts receivable and other assets which turned out to be fictitious.

* * *

The two causes of action will be considered in succession, first the one for negligence and second that for fraud.

1. We think the evidence supports a finding that the audit was negligently made, though in so saying we put aside for the moment the question whether negligence, even if it existed, was a wrong to the plaintiff.

We begin with the item of accounts receivable. At the start of the defendant's audit, there had been no posting of the general ledger since April, 1923. Siess, a junior accountant, was assigned by the defendants to the performance of that work. On Sunday, February 3, 1924, he had finished the task of posting, and was ready the next day to begin with his associates the preparation of the balance sheet and the audit of its items. The total of the accounts receivable for December, 1923, as thus posted by Siess from the entries in the journal, was $644,758.17. At some time on February 3, Romberg, an employee of the Stern Company, who had general charge of its accounts, placed below that total another item to represent additional accounts receivable growing out of the transactions of the month. This new item, $706,843.07, Romberg entered in his own handwriting. The sales that it represented were, each and all, fictitious. Opposite the entry were placed other figures (12–29), indicating or supposed to indicate a reference to the journal. Siess when he resumed his work saw the entries thus added, and included the new item in making up his footings, with the result of an apparent increase of over $700,000 in the assets of the business. He says that in doing this he supposed the entries to be correct, and that, his task at the moment being merely to post the books, he thought the work of audit or verification might come later, and put it off accordingly. The time sheets, which are in evidence, show very clearly that this was the order of time in which the parts of the work were done. Verification, however, there never was either by Siess or by his superiors, or so the triers of the facts might say. If any had been attempted, or any that was adequate, an examiner would have found that the entry in the ledger was not supported by any entry in the journal. If from the journal he had gone to the book from which the journal was made up, described as "the debit memo book," support would still have failed. Going farther, he would have found invoices, seventeen in number, which amounted in the aggregate to the interpolated item, but scrutiny of these invoices would have disclosed suspicious features in that they had no shipping number nor a customer's order number and varied in terms of credit and in other respects from those usual in the business. A mere glance reveals the difference.

The December entry of accounts receivable was not the only item that a careful and skillful auditor would have desired to investigate. There was ground for suspicion as to an item of $113,199.60, included in the accounts payable as due from the Baltic Corporation. As to this the defendants received an explanation, not very convincing, from Stern and Romberg. A cautious auditor might have been dissatisfied and have uncovered what was wrong. There was ground for suspicion also because of the inflation of the inventory. The inventory, as it was given to the auditors, was totaled at $347,219.08. The defendants discovered errors in the sum of $303,863.20, and adjusted the balance sheet accordingly. Both the extent of the discrepancy and its causes might have been found to cast discredit upon the business and the books. There was ground for suspicion again in the record of assigned accounts. Inquiry of the creditors gave notice to the defendants that the same accounts had been pledged to two, three, and four banks at the same time. The pledges did not diminish the value of the assets, but made in such circumstances they might well evoke a doubt as to the sol-

vency of a business where such conduct was permitted. There was an explanation by Romberg which the defendants accepted as sufficient. Caution and diligence might have pressed investigation farther.

If the defendants owed a duty to the plaintiff to act with the same care that would have been due under a contract of employment, a jury was at liberty to find a verdict of negligence upon a showing of a scrutiny so imperfect and perfunctory. No doubt the extent to which inquiry must be pressed beyond appearances is a question of judgment, as to which opinions will often differ. No doubt the wisdom that is born after the event will engender suspicion and distrust when old acquaintance and good repute may have silenced doubt at the beginning. All this is to be weighed by a jury in applying its standard of behavior, the state of mind, and conduct of the reasonable man. Even so, the adverse verdict, when rendered, imports an alignment of the weights in their proper places in the balance and a reckoning thereafter. The reckoning was not wrong upon the evidence before us, if duty be assumed.

We are brought to the question of duty, its origin and measure.

The defendants owed to their employer a duty imposed by law to make their certificate without fraud, and a duty growing out of contract to make it with the care and caution proper to their calling. Fraud includes the pretense of knowledge when knowledge there is none. To creditors and investors to whom the employer exhibited the certificate, the defendants owed a like duty to make it without fraud, since there was notice in the circumstances of its making that the employer did not intend to keep it to himself. . . . A different question develops when we ask whether they owed a duty to these to make it without negligence. If liability for negligence exists, a thoughtless slip or blunder, the failure to detect a theft or forgery beneath the cover of deceptive entries, may expose accountants to a liability in an indeterminate amount for an indeterminate time to an indeterminate class. The hazards of a business conducted on these terms are so extreme as to enkindle doubt whether a flaw may not exist in the implication of a duty that exposes to these consequences. We put aside for the moment any statement in the certificate which involves the representation of a fact as true to the knowledge of the auditors. If such a statement was made, whether believed to be true or not, the defendants are liable for deceit in the event that it was false.

• • •

The extension, if made, will so expand the field of liability for negligent speech as to make it nearly, if not quite, coterminous with that of liability for fraud. Again and again, in decisions of this court, the bounds of this latter liability have been set up, with futility the fate of every endeavor to dislodge them. Scienter has been declared to be an indispensable element, except where the representation has been put forward as true of one's own knowledge or in circumstances where the expression of opinion was a dishonorable pretense. . . . Even an opinion, especially an opinion by an expert, may be found to be fraudulent if the grounds supporting it are so flimsy as to lead to the conclusion that there was no genuine belief back of it. Further than that this court has never gone. Directors of corporations have been acquitted of liability for deceit, though they have been lax in investigation and negligent in speech. This has not meant, to be sure, that negligence may not be evidence from which a trier of the facts may draw an inference of fraud . . . but merely that, if that inference is rejected, or, in the light of all the circumstances, is found to be unreasonable, negligence alone is not a substitute for fraud. Many also are the cases that have distinguished between the willful or reckless representation essential to the maintenance at law of an action for deceit, and the misrepresentation, negligent or innocent, that will lay a sufficient basis for rescission in equity.

Our holding does not emancipate accountants from the consequences of fraud. It does not relieve them if their audit has been so negligent as to justify a finding that they had no genuine belief in its adequacy, for this again is fraud. It does no more than say that, if less than this is proved, if there has been neither reckless misstatement nor insincere profession of an opinion but only honest blunder, the ensuing liability for negligence is one that is bounded by the contract, and is to be enforced between the parties by whom the contract has been made. We doubt whether the average business man receiving a certificate without paying for it, and receiving it merely as one among a multitude of possible investors, would look for anything more.

2. The second cause of action is yet to be considered.

The defendants certified as a fact, true to their own knowledge, that the balance sheet was in accordance with the books of account. If their statement was false, they are not to be exonerated because they believed it to be true.

• • •

We think the triers of the facts might hold it to be false.

Correspondence between the balance sheet and the books imports something more, or so the triers of the facts might say, than correspondence between the balance sheet and the general ledger, unsupported or even contradicted by every other record. The correspondence to be of any moment may not unreasonably be held to signify a correspondence between the statement and the books of original entry, the books taken as a whole. If that is what the certificate means, a jury could find that the correspondence did not exist, and that the defendants signed the certificates without knowing it to exist and even without reasonable grounds for belief in its existence. The item of $706,000, representing fictitious accounts receivable, was entered in the ledger after defendant's employee Siess had posted the December sales. He knew of the interpolation, and knew that there was need to verify the entry by reference to books other than the ledger before the books could be found to be in agreement with the balance sheet. The evidence would sustain a finding that this was never done. By concession the interpolated item had no support in the journal, or in any journal voucher, or in the debit memo book, which was a summary of the invoices, or in anything except the invoices themselves. The defendants do not say that they ever looked at the invoices, seventeen in number, representing these accounts. They profess to be unable to recall whether they did so or not. They admit, however, that, if they had looked, they would have found omissions and irregularities so many and unusual as to have called for further investigation. When we couple the refusal to say that they did look with the admission that, if they had looked, they would or could have seen, the situation is revealed as one in which a jury might reasonably find that in truth they did not look, but certified the correspondence without testing its existence.

In this connection we are to bear in mind the principle already stated in the course of this opinion that negligence or blindness, even when not equivalent to fraud, is none the less evidence to sustain an inference of fraud. At least this is so if the negligence is gross. Not a little confusion has at times resulted from an undiscriminating quotation of statements in Kountze v. Kennedy, supra, statements proper enough in their setting, but capable of misleading when extracted and considered by themselves. "Misjudgment, however gross," it was there observed, "or want of caution, however marked, is not fraud." This was said in a case where the trier of the facts had held the defendants guiltless. The judgment in this court amounted merely to a holding that a finding of fraud did not follow as an inference of law. There was no holding that the evidence would have required a reversal of the judgment if the finding as to guilt had been the other way. Even Derry v. Peek, as we have seen, asserts the probative effect of negligence as an evidentiary fact. We had no thought in Kountze v. Kennedy, of upholding a doctrine more favorable to wrongdoers, though there was a reservation suggesting the approval of a rule more rigorous. The opinion of this court cites Derry v. Peek, and states the holding there made that an action would not lie if the defendant believed the representation made by him to be true, although without reasonable cause for such belief. "It is not necessary," we said, "to go to this extent to uphold the present judgment, for the referee, as has been stated, found that the belief of Kennedy * * * was based upon reasonable grounds." The setting of the occasion justified the inference that the representations did not involve a profession of knowledge as distinguished from belief. . . . No such charity of construction exonerates accountants, who by the very nature of their calling profess to speak with knowledge when certifying to an agreement between the audit and the entries.

[10] The defendants attempt to excuse the omission of an inspection of the invoices proved to be fictitious by invoking a practice known as that of testing and sampling. A random choice of accounts is made from the total number on the books, and these, if found to be regular when inspected and investigated, are taken as a fair indication of the quality of the mass. The defendants say that about 200 invoices were examined in accordance with this practice, but they do not assert that any of the seventeen invoices supporting the fictitious sales were among the number so selected. Verification by test and sample was very likely a sufficient audit as to accounts regularly entered upon the books in the usual course of business. It was plainly insufficient, however, as to accounts not entered upon the books where inspection of the invoices was necessary, not as a check upon accounts fair upon their face, but in order to ascertain whether there were any accounts at all. If the only invoices inspected were invoices unrelated to the interpolated entry, the result was to certify a correspondence between the books and the balance sheet without any effort by the auditors, as to $706,000 of accounts, to ascertain whether the certified agreement was in accordance with the truth. How far books of account fair upon their face are to be probed by accountants, in an effort to ascertain whether the transactions back of them are in accordance with the entries, involves to some extent the exercise of judgment and discretion. Not so, however, the inquiry whether the entries certified as there, are there in very truth, there in the form and in the places where men of businss training would expect them to be. The defendants were put on their guard by the circumstances touching the December accounts receivable to scrutinize with special care. A jury might

find that, with suspicions thus awakened, they closed their eyes to the obvious, and blindly gave assent. We conclude, to sum up the situation, that in certifying to the correspondence between balance sheet and accounts the defendants made a statement as true to their own knowledge, when they had, as a jury might find, no knowledge on the subject. If that is so, they may also be found to have acted without information leading to a sincere or genuine belief when they certified to an opinion that the balance sheet faithfully reflected the condition of the business.

[2]   Constructive Fraud Defined

Judge Cardozo's various formulations of fraud include:

(a)   "The pretense of knowledge when knowledge there is none";

(b)   "[A]n opinion . . . may be found to be fraudulent if the grounds supporting it are so flimsy as to lead to the conclusion that there was no genuine belief back of it";

(c)   A "reckless misstatement";

(d)   "[I]nsincere profession of an opinion"; and

(e)   Closing one's eyes "to the obvious" and "blindly" giving assent.

Of particular importance is Judge Cardozo's statement that negligence may be evidence from which a trier of fact may draw an inference of fraud. Judge Cardozo states that "negligence or blindness, even when not equivalent to fraud, is none the less evidence to sustain an inference of fraud. At least this is so if the negligence is gross."

¶ 4.06   Gross Negligence

Proof of a defendant's actual knowledge of the falsity of a representation is not easily proved for it involves a subjective standard, namely, what did *this* defendant know. It is the genius of the common law that judges recognized the difficulty of the burden of proof placed upon a plaintiff to meet this subjective test. Accordingly, the common law created the constructive fraud doctrine, which involves an element of objectivity, namely, the defendant's conduct is such a marked departure from reasonable norms or expectations that it suggests that the defendant knew of the falsity of his representation, or was outrageously indifferent to its truth or falsity.

But how far can the doctrine of constructive fraud be extended without becoming a contrivance or device to "end run" the limitations placed on a negligence action by non-client, third-party users of financial statements? Consider this question as you read the following decision by the same court that six years previously had decided *Ultramares*.

State Street Trust Co. v. Ernst
15 N.E. 2d 416 (N.Y. 1938)

FINCH, Judge.

[The plaintiff bank made a loan to the Pelz-Greenstein Co. based on a year-end annual balance sheet audited by the defendant accountants. Pelz-Greenstein was in the business of financing inventory for which it would receive assignments of accounts receivables as collateral. At trial, it was established that the officers of Pelz-Greenstein engaged in fraud whereby they made old and uncollectible accounts appear good. The officers also created fictitious accounts and inventory to cover up the fact that the company was "hopelessly insolvent."

The bank sued the accountants for fraud. The accountants appealed the jury's verdict in favor of the bank.]

Was the evidence introduced by plaintiff so inadequate that, resolving all contested issues and drawing all possible inferences in plaintiff's favor a jury could not find that defendants were *guilty of gross negligence raising an inference of fraud* [emphasis added] and that plaintiff relied upon the certified balance sheet prepared by defendants, thereby suffering damage?

• • •

With the certified balance sheet defendants issued the following certificate: "We hereby certify that we examined the books of account and record pertaining to the assets and liabilities of Pelz-Greenstein Co., Inc., New York City, as of the close of business December 31, 1928, and, based on the records examined, information submitted to us, and subject to the foregoing notes [not here material], it is our opinion that the above condensed statement shows the financial condition of the company at the date stated and that the related income and surplus account is correct."

On May 9, 1929, a month after supplying ten copies of the balance sheet to be used, to the knowledge of the defendants, to obtain credit, defendants sent a letter to the Pelz-Greenstein Company containing comments on and explanations of the balance sheet. Apparently only one copy of this letter was sent, and it did not come to the attention of plaintiff nor, so far as the evidence shows, to any one else until after the bankruptcy of Pelz-Greenstein. This accompanying letter contained statements of facts discovered by defendants in the course of their audit, and, therefore, known to them when they prepared the original certified balance sheet, but which were not mentioned therein. One of the defendants testified before trial that the certified

balance sheet was subject to the comments contained in the letter and the letter was sent for the purpose of trying to prevent any one from using this balance sheet without knowing the scope of the examination which was made.

• • •

At the time the accountants issued their audit report Pelz-Greenstein was hopelessly insolvent.

To what extent may accountants be held liable for their failure to reveal this condition? We have held that in the absence of a contractual relationship or its equivalent, accountants cannot be held liable for ordinary negligence in preparing a certified balance sheet even though they are aware that the balance sheet will be used to obtain credit. Ultramares Corporation v. Touche, 255 N.Y. 170, 174 N.E. 441, 74 A.L.R. 1139. Accountants, however, may be liable to third parties, even where there is lacking deliberate or active fraud. A representation certified as true to the knowledge of the accountants when knowledge there is none, a reckless misstatement, or an opinion based on grounds so flimsy as to lead to the conclusion that there was no genuine belief in its truth, are all sufficient upon which to base liability. A refusal to see the obvious, a failure to investigate the doubtful, if sufficiently gross, may furnish evidence leading to an inference of fraud so as to impose liability for losses suffered by those who rely on the balance sheet. In other words, heedlessness and reckless disregard of consequence may take the place of deliberate intention.

In Ultramares Corporation v. Touche, 255 N.Y. 170, we said with no uncertainty that negligence, if gross, or blindness, even though not equivalent to fraud, was sufficient to sustain an inference of fraud. Our exact words were: "In this connection we are to bear in mind the principle already stated in the course of this opinion that negligence or blindness, even when not equivalent to fraud, is none the less evidence to sustain an inference of fraud. At least this is so if the negligence is gross."

To emphasize our holding that active and deliberate fraud was not necessary to create liability, and that gross negligence, and even blindness to the obvious may be evidence to sustain an inference of fraud, we were careful to point out that the language in Kountze v. Kennedy, 147 N.Y. 124, saying that misjudgment, however gross, or want of caution, however marked, is not fraud, must be confined to the facts of that case, where the trier of the facts had found the defendants guiltless, and the ruling "amounted merely to a holding that a finding of fraud did not follow as an inference of law." Ultramares Corporation v. Touche, supra, page 191.

• • •

The record is, indeed, replete with evidence, both oral and documentary, to make a prima facie case against the defendants. In the first place, we have these accountants guilty of an act which is the equivalent of active misrepresentation. On April 2, 1929, they sent to Pelz-Greenstein the certified balance sheet, with ten additional copies, knowing that it was to be used to obtain credit. Not until thirty days later did the accountants send to Pelz-Greenstein a letter of explanation of this balance sheet, and then apparently only one copy. So important was this covering letter in the minds of defendants that, although the balance sheet attached to the covering letter was in other respects substantially identical with the original balance sheet, it contained the following notation, which did not appear at all on the original balance sheet released thirty days earlier: "This balance sheet is subject to the comments contained in the letter attached to and made a part of this report." One of the copartners, testifying before trial, said: "We want to try to prevent anyone using this balance sheet, without knowing the scope of the examination which we made, which is set forth in paragraph 2 of the full report. * * * We have had cases where our entire covering letter had been deleted from these reports and just the balance sheet used." Yet, in effect, these defendants themselves did just this. They held back this covering letter for thirty days and issued the balance sheet alone to the world of possible lenders. The loan by the plaintiff was made long before this important covering letter was even sent.

The above act of the accountants, in placing in circulation a certified balance sheet which they practically conceded should not be used without knowing the scope of the examination set forth in the covering letter, and then allowing a period of thirty days to elapse before sending the covering letter, and then only one copy, whereas there had been ten copies of the certified balance sheet issued, was itself gross negligence and an important piece of evidence raising an inference of fraud.

• • •

Turning now to the specific items. The second largest item in the balance sheet was the item:

Commission Accounts Receivable—secured by merchandise

Advances	$2,043,337.81
Less allowance	$ 19,767.15
	$2,023,570.66

The above item represented the advances made by Pelz-Greenstein to its borrowers to finance their operations in the purchase or manufacture of merchandise. These accounts, amounting to over one-fourth of Pelz-Greenstein's total assets, were shown on the certified balance sheet as good after deducting the $19,000 allowance. Yet, to the knowledge of defendants, according to their own statement, in the delayed covering letter, a very large proportion of these commission accounts receivable "were comparatively inactive during the year and appeared slow of collection." Out of the total of $2,043,000 an aggregate of $768,000, or over 38 per cent of the total amount, had unpaid advances at the end of the year 1928, amounting to 125 per cent of the total sales during the year. This meant that these borrowers owed Pelz-Greenstein more money at the end of the year than their total sales during the year by 25 per cent, thus indicating stagnation of inventories. Not only did these stagnant accounts represent over 38 per cent in amount, but they included 27 out of 55 borrowers. The defendants had knowledge of this condition as shown by the delayed covering letter, and this knowledge was brought home to them by their report for the prior year, when they referred in the following manner to similar accounts, although the percentage of advances to sales then was only 65 per cent, as compared with 125 per cent in 1928: "The following accounts had excessive advances as measured by their sales volume which indicated probably excessive or slow moving inventories." It was conceded that this was the third consecutive audit by the defendants of the books of Pelz-Greenstein.

One of the experts for the plaintiff testified without contradiction that the percentage of unpaid advances, amounting to 125 per cent of sales, indicated that the accounts were in an over-extended condition and were badly out of proportion to the amount of merchandise sold during the year, indicating that the inventories were either excessive, slow moving or unsalable. In his opinion this condition indicated the likelihood of excess losses. Furthermore, this expert testified unequivocally that the financial condition of Pelz-Greenstein could not be truthfully expressed without mention of this condition in the balance sheet. Professor Cole, the other expert called by plaintiff, testified that proper accounting practice required that defendants either establish a very large allowance for uncollectible accounts or indicate, in connection with the balance sheet, the existence of approximately $768,000 with a ratio of advances to sales of 125 per cent. The best corroboration of the testimony of both these experts is what defendants themselves said of this condition in the delayed covering letter. In spite of this a reserve of a mere $19,767.15 was set up against this account. This was to cover not only those accounts of $768,000, showing the stagnation of inventories described above, but all other commission accounts in a total of over $2,000,000.

This small reserve of $19,000 was practically absorbed in the one account of W. K. Wardener, which had gone into bankruptcy in 1924 and from which account Pelz-Greenstein had received nothing since May, 1924. Even if the accountants had not been informed that the Wardener account was in bankruptcy yet a warning that this account required a substantial reserve was given to them by the fact that an account upon which

nothing had been received since May, 1924, was being padded year after year by monthly interest charges. From a failure to note on the balance sheet the stagnant condition of over three-quarters of a million of these accounts and the setting up of a totally inadequate reserve, a jury might reasonably draw the inference that these defendants had no genuine belief in these figures in the balance sheet to which they certified.

We next come to a very substantial item entitled:

Commission Account Advances—Inactive and in Liquidation .... $215,124.72.

This item appeared on the certified balance sheet without any reserve. The books of Pelz-Greenstein showed on their face that many of the accounts included in this item had had no transactions for many years, neither sales nor realizations upon security. Furthermore, within this time the books showed systematic inflation of these accounts by steadily increasing interest charges. In fact, these charges were added to one account, even though the account appeared on the face of the books to have been in bankruptcy. The covering letter set forth the real condition of these accounts in detail, thus showing full knowledge on the part of the defendants. . . . The experts went on to testify without contradiction that from the facts as shown on the face of the books a reserve of at least $150,000 should have been set up against these accounts unless investigation showed them to be of full value.

The defendants urge that these defendants were excused from investigation because of a letter from Leon S. Pelz, treasurer of Pelz-Greenstein, in which he stated that Pelz-Greenstein had in its possession "sufficient salable merchandise to completely liquidate" these accounts. In other words, defendants were content to certify a balance sheet knowing it would be used to secure bank credit which contained an item of over $125,000 of apparently dead accounts on the uninvestigated and unsupported statement of the party seeking the credit that these accounts were amply secured, although it appeared on the face of the books that there had been no realization upon this security for years. Where the books indicate the likelihood of a substantial loss, a failure to indicate this on the balance sheet can be justified only by an actual check-up. It does not suffice to rely instead upon the statement of an officer of the firm the books of which are being examined. If an accountant may disregard a situation which indicates substantial losses because he is informed by the person whose books are being examined that there is adequate security, the balance sheet issued by the accountant, by its failure to point this out, contains a misrepresentation. The very purpose of the bank in seeking the balance sheet prepared by the accountant is to check any possible fraud on the part of the person seeking the loan. Yet these accountants contend that they may accept as true a statement by the party whose books are being examined, make no check-up or investigation on their own part, and issue a statement omitting entirely any mention of the reason why investigation of the security was omitted.

We have explicit expert testimony, uncontradicted, that under these circumstances it was improper accounting practice for defendants to accept a letter from Pelz-Greenstein, and that they should have investigated these accounts very fully to ascertain whether the companies were still in business and to ascertain definitely and independently what security, if any, Pelz-Greenstein held for the payment of these accounts.

. . .

The foregoing presents abundant evidence from which a jury could find that defendants knew facts which vitally affected the financial worth of Pelz-Greenstein, and which defendants totally suppressed on the certified balance sheet but disclosed to Pelz Greenstein alone in the one copy of the covering letter sent thirty days later. The jury further could have found that the computation of reserves on the certified balance sheet was a misrepresentation which did not reflect the facts as known to defendants, and which they in good faith should have revealed. Where the record shows acts on the part of the accountants, as outlined above, we cannot say, as a matter of law, that plaintiff has failed to make out a case for the jury.

[1] Judge's Role

What stops a plaintiff from devising an "end run" to the limitations on negligence actions by manipulating the doctrine of gross negligence? The trial judge.

In some cases it will be clear that acts of negligence do not constitute gross negligence from which an inference of fraud may be drawn reasonably. When confronted with this type of evidence a trial judge may properly prohibit the plaintiff from proceeding on a fraud claim.

Although the judge may exercise this power, it is often the case that the judge chooses not to use the power, reasoning that the issue is a factual question for the jury to decide.

¶ 4.07   Reckless Behavior

The question of whether reckless or grossly negligent conduct reaches the level of inferable fraud is not easily resolved. It is a question on which reasonable persons, including judges and juries, may and do differ. Conduct that one person may believe is reckless to the point of being fraudulent may be viewed by another person as simply inexcusable negligence.

The task of deciding whether evidence of reckless conduct gives rise to an inference of fraud is made more difficult if the court's definition of recklessness is unclear. The following cases reflect the lack of uniform and hence predictable treatment of this type of conduct.

[1]   Rule 10b-5 Recklessness: Further Defined

The U.S. Supreme Court in *Ernst & Ernst v. Hochfelder* left unresolved the question of whether reckless behavior could give rise to a lawsuit under Rule 10b-5. Subsequent federal court decisions have ruled that reckless behavior falls within the ambit of Rule 10b-5. As one federal court of appeals observed:

> At common law reckless behavior was sufficient to support causes of action sounding in fraud or deceit. Since there is no hint in *Hochfelder* that the Court intended a radical departure from accepted Rule 10b-5 principles, it would be highly inappropriate to construe the Rule 10b-5 remedy to be more restrictive in substantive scope than its common law analogs. . . . Therefore, we hold that a reckless omission of material facts upon which the plaintiff puts justifiable reliance in connection with a sale or purchase of securities is actionable under Section 10 (b) as fleshed out by Rule 10b-5.

Attempts at defining reckless behavior can often generate more confusion than clarity. Consider the following definition by a federal court of appeals:

> Apparently the only post-*Hochfelder* reported definition of recklessness in the context of omissions appears in *Franke v. Midwestern Oklahoma Development Authority*, . . .
>
>> [R]eckless conduct may be defined as a highly unreasonable omission, involving not merely simple, or even inexcusable negligence, but an extreme departure from the standards of ordinary care, and which presents a danger of misleading buyers or sellers that is either known to the defendant or is so obvious that the actor must have been aware of it.
>
> As the Supreme Court conceded in *Hochfelder*:
>
>> In certain areas of the law recklessness is considered to be a form of intentional conduct for purposes of imposing liability for some act.
>
> The *Franke* definition of recklessness is 'the kind of recklessness that is equivalent to wilful fraud'. . . .
> Indeed, the *Franke* definition of recklessness should be viewed as the functional equivalent of intent. . . . Under this definition, the danger of misleading buyers must be actually known or so obvious that any reasonable man would be legally bound as knowing, and the omission must derive from something more egregious than even 'white heart/empty head' good faith. While this definition might not be the conceptual equivalent of intent as a matter of general philosophy, it does serve as a proper legally functional equivalent for intent, because it measures conduct against an external standard which, under the circumstances of a given case, results in the conclusion that the reckless man should bear the risk of his omission.

With respect to the fraud defense that the conduct involves no more than "inexcusable negligence," the appellate court ruled:

> Thus if a trial judge found, for example, that a defendant genuinely forgot to disclose information or that it never came to his mind, etc., this prong of the . . . test would defeat

a finding of recklessness even though the proverbial 'reasonable man' would never have forgotten.

"Inexcusable negligence" shares a common character with pornography: we may not be able to adequately define it, but we know it when we see it—maybe!

[2]   Rule 10b-5 Recklessness: Split Decisions on Accountants

The following cases reflect that judges looking at the same case can differ markedly in their conclusions as to whether reckless conduct involves fraud or merely "inexcusable negligence."

[a]   *McLean v. Alexander* and Comments

McLean v. Alexander
599 F. 2d 1190 (3d Cir. 1979)

GIBBONS, Circuit Judge.

[Plaintiff McLean purchased all the outstanding stock of Technidyne, Inc., based on representations regarding the marketability of a laser-beam tool manufactured by Technidyne and distributed by AMVIT Company. Plaintiff relied on representations contained in the balance sheet audited by the defendant accountants regarding recent sales of the laser-beam tool known as the Model V Technitool. In fact, the sales representations were false and Technidyne was hopelessly insolvent at the time McLean purchased its stock.]

Cashman & Schiavi (C & S), a firm of certified public accountants, appeal from a final judgment awarding Malcolm P. McLean damages in his suit under Section 10(b) of the Securities Exchange Act of 1934, and Rule 10b-5, and under the Delaware common law of fraud. . . . The case was tried to the court without a jury. We conclude that the judgment against C & S must be reversed.

• • •

II. C & S's LIABILITY

From what has been said above, it is evident that McLean was induced to purchase the stock of Technidyne by representations concerning past sales, and future sales potential, of the Model V Technitool, and that those representations were false. Specifically, the representation that AMVIT had sold 114 Technitool units in 2½ years was false, as was the representation that 41 more units had been sold after the termination of the AMVIT distributorship. This fraud was substantial and pervasive.

The claim against C & S, however, is a much narrower one. C & S was not at any time privy to the negotiations between the stockholders and McLean, nor did it have any knowledge of the broad representations made during those meetings. So far as appears, the only contact between C & S and McLean was McLean's receipt, through Technidyne's management, of a copy of the November 30, 1969 Certified Report of Examination prepared by C & S, which contained an audited balance sheet dated November 30, 1969, the full text of which is set out. . . .

ASSETS		LIABILITIES	
Current Assets:		*Current Liabilities:*	
Cash	$ 7,544	Accounts Payable	$ 52,479
Accounts Receivable—		Note Payable—Bank of Delaware 8%—	
Considered Fully Collectible	73,733	Demand	200,000

ASSETS			LIABILITIES		
Inventories—At Lower of Cost or Market	66,111		Payroll Taxes Payable	667	
Notes Receivable— Stockholders	6,775		Accrued Expenses	1,604	
Refund Due from Prior Income Taxes Paid	13,392		Total Liabilities		$254,750
Prepaid Expenses	3,449		STOCKHOLDERS' EQUITY		
			Capital Assigned to Shares:		
Total Current Assets		$171,004	Common Stock— 1,000 No Par Shares Authorized of which 535 Shares are Issued and Outstanding	$ 25,316	
Property and Equipment—At Cost:					
Plant Equipment	$14,537		Retained Earnings (Deficit) (Exhibit B)	(91,647)	
Leasehold Improvements	2,749				
Office Equipment	3,902				
Total	$21,188		Total Stockholders' Equity		(66,331)
Less—Depreciation Taken To Date	3,873		Total Liabilities and Stockholders' Equity		$188,419
Net Property and Equipment		17,315			
Other Asset—Utility Deposit		100			
Total Assets		$188,419			

Only one item on this balance sheet—the statement of $73,733 in accounts receivable—was found at trial to be false or misleading. The report accurately showed a deficit in retained earnings of $91,647 and negative stockholders' equity of $66,331. It showed total assets of $188,419, and this figure is also substantially accurate, since if the accounts receivable were overstated the inventory of $66,111 was correspondingly understated.

McLean, however, was paying many times the total value of the assets shown on the balance sheet, and was primarily interested in sales potential. The district court found that McLean viewed the $73,733 figure "as representing almost entirely the accounts due and owing as a result of the 16 recent sales referred to in the Shields Report. . . ." It further found that

McLean and Jeter, relying upon the independence of the outside auditors, viewed the audit as confirming what they had previously been told and seen regarding the marketability of Technidyne's pipelaying tool.

It therefore stated the issue for trial as follows:

[T]he primary issue before the Court is whether the accountant proceeded in a deliberate, knowing or reckless manner in the preparation of his audit such that the plaintiff, relying on material information provided or omitted by defendant, incurred a loss protected by section 10(b) of the Securities Exchange Act of 1934.

The gravamen of McLean's complaint is that Schiavi knowingly or recklessly represented to McLean as a member of the investing public, that Technidyne had "hard" sales whereas in fact the underlying transactions were merely consignments or guaranteed sales.

The court then proceeded to determine that the audited statement of accounts receivable, as evidence of sixteen actual sales, was material to McLean's investment decision, that he relied upon that information, and that in purchasing the stock he acted with due diligence. . . .

The issue, then, is whether the plaintiff has made an affirmative showing that Shiavi acted with the scienter required to sustain a claim under §10(b). This in turn requires an inquiry into the governing standard of liability. Since the *Hochfelder* decision this court and other Courts of Appeals which have considered the issue reserved in *Hochfelder* have unanimously agreed that reckless conduct is actionable under §10(b). In *Coleco Industries, Inc. v. Berman*, . . . we approved Judge Huyett's statement that the scienter element in a §10(b) case required " 'a conscious deception or . . . a misrepresentation so recklessly made that the culpability attaching to such reckless conduct closely approaches that which attaches to conscious deception'."

In *Sundstrand Corp. v. Sun Chemical Corp.*, . . . the Seventh Circuit stated the minimum threshold for liability under §10(b) as follows:

> [R]eckless conduct may be defined as . . . highly unreasonable [conduct]; involving not merely simple, or even inexcusable negligence, but an extreme departure from the standards of ordinary care, and which presents a danger of misleading buyers or sellers that is either known to the defendant or is so obvious that the actor must have been aware of it.

The *Sundstrand* formulation of recklessness makes it clear, as did *Hochfelder*, that negligence—whether gross, grave or inexcusable—cannot serve as a substitute for scienter. At the same time, as applied to the somewhat specialized area of accountants' liability, that standard preserves a federal right of action for the kind of accountants' fraud that has been generally recognized as actionable at common law since the leading case of *Ultramares Corp. v. Touche*, 255 N.Y. 170, 174 N.E. 441 (1931). Judge Cardozo's opinion in *Ultramares* would have permitted recovery for fraud upon a showing that a misrepresentation was made knowingly or wilfully, or with reckless disregard for its truth

or falsity, or without a "genuine belief" in its truth. Further, fraud "includes the pretense of knowledge when knowledge there is none." As Judge Swan made clear in *O'Connor v. Ludlam*, 92 F.2d 50, 54 (2d Cir. 1937), also an accountants' liability case, in an action for fraud under the *Ultramares* standard:

> the issue [is] whether the defendants had an honest belief that the statements made by them were true. "If they did have that honest belief, whether reasonably or unreasonably, they are not liable. If they did not have an honest belief in the truth of their statements, then they are liable, so far as [scienter] is concerned."

We stress that to prove scienter the plaintiff need not produce direct evidence of the defendant's state of mind. Circumstantial evidence may often be the principal, if not the only, means of proving bad faith. A showing of shoddy accounting practices amounting at best to a "pretended audit," or of grounds supporting a representation "so flimsy as to lead to the conclusion that there was no genuine belief back of it" have traditionally supported a finding of liability in the face of repeated assertions of good faith, and continue to do so. In such cases, the factfinder may justifiably conclude that despite those assertions the "danger of misleading . . . [was] so obvious that the actor must have been aware of it." . . .

The district court took one line from the balance sheet, the reference to accounts receivable, and on that line built its finding that C & S was a joint tortfeasor. The line must, however, be placed in its context. The C & S opinion letter . . . states that its . . . "examination was made in accordance with generally accepted auditing standards, and accordingly included such tests of the accounting records and such other auditing procedures as we considered necessary in the circumstances. . . ." The representation was, then, an expression of opinion based upon generally accepted auditing standards. C & S could be held to have the necessary scienter only if the evidence supports an inference that when it expressed the opinion it had no genuine belief that it had the information on which it could predicate that opinion.

• • •

Although the defendants contended these sales had occurred, testimony by agents of L. B. Smith, Robbins, and Southern Laser established to the satisfaction of the court that the sixteen transactions were in the nature of consignments. There was no evidence that Schiavi, the C & S partner in charge of the audit, had actual knowledge of the consignment arrangements, or even that he was aware of the risk that they were consignment sales. Thus C & S could be held to have the requisite scienter only if the investigation it made, and the knowledge it had, give rise to an inference that it "must have been aware" of the risk that the accounts receivable item was misleading. Upon examination of the evidence bearing on Schiavi's investigation of the four questioned accounts, we conclude that such an inference was not permissible in this case.

The L. B. Smith Transaction

Schiavi examined purchase orders and invoices relating to the L. B. Smith transaction. With respect to that documentation, the district court found: "the underlying documentation does not clearly indicate that the transaction involving the five Model V Technitools was anything other than a sale, albeit an installment sale with an unspecified future delivery date." . . . The district court, however, concluded that several inconsistencies in the documentation should have put Schiavi on notice that the sale was in fact a consignment. Thus, the L. B. Smith purchase order, executed October 7, 1969, indicated that one unit was delivered at the time of purchase and that the remaining four were to be delivered "A.S.A.P." (presumably meaning "as soon as possible.") The district court concluded a Technidyne invoice dated November 30, 1969 and sent to L. B. Smith, was inconsistent with the A.S.A.P. notation, since it stated that these four units were still being

held in Technidyne's warehouse. From another perspective, however, the invoice was consistent with the purchase order, which also indicated that four of the five units were being held in Technidyne's warehouse, where Schiavi observed them. . . . The court also found that the L. B. Smith invoice was inconsistent with the purchase order, since the former called for one third payment within 60 days (*i.e.*, by December 6) while the invoice demanded payment in mid-January. Schiavi testified, however, that he was aware that Technidyne had had a bill and hold practice with AMVIT. The documentation was entirely consistent with such an arrangement with L. B. Smith.

Schiavi also made an effort to obtain confirmation of the accounts receivable by sending each customer a written confirmation request. . . . A telegram was sent from L. B. Smith:

> This will confirm our purchase order number BA51794 for 5 Number 5 Units of Technidyne.

The district court points out, correctly, that this telegram is not fully responsive to the C & S request for confirmation, in that it confirms a purchase order rather than an amount due and owing. The telegram was not, however, inconsistent with the Technidyne documentation of a sale. Finally, the district court noted the suspicious fact that the L. B. Smith invoice was dated November 30, 1969, the closing date of the audit. If we were applying a negligence standard we could affirm a finding that given the one month discrepancy in the due dates between the invoice and purchase order, the late issuance of the invoice, and the ambiguity in the telegraphic confirmation, Schiavi should have made further inquiry of management or of L. B. Smith before concluding that the account receivable was genuine. But we cannot hold that these factors, standing alone, were evidence that C & S was aware that it was without sufficient knowledge to form that opinion. Such a holding would obliterate the distinction between tortious conduct requiring scienter, which the *Hochfelder* construction of §10(b) demands, and negligence which *Hochfelder* found insufficient.

* * *

The Southern Laser Transaction

The Southern Laser purchase order and invoice, like those of L. B. Smith and Robbins, indicate an outright sale of ten units. While there were inconsistencies in the stated payment dates of the order and the invoice, Schiavi made inquiries of management regarding them. As in the case of L. B. Smith, the Southern Laser units were segregated in Technidyne's warehouse. C & S assumed that, as with AMVIT, Technidyne had a bill and hold arrangement with Southern Laser under which shipment would be made direct to its customers from that warehouse. A confirmation request was also sent to Southern Laser. When that request was not returned, a Technidyne salesman, Joe Daniel, received instructions from Technidyne to prod the customer to respond. Instead, Daniel called Western Union in Atlanta and caused a telegram to be sent to C & S as follows:

> Affirmation of order for 10 Model 5 Technidyne Lasers for $39,995.00 is correct—Tom Methvin Southern Laser Co.

C & S accepted the telegram as genuine, and as a confirmation of the underlying documents and the management representation. Like the L. B. Smith confirmation, this telegram is not literally responsive to the request for confirmation of an amount due. It is, however, entirely consistent with Technidyne's documentation of a sale, and no information was brought home to C & S that it was not genuine. The district court said of the Southern Laser telegram:

> However, in total and reckless disregard of the facts that he had never had any prior contact with, or knowledge of Southern Laser, that the telegram was a non sequitur in relation to the confirmations and that he had no way of knowing who sent it, Schiavi never bothered to contact Methvin.

With deference, we cannot believe that this is the standard of scienter which Judge Cardozo had in mind in *Ultramares*. At best, the retention of the units in the warehouse and the fact that the telegram referred to a purchase order rather than an amount due is evidence of possible negligence. It cannot support a finding that C & S knew it lacked the knowledge required to form the opinion that the Southern Laser account was genuine. The existing documentary evidence, the inquiries of management, the awareness of the past bill and hold practice, and the partial telegraphic confirmation simply cannot be characterized as "grounds . . . so flimsy as to lead to the conclusion that there was no genuine belief back of" Schiavi's representation to that effect.

* * *

The court also stressed the language in the C & S report describing the accounts receivable as "Considered Fully Collectible." Schiavi, as well as the expert witnesses who testified to standard of care, both testified that this language was a means of explaining the absence of a reserve for bad debts. McLean's fraud claim is not predicated upon the collectibility of the accounts receivable, but rather on their existence, as evidence of product acceptance in the marketplace. Thus had the "Considered Fully Collectible" language been omitted, or had C & S made a credit check on the four customers and included a reserve for bad debts, the effect on McLean's investment decision, given his theory of recovery, would have been slight. Insofar as the Considered Fully Collectible language assumes the accountant's underlying judgment that valid sales had occurred, McLean still must show that the evidence upon which Schiavi relied in reaching that opinion supports the conclusion that the figure of $73,733 was included with reckless disregard of the existence of the underlying accounts. We have indicated above that it does not. The accountant examined purchase orders and invoices which appeared genuine, received representations from management, took steps to obtain confirmation from the account debtors, and received partial confirmation of 15 of the 16 sales centrally in issue. C & S may have been negligent in not discovering management's fraud, but it did not act with reckless disregard for the truth.

Keep in mind that proof of a defendant's bad faith does not require proof of an "intent to deceive" or "motive to defraud," as one legal commentator has observed:

> The upshot is that common law fraud is and has been the test under 10b-5—plaintiff must prove a knowingly false statement or that the defendant was aware of facts, which, to a prudent man, would have made clear the probable falsity of the statement. Intent to deceive in the sense of wickedness or motive to defraud is irrelevant under *Hochfelder* as it has been in deceit for almost 200 years. Accountants who gullibly accept transparently fishy explanations from their clients of an obviously suspicious transaction are liable under 10b-5, no matter what their mental state. (Haimoff, *Holmes Looks at Hochfelder and 10b-5*, 32 Bus. Law. 14 (1976))

The *McLean* court relies upon the decision in *O'Connor v. Ludlam*, 92 F.2d 50 (2d Cir. 1937), which holds:

> Fraud presupposes not only an untrue statement but also a fraudulent intent. On the question of falsity of the representations the jury was told that the issue was whether the defendants' representations, "in the sense to be taken by an ordinary reasonable man," were, in fact, true or untrue—whether a true or a false impression was created. On the question of intent, the jury was told that fraud may be established by showing that a false representation has been made, either knowingly, or without belief in its truth, or in reckless disregard of whether it be true or false; and that the issue was whether the defendants had an honest belief that the statements made by them were true. "If they did have that honest belief, whether reasonably or unreasonably, they are not liable. If they did not have an honest belief in the truth of their statements, then they are liable, so far as this third element [scienter] is concerned." The jury was also told that an intent to deceive may be inferred from a lack of honest representation; and that, so far as alleged concealments or omissions were concerned, the issue was whether the omission to state certain matters was deliberate and intended to conceal. It was further charged that, if the audit made "was so superficial as to be only a pretended audit and not a real audit, then the element of knowledge of falsity of their representations is present, and they may be held liable." Reading the charge as a whole, it seems to be in strict conformity with the established law. *Ultramares Corp. v. Touche, Niven & Co.*, 255 N.Y. 170, 174 N.E. 411, 74 A.L.R. 1129.

[b]   *Oleck v. Fischer*

Oleck v. Fischer
623 F.2d 791 (2d Cir. 1980)

Before MANSFIELD and WATERMAN, Circuit Judges, and LEVAL, District Judge.

[Plaintiffs sold shares of stock to Sherwood Company in exchange for cash and Sherwood's promissory notes. Plaintiffs relied upon Sherwood's 1970 annual report, which was audited by the defendant accounting firm. The plaintiffs sued the accountants Arthur Andersen & Co. under Rule 10b-5, claiming that the financials were intentionally misleading in describing Sherwood's purchase and rapid divestiture in 1970 of the assets of a business known as U.S. Media.

As a result of this bad acquisition decision Sherwood had parted with $2.5 million in cash and had incurred contingent liabilities as guarantor of $2 million on notes issued by U.S. Media's successor company, New Media. Although Sherwood sold New Media back to its original owners for $500,000 in cash and New Media promissory notes of $2.57 million, Sherwood ultimately incurred substantial losses on this transaction when New Media filed for bankruptcy. As a result Sherwood defaulted on its promissory notes to the plaintiffs, who in turn sued the accountants.

In a bench trial the district court judge found in favor of the accountants. Plaintiffs appealed that decision to the court of appeals.]

It was Sherwood's desire by the divestiture to put itself as closely as possible in the financial position it had occupied before the acquisition. In several respects, however, the net effect of the two transactions left its position significantly changed. The most important changes were two:

> First, while Sherwood had parted with $3 million cash, $2 million to its seller and $1 million loaned to its U.S. Media subsidiary as working capital, it got back only $500,000 in cash in the divestiture, the remainder of the cash outlay being recoverable only over 8 years of monthly payments on the New Media notes;
>
> Second, Sherwood had incurred and retained a contingent liability of $2 million, as guarantor of U.S. Media's bank loan.

The extent of Sherwood's risk exposure during the eight years of gradual payment of the New Media notes depended in particular on New Media's receivables and collections. The receivables were valued by Andersen's auditors at $6 million as of September 30, 1970. These receivables were first pledged to secure New Media's bank debt of $2 million, which Sherwood had guaranteed. Upon satisfaction of the bank debt, the remainder of New Media receivables were pledged as security for Sherwood's notes. Sherwood accordingly had over $4 million exposure secured by these accounts receivables and the collections thereon.

Plaintiffs contend that the financial statements certified by Andersen on which plaintiffs relied in accepting Sherwood's long term notes were seriously misleading in their presentation of the Media transaction described above. The claim is not so much that the accounting entries were inaccurate, but rather that descriptive language, particularly in the lengthy footnote 11 to the financial statements, was designed to create the false impression that the acquisition had been "cancelled" in a manner which terminated

Sherwood's exposure. Plaintiffs contend that this language was designed to lull the reader to fail to appreciate Sherwood's continuing precarious $4 million exposure following the divestiture.

The portions [of footnote 11] which plaintiffs contend were particularly misleading are the statements that

> Sherwood and the selling shareholders [of the U.S. Media assets] agreed . . . to cancel the acquisition and return all consideration previously advanced . . .

and that

> [S]ince the result of this transaction is to effectively cancel the original acquisition, the results of operations of U.S. Media are not included in the accompanying financial statements for any period.

Plaintiffs also contended that Andersen's delivery of a "clean" (or unqualified) certifying opinion violated proper accounting principles and that the $500,000 reserve established on Sherwood's books against the possible uncollectibility of the New Media notes was so inadequate as to constitute a fraud.

· · ·

If Judge Haight's opinion is read as signifying that notes and financial statements must be read and evaluated in their entirety and should not be judged by citing words out of context, we agree. On the other hand, his opinion should not be misunderstood to suggest that liability for reckless or intentionally misleading use of palliative, soothing, or optimistic language can be avoided by the inclusion of numbers which, if studied and understood, would contradict the misleading verbal message. . . . An objective reader of the controversial footnote might well wonder whether the auditors had been overly accommodating to their client's desire to have the transaction look like a wash.

Judge Haight also found that plaintiffs had failed to demonstrate *scienter*, such as would satisfy the requirements established by the Supreme Court in *Ernst & Ernst v. Hochfelder*.

In seeking to interpret the kind and quality of *scienter* necessary to establish liability after *Hochfelder*, . . . this court has adhered to the proposition . . . that "reckless conduct will generally satisfy the *scienter* requirement."

Judge Haight concluded that recklessness would satisfy the *scienter* requirement in this case by reason of the foreseeability to the accountant that the certification would be relied on by third parties.

We need not pass on whether proof of recklessness is sufficient to make out a cause of action in view of Judge Haight's finding that no recklessness was shown.

Judge Haight found no reckless disregard for the truth. He concluded that Andersen's failures were at worst "judgmental," not rising "above the level of negligence," and thus non-actionable under *Hochfelder*. These findings were reasonably supported by the evidence.

Judge Haight found that Andersen's audit team had perceived the collectibility of the New Media notes as an important focus of inquiry which in turn depended for security on the extent and collectibility of New Media's receivables. Accordingly they devised a ten-step program to evaluate New Media in these respects.

Based on figures and projections furnished primarily by New Media, Andersen concluded that New Media had growing sales proceeding for the current year at a rate exceeding $17,800,000, with booked orders totaling $5,900,000 for the next four months. It observed that New Media's accounts were "mostly major firms."

A summary prepared by Andersen concluded that New Media's "cash projections [were] . . . reasonable and attainable . . . [and that the] cash flow shows the ability to pay principal and interest on the Sherwood notes without any detriment to its cash position." Andersen interviewed New Media's bankers and found "no plans to request payment against their $2,000,000 loan." The New Media receivables were found to be more than adequate security to cover the bank debt and the Sherwood notes. Andersen also obtained and relied on an opinion of Sherwood's counsel to the effect that Sherwood's lien on the Media receivables was enforceable. Based on these investigations, Andersen concluded that "a reserve for collectibility of $500,000 would be sufficient."

Judge Haight was convinced that Andersen made those investigations and observations in good faith and was justified in issuing a clean opinion.

Plaintiffs argued both here and below that Andersen could not reasonably have accepted and relied on the information furnished by New Media's executives and should have discredited the opinion of counsel which failed to acknowledge the 120 day gap during which Sherwood's lien would not take priority over New Media's other debts in case of New Media's bankruptcy. Those contentions were fully considered by Judge Haight who was not persuaded by them. His findings depended in significant part on his assessment of the credibility of Andersen's witnesses. Those findings were adequately supported by the evidence and may not be disturbed on appeal.

[c] *Adams v. Standard Knitting Mills* **and Comments**

Adams v. Standard Knitting Mills
623 F.2d 422 (6th Cir. 1980)

Before WEICK, ENGEL and MERRITT, Circuit Judges.

MERRITT, Circuit Judge.

[Plaintiffs were former shareholders of Standard Knitting Mills, Inc., who exchanged their stock for preferred stock issued by Chadbourn, Inc. The exchange took place on April 22, 1970, pursuant to a proxy solicitation which the plaintiffs claimed was false and misleading in violation of Rule 10b-5.

The plaintiffs sued the defendant accounting firm, Peat, Marwick, Mitchell & Co., based on the accountants' failure to disclose certain bank loan restrictions on dividend payments on Chadbourn preferred shares as well as restrictions on redemption of Chadbourn preferred. In a footnote to the audited financials, the accountants disclosed that the dividend restrictions were limited solely to Chadbourn's common stock.

In a bench trial, the trial judge found that the accountants' inaccurate footnote was the product of an intent to defraud. The accountants appealed from the district court's judgment of $3.4 million plus an award of $1.2 million for attorneys' fees.]

Chadbourn's financial statements as of August 2, 1969, and Peat's opinion, dated October 21, 1969, were published in the back of the March 27, 1970, Standard proxy statement. The liabilities and stockholders' equity side of the balance sheet was shown on page F-5 of the proxy statement. This page sets out amounts for current installments of long-term debt, the non-current portion of long-term debt, and "stockholders' equity," which referred in turn to certain notes, including footnote 7.

Footnote 7, paragraphs (c) and (d) erroneously described the two sets of restrictions as follows:

> (c) As to the note payable to three banks, the Company has agreed to various restrictive provisions including those relating to maintenance of minimum stockholders' equity and working capital, the purchase, sale or encumbering of fixed assets, incurrance [sic] of indebtedness, the leasing of additional assets and the payment of dividends *on common stock* in excess of $2,000,000 plus earnings subsequent to August 2, 1969.
>
> (d) . . . Further, the indenture has certain restrictive covenants but they are less restrictive than those contained in the note agreement with the three banks. (Emphasis added.)

The word "common" in paragraph (c) referring to the loan agreement was wrong because the relevant provision of the loan agreement restricted the use of retained earnings for the payment of dividends on "capital stock of any class," not just "common." Thus the restriction on retained earnings would apply to all distributions to pay dividends or redeem the preferred shares issued to Standard stockholders should they approve the merger.

Facts Respecting Peat's Negligence

The facts demonstrate that Peat's omissions were the result of negligence but did not arise from an intent to deceive, or *scienter*, as found by the District Court.

Peat failed to disclose fully in the financial statement the restrictive effect of the loan agreement and indenture on Chadbourn preferred stock. After each entry relating to long-term capitalization, the financial statement directs the attention of the reader to explanatory note 7. Note 7 alone pertains to Chadbourn's long-term debt. Missing from the note is any reference to limitations that the debt agreements placed on Chadbourn preferred stock.

Only in notes 7(c) and 7(d) does Peat mention the restrictive provisions. Note 7(c), which discusses the loan agreement, reports only that "the Company has agreed to various restrictive provisions including . . . the payment of dividends on common stock in excess of $2 million plus earnings subsequent to August 2, 1969." Note 7(d) describes the indenture. It says that "the indenture has certain restrictive covenants, but they are less restrictive than those contained in the [loan] agreement." Thus, there is no indication in either note that the long-term debt restrictions affected the redemption and earnings of preferred stock.

From notes 7(c) and 7(d), a reader easily could derive the following mistaken impression: The loan agreement contains certain restrictions on the payment of dividends by Chadbourn. As note 7(c) explicitly says, the loan agreement restrictions relate to the payment of dividends "on common stock." The indenture contains limitations that are "less restrictive" than those created by the loan agreement. Since the limitations of the loan agreement apply only to common stock, the reader mistakenly could reason that the "less restrictive" indenture constraints appear to have no broader sweep. What note 7 conveys to the reader is the erroneous notion that neither the loan agreement nor the indenture restrictions apply to Chadbourn preferred stock.

•   •   •

The finding of the District Court that Peat acted with scienter in making the omissions is nevertheless clearly erroneous. We find in the record nothing to indicate that a desire to deceive, defraud or manipulate motivated Peat to omit from the financial statement information regarding the applicability of long-term debt restrictions. Indeed, Stanwood Corporation, the successor to Chadbourn controlled by the former Standard shareholders, hired and retained as vice president and treasurer the Peat associate, Hugh Freeze, who the shareholders' counsel now claim sought to defraud them. If the shareholders and their representatives really believed Freeze intended to defraud them, it seems doubtful that they would have put him in charge of the financial affairs of the corporation.

At most the evidence supports a finding that Peat acted negligently in preparing the financial statements. Peat became aware that note 7 incorrectly described the debt limitation several weeks before the merger vote occurred. The Standard proxy statement was mailed to its stockholders on March 27, 1970. Between March 23, 1970, and April 1, 1970, Chadbourn's outside counsel telephoned Freeze, the Peat manager in charge of the Chadbourn audit, and told him that a description of restrictions relating to Chadbourn's stock had been inserted in the forepart of the Standard proxy statement prior to mailing. The lawyer called to his attention the difference in the description in the proxy statement and the footnote, pointing out that the footnote said "common" rather than "capital stock of any class." In the course of this conversation, Freeze took a copy of the preliminary Standard proxy statement and noted the change by hand in note 7(c). Thereafter, footnote 7(c) was not amended, and no effort was made to call the discrepancy to the attention of Standard stockholders or officials. Freeze did not foresee that the bottom would drop out of Chadbourn's earnings and that what appeared to be a minor error at the time would become a major bone of contention.

The evidence simply suggests a mistake, an oversight, the failure to foresee a problem. We find nothing in the record indicating an intent to deceive or a motive for deception. J. B. Woolsey, Standard's vice president for financial affairs, and presumably other Standard officers, knew of the restrictions and recommended the merger anyway. No stockholder testified that he was deceived. An erroneous statement cannot *ipso facto* prove fraud, and here we find no evidence of anything other than a negligent error.

• • •

Accordingly, the judgment of the District Court is reversed.

WEICK, Circuit Judge, dissenting.

• • •

It was not the province of an appellate court to review the factual findings of a trial judge *de novo* which is exactly what the majority did in the present case in many instances by stating that they were clearly erroneous when indeed they were not clearly erroneous, but were supported by substantial evidence, the testimony of many witnesses, including expert witnesses, depositions and credibility assessments made by the judge.

The District Court, after an extensive trial, following discovery and many proceedings in this complex case, filed its "Memorandum Decision" and also "Findings of Fact and Conclusions of Law." It specifically found that Peat had prepared a proxy statement which contained false and misleading financial statements which proxy statement was to be used in connection with the acquisition of Standard Knitting Mills, Inc. (Standard) a Tennessee corporation, by Chadbourn, Inc., (Chadbourn) a North Carolina corporation, to induce the shareholders of Standard to vote in favor of said merger and to be filed with the SEC.

• • •

In my opinion, the findings of fact adopted by the District Court are supported by substantial evidence and are not clearly erroneous. I would affirm the judgment of the District Court for the reasons herein set forth.

• • •

At the [April 22, 1970 special shareholders'] meeting Mr. Kramer, General Counsel and a Director of Standard, represented that there were no restrictions on the payment of dividends on the $.46⅔ cumulative and convertible preferred. This representation conformed to Footnote 7 of the Chadbourn financial statement contained in Standard proxy materials which was written and certified as correct by Peat.

. . .

The footnote incorrectly stated that the restriction upon the payment of dividends contained in the bank loan agreement applied only to Chadbourn common stock. Further, the exact provisions of the restrictive covenants of the Indenture are not set out but are characterized as "less restrictive than those contained in the note agreement with the three banks," implying that only restrictions on payment of dividends on common were contained in the Indenture. There is no mention of restrictions on the payment of dividends on Chadbourn preferred stock contained in the bank loan agreement or the Indenture, and there is no mention whatsoever of any restrictions on redemption of the preferred stock contained in either the bank loan agreement or the Indenture.

Approximately one month after the merger was approved plaintiffs received a proxy from Chadbourn soliciting their votes for approval of a loan and option agreement involving the acquisition of United Hosiery Mills by Chadbourn (the UHM proxy materials). Footnote 7(c) of the financial statement in the UHM proxy materials, which corresponded to footnote 7(c) contained in the Standard proxy materials, supra, had been altered so that the word "common" hereinbefore referred to was changed to the word "capital," thus indicating that restrictions on payment of dividends contained in the bank loan agreement applied to both common and preferred stock. This change was not brought to the attention of the reader in Peat's certification of the Chadbourn financial statement contained in the UHM proxy materials and the change was located on the 55th page of 77 pages of the UHM proxy materials.

Several months after plaintiffs received the UHM proxy materials plaintiffs received the 1970 Chadbourn Annual Report, which contained a financial statement for Chadbourn prepared by Peat. Footnote 6(c) of this financial statement returned to the use of the word "common." A quick reference to the 1969 Chadbourn Annual Report for the purpose of resolving this ambiguity would reveal that the pertinent footnote in the 1969 Chadbourn Annual Report used the word "common" as well. Footnote 7(c) in the UHM materials, therefore, was the only footnote in the certified financial statements in issue received by plaintiffs which indicated that restrictions on the payment of dividends in the bank loan agreement and Indenture applied to both common stock and preferred stock. The 1969 Chadbourn Annual Report, the financial statement in the Standard proxy materials, and the 1970 Chadbourn Annual Report uniformly indicated that the restrictions on the payment of dividends applied to common stock only, and none of the financial statements in issue, including the one in the UHM proxy materials, mentioned any existence of restrictions upon redemption contained in the bank loan agreement and the Indenture.

. . .

Chadbourn had to deal with approximately $18.5 million of new indebtedness before it could redeem plaintiffs' preferred as promised. Undisclosed was the fact that Chadbourn had to either earn approximately $16 million before taxes and $8 million after taxes, refinance the $18.5 million of indebtedness, or sell an additional $8 million of new equity securities.

It is clear that Peat had full knowledge of these restrictions when it prepared the Standard proxy financial statements and certified that the financial statements accurately described the financial condition and debt structure of Chadbourn. This certification was false and fraudulent as found by the District court. Furthermore, between March 23, 1970, and April 1, 1970, prior to the merger, Hugh Freeze, the Peat manager in charge of the Chadbourn audit, received a phone call from Chadbourn's attorney Herbert Browne, Jr., a member of the law firm of Helms, Mullis & Johnston, the firm that prepared parts of the proxy. Brown informed Freeze that the use of the word "common" in footnote 7(c) of the Peat audit was erroneous. Freeze then crossed out the word "common" on his copy of a preliminary draft of the Standard proxy footnote and wrote the word 'capital' underneath it. Peat, however, did not alter the proxy, or, if the proxy had already been mailed, Peat took no steps to notify Standard shareholders or the SEC to correct the alleged error before the Standard shareholders voted on the acquisition of Standard by Chadbourn. The District Court could rightly infer that the reason Freeze did not correct the original was because it would have defeated the merger as the Standard shareholders would not have approved it.

There is other direct evidence that Peat had actual knowledge of the alleged error in footnote 7 of the proxy statement before the merger vote was taken. At approximately the same time it was preparing the Standard proxy, Peat was also drafting a proxy containing the same financial statement for use in soliciting votes for the acquisition of Continental Strategies Corporation by Chadbourn (the Continental proxy materials). The Continental proxy, like the UHM proxy, contained the correct word "capital" in footnote 7(c). The Continental proxy was mailed on April 8, 1970, approximately two weeks before the vote on the Standard merger. The Continental proxy was not mailed to Standard shareholders because the Standard merger had not yet been consummated.

As indicated, *supra*, Peat also prepared the UHM proxy which contained the correct word "capital" in footnote 7(c). In a letter to the SEC dated April 20, 1970, two days before the Standard merger vote, counsel for Chadbourn sent to SEC copies of the UHM proxy containing the proper word.

Early drafts of the footnotes from the summer of 1969 when the audit was conducted indicate that Peat originally intended to disclose verbatim the Indenture restrictions on dividend payment. When the existence of the bank loan agreement for $6 million required a revision of the financial statement the following fall, Peat's auditing manager Freeze wrote footnote 7(c) using the word "common." For footnote 7(d) Freeze discarded the verbatim language of the Indenture restricting dividend payment and characterized the Indenture restrictive covenants as "less restrictive than those contained in the note agreement with the three banks." This characterization of the Indenture covenants

appeared in all of the certified financial statements in issue until counsel for Chadbourn stated the Indenture dividend restriction in full in the 1971 Chadbourn Annual Report and stated the Indenture restrictions on redemption as well.

Despite all this evidence of deliberate fraud, Peat has the audacity to assert that the false, untrue and misleading statements in footnotes 7(c) and 7(d) of its audit were only "lapsus calami" (Br. at 5), "slip of the pen" (Br. at 29), and a "footnote mistake" (Br. at i). It is unbelievable that the majority of this panel would swallow with hook, line and sinker such an outrageous and ridiculous proposition and to hold that Peat's misrepresentation was only negligent and use it as a basis for reversing a well reasoned opinion of the District Court thereby depriving the many shareholders of Standard of millions of dollars of compensation in which they were justly entitled because of the fraud perpetrated on them by Peat. If it originally was only a slip of the pen, it became a deliberate fraud when Chadbourn's own lawyer called this to the attention of Peat's manager in charge of the audit and the manager corrected the alleged mistake in his copy and did not correct the original because it would have defeated the merger. The characterization of Peat's misrepresentation as a "negligent misrepresentation" adds something new and unheard of in our jurisprudence.

The District Court characterized it differently. It found that Peat's Certificate that it had performed its 1969 Chadbourn audit in accordance with generally accepted accounting standards and auditing practices [to be] false and untrue and that Peat acted "willfully, with intent to 'deceive' and 'manipulate' and 'in reckless disregard of the truth' in respect to footnotes 7(c) and 7(d) in said audit. In my opinion, the majorities holding should be rejected and the factual findings of the District Court upheld.

In imposing liability the District Court followed the standards of *Ernst & Ernst v. Hochfelder*, 425 U.S. 185, 96 S.Ct. 1375, 47 L.Ed.2d 668 (1976) with respect to the necessity of proof of scienter as mere negligence is not enough to violate the Act. The District Court in finding scienter stated:

[n]otwithstanding this stringent element of proof, the court concludes that in all the facts and circumstances of this case, scienter on behalf of defendant has been established by a preponderance of the evidence. On two occasions when it counted most, with full knowledge of the correct term, Peat, deliberately, did not correctly describe the stock which was restricted in the payment of dividends by the bank loan which stock also was the particular class plaintiffs would receive by the merger. Furthermore, defendant never fully described either the dividend restrictions on preferred stock contained in the indenture or the redemption restrictions contained in the indenture or the redemption restrictions contained in the indenture and loan agreement.

• • •

The District Court was correct in finding that the deliberate misstatements and fraudulent omissions in the proxy statement were material. It is clear that no prudent Standard shareholder in his right mind would ever have voted for the merger if he had known of the restrictions on the payment of dividends and on the redemption of the cumulative preferred stock which he was to receive under the terms of the merger. The Standard stockholder had been receiving regular dividends on his Standard common stock. Because of the restrictions on the preferred stock which he was to receive in exchange he would not receive any dividends on the preferred stock for a long time and possibly he would never receive either the dividends or secure the redemption of the preferred shares.

Adams v. Standard Knitting Mills is an excellent example of the difficulty of determining whether negligence is merely negligence or much more, namely, fraud. In that case four scholarly, trained lawyers sitting as judges looked at the exact same facts and what did they conclude? Two judges said there was scienter and two said the conduct rose no higher than mere negligence.

The lesson of this case is simple: the "fine line" between conduct amounting to negligence and conduct sufficient to infer recklessness is often difficult to discern.

This case also demonstrates the unpredictability that sometimes attends litigation. The accountants ultimately prevailed in this case because the two judges who sided with them happened to constitute a majority of the appellate court. The alignment of the judges could easily have gone the other way.

Particularly interesting is the fact that this case was tried without a jury. This is referred to as a bench trial. The trial judge determines both the facts and law and applies the law to the facts. In a jury trial the jury applies the law as given by the judge to the facts as determined by the jury.

When a trial judge is the trier-of-fact his or her findings of fact are to be given substantial weight and are not to be overruled by appellate judges, unless they are "clearly erroneous." The rationale for this rule is the fact that the trial judge is usually more familiar with the case than the appellate judges who were not "eyewitnesses" to the trial. Most important, the trial judge observes firsthand the demeanor of witnesses who testify and from those observations draws conclusions as to the witness's credibility—a most important aspect of any trial involving allegations of fraud.

[3]   Common Law Recklessness: A Difference of Opinion

Differences of opinions regarding what type of conduct rises to the level of constructive fraud can result in certain inconsistencies and perhaps injustices. As long as human judgment must be brought to bear there will always remain the possibility for less than blind and evenhanded justice. Consider the following decisions by the same court from the state of New York.

Duro Sportswear, Inc. v. Cogen
131 N.Y.S. 2d 20 (Sup.Ct. 1954)

WASSERVOGEL, Special Referee.

Plaintiffs seek to recover from defendants the sum of $20,000 as damages allegedly resulting from malpractice by the defendant Cogen, a Certified Public Accountant, and the fraudulent representations by all defendants as to the financial condition of the plaintiff corporation as of December 1950.

Prior to January 6, 1951, plaintiff Schwartz and defendant Louis Leff owned the entire capital stock of the plaintiff corporation, the shares of which were registered in the names of their respective wives. On or about January 6, 1951, plaintiffs and the defendant Leff entered into a written agreement which provided, among other things that: (1) Schwartz would acquire all of the capital stock of the corporation; (2) Schwartz would loan $10,000 to the corporation without interest; (3) defendant Louis Leff would be relieved of certain liabilities then due and owing by him and would remain as an employee of the corporation at a fixed salary plus twenty-five per cent of its net profits; and (4) defendant Louis Leff would remain liable for one-half of the deficit of the corporation as it then existed. The defendant Cogen, a son-in-law of the defendant Leff, was employed to audit the books of account of the plaintiff corporation and to present to the parties a statement of its financial condition in order to determine the amount of deficit, in accordance with the terms of the above-mentioned agreement.

The record shows that when the agreement was entered into by the parties, the defendant Cogen, at the request of the individual plaintiff, certified as correct a statement of the financial condition of the corporation which fixed its deficit at $3,458.84. Subsequent thereto, however, and in or about March 1951, Cogen delivered to Schwartz a "Statement of Adjustments" which indicated that the deficit of the corporation was in-

creased to $5,534.84. It is plaintiffs' claim that Cogen and the other defendants knowingly caused the deficit of the plaintiff corporation to be understated by approximately $12,000 in order to induce the individual plaintiff to acquire all of the stock of the corporation and to relieve the defendant Louis Leff of certain liabilities, as set forth in the agreement entered into on January 6, 1951.

The documentary evidence and credible testimony adduced upon the trial clearly establish that Schwartz consented to acquire the stock of the corporation at a time when defendant Cogen advised him that its deficit was not in excess of $3,600, whereas, in fact, the deficit was greater than $9,000. The difference between the amount indicated in Cogen's original financial statement and the actual deficit consists, for the most part, of a series of bills which were not entered on the books of the corporation as of December 26, 1950, the closing date of the financial statement prepared by Cogen, but which were purportedly entered subsequent thereto. Plaintiffs, however, have failed to prove that defendants, or any of them, wilfully, deliberately, or fraudulently caused these bills to be omitted from either the original books of account or the financial statement prepared by Cogen. Contrary to plaintiffs' contention, it appears most unlikely that defendants could have fraudulently concealed any substantial bill which had to be paid by the corporation, inasmuch as the record shows that Schwartz was in charge of the office, made the purchases, paid the bils, made entries in the original books of account, kept a diary of due dates of bills, and, thus, had an independent source of knowledge of the finances of the corporation. The mere fact that plaintiff established that the defendant Louis Leff had failed to approve certain bills which were not entered in the corporate books of account prior to Cogen's audit thereof is insufficient to establish plaintiffs' claim of fraud, particularly in view of the evidence which shows that it was the practice of Schwartz and other employees of plaintiff corporation to delay the posting and entry of such bills for at least several weeks after they were received. In the absence of other proof, therefore, it necessarily follows that plaintiffs' second cause of action against all of the defendants, which is predicated upon allegations of fraud, must be dismissed upon the merits.

However, although there is not sufficient evidence to substantiate fraudulent intent on the part of any of the defendants, Cogen's unqualified certification of the financial statement and his method of preparing same is sufficient to sustain plaintiffs' claim that at the very least he is guilty of malpractice. It cannot be disputed that at the time the certified statement was delivered to plaintiffs, it did not accurately reflect the true financial condition of the corporation. Cogen's testimony that he took into consideration "all bills then available," is inconsistent with his certification, which was absolute and not qualified in any manner. There is sufficient evidence to establish that Cogen failed to fully investigate the probability that the original books of account did not reflect outstanding bills due as of the date of his financial statement, although such bills had been received by the corporation but had not been entered or posted by either the individual plaintiff, the defendant Louis Leff, or any employee of the plaintiff corporation. Cogen, however, was associated with the plaintiff corporation for a considerable length of time prior to his preparation of the financial statement. He, therefore, was fully familiar with the customary delay in posting and entering bills in the books of account. Despite his knowledge of this practice, he nevertheless failed to take it into consideration and qualify his certification accordingly. His apparent refusal to realize the effect of an absolute certification and his evident reckless disregard of the consequences of such action, in the opinion of the Court, is sufficient to constitute malpractice.

Moreover, it further appears that defendant Cogen, in April 1951, made a journal entry wherein he added $10,000 to the corporation's surplus account by crediting "Surplus" and debiting "Accounts Payable-Chic Style," a dress contracting business wholly owned by the individual plaintiff, his son and wife. It was Cogen's contention upon the trial that his authority for such entry was the January 6, 1951, agreement executed by the individual plaintiff and the defendant Leff. The record, however, establishes that Cogen did not post the $10,000 charge against the Chic Style account in the "Accounts Payable" ledger of the plaintiff corporation, as good accounting practice required. Likewise, the journal entry made by Cogen does not in any manner reflect a loan as contemplated by the parties at the time of the execution of their agreement. Nowhere in this agreement is there any provision which justifies the journal entry as made by Cogen, which, in effect, reflects a complete forgiveness of the money due and owing Chic Style by the corporation. If this journal entry had been correctly made and in accordance with the provisions of the January 1951 agreement, the total liabilities of the corporation would not have decreased by $10,000, which was the effect of Cogen's act. The individual plaintiff had merely agreed to make a loan to the corporation and a proper $10,000 loan entry would not have had the effect upon the capital, surplus, or deficit of the corporation as indicated in the financial statement prepared by Cogen. It clearly appears, therefore, that the defendant Cogen, as a Certified Public Accountant, improperly recorded the intention of the parties in the books of account and, at the very least, must be deemed negligent in the preparation of the financial statement relied upon by the parties prior to the actual execution of the agreement on January 6, 1951.

• • •

In a subsequent case, however, the Court of Appeals made it clear that under certain circumstances accountants may be held liable to third parties even where there is lacking deliberate or active fraud, State Street Trust Co. v. Ernst. . . . In order for Schwartz to recover damages, it would be necessary for the Court to find that Cogen was guilty of gross negligence rather than mere faulty judgment. In the opinion of the Court, the relevant facts of the instant action clearly require such finding.

Cogen's heedlessness and wanton disregard of the consequences of his incorrect financial statements take the place of a deliberate intention to defraud. Even under the principles set forth in the Ultramares case, "negligence or blindness, even when not equivalent to fraud, is none the less evidence to sustain the inference of fraud. At least this is so if the negligence is gross." As already stated, this Court has found that there is not sufficient evidence to warrant a specific finding of fraud. Nevertheless, the proof establishes that Cogen was derelict in his duty to thoroughly investigate the status of the corporate books of account prior to the preparation of his initial financial statement, and more particularly in view of the fact that he had personal knowledge of the practice of the corporation's bookkeepers to delay the entering and posting of such bills in these books of account. His unqualified certification and his failure to note the possibility of such unentered bills in the financial statement are matters which have not been explained to the satisfaction of the Court. As a licensed certified public accountant, Cogen must be deemed to be aware of the reliance which normally is attached to an absolute certification of a financial report. Moreover, it cannnot be denied that Cogen knew about specific unentered bills on or before March 25, 1951, at which time he delivered a supplemental financial statement to Schwartz. His repeated failure to include such bills in this statement is inexcusable, as is the fact that he incorrectly reflected Schwartz' loan of $10,000 to the corporation in the journal book of account. Thus, the record is replete with the foregoing evidence and other proof, both oral and documentary, showing Cogen's "refusal to see the obvious * * * and his failure to investigate the doubtful," which are sufficient to impose liability upon him for damage suffered by Schwartz. . . .

William Iselin & Co. v. Muhlstock, Elowitz & Co.
382 N.Y.S.2d 83 (App. Div. 1976)

Before MURPHY, J. P., and BIRNS, LANE and LYNCH, JJ.

[The plaintiff companies loaned money to Wash-Tex Inc., based on Wash-Tex financials that were prepared by the defendant accountants, Muhlstock, Elowitz & Co. In a jury trial the jury found that the accountants had not engaged in fraudulent conduct, although the jury believed that "the financial statements were materially misleading."

The plaintiffs appealed the jury's verdict. The appellate court affirmed the jury's verdict with one appellate judge issuing the following dissenting opinion.]

All concur except LANE, J., who dissents in the following memorandum:

The case was submitted to the jury, without objection, on the basis of the teachings of the seminal case of *State Street Trust Co. v. Ernst*, . . . The rule as articulated in *State Street* provides:

"Accountants, however, may be liable to third parties, even where there is lacking deliberate or active fraud. A representation certified as true to the knowledge of the accountants when knowledge there is none, a reckless misstatement, or an opinion based on grounds so flimsy as to lead to the conclusion that there was no genuine belief in its truth, are all sufficient upon which to base liability. A refusal to see the obvious, a failure to investigate the doubtful, if sufficiently gross, may furnish evidence leading to an inference of fraud so as to impose liability for losses suffered by those who rely on the balance sheet. In other words, heedlessness and reckless disregard of consequence may take the place of deliberate intention."

The facts in the case at bar, highlighted by the specific finding of the jury that the financial statement was "materially misleading," lead me to conclude that the verdict reached was against the weight of the credible evidence.

Muhlstock, in preparation of the financial statement, failed to verify independently the cash account, which verification would have revealed a shortage; failed to confirm the amount due from factors by direct correspondence; failed to confirm inventory; and failed properly to confirm accounts payable and receivable (since the former were understated and the latter overstated). Furthermore, Wash-Tex dealt primarily in the purchase of raw materials, known as greige goods, converting these items to a finished fabric, and selling the finished product to garment manufacturers.

The profits of Wash-Tex were tied to the sale of finished goods, although it also sold greige goods. Muhlstock reported separately to Wash-Tex as to the sales of greige versus finished goods but knowingly combined the sales of both under one heading ("Sales") on the December 31, 1962 financial statement. The net result of this unorthodox accounting maneuver was to mislead the plaintiffs into believing that the sales of Wash-Tex of its finished product were $5,365,531. As a matter of fact, more than one-half of these sales were of raw materials (greige goods) which were purchased by Wash-Tex from greige-goods manufacturers for the purpose of converting the same into a finished fabric for ultimate sale by Wash-Tex to garment manufacturers. Indeed, a substantial portion of the greige goods were sold at a loss.

Muhlstock's reporting method also concealed the fact that 22% of the finished goods sold were returned to Wash-Tex when, industry-wide, 5% was considered high.

In addition, the subordinated loan account, representing a capital investment by principals of the corporation, was misstated. This loan was demonstrated not to be available for corporate purposes but was reflected on the books only immediately before the preparation of the statement by Muhlstock, of which Muhlstock must have been aware since its own work papers revealed a deposit of funds at the end of December and withdrawal

of these same funds in the first week of January.

The use of an accepted auditing device known as a cash cut-off statement, which is a mid-month bank statement, would have revealed that the moneys deposited were withdrawn immediately after the statement date. The failure to use a cut-off statement by Muhlstock resulted in an improper confirmation by them of cash on hand and the viability of the subordinated loan.

Other items of which Muhlstock must have been aware were transactions in December 1962, valued at close to $50,000, involving companies wholly controlled by Wash-Tex. Wash-Tex had never engaged previously in such large transactions with its controlled corporations.

In one of the transactions, the goods were resold to Wash-Tex within two months of the sale. In the other transaction, payment to Wash-Tex was not made.

The recording of these intercompany transactions as bona fide and arm's-length resulted in the appearance of an increase in accounts receivable and a reduction in inventory. Muhlstock was the accountant for all the corporations involved and therefore must have had knowledge of the nature of the transactions and their purpose vis-à-vis the financial statement which was being prepared. These instances, albeit merely outlined in this dissent, reflect "a refusal to see the obvious" and "a failure to investigate the doubtful" sufficiently gross to lead to an inference of fraud (*State Street Trust Co. v. Ernst*, 278 N.Y. 104, 112, 15 N.E.2d 416, 419).

Implicit in the jury verdict is their finding that the plaintiffs relied on the "materially misleading" statement of Muhlstock. For the jury not to have inferred fraud based on these facts and not to award a verdict in favor of the plaintiffs is patently against the weight of the credible evidence.

CHAPTER 5

CRIMINAL LIABILITY

¶ 5.01 Sources of Criminal Liability

An accountant's exposure to criminal liability is a function of the extent to which an accountant's acts or omissions are contrary to an existing criminal statute. Criminal liability is exclusively statutory in nature, and the sources of statutory criminal liability are as diverse as the circumstances in which an accountant may render a professional service.

[1] Federal Statutes

The primary tools available to a prosecutor to combat "white-collar crime" are found in the following federal statutes.

[a] Securities Fraud. Section 24 of the 1933 Act imposes criminal responsibility upon any person who (1) "willfully" violates any section of the 1933 Act, including any rule or regulation thereunder, or (2) "willfully" files a materially false registration statement.

Section 32(a) of the 1934 Act subjects to criminal liability any person who (1) "willfully" violates any section of the 1934 Act, including any rule or regulation such as Rule 10b-5, or (2) "willfully and knowingly" makes or causes to make a material false statement in any document required to be filed under the provisions of the 1934 Act.

The penalties for violating the foregoing provisions include possible incarceration in prison up to five years and a possible fine of up to $100,000.

[b] Mail Fraud. The federal mail fraud statute, 18 U.S.C. § 1341, is violated by anyone who (1) devises or intends to devise a scheme or artifice to defraud by means of material false or fraudulent pretenses, representations, or promises, and (2) for purposes of executing or attempting to execute this scheme makes some use of the U.S. mail.

Violation of the federal mail fraud statute carries with it a fine of not more than $1,000 or imprisonment of not more than five years, or both.

[c] False Statements. The federal false statements statute, 18 U.S.C. § 1001, prohibits anyone in any matter involving any U.S. department or agency from knowingly and willfully (1) falsifying, concealing, or covering up a material fact, (2) making any false or fraudulent statement or representation, and (3) making or using any false writing or document.

This statute is sometimes used to prosecute false representations made during the course of an ongoing investigation, such as an IRS or SEC investigation. The federal false statements statute carries a penalty of imprisonment of not more than five years and a fine of not more than $10,000.

[d] False Statement to a Bank. To the extent an accountant assists in the preparation of a false loan application or assists in the submission of a false financial statement to a federally insured or affiliated financial institution, the accountant may be indicted under one of several statutes which prohibits such conduct. The federal statutes provide varying degrees of punishment including the possibility of a $10,000 fine and imprisonment of five years.

[e] Racketeer Influenced and Corrupt Organizations (RICO). A substantial prosecutorial weapon against white-collar crime exists under the so-called criminal Racketeer Influenced and Corrupt Organizations (RICO) statutes. The RICO statutes prohibit a person who is affiliated with an "enterprise" which affects or is engaged in interstate commerce from engaging in any of the following types of conduct:

(1) A person who has received any income derived directly or indirectly from a "pattern of racketeering activity" may not use or invest any of that income in the "enterprise";

(2) A person may not acquire or maintain any interest in or control of an "enterprise" through a "pattern of racketeering"; and

(3) A person employed by or associated with an "enterprise" may not conduct the affairs of the enterprise through a "pattern of racketeering."

An *enterprise* includes any association in fact or law and includes any individual, partnership, corporation, association, or other legal entity.

A *pattern of racketeering* is defined as a course of conduct which involves the commission of at least two "acts of racketeering activity" during a 10-year period. *Racketeering activity* is defined by statute to include:

(1) Bribery which is actionable under state felony law;

(2) Extortion which is actionable under state felony law;

(3) Fraud which is actionable under the federal mail fraud statute;

(4) Fraud which is actionable under the federal wire fraud statute; and

(5) Fraud which is actionable under the federal securities laws.

Criminal RICO has been used to supplant the use of mail fraud and securities fraud indictments. The criminal penalties under criminal RICO are substantial and include a fine of not more than $25,000 and imprisonment of not more than 20 years. In addition, the RICO statutes provide for forfeiture of any financial interest, assets or earnings that the defendant has acquired through the "pattern of racketeering activity."

Criminal RICO has been used against accounting practitioners. An accountant who is affiliated with an accounting firm or associated with a business concern, such as being the auditor for a company, may satisfy the requirement of being associated with an enterprise engaged in or affecting interstate commerce. To the extent the accountant engages in two or more acts of mail fraud in connection with his activities relating to the "enterprise," the ground work for criminal RICO has been laid.

Thus, an accountant could be subject to the following penalties:

(1) $25,000 fine;

(2)   Imprisonment for 20 years; and

(3)   Forfeiture of all monies that the accountant has made through his racketeering activities, including professional fees and potentially personal assets.

[f]   Internal Revenue Code.   Sections 7206 and 7207 of the Code prohibit various types of fraudulent conduct in connection with matters relating to the federal tax laws. The following types of conduct subject the individual wrongdoer to a fine of not more than $100,000, imprisonment of not more than three years, and the costs of prosecution:

(1)   Willfully making under penalty of perjury a false return, statement, or other document as to a material matter.

(2)   Willfully aiding, counseling, or advising regarding any matter under the Internal Revenue laws wherein there occurs fraudulent conduct regarding a material matter.

(3)   Removing or concealing assets with intent to defraud.

[g]   Conspiracy and Aiding and Abetting.   The federal conspiracy statute, 18 U.S.C. § 371, prohibits two or more persons from conspiring to commit an offense against the United States. A conspiracy is an agreement between two or more persons to engage in an unlawful course of conduct. Aside from the agreement between the parties, which may be inferred from the parties' actions and words, there must also be an act by one of the parties in furtherance of the conspiracy. A similar "associational crime" is the federal statute which prohibits aiding and abetting another person in the commission of a crime.

[2]   State Statutes

All states have criminal statutes that proscribe conduct, actions, and omissions that operate as a fraud. In some instances state statutes specifically criminalize the issuance of fraudulent financial statements and certain other types of financial documentation, such as loan applications.

¶ 5.02   A Practical Explanation of Criminal Liability: Attorney's Speech

Imagine that you have attended the annual meeting of the state society of accountants, where you have just witnessed a speech on accountant's criminal liability by the arrogant but brilliant criminal defense lawyer I. M. Good. From the subdued audience comes a question by an accounting practitioner, Doubting Thomas, which leads to the following colloquy:

MR. THOMAS: I find it hard to believe that we are exposed to any risk of criminal liability in our accounting, auditing, and tax practices. What the heck, I've never had any client ask me to do something dishonest. Why, if a client asked me to do that . . . I'd, I'd take a walk!

MR. GOOD: I find your attitude refreshing and healthy. Obviously, any accountant who knowingly does something illegal for his client is on a collision course with an indictment. But, let me ask you this, Mr. Thomas: What type of liability exposure does an accountant subject himself to if he "recklessly disregards the truth" or "closes his eyes to the obvious or that which he had a duty to see?"

MR. THOMAS: Well, I read the workshop book distributed here on accountant's liability just last night and, as I recall, that could be civil fraud, right? Yeah, civil fraud, the *Ultramares* decision by that famous judge. . . .

MR. GOOD: Cardozo. Yes, *Ultramares* clearly states that this type of conduct is a form of scienter sufficient to establish civil fraud. Would you believe that this same type of conduct would support a finding of criminal fraud?

MR. THOMAS: Naw! I don't believe it.

MR. GOOD: Well you have heard of the *National Student Marketing* case, have you not?

MR. THOMAS: I'm aware that the auditors there were convicted of a criminal violation of the federal securities laws. So what?

MR. GOOD: In that case the trial judge gave the following instruction of law to the jury, which I think you will find elucidating:

    While I have stated that negligence or mistake do not constitute guilty knowledge or intent, nevertheless, ladies and gentlemen, you are entitled to consider in determining whether a defendant acted with such intent if he deliberately closed his eyes to the obvious or to the facts that certainly would be observed or ascertained in the course of his accounting work or whether he recklessly stated as facts matters of which he knew he was ignorant.

If you find such reckless deliberate indifference to or disregard for truth or falsity on the part of a given defendant, the law entitles you to infer therefrom that that defendant willfully and knowingly filed or caused to be filed false financial information of a material nature with the SEC.

But such an inference, of course, must depend upon the weight and credibility extended to the evidence of reckless and indifferent conduct, if any.

I repeat: Ordinary or simple negligence or mistake alone would be insufficient to support a finding of guilty knowledge or willfulness or intent.

MR. THOMAS: Well, that decision by the trial judge will never survive an appeal.

MR. GOOD: The trial judge was a most eminent jurist. His instruction has already been affirmed by the U.S. Court of Appeals for the Second Circuit, an outstanding appellate court. Further, the U.S. Supreme Court declined to review the Second Circuit's decision.

MR. THOMAS: Well, that instruction has gotta be an aberration.

MR. GOOD: No, Mr. Thomas, it is the law and indeed merely restates a formulation of an accountant's criminal liability which dates as far back as 1963 to the decision of Judge Friendly, one of the preeminent judges of this country, in *United States v. Benjamin*.

MR. THOMAS: Are you telling us that there is absolutely no difference between an accountant's civil and criminal liability for fraud? I mean, there's gotta be some difference between them—why, the stakes alone are substantially different. It just can't be that an accountant can go to the slammer for reckless conduct— can it?

MR. GOOD: I am afraid so, Mr. Thomas. Essentially, conduct that will support a finding of civil liability under Rule 10b-5, for example, will also support a finding of a criminal violation of Rule 10b-5.

MR. THOMAS: If that is so, why haven't there been a whole lot of criminal prosecutions against accountants for violating Rule 10b-5?

MR. GOOD: The answer to that lies, I believe, in two factors. The first factor is what I refer to as certain substantive safeguards available to the defendant in a criminal case, including: (1) The presumption that a defendant is innocent until proven guilty. (2) The prosecutor's burden to prove a defendant's guilt beyond a reasonable doubt; in a civil fraud case a plaintiff must prove a defendant's fraud by clear and convincing evidence, a less-exacting burden of presenting and proving evidence. (3) A criminal defendant is entitled to a jury trial no matter how complex the case, and of course a defendant may not be called to the witness stand should he choose to invoke his constitutional right against self-incrimination.

The second factor that accounts for the sparseness of criminal fraud actions against accountants is really a function of the prosecutor exercising his discretion in light of his evaluation of the difficulty of proving a case, the fundamental fairness of prosecuting a case, and I suspect the deterrent value of a case—will it be an example to others, which will hopefully stem the tide of what might be perceived as the potential for similar wrongdoing.

I'm not sure that these are all of the reasons underlying a prosecutor's decision to seek an indictment. Needless to say, I don't and can't speak for the state's attorney or the U.S. Department of Justice. The policy reasons surrounding a decision to indict should really be explained by them.

What I can tell you is that there is absolutely no difference in the legal standards supporting a conviction for criminal fraud and a judgment for civil fraud. An accountant who has recklessly disregarded the truth or closed his eyes to the obvious not only sets himself up for a claim of civil fraud but also, in a bad case, for a criminal indictment.

MR. THOMAS: The bottom line—if I understand you—is that criminal and civil scienter are one and the same?

MR. GOOD: Yes, and that is why I say that an accountant's risk of exposure to criminal liability is greater than what most practitioners usually believe it to be. It is by no means limited to the practitioner who knowingly acquiesces in a client's wrongdoing, or the practitioner who is "on the take."

Mr. Thomas: [Following a momentary pause.] How can I learn more about this?

MR. GOOD: Read *United States v. Benjamin*, *United States v. Simon*, and the *National Student Marketing* case involving the auditors—they are in your workshop book in the Criminal Liability chapter.

MR. THOMAS: Oh, yeah, well I guess I sorta skimmed that chapter—you know, a light reading with a beer in one hand. Next time, I'll read those cases with a cup of coffee in hand.

MR. GOOD: I assure you, you will find it a very sobering experience.

¶ 5.03 Reckless Behavior: A Basis for Imposing Criminal Liability

Conduct that involves recklessness may be sufficient to support an inference of knowing wrongdoing. The origins of the doctrine that conduct less than actual knowledge may support a finding of criminal culpability were formulated as early as 1926 in *Bentel v. United States*, where the U.S. Court of Appeals for the Second Circuit observed:

> [D]uring the same time that statutory criminal responsibility for cheats has been growing, the civil responsibility for false pretense and fraudulent representation has received much study. It is now plain that one is more or less firmly held to knowledge of falsity by the circumstances under which he states that as true which is in fact false. Thus a man is supposed

and required to know matters pertaining to his own business, and one who makes representations, not knowing whether they be true or false, cannot be regarded as innocent, for a positive assertion of fact is by plain implication an assertion of knowledge concerning the fact asserted.

The matter is summed up by Lord Cairns in saying that a reckless statement of a fact of which the narrator is ignorant may be equivalent civilly to a statement of that which he knows to be false.

The measure or rule for what is evidence of the ultimate fact does not change in moving from the civil to the criminal side of the court; only the necessary quantum of probative force changes, and the just cited rules as to knowledge of falsity are applied, when what was once but a civil responsibility becomes by statute a criminal offense.

It always remains true that, when an intent or state of mind is a necessary ingredient of the offense charged, it must be averred and proved beyond a reasonable doubt; but it is just as true that, when that state of mind is a knowledge of false statements, while there is no allowable inference of knowledge from the mere fact of falsity, there are many cases where from the actor's special situation and continuity of conduct an inference that he *did* know the untruth of what he said or wrote may legitimately be drawn.

As the *Bentel* decision states, a defendant's knowledge regarding the falsity of a statement *may not* be inferred from the mere fact that a falsity was made. However, the *Bentel* decision observes that:

(a)   Because of the actor's "special situation" (e.g., the defendant's access to the facts and role with respect to disclosure of the facts), and

(b)   Because of the actor's "continuity of conduct" (e.g., a course of reckless indifference to the truth),

it may be inferred that the defendant knew of the falsity.

The following cases demonstrate that an accountant can easily find himself or herself in the role of an actor whose "special situation and continuity of conduct" allows the inference of fraud from reckless behavior.

[1]   *United States v. Benjamin* and Comments

United States v. Benjamin
328 F2d 854
United States Court of Appeals
New York
1964

FRIENDLY, Circuit Judge.
[In a bench trial, the auditor, attorney, and promoter of American Equities Corporation were convicted of mail fraud and of a conspiracy to defraud in the sale of securities in violation of Section 24 of the 1933 Act.

The auditor, Bernard Howard, prepared an "Auditor's Report," dated February 10, 1961, at the request of American Equities' promoter, Milton Mende, and American Equities' lawyer, Martin Benjamin. The auditor's report contained a "Pro-forma Balance Sheet as of December 31, 1960," which the trial judge found was materially false in that American Equities had no income or assets.

On March 6, 1961, Howard issued a second "Auditor's Report," which contained an income statement for the six months ended January 31, 1961. The trial judge found that this statement falsely stated material items of income.

The sole issue on appeal was whether Howard knew that the financials were materially false and misleading.]

In mid-January [of 1961] Benjamin invited Howard, a certified public accountant who had served Benjamin and his clients, to do some work for American Equities. Howard testified he received the November 30, 1960, "Pro Forma Balance Sheet," a yellow handwritten sheet of paper listing certain real estate holdings in Detroit, and balance sheets of corporations which Mende and Benjamin claimed were "owned or controlled" by American Equities. From these materials and without any examination of books and records, he prepared a paper dated February 10, 1961, and on the following day gave copies of this to Mende who handed one to Reiter. The latter testified that this was in Howard's presence.

The paper has a cover, on the stationery of Howard as a Certified Public Accountant, which bears the legend:

AMERICAN EQUITIES CORPORATION

DECEMBER 31, 1960

AUDITORS REPORT

This is followed by a two-page letter in which Howard advises the company that "After an examination of the books and records of the diversified holdings of your corporation for the period ended December 31, 1960," he is submitting a report of the company as at that date, consisting of "Exhibit 'A'—Pro-forma Balance Sheet as at December 31, 1960." Next comes a section entitled "COMMENTS" informing the company that it is "a diversified investment corporation with the following holdings." These were substantially the same as in the description accompanying the November 30 statement, with the Outpost Inn, Biesmeyer, Stanford and also California Molded Products now clearly listed among them. The comment on California Molded

Products anticipates 1961 sales of $2,000,000 with gross profit margin in excess of 30% and a net of better than 4%, but omits to limit the company's interest in these riches to 68%, the most that was claimed by the November 30 balance sheet. The comments say that "The statement which is pro-forma includes the disposition of $500,000 which a group of stockholders propose to advance to the corporation as a long term loan"; that $150,000 of this was to be advanced to subsidiaries for working capital and $71,000 "to repay an officer for the purchase of the assets of the Outpost Inn, Inc."; that "The assets are shown at actual cost and are calculated at the most conservative value," although "A recent appraisal of the real estate in Detroit shows an increase of approximately $2,500,000.00 over book value, which has not been reflected in the statement"; that "The accounts receivable, loans receivable, loans payable, and mortgages payable were not verified by direct communication" and inventories were taken as submitted by the management; and, finally, that "The statement reflects an accurate and true picture of the corporation's net worth after taking into consideration the proposed loan by the officers." The "Pro-Forma Balance Sheet as at December 31, 1960" showed total assets of $7,769,657.11 and a net worth of $3,681,049.70—this including $963,067.00 in the capital stock account. Howard received $200 for his two days of service in preparing the report.

Toward the end of February Mende asked Howard to come out to California; Mende's promise of a $200 advance remained unfulfilled despite Howard's repeated requests but Mende gave him a one-way air ticket. He stayed with Benjamin from February 27 to March 7 at the Beverly Hilton Hotel, which cut off food and telephone service for non-payment of bills and threatened to hold his baggage on departure. While in California, he made some examination of the books and records of California Molded Products, without investigating whether American Equities in fact owned 68% of the stock, and also of J. S. Lane & Co. which Mende said he was interested in buying for American Equities. Howard was given a copy of a statement, dated August 31, 1958, of Verdi Development Corporation; Kovaleski told him this was a dormant corporation which had been through a Chapter X proceeding and whose principal asset, a uranium mill, had been sold in foreclosure.

Under date of March 6, 1961, after the cut-off of food and telephone service, Howard rendered a second "Auditor's Report," which he left with Benjamin. This purportedly reflected "an examination of the books and records of the diversified holdings of your corporation for the period ended January 31, 1961." Although generally similar to his previous "Auditor's Report," it differed in some significant respects: Biesmeyer Boat and Plastic Co. and Stanford Trailer and Marine Supply Co. were no longer included; as Howard was later to tell the grand jury, the two boat companies "went down the river." Nevertheless the list grew from five to six through three additions. Plametron Corporation was included, without any investigation of its acquisition on Howard's part despite the personal knowledge he had gained. So also was J. S. Lane & Co.; Mende and Benjamin had been negotiating for the purchase of this company for $1,100,000 as Howard well knew since only a few days previously he had examined its books "to determine if the price they were offering was adequate * * *." As seems generally to have been the case, Howard's pro-forma report apparently makes no provision as to the acquisition cost. The comments also note the inclusion in the balance sheet of "Verdi Development Company * * * a mining company with various mills and claims in California, Utah and Nevada"; despite the age of Verdi's financial statement and what Kovaleski had told him, Howard reported as an asset "Unrecovered Development Costs" of $707,554.21, this being a major factor in the remarkable increase in American Equities' net worth from $3,681,049.70 to $4,609,560.07 in a single month. In addition to the $2,500,000 increment in the Detroit real estate from an appraisal previously reported, there is now an added $500,000 increase in the value of equipment. Nowhere was it suggested, unless by the naked word "pro-forma," that American Equities' acquisition of the mentioned companies had not yet been accomplished. To the contrary, a new paragraph recited:

> "A consolidated statement of income and profit and loss for the six months ended January 31, 1961 shows a net profit $399,623.94 on the basis of the last six months operations of the six corporations involved although they were all only recently acquired within the last few months. However, on the basis of a yearly projection of the six profits the corporation shows a net earnings of approximately 80¢ a share. With the contemplated expansion program under way, this should be increased."

This was supported by an exhibit entitled

AMERICAN EQUITIES CORPORATION CONSOLIDATED STATEMENT OF INCOME AND PROFIT AND LOSS FOR THE SIX MONTHS ENDED JANUARY 31, 1961.

American Equities stock continued to be sold until March 22, 1961, when, as a result of the SEC's action, trading stopped.

Howard's principal claim is that the evidence against him was insufficient to show the state of mind required for a criminal conviction. He says he was performing an accountant's duties innocently if inefficiently— and for a negligible compensation, that he sheltered himself with the label "pro forma," and that he did not know his reports were to help in stock peddling but thought they were to be used solely for management purposes. His own testimony belies the last claim; he admitted knowing that the promoters intended to use the stock as collateral for loans or as part of or collateral for the purchase price in various acquisitions and that his statements were shown to prospective lenders or sellers. Since his reports were little more than a regurgitation of material handed him by the "management" and related to properties that, as he had reason to know, were not owned, the judge could properly have regarded his claim that he thought them needed for "management" purposes as incredible in the last degree. But the evidence we have summarized shows directly that he knew his reports were being used with brokers who were selling the stock. Drattell, whom he knew to be a broker interested in American Equities, telephoned him in regard to his reports, and, on Reiter's testimony, he saw Mende hand a copy of his first report to Reiter whom he knew to be similarly interested.

The argument that reports which depicted American Equities as owner of properties and companies it neither owned nor had any firm arrangements to acquire were not false because they were stated to be "pro forma" involves a complete misconception of the duties of an accountant in issuing a report thus entitled. Although pro forma statements "purport to give effect to transactions actually consummated or expected to be consummated at a date subsequent to that of the date of the statements," "auditors consider it proper to submit their report and opinion on such statements only when the nature of the transactions effected is clearly described in the statements, and when satisfactory evidence of their bona fides is available, such as actual subsequent consummation or signed firm contracts." Montgomery, Auditing Theory and Practice (6th ed. 1940), 62–63; see also Prentice-Hall Encyclopedic Dictionary of Business Finance (1960), 485. It would be insulting an honorable profession to suppose that a certified public accountant may take the representations of a corporation official as to companies it proposes to acquire, combine their balance sheets without any investigation as to the arrangements for their acquisition or suitable provision reflecting payment of the purchase price, and justify the meaningless result simply by an appliqué of two Latin words.

It is true that the Government had not merely to show that the statements were false but to present evidence from which the judge could be convinced beyond reasonable doubt of Howard's culpable state of mind. But, as Judge Hough said for this court years ago, "when that state of mind is a knowledge of false statements, while there is no allowable inference of knowledge from the mere fact of falsity, there are many cases where from the actor's special situation and continuity of conduct an inference that he did know the untruth of what he said or wrote may legitimately be drawn." *Bentel v. United States*, . . . Any accountant must know that his obligations in certifying "pro forma" statements are not satisfied by any such arithmetical exercise as Howard performed. But, as our

description of the reports has indicated, there were further false assertions, some of them clearly known to Howard to be such; these constituted a basis for holding him that was independent of the falsity of the total report, as well as for discrediting his assertions of ignorance as to what was required of him. The Michigan real estate was represented to Howard not as properties to be acquired but as already owned; he claimed to have seen deeds for these properties but admitted that American Equities was not named as grantee. The statements that certain assets had not been "verified by direct communication" implied that with this qualification all assets had been verified by suitable means; they had not been. Howard made no examination of American Equities' books, which, indeed, were not available when he rendered his first report; even a most cursory inspection would have revealed that nothing had been paid when the capital stock account was written up ten-fold. His statement purported to reflect "an accurate and true picture of the corporation's net worth after taking into consideration the proposed loan by the officers"; at best it would have been accurate only if the corporation had had at least some contractual basis for the assertion of ownership, and even then only if proper provision had been made for the cost. The inclusion as an asset of over $700,000 of "Unrecovered Development Costs" of a dormant mining company known to have been through insolvency proceedings was wholly indefensible. Perhaps most damning of all was the making of a profit and loss statement including a positive assertion that the six companies were "acquired within the last few months," when Howard knew that at least some of them had not been acquired at all.

These and other items we could mention— and this in a setting where, at the very time that Howard was delivering his second report extolling the prospects of this $8,700,000 company, he had been unable to obtain a $200 advance and the hotel had turned off food and telephone service for nonpayment of bills—were quite sufficient to convince a trier of the facts beyond a reasonable doubt that Howard had actual knowledge of the falsity of his reports and deliberately conspired to defraud investors. As Judge Learned Hand said in a similar context, "* * * the cumulation of instances, each explicable only by extreme credulity or professional inexpertness, may have a probative force immensely greater than any one of them alone." . . .

In fact, however, the Government was not required to go that far. "Willful," the Supreme Court has told us, "is a word of many meanings, its construction often being influenced by its context." . . . We think that in the context of § 24 of the Securities Act as applied to § 17(a), the Government can meet its burden by proving that a defendant deliberately closed his eyes to facts he had a duty to see, . . . or recklessly stated as facts things of which he was ignorant. Judge Hough so ruled in Bentel v. United States, supra; although that case and the similar ruling in *Slakoff v. United States*, 8 F.2d 9 (3 Cir. 1925), were under the mail fraud statute, § 215 of the then Criminal Code, 35 Stat. 1130 (1909), the ancestor of 18 U.S.C. § 1341, which does not use the term "willfully," the Congress that

passed the Securities Act scarcely meant to make life easier for defrauders. Other circuits have gone further and have held the willfulness requirement of the Securities Act to be satisfied in fraud cases by proof of representations which due diligence would have shown to be untrue. . . . In our complex society the accountant's certificate and the lawyer's opinion can be instruments for inflicting pecuniary loss more potent than the chisel or the crowbar. Of course, Congress did not mean that any mistake of law or misstatement of fact should subject an attorney or an accountant to criminal liability simply because more skillful practitioners would not have made them. But Congress equally could not have intended that men holding themselves out as members of these ancient professions should be able to escape criminal liability on a plea of ignorance when they have shut their eyes to what was plainly to be seen or have represented a knowledge they knew they did not possess.

The decision in *United States v. Benjamin* was written by a highly regarded judge who attempted to mark the roadway for determining an accountant's liability for criminal wrongdoing. The following signposts were deeply planted:

(a) Congress did not mean that any misstatement of fact should subject an accountant to criminal liability simply because more skillful practitioners would not have made them.

(b) Members of these "ancient professions" may not escape criminal liability on a plea of ignorance when they have shut their eyes to what was plainly to be seen or have represented a knowledge they knew they did not possess.

Simple negligence is not enough to support a criminal indictment. However, to the extent an accountant engages in a course of conduct that involves several related acts of negligence, the cumulative effect may elevate the conduct to the level of recklessness sufficient to infer knowledge of wrongdoing.

[2]   *United States v. Simon* and Comments

United States v. Simon
425 F. 2d 796
(2d Cir. 1969)

Before WATERMAN, FRIENDLY and SMITH, Circuit Judges.
FRIENDLY, Circuit Judge:

Defendant Carl Simon was a senior partner, Robert Kaiser a junior partner, and Melvin Fishman a senior associate in the internationally known accounting firm of Lybrand, Ross Bros. & Montgomery. They stand convicted after trial by Judge Mansfield and a jury in the District Court for the Southern District of New York under three counts of an indictment charging them with drawing up and certifying a false or misleading financial statement of Continental Vending Machine Corporation (hereafter Continental) for the year ending September 30, 1962.

. . .

The trial hinged on transactions between Continental and an affiliate, Valley Commercial Corporation (hereafter "Valley"). The dominant figure in both was Harold Roth, who was president of Continental, supervised the day-to-day operations of Valley, and owned about 25% of the stock of each company.

Valley, which was run by Roth out of a single office on Continental's premises, was engaged in lending money at interest to Continental and others in the vending machine business. Continental would issue negotiable notes to Valley, which would endorse these in blank and use them as collateral for drawing on two lines of credit, of $1 million each, at Franklin National Bank ("Franklin") and Meadowbrook National Bank ("Meadowbrook"), and would then transfer to Continental the discounted amount of the notes. These transactions, beginning as early as 1956, gave rise to what is called "the Valley payable." By the end of fiscal 1962, the amount of this was $1,029,475, of which $543,345 was due within the year.

In addition to the Valley payable, there was what is known as the "Valley receivable," which resulted from Continental loans to Valley. Most of these stemmed from Roth's custom, dating from mid-1957, of using Continental and Valley as sources of cash to finance his transactions in the stock market. At the end of fiscal 1962, the amount of the Valley receivable was $3.5 million, and by February 15, 1963, the date of certification, it has risen to $3.9 million. The Valley payable could not be offset, or "netted," against the Valley receivable since, as stated, Continental's obligations to Valley were in the form of negotiable notes which Valley had endorsed in blank to the two banks and used as collateral to obtain the cash which it then lent to Continental.

By the certification date, the auditors had learned that Valley was not in a position to repay its debt, and it was accordingly arranged that collateral would be posted. Roth and members of his family transferred their equity in certain securities to Arthur Field, Continental's counsel, as trustee to secure Roth's debt to Valley and Valley's debt to Continental. Some 80% of these securities consisted of Continental stock and convertible debentures.

The 1962 financial statements of Continental, which were dismal by any standard, reported the status of the Valley transactions as follows:

ASSETS
Current Assets:
     *   *   *

    Accounts and notes receivable:
     *   *   *

Valley Commercial Corp., affiliate (Note 2)	$2,143,335
Noncurrent accounts and notes receivable:	
Valley Commercial Corp., affiliate (Note 2)	1,400,000

LIABILITIES
Current Liabilities:
     *   *   *

Long-term debt, portion due within one year	$8,203,788

     *   *   *

Long-term debt (Note 7)
     *   *   *

Valley Commercial Corp, affiliate (Note 2)	486,130

   *   *   *

Notes to Consolidated Financial Statements

2. The amount receivable from Valley Commercial Corp. (an affiliated company of which Mr. Harold Roth is an officer, director and stockholder) bears interest at 12% a year. Such amount, less the balance of the notes payable to that company, is secured by the assignment to the Company of Valley's equity in certain marketable securities. As of February 15, 1963, the amount of such equity at current market quotations exceeded the net amount receivable.

7. * * * The amounts of long-term debt, including the portion due within one year, on which interest is payable currently or has been discounted in advance, are as follows:

Valley Commercial Corp,
affiliate $1,029,475

The case against the defendants can be best encapsulated by comparing what Note 2 stated and what the Government claims it would have stated if defendants had included what they knew:

2. The amount receivable from Valley Commercial Corp. (an affiliated company of which Mr. Harold Roth is an officer, director and stockholder), which bears no interest at 12% a year, was uncollectible at September 30, 1962, since Valley had loaned approximately the same amount to Mr. Roth who was unable to pay. Since that date Mr. Roth and others have pledged as security for the repayment of his obligation to Valley and its obligation to Continental (now $3,900,000, against which Continental's liability to Valley cannot be offset) securities which, as of February 15, 1963, had a market value of $2,978,000. Approximately 80% of such securities are stock and convertible debentures of the Company.

Striking as the difference is, the latter version does not reflect the Government's further contention that in fact the market value of the pledged securities on February 15, 1963, was $1,978,000 rather than $2,978,000 due to liens of James Talcott, Inc. and Franklin for indebtedness other than Roth's of which defendants knew or should have known.

•   •   •

When Fishman visited Continental's office in early September 1962 in preparation for that year's audit, he was told that as of July 31 the Valley receivable had reached $3.6 million. He was told also that Continental was operating a check float in excess of $500,000 daily, that cash was "tighter than ever," and that Continental's Assistant Comptroller had spent most of July and August "juggling cash." Fishman reported this to Simon and Kaiser, noting that "all in all, it promises to be an 'interesting' audit."

The cash audit, conducted in early October 1962, showed how stringent cash had become. . . . The Valley receivable was found to be around $3.5 million and Fishman told Roth in late October that this was so large that "there could be a problem with the year-end audit." In answer to a question by Fishman in November why Valley needed so much money, Kalan, Continental's Assistant Comptroller, said that "Roth needed the money to maintain the margin accounts on the U. S. Hoffman stock and bonds and the Continental stock and bonds."

•   •   •

Meanwhile, according to Roth, he had contacted Simon in December and said that although Valley had a net worth of $2 million, it was not in a position to repay its $3.5 million debt to Continental as it had lent him approximately the same amount which he was unable to repay. He suggested that he secure the indebtedness with his equity in stocks, bonds and other securities of Continental and Hoffman International if this would be acceptable. Roth called Simon some ten days later and received the latter's assent. On December 31 Roth placed Arthur Field, counsel for Continental, in charge of preparing the assignments.

Late in January 1963 Fishman visited Roth and showed him a draft of Note 2 substantially identical with the final form; he told Roth that

Simon wanted to see him. They met in the Lybrand office on February 6. Defendants concede that at this meeting Roth informed Simon that Valley could not repay Continental and offered to post securities for the Valley receivable, and also to post as collateral a mortgage on his house and furnishings. Simon agreed that if adequate collateral were posted, a satisfactory legal opinion were obtained, and Continental's board approved the transactions, Lybrand could certify Continental's statements without reviewing Valley's, which still were not available.

* * *

The financial statements were mailed as part of Continental's annual report on February 20. By that time the market value of the collateral had declined some $270,000 from its February 15 value. The value of the collateral fell an additional $640,000 on February 21. When the market reopened on February 25 after the long Washington's birthday recess, it fell another $2 million and was worth only $395,000. The same day a Continental check to the Internal Revenue Service bounced. Two days later the Government padlocked the plant and the American Stock Exchange suspended trading in Continental stock. Investigations by the SEC and bankruptcy rapidly ensued.

* * *

On this dominating issue of Roth's diverting corporate funds we do not have a case where the question is whether accountants may be subjected to criminal sanction for closing their eyes to what was plainly to be seen. Fishman was proved to have known what was going on since 1958, Simon must have had a good idea about it from the spring of 1960 when Roth informed him that he had borrowed $1,000,000 from investment bankers to make a repayment to Valley, and the jury could infer that Kaiser also was not unaware. If Roth's testimony was believed, the defendants knew almost all the facts from December 1962. In any event they concede knowledge prior to the certification. Beyond what we have said, Field testified that at a meeting in February 1963 before the statements were certified, he, Simon and Kaiser discussed

"how was it possible for a man like Harold Roth * * * for a man like that to go wrong and to take out this money through the circuitous method of having it first go into Valley and then to withdraw it immediately by himself * * *." The jury could reasonably have wondered how accountants who were really seeking to tell the truth could have constructed a footnote so well designed to conceal the shocking facts. This was not simply by the lack of affirmative disclosure but by the failure to describe the securities under circumstances crying for a disclosure and the failure to press Roth for a mortgage on his house and furnishings, description of which in the footnote would necessarily have indicated the source of the collateral and thus evoked inquiry where the money advanced to Valley had gone.

Turning to the failure to describe the collateral, defendants concede that they could not properly have certified statements showing the Valley receivable as an asset when they knew it was uncollectible. That was why Roth proposed collateralization and they accepted it. As men experienced in financial matters, they must have known that the one kind of property ideally unsuitable to collateralize a receivable whose collectibility was essential to avoiding an excess of current liabilities over current assets and a two-thirds reduction in capital already reduced would be securities of the very corporation whose solvency was at issue—particularly when the 1962 report revealed a serious operating loss. Failure to disclose that 80% of the "marketable securities" by which the Valley receivable was said to be "secured" were securities of Continental was thus altogether unlike a failure to state how much collateral were bonds or stocks of General Motors and how much of U.S. Steel. Indeed one of the defense experts testified that disclosure would be essential if Continental stock constituted more than 50% of the collateral. Beyond this, we are not here required to determine whether failure to reveal the nature of the collateral would have been a submittable issue if the Valley receivable had constituted an advance made for legitimate business purpose. Defendants' conduct had to be judged in light of their failure to reveal the looting by Roth. Since disclosure that 80% of the securities were Continental stock or debentures would have led to inquiry who could furnish so much, the jury could properly draw the inference that the failure to reveal that the bulk of the pledged securities was of the one sort most inappropriate to "secure" the Valley receivable, rather than being a following of accepted accounting principles, was part of a deliberate effort to conceal what defendants knew of the diversion of corporate funds that Roth had perpetrated.

• • •

Defendants properly make much of the alleged absence of proof of motivation. They say that even if the Government is not bound to show evil motive, and we think it is not, . . . lack of evidence of motive makes the burden of proving criminal intent peculiarly heavy and the Government did not discharge this.

It is quite true that there was no proof of motive in the form usual in fraud cases. None of the defendants made or could make a penny from Continental's putting out false financial statements. Neither was there evidence of motive in the sense of fear that telling the truth would lose a valuable account. Continental was not the kind of client whose size would give it leverage to bully a great accounting firm, nor was it important to the defendants personally in the sense of their having brought in the business. One would suppose rather that the Continental account had become a considerable headache to the Lybrand firm generally and to the defendants in particular; they could hardly have been unaware of the likelihood that the many hours the firm had devoted to the 1962 audit would not be compensated and that another might never occur. Ordinary commercial motivation is thus wholly absent.

The Government finds motive in defendants' desire to preserve Lybrand's reputation and conceal the alleged dereliction of their predecessors and themselves in former years—the failure to advise Continental's board of directors of Roth's role in creating the Valley receivable, . . . the failure to expand the scope of the audit for those years to determine the nature and collectibility of the Valley receivable, despite the injunction in a well-known text originally authored by one of the founders of the Lybrand firm that receivables from affiliates must be scrutinized carefully to determine they "are what they purport to be"; and the certification of the 1961 statements despite Simon's warning to Roth that a further increase in the receivable would necessitate an examination of Valley's books. The apparent failure of the defendants to consult with the Lybrand executive committee, or with the partner in the firm to whom "problems" in audits were supposed to be referred, on what would seem highly important policy questions concerning the 1962 audit adds force to these arguments.

The main response is that if the defendants had wanted to cover up any past delinquencies they would not have insisted on financial statements so dismal in other respects. It is alleged that defendants demanded certain adjustments which good accounting practice permitted but did not require. It is said also that defendants must have known the statements were so unfavorable, even with the limited disclosure in Note 2, that Continental was bound to fold and a full investigation would follow. The argument is impressive but not dispositive. Defendants may have harbored the illusion that the dexterity of Continental's treasurer in "juggling cash" would enable it to survive. Moreover, men who find themselves in a bad situation of their own making do not always act with full rationality.

Even if there were no satisfactory showing of motive, we think the Government produced sufficient evidence of criminal intent. Its burden was not to show that defendants were wicked men with designs on anyone's purse, which they obviously were not, but rather that they had certified a statement knowing it to be false. As Judge Hough said for us long ago, "while there is no allowable inference of knowledge from the mere fact of falsity, there are many cases where from the actor's special situation and continuity of conduct an inference that he did know the untruth of what he said or wrote may legitimately be drawn." *Bentel v. United States*. . . . Moreover, so far as criminal intent is concerned, the various deficiencies in the footnote should not be considered in isolation. Evidence that defendants knowingly suppressed one fact permitted, although it surely did not compel, an inference that their suppression of another was likewise knowing and willful.

In addition to all that has been said on this score in the previous section of this opinion, a strong indication of knowing suppression lay in the evidence concerning the erroneous reduction of the Valley receivable by the $1 million of notes payable. Defendants say that this was mere negligence; that, beginning with Fishman's memorandum of November 12, 1962, they were "thinking net." But the jury was not bound to accept this. Even if the jury believed that Fishman had negligently slipped into error in November 1962, despite his peculiar awareness of the impossibility of netting, which it was not required to do, it truly taxed credulity to suppose that, with all the attention that was given to the Valley receivable over the next three months, none of these defendants, experienced in the business of Continental, ever mentioned to the others that the critical figure was not the net receivable but the gross, as indeed the body of the financial statements showed, so that $3 million of collateral would not secure the receivable. Indeed Simon and Kaiser swore in depositions taken in a civil suit brought by Continental's bankruptcy Trustee and before the grand jury that they had known in February 1963 that the Continental notes were pledged so that netting was impossible, and made the implausible contention, as did Fishman in his grand jury testimony, that Note 2 had not netted. Defendants' attempt to escape from all this by alleging that they learned of the pledges of the Continental notes only in discussions with a Valley employee in May 1963, may have made matters worse for them with the jury rather than better. For the employee denied the conversation and the story was incon-sistent with the failure to net in the financial statements themselves and with other evidence.

The Government furnished added evidence of criminal intent in the shape of conflicting statements by the defendants and contradictions by other witnesses. Simon and Fishman had testified before the Referee in Continental's bankruptcy proceedings that they had discussed, together with Kaiser, whether disclosure need be made of the nature of the collateral, and had rejected this as unnecessary. Yet Simon testified at trial that no consideration had been given to this and Fishman could not recall any discussion. Simon and Fishman swore to the Referee that they had not known of Roth's borrowings from Valley until March 1963. On the other hand, Fishman admitted before the grand jury that he had known of them as early as 1958; Roth testified to telling Simon about them in December 1962; all the defendants now admit they were fully informed before the certification in February 1963; and counsel for Continental's trustee testified that Simon had admitted knowing the facts "a long time" before that. When we add the delay in getting at the critical matter of the Valley receivable, the failure to follow up Roth's offer of a mortgage on his house and furniture and the last minute changes in the balance sheet, we find it impossible to say that a reasonable jury could not be convinced beyond a reasonable doubt that the striking difference between what Note 2 said and what it needed to say in order to reveal the truth resulted not from mere carelessness but from design. That some other jury might have taken a more lenient view, as the trial judge said he would have done, is a misfortune for the defendants but not one within our power to remedy.

1. In *United States v. Simon* the government conceded that "it had the burden of offering proof allowing a reasonable jury to be convinced beyond a reasonable doubt not merely that the financial statement was false or misleading in a material respect but that defendants knew it to be and deliberately sought to mislead." In order to prove the defendants' "intent" to defraud, the government prosecutors introduced evidence that demonstrated the defendants' "motive" to defraud.

With respect to proof of "motive," the *Simon* court held that the government was "not bound to show evil motive." The court noted, however, that "lack of motive makes the burden of proving criminal intent peculiarly heavy. . . . "

The court observed that:

> Even if there was no satisfactory showing of motive, we think the government produced sufficient evidence of criminal intent. Its burden was not to show that defendants were wicked men with designs on anyone's purse, which obviously they were not, but rather that they had certified a statement knowing it to be false.

2.   Although not necessary, proof of motive to defraud is important for it provides the background against which a defendant's conduct is scrutinized. To the extent that a motive to defraud exists, it colors the character of each and every act or omission to act by the defendant. Proof of motive facilitates proof of bad faith.

3.   The following types of evidence of motive have been used to prove intent to defraud:

Direct pecuniary gain or benefit such as increased professional fees;

Prevention of the loss of a major client;

"Cover-up" of prior professional failures to avoid being the subject of civil or criminal litigation or to avoid impairment of professional reputation.

[3]   *United States v. Natelli* and Comments

United States v. Natelli
527 F.2d 311
(2d Cir. 1975)

Before HAYS, MULLIGAN and GURFEIN, Circuit Judges.

GURFEIN, Circuit Judge:

[Defendant auditors, Natelli, the audit partner and Scansaroli, the audit supervisor, were convicted by a jury of criminal violations of the 1934 Act in conjunction with a proxy statement issued on September 27, 1969, by their audit client, National Student Marketing Corporation. The proxy statement contained a restated annual report for the fiscal year ending August 31, 1968, and an unaudited statement of earnings for the nine months ended May 31, 1969.

The restated annual report was audited by the defendants, who were charged with knowingly failing to disclose that more than 20 percent of Marketing's originally reported 1968 sales had been written off at the time the proxy statement was filed. At the time that the restated financials were issued in the proxy statement, the auditors knew that Marketing had written off $1 million of 1968 sales by subtracting $350,000 from fiscal-year 1969 sales, and by writing off $678,000 of 1968 sales. The write-off did not result in income reduction because the auditors determined that the reduction in earnings was offset by an extraordinary tax credit "that happened to be approximately the same amount as the profit to be written off."

The restated annual report contained Marketing's 1968 fiscal-year sales and earnings, as well as the pooled sales and earnings of seven companies acquired in 1969 by Marketing. A footnote to the restated audited financials deducted $1 million from 1968 sales of the pooled companies while allowing Marketing's 1968 sales to remain unchanged.

The auditors were also charged with preparing as part of the proxy statement an unaudited earnings statement for the nine-month period ended May 31, 1969, which they knew was false. The unaudited earnings statement materially overstated sales and reflected income when there was none.]

The Proxy Statement
A.   The Footnote

As part of the proxy statement, [the auditors] set about to draft a footnote purporting to reconcile the Company's prior reported net sales and earnings from the 1968 report with restated amounts resulting from pooled companies reflected retroactively. The earnings summary in the proxy statement included companies acquired after fiscal 1968 and their pooled earnings. The footnote was the only place in the proxy statement which would have permitted an interested investor to see what Marketing's performance had been in its preceding fiscal year 1968, as retroactively adjusted, separate from the earnings and sales of the companies it had acquired in fiscal 1969.

At Natelli's direction, Scansaroli subtracted the written-off Marketing sales from the 1968 sales figures for the seven later acquired pooled companies without showing any retroactive adjustment for Marketing's own fiscal 1968 figures. There was no disclosure in the footnote that over $1 million of previously reported 1968 sales of Marketing had been written off. All narrative disclosure in the footnote was stricken by Natelli. This was a violation of Accounting Principles Board Opinion Number 9, which requires disclosure of prior adjustments which affect the net income of prior periods.

B.   The False Nine-Months Earnings Statement

The proxy statement also required an unaudited statement of nine months earnings through May 31, 1969. This was prepared by the Company, with the assistance of Peat on the same percentage of completion basis as in the 1968 audited statement. A commitment from Pontiac Division of General Motors amounting to $1,200,000 was produced two months after the end of the fiscal period. It was dated April 28, 1969.

The proxy statement was to be printed at the Pandick Press in New York on August 15, 1969. At about 3 A.M. on that day, Natelli informed Randell [Marketing's president] that the "sale" to the Pontiac Division for more than $1 million could not be treated as a valid commitment because the letter from Pontiac was not a legally binding obligation. Randell responded at once that he had a "commitment from Eastern Airlines" in a somewhat comparable amount attributable to the nine-month fiscal period (which had ended more than two months earlier). Kelly, a salesman for Marketing, arrived at the printing plant several hours later with a commitment letter from Eastern Airlines, dated August 14, 1969, purporting to confirm an $820,000 commitment ostensibly entered into on May 14, just before the end of the nine-month fiscal period of September 1, 1968 through May 31, 1969. When the proxy statement was printed in final form, the Pontiac "sale" had been deleted, but the Eastern "commitment" had been inserted in its place.

Soon after the incident at Pandick Press, Douglas Oberlander, an accountant at Peat assigned by Natelli to review Marketing's accounts, discovered $177,547 worth of "bad" contracts from 1968 which were known to Scansaroli in May as doubtful, but which had not been written off. Oberlander suggested to Kurek [Marketing's controller] that these contracts and others amounting to over $320,000, in addition to the $1 million in bad contracts previously disposed of, be written off. Kurek consulted Scansaroli, who, after consulting with Natelli, decided against the suggested write-off.

The proxy statement was filed with the SEC on September 30, 1969. There was no disclosure that Marketing had written off $1 million of its 1968 sales (over 20%) and over $2 million of the $3.3 million in unbilled sales booked in 1968 and 1969. A true disclosure, which was not made, would have shown that without these unbilled receivables, Marketing had no profit in the first nine months of 1969.

Each [auditor] contends that the evidence was insufficient to support his conviction. We shall consider each [auditor] separately.

I
Natelli—Sufficiency of Evidence

It is hard to probe the intent of a defendant. Circumstantial evidence, particularly with proof of motive, where available, is often sufficient to convince a reasonable man of criminal intent beyond a reasonable doubt. When we deal with a defendant who is a professional accountant, it is even harder, at times, to distinguish between simple errors of judgment and errors made with sufficient criminal intent to support a conviction, especially when there is no financial gain to the accountant other than his legitimate fee.

Natelli argues that there is insufficient evidence to establish that he knowingly assisted in filing a proxy statement which was materially false. After searching consideration, we are constrained to find that there was sufficient evidence for his conviction.

The arguments Natelli makes in this court as evidence of his innocent intent were made to the jury and presented fairly. There is no contention that Judge Tyler improperly excluded any factual evidence offered. While there is substance to some of Natelli's factual contentions for jury consideration, we cannot find, on the totality of the evidence, that he was improperly convicted.

The original action of Natelli in permitting the booking of unbilled sales after the close of the fiscal period in an amount sufficient to convert a loss into a profit was contrary to sound accounting practice, particularly when the cost of sales based on time spent by account executives in the fiscal period was a mere guess. When the uncollectibility, and indeed, the non-existence of these large receivables was established in 1969, the revelation stood to cause Natelli severe criticism and possible liability. He had a motive, therefore, intentionally to conceal the write-offs that had to be made.

Whether or not the deferred tax item was properly converted to a tax credit, the jury had a right to infer that "netting" the extraordinary item against ordinary earnings on the books in a special journal entry was, in the circumstances, motivated by a desire to conceal.

With this background of motive, the jury could assess what Natelli did with regard to (1) the footnote and (2) the Eastern commitment and the Oberlander "bad" contracts.

A.   The Footnote

Honesty should have impelled appellants to disclose in the footnote which annotated their own audited statement for fiscal 1968 that substantial write-offs had been taken, after year end, to reflect a loss for the year. A simple desire to right the wrong that had been perpetrated on the stockholders and others by the false audited financial statement should have dictated that course. The failure to make open disclosure could hardly have been inadvertent, or a jury at least could so find, for appellants were themselves involved in determining the write-offs and their accounting treatment. The concealment of the retroactive adjustments to Marketing's 1968 year revenues and earnings could properly have been found to have been intentional for the very purpose of hiding earlier errors. There was evidence that Natelli himself changed the footnote to its final form.

That the proxy statement did not contain a formal reaudit of fiscal 1968 is not determinative. The accountant has a duty to correct the earlier financial statement which he had audited himself and upon which he had issued his certificate, when he discovers "that the figures in the annual report were substantially false and misleading," and he has a chance to correct them. See *Fischer v. Kletz*. . . . See also *Gold v. DCL Inc.* The accountant owes a duty to the public not to assert a privilege of silence until the next audited annual statement comes around in due time. Since companies were being acquired by Marketing for its shares in this period, Natelli had to know that the 1968 audited statement was being used continuously.

The argument that the disclosure was not material is weak, since applying write-offs only against pooled earnings, without further explanation, conceals the effect of the write-offs on the prior reported earnings of the principal company. It is the disclosure of the true operating results of Marketing for 1968, now come to light, that was material. Materiality is an objective matter, not necessarily limited by the accountant's own uncontrolled subjective estimate of materiality, see *United States v. Simon*. . . . In any event, the court charged that the earnings figures would have to be "known to be false in a material way"—a subjective test.

B. The Eastern Commitment and the Nine-Months Earnings Statement

The Eastern contract was a matter for deep suspicion because it was substituted so rapidly for the Pontiac contract to which Natelli had objected, and which had, itself, been produced after the end of the fiscal period, though dated earlier. It was still another unbilled commitment produced by Marketing long after the close of the fiscal period. Its spectacular appearance, as Natelli himself noted at the time, made its replacement of the Pontiac contract "weird." The Eastern "commitment" was not only in substitution for the challenged Pontiac "commitment" but strangely close enough in amount to leave the projected earnings figures for the proxy statement relatively intact. Marketing had only time logs of a salesman relating to the making of the proposals but no record of expenditures on the Eastern "commitment," no record of having ever billed Eastern for services on this "sale," and not one scrap of paper from Eastern other than the suddenly-produced letter. Nevertheless, it was booked as if more than $500,000 of it had already been earned.

Natelli contends that he had no duty to verify the Eastern "commitment" because the earnings statement within which it was included was "unaudited."

This raises the issue of the duty of the CPA in relation to an unaudited financial statement contained within a proxy statement where the figures are reviewed and to some extent supplied by the auditors. It is common ground that the auditors were "associated" with the statement and were required to object to anything they actually "knew" to be materially false. In the ordinary case involving an unaudited statement, the auditor would

not be chargeable simply because he failed to discover the invalidity of booked accounts receivable, inasmuch as he had not undertaken an audit with verification. In this case, however, Natelli "knew" the history of postperiod bookings and the dismal consequences later discovered. Was he under a duty in these circumstances to object or to go beyond the usual scope of an accountant's review and insist upon some independent verification? The American Institute of Certified Public Accountants, Statement of Auditing Standards No. 1—Codification of Auditing Standards and Procedures (1972), 1 CCH AICPA Professional Standards § 516.00, recognizes that "if the certified public accountant concludes [on] the basis of facts known to him that unaudited financial statements with which he may become associated are not in conformity with generally accepted accounting principles, which *include adequate disclosure*, he should insist . . . upon appropriate revision . . . " (emphasis added).

We do not think this means, in terms of professional standards, that the accountant may shut his eyes in reckless disregard of his knowledge that highly suspicious figures, known to him to be suspicious, were being included in the unaudited earnings figures with which he was "associated" in the proxy statement.

The auditor's duty is not as restricted as appellants urge where, as here, the auditors, rather than the company, controlled the figures, as is evidenced by Natelli's rejection of the Pontiac contract as one he would not accept for the subsequent audited financial statement for 1969, and where the erroneous figures had previously been certified by his firm. . . . We reject the argument of insufficiency as to Natelli, who could have pointed out the error of his previous certification and deliberately failed to do so, our function being limited to determining whether the evidence was sufficient for submission to the jury.

II
Scansaroli—Sufficiency of Evidence

The claim of Scansaroli with respect to insufficiency of the evidence is somewhat more difficult. As Judge Tyler noted after both sides had rested, "It is a close question, I think frankly as to Scansaroli, as I see it. Certainly if I were the factfinder, I would be more troubled with his case for a variety of reasons."

Scansaroli contends that there was insufficient evidence to prove beyond a reasonable doubt that (1) he participated in a criminal act with respect to the footnote or (2) that he made an accounting judgment permitting Marketing to include in sales certain contracts-in-progress with the requisite criminal intent. We hold that there was enough evidence to establish the former, but not the latter. For reasons relating to the form of the charge, we will reverse and remand for a new trial.

A.   The Footnote

The essence of Scansaroli's argument on his conviction with respect to the false footnote is that he was really convicted for his conduct during the 1968 audit, for which he was not indicted.

This misses the thrust of the Government's claim. The unjustifiable manner of treating the unbilled commitments in the 1968 audit bore upon the illegal acts connected with the 1969 proxy statement in two ways: (a) it created a motive to conceal the accounting errors made in the 1968 audit; and (b) the 1968 audited statement was part of the 1969 proxy statement and was not disclosed therein to have been wrong in the light of the subsequent known write-offs. In view of the established motive to conceal, the jury could properly find, as we have seen, that both the netting of the tax credit against earnings and the subsequent subtracting of the write-offs from the pooled earnings in the footnote without further explanation were done in order to conceal the true retroactive decrease in the Marketing earnings for fiscal 1968.

There is some merit to Scansaroli's point that he was simply carrying out the judgments of his superior Natelli. The defense of obedience to higher authority has always been troublesome. There is no sure yardstick to measure criminal responsibility except by measurement of the degree of awareness on the part of a defendant that he is participating in a criminal act, in the absence of physical coercion such as a soldier might face. Here the motivation to conceal undermines Scansaroli's argument that he was merely implementing Natelli's instructions, at least with respect to concealment of matters that were within his own ken.

We think the jury could properly have found him guilty on the specification relating to the footnote. Scansaroli himself wrote the journal entry in Marketing's books which improperly netted the tax credit with earnings, the true effect never being pointed out in the financial statement. This, with the background of Scansaroli's implication in preparation of the 1968 statement, could be found to have been motivated by intent to conceal the 1968 overstatement of earnings.

Scansaroli participated in the decision to subtract in the proxy statement footnote $678,000 of written-off Marketing sales from the figures for later-acquired pooled companies instead of from its own figures, without further disclosure. Even if Scansaroli did not write the footnote, he supplied the misleading computations and subtractions though he was conscious of the true facts.

B.   The Eastern Commitment

Having concluded that there was sufficient evidence to convict both appellants on the footnote specification, we turn to the nine-months earnings statement which, in turn, included two items, the Eastern contract and the doubtful commitments discovered by Oberlander. We put aside the decision to ignore Oberlander's questioning of certain commitments on the ground that, if it stood alone, the evidence would have been too equivocal to support proof beyond a reasonable doubt that this was not a mere error of judgment.

With respect to the major item, the Eastern commitment, we think Scansaroli stands in a position different from that of Natelli. Natelli was his superior. He was the man to make the judgment whether or not to object to the last-minute inclusion of a new "commitment" in the nine-months statement. There is insufficient evidence that Scansaroli engaged in any conversations about the Eastern commitment at the Pandick Press or that he was a participant with Natelli in any check on its authenticity. Since in the hierarchy of the accounting firm it was not his responsibility to decide whether to book the Eastern contract, his mere adjustment of the figures to reflect it under orders was not a matter for his discretion. As we have seen, Natelli bore a duty in the circumstances to be suspicious of the Eastern commitment and to pursue the matter further. Scansaroli may also have been suspicious, but rejection of the Eastern contract was not within his sphere of responsibility. Absent such duty, he cannot be held to have acted in reckless disregard of the facts.

III

Appellants contend that the trial court erroneously instructed the jury on the issue of knowledge. We do not agree.

The thrust of appellants' argument, as we understand it, is that the judge charged that each appellant could be convicted "if [his] failure to discover the falsity of [Marketing's] financial statements was the result of some form of gross negligence." We do not read the charge that way. It followed the charge of Judge Mansfield which was sustained in *United States v. Simon* . . .

It was a balanced charge which made it clear that negligence or mistake would be insufficient to constitute guilty knowledge. . . . Judge Tyler also carefully instructed the jury that "good faith, that is to say, an honest belief in the truth of the data set forth in the footnote and entries in the proxy statement, would constitute a complete defense here." On the other hand, "Congress equally could not have intended that men holding themselves out as members of these ancient professions [law and accounting] should be able to escape criminal liability on a plea of ignorance when they have shut their eyes to what was plainly to be seen or have represented a knowledge they knew they did not possess." *United States v. Benjamin* . . .

One of the bases for attack on the charge is that in charging "reckless disregard for the truth or falsity" or "closing his eyes," there must also be an instruction like "and with a conscious purpose to avoid learning the truth."

It is true that we have favored this charge in false statement cases, while noting that both phrases "mean essentially the same thing," and in cases involving knowledge that goods were stolen. . . . The dual instruction is not necessarily required, however, when the defendant is under a specific duty to discover the true facts, the facts tendered are suspect, and he does nothing to correct them. In *United States v. Benjamin*, . . . this court said, regarding an accountant, that "the Government can meet its burden by proving that a defendant deliberately closed his eyes to facts he had a duty to see." And *United States v. Simon*, . . . which affirmed the conviction of an accountant, as we have seen, sustained a charge in the very language Judge Tyler tracked.

While the facts in each case are not precisely the same, we think this appeal quite analogous to *Simon*, . . . because Natelli was suspicious enough of the Eastern contract to check it with Kelly, the account executive in house, but not to take the next step of seeking verification from Eastern, despite his obvious doubt that it could be booked as a true commitment. And with respect to the footnote, we think the language of this court in *Simon* to be quite pertinent, "The jury could reasonably have wondered how accountants who were really seeking to tell the truth could have constructed a footnote so well designed to conceal the shocking facts."

Appellants argue strenuously, however, that *United States v. Simon*, . . . involved an audited statement while the nine months statement here involved was an unaudited statement, and that, hence, the duties of appellants here were different from those enunciated in *Simon*. They urge as a corollary that the District Court failed to instruct the jury on the difference, and that his failure to do so was reversible error.

It is true that the point on appeal might have been eliminated if the judge had charged on the differences in the abstract. But in the circumstances he was not required to do so. As we have seen, *supra*, Point I, the duty of Natelli, given this set of facts, was not so different from the duty of an accountant upon an audit as to require sharply different treatment of that duty in the charge to the jury.

We agree with Judge Tyler when he charged the jury that they could find Natelli "knew" of the falsely material fact if he acted in "reckless disregard" or deliberately closed his eyes to the obvious. The issue on this appeal is not what an auditor is *generally* under a duty to do with respect to an unaudited statement, but what these defendants had a duty to do in these unusual and highly suspicious circumstances. . . . Nor was a proper charge requested.

The duly requested supplemental charge on Natelli's duty with respect to the unaudited earnings statement was properly denied. It read:

> "The defendants' *only* responsibility as to this statement [unaudited statement of earnings for the nine months ended May 31, 1969] was to be satisfied that, *as far as they knew*, the statement contained no misstatement of material facts" (emphasis added).

This requested charge was not correct, for even on an unaudited statement with which Natelli was "associated" and where there were suspicious circumstances, his duty went further, as we have seen. As the court correctly charged, Natelli was culpable if he acted in "reckless disregard" of the facts or if he "deliberately closed his eyes."

We expound no rule, to be sure, that an accountant in reviewing an unaudited company statement is bound, without more, to seek verification and to apply auditing procedures. We lay no extra burden on the normal activities of accountants, nor do we assume the role of an Accounting Principles Board. We deal only with such deviations as fairly come within the common understanding of dishonest conduct which jurors bring into the box as applied to the particular conduct prohibited by the particular statute.

It was not for Judge Tyler in his instructions to deal with the abstract question of an accountant's responsibility for unaudited statements, for that was not the issue. So long as we find that the Judge explicated the proper test applicable to the facts of this case, the duty inherent in the circumstances, and we do, we must also find that he gave the appellants a fair charge.

1.   In *United States v. Natelli* the court observed that it has "favored" an instruction to the jury that there must be both a "conscious purpose to avoid learning the truth," as well as "reckless disregard for the truth or falsity" or "closing his eyes." Yet the court in *United States v. Natelli* said that a "conscious purpose" is not required "when the defendant is under a specific duty to discover the true facts, the facts tendered are suspect, and he does nothing to correct them."

The court of appeals approved the following instruction given by the trial judge regarding "guilty knowledge":

While I have stated that negligence or mistake do not constitute guilty knowledge or intent, nevertheless, ladies and gentlemen, you are entitled to consider in determining whether a defendant acted with such intent if he deliberately closed his eyes to the obvious or to the facts that certainly would be observed or ascertained in the course of his accounting work or whether he recklessly stated as facts matters of which he knew he was ignorant.

If you find such reckless deliberate indifference to or disregard for truth or falsity on the part of a given defendant, the law entitles you to infer therefrom that that defendant wilfully and knowingly filed or caused to be filed false financial information of a material nature with the SEC.

But such an inference, of course, must depend upon the weight and credibility extended to the evidence of reckless and indifferent conduct, if any.

I repeat: Ordinary or simple negligence or mistake alone would be insufficient to support a finding of guilty knowledge or wilfulness or intent.

2.   The trial judge instructed the jury that "[o]rdinary or simple negligence or mistake alone would be insufficient to support a finding of guilty knowledge or wilfulness or intent." The court of appeals observed that:

> It is hard to probe the intent of a defendant. Circumstantial evidence, particularly with proof of motive, where available, is often sufficient to convince a reasonable man of criminal intent beyond a reasonable doubt. When we deal with a defendant who is a professional accountant, it is even harder, at times, to distinguish between simple errors of judgment and errors made with sufficient criminal intent to support a conviction, especially when there is no financial gain to the accountant other than his legitimate fee.

Although the line between negligent and intentional conduct may be brightly defined, the "bright lines" of demarcation tend to blur and fade when applied to facts. Distinguishing between errors of judgment and errors of intent is easier said than done.

3.   In *United States v. Natelli*, the court of appeals held that the audit supervisor, Scansaroli, could not be found guilty as to the nine-month unaudited earnings statement included in the proxy statement. The court reasoned that even if the audit supervisor was suspicious as to the accuracy of the unaudited statement, it was "not his responsibility" to determine whether adjustments were in order. The court held that the sole duty to make this determination rested with the audit partner.

With respect to the audited financials included in the proxy statement, the court of appeals upheld the finding of guilt as to the audit supervisor. The court stated that the supervisor "participated in the decision" to draft the proxy statement footnote in a misleading manner. The court also observed that the supervisor wrote an adjusting journal entry that improperly obscured the truth. The court further noted that the foregoing matters coupled with the supervisor's participation in the prior year's audit was a sufficient basis from which to conclude that the supervisor "could be found to have been motivated by intent to conceal the 1968 overstatement of earnings."

Unlike its analysis of the unaudited financial statement, the court of appeals declined to exculpate the audit supervisor from criminal liability on the basis that it was "not his responsibility" to determine whether adjustments were necessary to the *audited* financials. Thus, the court of appeals rejected the so-called defense of obedience to higher authority.

4.   *United States v. Natelli* is a classic example of how an accountant's breach of the "duty to correct" can give rise to subsequent charges of fraud, including a criminal indictment. The "duty to correct" is discussed in detail at ¶ 6.03.

5.   In *United States v. Natelli* the audit partner attempted to reverse that portion of his conviction relating to the unaudited nine-month's earnings statement. The audit partner sought an instruction that distinguished between an accountant's duty with respect to audited and unaudited financial statements.

The court of appeals rejected the audit partner's arguments holding that in "these unusual and highly suspicious circumstances" there was no basis to distinguish between audited and unaudited. See the discussion at ¶ 7.04[1] regarding an accountant's duties of inquiry and disclosure as they relate to unaudited financials, including those that are compiled or reviewed.

¶ 5.04   Good Faith Defense: Compliance with Professional Standards

The flip side of a prosecutor's attempt to prove a defendant's "bad faith" and intent to deceive is the defendant's efforts to prove that he acted in "good faith." *Good faith* is often described as a course of conduct resulting from a mistaken but honest belief. Thus, if a defendant has an "honest belief" that certain financial information is true and is not materially misleading, the defendant's "honest belief" or "good faith" would constitute a complete defense to a charge of criminal intent to defraud.

To demonstrate his good faith a defendant will draw on evidence of various types, including conversations, documents, and at times expert-witness testimony. This evidence will be offered to prove that the defendant's acts or omissions were not the result of an intent to defraud.

In criminal prosecutions against accountants the defense of good faith is often asserted based on the claim that the accountant complied with applicable professional standards. As the following cases demonstrate, compliance with professional standards may be "highly persuasive" but "not conclusive" evidence of a defendant's good faith.

[1]   *United States v. Simon* and Comments

United States v. Simon
425 F.2d 796
(2d Cir. 1969)
[See ¶ 5.03[2] for the facts]

The defendants called eight expert independent accountants, an impressive array of leaders of the profession. They testified generally that, except for the error with respect to netting, the treatment of the Valley receivable in Note 2 was in no way inconsistent with generally accepted accounting principles or generally accepted auditing standards, since it made all the informative disclosures reasonably necessary for fair presentation of the financial position of Continental as of the close of the 1962 fiscal year. Specifically, they testified that neither generally accepted accounting principles nor generally accepted auditing standards required disclosure of the make-up of the collateral or of the increase of the receivable after the closing date of the balance sheet, although three of the eight stated that in light of hindsight they would have preferred that the make-up of the collateral be disclosed. The witnesses likewise testified that disclosure of the Roth borrowings from Valley was not required, and seven of the eight were of the opinion that such dis-closure would be inappropriate. The principal reason given for this last view was that the balance sheet was concerned solely with presenting the financial position of the company under audit; since the Valley receivable was adequately secured in the opinion of the auditors and was broken out and shown separately as a loan to an affiliate with the nature of the affiliation disclosed, this was all that the auditors were required to do. To go further and reveal what Valley had done with the money would be to put into the balance sheet things that did not properly belong there; moreover, it would create a precedent which would imply that it was the duty of an auditor to investigate each loan to an affiliate to determine whether the money had found its way into the pockets of an officer of the company under audit, an investigation that would ordinarily be unduly wasteful of time and money. With due respect to the Government's accounting witnesses, an SEC staff accountant, and, in rebuttal, its chief accountant, who took a contrary view, we are bound to say that they hardly compared with defendants' witnesses in aggregate auditing experience and professional eminence.

Defendants asked for two instructions which, in substance, would have told the jury that a defendant could be found guilty only if, according to generally accepted accounting principles, the financial statements as a whole did not fairly present the financial condition of Continental at September 30, 1962, and then only if his departure from accepted standards was due to willful disregard of those standards with knowledge of the falsity of the statements and an intent to deceive. The judge declined to give these instructions. Dealing with the subject in the course of his charge, he said that the "critical test" was whether the financial statements as a whole "fairly presented the financial position of Continental as of September 30, 1962, and whether it accurately reported the operations for fiscal 1962." If they did not, the basic issue became whether defendants acted in good faith. Proof of compliance with generally accepted standards was "evidence which may be very persuasive but not necessarily conclusive that he acted in good faith, and that the facts as certified were not materially false or misleading." "The weight and credibility to be extended by you to such proof, and its persuasiveness, must depend, among other things, on how authoritative you find the precedents and the teachings relied upon by the parties to be, the extent to which they contemplate, deal with, and apply to the type of circumstances found by you to have existed here, and the weight you give to expert opinion evidence offered by the parties. Those may depend on the credibility extended by you to expert witnesses, the definiteness with which they testified, the reasons given for their opinions, and all the other facts affecting credibility, * * *"

Defendants contend that the charge and refusal to charge constituted error. We think the judge was right in refusing to make the accountants' testimony so nearly a complete defense. The critical test according to the charge was the same as that which the accountants testified was critical. We do not think the jury was also required to accept the accountants' evaluation whether a given fact

was material to overall fair presentation, at least not when the accountants' testimony was not based on specific rules or prohibitions to which they could point, but only on the need for the auditor to make an honest judgment and their conclusion that nothing in the financial statements themselves negated the conclusion that an honest judgment had been made. Such evidence may be highly persuasive, but it is not conclusive, and so the trial judge correctly charged.

Defendants next contend that, particularly in light of the expert testimony, the evidence was insufficient to allow the jury to consider the failure to disclose Roth's borrowings from Valley, the make-up of the collateral, or the post-balance sheet increase in the Valley receivable. They concentrate their fire on what they characterize as the "primary, predominant and pervasive" issue, namely the failure to disclose that Continental's loans to Valley were not for a proper business purpose but to assist Roth in his personal financial problems. It was "primary, predominant and pervasive" not only because it was most featured by the prosecution but because defendants' knowledge of Roth's diversion of corporate funds colored everything else. We join defendants' counsel in assuming that the mere fact that a company has made advances to an affiliate does not ordinarily impose a duty on an accountant to investigate what the affiliate has done with them or even to disclose that the affiliate has made a loan to a common officer if this has come to his attention. But it simply cannot be true that an accountant is under no duty to disclose what he knows when he has reason to believe that, to a material extent, a corporation is being operated not to carry out its business in the interest of all the stockholders but for the private benefit of its president. For a court to say that all this is immaterial as a matter of law if only such loans are thought to be collectible would be to say that independent accountants have no responsibility to reveal known dishonesty by a high corporate officer. If certification does not at least imply that the corporation has not been looted by insiders so far as the accountants know, or, if it has been, that the diversion has been made good beyond peradventure (or adequately reserved against) and effective steps taken to prevent a recurrence, it would mean nothing, and the reliance placed on it by the public would be a snare and a delusion. Generally accepted accounting principles instruct an accountant what to do in the usual case where he has no reason to doubt that the affairs of the corporation are being honestly conducted. Once he has reason to believe that this basic assumption is false, an entirely different situation confronts him. Then, as the Lybrand firm stated in its letter accepting the Continental engagement, he must "extend his procedures to determine whether or not such suspicions are justified." If as a result of such an extension or, as here, without it, he finds his suspicions to be confirmed, full disclosure must be the rule, unless he has made sure the wrong has been righted and procedures to avoid a repetition have been established. At least this must be true when the dishonesty he has discovered is not some minor peccadillo but a diversion so large as to imperil if not destroy the very solvency of the enterprise.

We are likewise unimpressed with the argument that defendants cannot be charged with criminality for failure to disclose the known increase in the Valley receivable from $3.4 to $3.9 million. Here again the claim that generally accepted accounting practices do not require accountants to investigate and report on developments since the date of the statements being certified has little relevance. Note 2 stated "As of February 15, 1963, the amount of such equity at current market quotations exceeded the net amount receivable." This means the net amount receivable as of February 15. If the receivable remained at the $3.9 million level it had attained at December 31, 1962, and there is nothing to indicate its reduction, the collateral of $2.9 million verified by Harris barely equalled even the "net" receivable, since the collateral, supplied long after September 30, 1962, although this also was not disclosed, concededly was security for advances after September 30 as well as before. The jury was thus entitled to infer that the failure to reveal the increase in the Valley receivable was part of an effort to create an appearance of collectibility which defendants knew to be false. Indeed one of the defense experts agreed that the increase in the receivable was a material event that required disclosure in the absence of sufficient collateral. Moreover, this issue, like the others, must be considered in context. The jury could find that failure to reveal the known increase in the Valley receivable, rather than being motivated by adherence to accepted accounting principles, was due to fear that revelation of the increase would arouse inquiry why a company in the desperate condition of Continental would go on advancing money to an affiliate and thus lead to discovery of Roth's looting.

1.   In *United States v. Simon* the court of appeals upheld the trial judge's instruction to the jury that:

> [T]he "critical test" was whether the financial statements as a whole "fairly presented the financial position of Continental as of September 30, 1962, and whether it accurately reported the operations for fiscal 1962." If they did not, the basic issue became whether defendants acted in good faith.

As to the question of the auditor's good faith, the court of appeals approved the trial judge's charge that:

> Proof of compliance with generally accepted standards was "evidence which may be very persuasive but not necessarily conclusive that he acted in good faith, and that the facts as certified were not materially false or misleading."

2.   The defendant auditors in *Simon* presented eight preeminent expert witnesses who testified that the defendants had not departed from generally accepted accounting principles

(GAAP) and generally accepted auditing standards (GAAS) and that the disclosures urged by the prosecutors were not required by GAAP or GAAS. The trial judge refused to give an instruction, requested by the auditors, which would have told the jury that a defendant could be found guilty only if according to GAAP the financials were materially misleading and the defendant willfully departed from GAAP. The court of appeals upheld the trial judge's rejection of the auditor's instruction, stating that "the judge was right in refusing to make the accountants' [expert] testimony so nearly a complete defense."

3. To the extent that an accountant relies upon a specific accounting principle, auditing procedure, or professional practice recognized as applicable, the accountant's compliance with the applicable professional standard will be highly probative evidence of good faith. To the extent that specific professional standards do not exist, an accountant will necessarily be compelled to draw on other forms of evidence to demonstrate his good faith.

The existence of professional standards is vital to successfully demonstrating good faith. At the same time, an accountant's failure to adhere to existing professional standards can be highly probative of "bad faith." Professional standards are thus a double-edged sword.

4. In *Simon* the trial judge rejected instructions tendered by the defendant. Jury instructions are a critical aspect of any trial by jury. Through the instructions the judge directs the jury regarding the nature of the applicable rules of law. The jury then determines what the facts are and applies the law to the facts to reach a verdict.

It is the practice in many courts to allow the jury to take the typed jury instructions with them to the jury room for reference during their deliberations. The instructions are therefore very important.

[2]   *United States v. Weiner* and Comments

United States v. Weiner
578 F.2d 757 (9th Cir. 1978)

Before CHOY and GOODWIN, Circuit Judges, and THOMPSON,* District Judge.

Julian Weiner, Marvin Lichtig, and Solomon Block appeal their respective convictions for securities fraud arising out of their employment as auditors of Equity Funding Corporation of America (Equity Funding) during the time covered by the indictment.

Equity Funding was incorporated in 1960 to sell life insurance, mutual funds, and "equity funding" programs. The company operated legitimately and profitably until 1964, when the government proved, it began to publish inaccurate and false financial statements. Equity Funding was accused of massive fraud in overstating its income and claiming non-existent assets in order to increase the market value of its stock.

Wolfson, Weiner, Ratoff, and Lapin were the independent public accountants for Equity Funding from 1961 until 1971. In early 1972, the Los Angeles branch of the Wolfson, Weiner firm joined with the accounting firm of Seidman & Seidman. The combined firm served as Equity Funding's independent public accountant until the exposure of the fraud in 1973.

• • •

The remaining inquiry is whether defendants approved of and concurred in the grossly misstated reports in the good faith belief that the statements were accurate representations or whether they knowingly and willfully acquiesced in the dissemination of false statements.. . . . As we discuss below, there was sufficient evidence from which the jury could find that defendants willfully and knowingly produced the documents containing erroneous information.

.   .   .

Each group of counts charged similar acts in different years. An erroneously recorded transaction in one year often persisted into the following years. Our count-by-count analysis is chronological, but in order to understand the full impact of particular actions a general examination is helpful.

Equity Funding's unorthodox bookkeeping began in the early sixties. Evidence of the manipulation before 1968 was presented to the jury. By 1968 a pattern had emerged in which the Funded Loans and Accounts Receivable asset account (FLAR) was being used as an umbrella account for numerous and varying false entries. Other accounts, both assets and liabilities, were inflated or created as needed to present the desired picture of a healthy, growing corporation. Weiner and Lichtig had audited the company since the early sixties. After Lichtig became Equity Funding's Executive Vice President, Block became the audit manager. They were thus involved with the company's financial history almost from its inception. Weiner and Lichtig also helped engineer many of the "innovative" accounting techniques utilized over the years.

Various Equity Funding officials testified to the falsity of the figures that appeared on the financial statements and to the fact that in many instances no backup papers supported the entries. Therefore, if the auditors had attempted to confirm the information given to them they would have been unable to do so. The lack of backup and supporting schedules would have been a clear indication that something was wrong. Since such backup often was not even fabricated, the jury could infer that the auditors either completely failed to audit the areas, in disregard of GAAS, or consciously failed to audit in "cooperation" with the Equity Funding officials, thus purposely avoiding the false entries. If the questionable areas had been audited and no backup found, the failure of the auditors to reflect that fact in their report would have

clearly contravened GAAS and the purpose of an independent audit.

After the fraud was discovered in 1973, Touche, Ross & Co. was appointed to audit the financial statements of Equity Funding in accordance with GAAS and GAAP. Touche, Ross & Co. made substantial adjustments after finding it impossible to confirm properly many of the recorded transactions or upon finding that mathematical calculations were erroneous. Many of the adjustments related to transactions that occurred years before. The total final adjustment to the FLAR account alone was a deduction of $62,305,353 to eliminate the items related to false or improper entries. The remaining valid balance was approximately $44,000,000.

The testimony of William Simpson, an SEC accountant, further supported the findings of the auditors from Touche, Ross & Co., as did the testimony of the Equity Funding employees regarding the development of non-existent assets. The sheer magnitude of the adjustment, and the length of time over which Weiner, Lichtig, and Block were involved with the company, warrants at first consideration a strong inference that the defendant auditors either were totally inept or, more likely, were at least partly aware of the false inflation of Equity Funding's accounts. . . .

.   .   .

Summation

Defendants have contended that they were victims of the fraud perpetrated by the officers of Equity Funding, and that, although they might have been to some degree negligent or they might have erred in their judgment as auditors, their criminal participation was not proved. More accurate is the following comment of the trial judge made during the proceedings relating to defendant's motion for new trial:

> "The evidence, I think, does not show that the defendants were aware of the fraud in its early stages. I think they were the victims of the fraud for some period of time. * * * Even though the evidence is not altogether direct, it is largely circumstantial, it is overwhelming to the point where I cannot escape the conclusion that the defendants must have known and must have come to

a point where they knew of the fraud, and that they thereafter did acts in furtherance of the fraud."

The Equity Funding account was a large part of the business of Wolfson, Weiner, Ratoff and Lapin. Weiner and Lichtig had worked with Equity Funding almost from its inception. Weiner's participation in financial decision-making at critical stages was established. Lichtig moved into an executive position. By 1971, Block was also attempting to gain employment with Equity Funding. There is no question that a purposeful fraud was perpetrated by the officers of Equity Funding. The overwhelming scope of the fraud, its often complex but sometimes very simple mechanisms, and the failure of the auditors to find in any of the suspicious procedures cause to dig further into Equity Funding's financial records system all lead to the inescapable conclusion that defendants were involved. Even if they did not initially know or indeed learn the step-by-step fictitious entries and improper manipulations, their consistent failure to apply GAAS and GAAP after they knew some kind of a major fraud was afoot provided a basis from which the jury could reasonably infer defendants' knowing and willful participation in the fraud.

> "* * * Generally accepted accounting principles instruct an accountant what to do in the usual case where he has no reason to doubt that the affairs of the corporation are being honestly conducted. Once he has reason to believe that this basic assumption is false, an entirely different situation confronts him. * * *." *United States v. Simon*, 425 F.2d at 806.

P. Jury Instructions Dealing with Intent

We next dispose of defendants' contentions regarding certain jury instructions: those related to the question of the sufficiency of the evidence.

1. *Compliance with GAAS and GAAP*
Defendants first challenge the court's instruction on the rule of generally accepted auditing standards and generally accepted accounting principles in the jury's deliberations. . . .

We have not previously ruled on the propriety of instructions which state that compliance or noncompliance with GAAS or GAAP is relevant to the determination of a defendant's intent. The Second Circuit has dealt with similar instructions in *United States v. Simon*. . . . and *United States v. Natelli*. . . . In *Simon* three accountants appealed from their convictions on three counts arising out of their drawing up and certifying a misleading and false financial statement. The jury was instructed that the primary determination was whether the financial statements accurately reflected the company's condition, and, if not, whether the defendants acted in good faith. Proof of compliance with GAAS was deemed "evidence which may be very persuasive but not necessarily conclusive that he acted in good faith." . . .

The prosecution introduced into evidence the Statement on Auditing Standards (1973) issued by the Committee on Auditing Procedure, American Institute of Certified Public Accountants. The Statement outlines the general purpose of the independent audit, and § 110.05 explains the responsibilities of the individual auditor who finds fraud in the entity whose records are being examined:

> "In making the ordinary examination, the independent auditor is aware of the possibility that fraud may exist, * *. However, the ordinary examination directed to the expression of an opinion on financial statements is not primarily or specifically designed and cannot be relied upon, to disclose defalcation and other similar irregularities, although their discovery may result * * *. The responsibility of the independent auditor for failure to detect fraud (which responsibility differs as to clients and others) arises only when such failure clearly results from failure to comply with generally accepted auditing standards."

Under these standards the auditor is not "responsible" for fraud that has gone undetected despite his utilization of generally accepted auditing standards. In our case, failure to apply generally accepted auditing standards is relevant to the issue of knowledge and willfulness.

Sufficient evidence was introduced to raise the issue of conformity with GAAS and GAAP. During the trial several witnesses testified that many of the practices under consideration were not in conformance with GAAS and GAAP. Generally, no audit manual was prepared for each year's audit, no checks on internal controls were made, and basic standards for confirming accounts were not followed. The witnesses included Norman Grosman, a partner in Touche, Ross & Co.; Frank West, who worked on the audits from 1969 through 1972; and William Simpson and Benjamin Karchin, SEC employees who reviewed Equity Funding's books. The jury had evidence from which it could determine whether GAAS and GAAP were properly utilized and whether the failure to utilize them was such as to lead to a reasonable inference of criminal intent.

The judge's instruction, which stated that evidence regarding compliance with GAAS and GAAP was not conclusive but was relevant, was a proper statement. The weight to be given the evidence was for the jury's determination.

2.   *"Willfulness"*

Defendants also assert that the court erred in instructing the jury on the issue of knowledge. The jury was instructed that proof of negligence was insufficient to support a conviction, and that proof of good faith constituted a complete defense to the charges. The court went on to instruct the jury that, in determining intent, the jury could consider whether defendants acted in "reckless, deliberate indifference to or disregard for truth or falsity," and could infer from proof of such acts that defendants acted willfully and knowingly.

The instruction was given before our decision in *United States v. Jewell*, . . . where we held:

"To act 'knowingly,' therefore, is not necessarily to act only with positive knowledge, but also to act with an awareness of the high probability of the existence of the fact in question. When such awareness is present, 'positive' knowledge is not required."

The trial court's instruction in the present case followed closely the instruction approved by the Second Circuit in *United States v. Natelli*. . . . There the trial court had instructed the jury that, on proof of "reckless deliberate indifference to or disregard for truth or falsity," the jury could infer the defendants' willful and knowing participation in the filing of false financial information with the SEC. The defendants contended that the instruction erroneously failed to state also that there must be a concurrent, "conscious purpose to avoid learning the truth." The court approved the instruction and stated:

"The dual instruction is not necessarily required, however, when the defendant is under a specific duty to discover the true facts, the facts tendered are suspect, and he does nothing to correct them." . . .

The court properly instructed the jury on the need to find both deliberate avoidance and an awareness of impropriety. Defendants here, as auditors, had a duty carefully to investigate and review the information presented. Because the instruction stated that good faith constituted a complete defense, it was implicit in the instruction that, coupled with a finding of deliberate avoidance of knowledge, the jury also had to find bad faith.

As the Second Circuit stated in *United States v. Simon*:

"[W]hile there is no allowable inference of knowledge from the mere fact of falsity, there are many cases where from the actor's special situation and continuity of conduct an inference that he did know the untruth of what he said or wrote may legitimately be drawn.' * * * Evidence that defendants knowingly suppressed one fact permitted, although it surely did not compel, an inference that their suppression of another was likewise knowing and willful." . . .

In view of the defendants' duty because of their roles as auditors and financial officer of the company, the jury instruction was proper.

1.   Perhaps no financial fraud has received more public attention than the Equity Funding Corporation fraud. It is a significant example of how a prosecutor can use existing professional standards to prove bad faith on the part of an accountant.

2. The court of appeals held that the following instruction by the trial judge properly advised the jury regarding the conclusions they could draw from the defendants' deviation from generally accepted professional standards:

"One circumstance you are entitled to consider and weigh in determining whether the defendants Weiner, Lichtig, and Block acted willfully and knowingly while in their capacities as independent accountants in relation to Equity Funding is whether they followed or deviated from generally accepted auditing standards or accounting principles in effect at the times here pertinent.

"For example, in this case you may recall evidence of certain accounting principles or auditing standards which were talked about.

"The government points to evidence which they say establishes that, at various times each of the defendants deviated from sound accounting principles and auditing standards.

"Evidence on this issue is not conclusive, however, on the overriding issue of the defendant's [sic] knowledge and intent. The weight and credibility to be extended by you to such proof must depend among other things, on the weight you give to the opinion evidence offered by the Governments' [sic] witnesses.

"Generally, when a certified public accountant is engaged to perform an independent audit for a corporation such as Equity Funding, he represents and warrants that he will perform the audit and other accounting work in accordance with generally accepted auditing standards and generally accepted accounting principles and that he will render an opinion as to whether the financial statement of the company fairly represents its financial position and the results of its business operation.

"Proof, if any, that any of these defendants departed from such standards of auditing and accounting as were then applicable or participated in the preparation or approval of an audited financial statement that did not fairly present Equity Funding's financial position is evidence, though not necessarily conclusive evidence, that the individual defendant involved did not act honestly or in good faith, and that the financial statement prepared contrary to such standards may have been materially false or misleading."

3. With respect to the defense of "good faith," the Court of Appeals approved the following instruction:

"It is not enough, of course, merely to establish that a given defendant acted negligently or through error or mistake. Under our system of laws men are not punished criminally for mere mistakes in judgment, mismanagement, carelessness, negligence, or errors of judgment. They are punished only for intentional wrongdoing. The defendants are not on trial here for errors of judgment or mistakes or mismanagement or negligence, but are on trial for a criminal offense, and an essential element of that offense is an evil or criminal intent, which it is incumbent upon the government to prove to your satisfaction and beyond a reasonable doubt before you will be warranted in returning a verdict of guilty.

"The defendants argue that they acted in good faith in their activities relating to Equity Funding. Good faith, that is to say, an honest belief in the truth of the statement made, would constitute a complete defense here.

"If the evidence in the case leaves you with a reasonable doubt as to whether the accused in good faith believed the financial statements, auditors' certificates, and other written statements to be true at the time they were made, then you should acquit the accused.

"While I have stated that negligence or mistake does not constitute guilty knowledge or intent, nevertheless, ladies and gentlemen, you are entitled to consider in determining whether a defendant acted with such intent if he deliberately closed his eyes to the obvious or to the facts that certainly would be observed or ascertained in the course of his portion of the accounting works, or whether he recklessly states as facts matters of which he knew he was ignorant.

"If you find such reckless, deliberate indifference to or disregard for truth or falsity on the part of a given defendant when considered in the light of all other evidence relating to intent, you may, but you need not necessarily, infer therefrom that such defendant acted willfully and knowingly. Such an inference, of course, depends upon the weight and credibility extended to the evidence of reckless and indifferent conduct, if any."

¶ 5.05   A Few Questions for the Prosecutor

Imagine that you have bumped into a former college classmate who is now a federal prosecutor. After an exchange of pleasantries and an update on the status of mutual friends, you find yourself with the perfect opportunity to ask a federal prosecutor all those questions regarding an accountant's criminal liability that you were afraid to ask. With the appropriate caveat that you have no personal problems, you proceed to discuss accountant's liability on the following theoretical basis:

MR. ACCOUNTANT: I always read in the newspaper that the Federal Grand Jury is investigating this or that case. What exactly is the Federal Grand Jury?

MR. PROSECUTOR: The Federal Grand Jury is an investigative body which consists of no less than 16 and no more than 23 grand jurors who are selected from a cross-section of people in our community. Unfortunately, Grand Juries tend to consist solely of people who are either retired or unemployed. This is in part due to the time commitment needed on some cases. For example, some Grand Juries will sit as long as three years. These are called special Grand Juries. They often meet once a week throughout this period and assist in the investigation of complex crimes.

MR. ACCOUNTANT: What do Grand Jurors actually do?

MR. PROSECUTOR: The Grand Jury is primarily the body to whom a criminal case is referred by the U.S. Attorney's Office. The end product of a Grand Jury investigation is an indictment. In rare instances a Grand Jury will refuse to indict a subject of its investigation.

An indictment is nothing more than a claim. The evidence that is presented to the Grand Jurors to secure an indictment need not necessarily be evidence of the type that is admissible in court. Moreover, the prosecutor does not have to prove his case to the Grand Jury beyond a reasonable doubt. It is sufficient if enough evidence is presented to the Grand Jurors to prove that there is probable cause to believe that a crime has been committed.

MR. ACCOUNTANT: What do you mean, the evidence before Grand Jurors doesn't have to be the same as in court?

MR. PROSECUTOR: In Grand Jury proceedings the prosecutor can present evidence through witnesses that is hearsay in nature. For example, I can put an IRS Special Agent on the witness stand before the Grand Jury and have him tell the Grand Jurors what other witnesses have told him regarding the person or allegations under investigation. This type of evidence is hearsay and would not necessarily be admissible in a jury trial. However, the rules of evidence do not apply to Grand Jury proceedings, and thus it is appropriate to use hearsay evidence.

MR. ACCOUNTANT: Well wouldn't the subject of the investigation or his attorney object to this type of evidence?

MR. PROSECUTOR: No. In fact, the attorney who represents the subject of the Grand Jury's investigation is not entitled to be in the Grand Jury room during the course of the Grand Jury's proceedings. In fact, the only persons allowed to participate in the Grand Jury's investigation are the Grand Jurors, the federal prosecutor, and whichever witness is called to testify by the Grand Jury. Those are the only people allowed in the Grand Jury room. Otherwise, the entire Grand Jury proceeding is secret.

MR. ACCOUNTANT: Secret? That doesn't sound fair.

MR. PROSECUTOR: There has been and will continue to be considerable debate regarding the secrecy that surrounds the Grand Jury's proceedings. Proponents of Grand Jury secrecy claim that it is vital to assure the successful investigation of criminal activity, particularly criminal activity by organized criminal groups capable of intimidating witnesses.

MR. ACCOUNTANT: Is the Grand Jury's sole function to hear testimony from witnesses?

MR. PROSECUTOR: No. The Grand Jury is also empowered to issue subpoenas for documents and records relevant to its investigation. Moreover, the subpoena power of the Grand Jury is extremely broad. It is very difficult for a person to resist production of documents pursuant to Grand Jury subpoena. Indeed, short of asserting a Fifth Amendment privilege against self-incrimination, it is almost impossible to resist the production of documents based on the argument that the requested information is not relevant to the Grand Jury's investigation.

MR. ACCOUNTANT: Speaking of the Fifth Amendment, I recently heard a speech by a criminal defense lawyer who claimed that in matters involving so-called white-collar crime, the Fifth Amendment privilege poses some tactical dilemmas to a defendant?

MR. PROSECUTOR: It does indeed. I'll be frank, whenever a defendant invokes his Fifth Amendment privilege not to testify, he takes the chance that the jury will misconstrue the reasons for his failure to take the stand. Specifically, there are many prosecutors who believe that it is almost imperative in a white-collar crime case that an otherwise educated, articulate, and presentable defendant must take the stand and testify in his defense in a jury trial. Unfortunately, jurors sometimes fall prey to the reasoning that a defendant who does not testify on his own behalf must be guiltier than heck. Jurors often expect to hear from the defendant.

MR. ACCOUNTANT: That's not right!

MR. PROSECUTOR: I know its not right but that's the reality of jury-trial litigation. In fact, the courts where I prosecute cases are compelled to give an instruction to the jury, if requested by the defendant, to the effect that the defendant has an absolute right not to testify and that no adverse inference should be drawn from the defendant's failure to testify. You might be interested to know that many defense lawyers decline to use this instruction—they believe it only highlights the obvious problem when a defendant doesn't testify.

MR. ACCOUNTANT: So you're saying that a professional who has been indicted must always take the stand in his behalf?

MR. PROSECUTOR: No. There are instances where a credible defense can be orchestrated without the need for a defendant to take the stand. Moreover, you must keep in mind that in jury-trial litigation the perception of truth is as important as the realities of truth.

MR. ACCOUNTANT: Run that by me again.

MR. PROSECUTOR: Sure. To give you an example, you see it every day in life; it's sometimes called body language. Oftentimes we know someone is telling the truth, but it happens that because of the way they communicate it, there is a tendency to disbelieve them. It's sort of the old saying that it's not just what you say, but how you say it that counts. There are situations where a defendant frankly is not a very "presentable" witness. In those circumstances a defense lawyer has to make a judgment call as to the most appropriate method by which to present his defense. That judgment call might include the possibility of not putting a defendant on the stand merely because the jury may wrongly perceive his testimony.

MR. ACCOUNTANT: It sounds like what you're telling me is that there is a presumption of guilt in this country regarding white-collar criminals!

MR. PROSECUTOR: No, I'm not saying that. In fact, there is a presumption of innocence in this country that remains with the defendant throughout the case, until it is otherwise disproved by the government through evidence of guilt beyond a reasonable doubt. However, I'm not so naive as to discount the possibility that the dynamics of jury-trial litigation could result in a situation where more is expected, by society, of a white-collar defendant than, say, is expected from less-educated and less-fortunate persons who are alleged to have engaged in criminal wrongdoing.

MR. ACCOUNTANT: What is this racketeering statute that we are hearing so much about?

MR. PROSECUTOR: Criminal RICO is a statute that prohibits a person from affiliating with a criminal "enterprise," which is a defined term. Essentially the RICO statute, which is an acronym for racketeer influenced and corrupt organizations, prohibits a person from engaging in a pattern of racketeering, which is also defined.

MR. ACCOUNTANT: What could that possibly have to do with white-collar crime?

MR. PROSECUTOR: Many arguments have been made that criminal RICO was designed by Congress solely to eliminate organized crime. I'm not sure that Congress intended to limit the RICO statutes to a particular group of criminal offenders or to a particular type of criminal offense.

In fact, the cost of white-collar crime to the American public has been estimated to range from $40 billion to $100 billion annually. White-collar crime has been defined by the U.S. Justice Department to involve "those nonviolent offenses which principally involve elements of deceit, deception, concealment, corruption, misrepresentation, and breach of trust."

It is precisely these types of activities that have been proscribed by the RICO statutes as acts of racketeering.

For example, if a person engages in a series of mail fraud activities, he has engaged in a pattern of racketeering, as defined in the RICO statutes.

MR. ACCOUNTANT: Well, why not charge the person with mail fraud?

MR. PROSECUTOR: The answer to that is simple. The penalties for violation of RICO are substantial. They involve more than a mere slap on the wrists. They can include up to 20 years' imprisonment as well as forfeiture of a defendant's personal assets. It is precisely this type of "disincentive" to commit white-collar crime that many people believe is necessary to control and limit the growth of such crime in this country.

MR. ACCOUNTANT: What exactly is mail fraud?

MR. PROSECUTOR: There are two essential elements to proving a violation of the federal mail fraud statute: (1) a "scheme to defraud," and (2) use of the mail in furtherance of the "scheme." With respect to proving a scheme to defraud, it is not necessary for all aspects of an alleged scheme to be illegal in their separate parts, but rather only that the scheme as a whole involved fraudulent conduct. Moreover, it is not necessary that the fraud actually be successful; a crime is committed by an attempt to engage in a scheme to defraud.

MR. ACCOUNTANT: Well doesn't a mail fraud statute really apply only to substantial frauds where, for example, financial statements are being mailed out to several hundreds of people? I mean, surely not every fraud case becomes a "federal case."

MR. PROSECUTOR: To the contrary, our U.S. court of appeals system has ruled that the mail fraud statute "includes a broad proscription of behavior for the purpose of protecting society" and that "the 'law' puts its imprimatur on . . . accepted moral standards and condemns conduct which fails to match the 'reflection of moral uprightness, of fundamental honesty, fair play and right dealing in the general and business life of members of society.' "

MR. ACCOUNTANT: That sounds pretty broad to me!

MR. PROSECUTOR: You bet! The mail fraud statute has been used in our jurisdiction to prosecute individuals who have failed to disclose certain critical information in the course of a political or commercial relationship which was relevant in determining an appropriate course of action. Indeed, the mail fraud statute has been used to prosecute a law-firm partner who did not advise of his simultaneous conflicting representation of a client who was competing against another firm client for a New York City bus stop franchise. The mail fraud statute is thus not limited strictly to a scheme that involves a pervasive use of the federal mails. In fact, the use of the federal mails is merely a jurisdictional requirement. It is not even necessary or an essential element that the defendant actually mail anything himself. All that is necessary is the possibility that it was foreseeable that the mails would be used in some manner to facilitate the fraud. Thus, a simple letter may be sufficient upon which to predicate a federal mail fraud action.

MR. ACCOUNTANT: If allegations of criminal wrongdoing involving an accountant were brought to you, how would you go about making a decision whether to prosecute?

MR. PROSECUTOR: Very carefully. When allegations of serious wrongdoing regarding a professional are brought to my attention, I treat them with extreme caution and care. I am not insensitive to the great potential for harm that can be brought about to the reputation and character of a professional merely from the fact that he is the subject of a Grand Jury's investigation. Indeed, it is unfortunate but nevertheless true that in our society a Grand Jury indictment can often do irreparable injury to a professional's reputation, even if he is ultimately acquitted of the underlying charge.

MR. ACCOUNTANT:: Is that fair?

MR. PROSECUTOR: No. It's not right, it's not fair, but it's reality. Accordingly, I would undertake such an investigation with a great deal of care. The natural starting point would be the issue of the potential defendant's knowledge, that is, his state of mind.

Assuming that the accountant has been charged with some part of participation in a fraud, the question becomes the extent to which the accountant has knowingly participated in this scheme to defraud. The courts in our circuit define knowledge per the following instruction which is submitted to the jury:

When the word 'knowingly' is used in these instructions, it means that the defendant realized what he was doing and was aware of the nature of his conduct, and did not act through ignorance, mistake or accident. Knowledge may be proven by defendant's conduct, and by all the facts and circumstances surrounding the case. No person can intentionally avoid knowledge by closing his eyes to facts which should prompt him to investigate.

MR. ACCOUNTANT: What are you looking for in respect to knowledge?

MR. PROSECUTOR: Did the accountant act through "ignorance, mistake, or accident"? That is, did his acts or omission to act occur as a result of a good faith mistake or through an accident or out of sheer ignorance? Stated another way, was the accountant an unwitting dupe or fool, or did he participate in the alleged contrivance?

MR. ACCOUNTANT: That seems like a fairly clear-cut measuring line.

MR. PROSECUTOR: Unfortunately, the line tends to be blurred. This is particularly so when the issue of the accountant's involvement concerns matters dealing with professional standards and professional judgment. This is an area where I am particularly careful to enlist the aid of an expert witness to advise me as to what extent, if any, the accountant's conduct involves a substantial deviation from existing professional standards.

MR. ACCOUNTANT: Why is this important?

MR. PROSECUTOR: If I am convinced that all accountants do it this way, I am going to be pursuaded that perhaps the accountant under investigation exercised good faith. By the same token, if I am convinced that the accountant has done something that professional standards do not support or indeed professional standards condemn, then I will be equally convinced that the accountant has engaged in an intentional course of wrongful conduct. Either way my decision as to whether the accountant exercised good faith or bad faith is made easier.

I might also add that I do not rely upon the expert opinion of a government accountant alone. In making my decision, I seek out the independent, unbiased opinions of professionals who are actively involved in the day-to-day practice of accounting. It would be inappropriate to rely solely on the expertise of a government accountant or investigative agent who may not have the depth or breadth of experience that comes from being an on-line practitioner.

MR. ACCOUNTANT: That's encouraging!

MR. PROSECUTOR: There's no other way to do it! Keep in mind, however, that merely because the expert that I counsel with advises me that the conduct engaged in by the subject is not contrary to professional standards, the inquiry is not necessarily over. There are situations, although rare, where superficial compliance with existing professional standards is a subterfuge to disguise plainly wrongful activity. That is why the courts who have addressed this issue have ruled that compliance with professional standards is highly probative but nonetheless not conclusive of a defendant's guilt or innocence. The question becomes one for the jury.

MR. ACCOUNTANT: Don't juries make mistakes?

MR. PROSECUTOR: Sometimes, but not often. If, for example, an accountant was convicted on the testimony of a supposed expert witness who had absolutely no prior experience in the subject matter, and who had just recently graduated from school, it may be that the evidence is insufficient as a matter of law to find a defendant guilty beyond a reasonable doubt. Assume further that the defendant's evidence consists of the testimony of credible opinions of leading authorities in the profession of accounting. In such circumstances, it may be that the judge would be compelled to set aside the jury's verdict based on a ruling that there was insufficient evidence to find the defendant guilty. That is a power that the judge has throughout the course of a jury-trial proceeding. It is, however, a power that judges exercise with a great deal of caution and discretion. The jury-trial system tends to work. I believe that it works better than any other system.

MR. ACCOUNTANT: Is there ever a circumstance where you might decline to prosecute a case which involved a violation of the federal statutes?

MR. PROSECUTOR: Yes. Federal prosecutors are vested with a certain amount of discretion in determining whether to prosecute a case. There are various factors that are relied upon in exercising this so-called prosecutorial discretion. Among these are the quality of the evidence, the materiality of the wrongdoing, the defendant's background, factors in mitigation, and the deterrent value that would arise from a successful prosecution of the case. These are a few of the factors that we roll around before we make a decision to approach the Grand Jury. Frankly, we do not have an endless supply of law enforcement resources. Contrary to popular opinion, prosecutors are often overworked to the point of breaking. These scarce law enforcement resources have to be judiciously spent. As a result, it may be that the priorities are such that we will decline to prosecute a case that may have been prosecutable. This involves various value judgments which we all bring to bear regarding criminal law enforcement. That is, some people feel that the resources of a prosecutor's office ought to be directed more in the direction of apprehending and prosecuting violent criminal offenders. Other people believe that we cannot allow white-collar crime to go unchecked. I suspect that somewhere in between, an appropriate balance is struck.

MR. ACCOUNTANT: You must enjoy putting criminals in jail!

MR. PROSECUTOR: Not really! My only joy is ensuring that justice is done. That includes bringing the wrongdoer to justice and preventing an innocent person from being unjustly accused!

CHAPTER 6

SPECIAL LIABILITY PROBLEMS: DUTY TO CORRECT, DUTY TO UPDATE, AND DUTY TO WARN— WHISTLE-BLOWING

¶ 6.01 Special Liability Problems: Attorney's Speech

Imagine that you are a participant in a continuing education seminar on accountant's liability. The course instructor, Mr. Able Defense Attorney, has concluded his formal remarks regarding civil liability for negligence and fraud. Between the attorney and the audience, consisting of accounting practitioners, the following dialogue occurs:

MR. ACCOUNTANT: Mr. Attorney, let me see if I understand the rules of negligence and fraud. If I exercise due professional care, skill, and competence in my accounting practice, I have satisfied my duty of due care, correct?

MR. ATTORNEY: Yes.

MR. ACCOUNTANT: And if I conduct myself at all times in good faith, then I have satisfied the duty to avoid bad faith activity or fraudulent activity, correct?

MR. ATTORNEY: Yes, that is essentially a correct approach to avoiding reckless or fraudulent conduct.

MR. ACCOUNTANT: So as I understand it, I can successfully satisfy *all* legal duties and obligations by performing all my professional services with good faith and due care. Isn't that right?

MR. ATTORNEY: Mr. Accountant, the answer to that question is: sometimes you do and sometimes you don't!

MR. ACCOUNTANT: What do you mean by that?

MR. ATTORNEY: In certain circumstances more may be expected from an accountant than merely exercising good faith and due professional care in the course of rendering professional services or advice. In fact, these special circumstances can give rise to what I will call special liability considerations. These special liability problems can be generally referred to as involving (1) the duty to correct, (2) the duty to update, and (3) whistle-blowing, the so-called duty to warn.

MR. ACCOUNTANT: Mr. Attorney, I am not sure that I follow you. Just what do these duties and this whistle-blowing obligation have to do with negligence and fraud?

MR. ATTORNEY: Let's address each of these issues separately and see if we can't reach a better understanding as to just exactly what is involved.

[1]   Duty to Correct

MR. ATTORNEY: Let me see if I can explain the duty to correct. Usually, in determining whether an accountant has satisfied his legal duties of good faith and due care, the accountant's conduct is judged in light of all the facts and customary professional practice that existed *prior* to and *on the date* the professional service or advice was rendered. However, the duty to correct involves a different time frame. For example, what should an accountant do if subsequent to rendering professional service or advice he discovers a fact that would have materially affected his professional service or advice had it been known to the accountant *prior* to rendering the service or advice? What if the fact did not exist at the time the service or advice was rendered? What if the fact existed *prior* to the rendition of the service or advice?

As we will discuss in more detail, in certain circumstances an accountant has a legal duty to correct a previously performed professional service or advice that he subsequently discovers was wrong at the time it was rendered.

This duty is often referred to as the so-called duty to correct. The genesis for the duty to correct is a famous district court decision referred to as the *Yale Express* case, which is also known as *Fischer v. Kletz*. In that decision the federal district court held that the accountants there had a duty to correct previously issued audited financial statements that they subsequently discovered were materially inaccurate at the time they were issued.

The duty to correct is not limited to situations where an accountant issues an audit opinion. In fact, there are cases where accountants have rendered tax advice that they subsequently discovered was wrong at the time. The courts have held that in certain circumstances accountants have a duty to correct the faulty information and to take steps necessary to assure that innocent persons will not rely to their detriment on the incorrect information previously disseminated.

[2] Duty to Update

MR. ATTORNEY: In fact, be careful not to confuse the duty to correct with what has often been described as a duty to update. With the exception of Section 11 of the 1933 Securities Act, there is no legal obligation created by case law or statute that imposes upon an accountant a duty to update professional advice or services previously rendered. If the advice or service was materially accurate at the time rendered, the accountant's legal obligation terminates. There is no responsibility imposed on the accountant to continuously update advice or reports in the face of changing events.

That is not to say that the law would not impose such a duty on other persons or entities who may have primary responsibility for issuing financial information. For example, although an accountant may not be charged with a duty to update the financial information of a client, it may be incumbent upon the client to advise others of changing financial circumstances that have a material impact on the previously reported financial position or condition.

[3] Duty to Warn: Whistle-Blowing

MR. ACCOUNTANT: Mr. Attorney, you mentioned that sometimes special liability problems arise out of what you called whistle-blowing. What is the law trying to do, make accountants "cops on the beat"?

MR. ATTORNEY: The law hasn't gone quite that far, yet! However, whistle-blowing is a loose way of describing circumstances and conditions in which the accountant discovers material financial information that the client does not particularly want to be exposed to the public or third persons. For example, what should an accountant do in circumstances where before rendering a professional report or opinion he or she is aware of a substantial material fact that the client does not want disclosed to the public? If the accountant refuses to render a report or resigns, does the accountant still bear a duty to "blow the whistle" on the client in the event that no disclosure is made of that fact?

MR. ACCOUNTANT: Well, what's the answer to that question, Mr. Attorney?

MR. ATTORNEY: The answer is that the accountant must proceed very cautiously in the face of such circumstances, keeping in mind that the law is unclear and ever-developing in this particular area.

In a nutshell, accountants bear absolutely no obligation to blow the whistle on the client in circumstances where accountants have not held themselves out for reliance by the public. However, to the extent that accountants can be viewed as having assisted in some way the fraudulent conduct of the client, they may expose themselves to liability for fraud unless they either blow the whistle on the client or totally disassociate themselves from the client.

MR. ACCOUNTANT: That's sort of a general explanation isn't it, Mr. Attorney?

MR. ATTORNEY: I agree. In this particular area the signposts are far apart and unclear. The law continues to develop. Moreover, fraud cases tend to generate bad facts and bad facts in turn tend to beget bad law. In circumstances involving fraud, the best advice that can be followed by an accountant is to see his attorney. Together they can pick their way through the legal minefields that exist in any circumstance where an accountant knows that his client or ex-client is engaging or is about to engage in a course of conduct that could defraud others.

¶ 6.02   Special Liability Problems: The Accountant Visits His Attorney

Issues involving the duty to correct, the duty to update, and whistle-blowing frequently arise in circumstances where an accountant has issued or is about to issue an audit report on financial statements. To obtain a better understanding of the considerations involved in addressing these issues, let us follow three "days in the life" of John Q. Accountant as he and his attorney attempt to grapple with these special liability problems.

[1]   Day One: Duty to Correct

MR. JOHN: Mr. Attorney, I have a real problem. On March 1 of this year I issued an audit report on the financial statements of Rock Bottom Company for the prior calendar year.

MR. ATTORNEY: What type of opinion did you render?

MR. JOHN: I issued a clean opinion, and the audit was just that, fairly straightforward.

MR. ATTORNEY: Well, what's the problem, John?

MR. JOHN: Well, two days ago, on June 1, I received a telephone call from Rock Bottom's Controller advising that the financials overstated gravel inventory by $5 million, which is a very material amount!

MR. ATTORNEY: I see. Why don't you issue new financial statements?

MR. JOHN: Rock Bottom does not "see any sense in changing the financials and admitting they were wrong." I tend to agree with Rock Bottom, I mean, I don't want to bring any trouble on myself and I think that no harm will come from this.

MR. ATTORNEY: John, I think you better rethink that thought! To begin with, if anyone has relied on, is relying on, or is about to rely on that financial statement, you could have plenty of problems. That financial statement is materially inaccurate. You would agree, wouldn't you?

MR. JOHN: Yes, it was wrong at the time it was issued.

MR. ATTORNEY: There is no mistaking the fact that had you known that the gravel was overstated by $5 million, you would have insisted on it being corrected at the time your report was issued. Is that correct?

MR. JOHN: Absolutely!

MR. ATTORNEY: Well here's the rub, John: if you know that the financial statement is "alive," that is, people are still relying upon it or are likely to rely upon it, you have a legal duty to take steps necessary to correct the financial statements. You cannot sit back and hope that everything goes away without any problems. In fact, John, about the worst thing you could possibly do is sit back, with this knowledge, and do absolutely nothing.

MR. JOHN: Yeah, but if I make the corrections, don't I get myself caught in a situation where it is almost an admission of negligence!

MR. ATTORNEY: Absolutely not! In fact, John, it might be that the circumstances surrounding your failure to detect the overstatement were perfectly innocent and blameless. That is, it might be that you were not negligent in failing to detect and discover that the gravel account was overstated by $5 million. The problem is *now* you know it is overstated and you further know that people are relying upon or potentially could rely upon materially inaccurate information. Your conduct now reaches the level of knowing participation in a course of conduct which could be claimed to be fraudulent.

MR. JOHN: Fraudulent!

MR. ATTORNEY: Yes, fraudulent!

MR. JOHN: Holy cow!

MR. ATTORNEY: John, you must understand that the duty to correct by and large deals with a knowing failure to correct information that was materially inaccurate at the time it was rendered. The fact that you did not know of the inaccuracy at the time the financial statements were issued is really not relevant!

MR. JOHN: What do you mean it is not relevant?

MR. ATTORNEY: The duty to correct involves what you did or failed to do after you found out that the information was incorrect at the time originally issued. Thus, it is possible that you would not be subject to a lawsuit for negligence for what you did or failed to do *before* you issued the audit report. However, you could be subject to a lawsuit for fraud because you failed to correct information that you subsequently knew was false when issued.

MR. JOHN: Well, what should I do?

MR. ATTORNEY: That involves several questions, John, none of which are easy or susceptible to instant determination. We must determine who is or who may be relying upon the inaccurate financial statement, and then we must determine an appropriate method by which we can advise these people that the previous financial statement should no longer be relied upon. Hopefully, Rock Bottom will see its way clear on this issue and agree that corrections must be made.

MR. JOHN: What if they don't?

MR. ATTORNEY: If they don't, it is possible that we will have to take the initiative to bring the inaccuracy of the previous financial statements to the attention of those people who we know are relying or have relied upon the misleading financial statement. But let's not cross that bridge until we are absolutely sure that Rock Bottom will refuse to correct these inaccurate financial statements.

MR. JOHN: Yeah, I hope Rock Bottom understands that a failure to correct could mean a rocky road for all of us!

[2] Day Two: Duty to Update

MR. JOHN: Mr. Attorney, I hate to bother you but I think I have a problem.

MR. ATTORNEY: What's that, John?

MR. JOHN: Last night I was at a cocktail party enjoying a banana daiquiri when I was told by a business associate that my audit client, Top Banana, incurred extensive damage yesterday morning to its banana crop in the Banana Republic!

MR. ATTORNEY: That's too bad, John, but what's that got to do with you?

MR. JOHN: Well, you have to understand that this crop failure was due to a totally unprecedented and unforeseeable stampede of wild elephants!

MR. ATTORNEY: So what?

MR. JOHN: Well, because of this damage it is expected that Top Banana will suffer a material decline in its earnings for this calendar year. And I mean material, Mr. Attorney, like maybe a 60 percent reduction in earnings.

MR. ATTORNEY: John, I still don't understand your point. What's the problem?

MR. JOHN: The problem is that just one week ago, prior to this elephant stampede, we issued our audit report for the prior calendar year on Top Banana. That report reflects that Top Banana had a substantial profit from the banana business.

MR. ATTORNEY: Well, John, the report for last year was accurate wasn't it?

MR. JOHN: Yes.

MR. ATTORNEY: Then you have no concern arising out of this elephant stampede.

MR. JOHN: Yes, but how can I avoid not doing anything or not worrying in light of the fact that this damage by the elephants will adversely affect Top Banana's trend of earnings. Look, Mr. Attorney, anybody who reads last year's audit financial statements and sees the upward trend of earnings has got to be advised that the upward trend of earnings is not going to continue. Don't I have an obligation to pull my audit report and update it with this information?

MR. ATTORNEY: John, slow down a bit. To begin with, there is no duty imposed by law on an accountant to update an audit report that was accurate at the time it was released. You and I both know that audit reports are issued as of a given point in time. If they accurately measure financial conditions and operations as of the date they were released, there is no more that is required of an auditor in the way of constantly updating what everyone knows or should know is an ever-changing financial position and condition.

MR. JOHN: Yeah, but who is going to advise innocent investors that Top Banana's trend of earnings is not going to continue? I mean, there are going to be a whole lot of people out there who are going to slip on a banana peel if they invest in Top Banana thinking that their smashing earnings are going to continue!

MR. ATTORNEY: John, the duty to update previously issued financial information is imposed upon Top Banana, not you. Top Banana will have to take the necessary steps to assure that innocent investors are not misled because of the fact that this obviously material information was not disclosed to them. You bear no legal obligation to disclose this event.

MR. JOHN: I don't understand the law! Yesterday you told me that I had to go back and correct the overstated gravel inventory in those audited financial statements we issued for Rock Bottom. Today, you tell me that I have absolutely no obligation to correct the misleading impression that has been or will be created because of this elephant stampede. Where is the logic in all this!

MR. ATTORNEY: John, the logic is simple. Rock Bottom's situation involved what is called a duty to correct. There you had actually issued a report on financial statements that was materially inaccurate. Your name was associated with the document, which was wrong at the time it was released. It was therefore incumbent upon you to right the wrong. Here, Top Banana's financial statements were not inaccurate when you released your report on them. What has occurred is an update in financial information. The law does not require an accountant to continuously monitor a client's financial condition. Indeed, I dare say that you would never be able to satisfy a duty to update previously issued audited reports. The financial position of a client is ever changing. That is not to say that a duty to update might not be imposed in other areas where professional services are rendered. Let's just leave it at that, in this particular situation you have no obligation to correct the financial statements because they were not wrong at the time that you issued your report.

MR. JOHN: Well, Mr. Attorney, your explanation makes some sense. I just wanted to be sure that I did not have one foot on a banana peel, if you know what I mean!

[3]   Day Three: Whistle-Blowing

MR. JOHN: Sorry to bother you today, Mr. Attorney, but I think I've got a real problem: my audit of Waning Days Company.

MR. ATTORNEY: Oh yeah, that's the company whose board chairman is John Hardhead.

MR. JOHN: That's correct.

MR. ATTORNEY: What seems to be the problem, John?

MR. JOHN: Well, my bright young assistant, I. M. Inquisitive, rushed into my office today to advise me of an important "discovery" during our audit field work of Waning Days.

MR. ATTORNEY: What happened?

MR. JOHN: Well, Inquisitive discovered that the vice president in charge of Waning Days' sales has been illegally kicking back rebates to the purchasing agents for three of Waning Days' biggest customers. We concluded that the client must disclose these kickbacks.

MR. ATTORNEY: How did you reach that conclusion?

MR. JOHN: Well, it appears to us that the kickbacks are illegal acts . . .

MR. ATTORNEY: That's true . . .

MR. JOHN: And we also believe that disclosure is necessary because these illegal rebates may possibly impair future sales to these three substantial customers. We have concluded that both of these items are material disclosures which must be made in the soon-to-be-released audited financials for Waning Days.

MR. ATTORNEY: Your judgment does not appear to be particularly out of line in that respect; what's the problem?

MR. JOHN: Well, we confronted Waning Days' board of directors with the necessity of publicly disclosing this matter . . .

MR. ATTORNEY: Yes, and what happened?

MR. JOHN: I wish you would have been there, Mr. Attorney, you would not have believed the reaction by John Hardhead.

MR. ATTORNEY: What did he say to you?

MR. JOHN: These are his exact words: "We don't see any need to disclose this. Why, this is the way we've been doing business for years, and we're going to keep on doing it this way. No liberal bureaucrats or pencil-pushing bookkeeper or pious politicians are going to tell me how to run my business! And we are not going to tell anybody in any financial statement or in any other message that we're doing business this way. You take me for a fool? No way am I going to invite trouble."

MR. ATTORNEY: Was he that strong in his rejection of disclosure?

MR. JOHN: That strong! What do you think, Mr. Attorney? Do you think Hardhead will reconsider and disclose?

MR. ATTORNEY: I doubt it.

MR. JOHN: What recourse do I have if he doesn't disclose?

MR. ATTORNEY: Assuming that you believe that these disclosures are necessary to prevent the financial statements from being materially misleading—

MR. JOHN: I have that belief!

MR. ATTORNEY: Then you have very few options.

MR. JOHN: What are my options?

MR. ATTORNEY: Obviously, you could issue to the client a qualified audit report.

MR. JOHN: And obviously Hardhead will not accept such a report.

MR. ATTORNEY: Your other recourse would be to withdraw from the audit engagement and resign as the auditor for Waning Days.

MR. JOHN: What kind of trouble do I buy for myself with that course of action?

MR. ATTORNEY: Probably not as much as you would if you stayed with Waning Days and failed to disclose these material illegal acts and their potential impact on future revenues.

MR. JOHN: Don't I have an obligation to blow the whistle on Hardhead if he doesn't disclose this information?

MR. ATTORNEY: The law in this area is developing. The best advice that I can give you is that there is no legal obligation imposed on you to blow the whistle on a client in circumstances where you have totally disassociated yourself from the client and his misleading financial statements.

MR. JOHN: Aren't there risks involved that I might get sued even if I resign?

MR. ATTORNEY: Yes, there is always the possibility that an innocent third party who is victimized by any misleading financial statements may seek to assert a claim against you for failing to advise them of the fraud.

MR. JOHN: What will happen to me if such a lawsuit is brought?

MR. ATTORNEY: That is hard to predict, John. The law has historically held that an accountant has no legal responsibilities in circumstances where he does not hold himself out to the public for reliance or does not in any respect assist the fraudulent conduct of another. The problem arises out of the question of whether your conduct could be construed as knowingly assisting a fraud perpetrated by Waning Days.

MR. JOHN: How can you be guilty of assisting when you've done absolutely nothing and have resigned?

Mr. Attorney   Your arguments are good and they are the type that are often asserted by accountants in this situation. However, you must keep in mind that the law is evolving toward imposing more disclosure obligations on accountants, and it is possible that a court someday may impose a whistle-blowing obligation on an accountant in circumstances similar to this. The question is a tough one and the policy considerations underlying it both support and reject the whistle-blowing obligation.

MR. JOHN: There is something about this situation that bothers me.

MR. ATTORNEY: What's that, John?

MR. JOHN: How can I sit back and watch Waning Days engage in a course of conduct that may defraud other people and not say anything merely because I am no longer his accountant? It bothers me that I may choose to sit back and do nothing while innocent people could be victimized by relying upon the misleading financial statements.

MR. ATTORNEY: You must keep in mind, John, that there is a difference between being legally obligated to disclose this misleading financial information and being legally justified in disclosing this information.

MR. JOHN: Legal obligation and legal justification, that sounds like a lot of lawyers' double-talk.

MR. ATTORNEY: Possibly, but look at it this way. It may be that in certain circumstances, even though you are not obligated to advise others of a potential fraud, you may nevertheless permissibly communicate your advice to them. In such circumstances, the law may deem your conduct to be legally justified. Thus, you may not be liable to Waning Days Company for violation of your obligation to maintain client confidences. The question is an exceedingly complicated one and obviously involves a closer look at the facts than what we have done here.

MR. JOHN: Yeah, but I'll tell you, I just don't think I could sit back and watch someone be injured by the fraud of an ex-client in circumstances where I know I could have stopped it.

MR. ATTORNEY: I think your sentiments are valid, and I must say in other areas of the law whistle-blowing obligations have been imposed on professionals in circumstances where their former clients were about to engage in a course of conduct that could result in physical injury to another person. Specifically, there have been cases that held that a psychotherapist, for example, is under a legal obligation to notify a potential victim of threats made by the psychotherapist's client during the course of their psychiatrist/client relationship. Similarly, the legal profession is gravitating toward a rule that would apprise third-parties of information relating to their physical well-being that was obtained by the attorney from his former client during the course of their attorney/client relationship.

MR. JOHN: There appears to be very few directional signs in this area.

MR. ATTORNEY: That's correct. Moreover, the signs that exist point in one direction, disclosure of some type to prevent financial injury to innocent victims.

¶ 6.03   Duty to Correct

An accountant's legal "duty to correct" materially misleading financial statements that are "still alive" orginates from the decision in the case of *Fischer v. Kletz*, which is also known as the *Yale Express* case.

[1]   *Fischer v. Kletz* and Comments

Fischer v. Kletz
266 F. Supp. 180
(S.D.N.Y. 1967)

OPINION
TYLER, District Judge.

• • •

Sometime early in 1964, PMM, acting as an independent public accountant, undertook the job of auditing the financial statements that Yale Express System, Inc. ("Yale"), a national transportation concern, intended to include in the annual report to its stockholders for the year ending December 31, 1963. On March 31, 1964, PMM certified the figures contained in these statements. On or about April 9, the annual report containing the certification was issued to the stockholders of Yale. Subsequently, on or about June 29, 1964, a Form 10-K Report, containing the same financial statements as the annual report, was filed with the SEC as required by that agency's rules and regulations.

At an unspecified date "early in 1964", probably shortly after the completion of the audit, Yale engaged PMM to conduct so-called "special studies" of Yale's past and current income and expenses. In the course of this special assignment, sometime presumably before the end of 1964, PMM discovered that the figures in the annual report were substantially false and misleading.

Not until May 5, 1965, however, when the results of the special studies were released, did PMM disclose this finding to the exchanges on which Yale securities were traded, to the SEC or to the public at large.

Furthermore, during the course of PMM's special studies, Yale periodically announced to PMM an intention to issue several interim statements and reports to show the company's 1964 financial performance. In at least two instances, Yale was told by PMM that figures derived from the special studies could not be used as a basis for these interim statements; in addition, PMM recommended that the figures developed by Yale through its internal accounting procedures be used in the reports.

Yale thereupon issued several interim statements containing figures which were not compiled, audited or certified by PMM. As in the case of the annual and SEC reports, later developments revealed that the figures contained in these interim statements were materially false and misleading.

Plaintiffs allege that, from the compilation of figures for 1964 and its knowledge of the contents of the interim reports, PMM knew that the figures contained in those statements were grossly inaccurate. No disclosure of this finding has yet been made to the exchanges, the SEC or the public.

Within this alleged factual context, the plaintiffs assert that PMM is liable in damages for its failure to disclose not only that the certified financial statements in the 1963 annual report contained false and misleading figures but also that the interim statements issued by Yale were inaccurate. Because the bases for such claimed liability are grounded on distinctly different legal theories, the issues unique to each area will be discussed and analyzed separately.

I.
ANNUAL REPORT LIABILITY

Plaintiffs attack PMM for its silence and inaction after its employees discovered, during the special studies, that the audited and certified figures in the financial statements reflecting Yale's 1963 performance were grossly inaccurate. They contend that inasmuch as PMM knew that its audit and certificate would be relied upon by the investing public, the accounting firm had a duty to alert the public in some way that the audited and certified statements were materially false and inaccurate. PMM counters that there is no common law or statutory basis for imposing such a duty on it as a public accounting firm retained by the officers and directors of Yale.

• • •

It was, of course, during the conduct of the special studies that the inaccuracies in the audited and certified statements were discovered. The time of this discovery makes the questions here involved difficult and unique. On the basis of the Commission's *Touche, Niven* opinion, an accountant has a duty to the investing public to certify only those statements which he deems accurate.

This duty is not directly involved here, however, for the inaccuracies were discovered after the certification had been made and the 1963 annual report had been released. PMM maintains, therefore, that any duty to the investing public terminated once it certified the relevant financial statements. Plaintiffs, of course, contend to the contrary. Thus, the serious question arises as to whether or not an obligation correlative to but conceptually different from the duty to audit and to certify with reasonable care and professional competence arose as a result of the circumstance that PMM knew that investors were relying upon its certification of the financial statements in Yale's annual report.

A. Common Law Liability

Plaintiffs' claim is grounded in the common law action of deceit, albeit an unusual type in that most cases of deceit involve an affirmative misrepresentation by the defendant. Here, however, plaintiffs attack PMM's nondisclosure or silence.

It is Dean Prosser's view that, in contrast with the issues raised when an affirmative misrepresentation is involved, "a much more difficult problem arises as to whether mere silence, or a passive failure to disclose facts of which the defendant has knowledge, can serve as the foundation of a deceit action." Prosser, Torts 533 (2d ed. 1955). The law in this area is in a state of flux due to the inroads being made into the old doctrine of *caveat emptor*. Although the prevailing rule still seems to be that there is no liability for tacit nondisclosure, Dean Prosser adds the following important qualification: "to this general rule, if such it be, the courts have developed a number of exceptions, some of which are as yet very ill-defined, and have no very definite boundaries." Id. at 534. One of these exceptions is that

one who has made a statement and subsequently acquires new information which makes it untrue or misleading, must disclose such information to any one whom he knows to be still acting on the basis of the original statement * * *. (Ibid.)

Section 551 of the First Restatement of Torts, which is couched in the specific terms of "a business transaction", is in substantial agreement with Dean Prosser. The Restatement position in Section 551(1) is that

> one who fails to disclose to another a thing which he knows may justifiably induce the other to act or refrain from acting in a business transaction is subject to the same liability to the other as though he had represented the nonexistence of the matter which he has failed to disclose, if, but only if, he is under a duty to the other to exercise reasonable care to disclose the matter in question.

Section 551(2) lists the instances when the requisite duty to disclose arises. For present purposes, the following portion from that subsection is important:

> One party to a business transaction is under a duty to exercise reasonable care to disclose to the other before the transaction is consummated * * * (b) any subsequently acquired information which he recognizes as making untrue or misleading a previous representation which when made was true or believed to be so.

Although an exhaustive discussion of the cases supporting Dean Prosser and the Restatement is not necessary, an analysis of several typical authorities will illustrate the practical effects of the operation of the principles described above.

• • •

It sould be noted that, in *Loewer*, the information contained in one representation was made untrue as a result of a change in the performance of the brewery; while, in the instant case, the representation was rendered false not by a change in conditions but by a discovery that the information on which the representation was based was itself false and misleading. This distinction would not seem crucial, however, for the impact upon the person who relies on the representation is the same: he is induced to act in reliance upon a representation which the representer knows has become false. In short, the manner in which the representation is transformed into a misrepresentation should not determine

the right of a plaintiff to maintain an action for nondisclosure.

• • •

Generally speaking, I can see no reason why this duty to disclose should not be imposed upon an accounting firm which makes a representation it knows will be relied upon by investors. To be sure, certification of a financial statement does not create a formal business relationship between the accountant who certifies and the individual who relies upon the certificate for investment purposes. The act of certification, however, is similar in its effect to a representation made in a business transaction: both supply information which is naturally and justifiably relied upon by individuals for decisional purposes. Viewed in this context of the impact of nondisclosure on the injured party, it is difficult to conceive that a distinction between accountants and parties to a business transaction is warranted. The elements of "good faith and common honesty" which govern the businessman presumably should also apply to the statutory "independent public accountant."

PMM, of course, disputes the imposition of a duty to disclose and, for its purposes, properly emphasizes that the Restatement speaks in terms of "a business transaction" to which the alleged tortfeasor is a party and in which he has a definite pecuniary interest. Indeed, the cases discussed and cited heretofore involve instances where both plaintiff and defendant are economically affected by the defendant's nondisclosure.

PMM contends that the duty imposed on a party to a business transaction to disclose that a prior representation is false and misleading is "in no way pertinent to the standard of responsibility applicable to the independent auditor" (PMM's Reply Brief, p. 8) and that the obligation to disclose is contingent upon the presence of the opportunity for the accrual of personal gain to the nondisclosure party as a result of the nondisclosure.

The parties and the SEC have not supplied, nor has the court found, any cases which analyze the issue raised by this contention within a factual framework involving nondisclosure of information which makes a prior representation false. As the ensuing discussion will show, however, this does not mean that plaintiffs' cause of action for deceit must be dismissed at this stage of this litigation, nor does it preclude a rational analysis of the issue raised by defendant.

In cases involving affirmative misrepresentations, it is now the settled rule that a misrepresenter can be held liable, regardless of his interest in the transaction.

. . .

In my view, accepting the pertinent allegations of the complaint to be true, PMM must be regarded as bound at this preliminary stage of the litigation by this rule of law. Though concededly "disinterested" in the sense that it achieved no advantage by its silence, PMM is charged in the complaint for losses realized by plaintiffs as a result of its nondisclosure. This is sufficient, at least in the pleading sense, under the cases discussed, save for one remaining problem—whether or not plaintiffs must plead and ultimately prove intent by PMM to deceive by its silence.

. . .

Liability in a case of nondisclosure is based upon the breach of a duty imposed by the demands of "good faith and common honesty." The imposition of the duty creates an objective standard against which to measure a defendant's actions and leaves no room for an analysis of the subjective considerations inherent in the area of intent. Thus, to base liability in part upon subjective standards of intent of the nondisclosing defendant would blur and weaken the objective basis of impact of nondisclosure upon the plaintiff. In the alternative, if this rationale be deemed unacceptable, it can be persuasively urged that in a nondisclosure case, intent can be sensibly imputed to a defendant who, knowing that plaintiff will rely upon his original representations, sits by silently when they turn out to be false.

In light of the foregoing discussion, I find no sound reasons to justify barring plaintiffs from the opportunity to prove a common-law action of deceit against PMM. It is true that each case cited and discussed above is factually distinguishable from the case at bar.

But the distinctions create no presently discernible, substantial differences of law or policy. The common law has long required that a person who has made a representation must correct that representation if it becomes false and if he knows people are relying on it. This duty to disclose is imposed regardless of the interest of defendant in the representation and subsequent nondisclosure. Plaintiffs have sufficiently alleged the elements of nondisclosure on the part of this "disinterested" defendant. Accordingly, they must be given an opportunity to prove those allegations.

To conclude thus is not to ignore the manifold difficulties that a final determination of liability on the part of public accountants for nondisclosure would create for professional firms and other business entities (and, indeed, individuals) similarly situated. Some obvious questions can be briefly set forth as examples of such potential problems. How long, for instance, does the duty to disclose after-acquired information last? To whom and how should disclosure be made? Does liability exist if the after-acquired knowledge is obtained from a source other than the original supplier of information? Is there a duty to disclose if an associate or employee of the accounting firm discovers that the financial statements are false but fails to report it to the firm members?

These and similar questions briefly indicate the potentially significant impact upon accountants, lawyers and business entities in the event that a precise rule or rules of liability for nondisclosure are fashioned and recognized in the law. On the other side of the coin, however, as the bulk of the discussion hereinbefore has shown, investors in publicly-held companies have a strong interest in being afforded some degree of protection by and from those professional and business persons whose representations are relied upon for decisional purposes. In my view, resolution of the issues posed by the complaint allegations here in question must be made with these important but conflicting interests in mind. Proper reconciliation of these interests or policy considerations, however, can only be made after full development of the facts of this case during the discovery process and at trial.

1.   In *Fischer v. Kletz*, the accounting firm's defense was that "any duty to the investing public terminated once it certified the relevant financial statements." The district court judge rejected this defense.

The court stated that the issue before it was "whether or not an obligation correlative to but conceptually different from the duty to audit and to certify with reasonable care and professional competence arose as a result of the circumstance that [the accounting firm] knew that investors were relying upon its certification of the financial statements in Yale's annual report." The court found that such an obligation existed, namely, a "duty to correct."

2.   It is important to note the trial judge's statement that the duty to correct is separate and different from the duty to act with due care and professional competence. The duty to act with due care and professional competence relates to an accountant's conduct and knowledge *prior to and at the time of* rendering professional services. The duty to correct relates to an accountant's conduct and knowledge *following* the rendition of professional services. In *Fischer v. Kletz*, the trial judge focused on what the accounting firm did and failed to do after the firm knew that the audited financial statements were materially misleading. In finding that a duty to correct existed, the trial judge did not have to focus on the question of whether the accounting firm acted in good faith and with due care prior to releasing its audit report on the financial statements. Thus, it is possible that an auditor could audit with due care and professional competence and yet breach a duty to correct.

3.   In *Fischer v. Kletz* the accountants were sued for failing to disclose that the 1963 annual financials that they audited were materially misleading at the date of the issuance of the auditors' report on March 31, 1964. Subsequent to June 29, 1964, and prior to December 31, 1964, the auditors discovered that the financials were materially misleading as of the date of their issuance. No public disclosure of the falsity of the financials was made until May 5, 1965. In holding that a duty to correct existed under these circumstances, the trial judge noted that the "common law has long required that a person who has made a representation must correct that representation if it becomes false and if he knows people are relying on it."

The trial judge in *Fischer v. Kletz* relied on cases that imposed an ongoing disclosure obligation on parties to a business transaction not yet consummated to correct prior representations that had become false. Unlike those cases however, the auditors' representation in *Fischer v. Kletz* did not become false as a result of subsequent events or developments. Rather, the auditors' representation that the financials fairly presented Yale Express's financial condition was false *at the time it was made*.

4.   The duty to correct imposed by *Fischer v. Kletz* is not limited merely to circumstances involving audited financial statements. The duty to correct could arise in circumstances where management or tax advisory services were materially incorrect when rendered and were still being relied upon. In such a situation the accountant would bear a duty to correct the inaccurate advisory services.

It is possible that in certain factual circumstances, an accountant who renders a tax opinion may have a "duty to update" that opinion based on subsequently acquired information. See the discussion at ¶ 8.02.

[a] Duty to Correct: Its Contours.   In *Fischer v. Kletz* the court recognized that by imposing a duty to correct it was navigating into previously uncharted waters. As the court observed, many questions remained to be answered regarding the nature of the duty to correct:

> To conclude [that a duty to correct exists] is not to ignore the manifold difficulties that a final determination of liability on the part of a public accountant for nondisclosure would create for professional firms and other business entities (and, indeed, individuals) similarly situated. Some obvious questions can be briefly set forth as examples of such problems. How long, for instance, does the duty to disclose after-acquired information last? To whom and how should disclosure be made? Does liability exist if the after-acquired knowledge is obtained from a source other than the original supplier of information? Is there a duty to disclose if an associate or employee of the accounting firm discovers that the financial statements are false but fails to report it to the firm members?

Fischer v. Kletz left for further development three essential questions: (1) When does the duty to correct arise? (2) How long does the duty exist?, and (3) How may the duty be satisfied or discharged?

[2]   When Does the Duty to Correct Arise?

A threshold requirement to imposing a duty to correct is that the accountant must obtain knowledge that his previously rendered services were materially inaccurate and misleading when performed. In *Fischer v. Kletz* the accountants discovered the falsity of the audited financial statements while performing a management advisory services engagement for the client.

In the case of audited financial statements it is important to recognize that an auditor's duty of inquiry or investigation terminates with the release of the audit report. See the discussion at ¶¶ 6.04[1] and 7.03[3] regarding the duty of inquiry. Thus, the law imposes no obligation on an auditor to continuously audit a client to assure that previously issued financial statements were accurate at the time of their release. If the auditor obtains information subsequent to the release of his report that casts doubt on the accuracy of the financial statements, he must then take steps to determine whether the financial statements were in fact materially incorrect at the time of their release.

The question as to exactly when the duty to correct arises is in large part dependent upon the reliability of the information that comes to the auditor's attention. The reliability of information is in turn a function of the source of the information.

Some people question whether the duty to correct should be triggered based on information obtained from a source outside the client. For example, the trial judge in *Fischer v. Kletz* questioned whether liability would exist if "the after-acquired knowledge is obtained from a source other than the original supplier of information."

It is possible that inherently reliable information casting doubt on the accuracy of audited financial statements could be obtained from sources other than the client. Specifically, a duty to correct could arise in circumstances where a client's previously audited financial statements are discredited by reliable information obtained from (1) another client, (2) a newspaper article, or (3) possibly even cocktail-party hearsay. This is not to suggest that every wild-eyed hearsay rumor or innuendo that casts doubt on the credibility of audited financial statements will or should necessarily give rise to an in-depth inquiry by the auditor. The litmus test, however, should simply be: Is the information reliable given all the circumstances and facts surrounding it? If the auditor deems the information to be reliable, he must in turn take certain affirmative steps to verify whether in fact the previously audited financial statements must be corrected.

[a]   Case Example of Violations of the Antifraud Provisions

Securities and Exchange Commission v. Chatham
CCH Fed. Sec. L. Rep. ¶ 96,911
(D. Utah 1979)

[The defendant CPA, Nielsen, was sued by the SEC for violations of the antifraud provisions of the securities laws. The defendant had issued an unqualified audit report as of July 31, 1976, in connection with a public offering of securities by the defendant's client, Commercial Leasing Corporation.

The SEC charged that the CPA knew or discovered shortly after the release of his audit report that his client had created $200,000 of fictitious notes receivable from various related corporations who were affiliated with a company known as Chatham Securities Corporation and its president, Richard Chatham.

One of the companies to whom the fictitious loan was allegedly made was Cash Investment Corporation. The defendant CPA audited the financials of Cash Investment at the same time he audited Commercial Leasing. Cash Investment Corporation did not reflect in its financials any note payable to Commercial Leasing Corporation.]

•   •   •

8.   To make it appear as if funds had been obtained by Commercial Leasing from the public sale of its securities and also to make it appear as if funds thus obtained had been used by Commercial Leasing, $125,000 worth of fictitious notes payable to Commercial Leasing, all dated July 30, 1976, were created by Richard L. Chatham, Burke T. Maxfield, James A. Foster and Kit R. Hendrickson reflecting purported loans by Com-

mercial Leasing to World Investment Corp. ($50,000), Cash Investment Corp. ($25,000), B. F. D. Capital Corp. ($20,000), First Colorado Underwriters, Inc. ($16,000), Ogden Smelting and Refining, Inc. ($9,000), and Maxfield and Associates ($5,000).

Nielsen's Violative Conduct

9.   On or about July 30, 1976, Nielsen began an audit of Commercial Leasing's financial condition as of July 31, 1976. With respect to the Commercial Leasing loans to and notes receivable from World Investment Corp., Cash Investment Corp., B. F. D. Capital Corp., First Colorado Underwriters, Inc., Ogden Smelting and Refining, Inc., and Maxfield and Associates, Nielsen obtained confirmations of the obligations from all of said companies. The Cash Investment Corp. and First Colorado Underwriters, Inc. confirmations were signed by Richard L. Chatham, the president of Chatham Securities Corp., which company was the underwriter of the Commercial Leasing public offering of securities. . . . Nielsen knew that Richard L. Chatham was the president of Chatham Securities Corp.; that Chatham Securities Corp. was the Commercial Leasing underwriter.

•   •   •

10.   Nielsen did not perform any of the following functions with respect to the audit of Commercial Leasing begun on July 30, 1976:

(a) Obtain or examine bank records regarding the disbursement of the $200,000 from the Commercial Leasing stock sale escrow to Commercial Leasing.

(b) Obtain or examine notes, contracts or agreements relating to the Commercial Leasing loans of $50,000 to World Investment Corp., $25,000 to Cash Investment Corp., $20,000 to B. F. D. Capital Corp., $16,000 to First Colorado Underwriters, Inc., $9,000 to Ogden Smelting and Refining, Inc., and $5,000 to Maxfield and Associates.

(c) Obtain or examine cancelled checks or any other form of money transfer document to further verify that the amounts purportedly loaned to World Investment Corp., Cash Investment Corp., B. F. D. Capital Corp., First Colorado Underwriters, Inc., Ogden Smelting and Refining, Inc., and Maxfield and Associates were in fact loaned by Commercial Leasing to such companies.

11.   After his audit of the financial condition of Commercial Leasing, Nielsen gave his unqualified opinion that the July 31, 1976, financial statement of Commercial Leasing accurately reflected the financial condition of the company as of that date. In fact, such financial statement was erroneous. It showed the use of proceeds from the sale of Commercial Leasing securities, which proceeds were never received by the company, to make loans to six companies, which loans were fictitious.

• • •

15.   Nielsen conducted an audit of the financial condition of Cash Investment Corp. as of August 10, 1976, and gave his unqualified opinion that the Cash Investment Corp. August 10, 1976, financial statement accurately reflected the financial condition of the company as of that date. Nielsen testified that this date was inaccurate and that it should have been July 31, 1976. There was no mention whatsoever of the $25,000 obligation which Cash Investment Corp. purportedly owed Commercial Leasing in the liability section of the balance sheet or footnotes to the financial statement. On August 10, 1976, Commercial Leasing's books still reflected

that Cash Investment Corp. owed it $25,000. Nielsen did not qualify his opinion on the Cash Investment August 10, 1976, financials and he did not withdraw his certification of the Commercial Leasing July 31, 1976, financials. The court finds that Nielsen must have known of the gross discrepancy between his certified financial statements for those two companies since they were prepared nearly simultaneously.

16.   The signature of the president of Chatham Securities Corp., as well as the signatures of three employees of that corporation on confirmations of purported loans by Commercial Leasing of $125,000 from its securities offering proceeds to six corporate entities, imposed an obligation on Nielsen to extend his audit procedures to verify such loans, which he failed to do. The appearance of the signature of Richard Chatham on two confirmations raised the probability that those two loans constituted "related party transactions" which an auditor must carefully scrutinize by extending his audit procedures beyond what would normally be required. Such careful audit scrutiny of related party transactions is required by the Statements on Auditing Standards, published by the American Institute of Certified Public Accountants.

17.   Nielsen's failure to reconcile Commercial Leasing's bank account to verify the receipt of the $200,000 of offering proceeds by Commercial Leasing from the stock sales escrow and subsequent loan of $125,000 of such proceeds constituted a failure to perform a routine audit procedure.

18.   When Nielsen found that Cash Investment Corp. did not reflect a liability of $25,000 to Commercial Leasing Corp., he had an affirmative duty to go back and perform additional audit procedures to determine whether the $25,000 had ever in fact been loaned to Cash Investment Corp. If he found that such loan was never in fact made, he had the additional duty to withdraw his certification of the Commercial Leasing July 31, 1976, financial statement, and to notify the Commercial Leasing Board of directors and the appropriate regulatory authorities. These duties he failed to perform.

[b]   Reliable Information.   The decision in *SEC v. Chatham* demonstrates that an auditor may obtain reliable information from sources independent of his client's books and records that the client's financials were incorrect when issued. *Chatham* also presents a unique circumstance in that the court held that there existed a duty to correct the financial statements of one client based upon confidential information that the auditor obtained from another client. Thus, it is possible that an accountant may find himself enmeshed in a web of facts involving more than one client where he is compelled to make public disclosures of information without regard to any arguments or claims of client confidentiality. (For a more complete discussion regarding the ethical obligation of confidentiality, see ¶ 9.01[3].)

SEC v. Chatham also supports the view that the duty to correct comes into existence based on reliable information that indicates that the client's financials were incorrect when issued. To the extent that the information is reliable, it matters little from what source it is derived.

For example, an accountant may find himself engaging in a hearsay conversation at a cocktail party where he is advised of information that could give rise to a duty to correct regarding an audit client's financial statements. If the declarant of this hearsay information makes a statement that implicates himself in a scheme of wrongdoing, such an admission against one's interest would be credited with substantial trustworthiness in a court of law. It could be urged therefore that the information was sufficient to at least impose upon the accountant an obligation to ascertain whether correction of the previously audited financial statements was in order.

More difficult problems arise when an accountant is advised of possibly incorrect financial statements based on "an anonymous tip." Absent any other circumstances that corroborate the reliability of such a tip, there may be absolutely no basis upon which to ground a duty to correct or any duty of investigation to ascertain if a correction should be made.

The issues involved in this area may be complicated, and in large part they are totally dependent upon the quality and extent of the factual information available.

[3]   How Long Does the Duty to Correct Exist?

In *Fischer v. Kletz* one of the questions posed was how long the duty to correct lasts. In that case the court imposed a duty to correct in circumstances where financial statement users were still relying or would rely on the misleading audited financial statements. The duty to correct thus existed where the incorrect financials might still be relied upon.

In general, the duty to correct exists in circumstances where it is reasonable to conclude that the incorrect or misleading professional service, advice, or opinion is still "alive." If the accountant's professional service, advice, or opinion is a material element in another's investment, management, or business decision, the duty to correct continues to exist. Conversely, if the service, advice, or opinion is no longer a material factor, the duty to correct no longer exists.

For example, it is possible that two-year-old financial statements are no longer material in view of the passage of time. The financials may have become "stale" in view of more current and timely financial information that is available to the user. If a reasonable person would no longer rely upon the accountant's professional service, advice, or opinion, the duty to correct no longer exists.

[a] "Stale" Financials: A Difference of Opinion.   In determining whether a reasonable person might be relying on financials, reasonable people might reach different conclusions. Thus, the issue of whether a duty to correct exists is subject to the uncertainty of human judgment and the individual facts. Consider the following three district court decisions.

Ross v. A. H. Robins Co.
465 F.Supp. 904 (N.Y. 1979)

PIERCE, District Judge: This is a proposed class action brought by two shareholders of the defendant A. H. Robins Company, Inc. ("Robins") against that corporation and several of its directors for violations of Rule 10b-5, as well as for common law fraud and breaches of the fiduciary duties of the individual defendants. . . . In 1970, Robins, a manufacturer of pharmaceutical and consumer products, began to produce and market a contraceptive device known as the Dalkon Shield. On July 23, 1973, the plaintiffs purchased 100 shares of Robins common stock. During the period between the introduction of the Shield into the market and plaintiffs' purchase of Robins common stock, Robins published favorable statements concerning the safety, efficiency and marketability of the device. The Shield, however, did not perform as anticipated, and Robins was named as defendant in several products liability actions. Also, in 1972 a report was completed which indicated that the Shield was not as safe or effective as Robins had originally advertised. This report was not published, and Robins did not attempt to modify or correct the earlier statements that had been made concerning the Shield until July, 1974.

• • •

The essence of plaintiffs' claim is that Robins and the individual defendants knew of or recklessly disregarded unfavorable information concerning the Shield. They allegedly failed to correct or modify the original statements made by Robins concerning the Shield in breach of the duty imposed upon them by Section 10(b) and Rule 10b-5. Further, defendants allegedly made, or caused

to be made, statements concerning the Shield or Robins' financial condition without also stating that problems involving the Shield had arisen or that an unpublished report indicated that the Shield may not perform as well as originally stated.

• • •

The theory under which the plaintiffs seek recovery is not, however, so limited. They claim that the defendants failed to correct statements made in documents issued by Robins which were true when made but which became misleading by subsequent events. Specifically, plaintiffs claim that Robins made certain statements in its 1970 and 1972 Annual Reports and in a March, 1972 prospectus. All of these documents were issued during the period 1970 through 1972 and indicated that the Shield was a safe and effective means of contraception and that the device was becoming popular in use. However, in 1972, an unpublished research report indicated that the Shield was neither as effective nor as safe as earlier publicized studies indicated.

Plaintiffs claim that defendants knew of or recklessly disregarded these facts, and that they concealed and failed to make proper disclosure of these facts. The defendants also allegedly failed, until 1974, to disclose that Robins had been named as defendant in several products liability suits during the proposed class period. The effect of these nondisclosures coupled with the earlier Robins statements concerning the Shield, plaintiffs contend, presented a false and inflated picture of the operating and financial condition of Robins when they purchased Robins securities. Had the disclosure been made prior to plaintiffs' purchase, they say, the price of Robins securities would have been lower than that which they paid.

* * *

It is now clear that there is a duty to correct or revise a prior statement which was accurate when made but which has become misleading due to subsequent events. This duty exists so long as the prior statements remain "alive." . . . Consequently, the defendants owed a duty to plaintiffs to revise any such statements made in Robins' 1970 and 1971 annual reports and in its March, 1972 prospectus if those statements were "alive" at the time the plaintiffs purchased Robins securities. Defendants contend that these reports were ineffective once Robins issued its 1972 Annual Report. The 1972 report was allegedly issued some months prior to plaintiffs' purchase.

Both section 10(b) and Rule 10b-5 are silent as to the effect of time on the duty to correct, but logic compels the conclusion that time may render statements immaterial and end any duty to correct or revise them. In measuring the effect of time in a particular instance, the type of later information and the importance of earlier information contained in a prior statement must be considered. Thus, general financial information in a two-year-old annual report may be stale and immaterial. However, no general rule of time can be applied to all circumstances. Rather, a "particular duty to correct a specific prior statement exists as long as traders in the market could reasonably rely on the statement." 2A. Bromberg, *Securities Law, Fraud*, §6.11(543) (1977).

The prior statements at issue would appear to be of a nature that traders in the market might reasonably rely on them until publicly corrected. The 1970 Annual Report allegedly stated that clinical data indicated that the Shield "offers a low incidence of spontaneous expulsion, cramping and bleeding than other IUD's as well as greater protection against pregnancy. We feel it has great promise, in the international as well as domestic market. . . ." The 1971 Annual Report allegedly states that the Shield was "[o]ne of our most highly successful products during the year. . . . We are also actively developing overseas markets for the Dalkon Shield, in more than a dozen countries. The device already has been purchased for distribution abroad by the International Planned Parenthood Federation, and also by the Pathfinder Fund. . . ." Finally, the 1972 prospectus generally indicates that the device was marketed in the United States and Canada and was being introduced overseas. These statements indicate that the Shield was developing a significant market appeal and arguably projected a favorable future for the Shield. The mere passage of time would not alone deter the trader in the market from relying on these statements. Such reliance does not appear to this Court to be unreasonable. The defendants therefore had a duty to correct these prior statements when they became aware of subsequent events which rendered those statements misleading.

Shahmoon v. General Development Corp.
CCH Fed. Sec. L. Rep ¶ 94,308
(S.D.N.Y. 1973)

CARTER, District Judge: This litigation is a consolidated action combining for trial to the court two complaints brought against corporate and individual defendants under Section 10(b) of the Securities and Exchange Act of 1934 and Rule 10b-5.

* * *

The basic contention in respect of the corporate defendant is that it issued false and misleading statements as to its accounts receivable, its sales and earnings for the years 1960 and 1961, and that plaintiffs, in reliance on these false and misleading statements, were induced to purchase defendant's stock and debentures, suffering a consequential loss of approximately $150,000, which they seek to recover.

The plaintiff Hannah Shahmoon is the wife, and plaintiffs, Anne, Leah, Rachel Shahmoon and Rebecca Shahmoon Shank, are the daughters of Solomon Shahmoon ("Shahmoon"). Shahmoon, however, is the real party in interest in this action. He is an experienced and skilled businessman, now over 80 years of age. He has made, lost and recovered several fortunes in China, Europe and the United States. Shahmoon started his business career in China in 1912 and retired some ten years later as the largest exporter in that country. Subsequently, in 1948, his property was appropriated by the Peoples [*sic*] Republic of China.

· · ·

Defendant, General Development Corporation ("GDC"), is a Delaware corporation, and during the relevant period of this controversy its common stock was listed on the American Stock Exchange. GDC's principal business is the retail sale of homes and homesite lots in Florida and the development of planned communities. It sells these homes and homesite lots on an installment basis. In 1960 it owned approximately 190,000 acres of undeveloped land in Florida, much of it located in the vicinity of Cape Canaveral (now Cape Kennedy), the situs of the United States Space program development activities.

· · ·

Shahmoon contends that in making these purchases in 1962 he was misled by false statements in GDC's 1960 annual report and its prospectus dated November 21, 1961, one page of which he read. To be more precise, the contention is that these documents misstated GDC's accounts receivable and did not reveal that pursuant to its installment purchase contracts the purchaser was exempted from personal liability. Hence, it is contended that the 1960 annual report and November 21, 1961 prospectus did not accord

with generally accepted accounting principles in recording as sales the non-personal liability installment contracts upon receipt of the down-payment and first monthly installment, in fraudulently overstating GDC's accounts receivable, and in not making sufficient allowance for contract cancellation.

Shahmoon's testimony as to what he read and what he relied upon is somewhat confusing. It is clear enough, and I so find, that what he relied upon in making his purchases in 1962 and thereafter was GDC's extensive holdings in locations where land values were expected to skyrocket, and his own business judgment at the time that the safest and surest investment was in real estate located where land values are high and on the rise.

However, even taking his contentions as they were embellished at trial at face value, plaintiffs cannot prevail. Shahmoon only read the highlights summary of the 1960 annual report and the auditor's certificate. In the prospectus he only read the bottom line of the consolidated earnings. In October or November, 1963, Shahmoon, for the first time, learned that the installment purchase contracts exempted the purchasers from liability, and he contends that if he had known that accounts receivable listed in 1960 as $103,000,000 were not enforceable, he would not have invested the $200,000 which was expended for GDC's stock and debentures in 1962.

His actions belie his statement.

He made his purchases in 1962, relying upon a cursory reading of a 1960 annual report which in March, 1962, was obviously out of date. He also relied upon a November 21, 1961 prospectus, which I suppose could be called current. There is no testimony that he attempted, before making the purchases in question, to update the information on which he claims he relied.

Summer v. Land & Leisure, Inc.
571 F.Supp. 380
(S.D. Fla. 1983)

Between June 24, 1971 and January 3, 1973, plaintiff, Roger L. Summer, purchased a total of 9,500 shares of Land & Leisure

common stock in eleven installments at a total cost of $54,000.00. On February 23, 1978, Mr. Summer filed a complaint in the

United States District Court for the Southern District of Florida alleging violations of the federal securities laws under Sections 11, 12(2) and 17 of The Securities Act of 1933, and of Section 10(b) of The Securities Exchange Act of 1934. Mr. Summer also claimed that by reason of a conspiracy among the several defendants to defraud investors and to conceal the fraud, the defendants engaged in a fraud actionable at common law.

• • •

Defendant Arthur Young and Company's Motion to Dismiss

Arthur Young and Company, accountants, has moved to dismis plaintiff's complaint which alleges that plaintiff relied on a 1971 Land & Leisure offering prospectus containing financial statements reported on by Arthur Young before purchasing Land & Leisure securities.

• • •

As its second ground for dismissal of the complaint, Arthur Young alleges that Summer may not recover for his last seven purchases of Land & Leisure securities because there can be no justifiable reliance as a matter of law on the Land & Leisure prospectus, es-

pecially the financial statements contained therein after July 1972.

The prospectus relied upon by Summer in the purchase of his stock in Land & Leisure was issued in June, 1971. This prospectus contained accounting information and a certificate issued by Arthur Young & Company. Neither Land & Leisure nor Arthur Young provided to any shareholder of Land & Leisure any further information concerning the financial status of the company. Summer made his first purchase of Land & Leisure stock on June 24, 1971, and his last purchase on January 3, 1973, 18 months later. Arthur Young argues that due to the passage of time the prospectus became stale, and, as a matter of law, Summer cannot rely upon the prospectus for his later purchases.

In *Sharp v. Coopers & Lybrand*, the district court noted that under Section 10(b) of the Exchange Act and Rule 10b-5, a duty was imposed upon an accounting firm to correct an opinion letter after it learned that information contained in it was materially misleading, and that the failure to do so rendered the firm liable to subsequent investors.

This court finds that Arthur Young may not avoid this duty to correct materially misleading information by alleging that Summer's reliance upon the prospectus was no longer justified.

(i) The AICPA's View. The accounting profession's view regarding the existence of a duty to correct audited financial statements is detailed in Statement on Auditing Standards (SAS) Section 561, which is entitled "Subsequent Discovery of Facts Existing at the Date of the Auditor's Report." SAS Section 561 imposes a duty to correct only when the auditor "believes there are persons currently relying or likely to rely on the financial statements" which are materially misleading.

In determining whether there are persons "currently relying or likely to rely," SAS Section 561 states that "consideration should be given, among other things, to the time elapsed since the financial statements were issued."

[4] How May the Duty to Correct Be Discharged?

In the event that a duty to correct exists, the accountant should take whatever steps are necessary to prevent future reliance on the incorrect professional report, opinion, or advice.

[a] Audited Financial Statements. In the event that a duty to correct exists with respect to audited financial statements, the SEC, and AICPA explicitly direct the auditor to take all steps necessary to assure that future reliance on the auditor's report is prevented and that all parties known to be relying on the auditor's report should be advised to terminate their reliance.

(i)   The SEC's Position.   The SEC has stated its views regarding discharge of the duty to correct as follows:

> Auditors are required to make certain that there is disclosure of newly discovered facts, and their impact on the financial statements, to persons who are known to be currently relying on them or who are likely to do so. Indeed, the auditor should take whatever steps he deems necessary to satisfy himself that the client has made the disclosures, and, if the company refuses to make the disclosures, the auditor should notify each member of the board of directors of such refusal, and, in the absence of disclosure, take certain steps, including notifying appropriate regulatory agencies and stock exchanges to prevent future reliance on his report. [SEC Accounting Series Release (ASR) No. 227]

(ii)   The AICPA's Position.   The AICPA has taken the following position in SAS Section 561:

.06   When the auditor has concluded, . . . that action should be taken to prevent future reliance on his report, he should advise his client to make appropriate disclosure of the newly discovered facts and their impact on the financial statements to persons who are known to be currently relying or who are likely to rely on the financial statements and the related auditor's report. When the client undertakes to make appropriate disclosure, the method used and the disclosure made will depend on the circumstances.

•   •   •

.07   The auditor should take whatever steps he deems necessary to satisfy himself that the client has made the disclosures specified in paragraph .06.

.08   If the client refuses to make the disclosures specified in paragraph .06, the auditor should notify each member of the board of directors of such refusal and of the fact that, in the absence of disclosure by the client, the auditor will take steps as outlined below to prevent future reliance upon his report. The steps that can appropriately be taken will depend upon the degree of certainty of the auditor's knowledge that there are persons who are currently relying or who will rely on the financial statements and the auditor's report, and who would attach importance to the information, and the auditor's ability as a practical matter to communicate with them. Unless the auditor's attorney recommends a different course of action, the auditor should take the following steps to the extent applicable:

a.   Notification to the client that the auditor's report must no longer be associated with the financial statements.

b.   Notification to regulatory agencies having jurisdiction over the client that the auditor's report should no longer be relied upon.

c.   Notification to each person known to the auditor to be relying on the financial statements that his report should no longer be relied upon. In many instances, it will not be practicable for the auditor to give appropriate individual notification to stockholders or investors at large, whose identities ordinarily are unknown to him; notification to a regulatory agency having jurisdiction over the client will usually be the only practicable way for the auditor to provide appropriate disclosure. Such notification should be accompanied by a request that the agency take whatever steps it may deem appropriate to accomplish the necessary disclosure. The Securities and Exchange Commission and the stock exchanges are appropriate agencies for this purpose as to corporations within their jurisdictions.

[5]   Failure to Discharge the Duty to Correct: Fraud

If confronted with circumstances that may give rise to a duty to correct, the accountant may find himself wedged between the proverbial "rock and a hard place." In circumstances where innocent parties are relying on the incorrect professional opinion, report, or advice, a failure to advise them may lead to allegations of fraud on the part of the accountant.

Conversely, in circumstances where a client insists that correction is not necessary, the accountant will run the risk of liability if in fact the client is right and the accountant is wrong. For example, if creditors and others are advised not to rely on financials, a "bad call" by the accountant could lead to a lawsuit by the client (doubtless the ex-client).

An accountant caught in a possible duty to correct situation is potentially in a "no win" situation. If the accountant decides not to disclose, he risks a subsequent charge of civil, or possibly criminal, fraud.

[a]   Civil Fraud.   In *Fischer v. Kletz* the trial judge held that in a "nondisclosure case, intent can be sensibly imputed to a defendant who, knowing that the plaintiff will rely upon his original representations, sits by silently when they turn out to be false." The trial judge thus held that an intent to deceive could be inferred in any case where a duty to correct has been breached. Because a decision not to disclose an alleged error is a knowing, conscious decision, it becomes more difficult to defend against the claim that the nondisclosure was the result of an intent to defraud.

[b]   Criminal Fraud.   Failure to discharge a duty to correct not only lays the foundation for a civil fraud action but also a criminal fraud action such as that brought against the auditors in the *National Student Marketing* case. In *United States v. Natelli* the court of appeals upheld the jury's verdict that the auditors had fraudulently failed to disclose adjustments to previously audited and released financials, observing:

Honesty should have impelled appellants to disclose in the footnote which annotated their own audited statement for fiscal 1968 that substantial write-offs had been taken, after year end, to reflect a loss for the year. A simple desire to right the wrong that had been perpetrated on the stockholders and others by the false audited financial statement should have dictated that course. The failure to make open disclosure could hardly have been inadvertent, or a jury at least could so find, for appellants were themselves involved in determining the write-offs and their accounting treatment. The concealment of the retroactive adjustments to Marketing's 1968 year revenues and earnings could properly have been found to have been intentional for the very purpose of hiding earlier errors. There was evidence that Natelli himself changed the footnote to its final form.

That the proxy statement did not contain a formal reaudit of fiscal 1968 is not determinative. The accountant has a duty to correct the earlier financial statement which he had audited himself and upon which he had issued his certificate, when he discovers "that the figures in the annual report were substantially false and misleading," and he has a chance to correct them. See *Fischer v. Kletz*. . . . The accountant owes a duty to the public not to assert a privilege of silence until the next audited annual statement comes around in due time. Since companies were being acquired by Marketing for its shares in this period, Natelli had to know that the 1968 audited statement was being used continuously.

¶ 6.04 Duty to Update

Updating a professional report, opinion, or advice involves a different situation entirely than *correcting* a professional report, opinion, or advice that was inaccurate when rendered. The latter situation involves the so-called duty to correct.

Updating professional services to reflect changing events that occurred *subsequent* to the performance of the professional service does not involve circumstances that give rise to a duty to correct. If the professional report, opinion, or advice was accurate at the time it was rendered there is nothing to "correct." However, the question may arise as to whether certain types of services performed by an accountant could carry with them a "duty to update." Moreover, it is possible that a "duty to update" may be imposed by statute in certain circumstances.

[1]   No Duty to Update Audited Financials

In many respects audited financial statements represent a "snapshot" in time of a client's financial position and operations. Financial position and conditions are not static. They necessarily change, sometimes drastically, within short periods of time.

An independent auditor bears a responsibility, along with the client, to assure that this snapshot in time is materially accurate at the time it is taken. The client also bears a responsibility to produce a "moving picture" of its financial affairs. Specifically, if a material financial event occurs subsequent to the client's release of its audited financials, the client may bear a legal duty to "update" its financial position and advise those persons who are or may be relying on its financial snapshot of the changed circumstances.

An independent auditor stands in a different position than his or her client with respect to updating financial statements. Absent a specific statutory obligation, the auditor's duties of inquiry and disclosure terminate when the auditor has issued a correct audit report. There is no duty to update what is otherwise a correct audit report on accurate financial statements. The following case is an excellent example.

Ingenito v. Bermec Corp.
441 F.Supp. 525 (S.D.N.Y. 1977)

[Plaintiffs purchased securities issued by Black Watch Farms, Inc., an entity that sold herds of cattle. Black Watch filed for bankruptcy in 1970. Defendant Arthur Andersen & Co. audited Black Watch during the period 1968–1970.]

Andersen first became involved with Black Watch in mid-1968. . . . It performed an audit of Black Watch for the fiscal year ending June 30, 1968. . . . These figures were certified on September 11, 1968 and were incorporated, along with unaudited figures for the six month period July 1–December 31,

1968, in the Black Watch prospectus and registration statement of March 20, 1969 and the amendment thereto which became effective May 26, 1969. (This is the May Prospectus).

A second audit of Black Watch for the year ending June 30, 1969 was completed in the Fall and certified on October 24, 1969. This report showed a drop in new herd sales from $12,339,000 in the first half of the fiscal year, July 1–December 31, 1968, to $8,224,000 in the second half, January 1–June 30, 1969. The significance of these figures is in sharp dispute. However, the trend worsened. In the three months ending September 30, 1969 Black Watch's unaudited figures showed new herd sales of only $1,600,000. Andersen recognized that Black Watch had a substantial problem, since new herd sales represented the company's principal source of cash flow. Accordingly, Andersen rendered its October 24th certification on the results of the '69 audit subject to a broad qualification, expressing its inability, because of the serious cash flow and liquidity problem caused by the drop in herd sales, to form an opinion as to the adequacy of a $6½ million reserve for possible losses.

The results of this audit were included in a proposed updated registration statement submitted to the SEC on November 26, 1969 in support of Black Watch's efforts to renew the registration for the sale of managed herds. (The May Prospectus was to expire on December 19, 1969.) However, the SEC refused to permit the superseding registration to become effective without substantial amendments. . . . The agency's concern stemmed in part from the breadth of the qualification of Andersen's opinion, and it solicited additional explanation of the reasons for the qualification in order to determine whether the financial statement properly could be considered "certified" as required by law.

Black Watch subsequently abandoned its attempt to comply with the SEC's requirements. Instead, it discontinued sale of new herds in late 1969.

B. Andersen's Alleged Failure to Update

The moving plaintiffs claim never to have seen the results of Andersen's audit for fiscal '69. Yet they seek summary judgment against Andersen for its failure to insure that the contents of this audit were disseminated to them. They claim that Andersen is liable for failure after October 24, 1969, to demand that Black Watch "make full disclosure in its circulating Prospectus [i. e. the May Prospectus] of the downturn in sales and earnings through September, 1969, the cash flow problems and the possibility of liquidation at significant losses." . . . They take the position that be-

cause Andersen knew of the continued use of the May Prospectus and knew further that the financial picture it portrayed no longer reflected the true state of affairs, Andersen owed a duty under established case law and prevailing professional standards to see that the figures in the May Prospectus were "updated," [by which they appear to mean supplemented with the results of the '69 audit,] or that the truth was somehow disseminated to the public. "Permitting such outdated material to circulate for so long a period sums up Andersen's breach of duty."

In support of this argument plaintiffs rely primarily on *Securities and Exchange Comm. v. Manor Nursing Centers, Inc.* . . . and *Gould v. American Hawaiian Steamship Co.* . . . Neither case is apposite. *Securities and Exchange Comm. v. Manor Nursing Centers, Inc.*, holds that sellers of securities must inform investors of developments subsequent to the effective date of a registration which render statements contained in the prospectus materially false and misleading. Although the case thus imposes a duty of continuous disclosure on the seller of securities, it says nothing with respect to the obligation of an independent public accountant in this regard. Plaintiffs' contention that the holding of the case "necessarily applies to every professional connected with a prospectus" . . . is entirely at odds with the cases dealing with accountants' liabilities. Not a single case cited in plaintiffs' extensive briefs on this point can reasonably be read to support their argument.

The task of an independent public accountant is fairly to report a company's financial status at a particular time.[17]

It is by now basic that when an accountant certifies a financial statement it represents to those who see the statement that the figures are accurate in all material respects; a relationship is thus created between the accountant and those who see the statement

---

[17] *See State Street Trust Co. v. Ernst*, 278 N.Y. 104, 113, 15 N.E.2d 416 419 (1938) ("[The auditor's] business is to ascertain and state the true financial position of the company at the time of the audit, and his duty is confined to that.")

which gives rise to certain duties of disclosure. . . . On the basis of this representation, the accountant may be held liable under Rule 10b-5 for the preparation of false or misleading financial statements which portray an inaccurate picture for the period covered by the report. . . . In connection with a registration statement, an accountant is under an additional obligation to conduct a reasonable inquiry, but not an audit, to discover whether events subsequent to the audit period up to the effective date of the registration require disclosure in order to maintain the integrity of the portrayal. . . . Where financial statements have been certified and released to the public, courts have imposed a continuous duty to disclose after-acquired information which casts doubt on the reliability of the certified figures with respect to the period covered by the audit.

• • •

Plaintiffs' argument on this branch of their motion brings none of these principles into play. Rather, they seek to impose on Andersen a continuing duty to keep investors apprised of adverse developments long after the date of the certified report. There is no basis for such a claim. The mere possession of adverse financial information regarding a public company does not require an independent auditor to disclose it.

• • •

This remains true even if the auditor previously has certified figures for a prior period, so long as the certified statement is still accurate as of the date of its issuance.

Yarvis, [a plaintiff] who saw neither the '69 financials nor the May Prospectus containing the figures for the prior year, contends that Andersen owed him a duty to insure that he was provided with a copy of the May Prospectus as well. This claim is based on equally chimerical grounds. His theory appears to be that Andersen "aided and abetted" Black Watch's "conscious determination" to withhold this data from the preprospectus purchasers. In particular, Yarvis complains that had he seen the prospectus, he would have learned of his right to rescind, which was discussed in Note 10 of the document.

[Plaintiff Yarvis] cites no authority whatsoever which supports his theory that accountants have a continuing duty to insure that all possibly interested persons are provided with financial statements which they prepare. And we know of none.

[2]   Section 11 of the Securities Act of 1933

A duty to update or supplement may be imposed by statute. The primary example of a statute that imposes an updating responsibility is Section 11 of the 1933 Act, which relates to the sale of securities pursuant to a registration statement.

The updating responsibilities imposed by Section 11 are contained within the provisions of Section 11(b), which address an accountant's liability in circumstances where his audit report is part of a registration statement. Specifically, the accountant is deemed to be an "expert" within the meaning of Section 11. As to that portion of a registration statement which has been "expertised," Section 11(b) provides:

> Notwithstanding the provisions of subsection (a) no person . . . shall be liable as provided therein who shall sustain the burden of proof—. . . (3) that . . . (B) as regards any part of the registration statement purporting to be made upon his authority as an expert . . . (i) he had, after reasonable investigation, reasonable ground to believe and did believe, *at the time such part of the registration statement became effective*, that the statements therein were true and that there was no omission to state a material fact required to be stated therein or necessary to make the statements therein not misleading. [Emphasis added.]

As the trial judge observed in *Ingenito v. Bermec Corp.* (see ¶ 6.04[1]), the language of Section 11(b) quoted here imposes upon an accountant "an additional obligation to conduct a reasonable inquiry, but not an audit, to discover whether events subsequent to the audit period up to the effective date of the registration require disclosure in order to maintain the integrity of the portrayal."

Absent a statutory updating obligation such as Section 11(b), an accountant's audit duties of inquiry and disclosure terminate on release of the audit report (see discussion at ¶ 7.03[3]). Under Section 11(b) an auditor bears a limited duty of inquiry and disclosure to determine whether there have been any material financial events subsequent to the date of his or her audit report that may render the financial statements misleading.

This duty of inquiry is not limited to looking for material financial information that "corrects" misleading financial statements. The duty also includes searching for material financial information that "updates" or "supplements" financial statements that were correct as of the date of the auditor's report. The following case is an example of this.

Escott v. BarChris Construction Corp.
283 F.Supp. 643 (S.D.N.Y. 1968)

[The facts of the case are reprinted at ¶ 3.03[1].]

McLEAN, District Judge.

• • •

Peat, Marwick

Section 11(b) provides:

Notwithstanding the provisions of subsection (a) no person * * * shall be liable as provided therein who shall sustain the burden of proof—

• • •

"(3) that * * * (B) as regards any part of the registration statement purporting to be made upon his authority as an expert * * * (i) he had, after reasonable investigation, reasonable ground to believe and did believe, at the time such part of the registration statement became effective, that the statements therein were true and that there was no omission to state a material fact required to be stated therein or necessary to make the statements therein not misleading * * *."

This defines the due diligence defense for an expert. Peat, Marwick has pleaded it.

The part of the registration statement purporting to be made upon the authority of Peat, Marwick as an expert was, as we have seen, the 1960 figures. But because the statute requires the court to determine Peat, Marwick's belief, and the grounds thereof, "at the time such part of the registration statement became effective," for the purposes of this affirmative defense, the matter must be viewed as of May 16, 1961, and the question is whether at that time Peat, Marwick, after reasonable investigation, had reasonable ground to believe and did believe that the 1960 figures were true and that no material fact had been omitted from the registration statement which should have been included in order to make the 1960 figures not misleading. In deciding this issue, the court must consider not only what Peat, Marwick did in its 1960 audit, but also what it did in its subsequent "S-1 review." The proper scope of that review must also be determined.

• • •

The S-1 Review

The purpose of reviewing events subsequent to the date of a certified balance sheet (referred to as an S-1 review when made with reference to a registration statement) is to ascertain whether any material change has occurred in the company's financial position which should be disclosed in order to prevent the balance sheet figures from being misleading. The scope of such a review, under generally accepted auditing standards, is limited. It does not amount to a complete audit.

Peat, Marwick prepared a written program for such a review. I find that this program conformed to generally accepted auditing standards. Among other things, it required the following:

> 1. Review minutes of stockholders, directors and committees. * * *
> 2. Review latest interim financial statements and compare with corresponding statements of preceding year. Inquire regarding significant variations and changes.

> •   •   •

> 4. Review the more important financial records and inquire regarding material transactions not in the ordinary course of business and any other significant items.

> •   •   •

> 6. Inquire as to changes in material contracts * * *

> •   •   •

> 10. Inquire as to any significant bad debts or accounts in dispute for which provision has not been made.

> •   •   •

> 14. Inquire as to * * * newly discovered liabilities, direct or contingent * * *.

Berardi made the S-1 review in May 1961. He devoted a little over two days to it, a total of 20½ hours. He did not discover any of the errors or omissions pertaining to the state of affairs in 1961 which I have previously discussed at length, all of which were material. The question is whether, despite his failure to find out anything, his investigation was reasonable within the meaning of the statute.

What Berardi did was to look at a consolidating trial balance as of March 31, 1961 which had been prepared by BarChris, compare it with the audited December 31, 1960

figures, discuss with Trilling certain unfavorable developments which the comparison disclosed, and read certain minutes. He did not examine any "important financial records" other than the trial balance. As to minutes, he read only what minutes Birnbaum gave him, which consisted only of the board of directors' minutes of BarChris. He did not read such minutes as there were of the executive committee. He did not know that there was an executive committee, hence he did not discover that Kircher had notes of executive committee minutes which had not been written up. He did not read the minutes of any subsidiary.

In substance, what Berardi did is similar to what Grant and Ballard did. He asked questions, he got answers which he considered satisfactory, and he did nothing to verify them. For example, he obtained from Trilling a list of contracts. The list included Yonkers and Bridge. Since Berardi did not read the minutes of subsidiaries, he did not learn that Yonkers and Bridge were intercompany sales. The list also included Woonsocket and the six T-Bowl jobs, Moravia Road, Milford, Groton, North Attleboro, Odenton and Severna Park. Since Berardi did not look at any contract documents, and since he was unaware of the executive committee minutes of March 18, 1961 (at that time embodied only in Kircher's notes), he did not learn that BarChris had no contracts for these jobs. Trilling's list did not set forth contract prices for them, although it did for Yonkers, Bridge and certain others. This did not arouse Berardi's suspicion.

Berardi noticed that there had been an increase in notes payable by BarChris. Trilling admitted to him that BarChris was "a bit slow" in paying its bills. Berardi recorded in his notes of his review that BarChris was in a "tight cash position." Trilling's explanation was that BarChris was experiencing "some temporary difficulty."

Berardi had no conception of how tight the cash position was. He did not discover that BarChris was holding up checks in substantial amounts because there was no money in the bank to cover them. He did not know of the loan from Manufacturers Trust

Company or of the officers' loans. Since he never read the prospectus, he was not even aware that there had ever been any problem about loans from officers.

During the 1960 audit Berardi had obtained some information from factors, not sufficiently detailed even then, as to delinquent notes. He made no inquiry of factors about this in his S-1 review. Since he knew nothing about Kircher's notes of the executive committee meetings, he did not learn that the delinquency situation had grown worse. He was content with Trilling's assurance that no liability theretofore contingent had become direct.

Apparently the only BarChris officer with whom Berardi communicated was Trilling. He could not recall making any inquiries of Russo, Vitolo or Pugliese. As to Kircher, Berardi's testimony was self-contradictory. At one point he said that he had inquired of Kircher and at another he said that he could not recall making any such inquiry.

There had been a material change for the worse in BarChris's financial position. That change was sufficiently serious so that the failure to disclose it made the 1960 figures misleading. Berardi did not discover it. As far as results were concerned, his S-1 review was useless.

[a]   The AICPA's Position.   The AICPA in Statement on Auditing Standards Section 711 makes the following observations regarding an auditor's Section 11 responsibility to update audited financial statements contained within a registration statement:

.05   Because a registration statement under the Securities Act of 1933 speaks as of its effective date, the independent accountant whose report is included in such a registration statement has a statutory responsibility that is determined in the light of the circumstances on that date. This aspect of responsibility is peculiar to reports used for this purpose. . . .

.10   To sustain the burden of proof that he has made a "reasonable investigation" . . . , as required under the Securities Act of 1933, an auditor should extend his procedures with respect to subsequent events from the date of his audit report up to the effective date or as close thereto as is reasonable and practicable in the circumstances. In this connection, he should arrange with his client to be kept advised of the progress of the registration proceedings so that his review of subsequent events can be completed by the effective date. The likelihood that the auditor will discover subsequent events necessarily decreases following the completion of field work, and, as a practical matter, after that time the independent auditor may rely, for the most part, on inquiries of responsible officials and employees. In addition to performing the procedures outlined in section 560.12, at or near the effective date, the auditor generally should

a.   Read the entire prospectus and other pertinent portions of the registration statement.

b.   Inquire of and obtain written representations from officers and other executives responsible for financial and accounting matters (limited where appropriate to major locations) about whether any events have occurred, other than those reflected or disclosed in the registration statement, that, in the officers' or other executives' opinion, have a material effect on the audited financial statements included therein or that should be disclosed in order to keep those statements from being misleading.

The Section 560.12 subsequent event procedures are as follows:

.12   In addition, the independent auditor should perform other auditing procedures with respect to the period after the balance-sheet date for the purpose of ascertaining the occurrence of subsequent events that may require adjustment or disclosure essential to a fair presentation of the financial statements in conformity with generally accepted accounting principles. There procedures should be performed at or near the completion of the field work. The auditor generally should:

a.   Read the latest available interim financial statements; compare them with the financial statements being reported upon; and make any other comparisons considered appropriate in the circumstances. In order to make these procedures as meaningful as possible for the purpose expressed above, the auditor should inquire of officers and other executives having responsibility for financial and accounting matters as to whether the interim statements have been prepared on the same basis as that used for the statements under examination.

  b. Inquire of and discuss with officers and other executives having responsibility for financial and accounting matters (limited where appropriate to major locations) as to:

    (i) Whether any substantial contingent liabilities or commitments existed at the date of the balance sheet being reported on or at the date of inquiry.

    (ii) Whether there was any significant change in the capital stock, long-term debt, or working capital to the date of inquiry.

    (iii) The current status of items, in the financial statements being reported on, that were accounted for on the basis of tentative, preliminary, or inconclusive data.

    (iv) Whether any unusual adjustments had been made during the period from the balance-sheet date to the date of inquiry.

  c. Read the available minutes of meetings of stockholders, directors, and appropriate committees; as to meetings for which minutes are not available, inquire about matters dealt with at such meetings.

  d. Inquire of client's legal counsel concerning litigation, claims, and assessments. [As amended, January 1976, by Statement on Auditing Standards No. 12.] (See section 337.)

  e. Obtain a letter of representations, dated as of the date of the auditor's report, from appropriate officials, generally the chief executive officer and chief financial officer, as to whether any events occurred subsequent to the date of the financial statements being reported on by the independent auditor that in the officer's opinion would require adjustment or disclosure in these statements. The auditor may elect to have the client include representations as to significant matters disclosed to the auditor in his performance of the procedures in subparagraphs (a) to (d) above and (f) below.

  f. Make such additional inquiries or perform such procedures as he considers necessary and appropriate to dispose of questions that arise in carrying out the foregoing procedures, inquiries, and discussions.

¶ 6.05 "Whistle-Blowing": Duty to Warn

[1] Definition of the Problem: Attorney's Speech

Let us join a question-and-answer session following a speech on accountant's liability at the annual meeting of the Society of CPAs.

MR. ACCOUNTANT: Mr. Attorney, I heard you say that an accountant has no obligation to blow the whistle on his client. What do you mean by the term *whistle-blowing*?

MR. ATTORNEY: First of all, I believe I said that in certain circumstances an accountant has no legal obligation or duty to blow the whistle on his clients. Before I describe the circumstances where there is no duty to blow the whistle, perhaps we should be sure that we have a common understanding of what we mean by whistle-blowing.

MR. ACCOUNTANT: I take it that whistle-blowing is an effort to turn an accountant into a "cop on the beat"!

MR. ATTORNEY: Well, I wouldn't go that far in describing the concept of whistle-blowing. Perhaps whistle-blowing can best be described by a series of questions: If an accountant knows that his client is about to issue false and misleading financial statements, must the accountant warn the financial statement users not to rely on the financials?

MR. ACCOUNTANT: Of course! There is no way that an honest practitioner can knowingly let false financials be issued under his or her report!

MR. ATTORNEY: What if the accountant issues no audit report and makes no representation regarding the financials?

MR. ACCOUNTANT: Well. . . .

MR. ATTORNEY: What if the client is an ex-client because the accountant has resigned rather than be part of a fraud? Should the accountant still advise the financial statement users not to rely on the false financials?

MR. ACCOUNTANT: Well . . . I don't know . . . what the heck can an accountant do once he's resigned?

MR. ATTORNEY: That's a good question!

MR. ACCOUNTANT: You are the attorney, tell me the answer!

MR. ATTORNEY: The law presently does not require the accountant who has resigned to do anything more than resign. If the accountant has not held himself out to the public for reliance and will not otherwise allow himself to be associated or identified with the misleading financial statements, the accountant's disclosure obligation terminates on withdrawal and dissociation. There is no obligation to blow the whistle in these circumstances.

MR. ACCOUNTANT: I'm glad to hear that the law has finally done something right when it comes to accountant's responsibilities. That's great!

MR. ATTORNEY: You believe that this legal principle is "great." Do you see any problems with it?

MR. ACCOUNTANT: Naw! Besides, who cares? I mean, that's the law, right?

MR. ATTORNEY: Right, that's the law as it's presently constituted. Keep in mind, however, that laws change, particularly when the results they yield may be unfair or inconsistent.

MR. ACCOUNTANT: What are you telling me, Mr. Attorney? Is this law going to be changed?

MR. ATTORNEY: It's always possible. In fact in recent years the courts have stated that an accountant may be liable for a client's fraud, although the accountant hasn't breached any duty of disclosure or held himself out to the public.

MR. ACCOUNTANT: What? How can you be liable for a client's fraud when you haven't issued any report or made any representation to the public?

MR. ATTORNEY:	You can be held under the legal theory of aiding and abetting a fraud.
MR. ACCOUNTANT:	Aiding and whatting a fraud?
MR. ATTORNEY:	Abetting.
MR. ACCOUNTANT:	Is this some esoteric legal theory?
MR. ATTORNEY:	No, it's a rule of law that prohibits a person from aiding another person's efforts to defraud an innocent person. Aiding and abetting involves those circumstances or "special relationships" where a person substantially assists the known fraud of another person.
MR. ACCOUNTANT:	How can an accountant "substantially assist" an ex-client's fraud when he has not issued any report or made any representation?
MR. ATTORNEY:	What if an accountant has prepared accounting books and records for a client and the accountant discovers that they are false and fraudulent. Assume that the accountant also knows that a bank will be relying on financials prepared by the client from these false financial records? Although the accountant has not issued any report, hasn't his conduct substantially assisted his client's fraud?
MR. ACCOUNTANT:	Possibly. But, in this situation the accountant has not issued any public report. . . .
MR. ATTORNEY:	Shouldn't the accountant nevertheless advise the bank not to rely on the *false* financial records, which the accountant helped prepare?
MR. ACCOUNTANT:	[Silence].
MR. ATTORNEY:	Let me give you another example of the problems involved with the doctrine of aiding and abetting. Assume that a client has materially overstated inventory. The accountant has prepared draft financials that contain this material overstatement. The client receives the accountant's draft financial statement, which bears the accounting firm's letterhead.
MR. ACCOUNTANT:	Okay. I follow you. What's next?
MR. ATTORNEY:	Assume that after sending the draft financials to the client the accountant discovers the material overstatement. The accountant advises the client of the discovery and the need to correct the draft. The client refuses to make the correction—and . . .
MR. ACCOUNTANT:	—I would quit right then and there. So what's the problem?
MR. ATTORNEY:	The problem arises when the accountant subsequently discovers that the client has sent a banker the draft financials, which are incorrect. The accountant knows that the banker will decide whether to continue to loan money to the accountant's ex-client based on this draft. That's how the banker has done it in the past. What should the accountant do? If he sits back and does nothing while the banker is being defrauded, has the accountant "substantially assisted" his ex-client's fraud?

MR. ACCOUNTANT: This is a difficult situation. Why not just tell the banker the draft financials are misleading and to not rely on them?

MR. ATTORNEY: What if the accountant is wrong? What if the draft financials are in fact correct; inventory was not overstated?

MR. ACCOUNTANT: What would happen to the accountant?

MR. ATTORNEY: The accountant could be sued for defamation. The accountant could also be sued by the ex-client for breach of the professional obligation of confidentiality.

MR. ACCOUNTANT: Hmmm . . . maybe the accountant should say nothing?

MR. ATTORNEY: Let's change one fact in this example. Assume that the accountant discovers that inventory is materially overstated but that the discovery occurs *one day after* the accountant has issued the final audit report.

MR. ACCOUNTANT: You mean the audit report has been released and the accountant now discovers the financials are incorrect?

MR. ATTORNEY: Yes.

MR. ACCOUNTANT: Isn't that the duty to correct situation?

MR. ATTORNEY: Yes. In those circumstances the accountant has a legal obligation to make sure that the bank no longer relies upon the misleading financials.

MR. ACCOUNTANT: The accountant has an obligation to blow the whistle on the client one day after the audit report is released?

MR. ATTORNEY: Yes.

MR. ACCOUNTANT: But the accountant does not have a legal obligation to blow the whistle on the client *before* the final false financials and audit report are released even though false draft financials have been issued by the client to its bank?

MR. ATTORNEY: It's possible.

MR. ACCOUNTANT: What do you mean "possible"? Does the accountant have an obligation or not?

MR. ATTORNEY: There is no yes-or-no answer to that question. Fraud issues are simply too explosive. They do not lend themselves to simple instructions regarding how to avoid being sued. It's possible that the accountant's failure to advise the bank not to rely on the false draft financials could be held to constitute substantial assistance of a known fraud.

MR. ACCOUNTANT: It sounds like the accountant should warn a potential victim of an impending disaster.

MR. ATTORNEY: That's the way the law is gravitating. You might call it a "duty to warn" of an impending financial crime.

MR. ACCOUNTANT: Why haven't the courts imposed an absolute duty to warn potential victims of financial crimes?

MR. ATTORNEY: I'm sure that one of the reasons relates to the impact that such a duty would have on the communications and relationship between an accountant and client.

MR. ACCOUNTANT: I'm sure that some of my clients would be reluctant to discuss sensitive matters with me if they believed that I could not preserve their confidences.

MR. ATTORNEY: That's one of the arguments. But it may not be enough to avoid imposition of a duty to warn. Simply stated: to the extent that a fraud would have been prevented or aborted by some type of warning to the unsuspecting financial statement user or to regulatory officials, an accountant's failure to warn will be seriously scrutinized and possibly challenged in court.

MR. ACCOUNTANT: Yeah, but if I have no legal obligation or duty to blow the whistle, won't I win?

MR. ATTORNEY: Remember this about fraud cases: fraud cases necessarily involve bad facts and, as the saying goes, "bad facts often beget bad law." Also remember the corollary saying that "bad facts often result in big liability."

MR. ACCOUNTANT: It sounds like you are saying that even when he should win an accountant caught in a client's fraud could lose.

MR. ATTORNEY: That's it, plus an accountant caught as a defendant in litigation must always realize that even when he wins, he still loses.

[2]   Perspective: An Accountant Should Not Bear the Role of a "Cop on the Beat"

When The Rules Say: "See Your Lawyer"[1]

• • •

Client's Unauthorized or Improper Use of the CPA's Name or Work Product and "Whistle-Blowing"

Many accountants encounter situations in which a client is using a CPA's name im-

---

[1] Charles Chazen, Richard L. Miller, Jr., and Kenneth I. Solomon, "When the Rules Say: 'See Your Lawyer,' " *Journal of Accountancy*, AICPA, January 1981. Copyright © 1981 by the AICPA, Inc. Opinions expressed in the *Journal of Accountancy* are those of editors and contributors. Publication in the *Journal of Accountancy* does not constitute endorsement by the AICPA or its committees.

properly, inaccurately, excessively or without authorization. This may take place in connection with projections, tax opinions, acquisition analyses or other types of limited purpose reports. Occasionally, clients will issue prematurely to third parties incomplete drafts of financial statements or other work products prepared by the CPA. In such cases, wouldn't it be wise for the CPA to seek advice of legal counsel on the course of action the CPA should pursue?

Apart from circumstances when, without prior authorization or approval, the client associates or identifies the auditor with potentially misleading information, what should an auditor do when a client intends to issue materially misleading information with which the auditor will not be identified because he has decided to withdraw and terminate the engagement? Even if the withdrawal decision was clear, isn't it equally clear that an attorney should be consulted regarding any legal loose ends which may lurk in the wake of withdrawal?

While professional standards direct in certain circumstances that the auditor would be "well advised to consult," or "should consider consulting" or "may wish to consult" with legal counsel, it is noteworthy that the SAS which has dealt most extensively with the need for consultation with legal counsel—SAS no. 17—interposes two different admonitions regarding seeking legal guidance. In the case of possible withdrawal from an engagement in connection with (1) illegal acts having a quantitatively material effect on the financial statements and (2) illegal acts which are qualitatively material because they bear adversely on management's integrity or the reliability of the client's books and records, SAS no. 17 recommends that the auditor *"may wish* to consult with his legal counsel." However, with respect to determining whether there is a need to notify parties other than personnel within the client's organization of an illegal act, SAS no. 17 directs that the auditor *"should* consult with his legal counsel." (Emphases added.)

This distinction between recommending and directing that the auditor obtain legal guidance is more than a mere editorial difference. The entire area of questionable and illegal acts (with the latter category by definition also including material management fraud) is an extremely sensitive one, requiring great care and prudence on the part of the auditor as well as those who advise him on appropriate conduct in the circumstances. Particularly sensitive is the concept of "whistle-blowing" to regulatory or law enforcement bodies, and that is why the professional statements direct, rather than suggest, legal counsel's input.

When an auditor has withdrawn from an engagement because the client (1) has declined to make disclosures necessary to prevent its financial statements from being materially misleading and (2) has otherwise refused to accept a qualified or disclaimed opinion audit report, the auditor is not affirm-atively obligated to "blow the whistle" on the former client to regulatory authorities or other parties. Any suggestion that a whistle-blowing obligation exists in such circumstances is without support in the Code of Professional Ethics, accounting principles, auditing standards or judicial decisions. Because the auditor will not hold himself out to the public for reliance and will not otherwise allow himself to be associated or identified with the financial statements, his disclosure obligation terminates on withdrawal and dissociation as auditor. As the court held in *Gold v. DCL Incorporated*,[2] "There is, however, no basis in principle or authority for extending an auditor's duty to disclose beyond cases where the auditor is giving or has given some representation or certification."

Quite apart from the lack of any sound legal basis on which to ground a whistle-blowing obligation in these circumstances,[3] there are very strong policy reasons militating against such an obligation. Not only might such an obligation cause clients to be reticent to discuss questionable matters with a professional adviser who is compelled to disclose such information to a regulatory agency, thus depriving the auditor of what could be essential information, but such an obligation could also create the potential for the greater harm that clients might take active steps to intentionally conceal information from the auditor relating to possibly sensitive and questionable matters. The unfortunate result in many cases could be a misleading financial presentation and report.

That a whistle-blowing obligation would have a chilling effect on auditor-client communications and could impair the entire audit process has been recognized by no less an authority than Securities and Exchange Commission Chairman Harold Williams, who has testified on this issue at Senate oversight hearings regarding the accounting profession:

---

[2] *Gold v. DCL Incorporated*, 339 F.Supp. 1123, 1127 (S.D.N.Y. 1973).

[3] In circumstances which will give rise to a duty to correct, as discussed on page 61, there may exist a whistle-blowing obligation. See SAS no. 1, *Codification of Auditing Standards and Procedures* (New York: AICPA, 1973). See also *AICPA Professional Standards*, AU sec. 561.08.

Senator Eagleton: What about the question of the accountant's obligation to disclose potentially criminal activity that the accountant discovers in the course of his audit? To whom should the accountant report such facts within the corporation?

Chairman Williams: The law is not totally clear, I suspect; but, from our standpoint, to the client, certainly the audit committee—

Senator Eagleton: To the audit committee.

Chairman Williams: Yes.

Senator Eagleton: Does the accountant have any further obligation to report it to any public body; for example, you, the Securities and Exchange Commission, or prosecutorial authorities?

Chairman Williams: No, sir. I think, under certain circumstances, he may well have an obligation to see to it that the information is disclosed in the financial statements or else to resign the account; but no obligation, under normal circumstances, to report it to either the prosecutorial authorities or the SEC.

Senator Eagleton: You are saying that is what his current obligation under the law is.

Chairman Williams: That is right.

Senator Eagleton: What do you think the law should be?

Chairman Williams: I think that is the way the law ought to be. I think there are certain circumstances where, when the auditor resigns, under the disclosure obligations, the resignation of the auditor is required to be disclosed. It may well come out in the wash. But I think that is the extent of the obligation. I think that is where the law ought to be.

We have to balance several things here. I think we have to balance on the one hand the desire that improper activity of the type you are describing be brought to light and dealt with. But, at the same time, I think we have to be concerned about—while we have to be sure that the auditors are independent, by the same token I think we need to be sure that the relationship, their ability to gain access or ability to get information from the corporation, which includes really the relationship and the quality and candor that exists between the management and the other people in the organization and the auditor, be one that is open. There is a balancing there between two public interests.

Senator Eagleton: So you think the auditor satisfies his obligation if he reports his findings and suspicions to the audit committee.

Chairman Williams: I think that is right, sir. And, under certain circumstances, as I say, either requires that the matter be disclosed by the company or resigns the account.

Apart from creating an unhealthy situation between the client and auditor, imposition of the onus for whistle-blowing on the auditor is unnecessary. Existing professional standards effectively place such a burden on the client. If the client declines to make disclosures necessary to prevent its financial statements from being materially misleading and refuses to accept a qualified or disclaimed opinion audit report, the auditor is then compelled to withdraw from the engagement. In such circumstances, withdrawal by an auditor is tantamount to whistle-blowing and results from the client's decision not to disclose. Such a system has as its virtues the preservation of client confidentiality and the free flow of client-auditor communications, while assuring that an isolated occurrence of material management fraud known to the disengaging auditor will not go unnoticed by a regulatory agency such as the SEC[4] or any successor auditor.

Although an auditor is not legally obligated to blow the whistle on a former client, there may exist circumstances, however, where the auditor is legally justified in making a disclosure to a regulatory agency or a nonclient third party, particularly when the auditor has concluded that the former or existing client may be perpetrating or is about to perpetrate a fraud or mislead individuals specifically known to the auditor. For example, if a client has distributed to a third party draft financial statements prepared by the CPA for internal use only, the CPA would be justified—but not necessarily obligated—in contacting the third party in the absence of the client's agreement to rectify the situation.

---

[4] SEC form 8-K requires (1) all registrants who file reports with the commission to disclose a change in auditors and the reasons therefor if the change was precipitated by a disagreement over matters of disclosure, accounting or auditing and (2) a corroborating letter from the auditors.

Similarly, an auditor may be justified in publicly disclosing the materially misleading nature of other client information contained within an annual report or a prospectus for which the auditor has not assumed responsibility and to which he has not consented, although his report on the financial statements is a part of the document.

Clearly, however, an auditor's decision to publicly disclose the materially misleading nature of client information published without the auditor's consent or assumption of responsibility should be the result of the exercise of his considered judgment in light of all the circumstances. In no instance should the auditor be absolutely obligated or otherwise bear a duty to make public disclosure when the misleading information was issued without the auditor's prior consent or active assistance.[5]

When the auditor has not done anything to facilitate or otherwise assist a client's misleading ways, the CPA has no obligation in such circumstances to be his client's keeper, and, accordingly, the CPA cannot be faulted for mere inaction. However, when the client has intentionally and without authorization associated or involved the CPA in its misleading conduct, the CPA should be fully justified in taking action to right the wrong. Given the legal complexities of such situations as well as possible consequences, the counsel of caution is clear, "See your attorney before you do anything!"

---

[5] The soundness of this principle is illustrated by *Wessel v. Buhler*, 437 F.2d 279, 283 (9th Cir. 1971), and *Mendelsohn v. Capital Underwriters, Inc.*, CCH Fed. Sec. L. Rep. [Current] ¶96,448 (N.D. Cal. 1979).

[a]   Comment: The Accountant Is a "Public Watchdog," Says the U.S. Supreme Court.

1.   The authors of the preceding extract contend that imposing a "whistle-blowing obligation" on auditors would have a "chilling effect on auditor-client communications and could impair the entire audit process." This same argument was made by the auditing profession to the U.S. Supreme Court in the case of *United States v. Arthur Young & Co.* (See ¶ 8.03[3] for the decision.)

In that case the auditing profession argued that the IRS should not be able to obtain the tax contingency (accrual) work papers prepared by the independent auditors. The auditors argued that providing IRS access to such confidential information would inhibit communications between the auditor and client.

The U.S. Supreme Court totally rejected the auditing profession's argument.

2.   In rejecting the auditing profession's request for a privilege covering the tax contingency work papers, the U.S. Supreme Court stated that auditors are "public watchdogs," holding:

Nor do we find persuasive the argument that a work-product immunity for accountants' tax accrual workpapers is a fitting analogue to the attorney work-product doctrine established in *Hickman v. Taylor, supra*. The *Hickman* work-product doctrine was founded upon the private attorney's role as the client's confidential advisor and advocate, a loyal representative whose duty it is to present the client's case in the most favorable possible light. An independent certified public accountant performs a different role. By certifying the public reports that collectively depict a corporation's financial status, the independent auditor assumes a *public* responsibility transcending any employment relationship with the client. The independent public accountant performing this special function owes ultimate allegiance to the corporation's creditors and stockholders, as well as to investing public. This "public watchdog" function demands that the accountant maintain total independence from the client at all times and requires complete fidelity to the public trust.

To insulate from disclosure a certified public accountant's interpretations of the client's financial statements would be to ignore the significance of the accountant's role as a disinterested analyst charged with public obligations.

We cannot accept the view that the integrity of the securities markets will suffer absent some protection for accountants' tax accrual workpapers. The Court of Appeals apparently feared that, were the IRS to have access to tax accrual workpapers, a corporation might be tempted to withhold from its auditor certain information relevant and material to a proper evaluation of its financial statements. But the independent certified public accountant cannot be content with the corporation's representations that its tax accrual reserves are adequate; the auditor is ethically and professionally obligated to ascertain for himself as far as possible whether the corporation's contingent tax liabilities have been accurately stated. If the auditor were convinced that the scope of the examination had been limited by management's reluctance to disclose matters relating to the tax accrual reserves, the auditor would be unable to issue an unqualified opinion as to the accuracy of the corporation's financial statements. Instead, the auditor would be required to issue a qualified opinion, an adverse opinion, or a disclaimer of opinion, thereby notifying the investing public of possible potential problems inherent in the corporation's financial reports. Responsible corporate management would not risk a qualified evaluation of a corporate taxpayer's financial posture to afford cover for questionable positions reflected in a prior tax return. Thus, the independent auditor's obligation to serve the public interest assures that the integrity of the securities markets will be preserved, without the need for a work-product immunity for accountants' tax accrual workpapers.

[3] *Gold v. DCL Inc.* and Comments

Gold v. DCL Inc.
399 F.Supp. 1123 (S.D.N.Y. 1973)

FRANKEL, District Judge: The plaintiff, a lawyer and experienced investor, claims to have been misled by material omissions affecting certain stock purchases so that he lost money rather than winning, as he had hoped to do. In a now common kind of action, he sues for himself and his alleged class under §§ 10(b), 20, and 27 of the Securities Exchange Act of 1934, and Rule 10b-5.

The securities involved are the common shares of defendant DCL Incorporated, of which plaintiff bought 500 on February 10 (at $10⅜), 500 on February 14 (at $10), and 1,000 on March 13, 1972 (at $9½).

DCL is in the business of short-term leasing of computers, primarily the System/360 series which it purchases from IBM. The short leases which DCL must offer to remain competitive with IBM do not afford sufficient return to recoup the purchase price of the computers. Consequently, it is essential that DCL remarket its equipment by securing lease renewals or new lessees, or by selling its computers. Obsolescence of a computer "portfolio," as the inventory appears to be called, is a major industrial threat to a remarketing program. It was, therefore, a matter of potential concern for DCL that in 1970 IBM announced its intention to introduce a new, more powerful computer line, the System/370.

During the year 1971 and until February 15, 1972, defendant Price Waterhouse & Co. served as DCL's independent auditing firm. In December 1971, Price Waterhouse informed DCL that it intended as of then to qualify its opinion of DCL's 1971 financial statements by making its opinion

> subject to the ability of the Company to fully recover the cost of its computer equipment by lease renewals, by attracting new lessees and by sale of equipment.

This became a subject of dispute that was to lead soon to severance of the relationship. DCL requested, perhaps demanded, that

Price Waterhouse study DCL's portfolio, re-marketing program, and depreciation sched-ule, as well as the computer leasing industry in general, in order to recommend steps which would enable Price Waterhouse to avoid qualifying its opinion. Price Waterhouse de-clined to do so, however, maintaining that its position rested upon considerations per-vading the computer leasing industry rather than factors peculiar to DCL. As has been noted, DCL discharged Price Waterhouse on February 15, 1972, having therefore (1) ob-tained the opinion of Touche Ross & Co. that there was no reason for DCL to change its policies concerning its portfolio of System/360 computers, and (2) arranged for the ser-vices of Lybrand, Ross Bros. & Montgomery as independent auditors. The latter firm ul-timately certified DCL's 1971 figures without any qualification of the kind Price Waterhouse had contemplated.

The problems of new leases and remar-keting as they affected companies like DCL appear not to have been secret during the period here in question and for some time before that. For example, such articles as "Computer-Leasing Firms Offer Discounts by Gambling on Long Lives for Machines" and "Computer Lessors Worried About Rental of Their Old Machines, Threat of New Ones," as well as others describing the industry structure and remarketing efforts, appeared in the Wall Street Journal on various dates in 1967, 1968, and 1970, and in the August 1968 issue of Datamation, an industry mag-azine. In addition, DCL's published state-ments, e.g., its original prospectus of August 27, 1968, its 1970 Annual Report, and a March 1, 1971, listing application to the American Stock Exchange, stressed remarketing prob-lems. Nevertheless, plaintiff's claim focuses on:

1. the failure to mention this problem at the key times involved here, and, seemingly more importantly,

2. the failure to mention on February 8, 1972, Price Waterhouse's intention to qualify upon grounds of this concern its certification of the 1971 figures.

The importance of the date February 8, 1972, for this lawsuit results from the fact that DCL on that day announced *unaudited* figures showing earnings per share of 96 cents for 1971 as compared with 48 cents for the prior year. "No mention was made that defendant Price Waterhouse had stated to defendant DCL that such earnings should be accompanied by a warning to investors that they were subject to the ability of de-fendant DCL to remarket certain of its in-ventory items." The cheerful 1971 figures, absent the Price Waterhouse caveat, are claimed by plaintiff to have caused the sus-taining of DCL's common stock price at a level substantially higher than what it would have been had that warning cloud been ex-posed. Continuing his account of the alleged wrongs, plaintiff tells that DCL's annual report, issued in April 1972, finally recounted the Price Waterhouse disagreement and dis-charge and that, "as a direct consequence thereof, defendant DCL's common stock fell drastically in price."

Upon the fuller allegations thus summa-rized, plaintiff makes two sets of claims:

1. against DCL and its directors named here as defendants for perpetrating a scheme and artifice to defraud the investing public by is-suing a misleading earnings statement in or-der to cause DCL's common stock to trade at an artificially high price; and

2. against Price Waterhouse for failing to "take steps to inform the public that the fi-nancial information disseminated by defend-ant DCL was, in its opinion, incomplete and misleading."

For reasons hereinafter outlined, the com-plaint will be dismissed as against Price Waterhouse, but the suit will be allowed to proceed as a class action against the re-maining defendants.

1.   Plaintiff, in a letter to this court, orig-inally characterized the issue of Price Water-house's liability as being one solely of law, concerning the duties and responsibilities of an independent auditor to the investing public. Now, however, plaintiff contends that his po-sition is based upon several material and disputed factual assumptions—namely whether Price Waterhouse was still DCL's independent auditor at the time of DCL's

earnings release; whether, in connection with its work for DCL, Price Waterhouse had obtained sufficient information to cause it to qualify its opinion; and whether Price Waterhouse performed services in connection with the earnings release.

Contrary to plaintiff's assertion, these subjects are either not issues or not material. As DCL's own documents (e.g., the 8-K form filed with the SEC on February 28, 1972) demonstrate, Price Waterhouse remained as DCL's independent auditor until February 15, 1972, when it was fired by DCL. Secondly, it is for reasons hereinafter outlined, neither important nor disputed that Price Waterhouse had reasons it deemed sufficient (though others disagreed) to warrant a qualification. Finally, plaintiff offers no support whatsoever for his contention, which he raised for the first time in the papers opposing the motion for summary judgment, that Price Waterhouse prepared the earnings figures released by DCL. Nor—what is dispositive in any case— does he even allege that the figures were erroneous. In any event, as can be seen from the discussion which follows, the issue is not material. The question of Price Waterhouse's liability is ripe for decision now.

Plaintiff seeks to hold this defendant liable either on the theory that (1) as DCL's auditor Price Waterhouse owed investors an independent duty to come forward, after DCL's press release, and disclose its intended qualification or (2) Price Waterhouse's failure to disclose the proposed qualification aided and abetted DCL's market manipulation. Both theories are bottomed on plaintiff's contention that the "investing public * * * had the right to infer that the 1971 earnings reported therein accurately reflected defendant Price Waterhouse's opinion as to earnings."

The parties agree that mere possession and nondisclosure of material facts does not alone create liability under Rule 10b-5; there must be, in addition, some relationship which generates a duty to inform.

In this case plaintiff contends that Price Waterhouse's duty arose from its status as DCL's independent auditor, making it responsible not just to its employer but to all persons relying on its figures. There is, however, no basis in principle or authority for extending an auditor's duty to disclose beyond cases where the auditor is giving or has given some representation or certification. Where it gives an opinion or certifies statements, an auditing firm publicly assumes a role that carries a special relationship of trust vis-à-vis the public. The auditor in such a case holds itself out as an independent professional source of assurance that the audited company's financial presentations are accurate and reliable. . . . The importance of the act of certifying is such that a continuing duty to disclose has been imposed where the auditor learns facts revealing that a certification believed correct when issued was actually unwarranted. *Fischer v. Kletz*, 266 F. Supp. 180 (S.D.N.Y. 1967).

In the vitally different circumstances of this case, Price Waterhouse issued no public opinion, rendered no certification, and in no way invited the public to rely on its financial judgment at or around the time in question. The earnings information of which plaintiff complains was disclosed by DCL, which specifically noted that the figures were unaudited. The situation is utterly lacking in the kind of special relationship which has heretofore imposed on auditors a duty of disclosure. The point is highlighted by the inconsistent positions assumed by the plaintiff in this case. Observing that he is "a practicing attorney" and "a well informed, sophisticated investor," he argues that the status of independent auditor, without more, creates a duty to disclose whether or not any opinion or certification is being rendered. On the other hand, plaintiff testified that at the time of his purchases he was not aware that Price Waterhouse had ever acted as independent auditors for DCL in connection with any of their consolidated financial statements. Similarly, he did not know whether the figures he read were audited or not, nor did he think this was of any consequence. If an investor is sophisticated enough to care who the auditor is, he must surely care whether or not the figures he reads have been audited. He cannot acknowledge indifference to this, and then conjure up a fiction of "reliance" on which to make the auditor bear any losses (without sharing any profits) he may later have realized.

As an alternative ground for his claim, plaintiff argues that Price Waterhouse's knowing failure to come forward after DCL has released its earnings figures aided and abetted DCL's alleged 10b-5 violation. . . . On precedents this court finds persuasive, this theory is rejected. *Wessel v. Buhler*, 437 F.2d 279 (9th Cir. 1971); *Fischer v. Kletz*, supra.

In his papers opposing the motion to dismiss plaintiff argues, for the first time, that Price Waterhouse may have compiled the figures released by DCL and thus may have actively aided DCL's alleged violation. Plaintiff has testified, however, that the information on which his complaint is based was obtained from DCL's annual report and proxy materials. Nowhere in these documents is there an indication that Price Waterhouse prepared the figures released by DCL. Nor has plaintiff presented any other evidence to support his speculation. Furthermore, there is no contention here that the figures were false or misleading.

Finally, the peculiar facts of this case make it impossible to characterize Price Waterhouse's silence and inaction as aiding and abetting. The press release, of course, labeled the figures unaudited and in no way indicated participation by Price Waterhouse. The omission complained of concerned an intent to qualify an opinion, which intent had already been disclosed to the SEC in December 1971. Furthermore, far from there being a tacit agreement not to disclose because of mutual benefit (as, say, in the case of an accountant agreeing to certify false figures in order to retain its client), it is undisputed that Price Waterhouse was fired by DCL because of the parties' disagreement over the validity of the intended qualification.

Lastly, in dismissing the complaint against Price Waterhouse, the court notes that plaintiff offers (and we have imagined) no realistic or sensible means by which Price Waterhouse could have been expected to "disclose" the planned qualification it never had occasion or opportunity to publish. It is at least mildly perplexing to speculate on the prospect of an accountant's public attack upon a client on the occasion of being discharged by the client for a divergence of opinion on proper accounting in an area where responsible accountants could (and did) responsibly differ. We need not go so far as to say Price Waterhouse could have been sued, or denounced for ethical impropriety, in order to hold, as we do, that this defendant's "nondisclosure" may not in such circumstances be held an actionable wrong to plaintiff.

1.   *Gold v. DCL Inc.* sets out two significant legal principles which bear on the issue of whistle-blowing. The court held that (1) there is "no basis in principle or authority for extending an auditor's duty to disclose beyond cases where the auditor is giving or has given some representation or certification," and (2) the defendant auditors in *Gold* did not "aid and abet" their ex-client's alleged fraud by their "silence and inaction."

2.   In holding that the auditors had no duty of disclosure, the *Gold* court reasoned that because the auditors had issued no "public opinion, rendered no certification and in no way invited the public to rely on its financial judgment" there was no "special relationship which has heretofore imposed on auditors a duty of disclosure." The court thus held that there was no direct duty of disclosure that could be imposed upon the auditors.

3.   The "silence and inaction" that the plaintiff attacked in *Gold* was the omission by the auditors to publicly disclose their intention to issue a qualified opinion before they were fired by the audit client. The court held that this type of silence and inaction could not be characterized as aiding and abetting. The court noted that there was no evidence of a "tacit agreement not to disclose because of mutual benefit." The court also observed that the misleading financial press release issued by the client was labelled

"unaudited" and did not identify the auditors by name and further did not contain any "indication that the [auditors] prepared the figures released by *DCL*."

[4]   Aiding and Abetting a Fraud

An accountant who aids and abets the fraudulent conduct of another person may be held liable to all persons who are defrauded. To aid and abet, an accountant must:

(1)   know that the conduct of another party constitutes a fraud and

(2)   *substantially assist* that party's fraudulent course of conduct.

     The question of what constitutes "substantial assistance" is a difficult one. Several cases declare that an accountant's mere silence and inaction cannot constitute aiding and abetting, absent either (1) a special relationship or (2) breach of a duty of disclosure. Other cases have held that substantial assistance may consist of a party's failure to disclose or failure to act which results from an "improper motive." Keep in mind these different standards as you read the following cases which have grappled with the issue of aiding and abetting.

[a]   *Fischer v. Kletz, Wessel v. Buhler*, and Comments

Fischer v. Kletz.
266 F.Supp. 180 (S.D.N.Y. 1967)

[The facts of the case are reprinted at ¶ 6.03[1].]

II.
Interim Statement Liability

During PMM's conduct of the "special studies" in 1964, Yale utilized its internal accounting procedures to compile figures which could be used to evaluate the company's 1964 performance on a continuing basis. These figures were then inserted in various interim statements and reports issued by Yale, which, Paragraph 22 of the Second Consolidated Amended Complaint alleges, "were widely circulated" and in which there were "gross overstatements" of the company's "earnings and revenues and forecasts thereof."

     Plaintiffs claim that PMM is liable for damages suffered as a result of their reliance upon these allegedly false and misleading statements and reports. The argument made by plaintiffs in their memorandum submitted for purposes of this motion can be summarized in the following manner: the dissemination of the interim statements and re-

ports constituted a violation by Yale of Section 10(b) of the 1934 Act in that it was a "manipulative or deceptive device" undertaken "in connection with the purchase or sale" of a security registered on the New York Stock Exchange. PMM knew as a result of its special studies that the figures disseminated were false and misleading but did not disclose its discovery thereof to anyone; moreover, PMM "recommended" to Yale that the false reports be issued. Plaintiffs conclude that, in light of these facts, PMM must be held liable under Section 10(b) for "aiding and abetting" Yale's scheme to defraud its investors. Urging that the complaint fails to succinctly state facts spelling out an actionable conspiracy and contending, that in any event, it owed no duty to the investing public in respect to the special studies, PMM moves to dismiss this claim.

•   •   •

     Essentially, plaintiffs claim that PMM aided and abetted Yale in two ways: first, by remaining silent when it was known that the interim reports were false and, second, by recommending or sanctioning the issuance of the reports. There is no allegation that PMM compiled, audited, or certified any of the interim statements, nor is there indication that any of the statements contained material which an investor could justifiably attribute or relate to PMM.

A. PMM's Silence and Inaction

The issue posed here was stated succinctly by the court in *Brennan v. Midwestern United Life Insurance Company*, *supra*

> Certainly, not everyone who has knowledge of improper activities in the field of securities transactions is required to report such activities. This court does not purport to find such a duty. Yet, duties are often found to arise in the face of special relationships, and there are circumstances under which a person or a corporation may give the requisite assistance or encouragement to a wrongdoer so as to constitute an aiding and abetting by merely failing to take action. * * The question raised by the motion at bar is whether the allegations in the complaint will permit evidence which may establish such circumstances in the instant case.

Discussion of two cases in which defendants have been subjected to possible liability as aiders and abettors under Section 10(b) for their silence and inaction is helpful to resolution of this issue.

In *Pettit v. American Stock Exchange*, 217 F.Supp. 21 (S.D.N.Y.1963), analyzed heretofore in the discussion relating to PMM's liability attendant to the 1963 annual report, defendant stock exchange and its officers were held accountable for their failure "to take necessary disciplinary action against abusive conduct and practices of which they knew or should have known." 217 F.Supp. at 28.

The case is, however, distinguishable from the one at bar. In *Pettit*, the exchange was under an independent duty, imposed by Section 6 of the Securities Exchange Act, to adopt and enforce just and equitable principles of trade. Liability was premised, of course, on the breach of that duty.

No similar independent duty can be found here by application of either statutory or common law principles. Contrary to plaintiffs' suggestion, issuance by Yale of the interim statements created no "special relationship" between the investors and PMM. In respect to the interim statements, PMM was not a statutory "independent public accountant" as it was during the audit and certification of the annual report. PMM made no representations which appeared in the statements, nor did it compile the figures contained therein. In sum, unlike the situation in *Pettit*, there is absolutely no basis in law for imposing upon PMM a duty to disclose its knowledge of the falsity of the interim financial statements.

The discussion of the court in *Brennan v. Midwestern United Life Insurance Co.*, *supra*, lends support to this conclusion. In that case, defendant was a corporation whose stock was sold by a broker. At the time of suit, the broker was bankrupt. In a class action, plaintiff purchasers of securities alleged that the defendant issuer aided and abetted the broker's violations of Section 10(b) and Rule 10b-5 by failing to disclose to either the SEC or the Indiana Securities Commission that it knew that the broker was making fraudulent representations in the course of the sales and was improperly using the proceeds from the sales.

Defendant moved to dismiss the action on the ground, *inter alia*, that the complaint failed to state a claim under the "aiding and abetting" theory. The motion was denied. The court reasoned that defendant Midwestern was an "insider" allegedly taking advantage of the broker's activities and, as such, was under a duty to disclose to the investors that the broker was acting improperly. By remaining silent, Judge Eschbach concluded, this duty was breached and the defendant was thereby subject to the "aider and abettor" claim.

As in *Pettit*, defendant's liability was premised upon the rationale that the failure to disclose constituted a breach of duty. But, as indicated, no such duty can be found in the context of those facts pleaded here. Absent such a duty, there is no basis for transforming silence into actionable aiding and abetting.

B. PMM's Acts of Recommending Release of the Statements

Plaintiffs contend that, in addition to failing to disclose that the Yale interim financial statements were false and misleading, PMM actively aided and abetted Yale's alleged violation of Section 10(b) by recommending or sanctioning the release of statements containing figures compiled by Yale's own accountants rather than figures developed by PMM during the course of the special studies. The basis for this claim is said to be found in answers given to plaintiffs' interrogatories (1st Series) by certain individual defendants who are former officers and directors of Yale. Specifically, the following statements are relied upon:

    16. Shortly before August 17, 1964, Robert G. Conroy of Peat, Marwick met with defendant Gerald W. Eskow, defendant Fred H. Mackensen and H. Kenneth Sidel at the Bon Vivant restaurant in New York City. At this meeting Mr. Conroy advised Mr. Eskow that the figures shown in the revised Peat, Marwick special study six month report could not be used as the basis of Yale's financial reports for the first half of 1964 and recommended that the corporation release instead the figures prepared by Mr. Mackensen as the head of its internal accounting operation.

    17. Mr. Conroy stated that he did not know whether or not Mr. Mackensen's figures were correct and said that the Peat, Marwick special study would not show this even when it was complete. Mr. Conroy also said that basing the six month report upon the Mackensen figures would have the advantage of being consistent with previous reports and that any inaccuracies in these figures would be picked up by Peat, Marwick in the course of its year-end audit at which time any necessary adjustments would be made.

. . .

    19. Shortly before November 5, 1964, said Robert G. Conroy [partner of Peat, Marwick] met with defendants Gerald W. Eskow and Fred H. Mackensen and Harold Rosegarten and H. Kenneth Sidel at a luncheon club in the Wall Street area. At this meeting Mr. Conroy told Mr. Eskow that the Peat, Marwick special study report for the first nine months of 1964 could not be used as a basis for Yale's financial reports for this period. Mr. Conroy recommended that these reports be made on the basis of the figures prepared by Mr. Mackensen, once again stating that while he did not know that these figures were accurate he could not say that they were inaccurate either and using them would be inconsistent with earlier reports.

The issue, of course, is whether or not PMM can be termed "aiders and abettors" as a matter of law if the interrogatory answers by certain defendants are established as a matter of fact. Conveniently, the Restatement of Torts provides the following standard by which PMM's putative liability can be measured:

> For harm resulting to a third person from the tortious conduct of another, a person is liable if he
>
>   *   *   *
>
> (b) knows that the other's conduct constitutes a breach of duty and gives substantial assistance or encouragement to the other so to conduct himself. . . . (Restatement, Torts § 876 (1939))

Assuming that PMM knew that Yale was breaching its duty to its investors by issuing false financial statements,[1] the question becomes whether or not PMM gave "substantial assistance or encouragement" to Yale's course of conduct.

From the facts pleaded in the complaint, even when buttressed by the aforementioned answers to interrogatories, it is difficult to characterize PMM's action as "assistance or encouragement" in the sense contemplated by the Restatement. Even if these labels fit

---

[1] Note the Eskows' statement that Mr. Conroy of PMM said that he did not know whether or not the Yale figures were correct. In an affidavit submitted to this court in support of this motion, Mr. Conroy states, *inter alia*, "Indeed, PMM during 1964 informed Yale's management, from time to time, that the interim figures which Yale's management had released, or was in the process of releasing, were materially different from interim unaudited statements which PMM had compiled from the special studies material. The decision to release the company prepared figures was made solely by management."

the pleaded facts, doubt remains as to whether or not the quantitative term "substantial" could be added to them.

It is, however, inappropriate to make a determination of the "aiding and abetting" issue at this time. Discovery is presently in a relatively inadvanced stage. While plaintiffs can now show only minimal interaction between PMM and Yale in relation to the interim statements, they must be given an opportunity to further explore this facet of the Yale-PMM relationship. "The very fact that this case arises in a newly developing area of law cautions that the court should refrain from abstract and premature legal determinations fashioned in an evidentiary vacuum." Brennan v. Midwestern United Life Ins. Co., 259 F.Supp. at 682.

The cross motion of PMM to dismiss paragraphs 25–25.3 is denied. It is so ordered.

Wessel v. Buhler
437 F.2d 279 (9th Cir. 1971)

Before ELY, HUFSTEDLER, and TRASK, Circuit Judges.

HUFSTEDLER, Circuit Judge:

Appellants, stockholders of Rocky Mountain Chemical Corporation ("RMC"), appeal from adverse portions of a judgment against L. M. Buhler, president of RMC, and from a judgment in favor of N. A. Jordan, an accountant, in their actions to recover damages for losses allegedly caused by the violations by Buhler and Jordan of Rule 10b-5 of the Securities and Exchange Commission.

Appellants initiated the action against Buhler, certain other officers and directors of RMC, and Jordan, on their own behalf and for some 4000 other stockholders who had purchased RMC's stock in reliance upon three prospectuses dated February 10, 1960, August 1, 1961, and March 11, 1963. . . . At the close of appellants' case, the court granted Jordan's motion for a directed verdict.

Buhler and his associates organized RMC in 1959 to produce alcohol from potatoes. Shortly thereafter RMC began selling its common stock to the public. Most of the stock was sold to Idaho residents, but some portions of the later issues were sold to out-of-state purchasers. Appellants variously bought stock under the first, the second, or all of the prospectuses. The financial condition of RMC was precarious from the outset. By 1962 its condition was worse and by 1963 it was desperate. RMC was adjudicated bankrupt in June 1964.

Jordan's Liability

Jordan, an independent certified public accountant, was retained on three separate occasions to prepare financial statements for RMC. In February 1962, Buhler asked him to prepare a financial statement to accompany RMC's application for a surety bond. Jordan examined the corporate records and found that they were seriously deficient. After he persuaded RMC to hire a bookkeeper, Jordan and the bookkeeper gathered enough financial data to permit Jordan to prepare an unaudited statement for the accounting period ending June 30, 1962. Jordan delivered the statement to RMC's Board, with a transmittal memorandum noting the dubious collectibility of the Spring Kist account receivable listed in the face amount of $272,000 and cautioning that physical assets were carried at the acquisition costs reflected in RMC's books without any independent appraisal or audit. The second statement, also unaudited, was a balance sheet prepared by Jordan in cooperation with RMC's bookkeeper in January 1963. The balance sheet was to accompany RMC's application to the Small Business Administration for a loan. The second statement picked up some of the asset figures from the 1962 statement, with various current adjustments. Cash on hand was shown at $345.72. An operating loss of $267,780.34 also appeared. The third statement was prepared in July 1963. That audited statement disclosed a net loss during the period January through July 1963 of $451,000 and an operating loss of $775,500.

Appellants have two theories to sustain their claims against Jordan: (1) Jordan's financial statements were in and of themselves misleading statements "in connection with the purchase or sale of any security," within the meaning of Rule 10b-5. (2) The misleading financial statements, as Jordan knew, or should have known, were used in preparing the prospectuses that, in turn, were used "in connection with the purchase or sale of any security."

For the purpose of discussing the first point we assume that all three financial statements were misleading. Despite that assumption, no liability under Rule 10b-5 could have been based on those statements because there was no proof that the statements alone were statements "in connection with the purchase or sale of any security."

None of the three financial statements was made "in a manner reasonably calculated to influence the investing public." None was publicly disseminated in any way. There was no evidence that any investor ever saw the statements until after the litigation began. The evidence was that Jordan delivered them to the Board for uses unconnected with stock issuance, and, as far as the evidence discloses, no one before suit ever saw them, except the officers and directors of RMC and the agencies to which they were directed. We decline to stretch Rule 10b-5 to cover Jordan's financial statements.

We turn to appellants' alternative theory. It is evident that Jordan had nothing to do with the first two prospectuses because they were issued before he reached the RMC scene. It is also evident that his third financial statement had nothing to do with the third prospectus because the third prospectus was issued before he prepared the third statement. Appellants' efforts to fasten responsibility upon Jordan rest upon connecting his first two statements with the production of the third prospectus.

Appellants attempted to show that Jordan participated in the creation of the prospectus by pointing to the use in the prospectus of some of the figures that appeared in Jordan's financial statements and by asking that an inference be drawn therefrom that Jordan was responsible for their appearance in the prospectus. Of course, we can infer from the presence of those figures in both instruments that whoever drew the prospectus took those figures from the earlier financial statements. But the further inference does not follow that the person who copied parts of the financial statements was Jordan. That inference is particularly untenable because other key

features of the prospectus had no counterpart in the financial statements. Thus, RMC's operating loss of $267,000, shown on the 1963 balance sheet, was completely omitted from the prospectus. Cash on hand was listed as $345.72 on the balance sheet, but on the prospectus the sum was raised to $10,345.72. The evidence demonstrated that whoever wrote the prospectus picked out the figures he found attractive in the balance sheet, discarded those he did not like, and simply made up the rest. The result was fiction, but there was no proof that Jordan created it.

The direct evidence from both Jordan and Buhler was that Jordan had nothing to do with the production of the third prospectus. Of course, the jury could have disbelieved the denials, but disbelief does not become a substitute for affirmative evidence.

Perhaps in recognition of their failure to prove any direct participation by Jordan in the production of the third prospectus, appellants argue that Jordan indirectly participated in the prospectus by aiding and abetting Buhler and the other officers and directors of RMC and that Jordan should thus be held liable as a principal for the commission of their wrong. The argument has two prongs. The first is that some of the figures that appeared in Jordan's financial statements and that reappeared in the prospectus were of themselves misleading; therefore, Jordan should be chargeable with liability for making those misleading statements in the prospectus. There was no evidence that the items appellants attack were not prepared in accordance with good accounting practice under the circumstances. But even if some inference might arise that those figures were misleading, as we have said, there was no evidence at all to prove that Jordan was in any way responsible for their appearance in the third prospectus.

The second prong is appellants' contention that Jordan owed a duty to prospective investors to disclose his knowledge of RMC's irregular financial conduct and of deficiencies in its financial records, and that his failure to perform that duty placed Buhler and his associates in a position to dupe the investors by launching stock with the third prospectus; therefore, Jordan aided and abetted Buhler and should be held as a principal. There is not a scrap of authority supporting this extraordinary theory of Rule 10b-5 liability, and we will not supply any in this case.

We find nothing in Rule 10b-5 that purports to impose liability on anyone whose conduct consists solely of inaction. On the contrary, the only subsection that has any reference to an omission, as distinguished from affirmative action, is subsection (2) providing that it is unlawful "to omit to state a material fact necessary in order to make the statements made * * * not misleading," *i.e.*, an omission occurring as part of an affirmative statement. . . . We perceive no reason, consonant with the congressional purpose in enacting the Securities and Exchange Act of 1934, thus to expand Rule 10b-5 Liability. . . . On the contrary, the exposure of independent accountants and others to such vistas of liability, limited only by the ingenuity of investors and their counsel, would lead to serious mischief.

We conclude that the district court properly directed the verdict in Jordan's favor.

1.   As the court in *Fischer v. Kletz* indicates, the legal claim that one may aid and abet a fraud arises from common law cases which hold that a person is liable for another's fraud if he "*knows* that the other's conduct constitutes a breach of duty and *gives substantial assistance or encouragement* to the other so to conduct himself." Under the aiding and abetting theory of liability it is not enough that a person knows of another's fraud, he must also "substantially assist" the perpetration of the fraud.

2.   In *Fischer v. Kletz* and *Wessel v. Buhler* the courts rejected the arguments that the accountants in those lawsuits aided and abetted their clients' fraud merely through "silence and inaction." Subsequent court decisions, however, have indicated a reluctance to go so far as to state that an accountant can never "aid and abet" merely by silence and inaction.

3.   In *Hochfelder v. Midwest Stock Exchange*, 503 F.2d 364, 374 (7th Cir. 1974), the court, after taking note of *Wessel v. Buhler*, stated:

> We are not prepared to hold that a claim for aiding and abetting solely by inaction cannot be made under Rule 10b-5. In invoking such a rule, however, we would not go so far as to charge a party with aiding and abetting who somehow unwittingly facilitates the wrongful acts of another. Rather, to invoke such a rule investors must show that the party charged with aiding and abetting had knowledge of or, but for a breach of duty of inquiry, should have had knowledge of the fraud, and *that possessing such knowledge the party failed to act due to an improper motive or breach of a duty of disclosure.* [Emphasis added.]

Under this approach an accountant could substantially assist a known fraud if the accountant fails to blow the whistle due to either (1) a breach of an existing duty of disclosure or (2) an improper motive.

[b]   Aiding and Abetting: Equity Funding.   Liability for aiding and abetting a fraud can extend to all persons who "substantially assist" the fraud, regardless of the nature of their relationship to the party who is perpetrating the fraud. For example, it is possible that an accountant may be held liable for aiding and abetting the fraud of a party who is not a client of the accountant.

Consider the relationship of the accountants in the *Equity Funding* litigation who settled a claim against them arising out of services that they performed for an insurance client who was doing business with Equity Funding.

(i)   The Settlement[1]

Peat Marwick to Pay $1.5 Million to Settle Equity Funding Suit

LOS ANGELES—Peat, Marwick, Mitchell & Co. agreed to pay $1.5 million to settle claims alleged in a class action suit in federal court here that it knew about but concealed the Equity Funding Corp. of America insurance fraud 16 months before the company finally collapsed.

The consolidated class action, brought by holders of Equity Funding's securities, charged that auditors from Peat Marwick's Houston office had "actual knowledge" or should have known as early as 1971 that Equity Funding's subsidiary, Equity Funding Life Insurance Co., was manufacturing bogus life insurance policies and selling them to reinsurers.

The suit said that Peat Marwick auditors learned of the fraud while doing several special examinations for Ranger National Life Insurance Co., a subsidiary of Anderson Clayton & Co. that was buying policies from

the Equity Funding unit. After the examinations, Peat Marwick auditors exchanged memoranda with such titles as "On (the) Possibility That Equity Funding Is Ceding Fraudulent Policies" and "'Regarding Possible Fraud" at Equity Funding. Eventually, though, Peat Marwick told Ranger that the policies bought from the Equity Funding unit appeared to be in order and declined to make further examinations.

Peat Marwick has denied vigorously that it had "actual knowledge" of fraud at Equity Funding, and the proposed settlement agreement said the $1.5 million payment was in the securities holders' best interests considering Peat Marwick wasn't the auditor for Equity Funding and the "absence of evidence that defendant Peat, Marwick had actual knowledge."

The Peat Marwick settlement, if approved by the federal court, would bring the total amount paid by defendants in the class action to $62 million, including $39 million by Haskins & Sells, Seidman & Seidman, and Wolfson, Weiner & Co., the three accounting firms that audited the results of Equity Funding or its life insurance unit. . . .

---

[1] As reported in the *Wall Street Journal*.

(ii)   The Court Decision Which Preceded the Settlement

In re Equity Funding Corporation of America Securities Litigation
416 F.Supp. 161 (C.D. Cal 1976)

LUCAS, District Judge.

On January 23, 1976, the Court denied PMM's motion to dismiss the complaint, by which PMM also sought sanctions against plaintiffs. PMM, in their motion denied any knowledge of the fraud at either EFCA or EFLIC, denied any duty, even if it possessed such knowledge, to disclose any information to plaintiffs, and denied any causal connection between any activities of PMM and any harm caused by plaintiffs.

The Court, in denying PMM's motion, at page 44 of its Order of January 23, 1976, stated:

The Court is extremely reluctant to dismiss, at this stage of the proceedings, any de-

fendant alleged to have known about major aspects of the fraud at EFCA or EFLIC because this case presents unique issues with regard to regulation of the national securities markets by means of private investor suits. . . . If PMM knew about the EFLIC bogus policy scheme but still allowed EFCA to use financial statements certified by PMM as a means of inflating the price of EFCA securities, it contributed substantially to the breakdown of this regulatory system. By such conduct, it knowingly allowed innocent investors, who relied on the prestige and reputation of all of the defendants here for protection of their financial interests, to suffer harm of the precise kind the 1933 Securities Act and the 1934 Securities Exchange Act were meant to prevent.

Thus, plaintiffs' allegations that PMM failed to disclose, in financial statements audited and certified by PMM for Liberty Savings and Loan Association, a subsidiary of EFCA, actual knowledge of the fraud at EFLIC, which PMM gained while conducting a special examination of EFLIC at the request of PMM's client Ranger National Life Insurance Co., (hereinafter "Ranger") were found by the Court, to sufficiently state a claim for relief against PMM.

With this background, the major issues on this motion for summary judgment can be stated as follows:

1. Whether a genuine issue of fact exists as to whether PMM had actual knowledge of the fraud at EFLIC, and

2. if no genuine issue of facts exists, whether PMM is entitled to judgment as a matter of law.

• • •

The defendant apparently concedes that, if the issue exists, it is a factual issue which can only be decided by a jury; however, PMM argues that plaintiffs have failed to present a scintilla of direct evidence to demonstrate that the factual issue exists.

Plaintiffs, in support of their position, necessarily rely upon circumstantial proof of knowledge. The question is such that all evidence thereon would be in the possession of the defendant. As indicated above, PMM's position throughout the litigation has been that there was absolutely no evidence to demonstrate that PMM had any knowledge, whatsoever, of the fraud at either EFCA or EFLIC. The discovery to date, as presented by plaintiffs, in opposition to this motion, bears out the fact that PMM's position is not well-taken.

PMM was engaged by its client Ranger for the specific purpose of conducting a special investigation of EFLIC to determine whether the life insurance policies being ceded to Ranger by EFLIC, pursuant to a Reinsurance Agreement between them, were valid. The facts presented by the plaintiffs demonstrate that problems encountered by PMM during this investigation consisted of continual delays in obtaining files of policyholders of EFLIC, inability to locate missing EFLIC files, and continued lack of cooperation from EFLIC personnel. Furthermore, as counsel for PMM indicated to the Court during oral argument, it appears likely that 85.5% of the EFLIC policies ceded to Ranger in 1971 were fictitious and, therefore, bogus. In December, 1971, PMM commenced its third special examination of EFLIC for the year ending September 30, 1971. After being met with delays, excuses and lack of cooperation, the investigation of EFLIC, during this critical year, was unexpectedly and abruptly halted, on December 16, 1971, by Fred Levin, the President of EFLIC. This interrupted special examination resulted in a memorandum dated December 28, 1971, authored by Mr. Fred Krenzke, a PMM employee involved in the EFLIC examination, which stated "[h]is position [Mr. Bill Suttle, PMM engagement partner] that this is exactly the kind of treatment we would have received if there was fraud." Exhibit 221-028.

PMM argues that each of these facts, and all others presented by plaintiffs, can be explained or refuted by other evidence. This argument, however, misses the mark because it is the very existence of the facts which raises, at least, one genuine issue of fact and, thus, prevents the Court from granting PMM summary judgment. The effect and weight of PMM's countervailing evidence is a decision for the trier of fact to make when deciding the factual issue raised.

A jury, when presented with the numerous indications to which plaintiffs point of PMM's knowledge of the EFLIC fraud, could find that PMM personnel knew and believed there was fraud at EFLIC and intentionally decided not to disclose that knowledge or belief to either its client, the Securities and Exchange Commission or the investing public. Such knowledge or belief by PMM plus a deliberate refusal to take steps to disclose that knowledge are facts which could permit a trier of fact to find an intent to deceive or recklessness sufficient to impose liability under Rule 10b-5.

[c] *Mendelsohn v. Capital Underwriters, Inc.* **and Comments**

Mendelsohn v. Capital Underwriters, Inc.
490 F.Supp. 1069 (N.D. Cal. 1979)

ORRICK, District Judge.

[Plaintiffs were defrauded by Gary DiGirolamo, president of Capital Underwriters, Inc. (CU), who sold plaintiffs interests in limited partnerships allegedly established to finance real estate developments in Hawaii. DiGirolamo used the investors' funds for his personal expenses and to pay profits and capital to earlier investors in this investment scheme.

The plaintiffs sued CU's accounting firm, Harris, Kerr, Forster & Co. (HKF) and the manager of HKF's Honolulu office, David Latham. The plaintiffs claimed that the defendant accountants aided and abetted DiGirolamo's fraud in violation of Rule 10b-5.

The district court trial judge granted the accountants' motion for summary judgment and dismissed the case. The court issued the following opinion.]

Neither Latham nor anyone else at HKF ever met with or spoke to any of the named plaintiffs or anyone else contemplating an investment in CU or in any related entities. Latham made no representations to anyone concerning such investments. Neither HKF nor Latham did work in connection with, or prepared material knowingly for inclusion in, any prospectus or offering circular issued by CU or by any limited partnership affiliated with it.

The services performed by HKF for CU are detailed as follows:

a. From August, 1972, through February, 1973, HKF set up certain bookkeeping records, in particular a general ledger and a cash receipts and disbursements journal based on the information provided it by CU. Using this same information, HKF prepared tax returns for CU during March and April, 1973.

b. In November, 1972, HKF prepared a projection of possible income from the Sherilani Apartments in Honolulu, a project unrelated to this suit.

c. In March, 1973, HKF made some preliminary income calculations for the Morgan Hill project, also a project unrelated to the instant suit.

During the relevant time period, from the time HKF first performed services for CU in August, 1972, through October, 1973, when plaintiffs' last investments were made, HKF's time records show that it spent 687 hours on the CU account over a nine-month period (August 1972–April 1973).

d. In February, 1974, HKF prepared a partnership tax return for Kahaluu Plantation, one of the projects of which several of the named plaintiffs now complain, but in which they had already invested well *before* HKF prepared the above-mentioned tax return.

e. In July and August, 1974, likewise after the time period in which the investments which are the subject of this suit took place, HKF prepared a financial statement for the Kinau joint venture project.

f. In July, 1974, HKF wrote two letters to Charles Slocum, the treasurer of CU, answering certain questions propounded by him regarding the deductibility of certain items for income tax purposes.

g. In September, 1974, HKF completed tax returns for CU based on the information which it had received from the company.

• • •

HKF never prepared audited or unaudited financial statements for CU or for any entity allegedly related to it with the exception of the above-mentioned Kinau project and another project similarly unrelated to this suit. Apart from those two financial statements, HKF never expressed any opinion on the financial condition of any entity related to CU.

The Second Circuit has recently formulated the following three elements of a cause of action for aiding and abetting a 10b-5 violation: (1) the primary party's violation of Rule 10b-5; (2) the alleged aider and abettor's knowledge of the primary fraud; and (3) the aider and abettor's performance of acts that substantially assist the violation.

• • •

Plaintiffs maintain that HKF aided and abetted DiGirolamo's fraudulent course of business by (1) providing knowing and substantial assistance to the principal violators, (2) letting the violators know that HKF would be available to cover up the scheme, and (3) subsequently participating in a cover-up. Plaintiffs also urge aiding and abetting liability based on alleged misrepresentations or misleading omissions contained in certain CU prospectuses regarding the tax deductibility of partnership expenses, and based on HKF's alleged participation in the preparation of the partnership tax returns.

HKF concedes that it knew from the start that CU was without a set of accounting books and that DiGirolamo had received funds without adequate documentation, commingled the funds raised for the various partnerships, and borrowed over $300,000 from CU. In drawing from these facts the inferences most favorable to plaintiffs, this Court must assume for the purposes of this motion that HKF knew of, or at least was recklessly indifferent to, DiGirolamo's fraudulent activity, and that HKF remained in DiGirolamo's employ and did nothing to put a halt to the fraudulent scheme. Nevertheless, HKF cannot be held liable for aiding or abetting the alleged violation of Rule 10b-5 because (1) HKF's work for CU did not substantially assist the alleged violation, and (2) HKF owed no duty to prospective investors to disclose any knowledge of DiGirolamo's irregular financial conduct or of the deficiencies in CU's financial records.

Under Section 10(b) and Rule 10b-5, knowing assistance of or participation in a fraudulent scheme gives rise to liability equal to that of the perpetrators themselves. . . . Various circuits have recognized, however, that Section 10(b) and Rule 10b-5 were not intended to reach all levels of participation. The courts generally draw the line between substantial and insubstantial assistance. . . . Though the Ninth Circuit has yet to delimit the extent of liability for aiding and abetting

a 10b-5 violation, from the above decisions it seems clear that, not only must the alleged aider and abettor be aware of the violation and of his own role in it, he must also render substantial assistance.

For the meaning of "substantial assistance," other circuits have looked to common law tort principles. As noted by the court in *Landy v. Federal Deposit Insurance Corp.*, . . . the Restatement does not define the concept of "substantial assistance," but explains that

> If the encouragement or assistance is a substantial factor in causing the resulting tort, the one giving it is himself a tortfeasor and is responsible for the consequences of the other's act. Restatement, Torts § 436.

Thus, there must be a substantial causal connection between the culpable conduct of the alleged aider and abettor and the harm to the plaintiff. Specifically, in order to defeat a motion for summary judgment, a plaintiff must make some factual showing that the assistance provided by the alleged aider and abettor was a substantial factor in bringing about the violation. Viewing the facts in the instant case in the light most favorable to plaintiffs, it is apparent that HKF's services were not a substantial factor in causing the alleged 10b-5 violation. HKF had no authority to influence the affairs of CU and, had HKF quit upon learning of CU's irregular financial practices, CU could simply have hired a less astute accountant or bookkeeper. Unlike the defendant in *Anderson v. Francis I. duPont & Co.*, . . . HKF is not alleged to have allowed CU to obtain customers by trading on the use of HKF's established reputation. The defendant brokerage houses in *Anderson* had allegedly given the offending dealer office space, endorsed his skill and standing as a commodities trader, and held him out as a favored and valued customer. HKF did not publicly endorse CU. Plaintiffs admit that they did not rely on HKF's reputation in making the investments in question, and all but one has stated in answers to interrogatories that he never heard of HKF or Latham in connection with his investment.

Plaintiffs' characterization of HKF's assistance as "extensive" is conclusory and fails to create a genuine issue of fact. Likewise, referring to the books HKF set up as the "accounting apparatus" whereby investors were duped does not dispute the nature of the services HKF actually performed for CU. Plaintiffs have not shown that setting up books to faithfully record DiGirolamo's dubious transactions in any way facilitated the alleged fraud or encouraged its perpetrators. To the contrary, HKF's work only made exposure more likely. This Court holds that the accounting services HKF performed, the nature and extent of which are not in genuine dispute, were not substantial enough to render HKF liable as an aider and abettor of the alleged fraud.

Plaintiffs' second contention, that by setting up the books HKF let DiGirolamo and CU know it sanctioned the scheme, would be available to assist in it in the future, and "would not blow the whistle," is merely a different formulation of plaintiffs' argument that HKF lent substantial assistance to DiGirolamo's and CU's illegal operations. This Court is not aware of any authority for the proposition that recording a series of fraudulent transactions constitutes substantial encouragement of the fraud. In *Odetie v. Shearson Hammill & Co.*, . . . the district court for the Southern District of New York found an allegation that the defendant bank had falsified its own books to corroborate a corporation's financial statements to the public sufficient to allege substantial assistance and encouragement of the alleged securities violation. There is no allegation in the instant case that HKF falsified either its own books or those of CU. Without evidence that HKF did some affirmative act tending to cover up the fraud, this Court would hesitate to find substantial encouragement based on evidence of equivocal acts accompanied by mere allegations of undisclosed psychic support. Viewing the facts in the light most favorable to plaintiffs, the evidence is insufficient to create an issue of fact as to whether HKF gave DiGirolamo substantial encouragement in the form of reassurance that HKF was ready to help conceal the fraud.

Plaintiffs' third contention, that HKF actually engaged in a conspiracy to cover up the fraud from early 1974 to November, 1974, is not material to the issue of liability for aiding and abetting the fraudulent securities transactions which are the subject of this suit. As stated above, there must be a substantial causal connection between the culpable conduct of the alleged aider and abettor and the harm done to the plaintiff. The investments in question were made during the time period October, 1972, through October, 1973, and the subsequent cover-up in which HKF allegedly participated could not have been a substantial factor in causing those fraudulent transactions to take place.

Having disposed of plaintiffs' contention that HKF aided and abetted the principal defendants by substantially assisting in the overall scheme to defraud, the Court now turns to plaintiffs' second theory of aiding and abetting liability: that HKF participated in making misrepresentations to plaintiffs. Presumably relying on subsection (b) of Rule 10b-5 to support this theory of liability, plaintiffs urge that HKF participated in making representations to them regarding the tax deductibility of certain purported partnership expenses, which representations omitted a material fact necessary to make the statements not misleading, namely, that there were no legitimate deductions available because the money was not legitimately invested.

According to Latham's affidavit, neither HKF nor Latham did any work in connection with, or prepared material knowingly for inclusion in, any prospectus or offering circular issued either by CU or by any limited partnership affiliated with it.

Even assuming that plaintiffs succeeded in creating a *bona fide* dispute as to whether HKF assisted in preparing *all* of the tax opinions that appear in the prospectuses, the mere presence of an accountant's work in a prospectus provides no basis for Rule 10b-5 liability without some proof that the accountant was responsible for or consented to it. . . . That various CU prospectuses contained tax opinions is no evidence that HKF took part in their preparation, much less that it then consented to their inclusion.

• • •

In light of this Court's holding that HKF's affirmative act of providing accounting services for CU does not establish its liability as an aider and abettor under Rule 10b-5, it is necessary to reach the issue whether HKF's silence and inaction alone suffice. In *Wessel v. Buhler, supra*, the Ninth Circuit refused to find liability under Rule 10b-5 based on an accountant's silence and inaction in a factual situation very similar to the case at bar.

The holding in *Wessel v. Buhler* at first appeared to be *contra* to decisions in other circuits which had found that silence or inaction alone could create liability for aiding and abetting. *See, e.g., Brennan v. Midwestern United Life Insurance Co., . . .* The Ninth Circuit eased the apparent contradiction in *Strong v. France*, 474 F.2d 747 (9th Cir. 1973), in which the court held that liability for silence or inaction can arise, but "only when a duty to disclose has arisen." *Id.* at 752. It is the opinion of this Court that HKF owed no duty to prospective investors to disclose its knowledge, if any, of the ongoing fraud, and therefore cannot be held liable for its failure to do so.

The instant case does not involve any of the circumstances which in the past have been held to give rise to a duty to disclose. HKF did not attempt to use any "inside information" to trade for its own account in the securities of the corporation in question, as did the defendant in *Securities & Exchange Commission v. Texas Gulf Sulphur Co., . . .* As this Court has found, HKF did not substantially assist the fraud in question as did the defendant in *Anderson v. Francis I. duPont & Co., supra. Brennan v. Midwestern United Life Insurance Co., supra*, often cited for the proposition that Rule 10b-5 imposes a duty to disclose information on deceptive practices, should be distinguished. In *Brennan*, the defendant corporation had failed to disclose its knowledge of a broker's fraudulent trading in that defendant's own stock, even though customers of the broker had directed specific inquiries to the defendant regarding the matter. HKF, on the other hand, was not an officer or part-owner of CU, and had no contact whatsoever with any of the named plaintiffs.

Plaintiffs argue that HKF's work for CU in late 1972 and early 1973 supplies a "special relationship" requiring disclosure to prospective investors. The proposed authority for their argument, *In re Equity Funding Corp. of America Securities Litigation*, 416 F.Supp. 161 (C.D. Cal. 1976), is distinguishable. The various accountants involved in that case were alleged to have audited and certified false and misleading financial statements, allowing innocent investors to rely on the accountants' prestige and reputations. The undisputed facts in the instant case are that no plaintiff knew of HKF's engagement by CU, much less relied on HKF's prestige and reputation in making the investments in question, and that HKF did not prepare any false or misleading financial statements. As discussed above, there is no genuine issue with respect to HKF's lack of participation in or responsibility for the appearance of misleading tax opinions in various CU prospectuses. Another case on which plaintiffs rely to impose a duty to disclose on HKF, *Kerbs v. Fall River Industries Inc., . . .* is likewise not factually on point. In *Kerbs*, the defendant, as president of the corporation whose stock was involved, was a corporate "insider" possessed of information material to the legitimacy of the transactions in question, and was present at meetings during which plaintiff and the principal defendant arranged and discussed the fraudulent transaction. As noted previously, HKF did not attempt to make use of any "inside information" to trade for its own benefit, and did not come into contact with any of the plaintiffs. In such a situation there is no authority for imposing a duty on HKF to disclose any knowledge it may have had concerning the alleged fraud.

Plaintiffs' attempt to distinguish *Wessel v. Buhler, supra*, must fail because, despite plaintiffs' assertion to the contrary, there was as much evidence in *Wessel* that the accountant knew of the fraud in question as there is in the instant case with respect to HKF. Jordan's knowledge of RMC's questionable financial conduct in *Wessel* was clear. Yet, in directing the verdict in favor of Jordan, the district court necessarily found that no issue of material fact remained for the jury. This Court interprets *Wessel*, as refined in *Strong v. France, supra*, to mean that whether or not the accountant knew of the fraud was not a material fact in the absence of a duty to disclose. This Court finds that HKF owed no duty to prospective investors in CU to disclose whatever it knew of the corporation's questionable financial conduct, and, accordingly, the extent of HKF's knowledge of the fraud is not a material fact which the Court must consider in granting HKF's motion for summary judgment.

1. The *Mendelsohn* court attempts to distinguish the result reached by the district court judge in the *Equity Funding* litigation by stating that in *Equity Funding* innocent investors relied on the prestige and reputation of the accountants involved there, while the plaintiffs in *Mendelsohn* did not know of, much less rely on, the auditors' prestige and reputation. Are the two decisions that easily distinguishable?

Consider the fact that the auditors involved in the *Equity Funding* decision were only one of several auditing firms sued and were not sued because of any failure on their part to adequately audit Equity Funding Corporation of America. Indeed, they were not even the auditors of Equity Funding Corporation of America. They were auditors for an insurance company, Ranger National Life Insurance, a corporation totally unrelated to Equity Funding that had entered into a reinsurance agreement with Equity Funding.

At Ranger's request, the auditors performed a special management advisory services examination to investigate the validity of the insurance policies ceded by Equity Funding to Ranger pursuant to their agreement. It was in these circumstances that the trial court held that the auditors for Ranger had a duty to blow the whistle on Equity Funding if, based on their limited special examination, conducted solely for Ranger's benefit, they "knew and believed there was fraud" at Equity Funding.

2. The trial judge in *Mendelsohn* held that "without evidence that [the accountants] did some affirmative act tending to cover up the fraud, this Court would hesitate to find substantial encouragement based on evidence of equivocal acts accompanied by mere allegations of undisclosed psychic support." In circumstances where an accountant knows of a fraud but has not issued any public report or otherwise been identified or associated with the client, a plaintiff may attempt to prove "substantial assistance" in one of the following ways:

A plaintiff will search for evidence that the accountant facilitated the fraud by some means that was a necessary element to perpetration of the fraud. For example, an accountant who prepares false accounting records of a company may by this conduct alone substantially assist the fraud of the company.

A plaintiff will attempt to ascertain whether the accountant assisted in efforts to cover up the fraud or prevent its detection or discovery. For example, substantial assistance may occur where an accountant falsifies the financial records of a company and thereby covers up fraud by the company.

A plaintiff will search for evidence indicating that the accountant had a personal motive to facilitate the fraud or prevent its detection. Motive may be proved by evidence that an accountant directly or indirectly benefits financially by facilitating the fraud. For example, an accountant's motive may be suspect in circumstances where the accountant's silence and inaction resulted from a concern over loss of business and fees or a concern that he would be sued for past actions.

3.   The aiding and abetting doctrine is often used by those plaintiffs who have not read or otherwise relied upon any representations made by the accountants. In *Hochfelder v. Ernst & Ernst* the plaintiffs freely admitted that they did not even know of or rely upon Ernst & Ernst or any of that accounting firm's audit reports issued over the 23 years they were auditors for First Securities.

Despite this lack of reliance, the court of appeals allowed the plaintiffs to sue Ernst & Ernst for aiding and abetting the fraud perpetrated on the plaintiffs by First Securities' president, Leston Nay. The court of appeals' theory was simple: but for Ernst & Ernst's breach of duties of inquiry and disclosure, Nay's fraud would have been prevented and/or detected, and thus plaintiffs would not have been defrauded.

4.   The trial judge in *Mendelsohn* makes the sweeping statement that

[W]hether or not the accountant knew of the fraud was not a material fact in the absence of a duty to disclose. This Court finds that [the auditors] owed no duty to prospective investors in Capital Underwriters to disclose whatever it knew of the corporation's questionable financial conduct.

If a corporation's "questionable financial conduct" consists of a massive fraud, such as in *Equity Funding*, it may be small solace for an accountant to defend a decision not to warn of the fraud based on the arguments that there was no duty to disclose and that the accountant's knowledge of the fraud was irrelevant.

[5]   Whistle-Blowing: Criminal Liability

An accountant's knowing participation in the fraudulent activities of another could subject the accountant to civil and criminal liability. In circumstances where an accountant does not participate in the fraud but subsequently discovers that a fraud has been perpetrated, a question arises: Does the accountant bear a duty to disclose this information regarding a completed crime to law enforcement officials?

Criminal law makes it a crime to conceal a felony committed by another person. This crime is referred to as misprision of a felony and requires proof of the following elements:

(a)   Knowledge of the actual commission of a felony

(b)   Concealment of the committed felony

(c)   Failure to disclose the felony to law enforcement officials

The element of concealment requires an affirmative act of concealment. Knowledge of a committed crime and inaction are not enough to support a criminal charge of misprision of a felony. For example, assume that an accountant discovers that the treasurer of a corporate audit client has embezzled money from the corporation. The accountant's decision not to advise law enforcement officials of the embezzlement does not consititute misprision of a felony. It may be, however, that the embezzlement will constitute an illegal act that must be disclosed in the corporation's financial statements pursuant to the requirements of GAAP and GAAS.

CHAPTER 7

DEFENSES TO LIABILITY
OTHER THAN LACK
OF PRIVITY

¶ 7.01 A Practical Explanation of the Duty of Inquiry and the Duty of Disclosure: Dinner with Your Attorney

Let us eavesdrop on a dinner discussion between two friends, Able Accountant and Justice Attorney, as they engage in a discussion before dessert regarding accountant's liability:

MR. ACCOUNTANT: Justice, there's no justice in this world. I see that another state supreme court has held that accountants can be sued for negligence by third parties. What was the defense that accountants used to assert successfully?

MR. ATTORNEY: Lack of privity—essentially an accountant could defend against negligence suits by contending that he owed no duty of due care to persons with whom he had no "privity of contract."

MR. ACCOUNTANT: That's my kind of rule!

MR. ATTORNEY: Well, pal, I'm sorry to say but there's not much left of that rule. In fact in just about all courts nonclient third-parties can sue accountants for negligence. The only question is how large a class of third-parties should be able to sue.

MR. ACCOUNTANT: I guess that accountants can pretty much throw in the towel if they are sued for negligence. It seems we are virtually defenseless.

MR. ATTORNEY: Wrong! As the courts have become more knowledgeable regarding what it is that accountants do, the courts have developed new legal defenses to liability. The courts recognize that accountants should not be held to a standard of strict liability or liability without fault.

MR. ACCOUNTANT: What are these legal defenses to liability?

MR. ATTORNEY: The defenses to legal liability fall under three general categories which I refer to as involving (1) the duty of inquiry, (2) the duty of disclosure, and (3) unjustified reliance.

[1]   Separate but Related Duties: Inquiry and Disclosure

MR. ACCOUNTANT: What are the duties of inquiry and disclosure?

MR. ATTORNEY: To answer that question let me ask you a question: What type of professional services do you perform?

MR. ACCOUNTANT: Well, I do a significant amount of reports on clients' financials.

MR. ATTORNEY: You issue audit reports, as well as compilation and review reports?

MR. ACCOUNTANT: Yes. I also perform certain management and tax advisory services.

MR. ATTORNEY: You advise clients on matters in these areas. For example, I take it that tax advisory services include rendering advice, or opinions, on the effect of the tax laws.

MR. ACCOUNTANT: Yes. And my management advisory services include giving recommendations regarding accounting and computer systems. What's all this have to do with these duties of inquiry and disclosure?

[2]   Duty of Inquiry

MR. ATTORNEY: The duty of inquiry deals with facts. You render your professional services and advice based on facts, correct?

MR. ACCOUNTANT: Correct.

MR. ATTORNEY: You would agree that seldom is a professional service or advice rendered in the abstract without regard to any facts?

MR. ACCOUNTANT: Yes, you're right.

MR. ATTORNEY: An accountant's duty of inquiry to ascertain the relevant, material facts necessary to render a professional service or advice varies depending on several factors.

MR. ACCOUNTANT: I'm not sure I follow you.

MR. ATTORNEY: The extent to which an accountant must make an examination or inquiry regarding the existence or nonexistence of facts before he successfully renders his professional service or advice is a function of the following factors:

    (a)   The nature of the accountant's engagement (e.g., is it an audit, a review, or a compilation?)

    (b)   The nature of any specific agreements with the client regarding the accountant's inquiry (e.g., the accountant may render tax advisory services based on agreed-upon assumptions that certain facts do or do not exist)

      (c) Applicable professional standards and practice governing and establishing the extent of inquiry

      (d) Any applicable statutory obligations of inquiry (e.g., an accountant may agree to perform an audit examination in accordance with the requirements of a statute which governs the audit client)

MR. ACCOUNTANT: This "duty of inquiry" seems to be a fancy way to describe the process by which an accountant gathers his facts to do his work.

MR. ATTORNEY: It's that and more. You see, it may be that in a particular situation an accountant was not aware of facts that would have a material impact on his advice or service. The accountant's failure to know these facts may not be the result of any negligence, for it is possible that the courts would determine he had no duty of inquiry regarding these unknown facts and thus cannot be held liable for failing to discover them.

MR. ACCOUNTANT: Can you give me a specific example of this?

MR. ATTORNEY: Sure. When you audit a client you confirm certain of its accounts receivable. When a customer confirms that it owes your client a certain amount, do you carry your inquiry further to determine whether the customer has the ability to pay the amount owed?

MR. ACCOUNTANT: Not usually. My examination normally stops with the confirmation. I don't audit the customer if that's what you're driving at. I don't have to . . . no one audits the customers.

MR. ATTORNEY: Your duty of inquiry does not extend that far. If you were challenged in a lawsuit regarding your failure to discover that a customer of the client was insolvent and was thus improperly reflected as an account receivable, your defense would be simple: no duty of inquiry.

MR. ACCOUNTANT: That's slick. Does this duty of inquiry work in any other ways?

MR. ATTORNEY: Yes. For example, there is a time limit on your duty of inquiry. When you perform an audit your duty of inquiry terminates on the day you issue your audit report. You have no duty of inquiry regarding events which occur subsequent to your audit report.

MR. ACCOUNTANT: Makes sense. Any other limits on my duty of inquiry?

MR. ATTORNEY: The duty of inquiry imposes an obligation to search only for those facts that are relevant and material to the successful performance of your engagement. For example, when you audit a company you do not audit each and every transaction. You would be there all year auditing and the costs would outweigh the benefits. Consequently, considerations of "materiality" govern the nature of your audit examination. In my view your duty of inquiry on an audit

	examination is limited to ascertaining those facts that are relevant and material to rendering your audit report.
MR. ACCOUNTANT:	I'll drink to that. Can you think of any other limits on my duty of inquiry?
MR. ATTORNEY:	The duty of inquiry is a safeguard against attempts to impose on an accountant financial and business reporting responsibilities that should be borne only by the accountant's client. For example, when a client issues a prospectus it discloses significant nonfinancial information that will ultimately have a financial impact on the company's business fortunes. Disclosure of marketing and management policies are important, but they are not the responsibility of the independent accountant. There is no duty of inquiry to ascertain the existence and validity of these types of management disclosures.
MR. ACCOUNTANT:	Are you saying that an accountant's duty of inquiry should be limited to the financials upon which he reports?
MR. ATTORNEY:	Essentially, yes.

[3] Duty of Disclosure

MR. ACCOUNTANT:	What is the duty of disclosure?
MR. ATTORNEY:	The duty of disclosure is related to but distinct from the accountant's duty of inquiry to ascertain the material facts. The duty of disclosure deals with the question of what the accountant should report or advise based upon the facts.
MR. ACCOUNTANT:	How does the duty of disclosure affect an accountant's risk of liability?
MR. ATTORNEY:	With respect to professional services that involve rendering an opinion or representation, the question becomes: Based on all the facts known or that should have been known, did the accountant render a materially accurate and complete opinion or representation? Or, did the accountant fail to disclose a fact necessary to render his opinion or representation materially accurate and complete? Was the accountant's opinion or representation false or misleading because he breached a duty to disclose a material fact?
MR. ACCOUNTANT:	How does the duty of disclosure limit an accountant's liability?
MR. ATTORNEY:	The duty to disclose requires disclosure of only those facts that are material. There is no duty to disclose the immaterial.
	In some instances an accountant may know of financial information that is material. It does not necessarily follow that an accountant bears a duty to disclose this material financial information.
MR. ACCOUNTANT:	I lost you. Give me an example of what you are talking about.

MR. ATTORNEY: An accountant resigns as auditor for a client who refuses to make certain disclosures in the annual financials. The ex-client issues the materially misleading financials. Although the accountant knows of the material inaccuracy in the financials, the accountant bears no duty of disclosure.

MR. ACCOUNTANT: No liability?

MR. ATTORNEY: No liability! There are other instances where the duty of disclosure may limit an accountant's liability.

An accountant may know of certain nonfinancial information that may have a long-range effect on a company's success. For example, the company's internal controls may not be adequate, indeed they may be materially inadequate. A court may nevertheless determine that an accountant who renders an audit report has no duty to publicly disclose in his report that the company's internal controls are materially inadequate.

MR. ACCOUNTANT: Justice, you said that the duties of inquiry and disclosure are separate but related. I can see how they are separate. How are they related?

MR. ATTORNEY: In analyzing an accountant's responsibility in circumstances involving the rendition of a professional opinion or representation, two questions must be answered:

(a)   What was the accountant's duty of inquiry to ascertain the material facts? and

(b)   Based on the material facts that the accountant either knew or, but for a breach of duty of inquiry, should have known, did the accountant breach any duty of disclosure?

The answers to these questions will be determinative of an accountant's liability.

[4]   Unjustified Reliance

MR. ACCOUNTANT: If an accountant breaches his duties of inquiry and disclosure, what does he do next—take out the checkbook?

MR. ATTORNEY: Not necessarily.

MR. ACCOUNTANT: What possible defense to liability could exist?

MR. ATTORNEY: Unjustified reliance.

MR. ACCOUNTANT: What's that?

MR. ATTORNEY: It's a general characterization which I use to describe circumstances where the party suing the accountant has contributed to his own injury in whole or part through his own efforts. For example, the party may have engaged in conduct that I call "contributory fault," which will bar the party's lawsuit against the accountant.

It is also possible that a party's reliance on an accountant's report or advice was unjustified. In certain circumstances the party's knowledge of all the facts may demonstrate that the party did not rely on the accountant's work product. It may be that the courts would hold that the party's claim of reliance on the accountant was simply unjustified or untrue.

MR. ACCOUNTANT: Can you give me an example of how this defense works?

MR. ATTORNEY: Sure. Assume an accountant issues a compilation report with the appropriate disclaimer of responsibility. Subsequently, the accountant is sued by a bank who relied on the financials, which it turns out were materially wrong. The misleading nature of the financials would have been discovered *only if* the accountant had performed an audit examination.

MR. ACCOUNTANT: Won't the compilation disclaimer protect the accountant?

MR. ATTORNEY: It may. Some courts might hold that the bank's reliance on the financials as if they were audited was unjustified. Other courts might hold that in light of the bank's knowledge of the fact that the financials were merely compiled, the bank did not rely on the financials. Still other courts might hold that the issue of the reasonableness of the bank's reliance is a fact question to be decided by the jury or trier of fact. There may be some courts who hold that given the limited nature of the accountant's compilation engagement, there were no duties of inquiry and disclosure regarding the undiscovered financial information.

Shall we order dessert?

MR. ACCOUNTANT: Yes, I suddenly regained my appetite.

¶ 7.02 Duties of Inquiry and Disclosure: A Practical Application

Imagine that we have been invited to a meeting of professional advisors to I. M. Gadfly, the surly but brilliant investor and stock speculator. Gadfly has recently suffered a major financial loss caused by the drastic decline of the market value of the stock of Bubbling Balloon Company.

Bubbling Balloon is a major manufacturer of balloons that bear imprinted greeting messages. Gadfly was so impressed with Bubbling's business prospects that on March 15 of this year he purchased 10,000 shares of Bubbling at $100 per share. Less than three weeks after his purchase the market value of Bubbling's stock fell to $1 a share.

This meeting has been called to discuss a possible lawsuit to "right the wrong" done to Gadfly. Among those attending are Gadfly's attorney, I. Suem, and Gadfly's public relations employee, John Mouthpiece. Suem has also invited Arthur A. Auditor for his advice regarding potential liability on the part of the accountant for Bubbling Balloon Company.

We join the discussion in Suem's conference room in the Skyscraper Building, where you can view the city from on high, as the gods at Olympus:

MR. SUEM: Gentlemen, as financial advisors and consultants to Mr. Gadfly, each of you has been invited here to discuss the advisability of filing a lawsuit in light of the $990,000 loss recently suffered by our client. Before we get to the merits of any lawsuit, I believe it is essential that we agree that there is only one real target of any lawsuit, namely, Bubbling Balloon's accounting firm. Are we agreed?

MR. MOUTHPIECE: Of course. If you can't rely on accountants to predict these kinds of things, who can you rely on?

MR. GADFLY: Well said, John. Besides, the accounting firm is the deep pocket— I mean, Bubbling is so bankrupt, I'll bet they can't even afford the bankruptcy filing fees! Ha ha!

MR. SUEM: Very good. Now that we are agreed that the accountants ought to be sued, how can we sue them. . . . I should say, what grounds do we have to sue them? Just what is it that they did or failed to do?

MR. GADFLY: Well, I'm not sure. All I know is that on March 15 I bought 10,000 shares, relying on Balloon's annual report for the past calendar year. Balloon's accountant, John Q. Accountant, had something to do with those financials.

MR. SUEM: Were the financials audited? Did John Q. Accountant issue an audit report?

MR. GADFLY: I can't remember. I've got the statement somewhere in my office. In any event, I do remember reading the financials and I can recall that the financials painted a very rosy future picture—earnings and profits were up, yielding a rate of return on assets that is considered exceptional. Bubbling Balloon was really on the rise, if you get my drift!

MR. SUEM: Well, what caused Bubbling to burst?

MR. GADFLY: I'll tell you. On April 1, Bubbling issued a press release that indicated that Bubbling's president, Harry Hotair, had resigned!

MR. SUEM: So what?

MR. GADFLY: So what! Great Scott, man, do you have your head stuck in the clouds of Olympus?
                 Harry Hotair was solely and single-handedly responsible for the fast rise of Bubbling Balloon. Why, it was Hotair who was responsible for creating all the witty greetings on the balloons that they marketed.
                 Without Hotair, Bubbling Balloon's value deflated!

MR. SUEM: What happened to Hotair?

MR. GADFLY: He resigned to join a monastery in the Himalayas. He tendered his resignation last December, effective April 1. He had to wait four months to get into the monastery. Anyway, if I had known that Hotair was leaving, I would have never bought into Bubbling.

Frankly, without Hotair, Bubbling's financial statements weren't worth the paper they were written on!

MR. MOUTHPIECE: Mr. Gadfly, you don't know the full story behind Hotair's departure.

I have it from reliable sources that Hotair offended the wife of one of his biggest buyers. Apparently, he sent a new product to the buyer's wife, a happy-birthday greeting paper sack with the saying: "From One Bag to Another."

The greeting went over like a lead balloon, and as a result, Bubbling lost the account, which represented 25 percent of the company's sales revenue.

MR. GADFLY: When did this occur?

MR. MOUTHPIECE: I am told that Hotair was advised in December of the termination of business.

MR. GADFLY: Well, Hotair was brilliant. He would have been able to rise above this incident.

MR. MOUTHPIECE: Maybe, that's not all, however. I also heard that in December Hotair received a government subpoena regarding an investigation into a possible payoff by Hotair to employees of the company that supplied the balloons on which Hotair imprinted his greeting messages.

Apparently, Hotair was told in December by his supplier that they would no longer sell balloons to him. Hotair could not find a suitable replacement source because nobody makes balloons like these.

MR. GADFLY: If Bubbling's accountant had made sure these facts were disclosed in the annual report, I would have never bought any stock in this company!

MR. MOUTHPIECE: Mr. Gadfly, I'm not sure that even Bubbling's accountant knew any of this information.

MR. GADFLY: Well, they should have known. What are these people being paid to do?

MR. SUEM: Well, let's ask the accountant who we have invited to this meeting. Arthur Auditor, tell us:

Do we have a case against John Q. Accountant? What should the accountant have known and what should he have disclosed?

MR. AUDITOR: I need to know whether John Q. Accountant performed an audit, review, or compilation.

MR. GADFLY: What difference does that make? The accountant was associated with these financials and that's all that counts.

MR. AUDITOR: The nature of the accountant's engagement and report will have a direct bearing on the accountant's duty of inquiry and duty of disclosure.

MR. GADFLY: Duty of what?

MR. AUDITOR: Inquiry and disclosure. Look, if an accountant performs a review or compilation, his duty of inquiry to ascertain or investigate the facts is limited.

   On the other hand, if the accountant performed an audit, his duty to examine and ascertain the material facts is broader and more extensive than the duty of inquiry which attends a compilation or review.

MR. SUEM: How does this affect Mr. Gadfly's lawsuit?

MR. AUDITOR: He may not have a suit if all that was released was a compilation. The accountant's duties of inquiry and disclosure are limited in those types of engagements. John Q. Accountant may not have breached his duty of inquiry.

MR. SUEM: Mr. Auditor, let's assume that John Q. Accountant issued an audit report. If that's the case, were any duties violated?

MR. AUDITOR: If an audit report was issued, I still have a problem finding a breach of the duties of inquiry and disclosure.

MR. SUEM: Let's take the disclosure deficiencies item-by-item. Shouldn't the accountant have reported Harry Hotair's December resignation?

MR. AUDITOR: I think that was something that Bubbling Balloon should have disclosed, but it was not John Q. Accountant's responsibility to disclose. In fact in performing an audit, I do not see how you could argue that the auditor had a duty of inquiry to ascertain if any directors or officers resigned.

MR. SUEM: What about the December termination of the sales account that represented 25 percent of Bubbling's revenue? Surely, an auditing firm must disclose that type of information if the financials are not to be misleading?

MR. AUDITOR: I do not believe that John Q. Accountant had a duty of inquiry to ascertain whether future revenues of the company would be impaired or discontinued. John Q. Accountant could never discharge a duty of inquiry that would involve investigation into nonfinancial affairs—

MR. SUEM: But this is very much a financial affair—revenues were decreased by 25 percent!

MR. AUDITOR: I'm not saying that there was no duty to disclose this information if known. I'm saying that John Q. Accountant cannot be charged with a breach of duty of inquiry if he was unaware of the termination of sales.

MR. SUEM: What if John Q. Accountant knew of the 25 percent loss of revenues *before* he issued his audit report?

MR. AUDITOR:	It's possible that a court would impose a duty to disclose this type of financial information if John Q. Accountant knew of it.
MR. SUEM:	Should John Q. Accountant have disclosed the loss of Bubbling's sole balloon supplier and the related government investigation regarding payoffs by Hotair?
MR. AUDITOR:	Possibly.
MR. GADFLY:	Be specific, was there a duty of inquiry?
MR. AUDITOR:	In performing an audit examination, the auditor's duty of inquiry may bring to his attention illegal acts by the client. The further removed an illegal act is from the events and transactions reflected in the financials, the less likely it is that the auditor's inquiry will discover or recognize the illegal act.
MR. GADFLY:	If these improper payments were recorded in the books of the company, should they have been discovered?
MR. AUDITOR:	It's possible. I need to know more facts. Suffice it to say there is a duty of inquiry regarding illegal acts.
MR. SUEM:	Let's assume that John Q. Accountant knew, or in the exercise of due professional care, skill, and competence, should have known, of these illegal payments.
MR. AUDITOR:	Okay.
MR. SUEM:	In those circumstances, shouldn't John Q. Accountant disclose these illegal acts?
MR. AUDITOR:	There is a duty of disclosure regarding illegal acts that create significant unusual risks associated with a material amount of revenues or earnings, such as the loss of a significant business relationship.
MR. SUEM:	The balloon supplier had a significant relationship with Bubbling, correct?
MR. AUDITOR:	Yes.
MR. SUEM:	And there was a significant loss of revenues and earnings caused by not having the product to sell, correct?
MR. AUDITOR:	It appears to be so.
MR. SUEM:	It looks like if John Q. Accountant knew of this government investigation and the loss of the supplier, he should have insisted on disclosure in the financials.
MR. GADFLY:	Yes, I would say John Q. Accountant breached his duty of disclosure.
MR. AUDITOR:	You still have a problem with your proposed lawsuit, Mr. Gadfly.
MR. GADFLY:	How?
MR. AUDITOR:	You said you don't recall ever reading John Q. Accountant's report which accompanied the financials.

MR. GADFLY:	So what?
MR. AUDITOR:	How can you contend you relied on the report if you did not read it?
MR. GADFLY:	I'll let my lawyer handle that.
MR. SUEM:	Mr. Auditor, there are rules of law which provide that in some instances a plaintiff need not prove actual reliance if the fraud complained of is a material omission. Reliance will be presumed.
MR. AUDITOR:	What if John Q. Accountant issued an audit report in which he qualified or disclaimed an opinion regarding the financials.
MR. SUEM:	A qualification or disclaimer by itself will not extricate John Q. Accountant from responsibility for a misleading disclosure. The accountant's report must state the reasons underlying the qualification or disclaimer. To be effective, John Q. Accountant would have to qualify his opinion regarding any financial uncertainty relating to the illegal acts and the government's investigation.
MR. AUDITOR:	And if these reasons are not stated. . . .
MR. SUEM:	Then the simple qualification without more will not extricate John Q. Accountant from his breach of the duty of disclosure.
MR. GADFLY:	It sounds like John Q. Accountant's balloon may have burst!

¶ 7.03   Duty of Inquiry: Limitations

The duty of inquiry to ascertain and examine the facts prior to rendering a professional report or advice must be limited in terms of the (1) scope of inquiry and (2) the time period in which the inquiry is undertaken. If the duty of inquiry were unlimited in terms of scope and time, it could never be successfully discharged even if the accountant otherwise acted in good faith and with due professional care, skill, and competence.

The duty of inquiry will be established by several factors including:

(a)   What the accountant agreed to do

(b)   What the accountant represented he had done

(c)   What existing professional standards, custom, and practice required to be done

In the final analysis the courts may determine the nature of an accountant's duty of inquiry as it relates to the facts of the case before the court. Consider the following cases:

[1] *Hochfelder v. Ernst & Ernst* and Comments

Hochfelder v. Ernst & Ernst
503 F.2d 1100 (7th Cir. 1974)

Before SWYGERT, Chief Judge, CASTLE, Senior Circuit Judge, and SPRECHER, Circuit Judge.

SWYGERT, Chief Judge.
[Plaintiffs were defrauded by Leston Nay, president of First Securities Company, in vi-

olation of Rule 10b-5. First Securities was a broker-dealer in securities through which Nay induced the plaintiffs to invest in fictitious "escrow accounts" created by him.

Defendant accountants, Ernst & Ernst, audited First Securities throughout the period of Nay's fraud. The plaintiffs contended that the auditors aided and abetted Nay's fraud by failing to discover and disclose the existence of Nay's so-called mail rule. The mail rule was an office rule imposed by Nay on all employees of First Securities, whereby all mail addressed to Nay or to the company for his attention was to be opened only by Nay, and when Nay was away from the office the mail was to remain unopened regardless of the duration of his absence from the office. The plaintiffs contended that the mail rule was the "key to concealment of his fraudulent escrow scheme" and that the auditors bore a duty of inquiry to investigate this practice. The plaintiffs further contended that the mail rule constituted a material weakness in internal controls which the auditors should have discovered and disclosed.]

With respect to the existence of a duty of inquiry it is clear that Ernst & Ernst's contractual arrangement whereby it undertook to audit First Securities gave rise to a common law duty of inquiry. The extent and scope of that duty will be the subject of additional analysis; for present purposes, however, it is sufficient to state that Ernst & Ernst's audit engagement imposed a common law duty of inquiry.

In addition, having undertaken the contractual duty to audit First Securities and prepare SEC Form X-17A-5 pursuant to section 17(a) of the Securities Exchange Act and SEC Rule 17a-5 thereunder, a statutory duty of inquiry is properly imposed on Ernst & Ernst. Section 17(a) and its corollary Rule 17a-5 require a member of a national securities exchange to file with the SEC an annual report of financial condition certified by an independent certified public accountant, which report meets the requirements of Form X-17A-5. In accordance with the provisions of section 17(a) and Rule 17a-5 First Securities retained Ernst & Ernst. Thus, we find

Ernst & Ernst chargeable additionally with a statutory duty of inquiry.

• • •

In determining whether Ernst & Ernst breached its statutory duty of inquiry our examination is twofold: (1) the scope of Ernst & Ernst's duty of inquiry must be ascertained; and (2) the standard of conduct by which Ernst & Ernst executed its duty must be delineated.

Going first to the last element, we are of the view that when accountants undertake to perform an audit, they are required to meet only the standard of care reasonably expected of persons holding themselves out as skilled accountants. We agree with Judge McLean that, in general "accountants should not be held to a standard higher than that recognized in their profession." *Escott v. Barchris Construction Corp.*, 283 F.Supp. 643, 703 (S.D.N.Y. 1968). Accordingly, the standard of care which generally prevailed in the accounting profession during the years of Ernst & Ernst's audits of First Securities is the standard to which Ernst & Ernst must be held.

The extent or scope of Ernst & Ernst's statutory duty of inquiry imposed by section 17(a) and Rule 17a-5 is clearly set forth in Form X-17A-5:

> "The audit shall be made in accordance with generally accepted auditing standards and shall include a review of the accounting system, the internal accounting control and procedures for safeguarding securities including appropriate tests thereof for the period since the prior examination date. It shall include all procedures necessary under the circumstances to substantiate the assets and liabilities and securities and commodities positions as of the date of the responses to the financial questionnaire and to permit the expression of an opinion by the independent public accountant as to the financial condition of the respondent at that date."

This duty to audit in accordance with generally accepted auditing standards does not differ from the duty which is otherwise imposed by law, *Wessel v. Buhler. . .* ; *Caddell v. Good-*

body & Co. . . . ; or the accounting profession itself. American Institute of Certified Public Accountants, *Audits of Brokers and Dealers in Securities* (1956).

Moreover, with regard to accountants' duty to uncover fraud or irregularities, we think that in general it is properly stated that:

> In making the ordinary examination, the independent auditor is aware of the possibility that fraud may exist. Financial statements may be misstated as the result of defalcations and similar irregularities, or deliberate misrepresentation by management, or both. The auditor recognizes that fraud, if sufficiently material, may affect his opinion on the financial statements, and his examination, made in accordance with generally accepted auditing standards, gives consideration to this possibility. However, the ordinary examination directed to the expression of an opinion on financial statements is not primarily or specifically designed and cannot be relied upon, to disclose defalcations and other similar irregularities, although their discovery may result. Similarly, although the discovery of deliberate misrepresentation by management is usually more closely associated with the objective of the ordinary examination, such examination cannot be relied upon to assure its discovery. The responsibility of the independent auditor for failure to detect fraud (which responsibility differs as to clients and others) arises only when such failure clearly results from failure to comply with generally accepted auditing standards.

With this statement in mind, the statutory duty of inquiry was breached if it can be shown that Ernst & Ernst in failing to attain the professional standard of care did not conduct its audit of First Securities in accordance with the requirements set forth therein.

• • •

Plaintiffs further contend that Ernst & Ernst was under a duty of inquiry to detect and report First Securities' noncompliance with Rule 27(c) of Article III of the Rules of Fair Practice of the National Association of Se-

curities Dealers, Inc. (N.A.S.D)[1] In *Securities & Exch. Com'n v. First Securities Co. of Chicago*, 463 F.2d 981 (7th Cir. 1972), we held that First Securities' enforcement of Nay's "mail rule" was sufficient without more to constitute a violation of Rule 27. Accordingly, we found First Securities, a member of the N.A.S.D., liable for Nay's fraud, due to its failure to enforce Rule 27. In *Hochfelder, et al. v. Midwest Stock Exchange*, 503 F.2d 364 (1974) plaintiffs raised a contention, somewhat similar to the one they raise here, that the Midwest Stock Exchange was under a duty to enforce the rules of the N.A.S.D. In response to that contention we observed (at pp. 373, 374):

> In this action plaintiffs request that we place a duty on Midwest as a national securities exchange to enforce the rules of another self-regulatory organization, namely, the N.A.S.D., a national securities association. Without facing the question whether even the N.A.S.D. as promulgator of Rule 27 could be liable because of its member's noncompliance, plaintiffs would have us place an additional burden on Midwest to enforce the rules of another self-regulatory body. There is nothing in the 1934 Act which

---

[1] Rule 27 in pertinent part provides:

"(a)   Each member [of the Association] shall establish, maintain and enforce written procedures which will enable it to supervise properly the activities of each registered representative and associated person to assure compliance with applicable securities laws, rules, regulations and statements of policy promulgated thereunder and with the rules of this Association.

(b)   Final responsibility for proper supervision shall rest with the member.

(c)   Each member shall be responsible for keeping and preserving appropriate records for carrying out the member's supervisory procedures. Each member shall review and endorse in writing on an internal record, all transactions and all correspondence of its registered representatives pertaining to the solicitation or execution of any securities transaction."

mandates this unique theory. Indeed, the imposition of such a burden of enforcement would be unduly onerous and result in a wasteful duplication of actions in that Midwest would be expected to enforce the rules of all self-regulatory organizations to which a member firm might belong. This would be contrary to the avowed intention of Congress and the Securities and Exchange Commission that there be more coordination and less duplication of self-regulatory activities. We hold that Midwest was under no duty to enforce Rule 27(c) of the Rules of Fair Practice of the N.A.S.D.

In the instant action the posture of plaintiffs' contention that Ernst & Ernst was under a duty to examine First Securities' compliance with the Rules of Fair Practice of the N.A.S.D. and in particular Rule 27(c) is: Public accountants are chargeable with a general duty of examining N.A.S.D. member firms for compliance with N.A.S.D. rules in view of the fact that the self-regulatory organization which promulgated the rules, the N.A.S.D., has failed to conduct examinations verifying compliance with its rules. Moreover, plaintiffs in effect claim that the duty to investigate compliance with the N.A.S.D. Rules of Fair Practice is necessarily encompassed within the body of generally accepted auditing standards. Ernst & Ernst makes the counter argument that neither SEC Rule 17a-5, Form X-17A-5, nor generally accepted auditing standards require that an auditor of a securities broker or dealer who is also a member of N.A.S.D., has any duty to review compliance by the broker or dealer with the rules of the N.A.S.D. It is claimed that such an examination for compliance with N.A.S.D. rules is entirely outside of the scope of an audit.

A fair reading of SEC Rule 17a-5 and Form X-17A-5 indicates that no duty is imposed on an auditor to ascertain compliance with N.A.S.D. rules. Moreover, it appears that the perceptible body of generally accepted auditing standards does not embrace such a requirement of audit review. In addition, even if plaintiffs were to be heard to complain of a contractual breach of duty by Ernst & Ernst, it is clear that Ernst & Ernst was not retained to verify First Securities' compliance with the N.A.S.D. Rules of Fair Practice.

Although plaintiffs' proposition is somewhat novel, we recognize, in agreement with the accounting profession, that it is not entirely devoid of merit. In the American Institute of Certified Public Accountants' industry audit guide on *Audit of Brokers and Dealers in Securities* the admonition is given (at p. 3):

> In addition to a familiarity with the above rules of the Securities and Exchange Commission, it is necessary for the independent public accountant to have a working knowledge of Regulations T and U of the Board of Governors of the Federal Reserve System, and, if his client is a member of a stock exchange or the National Association of Securities Dealers, Inc., he should be familiar with the pertinent rules of those organizations. It is also considered advisable to review the applicable Accounting Series and other releases which are published from time to time by the Securities and Exchange Commission.

And, although the defendant correctly states that generally accepted auditing standards do not ordinarily require such investigation, we do not find that entirely compelling. The teaching of *The T. J. Hooper*, 60 F.2d 737 (2d Cir. 1932), is not lost to us for we recognize that we are not constrained to accept faulty standards of practice otherwise generally accepted in an industry or profession.[2] Moreover, the potential for imposition of liability on a broker or dealer for noncompliance with N.A.S.D. rules would seem to undermine the

---

[2] Judge Learned Hand aptly stated in *The T. J. Hooper* decision:

> There are, no doubt, cases where courts seem to make the general practice of the calling the standard of proper diligence; we have indeed given some currency to the notion ourselves. . . . Indeed in most cases reasonable prudence is in fact common prudence; but strictly it is never its measure; a whole calling may have unduly lagged in the adoption of new and available devices. It never may set its own tests, however persuasive be its usages. Courts must in the end say what is required; there are precautions so imperative that even their universal disregard will not excuse their omission. 60 F.2d at 740.

auditor's ability to represent that the financial statements fairly reflect the financial position of the broker or dealer unless some sort of inquiry were made into compliance with those rules.

To countenance the duty of inquiry advocated by plaintiffs, however, would in our judgment be inappropriate. To direct full examination for compliance with the various rules of all the self-regulatory organizations to which a broker or dealer might belong would be to impose a burden of inquiry—otherwise not demanded by contract, statutory law, or professional practices—of indefinable proportions which arguably could never effectively and completely be implemented. We cannot subscribe to a situation whereby the accountant has the burden of an investigation which is unascertainable and everchanging.

In summary, the burden of inquiry as to compliance with N.A.S.D. rules is placed with the N.A.S.D., where it should properly repose, for it is the promulgator of those rules and as such should command adherence thereto. Ernst & Ernst, as auditor of a member firm of the N.A.S.D., need have only inquired as to whether the member firm received an adverse report following an examination by the N.A.S.D. Having carried the inquiry that far, Ernst & Ernst cannot be charged with more.

1. Although the U.S. Supreme Court reversed the court of appeals decision in *Hochfelder v. Ernst & Ernst*, the court did not reverse the court of appeals' analysis regarding an auditor's duty of inquiry. With respect to the duty of inquiry the court of appeals held in *Hochfelder* that the "duty of inquiry advocated by plaintiffs" would impose a burden of inquiry of "undefinable proportions which arguably could never effectively and completely be implemented." The court of appeals concluded that it could not "subscribe to a situation whereby the accountant has the burden of an investigation which is unascertainable and everchanging."

2. The rejection of a duty of inquiry of "undefinable proportions" is consistent with the notion that an auditor's duty of inquiry should be governed by consideration's of materiality and cost/benefit. An auditor could set out to audit the entire universe of facts that might bear on his client's financials. It is doubtful whether an auditor could complete his audit of the "universe" of facts within his lifetime, let alone on any basis that would make timely use of the financials. Moreover, there is little question that the expense of auditing the "universe" of facts would not be justified by any benefit derived from such an audit.

3. In *Hochfelder* the court of appeals observed that the audit duty proposed by the plaintiff was "not demanded by contract, statutory law, or professional practices." The court of appeals also observed that it was not "constrained to accept faulty standards of practice otherwise generally accepted in an industry or practice." The message communicated by the court to the auditing profession was simple: We agree with the auditing profession that the audit duty of inquiry proposed by plaintiff is no good; but keep in mind that just because a whole profession engages in a certain practice, don't expect the courts to automatically accept the practice as evidence of due care.

4. The plaintiffs in *Hochfelder v. Ernst & Ernst* also sued the Midwest Stock Exchange for failure to regulate First Securities and Leston Nay. In *Hochfelder v. Midwest Stock Exchange* the U.S. court of appeals rejected the plaintiff's attempt to impose a far-reaching duty of inquiry on Midwest to examine Nay's personal financial affairs. The court rejected this duty of inquiry, holding:

We are not prepared to place a burden of inquiry on an exchange which would effectively require scrutiny and investigation into all the personal affairs and activities of member nominees or the personal, business, and financial affairs of those individuals closely associated with member organizations. In this same vein plaintiffs contend that as part of the duty of self-regulation it was incumbent on Midwest to obtain and examine copies of Nay's federal income tax returns, which it is asserted would have uncovered Nay's fraudulent escrow scheme. As is true of the contention that Midwest should have investigated the reasons for Nay's personal loan, to require Midwest to inspect Nay's personal tax returns would impose a burden on Midwest to investigate into events not related to matters reflected in a member organization's books and records. Although Midwest used a protective system to assure responsibility and integrity in the handling of public customer business which focused primarily on the books and records reflecting the activities of member organizations, plaintiffs argue that the system was insufficient because it failed to go beyond the member organization and investigate personal books and records, if any, reflecting the personal activities and affairs of member nominees. This asserted burden of inquiry would be applicable not solely to those individuals similarly situated to Nay; rather, the burden of inquiry would likewise be applicable to everyone associated with any member organization who might possibly be engaged in a personal, remote, and carefully concealed fraudulent scheme. To place such a burden on Midwest to inquire into affairs unrelated to the activities of the Exchange would be tantamount to making the Exchange a guarantor of losses resulting from every fraudulent, personal scheme engaged in by individuals associated with member organizations. Indeed, the implementation of such a burden of inquiry might well be counter-productive in that it would dissipate resources which are limited and needed for the basic self-regulatory actions in scrutinizing matters pertaining to member organization activities and affairs.

The *Hochfelder v. Midwest Stock Exchange* decision is one way a court might decide the issue of whether an auditor has a duty of inquiry to "investigate into events not related to matters reflected in a [client's] books and records."

5. In *Hochfelder v. Midwest Stock Exchange* the court of appeals observed that to "place such a burden on Midwest to inquire into affairs unrelated to the activities of the Exchange would be tantamount to making the Exchange a guarantor of losses resulting from every fraudulent, personal scheme engaged in by individuals associated with member organizations." It is clear that auditors are not guarantors of their client's financials. A duty of inquiry that would make an auditor a "guarantor" would not be appropriate.

[2] *Oleck v. Fischer* and Comments

Oleck v. Fischer
CCH Fed. Sec. L. Rep. ¶96, 898 (S.D.N.Y. 1979)

[The facts of this case are set out at ¶ 4.07[2][b].]

HAIGHT, District Judge: In March of 1971 plaintiffs Lawrence and Theodore Oleck, brothers and business partners, sold the stock of their Blue Circle Telephone Answering Service, Inc. to Sherwood Diversified Services, Inc., in exchange for cash and a series of promissory notes executed by Sherwood. The notes, plus interest, were payable through 1976. Sherwood filed a petition under Chapter XI of the Bankruptcy Act in March, 1973, leaving substantial amounts due to the Olecks under the notes. The Olecks commenced this action pursuant to §§ 10(b) and 27 of the Securities Exchange Act of 1934, 15

U. S. C. §§ 78(a) *et seq.*, and Rule 10b-5 of the Securities and Exchange Commission, 17 C. F. R. 240.10b-5, against former officers and stockholders of Sherwood, and an individual described as Sherwood's principal negotiator on the transactions, as well as his company. The complaint was amended to add a cause of action against Arthur Andersen & Co., the accounting firm that audited Sherwood's 1970 financial statements, upon which plaintiffs allegedly relied in selling Blue Circle to Sherwood.

· · ·

Plaintiffs' charges against Andersen, put forward in the testimony of its expert witness Rehmet, may be summarized as follows:

(a)   Footnote 11 to the 1970 Sherwood annual report was misleading, in that it did not adequately describe the risks to Sherwood inherent in its investment and obligations with respect to U.S. Media and

(b)   Andersen violated generally accepted auditing standards by issuing an unqualified opinion to Sherwood, in that Andersen did not obtain sufficient competent evidential matter with respect to the realizability of Sherwood's investment in USM to justify such an opinion; and the evidence Andersen did obtain should have given rise to substantial doubt requiring a qualified opinion or disclaimer of opinion. Plaintiffs' expert contended, to recapitulate, that even if Andersen considered footnote 11 was fair, it should nonetheless have issued a qualified opinion because of the insufficiency of evidential matter demonstrating the realizability of the USM notes; alternatively, and consistent with plaintiffs' contention that the footnote was misleading, Andersen should have further qualified its opinion, or issued an adverse one.

Plaintiffs' first criticism of Andersen's clean opinion is that it was issued with insufficient evidential support. Their expert witness, Ralph A. Rehmet, gave his opinion that Andersen issued an unqualified opinion "without also having obtained sufficient competent evidential matter to provide the firm with a rea-

sonable basis for providing such an opinion under the circumstances." However, that conclusion is based upon a relatively narrow point. His criticism, was limited to Andersen's work relative to "the value of the note [i.e., the USM promissory notes] when it was issued." As to that, Rehmet did not quarrel with the steps Andersen took (see ¶40, *ante*); his view was that "the due care standard required Arthur Andersen to delve beyond ordinary procedures." The only specific step Rehmet said Andersen should have taken which it had not taken was to obtain a third party assessment of the value of the notes, from a potential investor such as a factor, or a lending institution such as a bank. That is the sum and substance of plaintiffs' argument on the point, as put forward by their expert witness; the limited scope of the criticism appears clearly from Rehmet's testimony, set out in the margin.[1] I find, however, that generally accepted auditing standards did not require Andersen, in the circumstances of the case, to obtain such a third party evaluation of USM's receivables [which were the collateral underlying USM's promissory notes to Sherwood]. Rehmet himself acknowledged that generally speaking, auditors do not obtain third party appraisals of trade accounts receivable in the absence of special circumstances, such as a slow paying major account; a "break in the pattern of payments"; or indications that the client company was "having financial problems" of such a magnitude that the auditors needed to consider the issuance of a qualified opinion "as to the continuation of the business as a going con-

---

[1] Rehmet testified on direct examination:

"In my opinion, the evidence gathered by Andersen should have created substantial doubt as the collectability of $2,570,000 of notes from U. S. Media. In view of Andersen's admittedly heavy reliance on the collateral, coupled with that collateral's insufficiency in meeting standards set by the Continental Bank in their lending to [Sherwood], this should have required Andersen to either obtain competent advice from experienced lenders as to the soundness of Media's $2,570,000 collateralized debt to Sherwood or result in a qualified or disclaimed opinion.

cern," in which event they might "ask the client to get an evaluation of its lending capability to see whether or not the client did have the capability to obtain sufficient future financing to stay in business." None of these circumstances was present here. To the extent that they were identified in the evidence, USM's creditors were responsible companies; there was no evidence of major problems arising out of slow payments. Some "breaks in the pattern of payments" were detected, but Andersen inquired and was satisfied with the explanations, such as a prolonged strike affecting a major USM client, National Airlines, which interrupted billings. As to USM's inability as a going concern, Andersen did not have before it during the 1970 audit (the only pertinent time) indications of so serious a decline as to necessitate "an evaluation of USM's lending capability" to see if it "could stay in business." Thus even on the analysis of plaintiffs' expert I decline to find that Andersen should have sought a third party evaluation of USM's trade account receivables. In any event, I prefer and accept the opinion of Andersen's expert witness, William Badecker, to the effect that Andersen's inquiries into the "carrying value" of the USM notes "complied with the standard of obtaining sufficient

evidential matter,"[2] further taking into consideration the establishment of a reserve for collectability. I find, in accordance with Badecker's testimony, that it was not the general practice for auditors to obtain third party evaluations of such notes or their underlying collateral, and that Andersen was not required to do so by the circumstances of this case.

---

[2] Q. "And in your opinion, in evaluating the collateral which consisted of accounts receivable, should Andersen have extended its auditing procedures by insisting that Sherwood engage an outside financial institution to value the notes?"

A. "No, sir. In the kind of collateral that supported these notes, Andersen did everything that generally accepted auditing standards required them, and I would add that in my 28 years of experience, at times there have been occasions where I have had to look at collateral, where the collateral is accounts receivable, that I have never had to look to outside specialists or to get an opinion of a banker or a factor with respect to accounts receivable."

Q. "What is the general practice in the auditing profession when auditors became concerned with long-term notes receivable, themselves secured by accounts receivable, to engage a factor or a financial institution to assist in the evaluation?"

A. "No, that is not general practice." Tr. 703-4.

1. *Oleck v. Fischer* involves the limitation on the scope of an auditor's duty of inquiry. The trial court held that the auditors did not have to examine the collectability of notes receivables from a company, U.S. Media, to the audit client, Sherwood, which notes were collateralized by U.S. Media's accounts receivables. Specifically, the court held that the auditor's duty of inquiry did not require them to "audit" the value of U.S. Media's notes and underlying collateral by obtaining an evaluation from a third-party such as a factor or a lending institution.

2. The *Oleck v. Fischer* case demonstrates the importance which expert-witness testimony plays in litigation involving an accountant's professional responsibilities. The trial court decided that it was "not the general practice for auditors to obtain third party evaluations of such notes or their underlying collateral."

In reaching this conclusion the trial court relied upon the testimony of the auditor's expert witness, who testified there was no duty of inquiry. The plaintiffs' expert witness had testified to the contrary. In resolving the conflict in testimony the trial judge observed:

> While not intending to denigrate plaintiffs' expert Rehmet, I am bound to say that Mr. Badecker's opinions impressed me because of his demeanor and his experience, particularly his service between 1974 and 1977 on the Audit Standards Executive Committee of the American Institute of Certified Public Accountants. That is the committee designated by the

profession to set the auditing standards which lie at the heart of this case. On the precise issue presented, the necessity of a third-party evaluation, it is not that clear that Mr. Rehmet's testimony, when the special circumstances he described are analyzed, is at variance with that of Mr. Badecker.

3.   Expert-witness testimony can become critical on issues such as the appropriate scope of the duty of inquiry. If an expert, who is well recognized and received, testifies that an auditor has a duty of inquiry, the trier of fact (which could be judge or a jury) may be highly persuaded.

Cross-examination may reduce the persuasiveness of the expert's opinion. Likewise, the opposing party may put on his own expert who will persuasively refute and contradict the position taken by the other party's expert.

If the opposing experts contradict each other, this "Mexican standoff" may be resolved by the trier of facts' reliance upon the myriad of intangible factors involved in determining the credibility of a witness, such as:

The witness's demeanor on the stand (e.g., surly arrogance versus the "nice guy" versus the straightforward, no-nonsense type)

The witness's experience (e.g., theoretical training but no experience in the field versus signficant experience in the field but weak technical skills and understanding)

The color of the witness's shirt and tie (the "good vibrations" factor)

4.   With respect to the duty of disclosure, the opinions of expert witnesses take on less significance. This is especially true when the issue involves questions of fraud. The textbook example of the insignificance of expert opinions in a fraud case is the criminal conviction of the auditors in *United States v. Simon*, which is discussed at ¶ 5.03[2] and 5.04[1].

When it comes to a question of whether all the facts have been disclosed in order to provide the complete "big picture," expert opinions may be helpful to the trier of fact but not dispositive.

[3]   *Katz v. Realty Equities Corp.* and Comments

Katz v. Realty Equities Corp.
406 F.Supp. 802 (S.D.N.Y. 1976)

POLLACK, District Judge.

The defendants Alexander Grant & Co. and Klein, Hinds, & Finke, (hereafter "Grant" and "KHF"), two public accounting firms, have moved for summary judgment.

The complaints involving the . . . defendants allege that Republic and Realty defrauded investors by engaging in a series of transactions which were designed to artificially inflate the reported income and assets of the two companies. . . . KHF served as Realty's independent certified public accountant for a number of years prior to September 1, 1969; Grant succeeded KHF in that capacity after that date, when the two defendants combined practices.

The complaints allege that the two defendants "discovered or knew of the material problems between Realty and Republic," and that "both firms failed in their obligations to the public and to the SEC to fully disclose such facts and to alert responsible authorities thereto." The defendants are also charged with aiding and abetting violations of the securities laws.

It is uncontroverted that KHF's work for Realty did not encompass any activity involving Realty's operations or transactions subsequent to the fiscal year ending March 31, 1969, and that Grant's responsibility did not extend beyond the fiscal year ending March 31, 1970. The defendants had no duty of inquiry, and consequently no duty of disclosure, in regard to Realty transactions and operations which occurred subsequent to the periods during which they acted as Realty's independent certified accountants.

Plaintiffs' allegation must therefore be limited to the non-disclosure of material facts which the defendants knew of during the period they acted as Realty's independent accountants. To survive the instant summary judgment motion, there must appear to be a genuine issue that the defendants during the relevant period were aware of, and did not disclose, information which would have been material to the plaintiffs' investment decisions. As is shown below, there is no such genuine issue of fact.

The complaints do not allege any specific transactions as grounds for relief which occurred during KHF's tenure as Realty's accountant. Hence, KHF cannot be held responsible for a material non-disclosure; there can be no genuine issue and summary judgment is appropriate as to KHF.

1.   The trial judge quite sensibly held that the accounting firm that audited Realty Equities Corp. up to September 1, 1969, had no duty of inquiry and consequently no duty of disclosure subsequent to that date. This principle limits the duty of inquiry to the period during which the auditor has access to the client's books and records. If the auditor no longer has access to the client's financial records, there should be no imposition of a duty of inquiry.

2.   The fact that the accountant no longer has access to the client's records does not rule out the possibility that a duty of disclosure still might be imposed. For example, the duty to correct (discussed at ¶ 6.03) is imposed whenever the accountant becomes aware that previously issued audited financials were materially wrong at the time the auditor issued the report. The auditor has no duty of inquiry to continously examine financials, but he does bear a duty to correct whenever the false financials are still "alive" and being relied upon.

¶ 7.04   Duty of Inquiry: Compilation and Review Services

[1]   The "Unauditor" Confronts "Suspicious Circumstances"— A Duty of Inquiry

When an accountant agrees to perform an audit examination in accordance with GAAS, the accountant assumes a duty of inquiry to ascertain and analyze the material facts relating to the client's financials. This duty of inquiry will be coextensive with the standards and practices of the profession.

If an accountant merely agrees to compile financial statements, does he have any duty of inquiry? If the accountant has agreed to review financial statements, how extensive is his duty of inquiry?

The accountant who is associated with compiled or reviewed financials may be referred to as the "unauditor." The unauditor does not bear a duty of inquiry that is identical to an auditor's duty of inquiry.

It is possible that an unauditor may bear a duty of inquiry when he becomes aware of "suspicious circumstances" that call into question the accuracy and substance of the financial statements. The duty of inquiry to investigate and resolve questions relating to the "suspicious circumstances" may be extensive—even if the unauditor has agreed only to compile the financials.

[a] *1136 Tenants' Corp. v. Max Rothenberg & Co.* and Comments

1136 Tenants' Corp. v. Max Rothenberg & Co.
319 N.Y.S.2d 1007 (App. Div. 1971)

Before STEVENS, P. J., and CAPOZZOLI, NUNEZ, McNALLY and STEUER, JJ.

PER CURIAM.

[The plaintiff corporation owned a cooperative apartment building which was managed by Riker. At trial it was established that Riker embezzled monies that belonged to the plaintiff and were intended to pay the expenses of the cooperative.

The defendant accounting firm was hired by Riker to perform services with respect to the cooperative's financial books and records. The accountants contended that they were hired to "write up" the books and records for which they charged a fee of $600. The accountants prepared financial statements that were marked "unverified" and stated that "no independent examination had been made."

The plaintiff corporation contended that the accountants had been hired to perform an audit of the cooperative's books and records. The plaintiff corporation claimed that had the accountants performed their audit with due care, they would have discovered Riker's defalcations.

The trial judge ruled that the accountants had been engaged to perform an audit. The trial judge also held that had the accountants performed a "minimal amount of internal auditing procedures," the fraud would have been discovered.

The trial judge assessed damages against the accountants in the amount of $237,278.33. The accountants appealed the trial judge's decision to the Supreme Court, Appellate Division.]

The record amply supports the Trial Court's findings that defendant was engaged to audit and not merely "write-up" plaintiff's books and records and that the procedures performed by defendant were "incomplete, inadequate and improperly employed." One of defendant's senior partners admitted at the trial that defendant performed services for plaintiff which went beyond the scope of a "write-up" and that it actually performed some auditing procedures for plaintiff. Defendant's worksheets indicate that defendant did examine plaintiff's bank statement, invoices and bills and, in fact, one of the worksheets is entitled "Missing Invoices 1/1/63–12/31/63" (plaintiff's exhibit 16-B-6). That sheet alone indicates invoices missing from the records of Riker & Co. which totalled more than $44,000.

Utilization of the simplest audit procedures would have revealed Riker's defalcations. Moreover, *even if* defendant were hired to perform only "write-up" services, it is clear, beyond dispute, that it did become aware that material invoices purportedly paid by Riker were missing, and, accordingly, had a duty to at least inform plaintiff of this. But even this it failed to do. Defendant was not free to consider these and other suspicious circumstances as being of no significance and prepare its financial reports as if same did not exist.

The questions of fact presented in this case were ably discussed in the decision of the Court below and there is no reason why we should interfere with the result reached by that Court.

1. In the *1136 Tenants' Corp.* the parties were at issue as to the scope of the accountants' engagement. The trial judge held that the accountants had agreed to perform an audit. The appellate court sidestepped that issue by holding that even if the accountants were not hired to perform an audit, they nevertheless bore a duty of inquiry to either examine the "suspicious circumstances" or inform the client of the suspicious circumstances.

The suspicious circumstance was the fact that the accountants had discovered that invoices totaling more than $44,000 were missing. The accountants prepared a worksheet entitled "Missing Invoices." They did not investigate further the reasons relating to why these invoices were missing. The accountants did not advise the plaintiff corporation of their discovery.

2. The trial court in the *1136 Tenants' Corp.* case found that the accountants had been engaged to perform an audit, reasoning that (1) the $600 retainer paid to the accountants was a "sufficient and adequate retainer" to perform an audit; (2) the accountants' claim that "were an 'audit' involved, the fee would be much larger, is gratuitous and unfounded"; and (3) the trial court credited the testimony of a witness for the plaintiff who testified that he had orally retained the accountants to perform an audit—an audit that would have discovered the witness's defalcation.

[b]   *United States v. Natelli* and Comments

United States v. Natelli
527 F.2d 311 (2d Cir. 1975)

[The facts of the case are set out in more detail at ¶ 5.03[3]. The audit partner and supervisor responsible for the examination of National Student Marketing were found by a jury to be guilty of criminal fraud. The auditors appealed their criminal conviction to the U.S. Court of Appeals.

On appeal the auditors challenged that portion of their conviction that related to an unaudited nine months' earnings statement, which was part of the misleading financial information contained in a proxy statement issued by National Student Marketing.

The audit partner, Natelli, contended that he had no duty of inquiry to determine whether the nine months' earnings statement was accurate or false. Natelli further contended that the evidence did not demonstrate that he "knew" that the earnings statement was false and in particular that a "booked" contract from Eastern Airlines was fictitious.]

B. The False Nine Months Earnings Statement

The proxy statement also required an unaudited statement of nine months earnings through May 31, 1969. This was prepared by the Company, with the assistance of Peat on the same percentage of completion basis as in the 1968 audited statement. A commitment from Pontiac Division of General Motors amounting to $1,200,000 was produced two months after the end of the fiscal period. It was dated April 28, 1969.

The proxy statement was to be printed at the Pandick Press in New York on August 15, 1969. At about 3 A.M. on that day, Natelli informed Randell that the "sale" to the Pontiac Division for more than $1 million could not be treated as a valid commitment because the letter from Pontiac was not a legally binding obligation. Randell responded at once that he had a "commitment from Eastern Airlines" in a somewhat comparable amount attributable to the nine months fiscal period (which had ended more than two months earlier). Kelly, a salesman for Marketing, arrived at the printing plant several hours later with a commitment letter from Eastern Airlines, dated August 14, 1969, purporting to confirm an $820,000 commitment ostensibly entered into on May 14, just before the end of the nine-month fiscal period of September

1, 1968 through May 31, 1969. When the proxy statement was printed in final form, the Pontiac "sale" had been deleted, but the Eastern "commitment" had been inserted in its place.

The Eastern contract was a matter for deep suspicion because it was substituted so rapidly for the Pontiac contract to which Natelli had objected, and which had, itself, been produced after the end of the fiscal period, though dated earlier. It was still another unbilled commitment produced by Marketing long after the close of the fiscal period. Its spectacular appearance, as Natelli himself noted at the time, made its replacement of the Pontiac contract "weird."[1] The Eastern "commitment" was not only in substitution for the challenged Pontiac "commitment" but strangely close enough in amount to leave the projected earnings figures for the proxy statement relatively intact. Marketing had only time logs of a salesman relating to the making of the proposals but no record of expenditures on the Eastern "commitment," no record of having ever billed Eastern for services on this "sale," and not one scrap of paper from Eastern other than the suddenly-produced letter. Nevertheless, it was booked as if more than $500,000 of it had already been earned.

Natelli contends that he had no duty to verify the Eastern "commitment" because the earnings statement within which it was included was "unaudited."

This raises the issue of the duty of the CPA in relation to an unaudited financial statement contained within a proxy statement where the figures are reviewed and to some extent supplied by the auditors. It is common ground that the auditors were "associated" with the statement and were required to object to anything they actually "knew" to be materially false. In the ordinary case involving an unaudited statement, the auditor would not be chargeable simply because he failed to discover the invalidity of booked accounts receivable, inasmuch as he had not under-

taken an audit with verification. In this case, however, Natelli "knew" the history of post-period bookings and the dismal consequences later discovered. Was he under a duty in these circumstances to object or to go beyond the usual scope of an accountant's review and insist upon some independent verification? The American Institute of Certified Public Accountants, Statement of Auditing Standards and Procedures (1972), 1 CCH AICPA PROFESSIONAL STANDARDS § 516.00, recognizes that "if the certified public accountant concludes on the basis of facts known to him that unaudited financial statements with which he may become associated are not in conformity with generally accepted accounting principles, *which include adequate disclosure*, he should insist . . . upon appropriate revision . . ." (emphasis added).

We do not think this means, in terms of professional standards, that the accountant may shut his eyes in reckless disregard of his knowledge that highly suspicious figures, known to him to be suspicious, were being included in the unaudited earnings figures with which he was "associated" in the proxy statement.

Appellants contend that the trial court erroneously instructed the jury on the issue of knowledge. We do not agree. . . . In *United States v. Benjamin, supra,* 328 F. 2d at 862, this court said, regarding an accountant, that "the Government can meet its burden by proving that a defendant deliberately closed his eyes to facts he had a duty to see." And *United States v. Simon,* which affirmed the conviction of an accountant, as we have seen, sustained a charge in the very language Judge Tyler tracked.

While the facts in each case are not precisely the same, we think this appeal quite analogous to *Simon,* because Natelli was suspicious enough of the Eastern contract to check it with Kelly, the account executive in house, but not to take the next step of seeking verification from Eastern, despite his obvious doubt that it could be booked as a true commitment. And with respect to the footnote, we think the language of this court in *Simon* to be quite pertinent, "The jury could reasonably have wondered how accountants who were really seeking to tell the truth could

---

[1] Natelli's explanation that only the suggestion of Randell for *complete* replacement of the Pontiac contract *without changing the figures at all,* was "weird" is not convincing. Certainly the jury could find otherwise.

have constructed a footnote so well designed to conceal the shocking facts."

Appellants argue strenuously, however, that *U.S. v. Simon* involved an audited statement while the nine months statement here involved was an unaudited statement, and, that hence, the duties of appellants here were different from those enunciated in *Simon*. They urge as a corollary that the District Court failed to instruct the jury on the difference, and that his failure to do so was reversible error.

It is true that the point on appeal might have been eliminated if the judge had charged on the differences in the abstract. But in the circumstances he was not required to do so. As we have seen, *supra*, Point I, the duty of Natelli, given this set of facts, was not so different from the duty of an accountant upon an audit as to require sharply different treatment of that duty in the charge to the jury.

We agree with Judge Tyler when he charged the jury that they could find Natelli "knew" of the falsely material fact if he acted in "reckless disregard" or deliberately closed his eyes to the obvious. The issue on this appeal is not what an auditor is *generally* under a duty to do with respect to an unaudited statement, but what these defendants had a duty to do in these unusual and highly suspicious circumstances. . . . Nor was a proper charge requested.

The duly requested supplemental charge on Natelli's duty with respect to the unaudited earnings statement was properly denied. It read:

"The defendants' *only* responsibility as to this statement [unaudited statement of earnings for the nine months ended May 31, 1969] was to be satisfied that, *as far as they knew*, the statement contained no misstatement of material facts." (emphasis added).

This requested charge was not correct, for even on an unaudited statement with which Natelli was "associated" and where there were suspicious circumstances, his duty went further, as we have seen. As the Court correctly charged, Natelli was culpable if he acted in "reckless disregard" of the facts or if he "deliberately closed his eyes."

We expound no rule, to be sure, that an accountant in reviewing an unaudited company statement is bound, without more, to seek verification and to apply auditing procedures. We lay no extra burden on the normal activities of accountants, nor do we assume the role of an Accounting Principles Board. We deal only with such deviations as fairly come within the common understanding of dishonest conduct which jurors bring into the box as applied to the particular conduct prohibited by the particular statute.

It was not for Judge Tyler in his instruction to deal with the abstract question of an accountant's responsibility for unaudited statements, for that was not the issue. So long as we find that the Judge explicated the proper test applicable to the facts of this case, the duty inherent in the circumstances, and we do, we must also find that he gave the appellants a fair charge.

1. If an "unauditor" encounters suspicious circumstances in preparing unaudited statements, the duty of inquiry that arises may not differ at all from an auditor's duty of inquiry in the same circumstances.

2. In *United States v. Natelli* the AICPA filed a brief arguing that:

> The trial court committed prejudicial error in its instructions to the jury by failing to instruct it as to the distinct differences between the responsibility of an independent accountant with respect to financial statements he has audited and reported on and his very limited responsibility with respect to financial statements which he has not audited and on which he has not reported.

To this argument the court of appeals responded:

> It is true that the point on appeal might have been eliminated if the judge had charged on the differences in the abstract. But in the circumstances he was not required to do so. As

we have seen, the duty of Natelli, given this set of facts, was not so different from the duty of an accountant upon an audit as to require sharply different treatment of that duty in the charge to the jury.

We agree with Judge Tyler when he charged the jury that they could find Natelli "knew" of the falsely material fact if he acted in "reckless disregard" or deliberately closed his eyes to the obvious. The issue on this appeal is not what an auditor is generally under a duty to do with respect to an unaudited statement, but what these defendants had a duty to do in these unusual and highly suspicious circumstances.

3.   Breach of the duty of inquiry in suspicious circumstances may result not only in civil liability but criminal liability. The unauditor's exposure to risk may be great if he consciously ignores "suspicious circumstances."

4.   In *United States v. Natelli* the court of appeals held that the defendant Scansaroli bore no "duty in the circumstances to be suspicious," because as an audit supervisor he was Natelli's subordinate. The court of appeals stated:

> With respect to the major item, the Eastern commitment, we think Scansaroli stands in a position different from that of Natelli. Natelli was his superior. He was the man to make the judgement whether or not to object to the last-minute inclusion of a new "commitment" in the nine-month statement. There is insufficient evidence that Scansaroli engaged in any conversations about the Eastern commitment at the Pandick Press or that he was a participant with Natelli in any check on its authenticity. Since in the hierarchy of the accounting firm it was not his responsibility to decide whether to book the Eastern contract, his mere adjustment of the figures to reflect it under orders was not a matter for his discretion. As we have seen, Natelli bore a duty in the circumstances to be suspicious of the Eastern commitment and to pursue the matter further. Scansaroli may also have been suspicious, but rejection of the Eastern contract was not within his sphere of responsibility. Absent such duty, he cannot be held to have acted in reckless disregard of the facts.

[2]   Perspective: Compilation and Review Services

[a]   Compilation and Review: The Safety Factor[1]

An accountant's exposure to the risk of legal liability results in part from an "expectation gap" between the perceived and the actual responsibilities assumed by an accountant in performing compilation and review services. This article analyzes (1) client and third-party users' expectations and (2) the extent to which the institution of compilation and review services has effected new or increased professional responsibilities.

Users' Expectations

Accountants' past experiences with liability may foreshadow future expectations of users of compilation and review services.

Two landmark cases from which lessons still can be learned and which demonstrate the difficulties encountered by users and by the courts in perceiving the nature and degree of an "unauditor's" undertaking are *1136 Tenants' Corporation v. Max Rothenberg & Company* and *U.S. v. Natelli.*

---

[1] Kenneth I. Solomon, Charles Chazen, and Richard L. Miller, Jr., "Compilation and Review: The Safety Factor," *Journal of Accountancy*, July 1983. Copyright © 1983 by the AICPA, Inc. Opinions expressed in the *Journal of Accountancy* are those of editors and contributors. Publication in the *Journal of Accountancy* does not constitute endorsement by the AICPA or its committees.

In *1136 Tenants'*, the trial court demonstrated a fundamental misunderstanding of an unauditor's role when it held that "even though the sterile procedure of a write-up differs markedly from the professional expertise required and necessitated by an audit . . . the need for a certain amount of auditing procedures is required even in a 'write-up.' " It also held that "a CPA can make an examination which constitutes an audit without making independent verifications."

The appellate court in *1136 Tenants'* affirmed the trial court under a different approach, holding that

> Even if defendants were hired to perform only write-up services, it is clear, beyond dispute, that the [accountants] did become aware that material invoices purportedly paid by the [co-op's manager] were missing, and accordingly, [the accountants] had a duty to at least inform plaintiff of this. But even this they failed to do. The accountants were not free to consider these and other suspicious circumstances as being of no significance and prepare their financial report as if same did not exist.

The perception of an unauditor's role held by *1136 Tenants'* was not limited merely to a state court on the eastern side of the country. In 1972, a federal district court in Oregon held in *Blakely v. Lisac* that

"Even when performing an unaudited write-up, an accountant is under a duty to undertake at least a minimal investigation into the figures supplied to him. He is not free to disregard suspicious circumstances."

One of the most recent and authoritative decisions that attempts to grapple with the distinction in roles and responsibilities between an auditor and an unauditor is the U.S. Court of Appeals decision in *U.S. v. Natelli*. Among the several issues that the second circuit dealt with in the appeal of that criminal action against an audit partner and supervisor was the issue of the trial judge's refusal to give a jury instruction which distinguished an accountant's responsibility for audited and unaudited financial statements.

With respect to the nine-month unaudited financial statements that were allegedly misleading, the accountants had requested that the jury be instructed that

"The defendants' only responsibility as to this statement [the unaudited statement of earnings for nine months] was to be satisfied that, as far as they knew, the statement contained no misstatement of material facts."

The second circuit stated that "this requested instruction was not correct," observing that the audit partner's duty went further when there were "suspicious circumstances" involving the unaudited financial statements. The court held that "the duty of the audit partner, given this set of acts, was not so different from the duty of an accountant upon an audit." Accordingly, the court held that there was no reason to distinguish between the two services in the instructions to the jury.

In a recent decision of the Supreme Court of New Hampshire (*Spherex, Inc. v. Alexander Grant & Company*), the court included the following comment: "We are unable, as a matter of law, to consider it unreasonable for a third party to rely upon information presented in an unaudited financial statement prepared by the defendant accountant, or to rely upon an accountant to verify the substantive accuracy of the information presented in an unaudited financial statement. . . . 'Their liability must be dependent upon their undertaking, not their rejection of dependability. They cannot escape liability for negligence by a general statement that they disclaim reliability.' "

The foregoing history reflects that user and court confusion has and can occur regarding the responsibilities of the accountant in his varying roles. Indeed, most of this confusion arose at a time when users had to concern themselves with only two basic forms of report—the audited and the unaudited.

It's evident to us that users' expectations are influenced by two assumptions:

1. That financial statements are either materially fair and "accurate" depictions of financial position and results of operations or they are not.

2. That an accountant's identification or association with a financial statement is designed to add credibility to and invite some degree of user reliance on that financial statement.

The interplay of these two factors will influence the manner in which many, perhaps most, users of compiled or reviewed financial statements will construe and perceive the role of an accountant and his attendant responsibilities. And with the occurrence of adverse economic consequences, users' perceptions will become users' expectations.

Actual Responsibilities Assumed

When the expectations of users of compiled and reviewed financial statements exceed those warranted by the responsibilities actually undertaken by the accountant, a risk of a lawsuit results. To the extent the variance is material, the risk of liability may be deemed unreasonable. All practitioners do not have the same conception of compilation and review responsibilities, and, to the extent that there are differences within the profession itself regarding actual responsibilities undertaken, the expectation gap may be unbridgeable.

Compilation responsibilities. In a compilation engagement, SSARS no. 1, *Compilation and Review of Financial Statements*, provides that the accountant must, as an integral part of the engagement, establish an understanding with the client regarding the services he will perform. In addition, SSARS no. 1 requires the accountant to be knowledgeable about the generally accepted accounting principles applicable to the client's industry and to possess a general understanding of how the entity accumulates its information to enable the accountant to present it in the form of financial statements. Although this requirement goes beyond earlier standards, the obligation imposed is simply to become "streetwise" regarding the compilation client.

SSARS no. 1 also imposes a duty of inquiry when the accountant becomes aware of suspicious circumstances. This is not a new requirement. Earlier professional standards required an accountant associated with unaudited financial statements to verify the accuracy of unaudited data that was of questionable reliability based on suspicious circumstances known to the accountant.

Although an accountant makes no express representations when issuing a compilation report, we believe several implied representations attend the issuance of the compilation report:

1. The accountant does not know of any circumstances or evidence that indicates that the financial statements may be materially misleading or false.

2. If the financial statements purport to omit substantially all disclosures, the accountant has no knowledge that such omission was undertaken with the intent to mislead users.

3. The accountant has no reason to believe that the financial statements do not follow GAAP or another comprehensive basis of accounting.

Liability problems arise when facts exist that are contrary to the foregoing implicit representations and the accountant (a) either knew of these facts or (b) in the exercise of reasonable care within the terms of a compilation engagement should have known.

While these vistas of liability that attend compilation engagements are not new, SSARS no. 1 compilation standards certainly have not reduced the unauditor's liability exposure.

Review responsibilities. SSARS no. 1's review standards track the compilation standards in the following respects: (1) a requirement exists to establish an understanding with the client regarding the services to be performed, (2) a requirement to be streetwise exists regarding the review client and (3) a duty of inquiry is imposed when the accountant becomes aware of suspicious circumstances.

SSARS no. 1's review standards go beyond the compilation standards by imposing on the accountant a duty of inquiry and the application of analytical procedures. SSARS no. 1 states that an accountant's review inquiry needs to extend as far as is necessary to provide him with a reasonable basis for expressing limited assurance that there are no material modifications that should be made to the financial statements for them to be in conformity with GAAP.

SSARS no. 1 states that a review does not contemplate an audit or impose an audit duty of inquiry. Yet, the question occurs: How much inquiry is enough inquiry to afford a basis for representing or expressing limited assurance that no material modifications are necessary?

We believe that SSARS no. 1 opens the door to potential problems by stating that "inquiries to be made in a review of financial statements are a matter of the accountant's judgment." The objective judgment of reasonable accountants may differ regarding the applicability of any of the required review procedures, especially when one of these accountants is a plaintiff's expert offering his opinion with the benefit of hindsight.

In addition to the inquiry issue, SSARS no. 1 raises questions about the extent and nature of the reliance invited by the review report on the financial statements. In issuing a review report, an accountant expressly represents that

1. He has reviewed the financial statements in accordance with standards established by the profession.

2. Based on this review, he knows of no material modifications necessary to make the financial statements comply with GAAP.

The following questions may arise with regard to the second representation: What type of reliance is the accountant inviting when he issues a review report? What is the nature of the accountant's limited assurance?

How will the unsophisticated user of a reviewed financial statement perceive the accountant's responsibility? Will the unsophisticated, or even the sophisticated, user be able to perceive the qualitative difference between an audit and a review? Moreover, even if the user understands the difference, will the user necessarily calibrate his reliance based on the degree of assurance offered by the accountant? Should the user's reliance mirror the accountant's assurance? We believe that from a user's perspective there can be no middle ground between reliable and unreliable financial statements—that in the real world "semi-reliable" just does not exist.

Risk Prevention

The answers to the foregoing questions remain to be determined. To a certain degree users' perceptions of the accountant's role are shaped by the language and warnings within the report he renders on unaudited financial statements, which communicate to the public the limited extent and nature of his undertaking and responsibilities.

Given the risks, some of which are outside the profession's control, that may arise from a user's overreliance on such a report, we believe that the profession must eliminate those risks directly within its control. Specifically, this means answering all of the questions that exist regarding how much inquiry is enough and retooling certain SSARS standards that we believe to be inadequate.

¶ 7.05   Duty of Inquiry: Management Fraud

Management fraud may range from "employee fraud," which involves conversion of cash or other assets for the employee's direct benefit, to a wider spectrum of "performance fraud," a course of conduct designed to fraudulently inflate earnings or to cover up a decline in earnings or insolvency.

The extent of the auditor's duty of inquiry to detect material management fraud has been the subject of considerable debate and controversy. Many users of financial statements believe that detection of fraud is a significant objective of an audit. The accounting profession's view of its duty to detect fraud has been more restrictive than what appears to be the expectation of users of financial statements.

[1]   Discovery of Management Fraud: Limitations on an Auditor's Duty of Inquiry

As early as 1960 the auditing profession described its duty of inquiry relating to fraud in Statement on Auditing Procedure No. 30 as follows:

> The ordinary examination directed to the expression of an opinion on financial statements is not primarily or specifically designed, and cannot be relied upon to disclose defalcations and other similar irregularities, although their discovery may result. Similarly, although the discovery of deliberate misrepresentation by management is usually more closely associated with the objective of the ordinary examination, such examination cannot be relied upon to assure its discovery. The responsibility of the independent auditor for failure to detect fraud. . . . arises only when such failure clearly results from failure to comply with generally accepted auditing standards.

In 1963 the auditing profession refined its position on the duty of inquiry relating to management fraud by issuing the following position on the issue in Statement on Auditing Procedure No. 33:

> In making the ordinary examination, the independent auditor is aware of the possibility that fraud may exist. Financial statements may be misstated as the result of defalcations and similar irregularities, or deliberate misrepresentation by management or both. The auditor recognizes that fraud, if sufficiently material, may affect his opinion on the financial statements, and his examination, made in accordance with generally accepted auditing standards, gives consideration to this possibility. However, the ordinary examination directed to the expression of an opinion on financial statements is not primarily or specifically designed and cannot be relied upon to disclose defalcations and other similar irregularities, although their discovery may result. Similarly, although the discovery of deliberate misrepresentation by management is usually more closely associated with the objective of the ordinary examination, such examination cannot be relied upon to assure its discovery. The responsibility of the independent auditor for failure to detect fraud (which responsibility differs as to client and others) arises only when such failure clearly results from failure to comply with generally accepted auditing standards.

The auditing profession's 1963 view of its duty of inquiry regarding management fraud was a composite of the following positions:

(a)   There was no absolute duty to detect management fraud.

(b)   There was a duty to be "aware of the possibility that fraud may exist" and to perform the audit examination with that possibility in mind.

(c)   Failure to detect material management fraud was not tantamount to a breach of the auditor's duty of inquiry. The duty of inquiry was breached only if the failure to detect the fraud clearly resulted from a failure to comply with GAAS.

The auditing profession's 1963 position went unchecked until the advent of the 1970s when several major instances of material management fraud renewed the debate regarding the auditor's duty of inquiry to detect fraud. Ironically, the one case in the 1970s which caused the greatest concern for the accounting profession, namely, the court of appeals decision in *Hochfelder v. Ernst & Ernst*, was favorably disposed to accepting the 1963 position of the auditing profession.

With the increased debate, the auditing profession once again redefined its duty of inquiry relating to management fraud with the release in January 1977 by the AICPA of SAS No. 16, which was entitled, "The Independent Auditor's Responsibility for the Detection of Errors or Irregularities." In that statement material management fraud was defined to be a material "irregularity."

With respect to the detection of material management fraud the auditing profession's position is:

> The auditor's examination, based on the concept of selective testing of the data being examined, is subject to the inherent risk that material errors or irregularities, if they exist, will not be detected. (§ 327.11)

> An independent auditor's standard report implicitly indicates his belief that the financial statements taken as a whole are not materially misstated as a result of errors or irregularities. (§ 327.05)

> In view of . . . limitations on the effectiveness of auditing procedures, the subsequent discovery that errors or irregularities existed during the period covered by the independent auditor's examination, does not, in itself, indicate inadequate performance on his part. The auditor is not an insurer or guarantor, if his examination was made in accordance with generally accepted auditing standards he has fulfilled his professional responsibility. (§ 327.13)

> The independent auditor's plan for an examination in accordance with generally accepted auditing standards is influenced by the possibility of material errors or irregularities. The auditor should plan and perform his examination with an attitude of professional skepticism, recognizing that the application of his auditing procedures may produce evidential matter indicating the possibility of errors or irregularities. The scope of the auditor's examination would be affected by his consideration of internal accounting control, by the results of his substantive tests, and by circumstances that raise questions concerning the integrity of management. (§ 327.06)

There are many within the auditing profession who believe that an audit should be designed to provide reasonable assurance that the financial statements are not affected by material fraud.

The auditing profession's most recent statement is a partial response but it is limited in two important respects:

1.   The statement provides that within the framework of a GAAS audit, an auditor should plan his examination so as to be aware of and search for material management fraud. The inquiry obligation imposed is not a duty to detect the existence of fraud. The "duty" is merely to search for fraud while performing a GAAS audit.

2.   The statement provides that the auditor, by issuance of his standard report, indicates his belief that the financial statements are not materially misstated as a result of management fraud. This is not a representation that *in fact* material management fraud is nonexistent.

[2]   1985 Congressional Hearings

In 1985 the U.S. House of Representatives Subcommittee on Oversights and Investigations conducted hearings on the performance of the public accounting profession and in particular whether the present audit system meets the public's reasonable expectations. An issue of concern to the congressional subcommittee was business failures and the audit function.

The AICPA addressed the question of an auditor's duty to detect management fraud in the following testimony submitted to the congressional subcommittee:

Business Failures and the Audit Function

Failures of large business enterprises invariably are accompanied by multi-million dollar lawsuits against their independent auditors on behalf of shareholders and creditors. Indeed, the suits often focus on the CPA firms because they are usually the "deepest pockets" available in the financial rubble of a failed company. Asserting their reliance on the audited financial statements, the plaintiffs allege that the statements were misleading and that the auditors failed to comply with professional standards in examining and reporting on them. The extensive media coverage of these events often conveys the impression that an actual audit failure has occurred.

To be sure, while the objective of CPAs is to prevent all audit failures, auditors are human and performance failures can and do occur. But a business failure or the filing of a lawsuit or media notoriety does not necessarily mean that there has been an audit failure. Even payments made by CPA firms in settlement of lawsuits are not proof of an audit failure. Such payments may be made simply because they are less than the potential legal and other costs of defending the firm in litigation.

Businesses fail for a variety of reasons that are unrelated to the financial reporting process. Poor management, societal or technological developments, domestic and foreign competition, and changes in the economy are some of the major causes of business failures.

Investors and creditors are responsible for assessing the risk of investing in or lending to a company. Accordingly, in making that judgment, they need to consider a wide range of information in addition to the historical financial information included in audited financial statements. The quality of management, developments in the industry, labor relations, marketing and product development plans, and the state of the economy are some of the factors that may be as relevant or even more relevant than historical financial statement information. As a result, investors and creditors can make bad judgments about a company and its future prospects even though the audit of the historical financial statements is without fault.

The role of the independent auditor is not to guarantee that investors and creditors will not make bad judgments and suffer losses. Neither is it to advise users of financial statements on the desirability of investing in or lending to a company.

The proper, long-standing role of the independent auditor is to provide the public with reasonable assurance that the representations of management reflected in the company's financial statements and the related disclosures comply with generally accepted accounting principles. The independent audit should bring a trained, experienced, professional oversight to the financial reporting process and, thus, serves to deter the issuance of misleading financial statements by management.

Indeed, in a January 1985 Pace University survey of Fortune 500 and private companies, 107 of the 117 respondents indicated that they would have an annual audit by a public accounting firm even if it were not required. The most frequently cited reasons were that the independent audit imposes discipline on the entire financial system and that an independent audit is required for credibility of financial statements.

The broad question of whether independent auditors are satisfactorily fulfilling their intended role leads to a number of inquiries:

1. Do the current reports of alleged audit failures indicate a deterioration of audit quality?

2. Is there sufficient regulation of independent auditors to safeguard against negligence or lack of objectivity or integrity?

3. Would changes in the present system of establishing financial accounting and auditing standards reduce the incidence of business and audit failures?

4. Is the performance of management advisory services for audit clients impairing the independence, integrity, or objectivity of auditors?

Alleged Audit Failures and Audit Quality

Professional standards require the auditor to plan his examination to search for misstatements that would have a material effect on the financial statements, but they do not call for extended auditing procedures to detect fraud unless the auditor's examination causes him to believe material fraud may exist. This is because the cost of an audit must be reasonable in relation to the expected benefits. However, auditors can and do detect fraud in the course of audit engagements. An independent auditor's standard report implicitly indicates his belief that the financial statements taken as a whole are not materially misstated as a result of error or irregularities.

As previously discussed, business failures are not caused by audit failures. Business failures may be caused, or hidden, by a material management fraud that goes undetected by the independent auditor until severe financial difficulties or some other events cause the fraud to be revealed. In these situations, notwithstanding the auditor's compliance with generally accepted auditing standards, forgery, unrecorded transactions or extensive collusion can make some management frauds exceedingly difficult if not impossible for auditors to detect.

The detection of management fraud is one of the most difficult problems faced by independent auditors, one that has received and continues to receive a great deal of attention by the profession.

Professional auditing standards have long included the concept of selective testing. Consistent with that concept, auditors rarely audit all of the transactions that compose an individual item (for example, accounts receivables) in the financial statements because the cost to do so would be prohibitive. Because of cost considerations, a sampling method is also used by the Internal Revenue Service in auditing tax returns and by the Securities and Exchange Commission in reviewing filings by registrants.

Auditors study and evaluate a company's system of internal control to decide on the nature, timing, and extent of tests to be performed. Nevertheless, it is possible for any control system to be circumvented, in which case even an audit of all transactions may fail to disclose the fraud. Thus, rather than being indicative of a general problem with audit quality in the profession, the failure to detect management fraud is more likely to be the result of the sophistication with which the fraud was carried out or the result of a human error on the part of the individual auditor. Also, to be frank, courts have concluded in rare cases that the conduct of an individual auditor was felonious. But in all of these situations, the auditing firm is as much the victim of fraud as are the investors and creditors.

In addition to undetected fraud, there are other circumstances that give rise to perceptions of audit failure and concerns about audit quality. For example, a company, with the auditor's knowledge and consent, may have selected an acceptable accounting treatment that presents its financial condition and operating results in the most favorable light. If the business subsequently fails or encounters severe financial problems, the auditor's acceptance of that treatment is questioned in the light of hindsight.

Since these situations are not cases of oversight by the auditor, they are not "audit failures" in the sense that errors or irregularities were not detected. But some critics of the profession contend that cases involving accounting treatment questions are even more serious because they see them as involving faulty judgment or, even worse, a lack of objectivity or integrity on the part of the auditor.

Auditors do insist on accounting changes when the appropriate accounting is clear. But what accounting standard is appropriate in a particular circumstance is not always clear. Accounting standards require the application of judgment. This stems from the fact that most important items in financial statements cannot be measured precisely but have to be estimated. For example, the preparer of financial statements has to estimate the amount of accounts receivable that will not be collected because goods may be returned or customers may default, the amount of inventory that should be considered obsolete, the useful lives of property and equipment, the amounts of possible losses from such things as product warranty claims or lawsuits, and whether and how revenue should be recognized as, for example, in a construction project extending over several years.

Thus, although financial statements are presented as numbers that may appear to be precise, the amounts are and can be only reasonable approximations of the results of a company's transactions. Complete accuracy is rendered impossible by the fact that financial statements are issued at regular points in time while certain of the underlying transactions are still not complete and important events that will have an effect on those statements have not or may not yet have taken place. Therefore, the fact that an accounting judgment made at the time of the audit may be shown by subsequent events to have been overly optimistic or conservative does not mean that the auditor's and management's judgment or conduct was flawed.

Understandably, auditors sometimes differ in their judgments about the accounting treatment that is appropriate when applying accounting standards to complex transactions. Concerns arise when companies, especially those in financial trouble, take advantage of the differences in judgments among CPA firms to seek the answer most favorable to them. This practice places added pressure on auditors. But few auditors would knowingly risk such severe penalties as legal liability or loss of reputation for independence

and integrity by agreeing to accounting treatments that were not consistent with their firmly-held professional convictions.

Another source of concern stems from cases where accounting measurement and disclosure standards are fully complied with and no fraud is involved, but a company unexpectedly fails. Critics generally insist that auditors should issue an explicit warning when a company is in a precarious condition.

As previously indicated, the auditor's role is to express an opinion on the conformity of the financial statements and related disclosures with generally accepted accounting principles. Those principles call for disclosure of uncertainties and contingencies in appropriate circumstances. Investors and creditors are expected to study, among other things, the financial statements and to assess the company's financial condition in the light of their own objectives and their tolerance for risk. Of course, auditors do qualify their opinions when questions about the ability of a company to continue in existence raise significant doubts about the amounts and classification of assets and liabilities. Such a qualification involves complex professional judgments and should be given only when circumstances demand.

In summary, a business failure is not the same as an audit failure, and actual audit failures need to be carefully distinguished from perceived failures. Perceived audit failures often stem from a lack of understanding of what reasonably can be expected to be achieved by audits or of the facts in a particular case. Misunderstandings of the nature, purpose, and limitations of financial statements also contribute to misperceptions that audit failures have occurred.

Actual audit failures are generally the result of honest human error on the part of individual auditors rather than a reflection of the general quality of work by their firms or the profession. Such errors may involve failing to detect material errors or irregularities or making good-faith judgments on accounting matters that are proven faulty by subsequent events.

Financial statements are necessarily only a reasonable approximation of a company's financial condition and results of operations. For this and other reasons, independent audits do not and cannot provide absolute assurance on the accuracy of financial statements. However, independent audits do provide a considerable measure of assurance that financial statements are not misleading within the context of generally accepted accounting principles. Therefore, it is important to all users of financial statements that audits be performed as effectively as possible. This is an objective not only of the SEC and of Congress, but is of prime importance to the AICPA.

¶ 7.06   Duty of Disclosure: Limitations

[1]   Duty to Disclose Only the Material Facts—Not the Immaterial and Irrelevant

In issuing a professional report or advice an accountant is not compelled to disclose every fact which he discovers in the course of his engagement. An accountant's duty to disclose is limited to those facts that are material to the report or service rendered. An accountant has no duty to disclose facts that are immaterial and irrelevant to the report or service that he renders.

[a]   Materiality Defined.   A material fact is one to which a reasonable person would attach significance in making a decision. The concept of *materiality* has been the subject of considerable attention in the area of the federal securities laws where the courts have crafted the following definitions of a "material fact":

> The basic test of materiality . . . is whether a reasonable man would attach importance [to the fact misrepresented] in determining his choice of action in the transaction in question.
>
> Any fact [is material] which in reasonable and objective contemplation might affect the value of the corporation's stocks or securities.
>
> Materiality, therefore, depends on whether a reasonable man in plaintiff's position might well have acted otherwise than to purchase if informed of the crucial facts.

Materiality is not a boundless concept; it has limits as reflected in the U.S. Supreme Court's decision in *TSC Industries, Inc. v. Northway, Inc.* (1976). That case involved omissions of facts from a company proxy statement which the plaintiffs claimed were material omissions.

The U.S. Supreme Court observed that the "question of materiality . . . is an objective one involving the significance of an omitted or misrepresented fact to a reasonable investor." The U.S. Supreme Court rejected the court of appeals' test of materiality, which embraced "all facts which a reasonable shareholder *might* consider important," noting that

> if the standard of materiality is unnecessarily low, not only may the corporation and its management be subjected to liability for insignificant omissions or misstatements, but also management's fear of exposing itself to substantial liability may cause it simply to bury the shareholder in an avalanche of trivial information—a result that is hardly conducive to informed decision-making.

The U.S. Supreme Court fashioned a "general standard of materiality," which provides that "an omitted fact is material if there is a substantial likelihood that a reasonable shareholder would consider it important in deciding how to vote [his proxy]." The U.S. Supreme Court held "there must be a substantial likelihood that the disclosure of the omitted fact would have been viewed by the reasonable investor as having 'significantly' altered the 'total mix' of information made available."

[b]   Qualitative and Quantitative Materiality.   When an accountant undertakes to report on the adequacy of financial accounting disclosures, the concept of materiality may be refined to two levels of scrutiny: (1) quantitative materiality, and (2) qualitative materiality.

Quantitative materiality deals with those facts which have primarily a quantitative significance. A fact such as a financial item or transaction may be quantitatively material because of the magnitude or financial effect of the matter in relation to net income or net worth. For example, an asset which in value represents 30 percent of a company's assets would be a material financial item.

Even if a matter is not quantitatively material it may nevertheless be qualitatively material "if there is a substantial likelihood that a reasonable shareholder would consider it important." *TSC Industries, Inc. v. Northway, Inc.*, 926 U.S. 438 (1976). For example, financial statement reporting may include footnote disclosure regarding pending litigation against the client. Although a loss contingency cannot be immediately quantified, the facts relating to the potential liability may indicate that an asset has been impaired or a liability incurred. These facts are qualitatively material and should be disclosed despite the absence of a quantifiable loss.

Qualitative materiality deals with those facts that may have a quantitative significance at some future point in time. For example, violation of a contract or statute which could result in a liability to the audit client or a loss of a significant component of revenues may be a material fact to a reasonable person relying on the financials. Qualitative materiality may be the basis for disclosure of illegal acts of the client that have no quantitative significance but that otherwise reflect adversely on the reliability of the client's financial records. (See the discussion ¶ 7.06[2] regarding illegal acts).

(i)   **McLean v. Alexander** *and Comments*

McLean v. Alexander
599 F.2d 1190 (3d Cir. 1979)

[The court's decision is reprinted at ¶ 4.07[2].]

1.   *McLean v. Alexander* involves a situation where a material misrepresentation was made by the auditors regarding a $73,733 line item for accounts receivable in the balance sheet. The trial court held that the accounts receivable were really consignments, not sales, and thus not properly reflected as accounts receivable. The court of appeals held that there was no evidence that the misrepresentation resulted from fraud on the part of the auditors, which was the charge against them.

2. *McLean v. Alexander* is an example of the application of qualitative materiality to test the adequacy of financial statement disclosures. The plaintiff McLean paid $1.950 million for a company that had assets of $188,419 and a retained earnings deficit of $91,647. As the court of appeals noted, "it is clear that the purchase price reflected McLean's interest in future sales rather than in present assets or past earnings."

3. The misstated $73,733 in accounts receivable was not "quantitatively" material. The plaintiff did not spend $1.950 million to purchase $73,733 of accounts receivable. The accounts receivable were qualitatively material because they represented "sales potential."

The court of appeals stated that "McLean and Jeter, relying upon the independence of outside auditors, viewed the audit as confirming what they had previously been told and seen regarding the marketability of Technidyne's pipelaying tool." The trial judge had ruled that "the audited statement of accounts receivable, as evidence of sixteen actual sales, was material to McLean's investment decision. . . ."

Qualitative materiality can work in strange ways.

(ii) Greenapple v. Detroit Edison Co. *and Comments*

Greenapple v. Detroit Edison Co.
618 F.2d 198 (2d Cir. 1980)

[Plaintiff purchased stock of defendant Detroit Edison Co., a public utility, relying on Detroit Edison's financial disclosures in a prospectus. Plaintiff contended that defendant's accounting treatment of the cost of obtaining construction financing was materially misleading.

The allegedly misleading accounting concept was referred to as the *allowance for funds used during construction (AFDC)*. The AFDC was a mandated federal regulatory accounting concept under which the cost of construction financing was carried as an item of "other income."]

Appellant charges that the inclusion of AFDC in the "net income" figure in the Consolidated Statement of Changes in Financial Position buttressed the misimpression that AFDC was interchangeable with cash and constituted a violation of applicable accounting principles. . . ., these objections do not withstand analysis.

It is undisputed that the inclusion of AFDC as an element of income did not distort the bottom line of the statement; the ultimate net profit figure was not affected, and indeed the Consolidated Statement of Changes in Financial Position showed a decrease in working capital. It may be argued, of course, that notwithstanding this bottom line accuracy, the portrayal of AFDC as a component of net income was misleading because it artificially inflated the apparent cash flow into the company, a signal consideration in the eyes of some potential investors. It postulates the existence of investors who are at once savvy enough to appreciate concepts such as cash flow and yet unable to comprehend the definition of AFDC fairly and accurately set forth earlier in the prospectus. In determining the adequacy of disclosure, we are required to view the prospectus from the standpoint of the reasonable, not schizophrenic, investor.

In judging the prospectus challenged in this case we are guided by general principles governing the mode of the portrayal of material information in a prospectus. Of course, the SEC's own detailed forms govern the manner of presentation of much material information. Thus, accounting computations relating to an issuer's balance sheet must be set forth in a consolidated income statement and in such other tables as are prescribed. In evaluating the appropriateness of portraying other significant matters whose mode and extent of disclosure are not dictated by these mandatory forms, however, consideration must be given to the function of the document in issue, the persons to whom it will be distributed and the underlying policies of the Securities Act of 1933.

The objective of a prospectus is to solicit investment by the general public. Mandatory registration of such materials with the SEC is intended to ensure that the factors entering into prudent investment decisions are depicted in a standardized, comprehensible, and accurate manner. Thus, the intended audience will be extremely broad, encompassing both sophisticated financial analysts and untutored lay persons. As the principal goal of the Securities Act is disclosure, *SEC v. Capital Gains Research Bureau, Inc.*, . . . close questions will generally be resolved in favor of the inclusion of information.

Given these factors, disclosure in a prospectus must steer a middle course, neither submerging a material fact in a flood of collateral data, nor slighting its importance through seemingly cavalier treatment. The import of the information conveyed must be neither oversubtle nor overplayed, its meaning accurate, yet accessible. Compare *Gerstle v. Gamble-Skogmo, Inc.* . . . ("it is not sufficient that overtones might have been picked up by the sensitive antennae of investment analysts") with *Richland v. Crandall*, . . . ("corporations are not required to address their stockholders as if they were children in kindergarten"). . . . The disclosure must be capable of being perceived as material and its significance—that is, its relationship to other aspects of the company's condition—susceptible to common understanding.

In our view the AFDC concept was properly set forth in the challenged prospectus, and was neither so obscure nor confusing as to constitute a misstatement of material fact within the meaning of Section 11. The initial explanatory note concisely yet accurately defines AFDC, stating explicitly that it is an item of cost. It goes on to highlight the dramatic increases in AFDC over the past five years, indicating the interest rates upon which these figures were calculated, and attributing this steady rise to an expanded construction program. The increased prominence of AFDC is again called to the reader's attention in the passage found in the text dealing with the consequences of the breakdown of one of the utility's generators. In this fashion the cost allocation function of AFDC and its noncash, cost nature is well illustrated.

Thus, the criteria for proper presentation of a material fact are fully satisfied; AFDC is portrayed as being of considerable importance to Detroit Edison, and its significance and relationship to the utility's financial condition as a whole can be appreciated by the diligent investor. Comprehended as it should be at the outset, the reasonable reader is not likely to be misled by later references to it in the prospectus.

We do not intimate that appellant's critique of the AFDC presentation is entirely unfounded. To be sure, the quality of the disclosure could have been improved. But the advisability of revision does not render what was done deceptive or misleading. The question is whether the prospectus, as written, adequately apprises the reader of the essential nature of a material facet of the issuer's financial condition. The fair and intelligible definition of AFDC set forth in Note (b) satisfies this basic requirement: the additional analysis proposed by appellant is not an essential increment to the investor's understanding without which comprehension is not possible. Indeed, the initial explanation establishes a point of diminishing returns. To demand more would open the door to unceasing and unreasonable clamorings for all manner of tutoring in basic corporate accounting, which would afford a bonanza to lawyers and regulators with no corresponding benefit to the actual investor.

---

1.   The court of appeals upheld the trial judge's ruling that the accounting disclosure was not materially misleading. The trial judge applied the following definition of materiality:

A fact is material if there is a substantial likelihood that under all the circumstances, a reasonable investor would consider it important in reaching an investment decision.

2. The trial court held that the accounting concept applied was explained with sufficient clarity in Detroit Edison's prospectus, observing that the "securities laws . . . do not require that an issuer include an in-depth explanation of widely used accounting terms and principles every time it disseminates a financial statement employing such terms and principles to the investing public."

3. The court of appeals upheld the trial court's decision, noting that:

> Disclosure in a prospectus must steer a middle course, neither submerging a material fact in a flood of collateral data, nor slighting its importance through seemingly cavalier treatment.

> The objective of a prospectus is to solicit investment by the general public. . . . As the principal goal of the Securities Act is disclosure . . . close questions will generally be resolved in favor of the inclusion of information.

[c] Relevance Defined. An accountant who reports on the adequacy of a client's financial accounting disclosure has no duty to disclose facts and matters that are not relevant to the accountant's report on the financial statements. Because *materiality* is a broad concept that could include matters not directly related to the financial statements, courts have been reluctant to impose on independent accountants a duty to disclose matters not directly relevant to the financials.

Efforts to impose a duty to disclose nonfinancial information have arisen in connection with faulty disclosures in those portions of a prospectus or registration statement for which the accountant has no responsibility or authority to demand changes. Questions that arise in this "twilight zone" of financial reporting are sometimes difficult to resolve. It is possible that many items for which the auditor should have no disclosure responsibility may be successfully claimed to be qualitatively material for purposes of financial statement disclosure (see the discussion at ¶ 7.06[3]).

[2] Qualitative Materiality: Illegal Acts and Management Fraud

An accountant may have a duty to disclose illegal acts by the client, and management fraud, in circumstances where there may be no quantitative significance to the matters. Disclosure would be mandated in these circumstances based on the qualitative significance of the matter or transaction.

Two areas in which the character of an event or transaction may be qualitatively significant include those events or transactions that

(a) reflect adversely on the quality and integrity of management or

(b) indicate doubt as to whether the client's accounting books and records may be relied upon.

These views of qualitative materiality were expressed by the SEC in a report made to the U.S. Senate on May 12, 1976, regarding questionable and illegal corporate payments and practices.

With respect to illegal acts performed by the client, the auditing profession has imposed a duty to disclose the circumstances and consequences of an illegal act where the potential effect of an illegal act is the impairment of a material amount of future revenue or earnings, or the loss of a significant business relationship. Even if the illegal act is quantitatively immaterial, disclosure may still be mandated if the future economic consequences of this act could be material. The test of qualitative materiality is met "if there is a substantial likelihood that a reasonable shareholder would consider it important."

Aside from the category of illegal acts that "benefit" the client, such as bribes, slush funds and facilitating payments, instances occur where management of a client engages in illegal acts that benefit only the individual employees of the client. The duty to disclose known management fraud may be absolute. To the extent that the integrity of management is seriously impaired, disclosure may be imperative without regard to the quantitative significance of the matter.

A classic statement of the importance of disclosing acts constituting management fraud is the decision by the court of appeals in *United States v. Simon* (see ¶ 5.03[2]), which was written by Judge Henry Friendly, a highly regarded jurist. The *Simon* case involved the criminal conviction of the auditors of Continental Vending Machine Co. Among the acts charged was the auditors' knowing failure to disclose that Continental Vending's president, Roth, was embezzling money from Continental. Roth accomplished his scheme through a series of related party transactions in the form of loans by Continental to Valley Commercial Corporation. Valley in turn loaned the money to Roth for his personal use.

In upholding the auditors' conviction for criminal fraud, the court of appeals held:

> Defendants next contend that, particularly in light of the expert testimony, the evidence was insufficient to allow the jury to consider the failure to disclose Roth's borrowings from Valley, the make-up of the collateral, or the post-balance sheet increase in the Valley receivable. They concentrate their fire on what they characterize as the "primary, predominant, and pervasive" issue, namely the failure to disclose that Continental's loans to Valley were not for a proper business purpose but to assist Roth in his personal financial problems. It was "primary, predominant, and pervasive," not only because it was most featured by the prosecution but because defendants' knowledge of Roth's diversion of corporate funds colored everything else. We join defendants' counsel in assuming that the mere fact that a company has made advances to an affiliate does not ordinarily impose a duty on an accountant to investigate what the affiliate has done with them or even to disclose that the affiliate has made a loan to a common officer if this has come to his attention. But it simply cannot be true that an accountant is under no duty to disclose what he knows when he has reason to believe that, to a *material extent*, a corporation is being operated not to carry out its business in the interest of all the stockholders but for the private benefit of its president. For a court to say that all this is immaterial as a matter of law if only such loans are thought to be collectible would be to say that independent accountants have no responsibility to reveal known dishonesty by a high corporate officer. *If certification does not at least imply* that the corporation has not been looted by insiders so far as the accountants know, or, if it has been, that the *diversion has been made good beyond peradventure or adequately reserved against and effective steps taken to prevent a recurrence*, it would mean nothing and the reliance placed on it by the public would be a snare and a delusion. Generally accepted accounting principles instruct an accountant what to do in the usual case where he has no reason to doubt that the affairs of the corporation are *being honestly conducted*. Once he

has reason to believe that this basic assumption is false, an entirely different situation confronts him. Then, as the Lybrand firm stated in its letter accepting the Continental engagement, he must "*extend his procedures to determine whether or not such suspicions are justified.*" If as a result of such an extension or, as here, without it, he finds his suspicions to be confirmed, *full disclosure must be the rule, unless he has made sure the wrong has been righted and procedures to avoid a repetition have been established.* At least this must be true when the *dishonesty* he has discovered is not some minor peccadillo but a diversion so large as *to imperil if not destroy the very solvency of the enterprise.* [Emphasis added.]

[3]   Nonfinancial Statement Information

It is not uncommon that a client's annual financial report, or a client's prospectus or registration statement, will contain nonfinancial business disclosures as well as audited financial statements. Nonfinancial statement business disclosures are often referred to as "other information."

Other information will be disclosed by the client because the information is considered relevant and material information that should be provided for shareholders, investors, creditors, and other interested parties. The decision to disclose this other information is made by the client. The client bears responsibility for any material omissions or misrepresentations that may occur in disclosing this other information.

In some instances other information is closely related to the financial information that is disclosed in the client's financial statements. When an accountant issues an audit report he has a duty to disclose all relevant, material facts necessary for purposes of full, fair, and complete financial statement disclosure. The accountant does not undertake to disclose and has no duty to disclose information that is not directly relevant to the financial statements.

The problem arises regarding finding a clear line of demarcation between financial statement information and nonfinancial statement information which is otherwise relevant and should be disclosed by the client. In some instances the information falls into the "twilight zone of disclosure." That is, reasonable minds could differ in deciding whether the information falls inside or outside the scope of financial statement information.

The following cases reflect the problems that arise in attempting to grapple with the question of the extent of an accountant's duty to disclose business information that is patently material to an investment decision.

[a]   *Seeburg-Commonwealth United Litigation* and Comments

Seeburg-Commonwealth United Litigation
CCH Fed. Sec. L. Rep. ¶ 93,802 (S.D.N.Y. 1972)

MCFADDEN, District Judge: This matter is before the Court on the motion of defendant, Arthur Young, for summary judgment. . . .

This is a shareholder derivative action on behalf of Commonwealth United Corporation against officers and directors of Common-wealth and Kleiner, Bell & Co., Inc., investment banker and financial consultant to Commonwealth (hereinafter all the preceding defendants shall be referred to collectively as the "Rozet-Kleiner Bell Group") and Arthur Young & Company (hereinafter referred to as "Arthur Young"), Commonwealth's accountants.

The amended complaint alleges that, while acting as Commonwealth's accountants, Arthur Young prepared and certified false and misleading financial statements and by failing to demand that Commonwealth's management make required truthful disclosures and by itself failing to make those disclosures enabled the Rozet-Kleiner Bell Group to perpetuate itself in control of Commonwealth and aided and abetted the Rozet-Kleiner Bell Group in wasting the corporation's assets. The complaint as supplemented by the statements of claims asserts the following specific claims:

1. Sometime prior to June, 1969, the Commonwealth management entered into an agreement with Dart Industries, Inc., for the sale of the Rexall Drug operations from Dart to Commonwealth and made a $5 million down payment on the purchase after Arthur Young furnished false and misleading information and financial statements to Commonwealth and Dart indicating that the balance could be financed. One of the conditions of sale, which was to be closed on August 8, 1969, was approval by the Commonwealth stockholders of the issuance of one million shares of a new series of convertible preferred stock, which were to be conveyed to Dart at closing as a part of the consideration. Commonwealth's management solicited stockholder approval of this transaction by a proxy statement dated June 24, 1969, which contained false and misleading financial statements furnished and certified by Arthur Young. However, because it could not obtain the necessary financing, Commonwealth defaulted on the Rexall sale, and Dart retained the $5 million down payment as liquidated damages.

2. Based on Arthur Young's advice to the Rozet-Kleiner Bell Group that unregistered and unmarketable common stock of Perfect Film and Chemical Corporation could be carried on the books at $7,000,000, a grossly inflated value, Commonwealth purchased at $7,000,000 eighty-six thousand shares of said stock in March, 1969, and these shares were

listed at their inflated value in the financial statements certified by Arthur Young and contained in the Commonwealth proxy statement dated June 24, 1969.

3. Upon receiving assurances from Arthur Young that it was prepared to include in Commonwealth's operating income gains to be realized therefrom, in 1968 Commonwealth sold to four individuals, who are principals of Kleiner Bell, two office buildings in Worcester, Massachusetts, and certain land located in Hawaii. Commonwealth had purchased the Massachusetts land earlier that same year and as part of the consideration therefor had delivered Commonwealth stock, valued at $1,500,000, to the seller. The purported gains from these sales were in fact listed as operating income in various financial statements, including those in the Commonwealth Annual Report for 1968, interim reports during 1969, and the Commonwealth proxy statement dated June 24, 1969. These same financial statements also failed to disclose Commonwealth's obligation to repurchase said properties at the option of the buyers at the same or a higher price and failed to disclose that the gains were unrealized, represented by promissory notes of questionable value. The net effect of this transaction was the issuance by Commonwealth of its stock worth $1,500,000, for $281,400 cash and other grossly inadequate consideration.

4. In January, 1969, Commonwealth acquired for a price greatly in excess of their value all of the outstanding shares of preferred stock of George A. Fuller Co., Inc., after Arthur Young had assured the Rozet-Kleiner Bell Group that it would report the cost of this purchase as being some $10 million less than it actually was. Arthur Young so reported the cost of the Fuller transaction in subsequent financial statements, including the one contained in the Commonwealth proxy statement dated June 24, 1969.

5. Arthur Young made numerous other false and misleading representations in the financial statements contained in the Commonwealth proxy statement dated June 24, 1969.

Plaintiffs contend that these allegations state a claim against defendant Arthur Young arising under Sections 10(b) and 14(a) of the Securities Exchange Act of 1934 . . . and Rules 10b-5 and 14a-9 promulgated thereunder.

Arthur Young argues that plaintiffs have not stated a claim under Rule 10b-5 or Rule 14a-9, because it appears therefrom that the corporation itself, acting by and through its officers and directors, was never deceived by Arthur Young, and whatever injury the corporation may have sustained by the series of transactions complained of were not caused by defendant's alleged misrepresentations.

The fundamental allegations against Arthur Young are that it misrepresented important financial facts to the Commonwealth stockholders in the proxy statement dated June 24, 1969, and previously had failed to inform the stockholders of these material facts which it knew the Rozet-Kleiner Bell management was misrepresenting to them. Plaintiffs do not contend that Arthur Young defrauded Commonwealth's management, but rather that by failing to report the misrepresentation it prevented the stockholders from taking timely action to prevent the transactions. No allegation sets forth the form of this action. While plaintiffs' contentions are cast in "but for" language of causation, they come down in the final analysis to an assertion that Arthur Young aided and abetted the CUC management in a scheme of corporate waste, mismanagement and breach of fiduciary duty. Plaintiffs attempt to bring the transactions under Rule 10b-5 because some of them involved the purchase and sale of securities by the corporation.

It appears therefore that the instant complaint against Arthur Young fails to state a 10b-5 derivative claim, since the alleged false and misleading proxy statement dated June 24, 1969, was not promulgated "in connection with the purchase or sale of any security," and there is an absence of any showing of a causal connection between any fraud alleged and the purchase or sale of a security. It should be noted that much of what plaintiffs complain of was not a part of the financial statements prepared by Arthur Young, but

the Court does not find it necessary to deal with that aspect of the case since the required elements of a Securities Act case have not been met assuming the participation of Arthur Young in the alleged fraud.

Plaintiffs cannot elevate their claims of corporate waste to the level of a Rule 10b-5 action merely by allegations that this was a part of a scheme to aid and abet the management in a program of corporate waste. The "security" transactions were incidental to a larger scheme of corporate mismanagement and waste and the alleged facts and those revealed by the proxy statement do not constitute a misrepresentation within the purview of Rule 10b-5.

Plaintiffs' contentions are not sustained by *Fischer v. Kletz*, . . . on which they heavily rely. That case involved an accounting firm which acquired information showing that its previously certified financial statements were not true. The Court declined to dismiss the complaint brought by shareholders who had purchased securities after the issuance of the false financial statements. [That] situation is quite different from that presented in this derivative action based on Arthur Young's actual or constructive knowledge of mismanagement and waste by management and its failure to reveal this knowledge to the shareholders. Accountants have a duty to accurately and fairly review and report the financial condition of the company, but the Court does not believe that *Fischer* or any other case places a duty on them to search out and reveal errors or omissions in management's proxy material for which they have no responsibility as auditors. The Court is also of the opinion that accountants are not required to search out and report acts of mismanagement or corporate waste, except to the extent that it is revealed in the financial information certified by them. This would place the responsibility of management squarely on the accountants without the prerogatives thereof and the law is not and could not be that sweeping. Such a result would make them liable for events over which they could have no control.

1.   In *Seeburg-Commonwealth* the trial judge ruled that the claims against the auditors involved matters relating to "corporate waste, mismanagement and breach of fiduciary

duty." The trial judge held that "much of what plaintiffs complain of was not a part of the financial statements prepared by Arthur Young."

2.   The trial judge stated that an accountant's duty of inquiry was limited to the financial statements, holding that accountants "have a duty to accurately and fairly review and report the financial condition of the company." The trial judge stated that there was no duty "to search out and reveal errors or omissions in management's proxy material for which they have no responsibility as auditors." The court's analysis begs the question, for the plaintiffs contended that the auditors had responsibility for the omitted disclosures which clearly dealt with material financial matters.

3.   The trial judge also makes a curious ruling regarding the auditor's duty of disclosure relating to "acts of mismanagement or corporate waste." The trial judge held that "accountants are not required to search out and report acts of mismanagement or corporate waste, except to the extent that it is revealed in the financial information certified by them."

In view of the breadth of the quantitative and qualitative materiality standards, it is difficult to accept the court's analysis. It should be noted that this decision was rendered in 1972, several years before the application of qualitative materiality by the SEC to corporate transactions involving waste and mismanagement.

The trial judge states that there is a duty to disclose mismanagement and corporate waste when it is "revealed in the financial information certified by them." The question left unanswered by the court is: When should corporate waste and mismanagement be revealed in the audited financials? See the following *Seiffer v. Topsy's International* case for another court's view on this matter.

[b]   *Seiffer v. Topsy's International Inc.* and Comments

Seiffer v. Topsy's International, Inc.
487 F.Supp. 653 (D. Kan. 1980)

[This lawsuit was brought by investors who purchased Topsy's International Inc. common stock and debentures during the period September 28, 1968 to March 10, 1970. Although the defendants in this lawsuit included Topsy's management, underwriters, attorneys, and auditors, only the auditing firm, Touche Ross & Co., chose to try the case rather than settle.

Plaintiffs claimed that they relied on various false financial information issued by Topsy's International, including:

1.   False prospectus disclosures in Topsy's registration statement,

2.   False management disclosures in Topsy's annual financial report,

3.   False quarterly reports to shareholders and the SEC, and

4.   Various other false public statements including information provided to the financial press.

In addressing the accountants' liability, the trial judge, who was the trier of fact in this case (a jury trial was not requested), was confronted with a situation where the false and misleading statements were part of management's disclosures and were not part of the audited financial statements. Thus, the trial judge was confronted with issues regarding the accountants' duties of inquiry and disclosure regarding this nonfinancial statement information.]

This action was brought by a number of purchasers of common stock and convertible subordinated debentures issued by Topsy's

International, Inc. Plaintiffs have alleged that defendants violated Section 17(a) of the Securities Act of 1933 . . . Section 10 of the Securities Exchange Act of 1934 . . . and the Kansas Blue Sky Law . . . in that they participated in a scheme to create an active and rising market in Topsy's stock up to the date of the public offering of stock and debentures, by means of statements which contained misrepresentations or were misleading because they omitted material facts. Plaintiffs have further alleged that thereafter defendants concealed the misstatements and omissions to maintain a market price for Topsy's securities above that which would have prevailed if accurate information had been disclosed.

The alleged misrepresentations and omissions center on SaxonS, an Ohio corporation in the business of franchising roast beef sandwich shops, purchased by Topsy's in the summer of 1968. On February 4, 1969, Topsy's made a public offering of $6,000,000.00 5 ¾% convertible subordinated debentures due February 1, 1984, and 104,796 shares of Class A Common Stock owned by three Topsy's officers—Jerry D. Berger, James T. House, and Harry Nuell. The final prospectus for the offering stated that the net proceeds from the sale of debentures would be used "to finance the acquisition, construction and development of sites for SaxonS Sandwich ShoppeS." Information disseminated to the public was generally favorable until March 6, 1970, when a letter from Topsy's to its shareholders reported that Topsy's had repurchased three SaxonS franchised units, which resulted in a reduction in second quarter earnings in the amount of $292,000.00. In a letter to shareholders of June 24, 1970, Topsy's reported that it was discontinuing its SaxonS operations.

• • •

1. *Topsy's 1968 Annual Report.* Topsy's annual report was distributed to shareholders in late October 1968. It contained financial statements audited by Touche Ross for the fiscal year ended July 31, 1968. The accountants' report did not express an opinion regarding any financial statements of SaxonS and referred to SaxonS only in Note 10, Subsequent Events: "On August 1, 1968, the Company acquired all the out-standing stock of SaxonS Sandwich ShoppeS, Inc., a company engaged in the development of a chain of specialty sandwich shops. The Company purchased the stock of SaxonS for $203,915 cash and 6,684 shares of Class A Common Stock." There are no allegations that these certified financials contained any misrepresentations.

The Message From Management section of the report stated that SaxonS received a $10,000.00 fee from each unit franchised. It has been suggested that this was misleading because no mention was made of the fact that not all franchise fees had been collected, $7,500.00 of the franchise fee was refundable, and several refunds had been made, in some cases the entire $10,000.00 previously paid and in others only the $7,500.00 refundable under the franchise agreement. We do not believe the omission makes the statement made materially misleading. Details about actual refunds would not have been expected in the context of the one-page Message From Management. Furthermore, were the statement misleading, Touche Ross cannot be charged with responsibility for it. Its legitimate concern was with statements in the annual report that might be inconsistent with the certified financials, and footnote 10 was the only aspect of the financials dealing with SaxonS. While some Touche Ross personnel were aware of the refund situation, Touche Ross cannot be charged with being management's keeper.

• • •

5. *The Final Prospectus.* The final prospectus, dated February 4, 1969, contained numerous statements, almost all of which appeared in the preliminary prospectus, that plaintiffs claim were misleading.

One preliminary matter must be considered before examining particular representations and omissions. Note (11), Subsequent Events, of the July 31, 1968 certified financial statements of Topsy's read as follows: "For information relating to the subsequent acquisition of all the outstanding stock of SaxonS Sandwich ShoppeS, Inc. see 'SaxonS Sandwich ShoppeS, Inc.' under 'Business' elsewhere in this Prospectus." Plaintiffs argue that the footnote operated as an incorporation by reference of the SaxonS section of the "Business" portion of the prospectus into the certified financials. Were this the case, Touche Ross would be directly liable for misrepresentations and misleading statements resulting from omissions in the SaxonS narrative.

∙ ∙ ∙

We find the approach taken in *Escott* to be the correct one and hold that Touche Ross has no direct responsibility for the SaxonS narrative as a result of note (11). The footnote does not serve to incorporate that portion of the narrative into the certified financial statements. This does not, of course, mean that Touche Ross may not be liable secondarily, as an aider-abettor, for misrepresentations in or omissions from narrative portions of the prospectus.

(a) *The SaxonS Section of the Prospectus*.   Material about SaxonS appeared on pages 10 and 11 within the "Business" portion of the prospectus. It stated that "[a]lthough SaxonS has been open less than two years, it has ten sandwich shops open and operating in Cleveland and Columbus, Ohio, West Palm Beach, Pompano Beach, Fort Lauderdale and North Palm Beach, Florida, and Waco, Texas."

The prospectus states further: "Two units are presently Company-owned and operated, including the pilot unit in Columbus, Ohio, adjoining SaxonS home office building."

The prospectus indicates that the pilot unit in Columbus had gross sales of approximately $413,000.00 in its first year of operation. No sales figures are given for other units. The parties apparently agree that the sales figure given is accurate. Plaintiffs, however, argue that the statement is misleading because the annual volume of $413,000.00 was not representative of other units open and operating at that time, and because the trend in sales at the pilot unit had been downward from its opening date in July 1967, and all SaxonS shops had a similar trend.

∙ ∙ ∙

The question is whether the downward trend of sales at the pilot unit and other units was an omission of material fact necessary to make the statement made not misleading. In light of the limited significance of the isolated sales figure given, and the short operating history of SaxonS, we are reluctant to find the omission of the sales trend material. Additionally, were it material, responsibility must fall on management and the attorneys who drafted the narrative portions of the prospectus. There is nothing to indicate that Touche Ross contributed to the decision to include the reference to first-year sales of the pilot unit or the decision, if such was consciously made, to omit an explanation of sales trends of the pilot units and other units. While there was conflicting testimony as to who "supplied" the dollar amount that appears in the prospectus, we find that West [CEO of SaxonS] originally provided pilot unit sales figures to Tucker [a Topsy's attorney], Berger, and House when he visited them in Kansas City in July 1968. All of the figures relevant to this statement and the alleged omission were clearly within the province of Topsy's management and its attorneys. While on a particular occasion, Touche Ross may have been asked for or volunteered a specific figure from the materials it had assembled, that does not mean that Touche Ross is responsible for the inclusion of that figure in the narrative portion of the prospectus. Such activity would not constitute the significant assistance that is the earmark of aiding-abetting liability.

∙ ∙ ∙

We are faced with the same problem in considering the statement in the prospectus describing the services which SaxonS provided to its franchisees:

> SaxonS provides each franchisee with a wide range of services, including a comprehensive purchasing program, a planned monthly advertising program, modern cost control and accounting procedures, public and employee relation aids, continual management supervision and assistance, and a field inspection service designed to maintain a high standard of uniformity and quality.

Jouras [a Topsy's attorney] obtained the information in these statements from West; Berger and House were familiar with the operation and in a position to know whether they presented a fair picture. There is no evidence that Touche Ross had any knowledge that the statements did not fairly present the services provided to SaxonS franchisees.

• • •

Plaintiffs argue that the Use of Proceeds section contained a misrepresentation because the proceeds were in fact used for the purchase of SaxonS. The offering closed on February 11, 1969, and a part of the proceeds were deposited in Topsy's regular bank account in Kansas City. On February 12, 1969, the account was debited $402,980.56, as a payoff to the bank's loan department of the $400,000.00 loan obtained in connection with the purchase of the Ft. Lauderdale and Waco properties. Without the proceeds, the Topsy's account was not sufficient to make that payment. At the time the revised Use of Proceeds section was submitted to the SEC, Topsy's intended to pay off the loan with part of the proceeds.

Plaintiffs' reasoning is apparently as follows: (1) The acquisition of SaxonS included the purchase of the Waco and Ft. Lauderdale properties; (2) Topsy's told the SEC that proceeds would not be used for the acquisition of SaxonS, either directly or indirectly; (3) Repayment of the $400,000.00 bank loan was using the proceeds indirectly for the purchases of the Waco and Ft. Lauderdale properties, and hence for the acquisition of SaxonS; (4) Therefore, the Use of Proceeds section was a misrepresentation. We have come to essentially the same conclusion, but have reasoned differently. The preliminary prospectus stated that part of the proceeds would be used to replace working capital expended in the purchase of the Waco and Ft. Lauderdale properties. The final prospectus changed the Use of Proceeds section, and thus implied that the proceeds would not be used as stated in the preliminary prospectus, that is, would not be used for the Waco and Ft. Lauderdale properties. But in fact, part of the proceeds was used indirectly for purchase of the Waco and Ft. Lauderdale properties. This use was intended by Topsy's when the final prospectus was issued. The Use of Proceeds section of the final prospectus was misleading. Responsibility for this rests with Topsy's management. . . . there

is no evidence from which the court can reasonably infer that anyone from Touche Ross was aware that Topsy's intended to use the proceeds to pay off the bank loan.

• • •

(c) *The "Management and Principal Stockholders" Section of the Prospectus.*

• • •

This particular section of the prospectus also sets forth the aggregate direct remuneration paid by Topsy's to certain officers and directors during the fiscal year ended July 31, 1968, as follows:

Jerry D. Berger	Chairman-Board of Directors- Director	$ 36,400.00
James T. House	President- Director	$ 35,100.00
All Officers & Directors as a Group	(12 persons)	$159,877.00

Plaintiffs do not claim that this statement is false, but rather that it is misleading because, at a meeting of Topsy's board on July 19, 1968, salary increases were authorized for the year beginning August 1, 1968. Berger's salary was raised to $50,000, House's to $45,000.00.

We do not believe the salaries statement in the prospectus was misleading. It specifically spoke to salaries for the fiscal year ended July 31, 1968. A reasonable investor would quite likely assume that salaries would be increased for the following year. Touche Ross had no responsibility for the failure of the prospectus to describe salaries for the fiscal year beginning August 1, 1969. It would not have been expected to note this, because its concern was with statements in the narrative portion of the prospectus which might be in conflict with the audited financials. The accountants' report did not cover the post-July 31, 1968 period, except for significant subsequent events. Salary increases would not have been so classified.

• • •

5. *Quarterly Report to Shareholders, June 20, 1969.* The report, in letter form, described Topsy's net sales and net earnings

for the quarter ended April 30, 1969, as $3,073,849.00 and $78,250.00 respectively. Herbert Martin, Topsy's controller, testified that when he initially drafted the financial statement it showed $150,000.00 less in pre-tax profits and a net loss for the quarter. He testified further that when he showed the statement to Berger, Berger told him that SaxonS had received $150,000.00 in pre-tax income not reflected in the statement, which resulted from the sale of three SaxonS franchises, each with a $50,000.00 franchise fee. . . . The inclusion of $150,000.00 in un-supported earnings in the letter to share-holders was a misrepresentation, and was the result of intentional false statements bla-tantly made by Berger and Tucker. There is no indication that Touche Ross had anything to do with this situation, however.

4.   *The 1969 Audit and Annual Re-port.*   Touche Ross performed an audit of Topsy's and its subsidiaries as of August 2, 1969, and expressed its unqualified opinion, dated November 14, 1969, on Topsy's con-solidated financial statements for fiscal 1969. Sharlip was the partner in charge of the 1969 audit and Miller, Eppenaur, and others worked with him. The consolidated financial state-ments were first published in the Annual Re-port issued on November 26, 1969. Tucker [a Topsy's attorney] drafted the Message from Management section of the report based on information obtained from Berger and House.

The Message from Management reported an increase in revenues from $8,256,000.00 to $11,823,000.00 but a decrease in earnings from $399,000.00 to $370,000.00 and stated:

> The lower earnings were due largely to the increase in expenses in developing the SaxonS franchise package and lower than estimated revenues in the SaxonS division, due to tight money and labor stoppages. Earnings for the nine months was previously reported at $439,000.00 Since then two SaxonS franchise agreements were repur-chased, causing a reduction in income. These franchises were resold in October.

It was also reported that there were twenty SaxonS units in operation and three more expected to open within the next quarter. A temporary slowing of plans for SaxonS was attributed to the extremely high cost of money. The Message from Management section ended on a positive note: "Your company is on a sound financial basis and looking forward to continued growth."

The Message from Management did not explain SaxonS' operating difficulties as a reason for declining earnings. Eppenaur's 1969 audit memorandum summarized the year's activities of SaxonS as follows:

> During the past year much money and effort on the part of management was spent on the following:
>
> **1.**   Redesign of building: making it smaller and less costly to build.
>
> **2.**   Negotiating with unhappy franchisees.
>
> **3.**   Operating units taken over.
>
> **4.**   Developing a new franchise agreement.
>
> **5.**   Finding new and capable management.
>
> The result of all this has been an unprofitable year coupled with an uncertain future. Man-agement has scaled down expansion due to the tight money market and uncertain nature of the "fast food industry." During this breathing period they intend to pay more attention to current operations, negotiate settlements with franchisees and landlords on unprofitable bad locations, and generally "clean house." Management contends that units which are unprofitable as a sandwich shop can be turned around by changing the menu to include hamburgers, etc. A menu change has recently been imple-mented in some shops. However, it is still too soon to see what effect this has on overall volume and profits.

It is clear that Topsy's was re-evaluating its expansion plans for SaxonS in light of the operating problems SaxonS was experienc-ing. Rapoport, who came on as SaxonS' president in August 1969, wanted to con-centrate on SaxonS in the Kansas City area and close scattered units like Waco, in order to make more effective use of television ad-vertising. Although it appears that Berger may have intended for Topsy's to pull out of SaxonS altogether, he did not communicate his intentions widely. Martin, who left Topsy's in October 1969, was unaware of any decision to discontinue the SaxonS' operation. As Ep-penaur's memorandum shows, he was not aware of a decision to cease expansion. Under the circumstances, we fail to see that Touche Ross had any responsibility to monitor the Message from Management section of the annual report.

. . .

The Message from Management section of the Annual Report spoke of the repurchase of two franchise agreements "causing a reduction of earnings." These were the Poulos franchises. Topsy's had reported net income of $439,300.00 for the first three quarters of fiscal 1969. Without the Poulos earnings, there was a loss in the fourth quarter. As a result, net earnings for the whole year were lower than reported for the first three quarters.

The position that Touche Ross took with respect to these transactions was fully in accord with generally accepted accounting principles. The transactions were irrelevant to the audited financials and no mention of this situation would have been expected in the financials. Touche Ross had no duty to monitor the message from Management section or to make any determination that the transactions should have been explained therein.

5. *Quarterly Report to Shareholders, November 28, 1969.* This report showed revenues, net earnings, and earnings per share for the twelve weeks ended October 25, 1969, as $2,842,000.00, $208,000.00, and 23 cents respectively. It also contained the following statement: "Included in the 1969 earnings is non-recurring income, net of income taxes, of $47,000.00 (5 cents per share)." Ben Schifman's column in the *Kansas City Times* of December 2, 1969, contained a summary of the report and also described $47,000.00 as non-recurring income. Plaintiffs claim that the report and article were misleading because they did not state that the non-recurring income resulted from Topsy's repurchase of some debentures. Despite the fact that Touche Ross had discussed the repurchases with Topsy's, it had no responsibility for statements made by Topsy's management in the quarterly report, and no responsibility for the summary of the report

that appeared in the *Kansas City Times.* Touche Ross' knowledge gave rise to no duty to review or explain these items.

7. *Quarterly Report to Shareholders, March 6, 1970.* This letter showed the following results for the twelve weeks ended January 17, 1970:

Revenues	$2,926,000
Net Earnings (Loss)	(20,000)
Earnings (Loss) per share	(2 cents)

The letter stated in part:

> Results for the quarter ended January 17, 1970, include charges made to reflect the repurchase of three SaxonS franchised units. The sale of one of these units was reported in the last quarter of fiscal 1969; sales of the other two units were included in the first quarter of this fiscal year. The effect of these repurchases was a reduction of second quarter earnings in the amount of $292,000, which had been included in earnings of prior periods. The Company is pursuing a policy of reacquiring certain of its franchised units. If additional units are repurchased, subsequent charges for earnings reported in previous quarters will be required.

From the letter it seems clear that a decision not to expand SaxonS had been made.

On March 19, 1970, Berger, House, Rapoport, Farmer, and Tucker met with two Kansas City attorneys in order to determine "[h]ow to terminate SSS [SaxonS] quickly, preserving for Topsy's its security represented by real estate mortgages, and securing interests in equipment, and at the same time exposing Topsy's as little as possible to litigation and unfavorable publicity." As a result of the meeting, Rapoport went into the field seeking to cancel or terminate franchises, and representing to franchisees that SaxonS had not been able to provide the help or assistance contemplated by the franchise agreements. Along with cancellations, he attempted to obtain releases running to SaxonS and Topsy's. His presentation to franchisees was basically "Look, we won't do anything for you or to you, and you agree to do the same for us. You operate, buy your own supplies, do your own advertising, pay your own rent to the landlord, and we will stay out of it, and you have no obligation to us; we have none to you."

There is no evidence that Touche Ross was aware at the time of these activities. The memorandum by Eppenaur dated September 2, 1970, on the history and status of SaxonS stated:

> Immediately subsequent to August 2, 1969, and after opening five new SaxonS's shops which had been under construction as of August 2, 1969, management decided to scale down expansion due to the tight money market and the uncertain nature of the "fast food industry." During this "breathing" period, management intended to give closer attention to current operations, negotiate settlements with franchisees and landlords on unprofitable locations and generally "clean house." Management felt that some of the units which were unprofitable as a pure sandwich shop, could be turned around by changing the menu to include hamburgers, etc. However, it soon became evident that the probability of turning SaxonS into a profitable operation was slim, thus management decided to buy back all franchises at whatever cost, negotiate unconditional releases with franchisees and landlords and basically "get out of the business." Thus, in February of 1970 they set the wheels in motion to accomplish this end.

This appears to be a fair analysis of the situation in late February and March 1970.

While the quarterly report was less than candid about plans for SaxonS, Touche Ross had no responsibility for it and no duty to monitor management's public statements in it. Similarly, Touche Ross had no responsibility

for the *Kansas City Times* article of March 10, 1970, which reported the letter to shareholders.

• • •

Earlier in the opinion we analyzed the statements individually about SaxonS in the final prospectus. Considering them separately, we concluded that, except for the Use of Proceeds section, they did not contain material misrepresentations or omit facts necessary to make what was said not misleading. We believe that this may be a case where the whole may be greater than the sum of its parts, that is, while individual items may be substantially accurate, the SaxonS' material *in toto* might be said to be misleading. The picture of SaxonS painted by the prospectus and pre-prospectus public statements is entirely positive, yet Topsy's management was aware of operational problems, franchise fee refunds, and a decline in sales for virtually all units. We are completely satisfied, however, with our conclusion that Touche Ross cannot be held responsible for these statements about SaxonS. With respect to the Use of Proceeds section, we believe that plaintiffs have not proven that Touche Ross was aware of Berger's intention to use the proceeds otherwise or, that by presenting management's case to the SEC, Touche Ross was assisting in the fraud being perpetuated by Topsy's management. . . .

In summary, we conclude that while plaintiffs have shown that there were securities laws violations, they have not proven that Touche Ross knew of the violations and of its possible implication in the scheme or that Touche Ross knowingly aided and assisted substantially in the violations.

---

1.   In *Seiffer* the audited financial statements were not vigorously challenged as misleading. As the trial court observed, "financial statements certified by an accountant for presentation to investors give rise to a direct duty to the public." The trial judge's scrutiny of Topsy's auditors was not concerned with violations of the "direct duty" or violations by the auditors as "primary wrongdoers."

The *Seiffer* case involved the court's consideration of allegations that the auditors were "aiders and abettors" of Topsy's fraud. The trial judge acknowledged that the auditors could be "classified as secondary wrongdoers" by "knowingly and substantially" assisting Topsy's fraud.

2.   With respect to the charge that the auditors were "aiders and abettors," the trial judge made the following observation regarding the application of professional standards as a defense to liability:

> [T]he question of an accountant's adherence to generally accepted auditing standards and generally accepted accounting principles is of limited importance. An accountant, who knows that by complying with these standards and principles he is substantially assisting in a fraud, is not protected. On the other hand, an accountant who relies on the profession's standards and principles without knowledge that by doing so he is playing a role in furthering a fraud will not be held liable.

3.   The plaintiffs contended that the reference in a financial statement footnote to Topsy's misleading management narrative imposed a "direct duty" of disclosure on the auditors as if the management narrative was incorporated into the financials. The trial judge, following *Escott v. BarChris Construction Corp.*, rejected any direct duty. The trial judge ruled, however, that rejection of a direct duty of disclosure "does not, of course, mean that Touche Ross may not be liable secondarily, as an aider-abettor, for misrepresentations in or omissions from narrative portions of the prospectus."

The court's statement is a curious twist for it could be viewed as (1) imposing no direct duty of disclosure regarding management disclosures but (2) imposing an indirect duty of disclosure regarding management disclosures to avoid liability as an "aider and abettor." If this is what the court intended, it is not in fact the standard of liability that it applied against the auditors.

4.   With respect to the various quarterly reports issued by Topsy's to its shareholders, the trial judge held that the auditors "had no responsibility for statements made by Topsy's management in the quarterly report." The trial judge further held that the auditors had "no duty to review" or "monitor management's public statements" in the quarterly reports. The trial judge thus held that the auditors had no duty of inquiry or disclosure regarding these management disclosures.

5.   With respect to management disclosures which accompanied the audited financial statements, the trial judge was confronted with a situation where the auditors had reviewed certain management "narrative" disclosures to "assure themselves that nothing in those portions was inconsistent with the audited financial statements of Topsy's." Thus, pursuant to professional standards the auditors had assumed "some" responsibility regarding management's disclosures, namely, to assure they were not inconsistent with the financials.

The trial judge held that the auditors' duty of inquiry was limited to "statements in the narrative portion of the prospectus which might be in conflict with the audited financials." Thus, the court held that the auditors had "no responsibility" for several alleged material omissions and misrepresentations in management's disclosures.

The trial judge further held that certain financial "transactions were irrelevant to the audited financials and no mention of this situation would have been expected in the financials." Although the auditors had no duty to disclose these transactions, management did bear a disclosure obligation which they breached.

[c]   *IIT, an International Investment Trust v. Cornfeld* **and Comments**

IIT, an International Investment Trust v. Cornfeld
619 F.2d 909 (2d Cir. 1980)

Before FRIENDLY, OAKES and NEWMAN, Circuit Judges.

FRIENDLY, Circuit Judge:

[Plaintiff IIT, an International Investment Trust, was an investment company controlled and managed by IIT Management Company (Management). Management was in turn controlled by its parent, Investors Overseas Services, Ltd. (IOS).

Between January 16, 1969 and October 26, 1969, IIT purchased various securities of related companies controlled by John M. King. King controlled King Resources Company (KRC), the Colorado Corporation (TCC), and a subsidiary known as King Resources Capital Corporation (KRCC).

IIT suffered substantial losses from these investments, which gave rise to a lawsuit alleging a conspiracy between those in control of IOS, Management, and the King-related companies. IIT contended that the King-related companies needed vast sums of money and to that end the individuals in control of IOS and Management agreed to "raid IIT for the benefit of the King complex."

IIT contended that it relied upon various false and misleading statements or nondisclosures in connection with its purchases of KRCC debentures and KRC common stock. IIT sued Arthur Andersen & Co., the auditors for both IOS and the King-related companies. IIT contended that Andersen aided and abetted the conspiracy "because of its accounting work on the false and misleading prospectus" of KRC.

IIT further charged that "Andersen's role as auditors for both the King and the IOS companies put it in a unique position to see the developing relationship between the two groups, yet it never informed either the IIT fundholders or the appropriate regulatory bodies."]

(2) *Scienter.* . . . reckless conduct will generally satisfy the *scienter* requirement. However, there are special considerations in applying this general principle to aiders and abettors. . . . We find it hard to see how these allegations that Andersen knew or should have known that something was "wrong," not in the financial statements in the prospectuses but in the general relationship between IIT and King—some of Andersen's alleged "concerns" relating to events subsequent to IIT's purchases—met the requirement for aider and abettor liability under the circumstances. Here we find helpful Judge Goldberg's statement in *Woodward v. Metro Bank of Dallas* that:

> When it is impossible to find any duty of disclosure, an alleged aider-abettor should be found liable only if scienter of the high "conscious intent" variety can be proved. Where some special duty of disclosure exists, then liability should be possible with a lesser degree of scienter.

The complaint does not allege any special duty of disclosure by Andersen. Although Andersen may have had a duty of disclosure as to errors which it found in the financial statements, the complaint does not allege any failure to disclose as to these statements, or even that Andersen ever knew that the statements were false or misleading. The failure to disclose concerned more general "wrongs" not dependent on or tied to Andersen's previous role as an accountant. As to the financial statements themselves nothing more than negligence is alleged. As to the general failure to disclose, the complaint does not charge "*scienter* of the high 'conscious intent,' " or "something closer to an actual intent to aid in the fraud."

(3) *Substantial assistance.*

• • •

The substantial assistance claimed on the part of Andersen is twofold, its activity in connection with the preparation of the prospectuses and its failure to inform either the IIT fundholders . . . or United States authorities of what was afoot. As we have seen, the former ground fails because of the lack of any allegation of scienter. The question how far mere inaction, here Andersen's failure to inform, can fulfill the requirement of substantial assistance is unsettled.

Several cases in other circuits refuse to impose aiding and abetting liability for inaction except when there existed an independent duty to disclose. . . . While here Andersen did prepare and certify the financial statements appearing in the fraudulent prospectus, there is, as we have noted, no adequate allegation of *scienter* by Andersen in that activity. Other courts have taken the view that mere inaction can constitute substantial assistance even in the absence of an independent duty to disclose if but only if there was a "conscious intention" to forward the violation of Rule 10b-5. . . . We approached this position in *Edwards & Hanly* . . . where Judge Gurfein, in dealing with an alleged failure to discover, stated that "[f]inding a person liable for aiding and abetting a violation of 10b-5, as distinct from committing the violation as a principal, requires something closer to an actual intent to aid in a fraud, at least in the absence of some special relationship with the plaintiff that is fiduciary in nature." Perhaps the leading example of "actual intent" aiding and abetting by what came close to mere inaction is *Brennan v. Midwestern United Life Insurance Co.* . . . A number of courts have read *Midwestern* as a case of mere inaction. . . . Even so viewed, *Midwestern* upholds aider and abettor liability in the absence of some independent duty to act only when there is clear evidence of the required degree of *scienter*, . . . and a conscious and specific motivation for not acting on the part of an entity with a direct involvement in the transaction.

Here plaintiffs do not allege that Andersen intended by its silence to forward completion of the fraudulent transactions in the expectation of benefiting from the success of the fraud. Moreover, application of the [aiding and abetting] test should not obscure the basic proposition that mere bystanders, even if aware of the fraud, cannot be held liable for inaction since they do not, in Judge Hand's words, associate themselves with the venture or participate in it as something they wish to bring about. Apart from a case like *Midwestern*, inaction can create aider and abettor liability only when there is a conscious or reckless violation of an independent duty to act. . . . Accountants do have a duty to take reasonable steps to correct misstatements they have discovered in previous financial statements on which they know the public is relying. See *Fischer v. Kletz*, . . . Paragraph 52(C) of the complaint alleged failure of the KRC and KRCC prospectuses to disclose the conspiracy with IOS as a material omission, and arguably alleged that Andersen acquired knowledge of this after the prospectuses had been issued. However, the omission alleged in ¶ 52(C) does not relate to that portion of the prospectus, the financial statements, over which Andersen had responsibility. Andersen had no independent duty to see to the correction of portions of the prospectus other than the financial statement it prepared. Even if we should assume adequate allegations of *scienter* on the part of Andersen with respect to other wrongs claimed by plaintiffs, the complaint fails because it neither alleges a conscious and specific motivation for not acting, as in the *Midwestern* case, nor alleges an independent duty to report.

1. In *IIT* the auditors issued an audit report which was part of a prospectus alleged to be misleading. Among the alleged material omissions from the prospectus was the failure to disclose a conspiracy to defraud, of which the auditors were knowledgeable, the plaintiffs contended.

With respect to this alleged omission the court of appeals held:

> [T]he omission . . . does not relate to that portion of the prospectus, the financial statements, over which Andersen had responsibility. *Andersen had no independent duty to see to the correction of the portions of the prospectus other than the financial statement it prepared.* [Emphasis added.]

2.   The court of appeals' decision states that even if the auditors were knowledgeable regarding the various acts of wrongdoing, the complaint against the auditors "fails because it [does not allege] a conscious and specific motivation for not acting." The court held that to impose liability on the auditors as aiders and abettors there had to exist a motive on the auditors' part to cover up the fraud and not blow the whistle on their client.

The court of appeals stated that "mere bystanders, even if aware of the fraud, cannot be held liable for inaction since they do not . . . associate themselves in the venture or participate in it as something they wish to bring about."

It is difficult to accept as true the proposition that all courts and judges would allow an auditor to issue an audit report that is accurate but that the auditor knows will be part of an otherwise fraudulent prospectus. An auditor caught in such circumstances may have great difficulty defending on the basis that he was a "mere bystander."

3.   The court of appeals ruled that the auditors "had no independent duty to see to the correction of the portions of the prospectus other than the financial statement it prepared." In effect the court ruled that with respect to a prospectus an accountant's duty of disclosure is limited solely to items properly disclosed in the financial statements.

With respect to the financial statements the court found that there was no claim by the plaintiffs of a breach of the duty of disclosure:

> The complaint does not allege any special duty of disclosure by Andersen. Although Andersen may have had a duty of disclosure as to errors which it found in the financial statements, . . . The failure to disclose concerned more general "wrongs" not dependent on or tied to Andersen's previous role as an accountant.

The court held that "we find it hard to see how these allegations that Andersen . . . knew that something was 'wrong,' not in the financial statements in the prospectuses but in the general relationship between IIT and King . . . met the requirement for aider and abettor liability. . . . "

4.   The court of appeals' decision suggests that the limits of an accountant's duty to disclose are capable of a black and white analysis. Unfortunately, the tough disclosure decisions fall into the gray zone where reasonable minds can disagree regarding the limits and scope of the duty to disclose. Indeed, even the auditing profession acknowledges that an auditor may not issue his report as part of a prospectus and totally disregard management's disclosures in the prospectus. (See the discussion at ¶ 7.06[3][d].)

It is possible that the court of appeals' decision is limited solely to circumstances where an auditor is unaware *at the time the prospectus is released* containing his audit report that management's disclosures are false. When the auditor subsequently discovers the fraud he has no duty to correct management's disclosures. If the court's ruling is limited to those circumstances, it is possible that accountants who consciously associate their accurate financials with a fraudulently inaccurate prospectus would be held liable for aiding and abetting a fraud. Isn't there an implied representation by accountants that they will never *knowingly* associate or identify themselves in any manner with a known fraud?

[d]   Accounting Profession's View of "Other Information."   The AICPA in its SAS defines *other information* to be everything published by an auditor's client other than the audited financial statements and the auditor's report. When other information is contained within a document that includes the auditor's report and the audited financials, a limited duty of inquiry arises relating to the other information.

Specifically, the auditor must read the other information to determine if it is "materially inconsistent" with the financial statements. If there is a material inconsistency a duty of disclosure arises:

> If the auditor concludes that there is material inconsistency, he should determine whether the financial statements, his report, or both require revision. If he concludes that they do not require revision, he should request the client to revise the other information. If the other information is not revised to eliminate the material inconsistency, he should consider other actions such as revising his report to include an explanatory paragraph describing the material inconsistency, withholding the use of his report in the document, and withdrawing from the engagement. The action he takes will depend on the particular circumstances and the significance of the inconsistency in the other information (SAS § 550.04).

The SAS acknowledges that in reviewing the "other information" the auditor may become aware of information that "he believes is a material misstatement of fact *that is not a material inconsistency.* . . . " The auditing profession gives the following guidance when the auditor knows that management disclosures are materially false:

> If the auditor concludes that a material misstatement of fact remains, the action he takes will depend on his judgement in the particular circumstances. He should consider steps such as notifying his client in writing of his views concerning the information and consulting his legal counsel as to further appropriate action in the circumstances (SAS § 550.06).

An auditor who reaches this point in the trail is given appropriate advice: "see his lawyer"!

[4]   Internal Controls

If in the course of auditing a client's financial statements an accountant discovers a material weakness or inadequacy in internal accounting controls, the accountant is obligated under existing professional standards to disclose the discovery to the client. Does the auditor have a duty to disclose this discovery to others—such as the client's shareholders, lenders, or creditors? The auditing profession has taken the position that an auditor has no duty to disclose to the public *any* weakness in internal controls.

The auditing profession's view of its duty to disclose known material weaknesses in internal controls is limited:

A duty to disclose to the client's management

No duty to disclose to the client's shareholders, lenders, and creditors as part of the footnote disclosure to the audited financials

The following cases will demonstrate that the courts and judges are not in total agreement regarding the limits of an auditor's duty to disclose known material weaknesses in internal accounting controls.

[a]   *Hochfelder v. Ernst & Ernst* and Comments

Hochfelder v. Ernst & Ernst
503 F.2d 1100 (7th Cir. 1974)

[The facts of the case are set out at ¶ 7.03[1].]

It is clear that as part of Ernst & Ernst's duty to conduct its audit in accordance with generally accepted auditing standards it was incumbent on it to investigate First Securities' system of internal accounting controls. The generally accepted auditing standards as approved and adopted by the membership of the American Institute of Certified Public Accountants provide in pertinent part:

Standards of Field Work

2. There is to be a proper study and evaluation of the existing internal control as a basis for reliance thereon and for the determination of the resultant extent of the tests to which auditing procedures are to be restricted.

Moreover, SEC Form X-17A-5, in directing that the accountant's audit be conducted in accordance with generally accepted auditing standards, emphasizes that those standards shall include a review of the internal accounting control. There is therefore no question but that Ernst & Ernst was under a duty to investigate the internal accounting controls of First Securities.

Ernst & Ernst says that there may be misapprehension about the function of internal accounting control. It contends that the function of internal accounting control is not to insure the detection of all irregularities, but rather to determine the extent to which an auditor can rely on the accounting records of the firm to produce a fair reflection of its financial condition and to provide reasonable assurance as to the safeguarding of assets against loss from unauthorized use or disposition.

Internal accounting controls, as defined by the American Institute of Certified Public Accountants (American Institute), comprise:

The plan of organization and all methods and procedures that are concerned mainly with, and relate directly to, safeguarding of assets and the reliability of the financial records. They generally include such controls as the systems of authorization and approval, separation of duties concerned with record keeping and accounting reports from those concerned with operations or asset custody, physical controls over assets, and internal auditing.

Moreover, as noted by the American Institute: "A function of internal control, from the viewpoint of the independent auditor, is to provide assurance that errors and irregularities may be discovered with reasonable promptness, thus assuring the reliability and integrity of the financial records." With respect to the prevention and detection of fraud the American Institute observes:

6.   Reliance for the prevention and detection of fraud should be placed principally upon an adequate accounting system with appropriate internal control. The well-established practice of the independent auditor of evaluating the adequacy and effectiveness of the system of internal control by testing the accounting records and related data and by relying on such evaluation for the selection and timing of his other auditing procedures has generally proved sufficient for making an adequate examination. If an objective of an independent auditor's examination were the discovery of all fraud, he would have to extend his work to a point where cost would be prohibitive. Even then he could not give assurance that all types of fraud had been detected, or that none existed, because items such as unrecorded transactions, forgeries, and collusive fraud would not necessarily be uncovered. Accordingly, it is generally recognized that good internal control and fidelity bonds provide protection more economically and effectively.

It is Ernst & Ernst's view that in light of the aforementioned purpose and function of internal accounting controls, Nay's mail rule was not relevant to the system of internal accounting control and that in any event First Securities maintained adequate internal accounting controls.

Plaintiffs meet Ernst & Ernst's contention with the affidavits of three former auditors. Fred J. Duncombe, past President of the Illinois Society of Certified Public Accountants and former Chairman of the Committee on Accountancy of the University of Illinois, stated in his affidavit: "If I had discovered in making an audit of a brokerage company that the President of the Company had established an office rule that all mail addressed to him or to the Company for his attention should not be opened by anyone but him; and that when he was away from the office for a few days, the mail addressed to him or to the Company for his attention piled up on his desk, I would not have regarded that brokerge firm as having adequate internal accounting control and would not have certified that a report based on such an audit fairly represented the financial position of the Company." To the same effect affiant Michael K. Garst, a national bank examiner of 25 years experience, indicated that under the circumstances he would have regarded Nay's "mail rule" as a possible violation of duality of control and would have appropriately commented on it. Likewise Gerhard Mayer, a certified public accountant with thirty years experience, comments in his affidavit: "If I had discovered in making an audit of a security brokerge business that its president had established an office rule that mail addressed to him at the business address, or to the company for his attention should not be opened by anyone but him, even in his absence; and that whenever he was away from the office such mail would remain unopened and pile up on his desk I would have to raise the question whether such rule or practice could possibly have been instituted for the purpose of preventing discovery of irregularities of whatever nature; would, as a minimum, have to undertake additional audit procedures to independently establish a negative answer to the latter question; also failing such an answer either withdraw from the engagement or decline to express an opinion on the financial statements of the enterprise."

The foregoing statements go directly to the adequacy of First Securities' system of internal accounting controls and the sufficiency of Ernst & Ernst's review of those controls. In essence they challenge Ernst & Ernst's contention that all audits of First Securities were performed in accordance with generally accepted auditing standards. That is, a negligent failure to discover a material inadequacy in internal accounting controls does not satisfy the generally accepted auditing standard that there "be a proper study and evaluation of the existing internal control." *Auditing Standards and Procedures*, Statement on Auditing Procedure No. 33, American Institute of Certified Public Accountants, at p. 16 (1963).

We realize that there never can be attainment of a perfect or a fail-safe system of internal accounting controls. The most sophisticated system of internal control may harbor inadequacies of some nature. Accordingly, the inadequacy in internal control is of signal importance only when it enters the realm of materiality. To that end we agree with the American Institute of Certified Public Accountants that:

> A material inadequacy [in internal accounting control] can be defined as a condition that would permit a person acting individually in the brokerage concern's organization to perpetrate errors or irregularities involving the accounting records, assets of the brokerage concern, and/or assets of customers that would not be detected through the internal control procedures in time to prevent material loss or misstatement of the concern's financial statements, or serious violation of rules of the regulatory agencies.

On the basis of the foregoing, therefore, there are genuine issues of material fact to be properly decided by a trial: (1) whether Nay's "mail rule" constituted a material inadequacy in First Securities' system of internal accounting control; and (2) whether Ernst & Ernst failed to exercise the due care required of a professional auditor in that it did not discover a material inadequacy in internal accounting control. An affirmative finding on both issues will therefore satisfy the third element of plaintiffs' claim of aiding and abetting, namely, a showing of a breach of duty of inquiry.

If it were found after a trial that Ernst & Ernst breached its statutory duty of inquiry by failing to exercise due care in coming to the knowledge of a material inadequacy in the internal accounting controls of First Securities, it would follow that Ernst & Ernst concomitantly breached an extant duty of disclosure. As we have previously stated, a breach of Ernst & Ernst's statutory duty of inquiry is a failure on its part to adhere with generally accepted auditing standards and as such clearly would not comport with the representation it made in its audit certificates that the audits were performed in accordance with generally accepted auditing standards.[1] To prevent such a misrepresentation and to comply with the disclosure requirement of Rule 17a-5(g)(2)(B), it would, at a minimum, be incumbent on Ernst & Ernst to disclose its departure from generally accepted auditing standards which of course it did not do.

More specifically, the duty, as part of generally accepted auditing standards to investigate internal accounting controls, necessarily implies that any material inadequacy in those controls will be disclosed. Indeed, it is our view that a material inadequacy in internal accounting controls is a matter to which the accountant must properly take exception and to that end we note the requirements of Rule 17a-5(i) which direct that: "Any matters to which the accountant takes exception shall be clearly identified; the exception thereto shall be specifically and clearly stated. . . ." Moreover, we note that the requirement to disclose a material inadequacy in internal accounting controls, which is at least implicit in Rule 17a-5 and Form X-17A-5, was made explicit by SEC Release No. 8172. As to reports of the financial condition of security brokers and dealers filed as of November 30, 1967 or thereafter, the audit requirements of Form X-17A-5 specifically directed that:

> Based upon such audit, the accountant shall comment upon any material inadequacies found to exist in the accounting system, the internal accounting control and procedures for safeguarding securities, and shall indicate any corrective action taken or proposed. These comments may be submitted in a supplementary certificate and filed pursuant to Rule 17a-5(b)(3).

Accordingly, under the circumstances, a finding of a breach of duty of inquiry requires a corollary finding of a breach of duty of disclosure.

---

[1] In its certificate Ernst & Ernst invoked the customarily used scope paragraph whereby the representation was made that Ernst & Ernst conducted its examination of First Securities "in accordance with generally accepted auditing standards." In addition, Ernst & Ernst expressly represented that their examination "included a review of the system of internal control."

1.   The court of appeals concluded in *Hochfelder* that the so-called mail rule of the president of the defunct First Securities brokerage house was possibly a "material inadequacy in internal accounting controls." The court of appeals ordered that the issue had to be tried by the trial court and not simply dismissed.

2.   The court of appeals ruled that the trial court had to decide two questions in reaching a determination regarding whether the auditors breached a duty of inquiry in failing to discover the mail rule.

First, it would have to be determined by the trier of fact whether the " 'mail rule' constituted a material inadequacy in First Securities' system of internal accounting contol." The court of appeals had ruled that "there never can be attainment of a perfect or a fail-safe system of internal accounting controls." And that the "most sophisticated system . . . may harbor inadequacies of some nature." Thus, the court ruled that "the inadequacy . . . is of signal importance only when it enters the realm of materiality."

Second, the trier of fact would have to determine whether "Ernst & Ernst failed to exercise the due care required of a professional auditor in that it did not discover a material inadequacy in internal accounting control." The court of appeals acknowledged the limited nature of the auditors' inquiry regarding internal controls. The limited duty of inquiry would be a circumstance taken into consideration in determining whether the auditors exercised due professional care, skill and competence.

3. The court of appeals in *Hochfelder* concluded that if the auditors breached their "duty of inquiry by failing to exercise due care in coming to the knowledge of a material inadequacy in the internal accounting controls of First Securities it would follow that Ernst & Ernst breached an extant duty of disclosure."

The court of appeals found a breach of a duty of disclosure by reason of an affirmative misrepresentation in the auditors' report and a material omission to disclose in the financials.

4. With respect to the affirmative misrepresentation in the audit report the court of appeals held that "a breach of Ernst & Ernst's . . . duty of inquiry is a failure on its part to adhere with generally accepted auditing standards and as such clearly would not comport with the representation it made in its audit certificates that the audits were performed in accordance with generally accepted auditing standards." The court of appeals observed that "Ernst & Ernst invoked the customarily used scope paragraph" in its audit report and had "expressly represented that their examination 'included a review of the system of internal control.' "

The court of appeals ruled that to prevent "such a misrepresentation . . . it would at a minimum be incumbent on Ernst & Ernst to disclose its departure from generally accepted auditing standards which, of course, it did not do."

5. The court of appeals ruled that failure to disclose a material inadequacy in internal controls was of itself a material omission to disclose. The court of appeals reasoned that "the duty, as part of generally accepted auditing standards to investigate internal accounting controls, *necessarily implies* that any material inadequacy in those controls will be disclosed." (Emphasis added.) Aside from "implication" of a duty to disclose, the court of appeals imposed a duty to disclose, stating: "Indeed, it is our view that a material inadequacy in internal accounting controls is a matter to which the accountant must properly take exception. . . ." The court of appeals also imposed a duty to disclose based on certain SEC reporting requirements which were imposed on security brokers and dealers by statute.

[b]   A Case of Conflicting Opinions: *Adams v. Standard Knitting Mills*.   *Adams v. Standard Knitting Mills* is a classic example of the differences of opinions which may exist among judges and courts regarding the extent of an auditor's duty to disclose to the public known material weaknesses in internal controls. Four judges looked at the facts in this case and heard the arguments — one federal trial judge and three federal appellate judges. The final vote: Two judges ruled there was a duty to disclose to the public a material weakness in internal controls. Two judges held there was no such duty. Fortunately for the auditors, the latter two judges comprised a majority of the appellate court, which reversed a $3.4 million judgment against the auditors by the trial judge.

The facts of this case are set out at ¶ 4.07[2][c]. Consider the opinions of both the trial court and the appellate court.

(i)   Trial Judge's Decision

BOLDT, District Judge:

Plaintiffs claim, . . . that defendant's [Peat's] failure to disclose or to compel Chadbourn's management to disclose that it had serious and continuing problems in electronic data processing (edp) was a material omission [in Chadbourn's financials].

2.   Failure to Disclose EDP Problems

The testimony of Dr. Larry Rittenberg [plaintiffs' expert witness] is replete with examples of gross deficiencies and errors, many of which were acknowledged by Peat's staff, in the Chadbourn edp both prior to, during and subsequent to the time Peat was conducting the 1969 audit. Among the more significant examples are:

1.   Mr. T. Marston, an employee of Peat, conducted a four-day review of Chadbourn's edp system prior to preparing a formal management letter to Chadbourn detailing edp deficiencies. In his work papers, in addition to finding other edp defects, Marston noted, "controls is out of control."

2.   Peat's management letter to Chadbourn dated September 17, 1969 contains a full identification of all the weaknesses of Chadbourn's edp system which, when combined, indicated serious edp deficiencies which urgently needed correction.

3.   Peat further noted in a later management letter dated December 30, 1969, edp weaknesses in the area of the Inventory Management File (IMF) control and cost accounting.

4.   In another management letter to Chadbourn dated December 22, 1970, Peat noted some improvement in Chadbourn's edp system but discovered the continuing existence of a number of deficiencies reported 15 months earlier in the September 17, 1969 management letter. Of this fact, Dr. Rittenberg said, ". . . we have gone now a year later and the data processing control problems still have not been solved, that there are basic pervasive types of control problems."

Plaintiffs contend that "Chadbourn's data processing created weaknesses in Chadbourn's system of internal control" which Peat relied on without reasonable or satisfactory verification. Defendant contends, . . . that only certain information and reports were utilized by Peat and that these reports did not suffer the same errors and weaknesses cited by plaintiffs in other of Chadbourn's edp reports and data output. Plaintiffs' testimonial and documentary evidence clearly established that in 1969 prior, during and subsequent to Peat's audit, Chadbourn's edp was suffering from significant errors in both input and output, as well as distinct shortcomings with respect to controls, to name but a few. These weaknesses were pervasive. Information fed into the computer could be printed out in a number of different reports and forms. From the fact that some significant errors in input and in reports were discovered, the court considers it a reasonable inference that errors not discovered were contained in reports and other output from the Chadbourn computer.

Defendant makes a belated attack on the qualifications and testimony of Dr. Rittenberg and moves to strike his testimony. The court found the qualifications of Rittenberg to be amply sufficient to admit his testimony, and to permit him to express opinions and conclusions on the edp problems and audit procedures of Chadbourn during the relevant time period. In fact, the court finds that in many instances Rittenberg's edp testimony was substantially more credible and convincing than the testimony of defendant's witnesses on the same subject matter. Accordingly, defendant's motion to strike the Rittenberg testimony is hereby denied.

In sum, the court finds and holds that in various particulars defendant failed to follow and apply general accounting principles which was essential for fair presentation of Chadbourn's financial position and the results of its operations, by not disclosing or compelling Chadbourn management to disclose its gross edp deficiencies.

(b) Material Misrepresentation

. . .

The edp deficiencies at Chadbourn were of such a pervasive nature and importance that their existence did, or at a minimum, could have significantly affected the entire operation of Chadbourn and would therefore most directly relate to matters contained in the financial statements.

Peat attempts to make a distinction between accounting controls and administrative controls to explain away Peat's reliance on Chadbourn's defective EDP system in the 1969 audit. Such distinction is overly technical and ignores the interrelatedness of the concepts in the real world.

No experienced accounting firm can report a company's financial position today and ignore what it may be tomorrow. This is especially true when as in this instance, the accountant has knowledge of adverse information and conditions which obviously may significantly jeopardize the client company's future performance. As noted previously, the independent auditor is under a duty to fairly present the financial position of a company and the "results of operations" in his financial statements. The court finds and holds that defendant . . . omitted to state . . . gross edp deficiencies at Chadbourn and failed to conduct the 1969 audit in compliance with GAAP and GAAS. The materiality of these misrepresentations and omissions will be discussed below.

Materiality, . . . is a determination to be made upon the facts and circumstances in each particular case. The test for materiality in the Sixth Circuit is ". . . whether a reasonable man would have attached importance to the undisclosed facts to determine his choice of action in the particular transaction in question."

Based upon the foregoing authority the court concludes that the defendant's misrepresentations and omissions, as fully set forth above, were material. This court has no doubt that, had Peat properly described and disclosed information it incorrectly described or failed to disclose, plaintiffs would have considered it important and would have significantly affected and influenced their investment decisions. This is not to say plaintiffs' ultimate decision to approve the merger might have been otherwise. At this time, it is now impossible to predict with certainty the actions

of the Standard shareholders in 1970 had defendant made a full and accurate disclosure in the Standard proxy statement; however, in all reasonable probability, some or all shareholders would not have voted for the merger, at least without important modifications or added conditions.

(ii)   *Appellate Judges' Majority Decision*

III. Computer Defects

Chadbourn used electronic data processing to record many of its financial records from sales to inventory on hand. The District Court found various deficiencies connected with these computer accounts which, it concluded, Peat should have disclosed in the notes accompanying the proxy statement.

The record contains evidence of poorly documented computer programs, a high level of computer personnel turnover, lack of security in the computer room, erroneously coded data, and poorly designed computer programs that failed to detect improperly coded data. Peat sent several memoranda to Chadbourn's management, documenting the computer weaknesses; and one internal Chadbourn memorandum not written by Peat stated that the company was "pushed . . . to the brink of bankruptcy" by the unreliability of computer-generated information. The District Court found that Peat's failure to disclose these weaknesses constituted fraud. We disagree.

An outside accountant examines the quality of a company's internal accounting primarily to determine the extent to which he must test a client's records. The more reliable the client's accounting system proves to be, the less testing the accountant must conduct. A by-product of this testing is the discovery of weaknesses in internal accounting. The accountant may bring such weaknesses to the attention of management but he is not always obligated to inform the stockholders. This is not to say that an accountant may keep a blind eye to all wrongdoing while walking through a client's corporate headquarters. He may be held liable to the extent that he intentionally or recklessly disregards the generally accepted, standard body of accounting knowledge. This is not the case here. Although we cannot say the District Court's inference, that faulty computer information materially impaired management's ability to manage, is clearly erroneous, there was no scienter in Peat's failure to disclose. The absence of an intent to deceive is fatal to plaintiff's claim.

According to the Statements on Auditing Procedure,[1] promulgated by the Auditing Standards Executive Committee of the American Institute of Certified Public Accountants (AICPA), the accountant may have a duty to direct management's attention to internal accounting weaknesses he has uncovered. But the Committee imposed no requirement that the notes to the certification of financial reports contain a similar disclosure of such weaknesses.

An auditor cannot always make an assessment of the effect of accounting weaknesses on the efficiency of a company. Often such an assessment requires a technical knowledge of a business in which accountants have no expertise. Peat's reliance on the AICPA's committee opinions is sufficient indication of good faith and lack of scienter.

Peat cannot be charged with knowledge of the interplay between poor or inefficient record-keeping procedures and mismanagement. Nor does the record disclose that Peat actually knew of Chadbourn's internal memoranda evaluating the effect of poor computer information upon management. Likewise, the evidence does not support a finding of recklessness.

Finally, undisputed testimony shows that by the time of the proxy solicitations, many of the computer problems had already been solved. The only relevant disclosure would

have been that, for the two quarters preceding the merger, Chadbourn's management may not have been sufficiently informed due to temporary computer deficiencies. Accountants are not liable for failing to speculate publicly about this subject.

(iii) Appellate Judge's Dissenting Decision

Although my dissent with respect to violations of section 10(b) of the Act and Rule 10b-5 is dispositive of the issue of liability, I also approve the findings and conclusions of the District Court as additional support with respect to Peat's false Certificate of the Chadbourn 1969 audit and the electronic data processing (edp).

The District Court found that Peat violated generally accepted auditing standards and generally accepted accounting principles (GAAS and GAAP) during the audit. Specifically, he found that Peat violated the following standards taken from Statements on Auditing Procedure No. 33 (SAP 33): the second and third general standards:

2.   In all matters relating to the assignment an independence in mental attitude is to be maintained by the auditor or auditors.

3.   Due professional care is to be exercised in the performance of the examination and the preparation of the report.

the second standard of field work:

> There is to be proper study and evaluation of the existing internal control as a basis for reliance thereon and for the determination of the resultant extent of the tests to which auditing procedures are to be restricted.

the third standard of field work:

> Sufficient competent evidential matter is to be obtained through inspection, observation, inquiries and confirmations to afford a reasonable basis for an opinion regarding the financial statements under examination.

[I] believe that there is substantial evidence in the record to support [the District Court's] findings, and that they are not clearly erro-

---

[1] See AICPA, Statement on Auditing Procedure, No. 33 at 32 (1963); AICPA, Statement on [Auditing] Standards No. 1 §§ 320, 640 (1973); Carmichael, *Opinions on Internal Control*, Journal of Accountancy 47 (1970). The AICPA in 1977 promulgated a rule that disclosure to management was required. See AICPA, Statement on [Auditing] Standards No. 20 (1977).

neous. With respect to the conduct of the audit, no working papers exist to verify that important auditing steps were performed during the audit. Peat's valuation of Chadbourn's inventory was poorly performed. Peat's employee Marston's working papers on the efficacy of Chadbourn's internal controls stated, "[c]ontrols is out of control!" Two letters from Peat to Chadbourn dated September 17, 1969, and December 22, 1970, show that Chadbourn's electronic data processing (edp) problems were widespread and pervasive in all internal accounting systems, yet Peat failed to adequately take these problems into consideration, or to demand a full manual audit at financial year end, only one month later, as required by Peat's own audit manual; indeed, Peat instead relied upon Chadbourn's internal accounting systems to adjust the audit figures so that the financial statement read as of August 2, 1969, instead of July 4, 1969.

• • •

In arriving at its factual findings with respect to the audit, the materiality of the omissions and misrepresentations by Peat and in internal control, the District Court was supported by the testimony of Larry E. Rittenberg, as assistant professor in the department of accounting of the University of Tennessee, and George J. Benston, a distinguished professor of accounting and finance at the University of Rochester Graduate School of Management.

• • •

The amicus brief of American Institute of Certified Public Accountants is noteworthy in its failure to discuss the main issue in this appeal, on which our decision is based, namely, the fraudulent footnote 7 of the Chadbourn financial statement contained in the Standard proxy materials written and certified as correct by Peat and mailed to Standard stockholders and filed with SEC. Instead, the Institute treats only one of the many issues in this case, namely, the liability of Peat for failure to disclose in its audit, weaknesses in the internal control of Chadbourn or require Chadbourn to make such disclosure.

If Peat desired to limit its liability it should have never attached to its audit the Certificate which it executed and was found by the District Court to be a false and fraudulent certification.

The District Court made a number of specific findings of fact with supporting record references with respect to Electronic Data Processing (EDP) deficiencies . . . and held that Peat had a duty to disclose them to Standard's stockholders as prudent investors would be entitled to this information. Peat's failure to disclose this material information on its audit constituted a breach of duty of disclosure.

(iv)   Comments on Adams v. Standard Knitting Mills

1.   The *Adams* case is arguably a "split decision" regarding its value as case precedent. It is not clear that the majority opinion by the court of appeals will be universally accepted by other courts. The *Hochfelder* decision is an example of how three federal appellate judges believed accountants have a duty to disclose to the public material weaknesses in internal controls.

2.   The trial judge's decision is an illustration of the application of the doctrine of "qualitative materiality." Although the financial statement disclosures were not quantitatively deficient (that is, the "bottom line" and the numbers in the financials were not assailed or otherwise proved wrong), the trial judge ruled that there was a qualitatively material disclosure omission, namely, the "gross electronic data processing (edp) deficiencies." The trial judge held:

The edp deficiencies at Chadbourn were of such a pervasive nature and importance that their existence did, or at a minimum, could have significantly affected the entire operation of

Chadbourn and would, therefore, most directly relate to matters contained in the financial statements.

In a classic statement of "qualitative materiality" the trial judge ruled:

> [N]o experienced accounting firm can report a company's financial position today and ignore what it may be tomorrow. This is especially true when as in this instance, the accountant has knowledge of adverse information and conditions which obviously may significantly jeopardize the client company's future performance.

3.   The majority decision by the court of appeals in *Adams* relied totally on the fact that the standards of the auditing profession did not compel public disclosure of known material weaknesses in internal controls. Thus, the appellate court made the auditors' reliance on professional standards a complete defense to the charge of fraud. (See *United States v. Simon* where the court took the contrary approach, ¶ 5.04[1].)

The appellate court does not attempt to refute or answer the trial judge's decision that the existence of material weaknesses in internal controls was a fact to which "a reasonable man would have attached importance." The appellate court's opinion is also silent regarding the issue of whether the auditors' representation that they conducted an audit in accordance with "generally accepted auditing standards" was materially false in view of the evidence that the auditors had violated the second and third standards of field work. In *Hochfelder v. Ernst & Ernst* the court of appeals held that "at a minimum" the auditors should have disclosed their "departure" from GAAS.

[5]   Foreign Corrupt Practices Act

In 1977 Congress enacted the Foreign Corrupt Practices Act (FCPA). The scope of the FCPA is not limited solely to the prohibition of certain payments of monies to foreign officials and others. The FCPA imposes accounting requirements on corporations that are subject to SEC reporting and regulation.

The corporate accounting provisions of the FCPA involve (1) recordkeeping requirements and (2) internal accounting control requirements. Both of these provisions have far-reaching implications on SEC reporting corporations and their independent auditors.

The recordkeeping provisions of the Act provide that those corporations subject to SEC authority shall:

> make and keep books, records, and accounts, which, in reasonable detail, accurately and fairly reflect the transactions and dispositions of the assets of the issuer.

The internal accounting control provisions, which are also applicable to all corporations subject to the authority of the SEC, provide that an issuer of securities shall:

> devise and maintain a system of internal accounting controls sufficient to provide reasonable assurances that:

(i)   transactions are executed in accordance with the management's general or specific authorization;

(ii)   transactions are recorded as necessary (1) to permit preparation of financial statements in conformity with generally accepted accounting principles or any other criteria applicable to such statements and (2) to maintain accountability for assets;

(iii)   access to assets is permitted only in accordance with management's general or specific authorization; and

(iv)   the recorded accountability for assets is compared with the existing assets at reasonable intervals and appropriate action is taken with respect to any differences.

The application of the foregoing accounting provisions of the FCPA raise several questions and points of consideration which must be addressed by an auditor's client.

[a]   Recordkeeping.   Among the considerations regarding compliance with the recordkeeping provisions are:

1.   What types of books, records, and accounts are necessary under the FCPA to "accurately and fairly" reflect the "transactions" and "disposition of assets" of the issuer. Should not the objective here be to require underlying financial data sufficient to allow a corporation to issue financial statements in accordance with generally accepted accounting principles? The legislative history of the FCPA indicates that the purpose of this provision is "to require that books and records are kept so that financial statements prepared in accordance with generally accepted accounting principles can be derived from them."

2.   Does the FCPA contemplate that a materiality standard should apply to considerations of (1) whether sufficiently detailed books and accounts have been created to account for the corporation's financial activities, and (2) whether the utilization of these accounts and books has been in conformity with the requirements of the Act? For example, there is some point where given the immateriality of a financial transaction, it is accounted for generally, without specific detail. Similarly, immaterial errors in recording financial transactions do not preclude the issuance of financial statements in accordance with generally accepted accounting principles. Evidence that Congress contemplated that a materiality standard should be the measure for application of the recordkeeping provision is suggested by Congress's use of the qualifying language that records and accounts be kept which in "reasonable detail" accurately and fairly reflect a corporation's financial transactions. The legislative history of the Act indicates that "the conference [committee] inserted 'in reasonable detail' before 'accurately and fairly' to make it clear that no absolute standard of precision is required or obtainable," and that:

> Standards of reasonableness must apply. In this regard, the term 'accurately' does not mean exact precision as measured by some abstract principle. Rather, it means that an issuer's records should reflect transactions in conformity with generally accepted accounting principles or other applicable criteria.

Any conclusion of what is reasonable under the circumstances involves a consideration of materiality for it is difficult to perceive that records and accounts which accurately reflect millions of dollars of transactions are rendered inaccurate and unfair by virtue of an improper recording of a transaction which is quantitatively and qualitatively immaterial (i.e., does not reflect adversely on the integrity of management or reliability of the books and records).

3. By requiring that an issuer shall "keep" books, records, and accounts, does the FCPA contemplate that an issuer shall have some type of records retention policy? If this was intended, what is the extent of such requirement? Would an issuer violate the Act by destroying certain accounting records one year subsequent to their use in preparing financial statements? Two years later? Twenty years later? Here also considerations of what is reasonable under the circumstances should apply.

[b]   Internal Accounting Controls.   With regard to the requirements of the FCPA's internal accounting controls provisions, several considerations and questions may be raised:

1. Since the source of the internal accounting control provisions is Section 320.28 of the AICPA's Statement on Auditing Standards No. 1, should not these prescriptions be construed in the entire context of the auditing literature from which it is drawn?

2. SAS 320.28 is a general statement which defines the objectives of a system of internal accounting control in order to safeguard the company's assets and assure the reliability of the financial records. The FCPA requires that a corporation's system of internal control shall provide "reasonable assurance" of meeting the broadly defined objectives of such a system. The concept of "reasonable assurance" as utilized by an auditor is defined in the context of a material weakness in internal accounting control:

> A material weakness means a condition in which the auditor believes the prescribed procedures or degree of compliance with them does not provide reasonable assurance that errors or irregularities in amounts that would be material in the financial statements being audited would be prevented or detected within a timely period by employees in the normal course of performing their assigned functions.

Such a concept, however, might not be sufficient in describing a level of assurance necessary for management for there may be situations where a weakness in internal accounting controls is not material for audit purposes but is otherwise unacceptable to management. For example, a weakness in internal accounting control may not preclude the potential misuse of a cash imprest fund of immaterial amount from the auditor's standpoint. Nevertheless, management may decide that such a weakness is significant and thus warrants corrective measures.

3. The concept of "reasonable assurance" from management's perspective is best related to § 320.32 of SAS 1 of which states:

> The definition of accounting control comprehends reasonable, but not absolute, assurance that the objectives expressed in it will be accomplished by the system. *The concept of*

reasonable assurance recognizes that the costs of internal control should not exceed the benefits expected to be derived. The benefits consist of reduction in the risk of failing to achieve the objectives implicit in the definition of accounting control. Although the cost-benefit relationship is the primary conceptual criterion that should be considered in designing a system of accounting control, *precise measurement of costs and benefits usually is not possible; accordingly, any evaluation of the cost-benefit relationship requires estimates and judgments by management.* [Emphasis added.]

This approach to analyzing the adequacy of a system of internal accounting controls reflects a pragmatic, flexible approach to implementing a system of internal controls, observing that (a) there can be no perfect, fail-safe system of internal controls; and (b) that even an almost perfect system of internal controls may be imperfect because the protections it affords are outweighed by the costs of its implementation.

The principles underlying the application of the "cost-benefit analysis" may be demonstrated by the following example. Assume a cash fund is inadequately controlled and contains $10,000. The cost of hiring an additional employee to remedy the potential weakness in control would be $15,000 annually. Here the incremental costs would arguably outweigh the incremental benefits of reducing the risk of misuse of corporate assets.

4. It appears clear that the "cost-benefit analysis" is the signpost by which a corporation is to test the adequacy of its system of internal controls under the FCPA. It is equally clear that such an analysis is to be grounded on the good faith judgment of management. The legislative history of the FCPA reflects that:

> The establishment and maintenance of a system of internal control and accurate books and records are fundamental responsibilities of management. The expected benefits to be derived from the conscientious discharge of these responsibilities are of basic importance to investors and the maintenance of the integrity of our capital market system. The committee recognizes, however, that management *must exercise judgment in determining the steps to be taken, and the cost incurred, in giving assurance that the objectives expressed will be achieved. Here, standards of reasonableness must apply.* In this regard, the term "accurately" does not mean exact precision as measured by some abstract principle. Rather it means that an issuer's records should reflect transactions in conformity with generally accepted accounting principles or other applicable criteria. While management should observe every reasonable prudence in satisfying the objectives called for in new paragraph (2) of section 13(b), *the committee recognizes that management must necessarily estimate and evaluate the cost/benefit relationships of the steps to be taken in fulfillment of its responsibilities under this paragraph.* [Emphasis added.]

Likewise, the SEC acknowledged the reasonableness of this approach in its Release No. 34-13185 where it proposed the regulatory antecedent to the existing internal accounting provisions, stating:

> The *design of any such system necessarily involves exercise of management's judgment, and entails the balancing of the cost of implementing any given internal accounting control against the benefit to be derived.* By requiring that a system provide reasonable assurance that the specified objectives are met, the Commission's proposed rule recognizes

that the issuer must, in good faith, balance the cost and benefits as they relate to the circumstances of that company. The definition of the term "reasonable assurance" in proposed Rule 13b-2 is, like the objective for a system of internal accounting controls, taken from existing accounting literature. See Statement on Auditing Standards No. 1, supra, Section 320.32. (Emphasis added)

Although the principle of cost-benefit analysis is clear in statement, it remains to be seen to what extent it remains clear in application. To that end, it can be expected that the accounting profession will attempt to provide appropriate guidance. However, the auditor's role with respect to review of internal accounting controls remains unchanged by the FCPA which places the burden for implementation of the provisions on management.

¶ 7.07   Unjustified Reliance

[1]   Plaintiff Must Prove Justifiable Reliance on the Accountant's Report, Advice, or Representation

A party who claims to have been misled by an accountant's report, advice, or representation must establish that the party justifiably relied on the false information provided by the accountant. Justifiable reliance is a necessary element in an action against an accountant for negligent misrepresentation or fraud. Justifiable reliance requires a plaintiff to prove:

(a)   That the plaintiff relied upon the report, advice, or representation which plaintiff claims was false and misleading, and

(b)   That plaintiff's reliance was not reckless or unreasonable in view of the plaintiff's knowledge of the facts and business sophistication.

A circumstance involving "no reliance" may occur where a plaintiff claims reliance but in fact the accountant's report, advice, or representation was not a factor in the plaintiff's decisional process. Unjustified reliance may exist where a plaintiff claims to have relied on an accountant's representation when in fact the plaintiff possessed knowledge of other facts from other sources which nullifies any claim of reliance on the accountant's false information or renders plaintiff's reliance "unreasonable" in the circumstances.

Unjustified reliance questions often arise in circumstances where a nonclient user of financial information claims reliance on financials on which the accountant has issued a qualified opinion or disclaimed an opinion. Questions relating to a plaintiff's justifiable reliance also arise in circumstances where an accountant makes written or oral representations that are not contained in any formal report to the client.

Disclaimers and qualified opinions will not of themselves limit an accountant's liability. A disclaimer or qualification will serve to limit the scope of an accountant's representation. To the extent the limited nature of the accountant's representation is clearly stated in his report, his liability may be limited. That is, a plaintiff may justifiably rely only on that which the accountant represents.

Problems sometimes arise in circumstances where an accountant makes written or oral representations which accompany a disclaimer. In such cases the written or oral representation may invite justifiable reliance on a plaintiff's part and thereby effectively "override" any disclaimer.

Liability problems sometimes arise despite the issuance of a qualified opinion. If the accountant fails to state all the material reasons underlying his qualification, the accountant's report may be found materially misleading. In such circumstances a plaintiff may claim justifiable reliance on a qualified opinion which omits to state material facts.

In certain situations the law does not require a plaintiff to prove reliance. For example, in a lawsuit brought under Section 11 of the Securities Act, a plaintiff who purchases a security need not prove reliance on the registration statement (see the discussion at ¶ 3.02[3]). Also, a plaintiff who sues an accountant as an aider and abettor of a fraud does not have to prove reliance. (See the discussion at ¶ 7.07[6].)

[2]   No Reliance, No Liability

If a plaintiff possesses a certain degree of business sophistication, the question may arise as to whether the plaintiff actually relied, as claimed, on the accountant's professional report, advice, or representation. If the plaintiff is highly sophisticated in business matters, the question of plaintiff's actual reliance will always be considered.

Aside from the plaintiff's business sophistication and intelligence, the plaintiff may have access to facts which call into question:

(a)   Whether the accountant's false report, advice, or representation was even a factor upon which the plaintiff relied in reaching a decision.

(b)   Whether the plaintiff knew that the accountant's report, advice, or representation was false, misleading, or incomplete.

If the plaintiff knew that the accountant's report was false, plaintiff's reliance would be "unjustified." If the plaintiff makes his decision based on other factors and simply did not care about or consider the accountant's report, there is no "actual" reliance. Consider these factors as you review the following case.

[a]   *Bunge Corp. v. Eide* **and Comments**

Bunge Corp. v. Eide
372 F.Supp. 1058 (D.N.D. 1974)

BENSON, Chief Judge.

[Plaintiff Bunge Corp. financed the operations of R.F. Gunkelman and Sons, Inc., which was engaged in the production and sale of grain and agricultural commodities. In 1970 Gunkelman was adjudicated bankrupt leaving an indebtedness of $1.5 million to Bunge.

The defendants were CPAs who audited Gunkelman. Bunge sued the auditors claiming that it relied on the CPAs' audit reports which were materially misleading.]

The credit extended to Gunkelman by Bunge was many times larger than that extended to any of the other financed accounts, and the account was considered to be unique. The account was supervised out of the Minneapolis regional office by Bunge's credit manager and a field man who traveled the territory. A friendly business and social relationship developed between the Gunkelman officers and Bunge's credit manager. By April 1, 1967, when a change in credit managers took place by reason of the retirement of the credit manager who had served in the position for about eight years, the Gunkelman indebtedness to Bunge had risen to $1,674,668.86.

The Gunkelman account was maintained as an open account, without stated limits and without security of any kind. The shippers contracts and the security agreements which Bunge required on its financed accounts had never been obtained from Gunkelman. There were no cross guarantees from the affiliated corporations, and no personal guarantees from the stockholder-officers. There were no controls of any kind on Gunkelman's management. There was no substantial seasonal reduction of the account.

• • •

Bunge failed in its efforts to get the Gunkelman account under control. The indebtedness rose to $3,153,000.00 at the end of April, 1969. Bunge thereafter asserted increased pressure on the account, but its efforts to get security agreements, financing statements, cross guarantees from affiliated corporations, personal guarantees from the stockholder-officers, and quarterly reports, were only partially successful. In November, 1969, stock pledges were secured from the officer-stockholders, but no personal guarantees were ever obtained.

• • •

In the years 1963 through 1968 inclusive, Gunkelman did a major business in sunflower seeds on which there was no quoted market. In their audit reports, defendants included unprocessed sunflower inventories under grain and valued them at local market. Bunge knew that sunflowers were included in the grain inventories and knew they were valued at local market.

Defendants' method of stating unprocessed sunflower inventories at local market was not in accordance with generally accepted accounting principles. In all other respects, the financial statements and reports and auditing procedures were in accordance with generally accepted auditing procedures. There is no evidence that the sunflower inventories were sold for less than the stated valuations, and there is no evidence that the defendants' financial statements and audit reports on Gunkelman did not fairly reflect the financial condition of the company for the period covered by the reports.

From the foregoing facts, the Court concludes the defendants did not materially misrepresent the financial condition of R. F. Gunkelman and Sons, and in extending credit, plaintiff's reliance was on Gunkelman principals and not on the reports of its accountants.

• • •

Specifically, the plaintiff contended that defendant in its audit reports from 1963 to 1968, valued sunflower seeds in the closing inventory at something more than cost in contravention of Statement 9 [of Accounting Research Bulletin No. 43] and as such, materially overstated net profits for those years. It is contended that Bunge placed great reliance on these audit reports in extending credit to Gunkelman.

Defendants, through the years in question, 1963 through 1968, consistently used the same method for arriving at a valuation for the unprocessed sunflower. Thus the value of the closing inventories from one year's report were the value of the beginning inventories of the succeeding year. There is no evidence that this resulted in a distortion in the reports of the financial condition of the company. . . . Even if the method used did overstate the value, the plaintiff's contention that it relied on those values and was misled to its detriment is not credible because the evidence conclusively established that it was fully aware that the value of unprocessed sunflowers was stated in the reports at local market. Bunge's attempt to draw a distinction between local market and "market escalation" is not persuasive. Defendant tested the "market escalation" values furnished by Gunkelman against local market as determined from sales inventories. One must therefore conclude that "market escalation" was local market as actually designated in the reports.

It was clearly established that the Gunkelman account went out of control by reason of Bunge's loose credit policy that existed prior to 1967. Thereafter, efforts to bring it under control were not successful. Its credit manager explained the continued extension of credit as having been required because if they had stopped "we would have put the business in jeopardy and Bunge would have suffered a loss." The credit manager also testified "to force them would put them out of business."

Bunge obviously did suffer a loss, but that loss was not the proximate result of any negligence of the defendants. It would seem to this Court that the objectives of the standards and guidelines of the American Institute of Certified Public Accountants is to correctly state the financial condition of a company. There is no proof that the defendants' reports failed to correctly state the financial condition of R. F. Gunkelman and Sons, Inc. There is much evidence that Bunge closed its eyes to the information disclosed by those reports and continued to extend credit without any of the normal controls and security that a prudent creditor usually requires.

1. The auditors were sued regarding their audit reports for 1963 through 1968. In 1969 the auditors disclaimed an opinion, stating: "Because of inadequate inventory procedures, we were unable to substantiate the correctness of inventory quantity, quality and prices." In a note to the 1969 financials the company's change of its method of valuing the unprocessed sunflower inventory was noted along with the observation that had this "method of valuation been used in the preceding year, the net loss for the current year would have been $149,536.00."

The trial judge ruled that the "Defendants' method of stating unprocessed sunflower inventories at local market was not in accordance with generally accepted accounting principles." In holding that the auditors were not liable to the plaintiff, the trial judge stated "in extending credit, plaintiff's reliance was on Gunkelman principals and not on the reports of its accountants."

2. The trial judge noted that the plaintiff lender extended credit to keep its borrower afloat. The trial judge held that "There is much evidence that Bunge closed its eyes to the information disclosed by [the auditors'] reports and continued to extend credit without any normal controls and security that a prudent creditor usually requires."

The trial court's finding that the plaintiff did not act as a "prudent" lender is an example of yet another defense to liability, namely, contributory fault. Under the contributory fault doctrine, even if the plaintiff relies on the accountant, the plaintiff's lack of due care may limit or bar completely any recovery from the accountant. That is, to the extent that a plaintiff's own negligent or faulty conduct contributes to his injury, the plaintiff's contributory fault may bar totally or partially a claim against the accountant. (See ¶ 7.08 for a discussion of contributory fault.)

[3] Disclaimed or Qualified Report: Unjustified Reliance

When an accountant issues a report on which he disclaims or qualifies an opinion, the accountant has put financial statement users on notice regarding the unreliability of certain material facts.

[a] Disclaimed Opinion

Katz v. Realty Equities Corp.
406 F.Supp. 802 (S.D.N.Y. 1976)

[The facts of the case are set out at ¶ 7.03[3].]

As to the defendant Grant, that firm did make disclosure of serious problems it uncovered during its examination of Realty. Indeed, it refused to certify the financial statements it prepared for Realty for the period ending March 31, 1970. That refusal was communicated to the SEC and Realty's shareholders as part of Realty's 1970 Annual Report. Furthermore, that report indicated that the transactions between Realty and Republic were among those that led to Grant's concern for the accuracy and reliability of the financial statements.

It thus appears that summary judgment is appropriate in favor of Grant. Even if Grant may not have disclosed all the information of which it was aware, the existence of any such non-disclosure would not be a fact material to the outcome of the litigation. In this action brought under § 10(b) of the Securities Exchange Act of 1934, . . . and Rule 10b-5 . . . a non-disclosure is "material" for summary judgment purposes only if it is an omission "to state a material fact necessary in order to make the statements made, in the light of circumstances under which they were made, not misleading." Given the disclosure which Grant did make in Realty's annual report, and especially in light of Grant's refusal to certify that report's financial statements, the failure to make any additional disclosure called for by the complaint could not possibly have affected a reasonable investor's decision-making. Grant put the public on notice that the financial statement was not reliable; its failure to reveal every detail which gave rise to the unreliability cannot possibly be a material omission.

1.   The auditors disclaimed an opinion which was communicated in the client's annual report. Despite the disclaimer, the auditors were sued.

2.   The trial judge dismissed the case against the auditors, holding that even if the auditors failed to "reveal every detail" that gave rise to their disclaimer, the auditors' disclaimer was sufficient to "put the public on notice that the financial statement was not reliable." See *Herzfeld v. Laventhol* ¶ 7.07[4] for a case where the auditors had qualified their opinion regarding the collectibility of a material contract and were found liable for not stating all the material reasons that underlay their decision to issue a qualified opinion.

[b] Qualified Opinions

(i) Stephens Industries Inc. v. Haskins & Sells *and Comments*

Stephens Industries Inc. v. Haskins & Sells
438 F.2d 357 (10th Cir. 1971)

Before BREITENSTEIN, HILL and SETH, Circuit Judges.

HILL, Circuit Judge.

[Plaintiffs Stephens Industries and Morris Stephens (referred to as "appellants" in the court's opinion) purchased shares of stock in a car-rental business which subsequently failed. The plaintiff purchasers and the stock sellers determined the stocks' purchase price based on an audit of the car-rental business by the defendant accountants, Haskins and Sells (the "appellees").

Shortly after Haskins and Sells was hired by the purchasers and sellers to perform an audit, it "became apparent that the accounts receivable records had been poorly maintained, and a significant discrepancy appeared between the accounts receivable ledger cards and the general ledger." Haskins and Sells advised their clients "of the added cost if the accounts receivables were to be audited." The clients advised Haskins and Sells not to audit the accounts receivable.

At trial the plaintiffs claimed that Haskins and Sells had "misrepresented the status of the accounts receivable in the audit."]

Specifically, it is urged that Haskins and Sells knew and should have disclosed the status of the accounts receivable to appellants. The basis for this contention springs from the Restatement of Torts § 552(a). A vital element of that rule which appellants fail to mention is that liability in those circumstances is contingent upon the failure "to exercise that care and competence in obtaining and communicating the information which its recipient is justifed in expecting." . . . Appellants' argument must fail. For the evidence is clear that Haskins and Sells did not fail to exercise the care and competence in disclosing the audit results which appellants were justified in expecting.

First, the evidence does not support the bald allegation that Haskins and Sells knew that certain accounts receivable were "obviously uncollectible" as of December 31, 1964. The undisputed testimony shows that until the accountants conducted the full audit on the accounts receivable, which they were instructed not to do, any conclusion about their uncollectibility would be irresponsible and in violation of accepted accounting procedures. Moreover, the accountants testified that they did not include in the book value figure any accounts receivable known to be uncollectible.

Second, the language in the purchase agreement between the car rental corporations and appellants leaves no doubt that the latter did not expect the accounts receivable to be adjusted to reflect uncollectibility. The obvious reason for Stephens' lack of concern here is the fact that he possessed a separate guarantee of accounts receivable from the sellers. Third, Morris Stephens twice testified that due to the expense of a full audit, and other representations of the then owners, the accounts receivable were not expected to be audited. And fourth, the care and competence of appellees is reflected in the notes attached to the balance sheet and in the separate accountants' opinion. In both places the accountants explicitly recited that the accounts receivable had not been adjusted to reflect collectibility.[1]

From this evidence, we are satisfied that appellees exercised the care and competence required of their profession. They followed the scope of audit as outlined by their clients, and carefully limited their work product results to coincide exactly with the undertaking. The charge that they consciously concealed crucial information from appellants simply will not stand under the evidence. The audit actually conducted by appellees was exactly what appellants bargained for with the sellers in the purchase agreement, and nothing less. Thus they have absolutely no grounds for saying they expected and had a right to receive more.

---

[1] In the Accountants' Opinion: "Our examination was made in accordance with generally accepted auditing standards, and accordingly included such tests of the accounting records and such other auditing procedures * * * as we considered necessary in the circumstances, excepting that in accordance with your instructions we did not request any of the customers to confirm their balances nor did we review the collectibility of any trade accounts receivable."

In the Notes to the Balance Sheet: "The balance shown on the balance sheets is the total of the daily accounts receivable records of the companies and has not been adjusted to reflect uncollectible accounts, the amount of which was not determined at December 31, 1964."

1.   The auditors noted in their report that the scope of their examination of accounts receivable had been limited, as requested by the client. The auditors did not represent they did more work than they had actually performed. Accordingly, the auditors made no representation regarding accounts receivable, which was the sole item plaintiff claimed was misrepresented.

2.   The court of appeals also ruled that the plaintiff did not rely on the accountants to audit accounts receivable. The plaintiff's own admissions belied any claim of reliance on the auditors.

(ii)   **C.I.T. Financial Corp. v. Glover** *and Comments*

C.I.T. Financial Corp. v. Glover
224 F.2d 44 (2d Cir. 1955)

Before CLARK, Chief Judge, MEDINA, Circuit Judge, and DIMOCK, District Judge.

CLARK, Chief Judge.

[Plaintiff C.I.T. Financial Corp. loaned M.T.C. Corp. $1,440,000. Defendant accountants issued audit reports on M.T.C.'s financial statements during the period that C.I.T. was lending money.

Following M.T.C.'s default on the loans, C.I.T. sued the accountants, alleging that it relied on the accountants' report of M.T.C.'s financial condition.]

The contentions of the parties as to the facts can be briefly summarized as follows. Plaintiff claimed that defendants' audits were fatally inadequate for failure to disclose overvaluation of M.T.C.'s loans to its debtors. Plaintiff argued that defendants should have pointed out the necessity for larger reserves due to the stagnancy of certain collateral, and due to its concentration in certain types of merchandise and in certain individual debtors, including Joseph Sachs, the brother of M.T.C.'s president, Alfred H. Sachs. This was the gist of the complaint, although reference was also made to alleged misclassification of particular items as accounts receivable, rather than as inventory loans.

The defense relied on the special nature of M.T.C.'s business and on plaintiff's knowledge of this. Defendants maintained that M.T.C. in its financial transactions had always relied primarily on the borrower's collateral, rather than on his general financial condition. Accurate appraisal of the value of such collateral in the event of the debtor's not infrequent insolvency and bankruptcy was always extremely difficult, and M.T.C.'s past income had resulted from Alfred H. Sachs' peculiar genius in such valuation. Defendants claimed that they had never asserted their own special competence to make such appraisals, but that they had inserted in their audit reports appropriate disclaimers qualifying their general assertions about M.T.C.'s financial stability. Further, they claimed that M.T.C.'s business was such that accountants had to rely to a great extent on management statements about the nature and the value of the collateral, and that, since the audit reports disclosed this reliance, defendants were not liable for whatever factual errors might have occurred. In addition, the defense asserted the factual correctness of the audits as made and claimed that plaintiff's inquiries of Sachs in response thereto showed adequate disclosure of M.T.C.'s weaknesses.

On all these points there was a sharp conflict of testimony. However we might ourselves have resolved this conflict, we cannot say that the jury's verdict [for the defendant accountants] was so clearly mistaken as to warrant reversal unless some error of law was committed.

In this connection the plaintiff strongly urges that the jury's verdict must have been based on the defendants' disclaimer, and that this issue should have been decided by the judge as a matter of law in plaintiff's favor. Each audit report had a disclaimer in these or similar words: "While it was not within our province to pass upon or assume responsibility for the legal or equitable title to the commercial receivables purchased by the companies or the valuation of any security thereto accepted and held by them, it was apparent from their books and records and by opinion of counsel, that their contractual and assignment forms are adequate for their legal protection in connection with the collection and liquidation of commercial receivables purchased." Plaintiff asserts that, as a matter of law, this disclaimer was limited to denying responsibility for the valuation of collateral and that, as a matter of law, defendants' responsibility for the valuation of receivables was unaffected by the disclaimer. But the jury could reasonably find that this dichotomy between face value and collateral was meaningless in the kind of transactions in which M.T.C. had been engaged, and that this fact had been adequately brought home to plaintiff, with the result that the disclaimer applied to the valuation of both collateral and receivables. With a proper charge, as given, the meaning of the disclaimer was therefore correctly left to the jury.

Plaintiff argues vigorously the importance of this case in holding accountants to strict liability for their audits, and, in effect, for increasing that liability. But we do not believe we should attempt to go beyond the standards of the market place, as reflected in current judicial decisions. So when, after a fair and carefully conducted trial under existing law, a jury has found for the defendants, the function of the courts should be considered fulfilled.

1. The auditors issued a "long form" report in which they inserted a disclaimer regarding the valuation of collateral. The disclaimer also contained language that appeared to disclaim any responsibility to evaluate the client's valuation of its receivables. The plaintiff contended that this disclaimer could not relieve the auditors of responsibility for the valuation of the receivables. The trial judge held that the "meaning of the disclaimer" was "left to the jury" to decide. The jury decided in this case for the auditors.

2. The court of appeals rejected the plaintiff's request to hold "accountants to strict liability for their audits." Effective use of a qualification or disclaimer can eliminate an auditor's liability as long as the standard is liability for fault—not liability without fault.

[4] Qualified and Disclaimed Report: Liability for Justified Reliance

[a] Qualified Report.   Not every qualified opinion will limit an accountant's responsibility or render a financial statement user's reliance unjustifiable. Consider the following cases.

(i) **Herzfeld v. Laventhol** *and Comments*

Herzfeld v. Laventhol
540 F.2d 27 (2d Cir. 1976)

Before: MOORE and TIMBERS, Circuit Judges and COFFRIN, District Judge.

[Plaintiff Herzfeld purchased securities of Firestone Group, Ltd. (FGL). Herzfeld relied on FGL's financials for the period ending November 30, 1969, which were audited by the defendant accountants, Laventhol.

Herzfeld contended that the financials were materially misleading based on the accounting treatment of two related real-estate transactions entered into by FGL prior to the close of the fiscal year. In those transactions FGL bought a group of nursing homes from Monterey Co. and then sold the nursing homes to Continental Recreation Co.]

This purchase and sale of nursing homes, if ever consummated, would have been the largest single transaction in the history of FGL. Placing these two purported agreements side by side, if the obligations therein were ever fulfilled in the future, FGL would have bought Monterey for $13,362,500 and sold it for $15,393,000, thus producing a profit, when, as and if the transactions were consummated, of $2,030,500, no part of which was even contemplated as having been received prior to November 30, 1969, and only payments of $5000 by FGL to Monterey and $25,000 from Continental to FGL may have been made.

A comparison of the financial condition of FGL with and without these transactions demonstrates the importance of them to FGL:

	Monterey Included	Monterey Excluded
Sales	$22,132,607	$6,739,607
Total Current Assets	6,290,987	1,300,737
Net Income	66,000	[169,000]
Deferred Profit	1,795,000	–0–
Earnings/Share	$0.10	[0.25]

Thus, the accounting treatment of these transactions determined the health of FGL's financial picture. Laventhol knew this was so. By this treatment, namely, immediate recognition of a so-called profit, Laventhol notes, dated November 30, 1969, reveal the conversion of estimated $772,108 losses into a $1,257,892 gain by the addition of the $2,030,500 "profit." These work papers contain the following entries:

Estimated loss 4 months ended 4/30/69	200,000
Estimated loss 7 months ended 11/30/69	572,108
Loss before sale to Continental Recreation	772,108
Profit on sale to Continental Recreation	2,030,000 [sic]
Profit before income taxes	1,257,892 [sic]

• • •

The first tangible results of Laventhol's accounting efforts appear in its audit enclosed in its letter to FGL, dated December 6, 1969. In the consolidated balance sheet as of November 30, 1969, the amount of $1,795,500 was recorded "as unrealized gross profit." The same characterization was given to this assumed profit in the income statement with a reference to an explanatory Note 4. This Note only explained the $1,795,500 by stating that "Because of the circumstances and nature of the transactions, $1,795,500 of the gross profit thereon will be considered realized when the January 30, 1970 payment is received." The $1,795,500 was apparently arrived at by first adding the $25,000 paid upon execution of the Continental agreement, the $25,000 not yet due (until January 2, 1970) and $185,000—a liquidated damage figure for non-performance. These amounts totalled

$235,000. They were apparently considered as received and were deducted from the then fictitious profit of $2,030,500, resulting in the figure of $1,795,500. This first December 6, 1969 report is marked "Withdrawn & Superseded."

The reason for the withdrawal is found in the testimony that FGL wanted the audit to reflect the entire amount of $2,030,500 as pre-November 30, 1969, income resulting from a sale by FGL to Continental. On December 4, 1969, [Laventhol partners] met with FGL officers. Firestone objected to the tentative accounting treatment of the Monterey transactions, and FGL threatened to withdraw its account and sue Laventhol if the private financing did not go through.

A second report (also dated December 6, 1969) was then submitted by Laventhol. In the income statement "unrealized gross profits (Note 4)" was changed to "Deferred gross profit (Note 4)" and Note 4 itself to read:

> Of the total gross profit of $2,030,500, $235,000 is included in the Consolidated Income Statement and the balance $1,795,500 will be considered realized when the January 30, 1970 payment is received. The latter amount is included in deferred income in the consolidated balance sheet.

It was this second report which was distributed to the investors, including Herzfeld.

Unlike the initial report, the opinion letter accompanying this second and final report was qualified. It stated:

> In our opinion, subject to collectibility of the balance receivable on the contract of sale (see Note 4 of Notes to Financial Statements) the accompanying consolidated balance sheet and related consolidated statements of income and retained earnings present fairly the financial position of [FGL]. . . .

Recognizing the difference between the [unaudited] financial statements (Exhibit B to the purchase agreement of November 10, 1969) and the Laventhol audit (December 6, 1969) submitted to Herzfeld and others, on December 16, 1969, FGL attempted to explain by a letter of that date the shift of $1,795,500 from a current to a deferred basis. The financial statements and the qualified opinion letter accompanied the FGL letter which purported to "explain" the distinctions between unaudited projections originally contained in the Agreement and Laventhol's report. No claim is made that Laventhol in any way participated in or was responsible for, this FGL letter.

● ● ●

Neither the Monterey nor the Continental transactions were consummated and somewhat over a year later FGL filed a petition under Chapter XI of the Bankruptcy Act.

The Trial Court first considered Herzfeld's claim under § 10(b) of the Securities Exchange Act of 1934, and Rule 10b-5 thereunder.

After analyzing the facts, the Court concluded that "the Laventhol report was materially misleading." . . . The Court found that Note 4, claimed by Laventhol to be fully explanatory, was misleading: (1) in not disclosing that Continental, obligated to pay almost $5,000,000, had assets of only some $100,000; (2) in affirmatively stating that FGL had "acquired" the nursing homes (when it had not); (3) in reporting that $1,795,500 was deferred income; and (4) in stating that there was a leaseback (when apparently no such lease existed). The Court's conclusion was that "the inclusion of the Monterey transaction in sales and income was misleading without a full disclosure by Laventhol of all the material facts about the transactions." Id.

● ● ●

Laventhol contends that the Court erred and would have us attribute Herzfeld's purchase of the securities to his own enthusiasm, his acquaintance's touting, the FGL letter which accompanied the Laventhol report— in short, to everything but the Laventhol material. As to the Laventhol material, Laventhol argues that Herzfeld ignored it and emphasizes that Herzfeld read neither the opinion letter nor footnote 4 to which both the opinion letter and the income statement referred. This, to Laventhol, is fatal because it contends . . . that the only statement made by an auditor upon which an investor is entitled to rely is the auditor's opinion letter. We agree with none of these arguments.

The Trial Court invoked the appropriate reliance test. Generally speaking, a plaintiff in a Rule 10b-5 damage action must prove that the misrepresentation was a "substantial factor" in his securities activities.

The Trial Court correctly applied the "substantial factor" test. Even assuming that persons other than Laventhol first aroused Herzfeld's interest in FGL, or that the FGL cover letter which accompanied the Laventhol material may have influenced Herzfeld somewhat, these considerations do not defeat Herzfeld's claim. Herzfeld was not required to prove that the Laventhol material was the sole and exclusive cause of his action, he must only show that it was "substantial", *i.e.*, a significant contributing cause.

The Laventhol material was clearly a substantial factor. . . . As the Trial Court observed "He paid particular attention to the earnings indicated and was very impressed by the deferred gross profit of $1,795,000. [sic] The latter figure, he understood, meant 'that this is a profit that the company had made and was going to pick up in a subsequent accounting period.' " In reliance upon this corroborative Laventhol financial statement, Herzfeld completed his investment in FGL securities.

The issue here is not one of negligence, but of the "materially misleading" treatment of facts known to Laventhol in its submitted audit.

The function of an accountant is not merely to verify the correctness of the addition and subtraction of the company's bookkeepers. Nor does it take a fiscal wizard to appreciate the elemental and universal accounting principle that revenue should not be recognized until the "earning process is complete or virtually complete", and "an exchange has taken place." Insofar as FGL's interest in the Monterey transactions is concerned, the earning process had hardly commenced, let alone neared completion. As of November 30, 1969, FGL had paid only $5,000 cash out of $13.2 million dollar purchase price and accepted a $25,000 "deposit" under a $15.3 million contract. Conditions for closing were unsatisfied. There remained the consummation of its purchase from Monterey, the furnishing to Continental of current title reports, and the delivery of the CC&R's and a copy of a lease. By the close of November 30, 1969, title had not passed. Nor was this the exceptional instance of a conditional sale or a long-term lease with purchase option, where the retention of title does not vitiate the economic reality of a consummated exchange.

Reference to the SEC's Accounting Series Release No. 95 ... ("ASR #95") points toward the same conclusion. That release lists several factors whose presence, according to the SEC, singly or in combination, raises a question of the propriety of current recognition of profit in real estate transactions. Not less than three of these factors inhere in the Monterey transaction, including (1) evidence of financial weakness of the purchaser (Continental's insignificant net worth relative to the resale property price); (2) substantial uncertainty as to amount of proceeds to be realized because of form of consideration—e. g., non-recourse notes; (3) small or no down payment. Because the FGL offer was a private placement, ASR #95 was not directly applicable to Laventhol's audit. But since ASR #95 merely codifies basic principles of accrual accounting theory, we do not reject its corroboration of our own independent conclusions.

If the hoped-for profit of $2,030,500 were ever to be realized, it could only come after the transactions had been consummated— and consummation was never even contemplated before the audit date, November 30, 1969. FGL's profit till for this transaction as of that date was as bare of profits as Mother Hubbard's cupboard, bare of bones.

An accountant should not represent on an audited statement that income and profit exist unless underlying facts justify that conclusion. Here, the underlying facts known to Laventhol dictated precisely the contrary course, namely, that income should not have been recognized for the accounting period ending November 30, 1969. And were it not for Laventhol's disregard of Statements on [Auditing] Procedure No. 33, Ch. 2, p. 16 (1963) ("SAP 33") it would have confronted additional evidence pointing in the same direction. SAP 33 states:

Sufficient competent evidential matter is to be obtained through inspection, observation, inquiries and confirmations to affirm a reasonable basis for an opinion regarding the financial statements under examination.

Laventhol knew that the issuance of FGL securities depended upon a correct ascertainment of that condition. It is undisputed that, without the Monterey-Continental transactions, for the eleven months preceding November 30, FGL had sustained a loss of $772,108. Query: by what accounting legerdemain was this figure converted into a substantial profit? The Monterey purchase added nothing to the FGL till. To the contrary, it reduced it by $5,000 (if the check was honored). The Continental sale produced a down payment of $25,000 (if made) but no profit. In fact, if the hoped-for profit of $2,030,500 were ever to be realized, it could only come after the transactions had been consummated—and consummation was never even contemplated before the audit date, November 30, 1969.

Laventhol points to the Trial Court's finding that the Monterey-Contental transactions were not "phony". This finding, however, only implies that there were signed agreements between the parties. By no stretch of the imagination does it imply that profits of $2,030,500 were realized therefrom before November 30, 1969, or would be at any time until consummation. In fact, both agreements showed on their face that the principal payments were to be made in 1970.

In such circumstances, the recognition of Monterey transactions was a materially misleading statement which, once included at the top of the income statement as a sale, resulted in, or necessitated, compensating adjustments which distorted all the financial figures which followed. A reasonable man in Herzfeld's position might well have acted otherwise than to purchase the FGL securities, had the truth been told and the Monterey transactions not been misleadingly represented as a consummated purchase and sale.

This misleading impression was aggravated by Laventhol's labeling of the $1,795,500 as "deferred" as opposed to "unrealized" gross profit. Such nomenclature conveyed the erroneous impression that all that profit was so much cash in hand and would be recognized periodically *in futuro* just as if it were prepaid interest or management fees. But as Laventhol well knew, net cash had increased only $20,000, and the transaction was still in doubt.

Having engendered its own quandary, it ill behooves Laventhol to seek the solace of SAP 33, which concerns the rendition of a qualified auditing opinion. But even assuming the propriety of allowing Laventhol to extricate itself by the simple expedient of disclaiming or qualifying its opinion of the very financial statements which it concocted, Laventhol did not follow the route proscribed by SAP 33. At Chapter 10, page 58, SAP 33 provides, *inter alia*:

> When a qualification is so material as to negative an expression of opinion as to the fairness of the financial statement as a whole, either a disclaimer of opinion or an adverse opinion is required.

> *   *   *

> When a qualified opinion is intended by the independent auditor, the opinion paragraph of the standard short-form report should be modified in a way that makes clear the nature of the qualification. It should refer specifically to the subject of the qualification and should give a *clear explanation of the reasons for the qualification* and of the effect on financial position and results of operations, if reasonably determinable. (emphasis added)

But Laventhol did not provide a *clear explanation of the reasons for the qualification*. A simple note would have sufficed saying in substance:

> Agreements for the purchase of Monterey Nursing Inns, Inc. for $13,362,500 and the sale thereof to Continental Recreation, Inc. for $15,393,000, have been executed. When, as and if these transactions are consummated, FGL expects to realize a profit of $2,030,500.

Instead, Laventhol chose to delete from its first so-called explanatory Note 4, the sentence "Because of the circumstances and nature of the transaction, $1,795,500 of the gross profit therein will be considered realized when the January 30, 1970 payment is received" and substituted therefor the sentence "Of the total gross profit of $2,030,500, $235,000 is included in the Consolidated Income Statement and the balance, $1,795,500 will be considered realized when the January 30, 1969 payment is received." The substituted note also changed "unrealized gross profit" to "deferred income". Even in the first Note, there is no explanation of what were the circumstances and nature of the transaction or, in the second Note, how or why $235,000 could qualify as gross profit or income as of November 30, 1969.

1.   The auditors qualified their opinion "subject to collectibility of the balance receivable on the contract of sale (see Note 4 of Notes to Financial Statements) . . . " Note 4 indicated that of the amount receivable, $235,000 was current income from the sale, while $1,795,500 was "deferred income."

The court of appeals held that the auditors' report was materially misleading because certain facts were misstated or omitted. The court of appeals also ruled no revenue should have been recognized from the sale because the transaction was not "consummated."

2.   The auditors argued that their report and the financials were not a "substantial factor" in the plaintiff's decision to make an investment. The auditors pointed to the fact that the plaintiff did not read the auditors' "opinion letter nor footnote 4 to which both the opinion letter and the income statement referred." The auditors contended that "the only statement made by an auditor upon which an investor is entitled to rely is the auditor's opinion letter." The court rejected this argument.

3.   The auditors defended their actions based on the fact that they qualified their report subject to the collectability of the sale contract. The court of appeals responded

by stating: "Having engendered its own quandary, it ill behooves Laventhol to seek the solace of SAP 33, which concerns the rendition of a qualified opinion."

The court went on to state: "But even assuming the propriety of allowing Laventhol to extricate itself by the simple expedient of disclaiming or qualifying its opinion of the very financial statements which it concocted, Laventhol did not follow the route proscribed by SAP 33."

The court held that the auditors had failed to provide a "clear explanation of the reasons for the qualification," as required by professional standards.

4. *Herzfeld* demonstrates that accountants may not associate with misleading financials and then hope to "extricate" themselves by the "simple expedient" of a disclaimer or qualification. A qualified opinion is tantamount to a representation that the financial statements "may be reliable." If there are material facts known to the auditors which cast doubt on the reliability of the financials, the auditors must take steps to disclose this information. As *Herzfeld* demonstrates, if the auditors have grave doubts regarding the financials, a qualified opinion will not "extricate" the accountants from responsibility unless they spell out the reasons for their qualification, including the "grave doubts."

[b] Disclaimer of Opinion. A disclaimer of opinion may lead to liability if the limits of the accountant's examination or the nature of his disclaimer are not adequately communicated. Consider the following case.

(i) **Rhode Island Hospital Trust National Bank v. Swartz** *and Comments*

Rhode Island Hospital Trust National Bank v. Swartz
455 F.2d 847 (4th Cir. 1972)

Before WINTER and BUTZNER. Circuit Judges, and DUPREE, District Judge.

WINTER, Circuit Judge:

[Plaintiff Bank extended credit to International Trading Corp. (referred to as "Borrower"), based on Borrower's representation that it had expended $212,000 for leasehold improvements to company facilities. In fact, the claimed leasehold improvements were totally fictitious.

Pursuant to the terms of their loan agreement, Borrower submitted its financial statements to the Bank. The financials reflected the fictitious leasehold improvements.

Borrower's financials were audited by the defendant accountants, who submitted a report to Borrower which in turn was given to the Bank.]

When Accountants transmitted the financial statements to their client they wrote a covering letter expressing certain reservations about the "fairness of the accompanying statements." They stated that they had reviewed the balance sheet and profit and loss statement of Borrower and "[o]ur examination included a general review of accounting procedures and such tests of accounting records as we were permitted to make."

The letter then discussed the crucial item concerned in this litigation—the leasehold improvements—and set forth the following:

Additions to fixed assets in 1963 *were found* to include principally warehouse improvements and installation of machinery and equipment in Providence, Rhode Island, Brunswick, Georgia, and Palm Beach, Florida. *Practically all of this work was done by company employees and materials and overhead was borne by the International Trading Corporation and its affiliates.* Unfortunately, fully complete detailed cost records were not kept of these capital improvements and no exact determination could be made as to the actual cost of said improvements. (emphasis added)

The total amount capitalized for leasehold improvements is as follows:

International Trading Corporation of Florida	$253,465.75
International Trading Corporation of Georgia	105,181.06
International Trading Corporation of New England	79,685.16
	$438,331.97

Management has obtained appraisals from the following companies, *which support* the amounts set up for leasehold improvements in the warehouses:

Kendall Construction Company
West Palm Beach, Florida
A. H. Leeming and Sons of Rhode Island, Inc.
109 Waterman Street
Providence 6, Rhode Island

Copies of their appraisals are attached hereto and are part of this report.[1] (emphasis added)

With reference to the appraisal from A. H. Leeming and Sons of Rhode Island, Inc., this report did not include engineering services, electrical service, crane service and concrete installation forms and drilling. Management was able to identify these items from invoices recorded on its books and are submitted herewith in conjunction with said appraisal. This work *was done* in Providence, Rhode Island. (emphasis added)

---

[1] While termed "appraisals" the documents attached to the letter are more correctly described as estimates of cost of construction. Specifically, there was an estimate from a general contractor to perform work at Palm Beach, Florida, and at Brunswick, Georgia, and another estimate of another general contractor to perform work at Providence, Rhode Island. The work to be performed at Palm Beach was estimated to cost $250,000.00, that at Brunswick to cost $105,000.00, and that at Providence to cost $69,144.00. The estimate for Providence was to do certain described items of work, and specified that it did not include silos or their foundations or any foundations under the walls which contain the cement, or any responsibility for the steel building column strength.

[The accountants' letter] concluded:

Because of the limitations upon our examination expressed in the preceding paragraphs and the material nature of the items not confirmed directly by us, we are unable to express an opinion as to the fairness of the accompanying statements.

Because of the death of the partner of Accountants who made the examination of Borrower's accounts the proof was not complete as to what examination and what inquiries had been made. The deceased partner's work papers were produced and they showed that the deceased had attempted to segregate the cost of labor, which Borrower had recorded as operating expenses, attributable to the purported leasehold improvements, but the work papers showed that no item of building material cost had been recorded.

• • •

By application of the rule stated, we think that Accountants are liable for negligence on either of the alternate theories.

From the Accountants' work papers and the other evidence in the case, either of two inferences may be drawn. First, Accountants, having identified some of the purported labor costs of the purported leasehold improvements, failed, from pressure of work or other reason, to search for material costs. Second, Accountants, having identified some of the purported labor costs of the purported leasehold improvements, searched for material costs and, not finding any, failed to conduct any independent investigation of the existence of the leasehold improvements and their value[2] and failed to disclose that there was no verification that the leasehold improvements were in being. In either event, Accountants certified the financial statements, saying overall only that they could not express an opinion with regard to their fairness. This

---

[2] It should be noted that Accountants did not hesitate to employ correspondents to verify the existence of inventories. Of course, the duty to investigate may arise only where the employment contract permits, Ryan v. Kanne, *supra*. But if the employment contract would not permit an independent investigation, at least the lack of verification should be disclosed.

disclaimer, however, followed other reference to the purported leasehold improvements which expressed no reservation about their existence but only about their precise value. We think that a fair reading of Accountants' covering letter and disclaimer indicates that while the leasehold improvements may have had a value of more or less than $212,000.00, there was no question but that they existed and that they had substantial value. Whether Accountants failed to look or, having looked, failed to find, they were guilty of actionable negligence if Bank, in reliance on the statements, made further loans.

Our conclusions with respect to the report and disclosure are reinforced by reference to industry standards of what should have been done in these circumstances. While industry standards may not always be the maximum test of liability, certainly they should be deemed the minimum standard by which liability should be determined. Brief references to American Institute of Certified Public Accountants, Statements on Auditing Procedure No. 33 (1963) are sufficient to prove the point. Chapter 10 ¶ 1 of the Statements reads, "[t]he report shall either contain an expression of opinion regarding the financial statements, taken as a whole, or an assertion to the effect that an opinion cannot be expressed. *When an overall opinion cannot be expressed, the reasons therefor should be stated....*" (emphasis added) When Accountants said only that "fully complete detailed cost records were not kept of these capital improvements and no exact determination could be made as to the actual cost of said improvements," we do not think that the reasons assigned were sufficiently stated. The documentary evidence shows that *no* cost records for material were kept, so that Accountants' statement, viewed even in the most charitable light, was a major understatement, whatever Accountants failed to do. Chapter 10 ¶ 9 reads "[w]hen a qualified opinion is intended by the independent auditor, the opinion paragraph of the standard shortform report should be modified in a way that makes clear the

nature of the qualification. It should refer specifically to the subject of the qualification and *should give a clear explanation of the reasons for the qualification* and of the effect on financial position and results of operations, if reasonably determinable." (emphasis supplied) Accountants failed to comply with this requirement, too, when they failed to disclose that the absence of any records for material purchases led them to resort to "appraisals." Had the absence of any records for material purchases been assigned as a reason for resort to "appraisals," Bank would have been charged with knowledge that the existence of the leasehold improvements might have been in question. The disclaimer, read in conjunction with the preceding paragraphs, conveyed the impression that the leasehold improvements unquestionably existed. Similarly, Chapter 10 ¶ 14, in dealing with disclaimer of opinion, states that when the independent auditor has not obtained sufficient competent evidentiary matter to form an opinion on the fairness of presentation of the financial statements as a whole he should state that he is unable to express an opinion on such statements. Paragraph 16 then reads, "[w]henever the independent auditor disclaims an opinion, he should give *all* substantive reasons for doing so. For example, when he disclaims an opinion because the scope of examination was inadequate, he should also disclose any reservations or exceptions he may have regarding fairness of presentation." (emphasis in original) This standard, too, Accountants failed to meet. Their disclaimer was to the effect that, because of limitations upon their examination, expressed in the covering letter, and the material nature of the items not confirmed by them, they could not express an opinion as to the fairness of the accompanying statements. They failed to state that they either did not look for or could not find evidence of material costs for the purported leasehold improvements, and either would have been more than a simple limitation upon their examination.

1.   The auditors disclaimed an opinion on the financials because of limitations on their audit relating to certain capitalized leasehold improvements. The auditors noted in

their report that "unfortunately, fully complete detailed cost records were not kept of these capital improvements and no exact determination could be made as the actual cost of said improvements." As the court of appeals observed, the "claimed 1963 leasehold improvements were totally fictitious."

2.   The court of appeals faulted the auditors for failing "to conduct any independent investigation of the existence of the leasehold improvements and their value." The court also criticized the auditors for failing "to disclose that there was no verification that the leasehold improvements were in being."

3.   With respect to the auditors' "duty to investigate" (duty of inquiry), the court ruled that the "duty to investigate may arise only where the employment contract permits." The court observed that "if the employment contract would not permit an independent investigation, at least the lack of verification should be disclosed."

If, by contract, the accountant's duty of inquiry is limited short of that required by professional standards, careful explanation and disclosure should be made of the limitations. See *Stephens v. Haskins & Sells* at ¶ 7.07[3] for an example of a properly disclosed limitation on the duty of inquiry.

Beardsley v. Ernst & Ernst, 191 N.E. 808 (Ohio App. 1934), is an example of a case in which the auditors successfully defended a fraud claim based on their explicit statement in their report of a limitation on their inquiry. In that case, the auditors relied upon the audit report of other auditors who had examined a foreign company whose financials were consolidated within the domestic parent audited by Ernst & Ernst.

In ruling that the auditors could not be charged with fraud for failing to detect and disclose financial wrongdoing which occurred in the foreign company segment, the court held:

> In the instant case, however, the certificate made by Ernst & Ernst clearly states that it is based both upon an examination of records and upon statements received from abroad with respect to the foreign constituent companies.
>
> The language used in these certificates gives rise to the indisputable inference that the accountants *had not examined* the books and records of the foreign constituent companies. The record does not establish fraud or any false or fraudulent statements in relation to the examination actually made of the books and records in this country. We do not think that the defendants can be charged with fraud under these certificates by the very language used therein, *when they in fact disclose that some of the information and statements came from abroad*. It is obvious that the accountants in this case could not know whether or not the information from abroad was accurate or inaccurate, and, inasmuch as they disclose that these certificates were based partly upon information so received, there was *no pretense of knowledge* as to the information received which would make defendants liable.

4.   With respect to the auditor's disclaimer, the court in *Swartz* held that it was ineffective. The court stated that "this disclaimer, however, followed other reference to the purported leasehold improvements which expressed no reservation about their existence but only about their precise value." The court held that a "fair reading" of the "disclaimer indicates that while the leasehold improvements may have had a value of more or less

than $212,000, there was no question but that they existed and that they had substantial value."

The auditor's disclaimer effectively represented that the fictitious leasehold improvements existed and had substantial value. The court held that the Bank was entitled to rely on these representations.

5.   The *Rhode Island Hospital Trust National Bank* case is a situtation where an auditor's express representation overrode the auditor's disclaimer. See the cases at ¶ 7.07[5] for other examples of a "representation override."

[c]   Use of a Qualified Opinion Instead of a Disclaimer: Possible Liability.   It is possible that a plaintiff could successfully argue that an auditor should have disclaimed an opinion rather than issue a qualified opinion. In such circumstances a plaintiff may claim that a disclaimer would have put investors or regulators on notice that the financials were "totally" unreliable as opposed to being "possibly" unreliable.

The following case demonstrates the differences in degrees of "unreliability" created by qualified as compared to disclaimed opinions.

Ingenito v. Bermec Corp.
441 F.Supp. 525 (S.D.N.Y. 1977)

[The facts of the case are set out at ¶ 6.04[1].]

C.   Andersen's Failure to Refuse Certification

As an alternative to their contention that Andersen owed a duty to "update" the financial data in the May Prospectus in the Fall of that year, plaintiffs contend that Andersen is liable for not refusing to certify the '69 figures altogether, an act they say would inevitably have precipitated the earlier demise of the Black Watch operation. The argument runs that had Andersen done so this would have precipitated the earlier demise of the Black Watch operation; and had Black Watch died sooner, late transactions occurring after that time would not have occurred.

Plaintiffs' argument amounts to an assertion that by failing to refuse certification, Andersen aided and abetted Black Watch's ongoing fraud, by aiding and abetting Black Watch's existence. They contend that if Andersen had withheld certification, the SEC would inevitably have been more concerned than it was and stepped in to terminate Black Watch's securities transactions. Thus, Andersen is charged with having rendered substantial assistance to the fraud. By issuing its qualified certification, instead of no certification at all, it enabled the business to stave off disaster for a longer period.

We cannot agree with Andersen that this claim is legally insufficient. . . . Each element of the claim is the subject of heated dispute. In order to prevail plaintiffs will have to show that Andersen knew of the fraud, intended to further it and actually rendered substantial assistance by deliberately qualifiedly certifying the '69 financials instead of refusing certification altogether. . . . Entirely apart from the questions of Andersen's knowledge of the fraud and intent to further its ends, the question whether it substantially assisted the fraud by issuing a qualified opinion raises a host of factual issues. A sample of the questions which spring immediately to mind is whether the qualified opinion, itself an important cause of the SEC's refusal to permit the updated registration to take effect, can in any way be considered to have *helped* Black Watch; whether, if Andersen really intended to further the fraud, it would have qualified the opinion it did give; and whether there is any reason to believe that an outright refusal to certify would have brought about an earlier end to Black Watch's affairs.

[5]   Liability for Representations by the Accountant Which Are Not Part of the Accountant's Report

An accountant's liability is not limited to those representations contained within the "four corners" of his professional report. An accountant may be held responsible for any material representations which he makes during the course of the engagement if the representation is the type which may be justifiably relied upon.

It is possible that the accountant may be held responsible for representations which are part of a letter issued by the accountant or are part of the accountant's workpapers. It is also possible that an accountant may be held responsible for "oral representations" that are communicated in circumstances conducive to reliance by a party.

A written or oral representation may effectively "override" any qualified or disclaimed report rendered by the accountant. Consider the following cases.

[a]   Letter Representations: Override of a Disclaimer

(i)   Ryan v. Kanne and Comments

Ryan v. Kanne
170 N.W. 2d 395 (Iowa 1969)

LARSON, Justice.

This action for accounting fees filed by plaintiff-accountants, with a counterclaim filed by one of the defendants, Kanne Lumber and Supply, Inc., was tried to the court without a jury and resulted in a . . . judgment in favor of Kanne Lumber and Supply, Inc. for damages in the sum of $38,685.81.

It appears without serious controversy that James A. Kanne owned and operated certain businesses including lumber companies in Carroll and Breda, Iowa, that he had incurred considerable indebtedness in connection therewith, that his accounting procedure left much to be desired, and that he was in need of further financing. It further appears that at the instance of officers of a creditor, the Mid-States Enterprises, Inc., he sought the services of the plaintiffs, who were certified public accountants and directed them to consult Mr. Feldmann of Mid-States, who was also a C.P.A., as to what was necessary in the financial statement requested. Particular attention to the item of Accounts Payable—Trade was directed and became the critical part of plaintiffs' undertaking. Feldmann discussed with Ryan the procedure recommended to determine that item in the ac-

counting, stating, "* * * we agreed that this would be the critical area, that we should do everything possible to find out what payables may exist." The witness Collison also testified, "* * * if I can correctly quote Bob Feldmann, he said, 'Use every conceivable means to determine the accounts payable.' " It appears Ryan agreed to follow the suggested investigative procedure to determine accounts payable, made some efforts to follow it, and guaranteed the accuracy of their statement as to that item within $5,000. He testified he felt very confident his balance sheet was correct within $5,000 at the time it was submitted.

It is defendant's contention that the evidence was sufficient to sustain a finding that plaintiffs were negligent in the investigation, preparation and submission of the accounts payable item in the financial statement rendered, that defendant relied thereon, to its detriment, and that it was entitled to recover the loss occasioned thereby. It contends, in view of the evidence as to the understood importance of the item of Accounts Payable—Trade, the assurance as to the work done in that regard, and the reliance placed on that item by the incorporators and the incorporation officials, it is unjust to minimize or overlook the plaintiffs' negligence or excuse it by any subsequent disclaimer.

Plaintiffs' financial statement, when submitted, was marked "Unaudited Statement." However, in the comments in the letter of submission attached thereto it is stated: "Accounts Payable—Trade. Confirmations were used to arrive at the balance due at the date of the balance sheet. The payee of each check issued during 1965 and the latter part of the calendar year 1964 was [contacted] to confirm if a balance was due at September 30, 1965. Also, a review of unpaid statements was made."

• • •

Pursuant to the submission of this financial statement, the defendant Kanne Lumber and Supply, Inc. was incorporated and took over the assets and liabilities of Kanne's lumber businesses. Defendant contends plaintiffs were aware of that purpose and plan when submitting the financial statement and failed to timely advise defendant of errors or discrepancies then known to them. When it became evident to the defendant corporation that the statement as to Accounts Payable—Trade was incorrect, it secured a re-audit of the lumber businesses. This audit disclosed a discrepancy of $33,689.22 in Accounts Payable—Trade.

Plaintiffs argue errors in their financial statement were due to Kanne's failure to cooperate as agreed, to the demand for haste and false information furnished as to various items, and that the proximate cause of defendant's injury was not their failure to carefully check Accounts Payable—Trade. They further contend defendant was guilty of contributory negligence in paying accounts after it was apparent an error was made and plaintiffs had advised payment be delayed until a recheck was made. Defendant disputed each of these contentions and the trial court, acting as a jury, rejected them and found that plaintiffs' negligence was the proximate cause of defendant's damage.

There is no merit in plaintiffs' contention that the court erred in not finding them relieved of liability when the issued financial statement as to the business operations was not certified and upon which they affirmatively stated they expressed no opinion. Although in this profession a distinction is made between certified audits where greater time and effort are expended to verify book items, and uncertified audits where greater reliance is placed on book items, it is clear to us that accountants, or any other professional persons, must perform those acts that they have agreed to do under the contract and which they claim have been done in order to make the determination set forth and presented in their report. Their liability must be dependent upon their undertaking, not their rejection of dependability. They cannot escape liability for negligence by a general statement that they disclaim its reliability. . . . [L]iability for professional negligence to third parties will not automatically result in injustice and financial ruin being levied upon accountants. Rather, the result will be to insure the use of professional standards. If, therefore, a party limits the investigation of an independent accountant, or if goods or work in progress cannot actually be seen, the accountant can note this in his report and thus limit the basis upon which an aggrieved party can obtain relief against him. It would at least indicate, as to certain items of a financial statement, that the accountant may thus escape liability for negligence if he does not certify the audit. As to other items which he agreed to and states he did investigate, but did not, we hold the lack of certification will not absolve him from liability. He must perform as agreed whether the work is certified or not. This being so, we have here fact questions as to the substance of the agreement between the parties, as to the care exercised in its performance, and as to the representation made, rather than whether the report was certified or uncertified.

Factually, the court found the plaintiffs had specifically contracted to determine in an agreed manner the amount of Kanne's Accounts Payable—Trade, and had assured its correctness within $5,000. The court did not hold them to strict accuracy as to other items in the financial statement, but found under the agreement that the plaintiffs were to accept the company's book figures and information furnished by Kanne, such as notes payable, accounts receivable, and work in process. The extent of this finding is evident in the court's amended judgment where it removed from liability a note improperly listed as Accounts Payable—Trade, as well as other minor items. Except, then, as to the item of Accounts Payable—Trade, the claim of "Unaudited Statement" was accepted by the court as effective to bar plaintiffs' liability to defendant. However, the determination that plaintiffs failed to properly perform the duty assumed under the contract as to Accounts Payable—Trade is binding upon us, and the court's conclusion that the accountants could not escape liability for negligence in that regard with an "Unaudited Statement" notation on the financial report is right.

1.   The accountants compiled a financial statement which they marked "unaudited." Accompanying the financials was the accountants' report in which they issued a disclaimer of opinion in the form required by existing professional reporting standards. In an accompanying letter, the accountants represented that they had confirmed accounts payable—trade and reviewed unpaid statements. This written representation was materially misleading in that the accountants were negligent in examining trade accounts payable.

2.   The accountants also agreed to "guarantee" the accuracy of trade accounts payable within $5,000 as stated in the financials. The accountants orally represented that the accounts payable were accurate within $5,000 when in fact they were materially understated. The court held that the accountants' oral representation was materially misleading.

3.   With respect to the effect of the accountants' disclaimer and the marking of the financials as "Unaudited," the Iowa Supreme Court held that accountants "must perform those acts that they have agreed to do under the contract and which they claim have been done. . . . Their liability must be dependent upon their undertaking, not their rejection of dependability."

The court further held that accountants "cannot escape liability for negligence by a general statement that they disclaim its reliability."

The *Ryan v. Kanne* case demonstrates that a disclaimer can be overriden by a written or oral representation. Stated another way, a disclaimer will not shield an accountant for any material misrepresentations made by the accountant which induce justifiable reliance by a party.

(ii)   **Seedkem, Inc. v. Safranek**

Seedkem, Inc. v. Safranek
466 F.Supp. 340 (D.Neb. 1979)

DENNEY, District Judge.

[Plaintiff corporation extended credit to Agri-Products, Inc., based upon that company's unaudited financial statements which were prepared by the defendant accountant. Following Agri-Products' inability to pay its $700,000 debt, plaintiff sued the defendant accountant contending that the unaudited financials were materially misleading.

The accountant filed a motion to dismiss the case arguing "that since this case involves both 'unaudited' reports *and* no direct representations [by the accountant], it falls outside of those cases which have found accountants liable." The district court denied the accountant's motion to dismiss for the following reasons.]

[T]he defendant argues that even if the Court finds the reasoning in *Ultramares* inapplicable, this case represents an extreme situation distinguishable from those cases which have rejected the privity requirement and found an accountant liable to a third party. Defendant points out that the cases cited by the plaintiff in support of its position all involved either certified or audited financial statements, . . . or express representations by the accountant to the third party as to the accuracy of the statements. *See, e.g., Ryan v. Kanne, supra; Bonhiver v. Graff, supra.* Defendant contends that this case, on the other hand, involves unaudited statements containing an express disclaimer of opinion without any contrary representation and is therefore thoroughly distinguishable.

The fact that the financial statements were expressly marked "unaudited" and contained an express disclaimer of opinion is not necessarily dispositive at this time. The observations and statements by the Iowa Supreme Court in *Ryan v. Kanne, supra,* are particularly persuasive:

> . . . Although in this profession a distinction is made between certified audits where greater time and effort are expended to verify book items, and uncertified audits where greater reliance is placed on book items, it is clear to us that accountants, or any other professional persons, must perform those acts that they have agreed to do under the contract and which they claim have been done in order to make the determination

set forth and presented in their report. Their liability must be dependent upon their undertaking, not their rejection of dependability. They cannot escape liability for negligence by a general statement that they disclaim its reliability.

> . . . He must perform as agreed whether the work is certified or not. This being so, we have here fact questions as to the substance of the agreement between the parties, as to the care exercised in its performance, and as to the representation made, rather than whether the report was certified or uncertified. . . .

Defendant accurately points out to the Court that there are no reported cases where an accountant's liability was founded on the circumstances presented at this point in the litigation; and the Court agrees that it should not adopt a theory beyond the ambit of those cases which have rejected the *Ultramares* rule and attempt such an extension of an accountant's duty. However, the Court believes that it would be wiser to defer a determination of the issue presented herein until further discovery proceedings can be undertaken in order to ascertain whether any express representations were actually made between the parties or any understandings existed between those involved.

(iii)   Spherex, Inc. v. Alexander Grant & Co.

Spherex, Inc. v. Alexander Grant & Co.
451 A.2d 1308 (N.H. 1982)

DOUGLAS, Justice.

This case, certified to us by the United States District Court for the District of New Hampshire (*Loughlin, J.*), requires us to decide an issue of first impression in this State: the extent to which an accountant may be held liable for damages in tort to third parties for negligent misrepresentation in an unaudited financial statement.

The facts certified by the district court are that the defendant, Alexander Grant and Company (Alexander Grant), a partnership with its principal place of business in Philadelphia, contracted to perform accounting services for General Home Products Corporation (GHP) of Pennsauken, New Jersey.

GHP engaged Alexander Grant to prepare an unaudited financial statement for the twelve-month period ending December 31, 1977, based on financial information provided by GHP. GHP submitted copies of this statement to the plaintiff, Spherex, Inc. (Spherex), a New Hampshire-based manufacturer of spoked wheels for baby carriages and shopping carts, for the purpose of obtaining credit. Spherex subsequently sustained a financial loss in its dealings with GHP and filed suit in United States district court alleging: that Alexander Grant either knew that the unaudited financial statement was inaccurate or was negligent in preparing the statement; that Alexander Grant knew GHP would show the statement to Spherex; and, that Spherex detrimentally relied on the statement in extending credit to GHP. Alexander Grant, in defense, contended its potential liability did not extend to a third-party creditor of GHP with whom Alexander Grant was not in privity. Alexander Grant further asserted it is unreasonable as a matter of law for a third party to rely upon an unaudited financial statement. . . .

We are unable, as a matter of law, to consider it unreasonable for a third party to rely upon information presented in an unaudited financial statement prepared by the defendant accountant, or to rely upon an accountant to verify the substantive accuracy of the information presented in an unaudited financial statement. Of course, whether an accountant was rendering merely a "compilation," rather than a "review," as those terms are commonly understood within the accounting profession, can make a difference as to the scope of service undertaken. It is for Spherex at trial

to adduce evidence as to any duty undertaken by the accounting firm in its engagement contract with the client, irrespective of the unaudited nature of the financial statement it prepared. "Their liability must be dependent upon their undertaking, not their rejection of dependability. They cannot escape liability for negligence by a general statement that they disclaim . . . reliability." *Ryan v. Kanne*. . . . Moreover, evidence of any express representation actually made by Alexander Grant to Spherex or any understandings existing between them would tend to modify Alexander Grant's duty, if any, towards Spherex, regardless of the fact that the financial statement allegedly relied upon by Spherex was unaudited. *See Seedkem, Inc. v. Safranek*. . . . The statement of facts certified to this court by the district court provides insufficient information to permit us to conclude, as a matter of law, that Alexander Grant owed Spherex no duty of due care.

[b]   Representations in Workpapers: Liability Despite the Absence of a Formal Report

(i)   Bonhiver v. Graff *and Comments*

Bonhiver v. Graff
248 N.W.2d 291 (Minn. 1976)

SHERAN, Chief Justice.

This is another case arising out of the 1965 collapse of American Allied Insurance Company.

The facts relevant to this appeal are as follows: Defendant Schwartz, Frumm & Company (hereafter Schwartz, Frumm) is a firm of certified public accountants with its office in Chicago, Illinois. Defendant Philip Graff, a duly certified public accountant, worked for Schwartz, Frumm from November 1960 to December 1964.

Prior to 1963, members and employees of Schwartz, Frumm had done some accounting work for Phillip Kitzer, Sr., . . . In May 1963, at the request of Kitzer, Sr., and Phillip Kitzer, Jr., Leonard Frumm and an employee, James Holly, journeyed from Chicago to Minneapolis to inspect the books of

American Allied Mutual Insurance Company (American Allied Mutual). The Kitzers were interested in purchasing American Allied Mutual for $100,000. Frumm and Holly spent about 10 hours inspecting American Allied Mutual's books, and reported to Kitzer, Sr., that American Allied Mutual was impaired. Frumm and Holly recommended to the Kitzers that they not purchase the company for the price requested, but they purchased it anyway for $20,000.

Upon purchasing American Allied Mutual, the Kitzers transferred its assets and liabilities to a newly formed stock company—American Allied Insurance Company (American Allied). . . . Thus, the Kitzers owned American Allied; American Allied in turn owned Allied Realty; Allied Realty in turn owned United States Mutual, Bell Mutual, and Bell Casualty.

In November 1963, Holly left Schwartz, Frumm to become a vice president of American Allied. In August 1964, Holly contacted Frumm and requested help in getting American Allied's books up to date as of June 30, 1964. Frumm sent Graff to St. Paul to do the work. Graff made various entries in the books and records of American Allied and prepared workpapers in the course of his work. On October 5, 1964, the commissioner of insurance of the state of Minnesota sent a team of examiners to examine the books of American Allied. Those examiners worked in the same room with Graff, examined his workpapers, and relied upon the entries he had made in the books, a standard practice. Graff at times personally furnished information to the examiners, and testified that he considered his work to be the "starting point" for the examiners. By his examiners' reliance upon Graff's entries, the commissioner was led to believe that American Allied was solvent, when in fact the company was insolvent. Had the examination disclosed that the company was insolvent, its continued operation would have been challenged by the commissioner. . . .

Because a number of Graff's entries were erroneous, the examination did not disclose American Allied's insolvency. During the existence of American Allied, the Kitzers embezzled over $2,000,000 from the company. Graff's errors involved his failure to investigate and discover the true nature of a number of transactions by which this fraud was taking place. Those errors, upon which the defendants' liability was established, . . . involved transactions between two companies wherein a payment would be recorded in one manner on American Allied's books and in a different manner on the books of the other party to the transaction. The books of the other parties—often related companies such as Bell Mutual, Bell Casualty, or United States Mutual—were readily available to Graff. The court found that his failure to examine those books was negligence.

Defendants dispute liability because they did not produce a complete, certified set of financial statements, but only a set of unaudited workpapers which were themselves incomplete.

Schwartz, Frumm was never asked to produce complete financial statements. It was engaged to bring American Allied's books up to date, a job which was never, in fact, completed.

All accountant malpractice cases called to our attention have involved accountants who prepare or certify completed financial statements. . . . No case cited by the parties passes on the liability of a certified public accountant when his work product is not a completed financial statement but is rather a set of unfinished workpapers and adjusting entries. Only one case passes on the liability of a certified public accountant with respect to an "unaudited" financial statement.

In *United States v. Natelli*, . . . the defendant accountants were convicted of making materially false statements in proxy statements filed with the Securities and Exchange Commission.

Natelli passed upon liability for an unaudited, but completed, financial statement. While no reported case has passed on the liability of an accountant for malpractice in producing workpapers and adjusting entries, it is our opinion that such liability must be imposed upon the defendants on the facts of this case.

This case is a most unusual one, Schwartz, Frumm had investigated American Allied Mutual in 1963 and found that it was impaired. This alerted them to the fact that they were dealing with a "sick cat." Then, in October 1964 Graff personally showed his workpapers and adjusting entries to the state examiners, and he knew that they were relying upon them in conducting their statutorily required examination of American Allied. This was a representation that the assets indicated by those entries were owned by American Allied and could be counted by the commissioner in his examination. The defendants' actual knowledge that the commissioner was relying upon these representations renders them liable for their negligence in making them.

Restatement, Torts 2d, Tent. Draft No. 12, § 552 provides as follows:

§ 552 Information Negligently Supplied for The Guidance of Others.

(1) One who, in the course of his business, profession or employment, or in a

transaction in which he has a pecuniary interest, supplies false information for the guidance of others in their business transactions, is subject to liability for pecuniary loss caused to them by their justifiable reliance upon the information, if he fails to exercise reasonable care or competence in obtaining or communicating the information.

(2)　Except as stated in subsection (3), the liability stated in subsection (1) is limited to loss suffered

(a)　By the person or one of the persons for whose benefit and guidance he intends to supply the information, or knows that the recipient intends to supply it; and

(b)　Through reliance upon it in a transaction which he intends the information to influence, or knows that the recipient so intends, or in a substantially similar transaction.

(3)　The liability of one who is under a public duty to give the information extends to loss suffered by any of the class of persons for whose benefit the duty is created, in any of the transactions in which it is intended to protect them.

The actions of the defendants fall within the above section. With respect to subsection (1), it is clear that defendants, in the course of their business, supplied false information to American Allied and the commissioner of insurance, that those parties justifiably relied upon the information, and that defendants failed to exercise reasonable care or competence in communicating it. With respect to subsection (2)(a), the defendants supplied the information to both American Allied and the commissioner; with respect to subsection (2)(b), these parties relied upon it in determining whether the operation of American

Allied could continue. Because of the continued operation, American Allied suffered an additional loss of $849,078.60 to the Kitzers.

The fact that no previous accounting malpractice case deals with liability for erroneous workpapers or adjusting entries does not unduly concern us, for in the normal case no representations are made by use of such work product; rather, the accountants prepare complete financial statements from their workpapers and distribute the completed statements. The workpapers remain the property of the accounting firm and not of the client. In this case, however, the defendants personally displayed their workpapers to the state examiners and knew that the examiners were relying upon them.[1]

Defendants not only had actual knowledge of the fact that representations were being made by use of the workpapers and adjusting entries, but they made those representations themselves—by personally handing over the workpapers and adjusting entries.

On the facts of this case, therefore, we hold that defendants can be held liable for negligent misrepresentation even though they had not produced an audited or completed financial statement.

---

[1] This is not a case where, unbeknown to defendants, American Allied employees displayed defendants' uncompleted workpapers to the examiners. In such a case, if such a display is not normally made, perhaps the accountants should not be held liable, as they would have had no idea that any representation would be made to anyone through the use of those papers or that anyone would be relying upon them.

1.　The Minnesota Supreme Court held that the state insurance examiners "justifiably relied" upon the accountants' workpapers. The court held that the workpapers contained a number of "entries" which were "erroneous" and that the workpapers did not disclose "American Allied's insolvency." The court held that it was not "unduly" concerned that liability was being imposed for "erroneous workpapers or adjusting entries."

2.　The court held that the accountants knew that "representations were being made by use of the workpapers and adjusting entries" and that "they made those representations themselves—by personally handing over the workpapers and adjusting entries" to the insurance examiners. The *Bonhiver* case demonstrates that the form of the representation is less important than the substance. That is, a material representation can be made by workpapers or a draft document which induces justifiable reliance to the same extent as if the representation was contained in a formal or final report.

3. The *Bonhiver* decision raises the possiblity that an accountant who knows that his draft financials are routinely disseminated by his client to other persons may be held liable to those parties for any justifiable reliance on the draft financials. The mere marking of a document "Draft—For Discussion Purpose Only" or "Draft—Not To Be Delivered to Nonclient Users" may not of itself be sufficient to avert "justifiable reliance" on the part of a nonclient. See the discussion at ¶ 7.07[5][a] regarding the effect of a disclaimer and marking a financial statement unaudited.

[c] **Oral Representations.** Oral advice and representations may induce a party's "justifiable reliance" as effectively as written advice and representations. The fact that a professional renders a "curbstone opinion" may be probative but not conclusive that the accountant's "advice" was not a factor in the party's decision-making process.

There has been more than one accountant's liability case which has gone to trial before the jury in circumstances when the "advice" rendered was informal to the point of being nonadvice. The following case is an example of a "nonadvice—nonreliance" case where the court found for the accountant.

Vernon J. Rockler & Co. v. Glickman
273 N.W.2d 647 (Minn. 1978)

ROGOSHESKE, Justice.

This is an appeal from an order and judgment in favor of defendants.

Plaintiff, a closely held corporation, is registered as a broker-dealer in securities with the Securities Exchange Commission and is licensed by the State of Minnesota. Defendant Glickman, Lurie, Eiger & Co. is a partnership comprised of certified public accountants engaged in the business of providing accounting, auditing, business planning, and tax planning services to the public, and has provided such services to plaintiff from 1961 to 1972.

Beginning in 1962 plaintiff maintained an investment account for which it purchased securities to be held as capital assets. These securities were segregated from those held in its inventory account for sale to customers in the ordinary course of business. Plaintiff reported profits realized from the sale of securities held in its investment account for more than 6 months at capital gains rates for income tax purposes. Plaintiff also maintained an inventory account through which it transacted approximately 95 percent of its business. Plaintiff maintained a separate inventory account for securities sold but not yet purchased. Such transactions are referred to by the parties as "short sales." Plaintiff hoped it would be able to purchase securities for this account in the marketplace for less than plaintiff had sold them. When plaintiff was able to do so, it realized gains; if it had to purchase the securities at a higher price, it suffered a loss. Plaintiff had lost considerable amounts on "short sales" at least three times between 1961 and 1967. Plaintiff reported all gains and losses from transactions in securities held in these accounts at ordinary income tax rates.

During the time in issue, plaintiff held many of the same securities in its investment account that it was selling short. Because of the rising market in many of these securities, plaintiff was in danger of losing money on its "short sales." Hence, plaintiff considered the possibility of transferring securities from its investment account to its inventory account to cover its short sales. Plaintiff's president, Vernon Rockler, claims he spoke with Mr. Serber of defendant firm concerning such transfers and their income tax effect some months prior to the end of the fiscal year ending June 30, 1968. Mr. Rockler testified that Mr. Serber advised him to transfer the securities by means of a general bookkeeping entry which would preserve their capital gains treatment. Mr. Serber denied that this conversation ever occurred.

In May or June 1968 Mr. Rockler directed plaintiff's bookkeeper to make general bookkeeping entries transferring certain securities from the investment account to the inventory account. When defendants audited plaintiff's books in the summer of 1968 in preparing plaintiff's income tax return, defendants relied on the schedules prepared by plaintiff and did not challenge such transfers.

In December 1968 Mr. Rockler met with Mr. Ephraim of defendant firm to discuss the possibility of "borrowing" securities which had not been held for 6 months from the investment account to cover certain "short sales." Mr. Ephraim told him there was no way to "borrow" such securities and maintain their capital asset status. He did advise Mr. Rockler that pursuant to Internal Revenue Code, 26 U.S.C.A. § 1236, there were two ways to preserve capital gains treatment—by direct sale from the investment account to the open market and by a general journal entry transferring securities from the investment account to the inventory account. He testified at trial:

> **The witness**: Well, my answer to it would be that I would have to know how long, or I would have to see what happened to the stocks that were then transferred into inventory. If the stocks were transferred into inventory and then right out on to the street, that would be one thing.
> BY MR. DAVIS:
> **Q**: Would that be okay?
> **A**: Yes, I think that would be okay. But that is just my thinking on it.
> **Q**: And that would not violate Section 1236 A-2, in your opinion?
> **A**: Yes, sir, that is correct; and they went directly out.
> **Q**: And they went directly out. You mean by that, suppose they went out against an account such as securities sold but not yet purchased?
> **A**: Well, as long as they weren't thereafter held.
> **Q**: In inventory?

> **A**: In inventory. If they went from the investment account to the inventory account to the street, I wouldn't like it as well as if they had gone directly to the street; but I would think that would be all right.
> **Q**: But that is in fact, exactly what you told Mr. Rockler in December of 1968, isn't it?
> **A**: Yes, I would think that probably is what I told Mr. Rockler. However, I would tell him that he has a very safe way of doing it, and that's to go directly to the street. But if he chooses to go through his inventory account, I just don't know what the results are going to be. I do know what the results are going to be if he goes directly to the street.

Between December 1968 and June 1969 plaintiff made numerous transfers from its investment account to its inventory account. Defendants audited plaintiff's records in the summer of 1969 in preparing plaintiff's income tax return. Defendants relied on schedules prepared by plaintiff and did not challenge these transfers.

In 1971 the Internal Revenue Service audited plaintiff's 1969 income tax return. The IRS disallowed capital gains treatment of these transfers and assessed a deficiency. Upon the advice of Walter Rockler, a tax attorney, plaintiff negotiated with the IRS and eventually settled the deficiency by paying capital gains tax rates on one-half the gain and ordinary income tax rates on the other half.

Plaintiff then brought suit against defendants to recover the amount of the deficiency assessment, interest and penalties, and for reimbursement of attorneys fees and costs incurred in protesting and settling the deficiency. The trial court found that the advice given by defendants did not constitute professional malpractice; that it did not warrant action in reliance thereon by plaintiff; that plaintiff did not actually rely on such advice.

The trial court found that the advice given was not a "clear-cut statement of advice such as to constitute professional malpractice." Mr. Ephraim's advice to plaintiff was based primarily on 26 U.S.C.A. § 1236, of the Internal Revenue Code, which was enacted to prevent broker-dealers from shifting securities from one account to another to obtain the most favorable tax treatment possible. The only way for a broker-dealer to obtain capital gains treatment under this section is to segregate securities in an investment account and never hold that security for sale to customers in the ordinary course of business.

The trial court also found that Mr. Ephraim's advice to Mr. Rockler in December 1968 was "nothing more than an expert opinion and not such as to warrant reliance thereon by plaintiff broker." Given Mr. Rockler's experience, the trial court found "it difficult to believe that plaintiff, Rockler, reasonably relied on the advice given, inconclusive and ambiguous as it was." In addition, the trial court found that plaintiff's decision to make the transfers from the investment account to the inventory account was caused by its need to cover its "short sales" not by defendants' advice.

The essence of the trial court's finding was that plaintiff did not rely on the advice, because there was an independent business reason for transferring these securities. The evidence, both oral and written, amply supports this conclusion. Plaintiff made similar transfers prior to the end of fiscal year 1968. Although plaintiff claims defendants advised it to make such transfers, defendants deny giving plaintiff such advice. In addition, plaintiff met with Mr. Ephraim on December 11, 1968, to discuss the possibility of "borrowing" securities which had been held for less than 6 months from its investment account not to seek advice on transferring securities which had already been held for 6 months. Only after Mr. Ephraim explained § 1236 did plaintiff question Mr. Ephraim about the consequences of such transfers.

The IRS Transmittal Report and District Conference Report indicated the IRS' belief that plaintiff used its investment account to protect against losses resulting from selling securities it had not yet purchased. This occurred because plaintiff did not always need to deliver the securities involved for a period of months. Therefore, at the same time plaintiff sold a security it had not yet purchased, it bought the same security for its investment account. If it was able to hold the security for 6 months in its investment account, it could obtain capital gains treatment when it sold that security. Because some of the securities became unobtainable, such as the securities of Ivey Corporation, or only obtainable at much-higher prices than plaintiff anticipated, plaintiff had no choice but to transfer the securities from its investment account to it inventory account to cover its "short sales." Failure to do this might have subjected plaintiff to large losses on its "short sales" or to the loss of its registration and license as a broker-dealer. Thus, even if the defendants had advised plaintiff to sell the securities in the open market and then repurchase them, plaintiff would not necessarily have followed such advice. The IRS determined that plaintiff held these securities for sale to customers in the ordinary course of business, because plaintiff's securities-sold-but-not-yet-purchased account was short throughout the taxable year in these securities, a window board in plaintiff's window indicated that plaintiff was a market maker in many of these securities, and plaintiff no longer traded in many of these securities when its investment account was depleted following the transfers to its inventory account.

Given the documentary and oral evidence, the trial court was justified in finding that plaintiff did not rely on defendants' advice and that such advice was not the factual cause of plaintiff's loss.

[6]   Nonreliance on the Accountant: The "But For" Substitute for Reliance— Aiding and Abetting

In some circumstances a plaintiff may not rely on an accountant's professional services. It is possible that an accountant may still be held liable to the nonrelying party based on a theory of aiding and abetting. (See ¶ 6.05[4] for a complete discussion of aiding and abetting liability.)

A party aids and abets the fraud of another party by:

(a)   knowing of the fraud; and

(b)   substantially assisting the fraud through some type of conduct which could consist of inaction, action, or a combination of both.

Hochfelder v. Ernst & Ernst is an example of how an accountant may be held liable as an aider and abettor despite the plaintiff's total unawareness of and nonreliance on the accountant. In that case the plaintiffs admitted that they had never once seen or read a financial statement audited by Ernst & Ernst. They also admitted that they did not rely on Ernst & Ernst. Based on these admissions, the U.S. court of appeals ruled:

> More important, however, is the plaintiff's admitted lack of reliance on the financial statements and reports prepared by Ernst & Ernst and Ernst & Ernst's certificate of opinion. The common law action against a public accountant independent of an action on the contract is grounded on negligent misrepresentation; this necessarily requires direct reliance of some sort by the plaintiff on the professional services rendered by the accountant.

Because the plaintiffs did not rely on the auditors' reports, the court held that the auditors could only be held liable as aiders and abettors. In place of plaintiffs' direct reliance the court of appeals substituted a "but for" theory of causation, namely, "but for" the auditors' breach of duties of inquiry and disclosure the client's fraud would have been discovered or prevented.

The court of appeals stated:

> The last element in plaintiffs' claim for aiding and abetting a Rule 10b-5 violation is proof of a causal connection between the breach of the duty of inquiry and disclosure and the facilitation of the underlying fraud. To that end it must be demonstrated that adequate inquiry and subsequent disclosure on Ernst & Ernst's part would have led to the discovery or prevention of Nay's fraud.
>
> Ernst & Ernst contends that plaintiffs would not be able to prove at trial a causal connection. It is urged that plaintiffs' theory of causation rests on utter speculation. On the state of the limited evidence before us and without passing on the extent of the weight and probative value of that evidence, it would not appear to be entirely outside of the realm of reasonableness for the fact finder to infer that adequate inquiry by Ernst & Ernst might not of itself have led to the discovery or prevention of Nay's fraud.[1] Moreover, with regard to the question of whether adequate disclosure by Ernst & Ernst of a material inadequacy in internal accounting controls would have precipitated action by the SEC or self-regulatory organizations leading to the discovery or prevention of Nay's fraud, we are inclined to the view that this is a matter properly left to full evidentiary development at trial and not disposable on a motion for summary judgment.

The "but for" theory of causation often exists in situations where an auditor's client is subject to some type of regulatory oversight and reporting. For example, the "but for"

---

[1] As we noted earlier, plaintiffs' [expert accountants] stated that at a minimum they would have made further investigation with respect to the mail rule to assure that it was not the vehicle for irregularity and, absent a satisfactory answer to such inquiry, would have withdrawn from the audit engagement or declined to issue an opinion on the financial position of First Securities.

theory would apply to insurance companies, banks, and companies reporting to the SEC. Under the "but for" theory the nonrelying party relies upon the regulatory organization to be a "watchdog" for him.

¶ 7.08   Contributory Fault

[1]   Defenses to Fraud, Negligence, and Contract Claims

In a lawsuit against an accountant, the plaintiff's conduct will be analyzed to determine whether the plaintiff's own actions contributed to the injury. If the plaintiff was at fault it is possible that plaintiff's contributory fault will bar partially or totally plaintiff's recovery.

The following defenses may be asserted to preclude a plaintiff's recovery against an accountant:

1.   An accountant's breach of contract is excused if the client hindered or failed to cooperate and thus prevented the accountant from performing the contract.

2.   In a negligence case, a plaintiff's negligence which causes his injury will prevent a negligence action. In some states, the courts have adopted a comparative negligence standard which bars a plaintiff's recovery on a percentage of total fault basis (e.g., the jury determines that 80 percent of plaintiff's damages were caused by defendant, the remaining 20 percent were caused by plaintiff's negligence, recovery is limited to 80 percent).

3.   In a fraud action, a plaintiff's negligence is not a defense. However, a participant in a fraud cannot sue for damages caused to him by the fraud. Plaintiff's participation in the fraud vitiates his reliance on any fraudulent representation.

4.   In Rule 10b-5 actions under the federal securities laws courts have required the plaintiff to exercise some degree of caution in his conduct. To the extent that the plaintiff does not exercise the required caution, the plaintiff's Rule 10b-5 action may be barred. The caution required of the plaintiff has included the following standards of conduct:

The securities laws were not enacted to protect sophisticated businesspeople from their own errors of judgment; investors must investigate the information available to them with the care and prudence expected of people with full access to information.

In a Rule 10b-5 action plaintiff's burden is to negate recklessness when the defendant puts that in issue.

Plaintiff must not act recklessly.

Plaintiff must act reasonably; defendant must prove plaintiff acted unreasonably.

[2]   Employee Fraud—Conduct That Benefits the Employer-Client

An auditor's negligent failure to detect and disclose a fraud by an employee of a client may not necessarily result in a finding of liability on the part of the auditor to the client.

Similarly, an auditor's *fraudulent* failure to disclose the fraudulent activities of employees of a client may not necessarily result in a finding of liability of the auditor *to the client*.

If the client is a corporation the acts of its employees may become the acts of the corporation if the employees were acting on behalf of the corporation. To the same effect, the acts of an agent may become the acts of his principal if intended to benefit the principal.

It is possible that the wrongful acts of the employees will preclude a lawsuit by the employer–client against the accountants. Consider the following case.

[a]   *Cenco, Inc. v. Seidman & Seidman* and Comments

Cenco, Inc. v. Seidman & Seidman
686 F.2d 449 (7th Cir. 1982)

Before BAUER, WOOD and POSNER, Circuit Judges.

POSNER, Circuit Judge.

[Plaintiff Cenco Inc. sued its former auditors, Seidman & Seidman, for failing to detect fraud by former members of Cenco's management. Between 1970 and 1975, Cenco's top management engaged in a massive fraud whereby Cenco's inventories and net worth were fraudulently inflated. The fraud inflated the value of Cenco's stock.

Those members of management "involved in the fraud were not stealing from the company, as in the usual corporate fraud case, but were instead aggrandizing the company (and themselves) at the expense of outsiders, such as the owners of the companies that Cenco bought with its inflated stock, the bank that loaned Cenco money, and the insurance companies that insured its inventories."

With the discovery of the fraud Cenco was sued by shareholders and creditors. Cenco in turn sued its auditors.]

The case went to the jury on the three remaining counts in Cenco's [claim] alleging respectively breach of contract, professional malpractice (negligence), and fraud. Cenco's evidence tended to show that in the early stages of the fraud Seidman had been careless in checking Cenco's inventory figures and its carelessness had prevented the fraud from being nipped in the bud; that as the fraud expanded, Seidman's auditors became suspicious, but, perhaps to protect the very high fees that Seidman was getting from Cenco (about $1 million a year, which was

70 percent of Seidman's total billings), concealed their suspicions and kept giving Cenco a clean bill of health at their audit reports; that one partner in Seidman, asked by Cenco's general counsel (who was not in on the fraud) whether Seidman suspected anything, answered: "No one suspects fraud. Dismiss that." Seidman's evidence tended to show, to the contrary, that Seidman had diligently attempted to follow up all signs of fraud but had been thwarted by the efforts of the large group of managers at all levels at Cenco who were in on the fraud to prevent Seidman from learning about it.

The jury found for Seidman on all three counts. Cenco appeals . . . from the judgment entered against it on the jury's verdict, which it contends was based on erroneous instructions.

This brings us to the main issue in the case—whether the district judge gave erroneous instructions to the jury. The challenged instructions relate to the question whether Seidman was entitled to use the wrongdoing of Cenco's managers as a defense against the charges of breach of contract, professional malpractice, and fraud. Despite the plurality of charges it is one question because breach of contract, negligence, and fraud, when committed by auditors, are a single form of wrongdoing under different names. The contract in question here (really a series of contracts) consists of the letters between Seidman and Cenco outlining the terms of Seidman's annual retention to audit Cenco's books. The material part of the letters is the incorporation by reference of general accounting standards which, so far as pertinent to this case, require the auditor to use his professional skill to follow up any signs of fraud that he discovers in the audit. The tort of negligence in the context of auditing is likewise a failure to use professional care and skill in carrying out an audit. And if such care and skill are not used, then the audit reports to the client will contain misrepresentations, either negligent or, if the auditor knows that the representations in the reports are untruthful or is indifferent to whether or not they are truthful, fraudulent.

Because these theories of auditors' misconduct are so alike, the defenses based on misconduct of the audited firm or its employees are also alike, though verbalized differently. A breach of contract is excused if the promisee's hindrance or failure to cooperate prevented the promisor from performing the contract. See Restatement (Second) of Contracts § 245 (1979). The corresponding defense in the case of negligence is, of course, contributory negligence. We need not consider to what extent that defense in an auditors' liability case may have been modified by the recent decision of the Illinois Supreme Court in a personal-injury case to replace contributory by comparative negligence. The court held that this change was not to apply to trials begun prior to the date of the decision, which was June 8, 1981.

Negligence is not a defense to an intentional tort such as fraud. . . . But a participant in a fraud cannot also be a victim entitled to recover damages, for he cannot have relied on the truth of the fraudulent representations, and such reliance is an essential element in a case of fraud. . . . If the misrepresentation is negligent rather than intentional, contributory negligence plays the same role it would play in an ordinary negligence case.

The jury instructions in this case stated these defenses accurately, but Cenco contends that the instructions should not have been given, because they related not to Cenco's conduct but to that of its managers. The judge was aware of the distinction but instructed the jury that the acts of a corporation's employees are the acts of the corporation itself if the employees were acting on the

corporation's behalf. If this instruction was correct, then the instructions which allowed the jury to consider Cenco's misconduct as a defense to Seidman's alleged wrongdoing were proper.

To determine the correctness of the instruction requires us to decide in what circumstances, if any, fraud by corporate employees is a defense in a suit by the corporation against its auditors for failure to prevent the fraud. Illinois precedent allows us to reject one extreme position on this question, which is that the employee's fraud is always attributed to the corporation by the principle of respondeat superior. This position, which would exonerate auditors from all liability for failing to detect and prevent frauds by employees of the audited company, was rejected in *Cereal Byproducts Co. v. Hall* . . . where a company's independent auditors were held liable for negligently failing to detect embezzlement by the company's bookkeeper. Auditors are not detectives hired to ferret out fraud, but if they chance on signs of fraud they may not avert their eyes—they must investigate. The references to keeping an eye out for fraud that appear in the accounting standards incorporated (by reference) in the retention letters between Cenco and Seidman would have little point if not interpreted to impose a duty on auditors to follow up any signs of fraud that come to their attention.

But this does not tell us what the result should be if the fraud permeates the top management of the company and if, moreover, the managers are not stealing from the company—that is, from its current stockholders—but instead are turning the company into an engine of theft against outsiders—creditors, prospective stockholders, insurers, etc. On this question the Illinois cases on auditors' liability provide no guidance. In fact, to our knowledge the question has never been the subject of a reported case. *Leeds Estate, Bldg. & Inv. Co. v. Shepherd* . . . described by Cenco in its main brief as "the one squarely applicable common law decision on accountants' liability," is nothing of the sort. The auditor in that case had failed to discover that the company's manager, by misrepresenting the profits of the company, had caused the company to pay out dividends, directors' fees, and bonuses for himself—all in violation of the charter—as a result of which the company went broke. This was stealing from, not for, the company.

In predicting how the Illinois courts might decide the present case, we assume they would be guided by the underlying objectives of tort liability. Those objectives are to compensate the victims of wrongdoing and to deter future wrongdoing. With regard to the first, we must refine our earlier statement that the "victim" of Seidman's alleged laxity was Cenco Incorporated. A corporation is a legal fiction. The people who will receive the benefits of any judgment rendered in favor of Cenco on its cross-claim against Seidman are Cenco's stockholders, comprising people who bought stock in Cenco before the fraud began, people who bought during the fraud period and either sold afterwards when the stock price fell or continue to hold the stock at a loss, and people who bought after the fraud was unmasked. A judgment in favor of Cenco on its claim against Seidman would not differentiate among these classes, but would benefit every stockholder as of the date of the judgment (or the date when a judgment was anticipated with some precision) in proportion to the number of shares he owned.

Once the real beneficiaries of any judgment in favor of Cenco are identified, it is apparent that such a judgment would be perverse from the standpoint of compensating the victims of wrongdoing. Among the people who bought stock in Cenco before the fraud began are the corrupt officers themselves. To the extent they are still stockholders in the company, they would benefit pro rata from a judgment in favor of Cenco. The other stockholders in this class are innocent in a sense, but of course it is they who elected the board of directors that managed Cenco during the fraud.

• • •

From the standpoint of deterrence, the question is whether the type of fraud that engulfed Cenco between 1970 and 1975 will be deterred more effectively if Cenco can shift the entire cost of the fraud from itself (which is to say, from its stockholders' pock-

ets) to the independent auditor who failed to prevent the fraud. We think not. Cenco's owners—the stockholders—hired managers (directly, in the case of the president and chairman, who were both members of the board of directors, indirectly in the case of the others) who turned out to be thoroughly corrupt and to corrupt the corporation so thoroughly that it caused widespread harm to outsiders. If Seidman had been a more diligent auditor, conceivably if it had been a more honest auditor, the fraud might have been nipped in the bud; and liability to Cenco would make Seidman, and firms like it, more diligent and honest in the future. But if the owners of the corrupt enterprise are allowed to shift the costs of its wrongdoing entirely to the auditor, their incentives to hire honest managers and monitor their behavior will be reduced. While it is true that in a publicly held corporation such as Cenco most shareholders do not have a large enough stake to want to play an active role in hiring and supervising managers, the shareholders delegate this role to a board of directors, which in this case failed in its responsibility. And not all of Cenco's shareholders were "little people." During the period of the fraud Curtiss-Wright Corporation owned between 5 and 16 percent of Cenco's common stock and had its own accounting firm conduct a study of Cenco's operations—without discovering the fraud.

Thus, not only were some of Cenco's owners dishonest (and, to repeat, to the extent they still own stock in Cenco they would benefit from any judgment in Cenco's favor against Seidman), but the honest owners, and their delegates—a board of directors on which dishonesty and carelessness were well represented—were slipshod in their oversight and so share responsibility for the fraud that Seidman also failed to detect. In addition, the scale of the fraud—the number and high rank of the managers involved—both complicated the task of discovery for Seidman and makes the failure of oversight by Cenco's shareholders and board of directors harder to condone.

Cenco tries to draw a sharp contrast between an innocent Cenco and a Seidman that was (or so the jury could have found) an intentional tortfeasor. But if Cenco may be divorced from its corrupt managers, so may Seidman from the members and employees of the firm who suspected the fraud. If Seidman failed to police its people, Cenco failed as or more dramatically to police its own.

Furthermore, we must assume that Cenco's corrupt managers were acting for the benefit of the company, not against it as in the *Cereal Byproducts* case. The jury was instructed that it could attribute the fraud of Cenco's managers to Cenco only if it found that the managers had been acting on Cenco's behalf, and the verdict for Seidman implies that the jury either so found or found that Seidman had not even committed a prima facie breach of duty to Cenco. The former assumption is more favorable to Cenco.

Fraud on behalf of a corporation is not the same thing as fraud against it. Fraud against the corporation usually hurts just the corporation; the stockholders are the principal if not only victims; their equities vis-à-vis a careless or reckless auditor are therefore strong. But the stockholders of a corporation whose officers commit fraud for the benefit of the corporation are beneficiaries of the fraud. Maybe not net beneficiaries, after the fraud is unmasked and the corporation is sued—that is a question of damages, and is not before us. But the primary costs of a fraud on the corporation's behalf are borne not by the stockholders but by outsiders to the corporation, and the stockholders should not be allowed to escape all responsibility for such a fraud, as they are trying to do in this case.

We need not go so far as to predict that the Illinois courts would hold that in any action by a corporation against its auditors an employee's fraud intended to benefit the company rather than the employee at the company's expense will be attributed to the corporation, however lowly the employee. It is true that the lower down the employee is in the company hierarchy, the less likely he is to commit fraud for rather than against the company. But there are overzealous employees at every level—many a corporation has paid heavy damages for antitrust violations committed by low-level sales managers who thought they were acting in the company's best interests as well as their own—and we think it premature as well as unnecessary to decide that an auditor is never liable for the frauds of loyal but misguided company employees that he could have prevented by taking care. But here the uncontested facts show fraud permeating the top management of Cenco. In such a case the corporation should not be allowed to shift the entire responsibility for the fraud to its auditors.

1. The court of appeals held that the trial judge properly instructed the "jury that the acts of a corporation's employees are the acts of the corporation itself if the employees were acting on the corporation's behalf." Thus, to the extent that the corporate management engaged in fraud, management's fraud *benefitting* the corporation was a complete defense for the auditors in a suit brought by the corporation against its auditors for failure to prevent the fraud.

2. A critical point is the court of appeals' ruling that the management fraud must *benefit* the corporation. The court observed that management at the highest level had turned the "company into an engine of theft against outsiders—creditors, prospective stockholders, insurers." The court noted that management was "not stealing from the company—that is, from its current stockholders." The court stated that "fraud on behalf of a corporation is not the same thing as fraud against it."

3. The court of appeals held that its ruling was not intended to imply that in "any action by a corporation against its auditors an employee's fraud intended to benefit the company rather than the employee will be attributed to the corporation, however lowly the employee." The court stated that the "lower down the employee is in the company

hierarchy, the less likely he is to commit fraud for rather than against the company." To the extent that an employee's fraud involves theft from the company, the employee's fraud should not be attributed to the corporation to bar a lawsuit by the corporation against its auditors.

One year after its decision in *Cenco* the same court of appeals expressed some additional thoughts on *Cenco* in issuing its opinion in *Schacht v. Brown* which was a civil RICO case alleging $300 million in trebled damages against auditors. *Schacht* qualified *Cenco*'s application. (See ¶ 10.03 for the *Schacht* case.)

4. The *Cenco* case involved an unusual situation where the company which had benefitted from management fraud had sued the auditors. The *Cenco* case did not involve a lawsuit by purchasers of Cenco stock during the period of the fraud when the stock price was inflated. Those shareholders had sued and received a sizeable settlement from the auditors. The fraud of Cenco's management could not be attributed to them.

[3] Employee Fraud—Conduct That Injures the Employer-Client

An auditor's negligent failure to discover an employee's embezzlement from the client-employer may subject the auditor to a lawsuit by the client for negligence. What if the employee's thefts occurred in part because the employer had failed to adequately supervise the employee or was negligent in some other respect which facilitated the embezzlement? Would the employer's contributory negligence preclude a lawsuit against the auditor for negligence?

The defense of contributory negligence is "theoretically" available in lawsuits by the client against the auditor for negligent failure to detect employee embezzlements. However, in practical application the courts have limited the use of contributory negligence as a defense against the client. The courts have held that negligence of the client is a defense only when it has contributed to the accountant's failure to perform his audit. Thus, if the auditor's negligent failure to perform an audit in accordance with GAAS was of the auditor's own doing, the client's negligence will not be a defense. Consider the following case.

[a] *Shapiro v. Glekel* and Comments

Shapiro v. Glekel
380 F.Supp. 1053 (S.D.N.Y. 1974)

CANNELLA, District Judge.

Defendant Ernst & Ernst's motion, [to dismiss] Count IV as against it, is denied.

Count IV of the complaint asserts that as a result of Ernst & Ernst's negligent performance of its auditing and accounting contract, Beck Industries, Inc. [hereinafter "Beck"] was allowed to overstate its earnings and financial condition in certain financial statements, and that these errors caused the fi-

nancial demise of Beck and Beck's petition for reorganization under Chapter X of the Bankruptcy Act. In essence, plaintiff alleges that Ernst & Ernst is liable to Beck, because Beck's financial statements for 1968 and 1969 were inaccurate and because the accountants negligently failed to detect such inaccuracies and report them to Beck's Board of Directors. It is further claimed that the accountants' failure to determine and report the true financial condition of Beck renders them legally responsible to the trustee [the plaintiff bankruptcy trustee] for permitting the Beck directors to engage in an ill-advised program of acquisitions. These claims against Ernst & Ernst are predicated upon both negligence and breach of [contract] theories.

[Ernst & Ernst] asserts that the plaintiff, by his statements in the pleadings, has conceded that the President and the Chairman of the Executive Board of Beck knew or should have known that Beck's earnings were materially less, and its financial condition was materially worse, than that represented in the financial statements and, therefore, that such knowledge and negligence on the part of Beck's two top officers precludes the trustee, who stands in the shoes of Beck, from suing the accountants for their negligence in permitting the overstatements in the financial reports to occur. Ernst & Ernst point to the following matters as supportive of their thesis: (1) that the President and Executive Committee Chairman of Beck (Messrs. Glekel and McDevitt) were aware or should have been aware of the fact that Beck's financial condition was materially worse than that reported in the financial statements; (2) that all the directors of Beck, "except defendants Glekel and McDevitt, were misled into believing that Beck was prospering, whereas it was not"; and (3) that the majority of Beck's directors, "except for defendants Glekel and McDevitt, and others, would have known of Beck's true financial condition" had Ernst & Ernst properly performed its duties. In short, [Ernst & Ernst] argues that assuming, as it must, the truth of the allegations made in the complaint, a recovery against Ernst & Ernst is here precluded as a matter of law because Beck was itself contributorily negligent and that, in any event, any negligence on the accountants' part was not, as a matter of law, the proximate cause of Beck's losses.

Contributory Negligence

In support of its position that the negligence of the employer precludes recovery against the accountants, Ernst & Ernst places reliance upon *Craig v. Anyon*. . . . In *Craig v. Anyon*

plaintiffs, a firm of stock and commodity brokers, were defrauded of more than $1,250,000 over a period of about five years by an employee (Moore) who was in charge of plaintiffs' commodities department. Plaintiffs brought suit on the theory that the accountants had negligently conducted an audit of plaintiffs' books, asserting that a proper audit would have uncovered the falsification of the books, led to the discharge of Moore, and prevented further losses. In affirming the trial court's reduction of the jury's verdict to the amount which had been paid to the accountants as compensation for their services, the [New York State Court] stated:

> [Moore's] various and diverse duties and powers put him in a position to keep records and papers, or cause them to be kept so as to deceive the accountants who relied on them. If it be assumed that they should not have done so, it is nevertheless true that the plaintiffs also relied upon them to an extent beyond all reason in view of the circumstances. They were guilty of the same kind of negligence of which they now complain. It may be true that a proper accounting would have put the plaintiffs on guard with reference to Moore's wrongdoing, but it is also true that, if the plaintiffs had attended to their business and, in view of the large transactions involved, had looked up Zabriskie's account when payments were being made to it, the dishonesty of Moore would have been discovered.
>
> There is no doubt in this case that plaintiffs could have prevented the loss by the exercise of reasonable care and that they should not have relied exclusively on the accountants.
>
> We think the damages cannot be said to flow naturally and directly from defendants' negligence or breach of contract. Plaintiffs should not be allowed to recover for losses which they could have avoided by the exercise of reasonable care. . . .
>
> The plaintiffs in effect contend that defendants are chargeable with negligence because of failure to detect Moore's wrongdoing, wholly overlooking the fact that, although they were closely affiliated with Moore, who was constantly under their supervision, they were negligent in failing properly to supervise his acts, or to learn the true condition of their own business and to detect his wrongdoing.

By a parity of reasoning, [Ernst & Ernst] here asserts that the conduct of Messrs. Glekel and McDevitt and their knowledge of Beck's true financial position is similarly preclusive of a recovery against the accountants in this litigation.

Plaintiff, on the other hand, in support of the position that a recovery against the accountants is not barred by the acts alleged to have been committed by Messrs. Glekel and McDevitt, places primary reliance upon the subsequent decision in *National Surety Corp. v. Lybrand.* . . . In that case, the defendant accountants were charged with negligence in failing to discover that Halle & Stieglitz, members of the New York Stock Exchange, had, for several years, been subject to embezzlements by their cashier. To this claim, the accountants asserted a defense of contributory negligence, offering evidence "that Halle & Stieglitz so conducted their business as to make possible [the cashier's] defalcations." In reversing the trial court, which had barred plaintiff's claim in reliance upon *Craig v. Anyon*, the [New York Court] stated:

> We are . . . not prepared to admit that accountants are immune from the consequences of their negligence because those who employ them have conducted their own business negligently. . . . Accountants, as we know, are commonly employed for the very purpose of detecting defalcations which the employer's negligence has made possible. Accordingly, we see no reason to hold that the accountant is not liable to his employer in such cases. *Negligence of the employer is a defense only when it contributed to the accountant's failure to perform his contract and to report the truth.* . . . That was the principle applied in *Craig v. Anyon* . . . where the embezzler had been negligently represented to the accountants as a person to be trusted. In the present case, the loss consisted of thefts by a cashier not so represented "whose own account of his receipts and payments could not reasonably be taken by an auditor without further inquiry. [Emphasis added]

The trustee contends that this narrower, more restrictive formulation of the contributory negligence defense, as it was expressed by the court in *Lybrand*, is here applicable and he asserts that viewing the conduct of Messrs. Glekel and McDevitt in a light most favorable to plaintiff, such cannot be said to have contributed to the accountants' failure to perform their contract and to report the truth.

> [C]ontributory negligence is the failure to use reasonable care in looking after one's own interest in certain circumstances. And here one of the circumstances is that the plaintiff has engaged defendant to help protect his interest. There can be nothing unreasonable about plaintiff's conducting his affairs on the assumption that defendant is doing his job properly. It should not be possible to base contributory negligence on a failure to take affirmative protective measures in reliance upon defendant's faithful performance. The New York [court] [in *Lybrand*] probably had the right idea. That is, contributory negligence must be accepted as a theoretical defense, but it applies only if the plaintiff's conduct goes beyond passive reliance and actually affects defendant's ability to do his job with reasonable care.

[T]he Court is convinced that the correct rule of contributory negligence applicable in accountant's liability cases, such as at bar, is that expressed in *Lybrand*, namely, that the "[n]egligence of the employer is a defense only when it has contributed to the accountant's failure to perform his contract and to report the truth. . . ." and that this rule must be followed here.

In addition, the Court finds significant policy considerations which are supportive of this approach. Accountants should not be allowed to avoid liability resulting from their own negligence except upon a showing of substantial negligence or fault by their employer—the *Lybrand* showing, at least. This view is particularly appropriate when, as here, public investors are involved and the accountants have been retained because of their professional standing and expertise. As was stated by Justice Clarke, speaking in dissent in *Craig v. Anyon*:

> The contract of audit was not one merely to discover if inadvertent clerical errors had been made in the bookkeeping, but was one of protection of the plaintiffs' firm from their own failure to find any error in their books of account. This contract the defendants failed to perform. Admitting the neglect of the plaintiffs to discover the embezzlement and falsification of the accounts through an examination of the books on

their own part, the defendants' work in pursuance of the contract, owing to the manner in which it was performed, failed to save plaintiffs from the consequences of such failure and neglect, which was the very subject of the contract.

Applying the above-stated principles to the matter at bar, the Court, viewing the facts in a light most favorable to the plaintiff, cannot conclude, as a matter of law, that the conduct of Messrs. Glekel and McDevitt "contributed to the accountant[s'] failure to perform [their] contract and to report the truth" and, therefore, that aspect of the instant motion which seeks relief on grounds of contributory negligence is denied.

1.   The *Shapiro* case accepted the principle of law that the "negligence of the employer is a defense only when it contributed to the accountant's failure to perform his contract and to report the truth." The *Shapiro* case rejected the view held by one court that "plaintiffs should not be allowed to recover for losses which they could have avoided by the exercise of reasonable care."

As the *Shapiro* court observed, the reasons for limiting the defense of contributory negligence include the fact that a client hires an auditor "to help protect his interest. There can be nothing unreasonable about plaintiff's conducting his affairs on the assumption that defendant [auditor] is doing his job properly." The *Shapiro* court noted that "it should not be possible to base contributory negligence on a failure [by the client] to take affirmative protective measures in reliance upon defendant's faithful performance."

2.   Unlike the *Cenco v. Seidman & Seidman* situation, the *Shapiro* case dealt with instances of theft from and injury to the corporate audit client. In such circumstances *Cenco* would not attribute the negligent and fraudulent acts of the wrongdoing employees to their corporate employer.

3.   An auditor may assert contributory negligence as a defense if the client has impaired the auditor's ability to examine the client's books and records resulting in the auditor's failure to discover the embezzlement. A client's "omissive" reliance on the auditor (i.e., the client's failure to take any protective or precautionary action aside from total reliance on the accountant) is not interfering conduct. An example of interfering conduct may be the client's intentional or negligent refusal to provide the auditor with complete access to the client's books and records.

[b]   *National Surety Corp. v. Lybrand*

National Surety Corp. v. Lybrand
9 N.Y.S.2d 554 (App. Div. 1934)

The defendants assert that they are not liable, no matter how negligent they may have been, because Halle & Stieglitz were guilty of contributory negligence. If it be true that Halle & Stieglitz so conducted their business as to make possible Wallach's defalcations, it did not necessarily excuse the defendants from the consequences of their negligence in failing to discover and report the facts. The action here, it must be remembered, is not to recover for the thefts committed by Wallach as it would be if it were against Wallach or against the surety. The action is for errors of the accountants in failing to discover Wallach's defalcations, thereby making further defalcations possible and rendering more difficult recovery for defalcations of the past. The measure of damages in two such classes of actions is not the same.

We are, therefore, not prepared to admit that accountants are immune from the consequences of their negligence because those who employ them have conducted their own business negligently. The situation in this respect is not unlike that of a workman injured by a dangerous condition which he has been employed to rectify. . . . Accountants, as we know, are commonly employed for the very purpose of detecting defalcations which the employer's negligence has made possible. Accordingly, we see no reason to hold that the accountant is not liable to his employer in such cases. Negligence of the employer is a defense only when it has contributed to the accountant's failure to perform his contract and to report the truth. Thus, by way of illustration, if it were found that the members of the firm of Halle & Stieglitz had been negligent in connection with the transfer of funds which occurred at about the time of each audit and that such negligence contributed to the defendants' false reports it would be a defense to the action for it could then be said that the defendants' failure to perform their contracts was attributable, in part at least, to the negligent conduct of the firm. That was the principle applied in Craig v. Anyon. . . . where the embezzler had been negligently represented to the accountants as a person to be trusted. In the present case, the loss consisted of thefts by a cashier not so represented "whose own account of his receipts and payments could not reasonably be taken by an auditor without further inquiry." Matter of Kingston Cotton Mill Company.

We are, therefore, of opinion that the plaintiff established a prima facie case. The question of the defendants' liability on the various theories set forth in the complaint should have been submitted to the jury.

[c] Client's Failure to Follow Accountant's Recommendation. A client's failure to follow the recommendations of its accountant may be held to be contributory negligence which precludes a claim against the accountant. For example, assume the accountant recommends certain changes in internal controls which are designed to prevent defalcations by employees. The client fails to follow the recommendations and as a result, an employee embezzles money and assets by a scheme which the recommended controls would have prevented. The client's failure to follow the recommendations is (1) negligence and (2) the legal proximate cause contributing to the client's injury. The following case is an example of this failure.

Stanley L. Bloch, Inc. v. Klein
258 N.Y.S.2d 501 (Sup. Ct. 1965)

[Plaintiff corporation sued its accountants for negligence in issuing a balance sheet containing material overstatements in plaintiff's inventory which was its most significant asset. Plaintiff claimed it relied to its injury on the overstated inventory item. The plaintiff contended that had it known its true financial status, it would have terminated its business and avoided further losses.]

With respect to plaintiff's cause of action sounding in negligence, however, although the proof leaves no doubt as to the professional carelessness of defendants, and while a proper audit would have revealed plaintiff's true financial condition, the record does not contain sufficient credible evidence to warrant the conclusion that defendants' errors or the omission of the qualifying statement were the proximate cause of all the damage for which plaintiff seeks recovery here (see Craig v. Anyon . . .). The proof adduced before me establishes that when discrepancies in their issued statement were later discovered by defendants, they then alerted plaintiff to these inaccuracies. Thereafter, plaintiff also continued to receive from defendants all the additional information concerning its inventory which an audited or unqualified balance sheet would have contained. Moreover, there is proof which indicates that despite defendants' recommendations and advice, plaintiff failed to hire additional or adequate clerical help to follow through on the inventory information supplied to it by defendants. Such recommendations, if accepted, would have eliminated or, undoubtedly, minimized any subsequent loss suffered by plaintiff. In my opinion, therefore, plaintiff's claim that it remained in business, with the consequent damage, *solely in reliance on the information set forth in the erroneous balance sheet* is without merit and unsupported by the credible proof.

All other claimed items of damage are denied. Plaintiff, as noted, has failed to prove that they flow naturally, directly and solely from defendants' negligence or their breach of contract (*Craig v. Anyon* . . .).

[4]   Rule 10b-5 Defenses

[a]   Sophisticated Investor Defense.   A plaintiff in a Rule 10b-5 action is required to exercise some degree of cautious conduct on his part. A sophisticated and astute business investor cannot blindly rely on fraudulent representations when the investor is aware of facts which militate against investment or which expose the misrepresented facts.

Courts have imposed varying standards of conduct on plaintiffs in Rule 10b-5 actions as a condition to their successful recovery, including the following standards:

A plaintiff put on notice of the questionable basis of a representation must investigate the available investment information with due diligence.

A plaintiff must not recklessly ignore or avoid facts relating to his investment decision.

(i)   **Rice v. Baron** *and Comments*

Rice v. Baron
CCH Fed. Sec. L. Rep. ¶ 97,200 (S.D.N.Y. 1979)

CARTER, District Judge. Plaintiffs, Henry Hart Rice and Abram Barkan contend that defendant Irwin Baron sold to each of them 190 shares of the common stock of James Feh & Co. ("JF") on June 2, 1971, without disclosing material facts concerning JF's putative liability for damages resulting from a fire on February 25, 1969, in a building managed by JF. They assert that this constituted withholding of material information in violation of Section 17a of the Securities Act of 1933 . . . Section 10b of the Securities Exchange Act of 1934 . . . and common law fraud as well.

Baron argues that plaintiffs were neither misled nor deceived in the June 2, 1971 transaction, and that these belated fraud assertions are fabrications of plaintiffs and their counsel in an effort to extract from him a contribution towards expenses plaintiffs incurred in connection with settlement of the claims against JF arising out of the 1969 fire.

Relevant Facts

On February 25, 1969, JF was managing agent of a building located at 595 Fifth Avenue, New York City, when a fire occurred which resulted in the death of 11 persons, personal injuries to 5 others and extensive property damage to the building. The fire was highly publicized. Barkan learned of it the day it occurred and telephoned Ralph Russ, the person at JF in charge of management properties. Barkan knew that JF managed the building. Rice was outside the country when the fire occurred and returned to New York on March 8.

Late in December, 1969, the first of a number of lawsuits ("fire action cases") against the owners of the building, JF and others, was commenced. These suits sought damages for wrongful death, personal injury and/or property damage. JF's own liability insurance did not cover managed property, and the only insurance protection available to JF was that policy coverage held by Acruem Associates ("Acruem"), the owners of the building.

JF had been founded in the early 1930's. It remained small but developed into a prestigious closely held real estate corporation that provided a wide variety of real estate services including consultation, appraisal, sales brokerage, management, mortgage servicing and brokerage, and leasing. Baron and Russ joined the company shortly after it commenced operations. Barkan started work at JF in 1936 as a messenger, and Rice came to the company in 1950 as head of its sales brokerage department.

Sometime in the 1960's the ownership of the organization passed to Baron and Russ with the former holding an 80% and the latter a 20% interest in the company. Baron became president and under the then by-laws, he was the chief executive officer of the company. In the meantime, Barkan had been rising in the organization. In 1956, he was made assistant vice president, in 1957, secretary, in 1965, director and vice president, and sometime prior to January 1, 1970, executive vice president. Rice was head of sales brokerage, a director and vice president from 1953 until January 1, 1970. Both Barkan and Rice were shareholders, at least since 1964.

Baron was born in 1902 and was thus 67 years old in 1969. At that time he began to consider a less active role in the company and had been grooming Barkan to take over as his successor. Beginning in 1969 and continuing into 1970, Baron began conferring with Proskauer, Rose, Goetz & Mendelsohn ("Proskauer"), his personal as well as JF's counsel, for advice on shifting the controlling interest in JF from himself to Barkan and Rice, and on the terms of an employment contract with JF as a consultant when he stepped down from active employment. On January 1, 1970, Barkan was made president, Rice became senior vice president, and Baron became chairman of the board. Russ remained treasurer. On January 12, 1970, the by-laws were amended creating the office of chairman of the board and according that

office the powers and duties of chief executive officer of the company which had heretofore been the function of the president.

On January 12, 1971, at a meeting of JF's board, Baron announced that he would be devoting less time to the company; that he was going to sell his controlling interest in JF to Barkan and Rice. In order to make the transfer less financially burdensome on them, the board agreed that 500 of Baron's shares would be sold to the company at once and that 190 shares each would be sold to Barkan and Rice the following June. An executive committee was formed consisting of Barkan, Rice and Russ to act for the board between meetings.

• • •

When Baron announced his intention to make Barkan president of JF in January, 1970, and subsequently to turn over a controlling interest in the company to Barkan and Rice effective in June, 1971, Barkan was, of course, delighted. On January 30, 1971, enroute to the Virgin Islands for vacation, after Baron's intention to sell him and Rice a controlling interest in JF on June 2, 1971, had been approved by the JF board, Barkan wrote Baron a warm and effusive letter of thanks "for the faith, encouragement and above all your friendship to me and all the Barkans during the past 35 years." . . . The letter goes on to state that his association with Baron had "molded" his life, that the "ethical manner in which both you and the late James Felt directed the firm left an indelible impression on me," and the communication closes with the hope that he, Barkan, "will find the strength and wisdom to maintain the ethical standards" set by Baron.

On June 2, 1971, agreements were signed giving Rice and Barkan control of the company through the purchase of Baron's shares. Payment was to be made over a 4-year period commencing in January, 1972. Baron remained in New York until November or December, 1971. Then he went to Florida for 4 to 5 months, returning to New York in April, 1972. This procedure was followed in each succeeding year during the period relevant to our determination. It is plaintiffs' testimony that Baron ran JF until November or December, 1971 despite the transfer of control to Barken and Rice on June 2, 1971.

• • •

The first of the fire action cases was instituted in December, 1969, naming JF as co-defendant. Therafter a number of such actions were filed, all naming JF as co-defendant. At first, John J. Bower, counsel for Acruem, represented JF's interests. As the cases accumulated, Bower suggested JF might desire separate counsel. Russ and Baron decided to retain Milton Lebe to represent JF in the fire action cases. Lebe's partner had prosecuted various collection suits for the firm. Russ, being in charge of management properties, was the JF official who was kept abreast of these cases. Throughout Russ was in communication with the attorneys and all papers on the cases were kept in a file on JF premises maintained by Russ.

At the outset Lebe's view was that JF's liability exposure was within the Acruem insurance coverage. He so advised JF accountants, and note g to the JF financial statement for the year ended January 31, 1970, refers to the pendency of the fire action litigation against JF and recites Lebe's advice that the Acruem insurance would be sufficient to cover damages being sought.

In March, 1970, apparently the number of actions had so multiplied that JF's liability exposure exceeded the insurance coverage, and JF was so advised. Lebe, however, while acknowledging this fact was, nonetheless, convinced that the law suits would either be settled or if they proceeded to trial that recovery would be kept within the insurance coverage on the building. He communicated this information to the accountants, and note g to the financial statement of JF for the year ended January 31, 1971, duly records this information. However, because of the uncertain nature of the matter, the accountants made a disclaimer on page one of this statement asserting among other things "because of the possible material effect of the law suit (note g), we are precluded from expressing an opinion on the accompanying financial

statements" (emphasis supplied. . . .). Both Barkan and Rice admit to seeing this statement, but both deny reading the disclaimer or note g.

Pursuant to the terms of the June 2, 1971 agreement, only one payment on the purchase of Baron's shares had been made by Rice and Barkan when the decision of Judge Tyler of this court was filed on March 31, 1972, holding JF negligent and liable for damages resulting from the fire. Nonetheless, Rice made the remaining payments on the purchase of the shares in 1973, 1974 and 1975 as required under the June 2, 1971 agreement. Barkan made the required payments in 1973 and 1974 but because of a fall off in business in 1975, he sought and secured from Baron permission to make his final payment over an extended period of time. He completed his payments in 1976.

• • •

Determination

This case required the expenditure of considerable time, talent, effort and money, but it is a case that should never have been brought. It is litigation structured on a theory that cannot be justified by the reality of the relationship among the parties involved. No extended argument need be made concerning the 17a, 10b and common law fraud claims. The claims simply have not been proved, and it is doubtful that a credible showing of fraud or misrepresentation could have been demonstrated given the manner in which the parties dealt with one another.

Barkan, Rice and Baron worked together for a number of years in JF. Baron was its chief executive. Rice was highly successful on the selling end, and Barkan was being groomed to take over as head of the firm when Baron stepped down. The firm consisted of approximately 12 officers and 12 secretaries, and the entire staff was housed on one floor of a building. These intimate physical arrangements in themselves would have made it extremely difficult for one JF official to withhold information concerning any matter of importance to the firm from another company official which the latter had an interest in knowing, and withholding such data over an extended period of time would have been even more difficult. Plaintiffs in their brief seek to depict Baron as controlling and keeping all information in his own hands and not allowing any free flow of information to others. There is nothing in the record to support this contention other than the assertion itself. At any rate, Russ, not Baron, was the JF official who was kept current on what was going on in the fire action cases.

In 1969, JF was confronted with fire damages in a building which it managed. It carried no liability insurance protection in re the property, and JF's liability coverage was through the insurance of the owner of the managed property. Russ, who was in charge of the management phase of JF, was aware of this. It is inconceivable that Barkan, who was being readied to become the firm's chief executive, and Rice, who was being prepared with Barkan to take over the controlling interest in JF, did not know this as well.

It may be true, as Rice testifies, that because of his absence from New York when the fire occurred that he learned nothing about the fire or JF involvement in it between the time of his return in March, 1969, and Judge Tyler's decision in March, 1972, which found JF guilty of negligence and liable for deaths, injuries and damage resulting from the fire. Yet, continued ignorance of the fire and of JF's involvement in it over such a long period of time in such a small organization is hard to credit. Acceptance of Rice's testimony, however, will not advance plaintiffs' contentions. Rice's testimony becomes plausible only by fully crediting the evidence that the JF officials who did know about the fire action cases were so confident that the firm had no negligent responsibility for any of the deaths, injuries or property damages caused by the fire that the cases were dismissed as unimportant and insignificant in JF operations.

When the fire action cases were first filed Baron and Russ felt that the damages would be covered by Acruem's insurance, and were content to have the attorney hired by the insurance company to represent Acruem's interests represent JF as well. When the damage claims exceeded the insurance coverage, JF retained separate counsel to represent its interest. JF's regular attorney and Baron's was Proskauer—one of New York City's most prestigious law firms. Baron and Russ, however, were sanguine in the belief that JF had not been negligent and felt so minimally threatened by the fire action litigation that Milton Lebe, a partner to a lawyer who had handled small collection claims for the company, was retained to represent and protect JF's interest. It is not to belittle Lebe's capabilities to conclude that if Baron and Russ had regarded JF's exposure in the fire action cases to have been a cause for serious concern Proskauer, rather than Lebe, would have been retained to represent the company. At the time Lebe was retained, Baron and Russ held between them virtually 100% ownership of JF. It is hard to believe that Baron and Russ would not have insisted on retaining the best lawyer they knew had they seriously thought that the fire action litigation posed a serious threat—as it later turned out—to JF.

While Russ was the official most involved in keeping up to date on the cases, both Baron and Barkan knew about the pending litigation. During the period between the fire and the June 2, 1971 sale of stock, Barkan had served as executive vice president and president of the firm. In both positions he was situated to learn whatever he wanted to know about the fire action cases and what action JF had taken in regard thereto. After he became president in 1970, Barkan had a twin burden of gratitude to Baron and a need to measure up to standards set by his predecessors. Under those circumstances, it would have been totally out of character for him to have failed to have made the effort to digest everything there was to know about JF's operations. Russ kept all information, communications from lawyers, complaints, subpoenas and other legal documents in a file in JF offices. These files were available to Barkan and Rice for study and inspection. Barkan must have known or should have known what was in those files before he and Rice consummated the June, 1971 agreement.

Even conceding, for purposes of argument, that Baron did dominate the organization and kept information about the fire litigation to himself, plaintiffs have another hurdle to surmount. The JF financial statement for the year ended January 31, 1970, made reference to the fire action cases. That reference, note g, was optimistic, in accord with information supplied the accountants by Lebe. Reference to the fire action cases is also contained in the financial statement for the year ended January 31, 1971. The note g reference in this document, while still optimistic—it quotes Lebe's belief that [the] matter would either be settled or if tried that damages would come within insurance limits—does state that the damage claims exceeded insurance coverage. Additionally, on the first page of this later statement the accountants warned that because of the uncertainty as to the impact the fire action claims might have on JF, they were "precluded from expressing an opinion" re the statement. This reservation was an admonition to a prudent investor to exercise due diligence to ascertain all the facts.

Rice and Barkan acknowledge receipt of that statement and that they saw and had copies of the January 31, 1971 financial statement before June 2, 1971, when they entered into the agreement to buy a controlling interest in JF. Both contend they either did not see the accountant's reservation and note g, or that they relied solely on Baron's good faith and paid no attention to what they did see. There is no contention, however, that Baron made any affirmative misrepresentations. The sole claim is a failure to disclose. However, when a party is provided with information which puts him on notice to exercise due diligence to inform himself, that available information must be investigated with due diligence before he can make a claim under the federal securities law. *Hirsch v. duPont*.

That the fire action claims against JF reached approximately 14 million dollars, that the fire resulted in death, injury and property damage, that the building in which the fire took place had been managed by JF, that JF had no liability insurance coverage of its own protecting it in re that property, and that JF was protected only to the extent of the insurance carried by the owners of the building were, at least as abstract propositions, all material facts—matters to which a reasonable man would have attached importance, *Mills v. Electric Auto-Lite Co.*, and would have viewed as significantly altering the total mix of information made available. *TSC Industries, Inc. v. Northway, Inc.* It is also clear that a deliberate and conscious failure to disclose these facts to the buyer of JF stock would constitute, under ordinary circumstances, an adequate basis for the 17a, 10b and common law fraud claims made here. However, whatever connotation we give the above stated facts in the abstract, this case must be determined on the basis of the actualities that existed in June, 1971, as disclosed by the record. Barkan and Rice contend that they did not know the true facts when they purchased Baron's shares and had they known what they argue Baron failed to disclose, they would not have gone through with the purchase. The evidence demonstrates that they knew all that any JF official in 1971 knew about JF's involvement and potential liability.

But again, giving them the benefit of the doubt and accepting the assertion of their lack of information, plaintiffs still cannot prevail. They certainly knew about JF involvement and exposure after learning of Judge Tyler's decision of March 31, 1972, which held JF responsible in damages for negligence. Nonetheless, Rice and Barkan continued to make payments due under the June 2, 1971 agreement until the total agreed upon purchase price for Baron's stock had been paid.

These acts belie plaintiffs' testimony that had they known all the facts about JF's exposure on or before June 2, 1971, they would not have made the purchases in question. In June, 1971, the known facts were that claims made in the fire action cases exceeded insurance coverage, and while there was a possibility that JF could be held, that possibility seemed remote at the time. As of March 31, 1972, JF was held liable in damages. That latter holding, however, did not deter Barkan and Rice from continuing to fulfill their part of the agreement. If they were not deterred by the grim reality of JF's having been found in 1972 negligent and liable in damages for death, injury and property damage caused by the 1969 fire, it is hardly likely that the more sanguine evaluations in 1970 and 1971 would have been regarded by them as material to their decision to buy Baron's stock. Their adherence to the agreement after March 31, 1972, evidences either that they were aware of the fire action litigation and JF's potential liability in those cases before the purchases or that these matters were not factors which would have altered the total mix of information on which they relied on June 2, 1971, in making the decision to buy control of JR from Baron. Their claim to the contrary is a sham.

1. The plaintiffs were sophisticated businesspeople who were in a position to be intimately familar with the corporate securities which they purchased—both plaintiffs were officers, directors, and shareholders of the company prior to the stock purchase which was at bottom of their Rule 10b-5 lawsuit. Thus, the court did not accept plaintiffs' argument that they had been misled regarding the materiality of the fire damages litigation against the company.

2. The court placed particular emphasis on the fact that the company's independent auditors disclaimed an opinion because of material uncertainty relating to the fire damages litigation. Footnote "g" to the financials detailed the fire litigation and was referred to in the auditors' disclaimer.

The plaintiffs stated that they received the auditors' report but did not read it or footnote "g." In response to the plaintiffs' argument that they relied solely on the "good faith" of the defendant and "paid no attention to what they did see," the trial judge ruled:

> When a party is provided with information which puts him on notice to exercise due diligence to inform himself, that available information must be investigated with due diligence before he can make a claim under the federal securities law.

[b] Estoppel. Estoppel is a defense to a claim of aiding and abetting a Rule 10b-5 violation. Under the estoppel doctrine, a claim may not be asserted where a plaintiff would benefit from his own inconsistent or misleading conduct on which the defendant has detrimentally relied.

The following case demonstrates the application of estoppel as a defense to liability.

Hochfelder v. Ernst & Ernst
503 F.2d 1100 (7th Cir. 1974)

[The facts of the case are set forth at ¶ 7.03[1].]

In accordance with generally accepted auditing standards, the basic audit procedure to determine the accuracy and correctness of the books and records of a broker or dealer in securities with respect to his customers' accounts is to request and obtain written confirmation from the customers with regard to their accounts.

Pursuant to these requirements, Ernst & Ernst mailed to some of the plaintiffs confirmation forms requesting that they verify the accuracy of the details stated in the confirmation forms as to the amount and composition of the customer's account. The confirmation expressly indicated that the customer was to note any differences and exceptions.

Admittedly, no confirmation of account sent by Ernst & Ernst to the plaintiffs at any time listed or referred to plaintiffs' escrow accounts. It is equally clear, however, that no plaintiff who received a confirmation request from Ernst & Ernst took exception to the failure of the confirmation to list his escrow account. On the basis of plaintiffs' failure to take exception to the confirmation requests, the trial judge held that they were estopped as a matter of law from pursuing their claims against Ernst & Ernst. The judge observed:

> Plaintiffs raise no factual issue that they failed to correct defendant's confirmation slips on their First Securities accounts, and it was only with respect to auditing First Securities Co. that defendant Ernst & Ernst had any responsibility. Therefore in the only direct dealings which plaintiffs had with this defendant, they misled defendant to its detriment in a very material respect. Had they not done so, we might infer that Ernst & Ernst would have been put on notice sufficiently to investigate further and perhaps perfect its audit, but its failure to do so was caused in part by the plaintiffs, for aught that appears in the record.

Estoppel is properly asserted as an affirmative defense to a claim of aiding and abetting a Rule 10b-5 violation. . . . It is a rule of fundamental fairness whereby a party is precluded from benefiting from his own inconsistent conduct which has induced reliance to the detriment of another. That is, where a plaintiff has, with knowledge of the facts, initially conducted himself in a particular fashion, he cannot thereafter assume a posture inconsistent with such conduct to the detriment of a defendant who has acted in material reliance upon that conduct.

Applying the estoppel rule to the instant case, if plaintiffs knew they were to report the escrow accounts as an exception on the confirmation and failed to do so, they ought not be heard to complain of Ernst & Ernst's failure to uncover or prevent the fraudulent escrow scheme, for the inference is strong that disclosure by plaintiffs to Ernst & Ernst of the existence of the escrow accounts would have led to the discovery of Nay's fraudulent scheme. Whether plaintiffs knew or as reasonable persons should have known that they were to report the escrow accounts as exceptions on the confirmation requests is a question to be properly decided by the fact finder. We cannot say as a matter of law that a reasonable investor of similar business sophistication and intelligence as plaintiffs would have reached no other conclusion but that disclosure of the escrow account was called for by the confirmation request. Nor can we conclude that a reasonable investor viewing the express language of the confirmation would have limited his verification to the amounts stated and noted no exceptions for the escrow account.

CHAPTER 8

TAX PRACTICE— RESPONSIBILITY AND LIABILITY

¶ 8.01 Introduction[1]

[1] Tax Practitioner Talks with His Attorney

Although there are few reported lawsuits involving tax practitioners, it does not follow that there is little or no legal risk attending an accountant's tax practice. Let's join a discussion between an accountant tax practitioner and his attorney regarding the liability problems which confront a tax accountant:

MR. ACCOUNTANT: I tell you, I'm glad I chose tax as my area of practice.

MR. LAWYER: Why?

MR. ACCOUNTANT: I can sleep at night without worrying about being sued. Those accountants who do audits have to constantly worry about lawsuits. I never worry about being sued.

MR. LAWYER: You're pretty confident, but did you know that the area of tax services generates almost more lawsuits than any other area of professional practice?

---

[1] *Tax Practice: The Nature of the Beast*: Even Judge Learned Hand, brilliant judge and jurisprudent that he was, found the Income Tax Act to be an onerous and frustrating piece of legislation to work with. In two of Judge Hand's opinions, he commented on the Act as follows:

[T]he words of such an act as the Income Tax, for example, merely dance before my eyes in a meaningless procession: cross-reference to cross-reference . . .

[and]

Some of the provisions it is true are almost too difficult for even the tax expert fully to understand . . . he must make that most inordinate expenditure of time that in many instances is necessary to a comprehensive understanding of them.

MR. ACCOUNTANT:	I don't believe it, where did you get that information from, the National Gossip Sheet?
MR. LAWYER:	No, from one of the largest insurers of accountants.
MR. ACCOUNTANT:	Why haven't we heard more about these types of lawsuits?
MR. LAWYER:	It is probably because many of these actions are settled. This is an area of practice where the "no harm, no foul" rule does *not* apply.
MR. ACCOUNTANT:	What's that?
MR. LAWYER:	No harm, no foul, is my way of describing the importance of concrete identifiable damages as a necessary condition to the bringing or settling of a lawsuit. If an auditor is negligent in auditing a company's financials which are otherwise accurately stated, there is "no harm" to a third party who relied on the accurate statement. If there is no harm, there is no foul, namely, a lawsuit.
MR. ACCOUNTANT:	So, what's that got to do with tax services?
MR. LAWYER:	In the area of tax practice, negligence by a tax practitioner has a tendency to have a most direct, identifiable and calculable impact on the client taxpayer. If an accountant is negligent, the taxpayer may perhaps pay too little tax through understatement of taxes or too much tax through lost tax benefits and savings. Either way there are ascertainable dollar costs which accompany the accountant's erroneous tax advice or service.
MR. ACCOUNTANT:	I have heard of accountants who have missed important tax filing dates and have cost their clients and ultimately the accountants dearly.
MR. LAWYER:	Those types of cases which involve what I call "errors in administration" are almost indefensible from an accountant's standpoint.
MR. ACCOUNTANT:	I agree. There is no excuse for errors involving timely elections, or timely filings of returns. These are not matters of judgment. They are matters of administrative execution which are the easiest areas of practice in which to exercise reasonable care—
MR. LAWYER:	And the hardest areas to defend if not performed.
MR. ACCOUNTANT:	Well, I have a comprehensive administrative "tickler system." I'm not afraid of that happening to me. Is there anything else that should concern me?
MR. LAWYER:	There are two areas of tax practice which frequently involve lawsuits: 1) preparation of and assistance in preparing tax returns; and 2) tax advisory services.
MR. ACCOUNTANT:	I can't imagine any of my clients suing me over any tax work which I have done on their tax returns!
MR. LAWYER:	You think you are another Marcus Welby, huh? Let me tell you, even Marcus Welby could be sued if the circumstances were right!

MR. ACCOUNTANT:	I don't follow.
MR. LAWYER:	The Internal Revenue Service has substantial powers to come after you and your client for a "substantial understatement of liability." In fact, if your client is a corporation you could be penalized $10,000 for aiding and abetting a substantial understatement. If your client gets tagged with substantial penalties for an understatement, you can bet the client's attorney will be paying you a visit.
MR. ACCOUNTANT:	O.K. O.K. I can live with that risk of liability. My tax returns are usually on target.
MR. LAWYER:	You do tax counselling or advisory services, don't you?
MR. ACCOUNTANT:	Yes. . . .
MR. LAWYER:	That is an extremely fruitful area for lawsuits involving "lost tax opportunities."
MR. ACCOUNTANT:	What's that? Give me an example.
MR. LAWYER:	A client goes to his tax advisor for advice on how to structure a proposed business transaction to minimize or save on taxes. If the advice is negligent and the client loses the opportunity to save on taxes, who should pay for this lost opportunity? Who should pay for the loss of tax benefits? The tax penalties? The interest payments? The tax deficiencies?
MR. ACCOUNTANT:	The client?
MR. LAWYER:	Guess again.
MR. ACCOUNTANT:	Well . . . the only party left is the tax advisor.
MR. LAWYER:	Right you are!
MR. ACCOUNTANT:	I haven't had any problems yet in my tax advisory services practice. What the heck, my clients usually call and ask for my opinion and I give it to them right on the phone and that's the last I hear of it!
MR. LAWYER:	Don't you document in writing your advice to them?
MR. ACCOUNTANT:	Sometimes, but its a real problem because I am so busy. I mean, why should I spend 15 minutes preparing a written memo of what was a five minute oral opinion.
MR. LAWYER:	If you don't you may be confronted with a question down the road as to 1) the scope of your engagement or the advice sought, and 2) the substance of your advice.
MR. ACCOUNTANT:	Huh?
MR. LAWYER:	The scope of your engagement involves the question of what you were hired to do. Did the client ask you for an opinion regarding a specific transaction and its tax implications, or was the advice sought broader, involving far more than what you agreed to or thought you were agreeing to? Also, the scope of your engagement

involves critical questions relating to the extent to which you agreed to investigate the existence of facts material to your tax advice. Is the engagement one in which the client asks you to assume the existence of certain material facts? Does the client ask you to make certain material assumptions which underlie your tax advice? These are often critical components of tax advice. It is imperative that you have an understanding with your client regarding your inquiry obligation.

MR. ACCOUNTANT: Is this what you have referred to as the "duty of inquiry?"

MR. LAWYER: Yes. Remember that it is also important to memorialize in writing your tax advice to the client should it subsequently be questioned regarding what you advised. It is almost impossible to reconstruct from memory the substance of tax advice rendered two or three years after the events occurred and the advice was given. Don't you advise hundreds of clients over the period of a year? Isn't it hard to remember the details of each engagement or the advice you gave?

MR. ACCOUNTANT: Yes. . . .

MR. LAWYER: A document made contemporaneously with your advice is the best way to protect yourself later on when your recollection of the events has faded. Moreover, a document recounting the events usually refreshes your recollection as to all the material details. In addition, if you have transmitted your advice in writing to your client, you should clearly state the extent to which you have investigated the existence and accuracy of the material facts upon which you are relying in rendering your tax advice. This avoids any misunderstandings as to the scope of your duty of inquiry . . .

MR. ACCOUNTANT: I see. . . . In the absence of investigating the existence and accuracy of the material facts, I should at least state that my advice is predicated on the assumption that certain facts exist.

MR. LAWYER: You got it! Keep in mind that the duty of inquiry relating to tax advisory services for the client is a matter of agreement between you and the client. However, when you prepare a tax return to be filed with the IRS, your duty of inquiry as a tax return preparer is also governed by the Internal Revenue Code and Treasury Regulations. In fact in the area of preparing tax returns, you have dual obligations relating to your client and the IRS.

MR. ACCOUNTANT: I know. The tax practitioner has to be sensitive to the IRS regulations involving the preparation of tax returns and the representation of a client before the IRS.

MR. LAWYER: Before I forget it, in the area of tax advisory services, you may have a "duty to warn" of the need for updated tax advice.

MR. ACCOUNTANT: The accounting profession has taken the position that there is no duty to update tax advice. We all know that tax advice changes with changes in tax laws.

MR. LAWYER: Do clients know when tax laws change?

MR. ACCOUNTANT: Probably not!

MR. LAWYER: How are clients going to know they need to update prior tax advice if they don't know the law has changed? Look, I know a nationally prominent tax practitioner who would testify as an expert witness that there is at least a duty to contact clients and advise of the need for review and possible revamping of their estate plans in light of changing laws.

MR. ACCOUNTANT: That's an interesting perspective, but it is not a professional standard . . .

MR. LAWYER: . . . . It may be a legal duty if successfully urged by a plaintiff's lawyer!

MR. ACCOUNTANT: I see. . . .

MR. LAWYER: One other aspect of this "duty of inquiry" question involves your role in tax planning engagements which include the cooperative work of an attorney, an accountant and possibly other professionals such as a bank trust officer or a life insurance representative.

MR. ACCOUNTANT: Many times I work with one or more of those types of professionals. So?

MR. LAWYER: Do you have a clear understanding as to your role versus their respective responsibilities? If you don't, you could be setting yourself up for a plunge through the "expectation gap!"

MR. ACCOUNTANT: Sounds ominous, what is it, a financial "Twilight Zone?"

MR. LAWYER: No, it is the breeding ground for a future lawsuit. I represented an accountant who was sued for work he performed in a major estate planning matter in which certain material facts did not exist. The accountant was sued along with the attorney, a trust officer, and a CLU—the whole team. Everyone pointed the finger at everyone else. No one had investigated the existence of the facts, everyone assumed erroneously that the facts existed. When the IRS subsequently pointed out the true state of the facts, the damage was done. The heirs of the estate paid $500,000 more in estate tax and penalties than they should have. And the professionals involved were sued because of the expectation gap.

MR. ACCOUNTANT: Sounds like a financial Twilight Zone to me!

MR. LAWYER: It was far worse. . . .

MR. ACCOUNTANT: How so?

MR. LAWYER: The professionals paid the $500,000 plus interest, plus their attorneys' fees, plus the cost of the diminution of their professional reputation.

MR. ACCOUNTANT: What a disaster, when you lose your reputation for competence as a tax advisor, you lose your clients too!

[2]   Liability Problems and Tax Practice

If you have adequately synthesized the preceeding chapters, this tax practice chapter will be largely a review for you. It will also afford you an opportunity to apply what you have learned about accountant's liability to tax practice; for virtually everything you have learned thus far applies to the accountant-tax practitioner with one notable addition, that is, the recovery by the government of civil extractions for various derelictions of duty. Referring back to Prosser's statement of the attributes of the reasonable person who is also a professional person ¶ 3.01, we can rightly conclude that we are now referring to a specialty (tax) within a specialty (accounting). Notice particularly that the attribute is phrased in terms of, "such superior skill and knowledge as the actor has, *or holds himself out as having*, when he undertakes the act." (Emphasis added.) Does this latter phrase create any distinct problems for the tax practitioner? You undoubtedly have already correctly surmised that defining the tax practitioner's duty precisely is probably impossible. Once again, the law can be stated in general terms only.

The same federal-state dichotomy we have examined in the previous chapters on negligence and fraud is present insofar as the liability of accountants who practice in the taxation area are concerned. In appropriate circumstances a tax practitioner may be sued under state law for breach of contract, negligence or fraud, or under the federal securities laws.

Additionally, criminal liability for tax fraud is always a possibility under federal or state law. Until 1976 civil liability for tax malpractice was almost exclusively the domain of state law and its courts, taking the form of an action by the client for breach of contract or negligence and possibly fraud. However, with the advent of mass merchandising of tax returns, coupled with long standing abuses and the exceptionally low level of expertise often encountered, Congress responded with legislation in 1976 as a part of the Tax Reform Act of 1976 which provided federal civil liability for improper tax return preparation. We shall first look at the state or common law rules and subsequently examine recent federal legislation.

One area of the accountant's duty to his or her client and also an area which is vital to the accountant, is concerned with working papers, privileged communication, summons by the IRS and grand jury subpoenas. We have saved this aspect of the accountant's rights and duties for this chapter since although it has great importance to all phases of accounting practice, it is particularly relevant to the tax practice and there is a 1984 landmark decision by the U.S. Supreme Court involving privileged communication in respect to the tax accrual file. This will be explored in the last part of this chapter. You will see that the duties owed by the tax practitioner are to the same parties who were suing the accountants in previous chapters. These include clients, the government, and to some extent third parties.

[3]   Duty of Inquiry: The I.R.C. Section 333 Disaster

Let us start with a hypothetical problem. The CPA firm of Criss & Cross are the auditors of Land Speculators, Inc. The corporation was founded in 1938. The stock of the corporation is primarily held by the founding family, current and past executives of the corporation, and the prior owners of Nexus Corp. that was merged into Land Speculators. Its assets, which consist mainly of real property, are well in excess of $25 million. For several years, stock dividends had been declared in order to preserve cash. The stated capital account had been credited to reflect the additional par value amounts as a result of the stock dividends. Due to factors not necessary to consider here, the board of directors has decided to liquidate the corporation. It would appear from the current balance sheet that there is a relatively insignificant amount of retained earnings. The fair market value of the real property held for investment and other capital assets is in excess of $10 million and has a basis of $3 million. Under the circumstances, the board of directors is considering a Section 333, one-calendar month liquidation, since the shareholders will be able to avoid paying capital gain tax presently on the appreciated investments the corporation owns. Couple this with the relatively small amount of retained earnings shown on the balance sheet which would be taxed as dividend to the shareholders, and the proposed Section 333 liquidation looks like a natural.

If the transaction qualifies, it is essentially a tax free, nonrecognition of capital gain insofar as the bulk of the gain inherent in the properties distributed is concerned.

Let us assume the worst for the sake of discussion. Criss & Cross was at the time in the peak period of its tax practice, consequently it assigned Newcomer, a relatively inexperienced staff member, to the engagement. In fairness to Criss & Cross, Newcomer was bright and had a fine academic background. In addition, the larger firm with which he was previously associated was a prominent firm with an excellent reputation. During lengthy interviews before and after he was hired, Newcomer held himself out as having had fairly extensive experience in corporate tax matters—including liquidations. This was not the case. In performing tax analysis of earnings and profits, Newcomer:

Did not determine whether the corporation was collapsible. Instead, he assumed it was not based upon its having been created in 1938 and the nature of its business.

Failed to properly include and ascertain the fair market value of certain stock and securities held by the corporation. He did check several stock acquisitions on a sample basis and found them to have been acquired prior to December 31, 1953. He assumed that all securities were so acquired, and therefore, concluded that since the amount of cash was small, the taxable income would be determined on the basis of the accumulated earnings and profits.

Used the balance sheet retained earnings figure as equivalent to earnings and profits for Section 333 purposes.

Newcomer was negligent, if not grossly negligent, in performance of the tax undertaking. The tax partner responsible for review of Newcomer's performance was hospitalized and another partner looked at the analysis, asked Newcomer a few questions, and accepted the end product virtually intact. Luckily for Newcomer, and more importantly for Criss & Cross, the corporation was not within the Section 341 definition of a "collapsible corporation." Regarding the question of securities to be distributed, Newcomer's conduct once again amounted to tax malpractice for and on behalf of the firm (*respondeat superior* applies to Criss & Cross). However, the difference proved to be immaterial.

The major error resulting from Newcomer's negligence relates to the computation of earnings and profits for the purpose of Section 333. Taking the balance sheet figure for earned surplus as earning and profits for tax purposes was negligent. Large additional amounts of earnings and profits were subsequently found to exist as a result of an IRS audit of the transaction. First, the source of the transfers to stated capital as a result of the stock dividends was retained earnings. Additionally, the retained earnings account failed to reflect a carryover of earnings and profits as a result of Land Speculator's prior acquisition of Nexus. Thus, Criss & Cross, as a result of Newcomer's negligence, is also negligent in the performance of the task undertaken. The concept of retained earnings resembles earnings and profits for tax purposes, but it is clear they are not identical. Several adjustments are normally required to be made to reconcile one with the other. To assume earned surplus or retained earnings are equivalent to earnings and profits without a careful analysis of all prior years, beginning with 1938, is to proceed at one's own risk. Any competent tax accountant would be aware of the distinction. Furthermore, stock dividends have no impact on earnings and profits, but they may affect retained earnings as was the case here.

The facts are not sufficient to determine the exact amount of damages. Criss & Cross would be held liable for any interest and penalties imposed upon the shareholders, and they might also be held liable for additional taxes incurred by the shareholders as a result of their erroneous advice. Obviously, this will vary from taxpayer-shareholder to taxpayer-shareholder. The major damage suffered is loss of the deferral part of the gain and the payment of additional tax at ordinary income tax rates instead of the ultimate tax which would be paid upon sale of the assets distributed. The transaction would appear to have been less costly tax wise had the typical liquidation been resorted to.

[4]   Responsibility to Whom?

Once again, the same cast of actor-plaintiffs is waiting in the wings ready to sue the accountant-tax preparer. These are the client, various third parties, and the federal, state, and possibly city governments. In the limited number of lawsuits brought by aggrieved parties regarding tax services, it is the client-plaintiff who is most often the litigant. It is surprising to discover the dearth of fully litigated, reported accountant liability cases in the tax area overall. This may be attributed to any number of causes. Liability and dollar damages are often clearcut, and therefore, the matter is settled. In some instances damages may be limited to any penalty assessed plus interest and thus not warrant litigation. In such circumstances the plaintiff may not recover the amount of additional tax payable if he would be obligated to pay the amount anyway without regard to the tax advisor's faulty conduct.

To put it another way, the tax practitioner will not be liable for the tax payment even if he erred, since the taxpayer was properly obligated to pay in any event. For example, a tax practitioner wrongfully categorizes a transaction as a capital gain. The IRS discovers the error and properly asserts ordinary income treatment, which results in additional tax, interest, and penalties. The liability is limited to interest plus penalties. Lastly, the absence of fully litigated tax malpractice lawsuits may arise from the fact that the vast majority of potential cases involve the client as the potential plaintiff. The better the client–accountant relations, the less likely a claim will be brought or fully litigated.

[5] Potential Liability and Applicable Theories

[a] Common Law—Contracts, Negligence, and Fraud. The potential liability and applicable theories have been extensively covered throughout the various chapters of the book. There is not much that has not been said already. Once again the breach of contract cause of action may be the only one available in the case of a total failure to perform or where the shorter tort statute of limitations has elapsed. Otherwise, the taxpayer usually has the option to sue for negligence as well as for breach of contract. The recovery will usually be the same since punitive damages for negligence are not available as is also the case in a breach of contract action. However, one very recent development regarding damages should be noted.

Fundamental to a plaintiff's right to recover is that he or she must have been damaged by the defendant's negligence. In addition, it must be the "right" kind of damage. Usually this is not a problem. Physical injury, damage to property, and financial loss satisfy the damages requirement and are recoverable as we have seen. There is one type of damages that may or may not be recoverable—mental suffering. Mental suffering is sometimes claimed in the tax area.[2] You can easily understand that this type of "damage" may be present or at least claimed in the case of many taxpayers who are audited or sued by the United States or the IRS. However, the unintentional (negligent) infliction of mental suffering was not recoverable in many jurisdictions until recently. Today the clear trend of the courts has been to recognize this type of damage as a sufficient basis for recovery. No case has held the CPA liable for such damage, but rest assured in those jurisdictions which permit recovery for this type of damage it will be asserted in a lawsuit by the plaintiff-client's attorney. No conclusion can presently be drawn on the applicability of this type of damages to tax malpractice actions.

Fraud does not seem to be a viable basis for imposition of liability on the tax accountant. Such is the case since the client is typically involved in the fraud or it inures to the client's benefit. It would seem to be clear to the accountant-fraud-doer that what is being done will without doubt create liability for the accountant if detected. However, it would appear that criminal tax fraud is the greater threat and not civil, common law liability to the client.

[b] Federal Securities Laws. Whenever audited financial statements are required under the Securities Act of 1933 or the Securities Exchange Act of 1934 there is potential

---

[2] *H&R Block, Inc. v. Testerman*, 338 A.2d 48 (Ct. App. Md. 1975).

liability in connection with that portion of the audit involving disclosure of existing or contingent tax liabilities. In addition, engagement by a party to an acquisition or merger which comes within one of the Acts can result in liability to the extent that proper care is not taken in rendering any opinions regarding the tax aspects of the transaction. A negligent performance of the tax part of the engagement subject to Section 11 of the 1933 Act may result in the imposition of substantial liability.

There is also the possibility of an action by a nonclient purchaser or seller of a security (e.g., a tax shelter investor), based upon fraud under Section 17 of the 1933 Act or more probably under Section 10(b) and Rule 10b-5 of the 1934 Act. The *Hochfelder* case applies and requires a showing of *scienter*. However, as is now obvious, actual knowledge is not required and a plaintiff will rely upon constructive fraud or gross negligence in order to satisfy this troublesome requirement and win the case. Finally, criminal fraud may be asserted by the appropriate governmental agency (the SEC, the IRS, and state and local tax or securities agencies). Chapter 5 painted a somewhat grim picture of the application of criminal fraud to situations where "actual" fraud on the accountant's part was not present.

[c]   Federal Tax Return Preparer Liability.   Prior to the Tax Reform Act of 1976, preparers of tax returns were subject to limited or narrow liability to the U.S. government. Prior law did not even penalize a tax return preparer if he or she failed to sign the return. The liability sanctions imposed by the Internal Revenue Code against a preparer dealt solely with criminal fraud, namely, fines not to exceed $5,000 and imprisonment not to exceed three years or both were provided for. These criminal sanctions remain. However, proof of criminal fraud is difficult to establish and this sanction was largely ineffective. Furthermore, there was nothing available to the IRS to police negligent preparation of a return or other objectionable practices.

The Tax Reform Act of 1976 substantially changed the liability imposed upon individuals who prepare income tax returns for compensation. In addition to disclosure requirements and ethical standards, the act imposed civil liability and penalties and empowered the government to obtain injunctive relief.

The basis for liability under the Tax Reform Act is primarily for an understatement of the taxpayer's federal income tax liability. A final determination by the IRS or the courts of the taxpayer's tax liability is not a necessary condition for establishing an understatement of that liability. Where the understatement is due to the negligent or intentional disregard of the income tax rules or regulations, the penalty is $100. The penalty does not extend to the employer of a tax return preparer solely by reason of the relationship. In the event of a trial of the question of the proper assessment of this penalty, the preparer has the burden of proving he was not at fault. This approach resembles that of the Securities Act of 1933 in respect to imposition of civil liability for a material misstatement or omission.

Where it is found that the preparer willfully understated the taxpayer's liability, the penalty is $500 per return. However, the IRS has the burden of proving that the understatement was willful. Where the willful understatement of liability also constitutes a negligent or intentional disregard for the rules and regulations, as it usually will, the combined penalty is a maximum of $500.

The 1982 Tax Act (TEFRA) added certain other liability provisions for tax return preparers, for example, where the preparer *knowingly* aids in the preparation of a return which results in an understatement of taxpayer's liability. The fine is $1,000 and it also imposed penalties on a person who promotes an abusive tax shelter. The 1984 Tax Reform Act also added additional obligations and another penalty. A return preparer is required to advise taxpayers of the requirements that adequate contemporaneous records must be kept in order to substantiate certain business expenses, and the preparer must obtain a written confirmation from the taxpayer that the requirements are met. Failure to comply with these requirements will result in a $25 penalty.

The 1976 Tax Reform Act also established new procedures for return preparers. Noncompliance with these procedures subjects the preparer to the following penalties:

$25 for failure to furnish a copy of the completed return to the taxpayer

$50 for failure to retain a copy of all returns prepared or alternately a list of all taxpayers and their identification number

$25 for failure to reflect the preparer's identification number on the tax return

$25 for failure to sign the return

$500 for each taxpayer's income tax check endorsed or otherwise negotiated by the preparer

Finally, the IRS has the power to seek injunctive relief, enjoining a preparer from engaging in prohibited practices or if there have been repeated violations of the proscribed practices, the guilty party may be enjoined from practicing as an income tax return preparer.

The specific practices of an income tax return preparer that can initiate an action to enjoin on the part of the IRS are:

(a)   Conduct subject to disclosure requirement penalties and understatement-of-taxpayer-liability penalties;

(b)   Conduct subject to criminal penalties under the Internal Revenue Code;

(c)   Misrepresentation of (1) the return preparer's eligibility to practice before the IRS or (2) his or her experience or education as an income tax return preparer;

(d)   Guarantee of payment of a tax refund or of allowance of a tax credit; and

(e)   Other fraudulent or deceptive conduct that substantially interferes with proper administration of the internal revenue laws.

(i)   Duty of Inquiry: Case of First Impression.   The United States Court of Appeals decision in *Brockhouse v. United States* is the first reported decision involving the tax return preparer penalties for negligent understatement.

Brockhouse v. United States and Comments
749 F. 2d 1248
(7th Cir. 1984)

Before COFFEY and FLAUM, Circuit Judges, and CAMPBELL, Senior District Judge.*

FLAUM, Circuit Judge.

This appeal raises the issue of whether the tax return preparer negligence penalty, section 6694(a) of the Internal Revenue Code,[1] can be assessed against a preparer who understates income tax liability because he relied solely on information supplied to him by the taxpayers. The Internal Revenue Service ("IRS") assessed a penalty against appellant John Brockhouse. Pursuant to section 6694(c), the appellant paid 15% of the penalty and sued for a refund. The district court, 577 F.Supp. 55, denied the refund. For the reasons stated below, we affirm.

I.

The appellant is a certified public accountant. In January 1979, he was hired by the CPA firm of Goldman, Weiss, Gelman & Sered ("Goldman, Weiss"). For several years Goldman, Weiss had prepared the income tax returns of Rubert-Busch, M.D., S.C., an Illinois professional corporation, and those of Dr. Robert Busch, the corporation's sole shareholder. The appellant's first contact with the tax affairs of Rubert-Busch and Dr. Busch was in March 1979.

The appellant prepared Rubert-Busch's corporate income tax return for its fiscal year ended February 28, 1979. He used a trial balance sheet prepared by the corporation's bookkeeper. The trial balance sheet showed loans to the corporation from Dr. Busch and

from a bank. It also showed that the corporation had made payments for interest expense; however, it did not show whether any of the interest had been paid to Dr. Busch.

The appellant also prepared the 1978 income tax return for Dr. and Mrs. Busch. Goldman, Weiss had adopted a procedure of sending a data questionnaire to its individual income tax clients. The client was either to complete and return the questionnaire or to use it as a guide in collecting the information necessary to prepare the return. The Busches chose not to complete a questionnaire. Rather, the information was supplied by the corporation's business manager or bookkeeper. The information was then entered on input sheets of an outside computer service. The appellant reviewed the sheets and compared them with the information supplied and the information shown on the Busches' 1977 return. There were no items shown on the 1977 return that were not accounted for in the 1978 return. The appellant signed the 1978 return and sent it to the Busches for signature and filing. The appellant never inquired whether any of the interest expense shown on the corporate trial balance sheet had been paid to the Busches.

In May 1980, an IRS agent began an examination of the corporate return. The agent requested an analysis of the corporation's interest expense account. The appellant went to the corporation's offices and examined the general ledger and disbursements journal. From this, he learned that the corporation had paid interest to Dr. Busch. The appellant promptly brought the omission to the attention of the IRS agent.

The corporation had paid Dr. Busch interest income in the amount of $15,291.20. The Busches had not reported the income on their 1978 return. This resulted in an underpayment of federal income taxes in the amount of $10,538.76.

The IRS assessed a $100 tax preparer penalty against the appellant. Pursuant to section 6694(c), the appellant paid $15 and

---

[1] Section 6694(a) provides: (a) Negligent or Intentional Disregard of Rules and Regulations.—If any part of any understatement of liability with respect to any return or claim for refund is due to the negligent or intentional disregard of rules and regulations by any person who is an income tax return preparer with respect to such return or claim, such person shall pay a penalty of $100 with respect to such return or claim.

filed a claim for refund. The refund was disallowed, and he filed suit in district court.

The district court denied the refund. It found that the appellant was negligent in omitting interest income from the return. The court found that he knew that the corporation had borrowed money from Dr. Busch and also that it had made interest payments. The court held that under these circumstances, a reasonable, prudent person would have made inquiries to determine whether any interest was paid to Dr. Busch. The court held that appellant was negligent in failing to obtain a completed data questionnaire from the Busches. Finally, the court relied on the factors listed in Revenue Procedure 80–40, which deals with liability under section 6694(a), to hold that the appellant had negligently disregarded a tax rule or regulation and thus was liable.

On appeal, the appellant argues that section 6694(a) does not apply to a tax return preparer's negligence in gathering facts from the taxpayer. He contends that section 6694(a) only applies where a preparer negligently misapplies a rule or regulation to a known item, and that where the preparer does not know of an item, he is not required to make inquiries or verify data. The appellant maintains that even if section 6694(a) does apply to a negligent failure to gather facts, his actions in this case were not negligent.

II.

Section 6694(a) allows a penalty of $100 to be assessed against an income tax return preparer whose negligent disregard of rules or regulations results in an understatement of tax liability.[2] The preparer has the burden of proving the absence of negligence. Treas.Reg. § 1.6694–1(a)(5).

Section 6694 was one of several provisions added by the Tax Reform Act of 1976 to regulate income tax return preparers. Congress generally was concerned with deterring abusive practices by preparers. Prior to 1976, preparers were subject only to criminal penalties for willfully aiding or assisting in the preparation of a fraudulent return. Congress found that these criminal penalties were inadequate. *See* H.R.Rep. No. 658, 94th Cong., 2d Sess. 273–76, *reprinted in* 1976 U.S.Code Cong. & Ad.News 2897 at 3169–71. Although Congress was concerned with abuses by "commercial" preparers—those who are not accountants or lawyers—it determined that regulation of all preparers was appropriate. *Id.* at 274–75, 1976 U.S.Code Cong. & Ad.News at 3169–70. Section 6694 was added primarily to deter preparers from engaging in negligent or fraudulent practices designed to understate tax liability. *Id.* at 278, 1976 U.S.Code Cong. & Ad.News at 3174. However, Congress did not limit the applicability of section 6694(a) to situations involving disregard of rules or regulations applicable to the facts as provided by the taxpayer. Rather, section 6694(a) applies generally to "negligent disregard." We therefore hold that a tax preparer negligently disregards a rule or regulation under section 6694(a) if his or her negligent failure to inquire into information provided by the taxpayer results in the filing of a return that violates a rule or regulation.

To determine whether a tax preparer's actions constitute negligence under section 6694(a), we must first determine the applicable standard of care. Negligence in this context is defined generally as a "lack of due care or failure to do what a reasonable and ordinarily prudent person would do under the circumstances." *Marcello v. Commissioner*, 380 F.2d 499, 506 (5th Cir.1967), *cert. denied*, 389 U.S. 1044, 88 S.Ct. 787, 19 L.Ed.2d 835 (1968); *see also Zmuda v. Commissioner*, 731 F.2d 1417, 1422 (9th Cir.1984).[3] The regulation under section 6694(b), relating to

---

[2] Section 6694(a) also applies to intentional disregard of rules or regulations. There is no claim that the appellant's actions were intentional, and thus we limit our discussion to negligent disregard.

[3] These cases were decided under § 6653(a), relating to disregard of rules or regulations by taxpayers on their own returns. Congress has indicated that § 6694(a) is to be interpreted in a manner similar to § 6653(a). *See* H.R.Rep. No. 658, 94th Cong., 2d Sess. 278, *reprinted in* 1976 U.S.Code Cong. & Ad.News 3174.

willful disregard of rules or regulations, expressly provides that a preparer may not rely without verification on information supplied by the taxpayer if that information appears incomplete or incorrect. Treas.Reg. § 1.6694–1(b)(2)(ii). The regulation under section 6694(a) does not contain such an express provision, but it does provide that a preparer is not negligent if he or she "exercises due diligence in an effort to apply the rules and regulations to the information given" to him or her. Treas.Reg. § 1.6694–1(a)(1). This due diligence requirement means that a preparer must act as a reasonable, prudent person with respect to the information supplied to the preparer. We hold that if the information supplied would lead a reasonable, prudent preparer to seek additional information, it is negligent not to do so. A reasonable, prudent preparer would inquire as to additional information where it is apparent that the information supplied was incorrect or incomplete and it is simple to collect the necessary additional information.

We find this standard of care to be consistent with the congressional purpose behind section 6694(a). Congress passed section 6694 as part of an attempt to curb abusive practices by preparers. For a preparer to ignore the implications of information furnished where the error is apparent and simple to correct would be an abusive practice. We note that the IRS has interpreted section 6694(a) to apply to situations where the preparer has reason to know that the information supplied is incomplete or incorrect. See Rev.Rul. 80–265, 1980–2 C.B. 378 (under section 6694(a), although the preparer is not required to audit information, "the preparer may not ignore the implications of information furnished to the preparer") (citing guidelines set forth in Rev.Proc. 80–40, 1980–2 C.B. 774–75).

Applying the standard of care outlined above to the facts in this case, we agree with the district court that the appellant was negligent in failing to inquire whether any of the interest paid by the corporation had been paid to Dr. Busch. The error involved was relatively apparent. The appellant was aware that Dr. Busch had made loans to the corporation and that the corporation had made interest payments.[4] This should have alerted him to the possibility that interest had been paid to Dr. Busch. The appellant also was aware that the Busches did not report any interest paid on the loans made to the corporation. This should have alerted him to the possibility that the information supplied to him was not complete. The fact that a loan from a shareholder to a corporation could bear interest and that such interest would be income to the shareholder is not uncommon. Moreover, the appellant could have discovered the error merely by asking the corporation or the Busches whether any of the interest paid by the corporation had been paid to the Busches or by requesting and examining the corporate ledger. A prudent preparer would have inquired about interest payments on the loans rather than ignoring the implications of the information furnished.[5] Appellant's negligent failure to inquire led him to disregard the applicability of section 61, which provides that gross income includes interest income.[6] Thus, appellant is liable under section 6694(a).

Affirmed.

WILLIAM J. CAMPBELL, Senior District Judge, dissenting.

---

[4] The appellant contends that there is no proof that he received the corporate trial balance sheet before he prepared the individual return. We do not regard the order in which he prepared the returns as significant. Even if he prepared the individual return first, the corporate trial balance sheet should have alerted him to the possibility of interest payments to Dr. Busch. At that time, he should have made the appropriate inquiries, recognizing that an amended individual return might be necessary.

[5] We do not regard the appellant's failure to obtain a completed data questionnaire from the Busches as significant in determining whether he was negligent. The parties stipulated that a client did not have to fill out the questionnaire but rather could use it as a guide. Stipulation of Facts ¶ 10.

[6] The appellant argues that § 7216, providing sanctions for unauthorized disclosure of information by tax return preparers, prohibited him from using information obtained from the corporate trial balance sheet in attempting to prepare the individual return. However, it appears that the regulations permit such disclosure. Tres.Reg. § 301.7216–2.

I regret that I cannot agree with the majority either in its construction of the statute or in its application to this case. The majority utilizes a general negligence analysis which is not justified by the language of the statute or the legislative history. In doing so it has given a broad interpretation to the statute in contravention of the principle that penal statutes are to be strictly construed. Furthermore, the majority has failed to present all the material facts and thus does not properly analyze the appellant's conduct. While the penalty assessed is quite modest, the sanction is important to the professional standing of the appellant. Moreover, this is the first published case involving this aspect of 26 U.S.C. § 6694(a). For these reasons, it is important that this case receive careful consideration.

The facts were presented to the district court in the form of a lengthy written stipulation. As noted by the majority, it is undisputed that the trial balance sheet indicated loans to the corporation from Dr. Busch and included entries for interest expense.[7] However, the balance sheet also noted that Rubert-Busch, M.D., S.C. borrowed money from the Michigan Avenue National Bank. The data submitted to Brockhouse did not indicate to whom the interest was paid as that information was irrelevant to the preparation of the corporate tax returns. Furthermore, the Busches' 1977 income tax return, which the appellant compared with the data for the 1978 return, accurately reflected no income from interest on loans to the corporation. These facts are crucial to an evaluation of appellant's conduct because they indicate that the information presented to him did not create the implication that Dr. Busch received interest income from the corporation in 1978. It is a common business practice for sole shareholders to make interest-free loans to their corporations. Such transactions can be compared to taking money out of one pocket and putting it in the other pocket. The data presented to Brockhouse was entirely consistent with this scenario. Therefore, I believe it is overstating the case to say that appellant ignored the implications of the information provided to him.

The majority notes that the appellant prepared the income tax return of Dr. and Mrs. Busch without requiring them to comply with the Goldman, Weiss data questionnaire procedure.[8] The district judge relied heavily on this fact as evidence of Brockhouse's lack of due diligence. However, the information was given to the appellant by Robert Eubank, the corporation's business manager and Dr. Busch's personal financial consultant. The data was prepared by the corporation's part-time bookkeeper who had a degree in law and business and was employed on a full-time basis by a national firm of certified public accountants. The fact that Brockhouse did not require compliance with the questionnaire procedure is not compelling, or even persuasive, evidence of negligence where the information was gathered by experienced specialists and not laypersons.

Turning to the statute in issue, the majority utilizes a general negligence analysis in determining the applicability of the penalty. They state:

> Congress did not limit the applicability of section 6694 to situations involving disregard of rules or regulations applicable to the facts as provided by the taxpayer. Rather, it applies generally to "negligent disregard." p. 1251

I do not understand what "negligent disregard" in the abstract is, but I do know that such a selective editing of the statute is not supported by the legislative history. The majority relies on *Marcello v. Commissioner*, 380 F.2d 499 (5th Cir.1967), *cert. den.*, 389 U.S. 1044, 88 S.Ct. 787, 19 L.Ed.2d 835 (1968), a case applying 26 U.S.C. § 6653(a), as authority for the application of a general negligence

---

[7] The stipulation of the parties reads: This trial balance sheet contained an item showing loans made by the Corporation to its sole shareholder. Stip ¶ 14. This is apparently an error as it is undisputed that Dr. Busch made the loans to the corporation.

[8] The majority indicates in footnote 6 that it did not consider this fact to be significant in evaluating Brockhouse's conduct. I agree with them on that point and I discuss the issue only because the district court found that evidence to be persuasive.

standard. The justification for such reliance is provided in a footnote:

> Congress has indicated that § 6694(a) is to be interpreted in a manner similar to § 6653(a). *See* H.R.Rep. No. 658, 94th Cong., 2d Sess. 278, *reprinted in* 1976 U.S.Code Cong. & Ad.News at 3174. fn. 4

This statement is an oversimplification. The penalty provision in § 6653 applies to tax-payers for under-payments "due to *negligence* or intentional disregard of rules or regulations" [Emphasis supplied]. The penalty provision in § 6694 applies to *"negligent* or intentional disregard of rules or regulations"* [Emphasis supplied]. Thus, under § 6653 two discrete standards of conduct are involved: general negligence and intentional disregard of rules or regulations, *see discussion Marcello, supra*, 380 F.2d at 505–507. However, under § 6694 there must be a disregard of rules or regulations (either negligent or intentional) in order to impose the penalty.

Whenever § 6653 is referred to in the legislative history of § 6694 its relevance is limited to the "disregard of rules or regulations" provision:

> The penalty applies generally to every negligent or intentional disregard of such regulations and rulings except that a good faith dispute by an income tax return preparer about an interpretation of a statute (expressed in regulations or rulings) is not considered a negligent or intentional disregard of rulings and regulations. The provision is thus to be interpreted in a manner similar to the interpretation given the provision under present law (sec. 6653(a)) relating to the disregard of rules and regulations by taxpayers on their own returns.

H.R.Rep. No. 94–658, 94th Cong. 2d Sess. 278, reprinted in 1976 U.S.Code & Admin.News at 3174; *see also*, S.Rep. No. 94–938, 94th Cong. 2d Sess. 355, reprinted in 1976 U.S.Code & Admin.News at 3784; H.R.Rep. No. 95–1800, 95th Cong.2d Sess. 284, reprinted in 1978 U.S.Code & Admin.News at 7279. The legislative history further indicates that Congress did not intend that all negligence would be subject to penalties under § 6694(a):

> [T]he bill establishes new penalties for certain negligent or willful attempts to understate a taxpayer's tax liability. H.R.Rep. No. 94–658, *supra* p. 278; *see also*, S.Rep. No. 94–938, *supra* p. 355.

Such a construction does not contravene the legislative purpose of the penalty:

> These penalties are primarily aimed at deterring income tax return preparers who prepare a large number of returns from engaging in negligent or fraudulent practices designed to understate a taxpayer's liability.

H.R.Rep. No. 94–658, *supra* p. 278; *see also*, S.Rep. No. 94–938, *supra* p. 355; *see, e.g., United States v. Ernst & Whinney*, 735 F.2d 1296 (11th Cir.1984).

In summary, the language of the statute does not provide that the penalty applies to all acts of negligence by an income tax preparer. While clearly § 6694(a) is modelled after § 6653(a) there is a significant difference in the terms of the statutes and we must assume that that distinction was intended by Congress. This conclusion is buttressed by a review of the legislative history. There is an additional consideration which reinforces, and to my mind solidifies, this analysis: *odioso restinjenda sunt* (translation: things odious must be strictly construed). This ancient principle of common law is so venerated that it is even applied to the tax gatherer:

> We are here concerned with a taxing Act which imposes a penalty. The law is settled that "penal statutes are to be construed strictly," *Federal Communications Commission v. American Broadcasting Co.*, 347 U.S. 284, 296, 74 S.Ct. 593, 601, 98 L.Ed. 699, and that one "is not to be subjected to a penalty unless the words of the statute plainly impose it," [Footnote and Citations omitted]. *Commissioner v. Acker*, 361 U.S. 87, 91, 80 S.Ct. 144, 147, 4 L.Ed.2d 127 (1959).

Thus, we are strictly limited to determining whether Brockhouse "disregarded a rule or regulation" either negligently or intentionally. The standard provided in the IRS's regulations is:

> A preparer is not considered to have negligently or intentionally disregarded a rule or regulation if the preparer exercises due

diligence in an effort to apply the rules and regulations to the information given to the preparer to determine the taxpayer's correct liability for tax. 26 C.F.R. § 1.6694–1(a).

In this case, there is no question that Brockhouse properly applied the rules and regulations to the information he received. The underpayment of tax occurred because he was not informed that Dr. Busch received interest on his loans to the corporation. The issue then becomes whether he was justified in relying on the information provided. Rev.Proc. 80–40 provides:

> .03 The penalty under section 6694(a) of the Code generally will not apply where a preparer in good faith relies without verification upon information furnished by the taxpayer. Thus, the preparer is not required to audit, examine or review books and records, business operations, or documents or other evidence in order to verify independently the taxpayer's information.

This language further exculpates the appellant. There is a caveat, however:

> [T]he preparer may not ignore the implications of information furnished to the preparer or which was actually known by the preparer. The preparer shall make reasonable inquiries if the information as furnished appears to be incorrect or incomplete. Rev.Proc. 80–40.

I have no quarrel with this standard of conduct, but I do not think the appellant violated it in this case. It is undisputed that Brockhouse did not have any personal knowledge of the financial operations of Rubert-Busch, M.D., S.C. Furthermore, I do not believe we can find that the information provided to him appeared incorrect or incomplete. The corporation's trial balance sheet, the Busches' income data, and their 1977 income tax return are all consistent with a situation in which a sole shareholder made interest-free loans to

his corporation. There was no data presented to Brockhouse which contradicted that common scenario. Thus, I do not believe that we can find that the appellant ignored the implication of the information provided to him.[9]

In conclusion, I believe there is no basis for finding that Brockhouse disregarded any rule or regulation of the IRS. That is the conduct described in the statute and that is the conduct that Congress intended to penalize. If Congress had intended to sanction all negligence by income tax preparers, it would have said so. But it did not and we should not redraft the legislation. We are duty bound to apply the plain language of the statute and to construe it narrowly. Under those guidelines I believe it is clear that the imposition of the penalty in this case is in error and the District Court should be reversed.

---

[9] Revenue Ruling 80–265 presents two factual situations similar to ours with slight, but significant, differences. In Situation 1, the income tax preparer had no knowledge of any loans by the sole shareholder to the corporation, although he did deduct an interest expense on the corporate return. Subsequently, it was determined by the IRS that the shareholder had loaned money to the corporation and received interest income on it. The Revenue Ruling concludes that the penalty provision of § 6694(a) does not apply to the income tax preparer in this situation. In Situation 2 the information relating to the corporation indicated that the shareholder had received interest on loans to the corporation. However, the data provided the income tax preparer with respect to the shareholder's individual return did not reflect interest income. The failure to report that item of income on the shareholder's tax return was determined to justify imposition of the penalty under § 6694(a). The reasoning was that in Situation 2 the income tax preparer had reason to believe that the information provided to him was incomplete, while in Situation 1 he did not. Our case falls in between those two situations and, utilizing the same analysis, the penalty should not apply.

1.   The court of appeals affirmed the decision of the district court which held that "under these circumstances, a reasonable, prudent person would have made inquiries to determine whether any interest was paid to Dr. Busch." The trial court also ruled that the tax return preparer was "negligent in failing to obtain a completed data questionnaire" from the taxpayers.

2. The district court ruled that it is the preparer's obligation to audit information provided by a client even though that information appears complete and correct. The tax return preparer urged the court of appeals to reverse the decision, arguing that a preparer "is not required to make inquiries or verify data." The court of appeals rejected the preparer's argument.

3. The court of appeals in *Brockhouse* v. *United States* held that the preparer breached a duty of inquiry in circumstances where "if the information supplied would lead a reasonable, prudent preparer to seek additonal information, it is negligent not to do so."

4. One of the more perplexing issues involves the question of whether a tax advisor in an accounting firm should be bound by relevant knowledge and information acquired by his audit partners during their audit of the taxpayer, but not communicated to the tax advisor. Shouldn't the tax advisor be bound by his firm's collective knowledge of the client's business affairs, particularly if this information would have a substantial impact on the tax services and advice rendered? Isn't there a duty of inquiry imposed on a tax advisor to follow-up with his partners regarding relevant, material client information which impacts on his tax advice? Many are the expert witnesses who will testify that an accounting firm's left hand should know what the right hand has done!

¶ 8.02   Tax Advisory Services: A Duty to Update?

In creating a duty to correct the court in *Fischer v. Kletz, supra (¶ 6.03[1])*, relied upon an established rule of law which provides that

> one party to a business transaction is under a duty to exercise reasonable care to disclose to the other before the transaction is consummated. . . . (b) any subsequently acquired information which he recognizes as making untrue or misleading a previous representation which when made was true or believed to be so.

With respect to the significance between updating versus correcting a representation which is known to be false, the court in *Fischer v. Kletz* stated that "this distinction would not seem crucial," holding:

> it should be noted that, in [the] *Loewer* [case], the information contained in one representation was made untrue as a result of a change in the performance of the brewery; while, in the instant case, the representation was rendered false not by a change in conditions but by a discovery that the information on which the representation was based was itself false and misleading. This distinction would not seem crucial, however, for the impact upon the person who relies on the representation is the same: he is induced to act in reliance upon a representation which the representer knows has become false. In short, the manner in which the representation is transformed into a misrepresentation should not determine the right of a plaintiff to maintain an action for nondisclosure.

In the areas of tax advisory services, difficult problems may arise when the advice given is no longer accurate because of materially changing conditions. For example, circumstances could arise where an accountant issues an opinion letter regarding the tax circumstances of a proposed investment. Assume that subsequent to the issuance of the opinion letter the accountant discovers that certain material facts upon which the advice was predicated have significantly changed and thus materially affect the opinion.

Although the accountant's tax opinion was correct when issued, the accountant now knows that anyone who relies upon it could be misled because of the changed factual conditions. If the accountant determines not to "update" the opinion letter, does the accountant buy a lawsuit? Isn't this a situation where an innocent investor "is induced to act in reliance upon a representation which the representor knows has become false." As the court held in *Fischer v. Kletz*, the "manner in which the representation is transformed into a misrepresentation should not determine the right of a plaintiff to maintain an action for nondisclosure."

The cases which follow further illustrate the duty of a tax advisor to disaffirm a prior opinion which others are relying upon, upon discovery of facts or changes in the law which render the opinion incorrect or invalid.

Sharp v. Coopers & Lybrand
491 F. Supp. 879 (1979) *aff'd* 649
F.2d 175 (1981) cert. denied 102 S. Ct. 1427 (1982)

JOSEPH S. LORD, III, Chief Judge.

Plaintiffs, investors in an oil drilling venture, alleged in this class action that the defendant, a major accounting firm, is liable to them for misstatements in several opinion letters which advised them as to the supposed tax circumstances of those investments.

Plaintiffs are persons who purchased limited partnership interests in oil wells to be drilled in Kansas and Ohio, of which Westland Minerals Corporation (WMC) was general partner and promoter. As a result of criminal fraud by WMC, many of these wells were never drilled and much of the invested money was diverted to WMC's own use. Economic Concepts, Inc. (ECI), the selling agent for these limited partnerships, and WMC sought to engage in April 1971 the services of defendant in rendering opinions as to the federal income tax consequences of these limited partnerships. In July the defendant decided to write such opinion letters, and on July 22, 1971, an opinion letter signed by a Coopers & Lybrand partner in its name was sent to Charles Raymond, president of WMC, stating that "based solely on the facts contained [in the WMC Limited Partnership Agreement] and without verification by us" a limited partner who contributed $65,000 in cash could deduct

approximately $128,000 on his 1971 tax return. That letter was drafted by defendant's employee Herman Higgins, who was at that time a tax supervisor working directly under the supervision of four partners of defendant. The letter was written specifically for the use of one Muhammed Ali, a potential WMC investor, with regard to reducing the amount of taxes that would be withheld from a fight purse. In early October 1971 Higgins told David Wright, a partner in the defendant firm, that copies of the July 22 letter had been shown to individual investors besides Ali, and Wright determined that a letter which would be seen by other investors should be more complete. Higgins redrafted the opinion letter, and on October 11, 1971, defendant sent another opinion letter, signed in defendant's name by Wright, and a covering letter to Raymond.

The jury found that the October 11 letter contained both material misrepresentations and material omissions, and that Higgins acted either recklessly or with intent to defraud in preparing the letters. Much of the evidence concerning those misrepresentations and omissions and their recklessness came from plaintiffs' expert witness, Professor Bernard Wolfman of the Harvard Law School, a specialist in federal income taxation. Most of his testimony was not rebutted by the defendant. Professor Wolfman explained the principles behind this tax shelter: a taxpayer who in 1971 contributed $25,000 to a partnership involved in a bona fide oil drilling venture, which then obtained for each $25,000 contribution an additional $25,000 bona fide bank loan that was fully secured by partnership property (the as yet undrilled wells) and then expended all of that $50,000 for drilling, could under the law applicable in 1971 deduct the full $50,000 from his taxable income. The effect would be to accelerate the tax deduction available to the investor in 1971. Professor Wolfman's expert testimony in concert with other evidence provided the basis for the jury's findings that the October 11 letter misrepresented or omitted to state material facts in at least three ways.

The jury concluded that, while Higgins caused the material misrepresentations and omissions in the October 11 letter recklessly or with an intent to defraud, no partner of the defendant firm caused any misstatements with such scienter. It also found no misrepresentations or omissions in the July 22 letter, so that liability is limited to those relying on the October 11 letter.

. . .

The jury found that the October 11 letter contained both material misrepresentations and material omissions, and that Herman Higgins, the defendant's employee who wrote the letter, acted either recklessly or with intent to defraud in preparing that letter. The jury also found that the July 22 letter did not contain material misrepresentations or omissions. We therefore stated . . . , although this matter was not briefed or raised, that "liability can arise only from reliance on the October 11 letter." . . . The plaintiffs have now argued, and we are persuaded, that those investors who purchased their securities *after* October 11, 1971 in reliance on *either* opinion letter may pursue their claims for damages. Careful analysis of the evidence presented at trial and of the jury's verdict compels this decision.

The plaintiffs' evidence, offered to prove that *both* opinion letters were fraudulent, fell into three categories. *First*, the plaintiffs of-

fered expert testimony that the letters were written recklessly because they failed to state certain material facts concerning the nonrecourse loan which the letter assumed lending institutions would make to Westland Minerals Corporation (WMC), the general partner and promoter of the venture in which the plaintiffs had invested. *Second*, the plaintiffs introduced evidence which showed that by October 11, 1971, Higgins had acquired certain knowledge of a fraudulent loan scheme entered into by WMC. The plaintiffs' expert testified that if Higgins had written the opinion letters with this knowledge, then they contained a number of material misrepresentations. *Third*, the plaintiffs established that by October 11, 1971, Higgins was working closely with Economic Concepts, Inc., (ECI), the selling agent for WMC. According to the plaintiffs' expert, Higgins' failure to disclose this relationship in his tax opinion letters was a material omission.

There is no question that the October 11 letter is nearly a verbatim copy of the July 22 letter, with the addition of two final paragraphs not relevant to the fraud which was perpetrated in this case. Thus, it is clear that the jury's finding that the October 11 letter contained material misrepresentations and omissions could not have been based on the first category of evidence (*see supra*), for *both* letters were identical in this respect. Therefore, the only rational explanation for the jury's verdict is that it was based upon the evidence concerning Higgins' knowledge of WMC's fraud and his connection with ECI, and that the jury found that Higgins acquired this knowledge and began working for ECI *after* July 22 but before October 11. In essence, the jury's verdict represents a finding that the July 22 letter did not contain material misrepresentations or omissions *when written*, but that the *same letter* became fraudulent by October 11 due to information acquired by the author between those two dates. In other words, the requisite scienter for §10(b) liability was missing on July 22, but was acquired by October 11.

The plaintiffs argue that reliance by an investor on the July 22 letter after October 11 should create liability, for after the latter date the author of the July 22 letter either knew it to be false or acted in reckless disregard of the truth. Given such knowledge, or reckless conduct, the author (and therefore the defendant) should be liable for a breach of the duty to correct, after October 11, what had *become* a fraudulent opinion letter. This duty to correct a previously truthful but now fraudulent opinion arises from §10(b) of the Securities Exchange Act of 1934. . . . The purpose of that statute, and the Rule promulgated thereunder, is to protect purchasers and sellers of securities from "*any* device, scheme, or artifice to defraud. . . ." Rule 10b-5(a) (emphasis added). As has been recognized, "[f]raud may be accomplished [not only] by false statements, [but also by] a failure to correct a misleading impression left by statements already made. . . ." *Cochran v. Channing Corp.*, 211 F. Supp. 239, 243 (S.D.N.Y. 1962).

The duty to correct a previously truthful but now false opinion was recognized in [a prior case]. In imposing 10b-5 liability, the district court in that case stated that

> The simple fact is that Thomas was induced by Lesser in January of 1968 to believe that his stock in Duralite was worthless, and worse still, that Thomas' position in Duralite had been transformed into a holding which, by reason of his personal loan and his company's (Edco) indebtedness, could be momentarily translated into a liability. This information, the evidence indicates, was accurate and truthful when Lesser gave it in January of 1968. It certainly was *no longer accurate* when Lesser, Thomas and Edwards met in April, and as of June 18, 1968, when the contract of sale was made, it was totally false. Yet Thomas sold his stock on the basis of the representation that Duralite still hovered on the edge of bankruptcy, and Lesser stood by silently and let him do so.

Similarly, on our case, the defendant's July 22 opinion, though truthful when made, became materially misleading and therefore fraudulent sometime on or before October 11, due to knowledge as acquired by the author after July 22. The failure by the author, and thus the defendant, to correct the impression given by the July 22 letter renders the defendant liable to those who invested after October 11 (the date the duty to correct arose) in reliance on the July 22 letter.

The defendant does not dispute the plaintiff's contention that the two letters are materially identical or that it violated its duty to correct the original letter once it was rendered fraudulent. Rather, it maintains that the plaintiffs' argument in favor of allowing those who relied on the July 22 letter after October 11 to recover damages is in reality an untimely motion for judgment n.o.v. We disagree; what the plaintiffs are now seeking from us is a ruling *in accordance* with the verdict. The above discussion of the verdict is the only rational explanation of the jury's distinction between two materially identical letters. The plaintiffs have not asked us to hold, nor do we now hold, that the July 22 letter, when written, contained material misrepresentations and/or omissions. Such a holding *would* be one not in accordance with the jury verdict, and prohibited as an untimely grant of judgment n.o.v. What we do now hold, however, is that the July 22 letter, although truthful when issued, became, according to the jury's verdict, fraudulent not later than October 11, and was unquestionably left uncorrected by the defendant. Therefore, any investor who purchased his or her limited partnership interest after October 11, 1971 in reliance on *either* the July 22 or October 11 opinion letter is now entitled to pursue his or her individual claim for damages.

Bancroft v. Indemnity Insurance Co.
203 F. Supp. 49
(W.D. La. 1962)

BEN C. DAWKINS, Chief Judge.

Presented here is an action for damages arising from an alleged breach of contract involving professional accounting services. It is brought by T. O. Bancroft, president of Bancroft Bag Factory, Inc., and his wife, of

Monroe, Louisiana, against the professional liability insurer of a firm of Certified Public Accountants practicing in Monroe.

The facts forming the basis of the suit occured during an accountant-client relationship which had existed between plaintiffs and defendant's insured since approximately 1938, the insured having been employed originally by plaintiffs while Bancroft was operating as an individual, then as a partnership, and later as principal stockholder of Bancroft Bag Factory, Inc., and Bancroft Paper Company, Inc.

May 23, 1955, Bancroft directed a letter to a member of the insured firm in which he explained that several stockholders in the bag factory, who were children of the Bancroft family, owed money to the bag factory and that a plan had occurred to him which possibly would effect a means of payment with minimum tax circumstances. The following question was asked:

> T. O. Bancroft, Sr. owns a certain amount of stock in the Bancroft Paper Company, Inc. This stock was acquired during the married life of T. O. Bancroft, Sr., and Vada Speed Bancroft, and is community property. Would it be possible, and not in violation of any law, for a sufficient amount of this stock to be sold to the Bancroft Bag Factory, Inc., and one-half of the sale price to be credited to Vada Speed Bancroft account on Bancroft Bag Factory, Inc. books, and one half sale price credited to T. O. Bancroft, Sr. on Bancroft Bag Factory, Inc. books, and these credits could set-off the debit charges by gifts from Vada and myself to the three children at the rate of legal gift limits per year until the accounts are balanced.
>
> The Bancroft Paper Company stock is Par $100.00 per share, and is maintained at that value by the distribution of dividends and bonuses each year.
>
> Please let me have your opinion in writing concerning this proposal.

The insured C.P.A. replied May 25, 1955, in a letter addressed to Bancroft, in the following language:

> Reply to your letter of May 23, 1955, is made as follows:
>
> You and Mrs. Bancroft propose to sell a certain amount of Bancroft Paper Company, Inc. stock at $100.00 per share to Bancroft Bag Factory, Inc. We understand that Bancroft Paper Company, Inc. stock has been kept at a book value of about $100.00 per share by the payment of dividends and that its selling price is $100.00 per share and your cost is the same amount per share. In our opinion, there would be no Federal or Louisiana income tax on the sale of the stock.
>
> We further understand that you are not to receive cash for the stock but that a credit will be set up for you and Mrs. Bancroft on the books of the Bancroft Bag Factory, Inc. Each calendar year you propose to make a gift of $3,000.00 to each of your three children by crediting their account due the Bancroft Bag Factory, Inc. and charging your account. Mrs. Bancroft will do likewise. The total gifts to the three children will be $18,000.00 annually. Such a transaction would not involve any Federal Gift Tax as a person may give $3,000 (the maximum annual exclusion) per year to as many individuals as he may choose without gift tax.

Relying on this advice, September 15, 1955, plaintiffs sold 410 shares of their stock in the paper company to the bag factory for $41,000.00; and October 18, 1957, they sold an additional 187 shares of paper company stock to the bag factory for $18,700.00. These two transactions were accomplished by bookkeeping entries on the accounts of the two corporations, the two sums being credited to plaintiffs' accounts on the books of the bag factory, thereby satisfying their children's indebtedness and leaving a credit balance. Following the 1955 transaction, plaintiffs' accounts in the bag factory were debited for $8,149.17 and the accounts of their children were credited with an equal amount to reflect gifts from the parents to the children.

In 1959, the Internal Revenue Service audited plaintiffs' income tax returns, including those for 1955 and 1957, and subsequently notified them that the two stock transactions were subject to the provisions of Section 304 of the 1954 Internal Revenue Code; that the sums received by plaintiffs from the sales of stock in 1955 and 1957 would be treated, for tax purposes, as dividends and taxed accordingly. The government's position was summarized in a letter dated December 1, 1959, from the office of the District Director, Internal Revenue Service, addressed to plaintiffs. After listing net adjustments (increases) to taxable income in the sum of $41,000.00 and describing them as "Dividends from Bancroft Bag Factory, Inc.," the letter explained:

> (1) The sale of 410 shares of stock of Bancroft Paper Co., Inc., in year 1955 to Bancroft Bag Factory, Inc., and the sale of 187 shares of stock of Bancroft Paper Co., Inc., to Bancroft Bag Factory, Inc., in year 1957, by the taxpayers, constitutes a distribution in redemption of the stock of Bancroft Bag Factory, Inc., in the amount of the sales proceeds. The proposed adjustment is to include in income the dividends resulting from the redemption. See Sec. 304 of the Internal Revenue Code of 1954. The assessment of additional tax in year 1955 is not barred by the statute of limitations because of the omission of over 25% of the amount of gross income stated in the return. See Sec. 6501 (e) of the Internal Revenue Code of 1954.

In an effort to reach an accord with the Internal Revenue Service and for purposes of securing a review of the adjustments, an informal conference was held among Bancroft, representatives of the Internal Revenue Service, the insured C.P.A், and D. C. Bernhardt, an attorney and certified public accountant then representing plaintiffs. The insured C.P.A. testified that all parties agreed that the assessment was owed for the stock sales in 1955 and 1957:

> Q You agreed to the assessment by the Federal Government and, in substance, told Mr. Bancroft he would have to pay it; isn't that right?
> A Yes, sir.
> Q When did you tell him he would have to pay it? Would that be before this conference or after it?
> A No, sir. In this conference we all agreed the tax was owed. I don't believe the computation was made that day, but we discussed the items to be included in the settlement and he later submitted a computation to me of the tax.
> Q That result, * * * was very different from the advice set forth in your letter of May 25, 1955, that there would be no tax?
> A It sure was.
> Q How do you account for the results you got—let us say, bad result?

> A I simply, in my research, missed the new law.
> THE COURT: What section was it you missed?
> A 304.
> THE COURT: Of the 1954 Code?
> A Yes, sir.
> BY MR. KING:
> Q Didn't you just, frankly, admit to Mr. Bancroft that you made a mistake?
> A Yes, sir.
> Q When you say you missed this Section 304, you were not aware of it, or what do you mean by that, * * * ?
> A I think when he posed the question, or rather outlining there was no profit or loss in the question, I simply didn't carry my research far enough.
> Q It was there.
> A The Section was there, yes, sir.
> Q Didn't the section fit this pretty much like a glove?
> A I would say so.
> Q Has there been any change in that law since then?
> A Not that I know of.

The insured further testified that he considered himself employed by Bancroft and his wife at the time the advice was given and when the 1955 stock transaction occurred. He also testified, as did Bancroft, that the latter paid the assessment on the strength of his opinion that the additional tax was due, Bancroft thus relying further, at least partially, at the date of the extra assessment, on the professional advice of the insured.

Following the conference, adjustments were made by I.R.S., including an allowance for the tax-exempt gifts from the parents to the children, and a total additional assessment for the years 1955 and 1957 was fixed at $35,419.74. This amount was paid to the government April 5, 1960, and is the sum sued for here.

Defendant denies liability to plaintiffs for the amount of the additional income tax paid on the grounds that, notwithstanding payment of the extra assessment, the taxes were not legally owed under Section 304 and related sections of the Internal Revenue Code of 1954; that its insured did not fall below the standard of reasonable care required of professional accountants in advising his clients as to their tax problems; that, assuming the advice given plaintiffs was erroneous and the result of professional negligence, plaintiffs were not "justified" in relying thereon in the transactions which occurred, in the first instance, approximately four months and, in the second, two years and five months after rendition of the written opinion; that the insured C.P.A. committed a criminal act within the meaning of [the state statute] by engaging in the unauthorized practice of law and, therefore, the terms of the professional liability policy did not extend coverage to include this.

• • •

As noted, defendant argues that plaintiffs were not "justified" in either instance in relying on the written opinion which was rendered some four months prior to the first stock sale and approximately two years and five months prior to the second. We find that plaintiffs were reasonable in their belief that the advice given four months earlier was correct and still reliable when the first sale occurred.

Not having been challenged about the first transaction by I.R.S., plaintiffs understandably followed the identical procedure in selling the stock in 1957. The insured having been retained as plaintiffs' C.P.A. and tax consultant for approximately seventeen years, surely plaintiffs were entitled to believe that, should a change in the Code have occurred within the four-months period, the insured would have notified them of it. Bancroft testified that in selling the stock in both 1955 and 1957 he relied on the advice of the insured. But for the insured's advice and the failure of the I.R.S. to question that transaction, presumably the 1957 stock transfer would not have been effected and that loss would not have occurred. It is reasonable to conclude, we think, that as time passed without objection from I.R.S. or notice from the insured Bancroft was justified in having confidence in the plan and in following the same procedure for sale of the additional stock in 1957.

[1]   The AICPA's Position: Updating Tax Advice

In *Bancroft v. Indemnity Insurance Co.*, the district court judge held that the plaintiffs were justified in relying on a tax opinion letter which was over two years old. The court also stated that "surely plaintiffs were entitled to believe that, should a change in the [Internal Revenue] Code have occurred within the four-month period [from the date of the issuance of the opinion letter], the insured [CPA] would have notified them of it." The trial court's holding clearly indicates that in certain circumstances an accountant may bear a duty to update tax advice which is materially affected by subsequent developments.

The American Institute of Certified Public Accountants has attempted to address this problem area with its Statement on Responsibilities in Tax Practice No. 8, entitled "Advice to Clients," which provides:

.03 The CPA may communicate with his client when subsequent developments affect advice previously provided with respect to significant matters. However, he cannot be expected to have assumed responsibility for initiating such communication except while he is assisting a client in implementing procedures or plans associated with the advice provided. Of course, the CPA may undertake this obligation by specific agreement with his client.

• • •

B. *Follow-up on Advice.* The CPA may assist clients in implementing procedures or plans associated with the advice offered. During this active participation, the CPA continues to advise and should review and revise such advice as warranted by new developments and factors affecting the transaction.

Sometimes the CPA is requested to provide tax advice but does not assist in implementing the plans adopted. While developments such as legislative or administrative changes or further judicial interpretations may affect the advice previously provided, the CPA cannot be expected to communicate later developments that affect such advice unless he undertakes this obligation by specific agreement with his client. Thus, the communication of significant developments affecting previous advice should be considered extraordinary service rather than an implied obligation in the normal CPA-client relationship.

C. *Precautionary Statement*. Experience in accounting and other professions indicates that clients understand that advice reflects professional judgment based on an existing situation. Experience has also shown that clients customarily realize that subsequent developments could affect previous professional advice. Some CPAs use precautionary language to the effect that their advice is based on facts as stated and authorities which are subject to change. Although routine use of such precautionary language seems unnecessary based on accepted business norms and professional relationships, the CPA may follow this procedure in situations he deems appropriate.

¶ 8.03   Tax Workpapers and Clients

[1]   Ownership

In *Ipswitch Mills v. Dillon*,[1] the leading case on the issue of the ownership of working papers, the Supreme Judicial Court of Massachusetts held that ownership rested in the accountants. The opinion of the court contained the following statement:

> With reference to . . . the letters addressed to the defendants [accountants], copies of letters written by the defendants, copies of returns furnished to the plaintiff, and work sheets relating to the tax case, are the sole property of the defendants, and this is true of the papers and reports collected by the defendants in the preparation of the tax case. The plaintiff is not jointly interested with the defendants in these documents. We do not understand that any of these reports, papers and returns were property of the plaintiff which had been placed in the defendants' custody by the plaintiff or merely delivered to the defendants. If there are any papers belonging to the plaintiff which were lent to the defendants, the plaintiff is entitled to them; but as we construe the record, the papers referred to [above] were gathered and collected by the defendants in the course of their business, and were not papers of the plaintiff placed by it in the defendants' possession.

Subsequent court decisions have unanimously affirmed the holding in the *Ipswitch Mills* case. In addition, some states have codified the rule as a part of their statutes which regulate accountants. Despite the fact that the accountant owns the working papers, he certainly cannot communicate their content to others. Confidentiality obviously overrides the ownership rights of the accountant. Furthermore, they are not inheritable upon the death of an accountant who is a sole practitioner. Finally and most importantly, they are subpoenable by the client in the event of litigation. Furthermore, the IRS may obtain

---

[1] 260 Mass. 453, 157 N.E. 604 (1927).

them by a summons. They may be subpoenaed by the grand jury and other government agencies, for example, the SEC may obtain them.

The major rationale behind the rule establishing possession in the accountant is to protect the accountant in the event of a lawsuit. The evidentiary value of the workpapers is obvious. Levy in his early work on *Accountants' Legal Liability* enumerated the relevancy of the working papers from an evidentiary viewpoint as follows:

1. The working papers will constitute a record of the audit work performed, both from a qualitative and quantitative standpoint. That is to say, they will constitute proof of what records were examined, what inquiries were made, what confirmations were undertaken, etc. At the same time they may constitute a record of the amount of testing and sampling that was performed, which, in the judgment of the accountant, was adequate in the circumstances.

2. The extent to which the audit work was properly planned and supervised may be evident from the working papers.

3. The nature and extent of the review of the client's system of internal control and its effective operation may appear in the working papers, and therefore the extent to which the accountant relied upon his appraisal of internal control in planning and carrying out his audit program.

4. The scope of his inquiries addressed to the client and the extent to which the accountant relied upon the client's representations may be recorded in the working papers.

5. Working papers may contain information which the plaintiff claims should have aroused the suspicion of the accountant and resulted in an extension of his audit procedures beyond the work which was done.

6. The working papers in their entirety may be offered by the accountant as evidence of his compliance with generally accepted auditing standards in support of the opinion expressed in his report.

7. The working papers may contain information which the plaintiff claims should have been disclosed and the omission of which, it is claimed, makes the report of the accountant misleading.

8. Where the genuineness of the accountant's belief in the opinion which he has expressed is put in issue, the working papers may offer persuasive evidence of the thinking of the accountant in the development and formulation of his opinion.[2]

[2] Obligations to the Client

The single most important duty of the accountant to the client in respect to the working papers is the preservation of *confidentiality*. This applies to other communications as well, for example, telephone conversations and communications which might not be technically included in the workpapers. Disclosure of a client's confidential data is prohibited unless:

Client consents

Disclosure is necessary to comply with GAAP or GAAS

---

[2] Levy, *Accountants' Liability* (1954), p. 53.

Disclosure is in compliance with an enforceable subpoena

Disclosure is necessary in connection with quality review under AICPA authorization

Disclosure is in response to a demand by an AICPA trial board

[3]   IRS Summons

[a]   Privileged Communication.   The case which follows is concerned with privilege and the attorney-client relationship. Although the case involves the use of evidence summoned by the Government, the requirements for successfully asserting the privilege are succinctly stated as are the policy factors which give rise to this exclusionary rule of evidence. The case holds that information transmitted by a client to an attorney for purposes of preparation of a tax return is not privileged information.

United States v. Lawless
709 F.2d 485
(7th Cir. 1983)

GRANT, Senior District Judge.

The Respondent-Appellee, J. Martin Lawless, an attorney in Peoria, Illinois, was retained by the co-executors of the estate to prepare the federal estate tax return of Edna E. Dieken, deceased. Petitioner-Appellant, Special Agent William C. McCormick, was assigned to investigate the correctness of the estate tax return. Summonses were issued to Lawless to testify regarding the tax return and to produce the following documents:

All books, papers, records, and other documents in your possession or control relating to the preparation or audit of the United States Estate Tax Return, Form 706, for EDNA E. DIEKEN. This is to include but is not limited to:
1.   Resource materials such as check lists or outlines of questions used in obtaining information from the executors.
2.   Memorandums, notes, or other such records made of the Executors' responses.
3.   Records furnished to you for use in preparation or examination such as savings passbooks, asset inventories, checking account statements, cancelled checks, loan records, accounts receivable, records of gifts and accounts payable.

(R. 1,p. 3). Lawless refused to comply with the summonses and enforcement proceedings were commenced.

At these proceedings, the Government limited the summonses to only those documents relating to or used in the preparation of the estate tax return. Lawless resisted the summonses upon the basis of attorney-client privilege. After an *in camera* examination of the six documents in dispute, the district court concluded that four of them were not privileged. However, with respect to documents 18 and 19, the district court ruled:

Number 18 is a letter from Charles Dieken [one of the executors] to Mr. Lawless's [sic] law firm containing a great deal of detailed financial information. I'm going to excuse production of that document as subject to the attorney-client privilege dated September 7, 1979, without any suggestion or knowledge as to how the data reported relates to data on the return.

I think it is the type of material that is entitled to be furnished to an attorney by the client on a confidential basis.

•   •   •

I will likewise excuse production of document No. 19, which is a hand written note [on an envelope] apparently to Mr. Lawless from the client in the handwriting of the client. Likewise subject to the privilege.

(R. 8, Transcript pp. 19-20)

The Government objected to the ruling, arguing that Lawless had made no showing that these documents were intended to be confidential, and that, from the description of the documents, they were intended for use in the preparation of the tax return. The district court explained the basis of its ruling to be:

> I didn't decide whether they were intended to be used in the preparation of the return or not or whether they were in fact used in the preparation of the return. I simply decided that they were the type of information which I think the client is privileged to furnish to his attorney and not have the attorney disclose to the extent they were used in the preparation of the return. The return shows them. I haven't made that determination. I assume very substantially from experience over a good many years with Mr. Lawless that any financial information applicable to the return furnished by the client which was applicable to the return was used in preparation of the return as shown on the return. I don't mean to be implying anything else.
> (R. 8, Transcript pp. 21-22)

The Government appeals from the district court ruling pursuant to 28 U.S.C. § 1291. The issue here on appeal is whether the district court erred in holding that the attorney-client privilege protected these two documents which had been transferred to an attorney in connection with the preparation of a federal estate tax return. Following oral argument of this case, we ordered the parties to transmit the documents held sealed by the district court for our examination *in camera*.

[1-3] This Court [has previously] adopted the general principles of attorney-client privilege as outlined by Wigmore:

> (1) Where legal advice of any kind is sought (2) from a professional legal adviser in his capacity as such, (3) the communications relating to that purpose, (4) made in confidence (5) by the client, (6) are at his instance permanently protected (7) from disclosure by himself or by the legal adviser, (8) except the protection be waived. 8 Wigmore § 2292.

(footnote omitted). *See also United States v. Tratner*, 511 F.2d 248 (7th Cir.1975). The party seeking to invoke the privilege has the burden of establishing all of its essential elements. *United States v. First State Bank*, 691 F.2d 332, 335 (7th Cir.1982). The claim of privilege must be made and sustained on a question-by-question or document-by-document basis; a blanket claim of privilege is unacceptable. *Id*. The scope of the privilege should be "strictly confined within the narrowest possible limits." 8 Wigmore, Evidence § 2291.

[4]   The district court in its ruling allowed the claim of privilege solely upon the basis of the intent for confidentiality by the client. When information is transmitted to an attorney with the intent that the information will be transmitted to a third party (in this case on a tax return), such information is not confidential.

[5]   The respondent argues that the information transmitted to him, as the attorney preparing the tax return, but which was not disclosed on the return, is protected by the privilege. If the client transmitted the information so that it might be used on the tax return, such a transmission destroys any expectation of confidentiality which might have otherwise existed.

Wigmore also indicated, for the privilege to apply, that the attorney must be acting in his capacity as a professional legal adviser at the time the information was transferred. Several courts have held that the preparation of a tax return, while it may require some knowledge of the law, is primarily an accounting service. *United States v. Davis*, 636 F.2d 1028, 1043 (5th Cir.), *cert. denied*, 454 U.S. 862, 102 S.Ct. 320, 70 L.Ed.2d 162 (1981); *United States v. Gurtner*, 474 F.2d 297, 299 (9th Cir.1973); *Canaday v. United States*, 354 F.2d 849, 857 (8th Cir.1966) ("merely as a scrivener"). Even assuming that the respondent here was giving legal advice, in addition to the preparation of the tax return (*In re Shapiro, supra*), no evidence was introduced to establish that the two disputed documents were given to Lawless for any other purpose. As the Government argued in its brief, these documents were submitted to the district court in response to a summons calling for all documents relevant to the tax return preparation. This Court has examined the documents and finds that both documents contain information which would be relevant to, and utilized in, a federal estate tax return. While this Court did not have the estate tax return before it, and the district court did not consider whether the information on the documents were in fact on the return, disclosure of tax information effectively waives the privilege "not only to the transmitted data but also as to the details underlying that information." *United States v. Cote*, 456 F.2d 142, 145 (8th Cir.1972). The district judge himself indicated that from his substantial experience with Lawless, any information applicable to a tax return was used in the preparation of the return.

This Court finds that the respondent has failed to sustain his burden regarding the elements of attorney-client privilege in order to invoke that privilege. We additionally find, from an examination of the documents submitted for *in camera* examination, that these documents contained information which would have been submitted for preparation of an estate tax return and reported in an estate tax return.

Following the precedence of other Circuits, . . . this Court now finds that information transmitted for the purpose of preparation of a tax return, though transmitted to an attorney, is not privileged information.

The holding of the district court is reversed and the documents are returned to the district court for enforcement proceedings consistent with this opinion.

1. In *United States v. Lawless* the United States Court of Appeals held that when "information is transmitted to an attorney with the intent that the information will be transmitted to a third party (in this case on a tax return), such information is not confidential."

2. The court of appeals also indicates that it is not necessary that the information actually be used on the tax return, "if the client transmitted the information so that it might be used on the tax return, such a transmission destroys any expectation of confidentiality which might have otherwise existed."

3. The *United States v. Lawless* decision reflects a clear policy of not allowing the use of a claim of privilege to block discovery of relevant, material information, particularly where there has been a partial "public disclosure" or waiver of the privilege such as occurs in the filing of a tax return. The same analysis and policy factors would weigh against an auditor who attempts to urge that tax accrual audit workpapers ought not be discoverable. Consider the decision in *United States v. Arthur Young* which follows.

[b] *United States v. Arthur Young* **and Comments.** *Res ipsa loquitur*, the case speaks for itself. The final "nail in the coffin" in respect to possible application of privileged communication to the accountant-client relationship has been driven home. In a unanimous nine justice opinion, the U.S. Supreme Court dispelled any hope that accountants might have had to assert at least a limited privilege in respect to the tax accrual files of a client. Since this is probably the most compelling situation for justification of the privilege from a fairness or equity standpoint, little or no hope remains after the decision. Any accountant's privilege will have to be the creature of state and federal legislation.

United States v. Arthur Young
104 S. Ct. 1495 (1984)

Chief Justice BURGER delivered the opinion of the Court.

We granted certiorari to consider whether tax accrual workpapers prepared by a corporation's independent certified public accountant in the course of regular financial audits are protected from disclosure in response to an Internal Revenue Service summons issued under § 7602 of the Internal Revenue Code of 1954 (Code), 26 U.S.C. §7602.

I
A

Respondent Arthur Young & Co. is a firm of certified public accountants. As the independent auditor for respondent Amerada Hess Corp., Young is responsible for reviewing the financial statements prepared by Amerada as required by the federal securities laws.[1] In the course of its review of these financial statements, Young verified Amerada's statement of its contingent tax liabilities, and, in so doing, prepared the tax accrual workpapers at issue in this case. Tax accrual workpapers are documents and memoranda relating to Young's evaluation of Amerada's reserves for contingent tax liabilities. Such workpapers sometimes contain information pertaining to Amerada's financial transactions, identify questionable positions Amerada may have taken on its tax returns, and reflect Young's opinions regarding the validity of such positions.

In 1975 the Internal Revenue Service began a routine audit to determine Amerada's corporate income tax liability for the tax years 1972 through 1974. When the audit revealed that Amerada had made questionable payments of $7830 from a "special disbursement account," the IRS instituted a criminal investigation of Amerada's tax returns as well. In that process, pursuant to Code § 7602, 26 U.S.C. § 7602,[2] the IRS issued an ad-

ministrative summons to Young, which required Young to make available to the IRS all its Amerada files, including its tax accrual workpapers. Amerada instructed Young not to comply with the summons.

The IRS then commenced this enforcement action against Young in the United States District Court for the Southern District of New York. See 26 U.S.C. § 7604.[3] Amerada intervened, as permitted by 26 U.S.C. § 7609(b)(1).[4] The District Court found that Young's tax accrual workpapers were relevant to the IRS investigation within the meaning

---

collecting any such liability, the Secretary is authorized—

(1) To examine any books, papers, records, or other data which may be relevant or material to such inquiry:

(2) To summon the person liable for tax or required to perform the act, or any officer or employee of such person, or any person having possession, custody, or care of books of account containing entries relating to the business of the person liable for tax or required to perform the act, or any other person the Secretary may deem proper, to appear before the Secretary at a time and place named in the summons and to produce such books, papers, records, or other data, and to give such testimony, under oath, as may be relevant or material to such inquiry, and

(3) To take such testimony of the person concerned, under oath, as may be relevant or material to such inquiry."

[3] Section 7604 of the Code, 26 U.S.C. § 7604, provides that:

"If any person is summoned under the internal revenue laws to appear, to testify, or to produce books, papers, records, or other data, the United States district court for the district in which such person resides or is found shall have jurisdiction by appropriate process to compel such attendance, testimony, or production of books, papers, records or other data."

[4] The IRS summons served upon Young sought the production of records concerning the business transactions and affairs of Young's client, Amerada. Accordingly, under Code § 7609(a)(1), 26 U.S.C. § 7609(a)(1), Amerada was entitled to notice of the IRS summons. Section 7609(b)(1) provides that "any person who is entitled to notice of a summons under subsection (a) shall have the right to intervene in any proceeding with respect to the enforcement of such summons under section 7604."

---

[1] See, e.g., Securities Exchange Act of 1934, § 12(b)(1)(J)–(L).

[2] Section 7602 of the Code, 26 U.S.C. § 7692, provides as follows:

"For the purpose of ascertaining the correctness of any return, making a return where none has been made, determining the liability of any person for any internal revenue tax or the liability at law or in equity of any transferee or fiduciary of any person in respect of any internal revenue tax, or

of § 7602 and refused to recognize an accountant-client privilege that would protect the workpapers. 496 F. Supp. 1152, 1156-1157 (SDNY 1980). Accordingly, the District Court ordered the summons enforced.

B

A divided United States Court of Appeals for the Second Circuit affirmed in part and reversed in part. 677 F. 2d 211 (1982). The Court of Appeals majority agreed with the District Court that the tax accrual workpapers were relevant to the IRS investigation of Amerada, but held that the public interest in promoting full disclosure to public accountants, and in turn ensuring the integrity of the securities markets, required protection for the work that such independent auditors perform for publicly owned companies. Drawing upon *Hickman v. Taylor*, 329 U.S. 495 (1947), and Fed. Rule Civ. Proc. 26(b)(3), the Court of Appeals fashioned a work-product immunity doctrine for tax accrual workpapers prepared by independent auditors in the course of compliance with the federal securities laws. Because the IRS had not demonstrated a sufficient showing of need to overcome the immunity and was not seeking to prove fraud on Amerada's part, the Court of Appeals refused to enforce the summons insofar as it sought Young's tax accrual workpapers.

One judge dissented from that portion of the majority opinion creating a work-product immunity for accountants' tax accrual workpapers. The dissent viewed the statutory summons authority, 26 U.S.C. § 7602, as reflecting a congressional decision in favor of the disclosure of such workpapers. The dissent also rejected the policy justifications asserted by the majority for an accountant work-product immunity, reasoning that such protection was not necessary to ensure the integrity of the independent auditor's certification of a corporation's financial statements.

We granted certiorari, _____ U.S. _____ (1983). We affirm in part and reverse in part.

II

Corporate financial statements are one of the primary sources of information available to guide the decisions of the investing public. In an effort to control the accuracy of the financial data available to investors in the securities markets, various provisions of the federal securities laws require publicly held corporations to file their financial statements with the Securities and Exchange Commission. Commission regulations stipulate that these financial reports must be audited by an independent certified public accountant in accordance with generally accepted auditing standards. By examining the corporation's books and records, the independent auditor determines whether the financial reports of the corporation have been prepared in accordance with generally accepted accounting principles. The auditor then issues an opinion as to whether the financial statements, taken as a whole, fairly present the financial position and operations of the corporation for the relevant period.

An important aspect of the auditor's function is to evaluate the adequacy and reasonableness of the corporation's reserve account for contingent tax liabilities. This reserve account, known as the tax accrual account, the noncurrent tax account, or the tax pool, represents the amount set aside by the corporation to cover adjustments and additions to the corporation's actual tax liability. Additional corporate tax liability may arise from a wide variety of transactions.[5] The presence of a reserve account for such contingent tax liabilities reflects the corporation's awareness of, and preparedness for, the possibility of an assessment of additional taxes.

The independent auditor draws upon many sources in evaluating the sufficiency of the corporation's tax accrual account. Initially, the corporation's books, records, and tax returns must be analyzed in light of the relevant Code provisions, Treasury Regulations, Revenue Rulings, and case law. The auditor

---

[5] For example, the characterization of the proceeds of a sale as capital gain instead of ordinary income, the claiming of an investment tax credit, and the attribution of a transaction to a future tax year are decisions requiring judgment calls in gray areas of the Code, any one of which might result in a recomputation of the corporation's outstanding tax liability.

will also obtain and assess the opinions, speculations, and projections of management with regard to unclear, aggressive, or questionable tax positions that may have been taken on prior tax returns. In exploring the tax consequences of certain transactions, the auditor often engages in a "worst-case" analysis in order to ensure that the tax accrual account accurately reflects the full extent of the corporation's exposure to additional tax liability. From this conglomeration of data, the auditor is able to estimate the potential cost of each particular contingency, as well as the probability that the additional liability may arise.

The auditor's tax accrual workpapers record this process of examination and analysis. Such workpapers may document the auditor's interviews with corporate personnel, judgments on questions of potential tax liability, and suggestions for alternative treatments of certain transactions for tax purposes. Tax accrual workpapers also contain an overall evaluation of the sufficiency of the corporation's reserve for contingent tax liabilities, including an item-by-item analysis of the corporation's potential exposure to additional liability. In short, tax accrual workpapers pinpoint the "soft spots" on a corporation's tax return by highlighting those areas in which the corporate taxpayer has taken a position that may, at some later date, require the payment of additional taxes.

III

In seeking access to Young's tax accrual workpapers, the IRS exercised the summons power conferred by Code § 7602, 26 U.S.C. § 7602, which authorizes the Secretary of the Treasury to summon and "examine any books, papers, records, or other data which may be relevant or material" to a particular tax inquiry. The District Court and the Court

---

[6] In *United States v. Powell*, 379 U.S. 48 (1964), the Court refused to impose a probable cause requirement in connection with the enforcement of an IRS summons under § 7602. Instead, the Court held that the IRS need show only "that the investigation will be conducted pursuant to a legitimate purpose, *that the inquiry may be relevant*

of Appeals determined that the tax accrual workpapers at issue in this case satisfied the relevance requirement of § 7602, because they 'might have thrown light upon' the correctness of Amerada's tax return."[6] Because the relevance of tax accrual workpapers is a logical predicate to the question of whether such workpapers should be protected by some form of work-product immunity, we turn first to an evaluation of the relevance issue. We agree that such workpapers are relevant within the meaning of § 7602.

As the language of § 7602 clearly indicates, an IRS summons is not to be judged by the relevance standards used in deciding whether to admit evidence in federal court. Cf. Fed. Rule Evid. 401. The language "may be" reflects Congress' express intention to allow the IRS to obtain items of even *potential* relevance to an ongoing investigation, without deference to its admissibility. The purpose of Congress is obvious: the Service can hardly be expected to know whether such data will in fact be relevant until it is procured and scrutinized. As a tool of discovery, the § 7602

---

to the purpose, that the information sought is not already within the Commissioner's possession, and that the administrative steps required by the Code have been followed. . . ." *Id.*, at 57–58 (emphasis added).

The relevance standard employed by the Second Circuit—whether the documents at issue "might have thrown light upon the correctness of the return"—appears to be widely accepted among the Courts of Appeals. See, *e. g.*, *United States v. Wyatt*, 637 F.2d 293, 300 (CA5 1981); *United States v. Turner*, 480 F.2d 272, 279 (CA7 1973); *United States v. Ryan*, 55 F.2d 728, 733 (CA9 1972); *United States v. Egenberg*, 443 F.2d 512, 15–516 (CA3 1971); *Foster v. United States*, 265 F.2d 183, 187 (CA2), *cert. denied*, 360 U.S. 912 (1959). In *United States v. Harrington*, 388 F.2d 520, 524 (1968), the Second Circuit amplified this test by stating that "the 'might in the articulated standard, 'might throw light upon the correctness of the return,' is . . . an indication of a realistic expectation rather than an idle hope that something may be discovered." But in *United States v. Coopers & Lybrand*, 550 F.2d 615 (1977), the Court of Appeals for the Tenth Circuit held that tax accrual workpapers not prepared in connection with the filing of a corporate tax return were not relevant within the meaning of § 7602.

summons is critical to the investigative and enforcement functions of the IRS, see *United States v. Powell*, 379 U.S. 48, 57 (1964); the service therefore should not be required to establish that the documents it seeks are actually relevant in any technical, evidentiary sense.

That tax accrual workpapers are not actually used in the preparation of tax returns by the taxpayer or its own accountants does not bar a finding of relevance within the meaning of § 7602. The filing of a corporate tax return entails much more than filling in the blanks on an IRS form in accordance with undisputed tax principles; more likely than not, the return is a composite interpretation of corporate transactions made by corporate officers in the light most favorable to the taxpayer. It is the responsibility of the IRS to determine whether the corporate taxpayer in completing a return has stretched a particular tax concept beyond what is allowed. Records that illuminate any aspect of the return—such as the tax accrual workpapers at issue in this case—are therefore highly relevant to legitimate IRS inquiry. The Court of Appeals acknowledged this: "It is difficult to say that the assessment by the independent auditor of the correctness of positions taken by the taxpayer in his return would not throw 'light upon' the correctness of the return." 677 F.2d, at 219. We accordingly affirm the Court of Appeals' holding that Young's tax accrual workpapers are relevant to the IRS investigation of Amerada's tax liability.

IV
A

We now turn to consider whether tax accrual workpapers prepared by an independent auditor in the course of a routine review of corporate financial statements should be protected by some form of work-product immunity from disclosure under § 7602. Based upon its evaluation of the competing policies of the federal tax and securities laws, the Court of Appeals found it necessary to create a so-called privilege for the independent auditor's workpapers.

Our complex and comprehensive system of federal taxation, relying as it does upon self-assessment and reporting, demands that all taxpayers be forthright in the disclosure of relevant information to the taxing authorities. Without such disclosure, and the concomitant power of the Government to compel disclosure, our national tax burden would not be fairly and equitably distributed. In order to encourage effective tax investigations, Congress has endowed the IRS with expansive information-gathering authority; § 7602 is the centerpiece of that congressional design. As we noted in *United States v. Bisceglia*, 420 U.S. 141, 146 (1975):

> The purpose of [§ 7602] is not to accuse, but to inquire. Although such investigations unquestionably involve some invasion of privacy, they are essential to our self-reporting system, and the alternatives could well involve far less agreeable invasions of house, business, and records.

Similarly, we noted in *United States v. Euge*, 444 U.S. 707, 711 (1980):

> [T]his Court has consistently construed congressional intent to require that if the summons authority claimed is necessary for the effective performance of congressionally imposed responsibilities to enforce the tax Code, that authority should be upheld absent express statutory prohibition or substantial countervailing policies.

While § 7602 is "subject to the traditional privileges and limitations," *id.*, at 714, any other restrictions upon the IRS summons power should be avoided "absent unambiguous directions from Congress." *United States v. Bisceglia, supra*, at 150. We are unable to discern the sort of "unambiguous directions from Congress" that would justify a judicially created work-product immunity for tax accrual workpapers summoned under § 7602. Indeed, the very language of § 7602 reflects precisely the opposite: a congressional policy choice *in favor of disclosure* of all information relevant to a legitimate IRS inquiry. In light of this explicit statement by the Legislative Branch, courts should be chary in recognizing exceptions to the broad summons authority of the IRS or in fashioning new privileges that would curtail disclosure under § 7602. Cf.

Milwaukee v. Illinois, 451 U.S. 304, 315 (1981). If the broad latitude granted to the IRS by § 7602 is to be circumscribed, that is a choice for Congress, and not this Court, to make. See *United States v. Euge, supra*, at 712.

B

The Court of Appeals nevertheless concluded that "substantial countervailing policies," *id.*, at 711, required the fashioning of a work-product immunity for an independent auditor's tax accrual workpapers. To the extent that the Court of Appeals, in its concern for the "chilling effect" of the disclosure of tax accrual workpapers, sought to facilitate communication between independent auditors and their clients, its remedy more closely resembles a testimonial accountant-client privilege than a work-product immunity for accountants' workpapers. But as this Court stated in *Couch v. United States*, 409 U.S. 322, 335 (1973), "no confidential accountant-client privilege exists under federal law, and no state-created privilege has been recognized in federal cases." In light of *Couch*, the Court of Appeals' effort to foster candid communication between accountant and client by creating a self-styled work-product privilege was misplaced, and conflicts with what we see as the clear intent of Congress.

Nor do we find persuasive the argument that a work-product immunity for accountants' tax accrual workpapers is a fitting analogue to the attorney work-product doctrine established in *Hickman v. Taylor, supra*. The *Hickman* work-product doctrine was founded upon the private attorney's role as the client's confidential advisor and advocate, a loyal representative whose duty it is to present the client's case in the most favorable possible light. An independent certified public accountant performs a different role. By certifying the public reports that collectively depict a corporation's financial status, the independent auditor assumes a *public* responsibility transcending any employment relationship with the client. The independent public accountant performing this special function owes ultimate allegiance to the corporation's creditors and stockholders, as well as to investing public. This "public watchdog" function

demands that the accountant maintain total independence from the client at all times and requires complete fidelity to the public trust. To insulate from disclosure a certified public accountant's interpretations of the client's financial statements would be to ignore the significance of the accountant's role as a disinterested analyst charged with public obligations.

We cannot accept the view that the integrity of the securities markets will suffer absent some protection for accountants' tax accrual workpapers. The Court of Appeals apparently feared that, were the IRS to have access to tax accrual workpapers, a corporation might be tempted to withhold from its auditor certain information relevant and material to a proper evaluation of its financial statements. But the independent certified public accountant cannot be content with the corporation's representations that its tax accrual reserves are adequate; the auditor is ethically and professionally obligated to ascertain for himself as far as possible whether the corporation's contingent tax liabilities have been accurately stated. If the auditor were convinced that the scope of the examination had been limited by management's reluctance to disclose matters relating to the tax accrual reserves, the auditor would be unable to issue an unqualified opinion as to the accuracy of the corporation's financial statements. Instead, the auditor would be required to issue a qualified opinion, an adverse opinion, or a disclaimer of opinion, thereby notifying the investing public of possible potential problems inherent in the corporation's financial reports. Responsible corporate management would not risk a qualified evaluation of a corporate taxpayer's financial posture to afford cover for questionable positions reflected in a prior tax return. Thus, the independent auditor's obligation to serve the public interest assures that the integrity of the securities markets will be preserved, without the need for a work-product immunity for accountants' tax accrual workpapers.[7]

---

[7] Indeed, rather than protecting the investing public by ensuring the accuracy of corporate financial records, insulation of tax accrual workpapers from disclosure might well undermine the public's confidence in the independent auditing

We also reject respondents' position that fundamental fairness precludes IRS access to accountants' tax accrual workpapers. Respondents urge that the enforcement of an IRS summons for accountants' tax accrual workpapers permits the Government to probe the thought processes of its taxpayer citizens, thereby giving the IRS an unfair advantage in negotiating and litigating tax controversies. But if the SEC itself, or a private plaintiff in securities litigation, sought to obtain the tax accrual workpapers at issue in this case, they would surely be entitled to do so.[8] In light of

the broad congressional command of § 7602, no sound reason exists for conferring lesser authority upon the IRS than upon a private litigant suing with regard to transactions concerning which the public has no interest.

Congress has granted to the IRS "broad latitude to adopt enforcement techniques helpful in the performance of [its] tax collection and assessment responsibilities." *United States v. Euge, supra*, at 716, n. 9. Recognizing the intrusiveness of demands for the production of tax accrual workpapers, the IRS has demonstrated administrative sensitivity to the concerns expressed by the accounting profession by tightening its internal requirements for the issuance of such summonses. See Int. Rev. Manual—Audit (CCH) § 4024.4 (May 14, 1981). Although these IRS guidelines were not applicable during the years at issue in this case, their promulgation further refutes respondents' fairness argument and reflects an administrative flexibility that reinforces our decision not to reduce irrevocably the § 7602 summons power.

---

process. The SEC requires the filing of audited financial statements in order to obviate the fear of loss from reliance on inaccurate information, thereby encouraging public investment in the nation's industries. It is therefore not enough that financial statements *be* accurate: the public must also *perceive* them as being accurate. Public faith in the reliability of a corporation's financial statements depends upon the public perception of the outside auditor as an independent professional. Endowing the workpapers of an independent auditor with a work-product immunity would destroy the appearance of auditor's independence by creating the impression that the auditor is an advocate for the client. If investors were to view the auditor as an advocate for the corporate client, the value of the audit function itself might well be lost. See generally A. Arens & J. Loebbecke, n. 13, *supra*, 55–58.

[8] See, *e. g.*, Securities Act of 1933, § 19, 48 Stat. 85, 15 U.S.C. § 77s(b) (for purposes of all "necessary and proper" investigations, SEC is empowered to "require the production of any books, papers, or other documents which the Commission deems relevant or material to the inquiry"): Securities Act of 1934, § 21, 48 Stat. 899, 15 U.S.C. § 78u(b) (same); Fed. Rule Civ. Proc. 26(b)(1) (parties may obtain discovery of "any matter, not privileged, which is relevant to the subject matter involved in the pending action").

V

Beyond question it is desirable and in the public interest to encourage full disclosures by corporate clients to their independent accountants; if it is necessary to balance competing interests, however, the need of the Government for full disclosure of all information relevant to tax liability must also weigh in that balance. This kind of policy choice is best left to the Legislative Branch. Accordingly, the judgment of the Court of Appeals is affirmed in part and reversed in part, and the case is remanded for proceedings consistent with this opinion.

It is so ordered.

There is not much that can be added to what has been said in the introduction with the exception of the relevancy question. In finding the workpapers to be relevant, the court clearly indicated that a liberal standard applied. In addition in footnote 6 (renumbered by the authors) the court rejects the relevancy limitation placed upon the IRS summons in situations where the workpapers are not actually used in preparation of a tax return. This was the ruling of the Tenth Circuit Court of Appeals in *United States v. Coopers & Lybrand*, 550 F.2d 615 (1977). Thus, this possible alternate basis for exclusion of the workpapers in similar situations has been effectively foreclosed.

[4]   Client Records

[a]   Discreditable Acts: Client Record Retention. *Rule 501—Acts discreditable* of the AICPA Code of Professional Ethics provides that an "accountant shall not commit an act discreditable to the profession." This "catch-all" provision has been interpreted to proscribe certain practices which are inconsistent with the goal of achieving and maintaining high standards of professionalism. For example, an accountant who negligently makes or permits another to make false and misleading entries in the financial statements or records of an entity commits an act discreditable to the profession. This type of conduct is prohibited without regard to whether the conduct may violate Rules 202 and 203 which deal with the application of GAAP and GAAS.

An act discreditable which routinely arises involves the accountant's retention of client records to secure payment for outstanding invoices for professional services rendered. The following article illustrates how the records retention issue poses legal and ethical questions for the accountant.

Client Records: To Hold Them or Not— an Ethical Dilemma[1]

The issue of whether a CPA may retain client records pending payment in full for professional services rendered poses legal and ethical questions. Let us join a telephone conversation between a CPA and his attorney as they puzzle through the problems which attend those circumstances where a client refuses to pay for services rendered:

CPA: I'm so mad I could file a law suit.
Attorney: Wait, before you throw good money after bad, let's talk about your options.
CPA: There's gotta be a law on the books that prevents gross injustices such as this. Not only did I compile my former client's financial statements, but I also prepared his federal income tax returns. He had no complaints regarding any of the services.

His only reason for changing accountants was that he said it could be done for less money. Isn't there a law that would give me a lien over the corporate books and records which I still have?
Attorney: Under Illinois law, there is no statutory lien which deals with professional services rendered by a CPA. Statutory liens have been created for other professions. For example, statutory or special liens as they

are often called have been created to cover services rendered by attorneys, dentists, and for services rendered by a physician in conjunction with injuries. In fact, there is a statutory lien for any person who is in the business of shoeing horses.
CPA: That's great! If I were a horse shoer I'd have a lien on my client's horse! I'll have to remember that if I ever decide to go into a new line of business! Isn't there any kind of equitable lien quite apart from the statutes?
Attorney: Under Illinois common law there is a so-called possessory lien in favor of an attorney for his fees. This possessory or "retaining lien" as it is also known was created by the Illinois Supreme Court in 1889 and has been acknowledged by the courts as recently as 1980.
CPA: Has the Illinois Supreme Court stated that a common law possessory lien exists in favor of accountants?
Attorney: No. In fact, the common law possessory lien is limited; it merely gives the attorney a right to retain the client's property and cannot be actively enforced by any judicial proceeding. This lien continues until the attorney's fees are either paid or the attorney surrenders the property with or without payment. Once the attorney surrenders the property, his retaining lien is lost.

Moreover, the case law that has developed in this area has recognized that the courts have inherent power to order an attorney to release property of the client in those cir-

---

[1] Richard L. Miller, *Illinois CPA Society News Journal*, 17–18 (December 1983).

cumstances where the interests of equity and fairness demand such a result. As a condition of releasing the client records, the courts can order the client to post some other alternative security to assure that the attorney will be paid.

If the attorney brings a law suit against the client for services rendered, some courts have held that the attorney may not refuse production of the client records during the pending law suit.

CPA: What kind of records can an attorney withhold from his client?

Attorney: The Illinois Supreme Court in its 1889 decision, which is still the law of this state, held that the "retaining lien" of the attorney exists on "all papers or documents of the client placed in the attorney's hands in his professional character or in the course of his employment."

CPA: You say that the Illinois Supreme Court has not created a retaining or possessory lien for CPAs?

Attorney: That's right.

CPA: Do you think they would be inclined to do so?

Attorney: It's hard to say. Needless to say, the policy reasons which persuaded the Supreme Court to create such a lien for attorneys' fees are arguably present for CPAs. That is, there is no reason to distinguish between a possessory lien for accountants and attorneys. What's allowable for one should be allowed for the other. However, there are cases which state that general or retaining liens are not favored under the common law. It is therefore possible that a court faced with the issue of creating a common law retaining lien in favor of a certified public accountant, may not be inclined to do so.

CPA: Are you telling me that its anybody's guess as to what a court might do?

Attorney: That's right. Let me couch it in typical legalese: It's unclear that a court addressing this issue in 1986 would find that there exists a common law retaining lien in favor of a CPA.

And you realize of course that quite apart from the legal issue, there remains the substantial ethical question as to the propriety of retaining client records.

CPA: Yes, I know that under Rule 501 of the Code of Professional Ethics, retention of client records pending payment of professional fees is deemed to be an act discreditable to the profession.

Attorney: Because the accounting profession considers the retention of client records to be an unethical act, I find it hard to believe that a court would create a common law retaining lien. Remember, the creation of these general retaining liens is not favored under the common law. To the extent that creating a lien would also facilitate conduct deemed to be unethical, it seems to me that a court would have a great deal of difficulty in siding with an accountant on this issue.

CPA: So what you're telling me is that my best tack is to turn over the records and sue my client for the unpaid professional fees?

Attorney: No! I'm advising you to turn over the records to avoid any violation of your profession's code of ethics. But I would not advise you to bring a law suit as a plaintiff seeking to collect for your professional fees. As a general rule, whenever an accountant sues as a plaintiff for unpaid professional services, I can almost guarantee that you'll become a defendant in the action as a result of a counterclaim being brought against you.

Also, I'm not advising you to turn over *all* records which you have. The only records to which a client is entitled are "client records" and not what I'll call the "accountant's records." There is absolutely no ethical obligation, for example, to turn over your workpapers which memorialize the work you performed.

CPA: What's the legal bottom line?

Attorney: The best course of action is to maintain a timely billing and collecting practice. Progress billing or a retainer arrangement often defuses a potential problem. In the long run this approach serves best the interests of both the CPA and the client.

[5]   Grand Jury Subpoena

It is 9:30 P.M. and John Accountant has received two visitors at his home, Special Agents of the Internal Revenue Service. They are investigating John's client who owns Atax

Company for possible criminal tax fraud violations. John has received a federal grand jury subpoena to testify and to bring financial books, records, and workpapers relating to all his work for his client and Atax. We join John's immediate telephone call to his attorney:

MR. ATTORNEY: Get a hold of yourself, John; the special agents told you that you are not the subject of the Grand Jury's investigation.

MR. ACCOUNTANT: I'm going to take the "Fifth," I don't want to testify. . . . I. . . .

MR. ATTORNEY: John, stop this nonsense . . . listen to me. To begin with you already talked to the Special IRS agents, right?

MR. ACCOUNTANT: Yes, I told them everything I know; I answered all their questions.

MR. ATTORNEY: Well you have already made yourself their witness to the extent you told them anything which will assist their investigation.

MR. ACCOUNTANT: Can't I take the "Fifth?"

MR. ATTORNEY: No! The Fifth Amendment is a privilege against "self-incrimination." There is no privilege when the incrimination is affecting someone else. Moreover, the Agents told you that you are not the subject of their investigation. If you were, they would have had to advise you of this fact.

Besides, we can ask the federal prosecutor in charge of this investigation for a "nonsubject letter."

MR. ACCOUNTANT: A what?

MR. ATTORNEY: A letter saying you are not the subject of the Grand Jury's investigation.

MR. ACCOUNTANT: Is that like immunity?

MR. ATTORNEY: Almost. It's a letter which reassures you and seeks your cooperation. It is not immunity because you are not deemed to be a party that would be prosecuted.

MR. ACCOUNTANT: What if they grant me immunity, can I still resist testifying in the Grand Jury? I mean . . . I'm . . . afraid to say anything . . . I don't want to be involved. . . .

MR. ATTORNEY: Look, you are involved. It's your client who is being investigated. If the prosecutor immunized you and you tried to resist testifying, you could go to jail for 18 months for contempt.

MR. ACCOUNTANT: What about the part of the subpoena which requests my workpapers and all the confidential client information. I can't turn that over, I have an ethical obligation to my client!

MR. ATTORNEY: You also have an obligation to respond to the Grand Jury's subpoena. Do you want to be held in contempt?

MR. ACCOUNTANT: No, what should I do?

MR. ATTORNEY:	The first thing we do is contact your client's lawyer and ask for his waiver of any ethical obligation. Also, because the Grand Jury subpoena does not request that we refrain from advising your client, we should immediately advise the client's attorney of the subpoena and the information requested.
MR. ACCOUNTANT:	What does that do?
MR. ATTORNEY:	It discharges your ethical obligations to the client. If the client wants to file a motion in court to quash the subpoena, he has at least been put on notice by you. If he doesn't make such a motion, you must appear before the Grand Jury with the documents and testify.
MR. ATTORNEY:	Can't I plead the client's Fifth Amendment? I mean what if some of these papers incriminate him?
MR. ATTORNEY:	You can't invoke any Fifth Amendment privilege that your client may have. In fact, if your client has given you any of his "personal papers," he has waived the privilege as to those papers in your possession.
MR. ACCOUNTANT:	Can't I give them back to my client so that he can assert the privilege?
MR. ATTORNEY:	No. That won't work, plus it could get you into a position where the prosecutor might claim that you tried to impede and impair the Grand Jury's investigation. In fact, if you give back to your client highly incriminating papers which he destroys and you know the Grand Jury wants these papers. . . .
MR. ACCOUNTANT:	It doesn't look so hot, does it?
MR. ATTORNEY:	It looks like obstruction of justice!
MR. ACCOUNTANT:	It's too bad these personal papers of the clients were given to me . . . I mean if they had been kept at his business, none of this would have been turned over to the Grand Jury.
MR. ATTORNEY:	That's not quite correct. The Fifth Amendment privilege has been substantially limited by the courts as it applies to financial books, records, and papers generated in conjunction with a business. Frankly, there is very little business documentation which can be protected from a Grand Jury subpoena.
MR. ACCOUNTANT:	Well, it looks like I made a mess of things by talking to the Special Agents. . . .
MR. ATTORNEY:	Look, you reacted the way anyone else would. In these matters the best approach is to cooperate by answering questions *provided you are not the subject of the investigation.* Before you answer questions you should probably contact your attorney.

This is particularly important in criminal investigations because it is often difficult for an accountant who is caught "in between." The accountant should cooperate with law enforcement officials, should not violate any ethical obligations to his client, and at the same time, the accountant must make sure the client does not attempt to implicate the accountant in a matter for which the accountant is blameless.

MR. ACCOUNTANT: Those are strong cross-currents!

MR. ATTORNEY: Strong enough to drown an unwitting accountant who does not seek his own attorney's advice!

CHAPTER 9

STATE, FEDERAL, AND PROFESSIONAL REGULATION OF ACCOUNTANTS

¶ 9.01   Regulatory Framework

[1]   Overseers of the Accounting Profession

Regulation of the accounting profession to assure high standards of professional practice occurs in the following ways:

Civil litigation brought by nongovernmental (private sector) plaintiffs for money damages. The involvement of courts in litigation has often given rise to upgrading professional standards of practice which are deemed inappropriate, incomplete, or simply lacking.

SEC injunctive actions and Rule 2(e) disciplinary proceedings are the primary tools by which the SEC regulates the accounting profession.

State disciplinary actions by the state board, department, or agency responsible for issuing licenses to practice public accounting.

Professional self-regulation through peer review programs and enforcement of the Code of Ethics of the accounting profession. The primary participants in this program of self-regulation are the AICPA and the several state societies of CPAs.

[2]   SEC Oversight

The SEC oversees and "regulates" the accounting profession by its use of injunctive actions and Rule 2(e) disciplinary proceedings. By the use of these powers, the SEC imposes its views regarding appropriate professional standards of practice which should govern the activities of *all* accountants who are subject to its power.

[a]   Injunctive Actions.   The federal securities laws give the SEC the authority to bring a lawsuit in federal court for an injunction against an accountant or accounting firm who has violated the federal securities law or is about to violate the securities law. In an injunctive action the SEC seeks to obtain a finding by the court that the defendant has violated the securities law. The relief sought by the SEC will include an injunction preventing the defendant from committing future violations of the federal securities law.

Although an SEC injunctive proceeding against an accountant does not seek money damages, it can nonetheless exact a heavy toll in several respects including: (1) the adverse publicity attending the public court proceedings and (2) a finding of a securities law violation in an injunctive action may legally bind the accountant in any pending civil action brought for money damages arising out of the same occurrence; that is, an accountant may be "collaterally estopped" from denying liability if sued for money damages under the federal securities laws.

The SEC can use its injunctive powers against accountants who do not "practice" before the SEC and are not, therefore, subject to a Rule 2(e) disciplinary proceeding. For example, an accountant associated with a scheme to defraud in violation of Rule 10b-5 may be sued by the SEC to enjoin his violation. It does not matter that the accountant's client is not a listed company reporting to the SEC. All that counts is the fact that Rule 10b-5 has been violated. The following case is an example of a SEC action.

(i) SEC v. Koracorp Industries *and Comments*

SEC v. Koracorp Industries
573 F.2d 692 (9th Cir. 1978)

HUFSTEDLER, Circuit Judge: The Securities and Exchange Commission ("SEC") brought these two suits to obtain injunctions preventing the defendants from committing future violations of the antifraud and reporting provisions of the federal securities laws. The district judge granted defendants' motions for summary judgment. . . . With respect to Andersen, [defendant Arthur Andersen] we conclude that there was no genuine dispute as to any material fact, summary judgment was permissible, and the district court acted within the scope of its discretion in denying the injunctive relief sought.

Defendant Koracorp Industries, Inc. ("Koracorp") is a corporation, engaged in a number of business enterprises, whose common stock is publicly traded on the New York and Pacific Coast Stock Exchanges. Defendant Koretec Communications, Inc ("KCI") was a wholly-owned subsidiary of Koracorp whose principal business was the publication of a controlled-circulation advertising magazine, "Homemaking with a Flair" ("Flair"), which was used for direct mail promotion. Defendant Weil was

the president of KCI, defendant Cunningham was a vice president and director of Koracorp, and defendant Helfat was chief executive officer and president of Koracorp.

According to evidence presented by the SEC, Weil was the chief architect of the fraud. Weil's compensation depended in part upon the volume of KCI's business. Weil was able to increase his compensation by causing to be placed and carried on KCI's books millions of dollars of uncollectible, and sometimes wholly fictitious, accounts receivable. The SEC claimed that Weil also used these overbooked receivables to conceal kickbacks that were paid to him by corporations with which KCI did business. KCI's financial statements were consolidated with Koracorp's. When KCI's stack of receivables collapsed, Koracorp had to reverse over five million dollars which had been improperly shown as income on its books.

Defendant Andersen, Koracorp's accounting firm, first became aware of irregularities in KCI's accounts receivable while preparing its audit of Koracorp's 1970 financial statement. Andersen received a poor response from selected KCI customers with whom it attempted to confirm receivables. When its examination of contracts and collections failed adequately to support receivables in the amounts recorded, Andersen insisted that KCI's 1970 reserves for uncollectible accounts be increased, and it furnished Koracorp with critical comments concerning the inadequate documentation of transactions at KCI. In its 1971 and 1972 audits, Andersen again attempted to obtain confirmation for KCI's receivables from its customers, and repeatedly cautioned Koracorp about the deficient control procedures and the inadequate written documentation of transactions at KCI. The SEC produced evidence that the principals of KCI, with the assistance, or at least the passive neglect, of one or more of the principals of Koracorp, tried to cover up the overbooked receivables of KCI. By early May, 1973, the accounts receivable of KCI had grown to almost six million dollars, of which five million dollars was long past due or had never been billed. Cunningham and Helfat were aware of the receivables debacle, and Helfat directed that an internal investigation be conducted.

Following that investigation, Weil, in early August, 1973, admitted to Helfat that almost all of KCI's 1972 accounts receivable from advertising were uncollectible. Koracorp directed Andersen to conduct a special investigation into the accounts receivable situation at KCI. Andersen learned that substantially all of the 1972 confirmed accounts were now disavowed by customers and that the information obtained during the 1972 audit had been misrepresented. On August 7, Koracorp informed the New York and Pacific Coast Stock Exchanges and the SEC, and on August 8, the SEC suspended all trading in Koracorp's securities. On September 10, 1973, Andersen withdrew its auditor's report on Koracorp's 1972 financial statement. The original 1972 financial statements reported earnings per share of $0.27. After restatement in early 1974, by which time five million dollars of improperly stated income of KCI had been reversed, the 1972 revised financial statement showed a loss of $1.02 per share. Trading in Koracorp's securities was not permitted to be resumed until early 1974.

Meanwhile, at a special Koracorp board of directors' meeting on August 7, 1973, the board was informed by Cunningham of KCI's overstated accounts receivable and by Helfat of Weil's offer to purchase Flair. The board agreed to the sale of Flair to Weil, contingent upon his resignation as president of KCI. On August 24, 1973, the Koracorp board of directors requested Helfat's resignation as president and director of Koracorp, but retained him as a special consultant at full salary with all fringe benefits. The board also removed Cunningham from his position as vice president, after he refused to resign. Cunningham remained as a director of Koracorp until May, 1975. Both Cunningham and Helfat received bonuses based upon Koracorp's original 1972 earnings of $0.27 per share.

. . .

The primary purpose of injunctive relief against violators of the federal securities laws is to deter future violations, not to punish the violators.

. . .

As Professor Loss points out: "The ultimate test is whether the defendant's past conduct indicates—under all of the circumstances and not merely in view of the time which has elapsed since the last violation—that there is a reasonable likelihood of further violations in the future." Both the SEC and Andersen filed motions for summary judgment, each contending that it was entitled to judgment and that there were no genuine issues of fact. The SEC charged Anderson with . . . failure to uncover the receivables fraud and with willful failure to disclose to the public the details of the KCI receivables fraud during the post-August, 1973, period, during the course of Andersen's special investigation.

Upon the basis of these facts, Andersen, solely for the purpose of summary judgment, conceded that the firm's failure to uncover the receivables fraud was due to simple negligence. The SEC accepted that concession as to Andersen's pre-August, 1973, activities. The SEC, however, also claimed that Andersen was guilty of willful failure to disclose to the public details of the KCI receivables fraud during the period from August, 1973, to February 28, 1974.

We first address the question whether Andersen's failure to disclose to the public its findings as it pursued its special investigation was a violation of the federal securities laws. It is uncontested that Andersen, along with Koracorp, informed the New York and Pacific Coast Stock Exchanges and the SEC of the overbooking of accounts receivable on August 8. Although Andersen had not completed its special investigation in September, Andersen advised the SEC that it was withdrawing its consent to the use of its prior auditor's report in connection with Koracorp's 1972 financial statement, and it confirmed its understanding that Koracorp would "notify the Securities and Exchange Commission forthwith and . . . promptly make appropriate disclosure to the public and to the New York Stock Exchange." In the interim, the SEC had suspended all trading in Koracorp's securities. Commencing in October, 1973, the SEC began its own extensive investigation of the Koracorp problems. The SEC deposed all of the key Andersen personnel involved in the Koracorp audits, obtained production of documents, including Andersen's work papers, memoranda, correspondence, and reports relating to those audits. Andersen and its personnel voluntarily cooperated with the SEC's investigation both as to document production and deposition testimony.

The SEC's argument that Andersen violated some kind of duty in reporting its findings during its special investigation is hard to follow. As nearly as we can ascertain, its claim of misconduct rests upon a contention that, in Andersen's September 10, 1973, letter to Koracorp and the SEC, withdrawing its consent to the use of its report on Koracorp's 1972 financial statement, Andersen was too cautious in its language. The Andersen letter stated that the information it had obtained "indicates the possibility that the consolidated financial statements of Koracorp Industries, Inc. for the year ended December 29, 1972, may require adjustments," and that "significant amounts of accounts receivable of that subsidiary (KCI) may have been included in these financial statements erroneously. . . ." The SEC argues that Andersen was engaged in a cover-up because it did not then and there state that "egregious management fraud

had occurred." The SEC cites no authority and we have found none that poses a duty upon an accountant in the middle of a special investigation to make a public announcement that the company whose affairs it is investigating is guilty of fraud. There was nothing in the record before the district court which permitted an inference that, under the circumstances of this case, Andersen was guilty of any kind of concealment. Moreover, there is nothing in the record suggesting that the alleged failure to disclose was material to investors. The fact of fraud had been revealed, even if it was not presented in language that the SEC might have chosen. Trading in Koracorp had been suspended for a month preceding Andersen's letter and remained suspended for another five months.

The only other fact to which the SEC points to support its contention that Andersen was guilty of a kind of culpable nondisclosure is that Andersen's February 28, 1974, report on Koracorp's restated 1972 financial statement said that "sufficient information is not available at present to determine the amount of the adjustment relating to this discontinued operation which may be applicable to periods prior to 1972." But the SEC points to nothing that casts any doubt about the accuracy of that statement. The SEC argues that the statement was misleading because it did not also tell investors either how or why the KCI receivables were improperly booked. Perhaps there may be situations in which a failure to report results of an ongoing investigation in greater detail may be misleading, but the record in this case does not support the inferences that the SEC asks us to draw. The SEC has not given us any reason why there was a substantial likelihood that a reasonable shareholder in 1974 would consider the omitted details of any significance. (*See TSC Industries, Inc. v. Northway, Inc.* . . .) By 1974, Andersen had already audited Koracorp's year-end 1973 report, trading in Koracorp had been suspended, and there had been substantial public disclosure with respect to the KCI scandal.

We are left then with the SEC's claim that Andersen's failure to detect the overbooking scheme before August, 1973, constituted simple negligence for which injunctive relief would be appropriate.

Unlike the Koracorp and KCI defendants, Andersen's conduct in these transactions was fully exposed, and its state of mind was not in issue. No triable issue of fact remained, as both the SEC and Andersen agreed below. The record thus presented to the district court on the cross-motions for summary judgment the issues: (1) Is injunctive relief under Section 10(b) and Rule 10b-5 available to the SEC against an independent auditor who was guilty of simple negligence, and (2) if the relief is available, did the district court abuse its discretion in refusing to grant injunctive relief? We need not reach the first question, which was specifically left open in *Ernst & Ernst v. Hochfelder* (1976), on this appeal because, even if we assume that simple negligence is enough to sustain the SEC's suit for an injunction, the district court was nevertheless free to exercise its discretion in denying equitable relief against Andersen. No *per se* rule requiring the issuance of an injunction upon the showing of past violation exists. The critical issue is whether there is a reasonable likelihood that the wrong would be repeated. The district court has a significant degree of latitude in making that determination.

Judgment in favor of Andersen is affirmed.

1.   The SEC charged the auditors with negligence and "willful failure to disclose to the public details of the . . . receivables fraud" after it was discovered and being investigated by the auditors. As to the "failure to disclose" the court of appeals held that there is no "duty upon an accountant in the middle of a special investigation to make a public announcement that the company whose affairs it is investigating is guilty of fraud."

At the time the court of appeals decided *SEC v. Koracorp Industries* it was an unanswered question whether "simple negligence" was enough to sustain an SEC suit for injunctive relief under Rule 10b-5. Subsequent to the *Koracorp* decision, the U.S. Supreme Court answered the question in *Aaron v. SEC*. The U.S. Supreme Court held that "scienter is an element of a violation of § 10(b) and Rule 10b-5, regardless of the identity of the plaintiff or the nature of the relief sought." The U.S. Supreme Court rejected the argument that a suit for injunctive relief brought by the SEC could be grounded on "mere negligence."

2.   In a SEC injunctive action, the issues of money damages and plaintiffs reliance are not elements which the SEC must prove to make its case. However, a critical element to obtaining an injunction is proof by the SEC that there is a reasonable likelihood of future violations of the securities laws by the defendant.

In *SEC v. Koracorp Industries* the trial judge concluded after reviewing all the evidence, that there was not a reasonable likelihood that the auditors would engage in future violations of the securities laws. Thus, the court refused to permanently enjoin the auditors from future violations of the federal securities laws.

3.   In assessing whether an injunction should be issued against "future securities laws violations," the court will look at the severity of the defendant's past wrongdoing. In *Aaron v. SEC*, 446 U.S. 680 (1980) the U.S. Supreme Court's Chief Justice observed in a concurring opinion:

It bears mention that this dispute, though pressed vigorously by both sides, may be much ado about nothing. This is so because of the requirements in injunctive proceedings of a showing that "there is a reasonable likelihood that the wrong will be repeated." *SEC v. Manor Nursing Centers, Inc.*, 458 F.2d 1082, 1100 (CA2 1975) . . . *SEC v. Keller Corp.*

323 F.2d 397, 402 (CA7 1963). To make such a showing, it will almost always be necessary for the Commission to demonstrate that the defendant's past sins have been the result of more than negligence. Because the Commission must show some likelihood of a future violation, defendants whose past actions have been in good faith are not likely to be enjoined. . . . That is as it should be. An injunction is a drastic remedy, not a mild prophylactic, and should not be obtained against one acting in good faith.

[b]   Rule 2(e) Proceedings.   The SEC exerts significant influence over the accounting profession by its use of what is called Rule 2(e) Proceedings. Rule 2(e) is a disciplinary rule contained within the SEC's Rules of Practice.

Under Rule 2(e) the SEC may deny temporarily or permanently an accountant's "privilege" of appearing or practicing before the SEC. Practicing before the SEC includes the accountant's preparation of any statement, opinion, or other paper which is included within any document filed with the SEC.

An accountant may be disciplined under Rule 2(e) if the SEC concludes that the accountant:

Does not possess the "requisite qualifications" to represent others;

Lacks "character or intergrity" or has engaged in "unethical or improper professional conduct"; or

Has "willfully violated, or willfully aided and abetted the violation of any provision of the Federal Securities Laws, or the rules and regulations thereunder."

Rule 2(e) proceedings are conducted by the SEC. The decision to discipline an accountant or an accounting firm is made by the SEC following a hearing. Rule 2(e) proceedings do not involve the courts prior to the SEC's decision. After an accountant is disciplined under Rule 2(e), the accountant may appeal the SEC's order of discipline to a federal district court for review.

Rule 2(e) has been criticized because the SEC wears three hats during a Rule 2(e) proceeding, namely, the SEC is not only the investigator but also the prosecutor and the judge. The greatest criticism of Rule 2(e) is its use by the SEC to "regulate" the accounting profession as a whole.

Rule 2(e) has been applied far beyond isolated instances of wrongdoing by accountants. The SEC has used Rule 2(e) to discipline an entire firm of accountants for the wrongdoing of a portion of their partners. In the process of its sweeping application of Rule 2(e) the SEC has publicly stated its expectations regarding appropriate professional standards of auditing practice and accounting disclosure. This "ad hoc" promulgation of professional standards by the SEC through the medium of a Rule 2(e) proceeding has been highly criticized as inappropriate.

The following article discusses the SEC's use of Rule 2(e) to regulate the accounting profession.

(i)   Distortion and Misuse of Rule 2(e)[1]

Introduction

Rule 2(e) of the Securities and Exchange Commission's Rules of Practice is one of the primary means by which the SEC exercises control over accountants and other professionals who practice before it. Recent Rule 2(e) proceedings against accountants demonstrate that the SEC has converted the Rule from one designed to serve the limited salutary purpose of exercising disciplinary authority over the incompetent, unethical, or dishonest accounting practitioner to a rule that has effectively been utilized to pervasively regulate accounting firms and the profession as a whole.

This expansion of the regulatory process has come without the benefit or inducement of any recent legislative enactment mandating such an approach and has brought into question not only the means by which the Commission has implemented Rule 2(e), but the fundamental issue of the existence and scope of the Commission's statutory authority to undertake any disciplinary action against accountants and other professionals practicing before it. This article will analyze these and other significant issues raised by the Commission's recent Rule 2(e) proceedings.

The Commission's Authority

Rule 2(e) (1) provides that the Commission may deny temporarily or permanently the "privilege" of appearing or practicing before it in any way to any person who is found by the Commission, after notice and hearing:

> (i)   not to possess the requisite qualifications to represent others;
> (ii)   to be lacking in character or integrity or to have engaged in unethical or improper professional conduct; or
> (iii)   to have willfully violated, or willfully aided and abetted the violation of any provision of the Federal securities laws, or the rules and regulations thereunder.

Practice is defined, under Rule 2(e), to include not only transacting business with the Commission but also the preparation of any statement, opinion, or other paper, by an accountant, which is included within any document filed with the Commission.

•   •   •

Rule 2(e) proceedings in recent years reflect that both the Commission's means and objectives in implementing the Rule have been anything but restrained.

Implementation of Rule 2(e)

The more expansive the Commission's application of Rule 2(e), the more pernicious becomes the deprivation of due process that results in such proceedings where the SEC is not only the investigator but the prosecutor and judge as well. Moreover, the "rudimentary requirements of fair play" which must attend any administrative adjudication are called into question when it becomes clear that the SEC is utilizing a Rule 2(e) proceeding to accomplish indirectly that which it is expressly prohibited from doing directly under the explicit provisions of the federal securities laws.

•   •   •

No Need to Prove Scienter

Beyond the foregoing infirmities of due process under Rule 2(e), the possibility exists under the standards of the Rule and the Commission's application thereof, that a Rule 2(e) proceeding may be adjudicated without regard to any standard of culpability or without regard to proof of fault on the part of the accounting practitioner. The Commission has long held that it need not prove scienter in a Rule 2(e) proceeding. In *In re* Haskins & Sells, it held:

---

[1] Richard L. Miller, *Securities Regulation Law Journal*

We accept respondents' assertion that they acted in good faith and accordingly do not find any willfulness in the sense referred to by them. However, in a disciplinary action under Rule II(e) we are not required to make such a finding. We are of the opinion that respondents' accounting work in connection with the Thomascolor registration statement was so deficient in the respects set forth above, as a result of their failure to give this professional undertaking the degree of care and inquiry it demanded under the circumstances, that disciplinary action is required.

Moreover, following the Supreme Court's decision in *Ernst & Ernst v. Hochfelder*, the Commission's General Counsel clearly stated that which had become the Commission's apparent practice in Rule 2(e) proceedings—simple negligence would serve as an appropriate basis to a finding of violation of Rule 2(e). The Commission's General Counsel observed in a memorandum to the chairman of the SEC which analyzed *Hochfelder* that the Supreme Court's decision strongly implied that the Commission would need to prove scienter in future injunctive actions brought under Rule 10b-5, and that as a result:

> it may be appropriate for the Commission to place greater reliance upon Rule 2(e) in the future as a means of preventing a recurrence of unethical or improper conduct.

In a subsequent memorandum to the chairman, the General Counsel stated:

> There may be cases where, as a consequence of *Hochfelder*, negligent conduct by an accountant or attorney which injured investors may not constitute a violation of Section 10(b) and Rule 10b-5, nor otherwise violate the securities laws, yet represent a substantial threat to the public interest if such conduct were to continue in the future. If this conduct would amount to a significant deviation from professional standards, a proceeding under Rule 2(e) to test the individual's fitness to continue to be permitted to practice before the Commission might be appropriate."

It appears clear therefore that the Commission views Rule 2(e) as a means whereby it may accomplish indirectly that which *Hochfelder* has arguably foreclosed it from doing directly.

The Commission's public Rule 2(e) proceeding against Touche Ross & Co. stands as testimony to this fact.

There, instead of joining Touche Ross in an injunctive action, which was brought against certain other defendants related to the audit client, the Commission chose to commence a Rule 2(e) proceeding and thereby avoid the risk that it would be held to the scienter standard of culpability. Nowhere in the order instituting the Rule 2(e) proceeding does the Commission allege that Touche Ross had any intent to deceive or defraud in connection with the audits it performed.[1] Moreover, by announcing publicly the commencement of the Rule 2(e) proceeding, the Commission did not deprive it of the benefit, from a settlement standpoint, which usually attends an injunctive action resulting from the publicity adverse to the professional.[2]

---

[1] *In re* Touche Ross & Co., Ad. Proc. File No. 3-5075, Order of Sept. 2, 1976.

In certain Rule 2(e) proceedings, it is questionable whether the Commission's contentions that an accountant was negligent would pass muster under judicial standards of due diligence and reasonable care. Indeed, in many Rule 2(e) proceedings the Commission merely states that an accountant has engaged in "improper professional conduct" by virtue of some Commission-determined departure from generally accepted auditing standards, and without elaboration or specific analysis or findings which clearly indicate that such departure was due to negligence or some level of conduct amounting to fault. See, e.g., Ernst & Ernst, Accounting Series Release No. 248 (1978), CCH Fed. Sec. L. Rep. ¶ 72,270; Haskins & Sells, Accounting Series Release No. 241 (1978), CCH Fed. Sec. L. Rep. ¶ 72,263. To be sure, the failure of an accountant to comply with generally accepted auditing standards, even under the Commission's view of those standards, is not necessarily tantamount to a lack of due diligence on the part of the professional. See AICPA Code of Professional Ethics, Rule 202.

[2] That this benefit is considerable has not gone unnoticed by one chairman of the SEC who observed that "if the proceeding is disposed of at the very time that it is begun, there normally will be only one round of adverse publicity. Otherwise, there may be two—or more. Lawyers should think about such things." Garrett, *A Look at the SEC's Administrative Practice* 10 (1974).

SEC Does Not Have to Show Likelihood of Future Violations

In addition to avoiding the scienter requirement, a Rule 2(e) proceeding also avoids the further judicial requirement that an injunction should not be entered and sanctions granted where there has been no showing by the Commission of the likelihood of any further violations or wrongdoing by the accounting firm. Under Rule 2(e), the Commission has not encumbered itself with such a requirement in determining whether sanctions are appropriate. Moreover, since the Commission's sanctions under Rule 2(e) are severe—temporary or permanent suspension from practice before the Commission—it effectively has at its command a range of sanctions, to be secured through settlements, which may be more farreaching than the ancillary relief afforded by the courts in injunctive proceedings.[3]

Procedural Unfairness of Rule 2(e)

Apart from these substantive infirmities in the means by which Rule 2(e) is implemented, there are also certain procedural aspects of Rule 2(e) proceedings that underscore the unfairness of its present usage as a vehicle to discipline and regulate the accounting profession. Unlike a judicial proceeding, discovery in a Rule 2(e) proceeding is not a matter of right but is subject to the discretionary approval of the administrative law judge, and in no event is the permissible scope of discovery as broad as that allowed under the Federal Rules of Civil Procedure.

The rules of evidence employed in Rule 2(e) proceedings are less rigorous than the governing rules of evidence in judicial pro-

ceedings. As a result, inherently unreliable hearsay and conjectural evidence are likely to be admitted and utilized as a basis for decision-making. Related to the quality of the evidence is the fact that although the SEC's staff has the burden of proof in a Rule 2(e) proceeding, it is a burden which in the Commission's view may be satisfied by a mere preponderance of the evidence and not by clear and convincing evidence, which is the governing standard in judicial proceedings where the "heavy sanction" of "deprivation of livelihood" may be imposed.

Thus, a Rule 2(e) proceeding is devoid of more than just an independent jurist attired in a black robe. As the foregoing indicates, many of the fundamental attributes of due process which attend judicial proceedings under the securities acts are totally lacking. In many types of administrative proceedings this would be objectionable. In this type of proceeding, which is tantamount to a "quasi-criminal proceeding" with the deleterious consequences of impugning the accountant's professional reputation and depriving him of his livelihood, the absence of fundamental concepts of fair play and due process is highly questionable.

Rule 2(e) Objectives

Beyond the Commission's facile and often repeated statement that the objective of Rule 2(e) proceedings is "to protect the public and the integrity of the Commission's own processes from incompetent, unethical or dishonest attorneys, accountants and other professionals and experts," there exist questions to what are the specific objectives of the SEC and its staff in administering Rule 2(e), and the effect of those objectives on the accounting profession as a whole.

At the outset of the Commission's increased enforcement activity under Rule 2(e), the Commission and its staff denied that

> it is the ultimate design of the Commission to create situations which would result in all the "Big Eight" being under . . . review procedures [monitored by the Commission]. Nothing could be further from the truth. There is no such plan or intent. As proceedings develop we will deal with them one at a

---

[3] In many Rule 2(e) proceedings, the Commission applies sanctions applicable to the nationwide practice of an accounting firm despite the Commission's acknowledgment that the alleged audit transgressions relate to a small percentage of the total number of audit engagements properly performed. See, e.g., Peat, Marwick, Mitchell & Co., Accounting Series Release No. 173 (1975), CCH Fed. Sec. L. Rep. ¶ 72,195, at 62,492; Seidman & Seidman, Accounting Series No. 196 (1976), CCH Fed. Sec. L. Rep. ¶ 72,218, at 62,542.

time, without plan or design to subject the profession to the thumb of the Commission.

Is the SEC Trying to Control the Accounting Profession?

Subsequent statements and actions by the Commission cast doubt on the notion that the present-day objective of the Commission is not to subjugate the accounting profession to the Commission's day-to-day control. In a memorandum to the SEC's chairman, the Commission's General Counsel observed:

> Admiral Rickover suggests that the Commission, periodically, should supervise audits of the performance of public accounting firms. Under its existing authority, and particularly Rule 2(e) of its Rules of Practice, the Commission has, where it finds substandard, unprofessional or questionable auditing practices, commenced and concluded disciplinary proceedings requiring the firm, at its expense, to undergo an independent quality control review. This approach has been employed in Commission disciplinary proceedings, involving some of the largest accounting firms, with the consent of the firms named as respondents in those proceedings. Variations of this procedure have also been used in settlements involving smaller accounting firms. Although some accounting firms apparently might argue otherwise, we believe the Commission's authority in this regard to be soundly based. The Commission has the authority to preclude accounting firms from practicing before it at all, and, accordingly, has the authority to condition an accounting firm's ability to practice before the Commission upon a thorough review of the firm's practices and procedures, and an undertaking by the firm to correct any deficiencies highlighted by such a review.
>
> While the Commission's authority would, in our view, permit the Commission itself to conduct this review of an accounting firm's performance and quality controls as Admiral Rickover has suggested, such an approach would be costly, time-consuming, and likely a less effective allocation of the Commission's limited resources in light of the results achieved in the cases discussed above, where the profession has undertaken to review its own performance, subject to Com-

> mission oversight. In these cases, of course, a condition of the settlement has been that the review performed be satisfactory to the Commission.
>
> Finally, Admiral Rickover suggested that, in the event an accounting firm does not meet minimum standards of professional performance and independence, the Commission should suspend the firm or revoke its license to audit publicly-held companies. This, of course, is the function of Rule 2(e) of the Commission's Rules of Practice.

The strongest evidence of the Commission's intention is the compiled record of the Commission's significant and "inordinate intrusion of government into professional activity." With few exceptions, virtually all the large public accounting firms practicing before the Commission have been the subject of recent Rule 2(e) proceedings and have succumbed to some form of sanctions with continuing Commission oversight, including:

1. The undertaking of peer reviews and quality-control inspections which are subject to Commission approval and oversight;

2. Imposition of continuing education requirements;

3. Prohibitions on a partner participating in a firm's activities in a partnership capacity;

4. Prohibitions on undertaking new business; notification of prospective clients of the SEC's findings;

5. Restrictions on a firm's merger activities; and inducements for a firm to merge with a larger firm.

No Authority to Set Auditing Standards

Although the above sanctions may be viewed as untoward by only those to whom the sanction applies,[4] the one sanction which appears most nettlesome to the accounting profession as a whole is the SEC's involvement in these proceedings in the ad hoc promulgation and

---

[4] The peer review of Peat, Marwick, the cost of which was borne by Peat, "assertedly cost over $1 million, and required in excess of 14,000 man hours." See Memorandum to Chairman Williams, note 36 *supra*, at 990 n.18.

implementation of what it views as generally accepted auditing standards.

That the Commission's regulatory effort in such situations is intrusive is clearly undeniable.[5] More important, however, is whether the Commission's ad hoc promulgation of generally accepted auditing standards is either authorized by statute or desirable.

Unlike the Commission's explicit statutory power to promulgate accounting principles generally acceptable in SEC practice, the Commission's power to promulgate auditing standards generally acceptable to SEC practice is notably absent from the securities acts. Despite the absence of express authority, the Commission finds such authority not only in the recesses of its antifraud authority and authority to define independence, but also as a part of its authority under Rule 2(e), which is itself highly suspect. Thus, the Commission's General Counsel has stated:

> In addition to its antifraud and definitional powers, Rule 2(e), as noted above, provides a ready vehicle for Commission articulation of standards of auditing practice not just as a means of treating specific instances of unprofessional or improper conduct, but also as a means, through the publication of its dispositions of such Rule 2(e) proceedings, of offering guidance to all auditors for their future audits.

Should the SEC Act in This Area?

Apart from the Commission's authority to promulgate auditing standards, there remains the question of the desirability of the Commission's enactment of such standards. The means by which the Commission "promulgates" auditing standards is, by the Commission's own concession, on an "ad hoc" basis through the medium of a Rule 2(e) proceeding. Thus the procedures which would

normally attend the enactment of a Commission rule or regulation (or the enactment of an auditing standard by the AICPA), including notice and publication of the proposal and a period for comment, are absent. Accordingly, the expression of such "guidance to all auditors for future audits" comes at the expense of the professional reputation of some auditor who should have known what the standards for "future audits" would be.[6]

Moreover, by making such proclamations of generally accepted auditing standards without the benefit of the views of those who actually are engaged in the day-to-day practice of auditing, the risk is created that a patently unrealistic standard will be the guiding light for avoidance of disciplinary activity under Rule 2(e). The danger of such an approach is amply demonstrated by the Commission's explication of an auditing standard in its Rule 2(e) proceeding in *In re Peat, Marwick, Mitchell & Co.*, involving that firm's examination of National Student Marketing Corporation. There, the Commission suggests the existence of a "whistle blowing" obligation in certain circumstances—an obligation which is not grounded on any ethical requirement, accounting principle, auditing standard, or judicial decision, and which was not subjected to the benefits of scrutiny by auditing practitioners and others, who might have addressed the extent to which that standard would have a chilling effect on auditor-client communications and could impair the entire audit process.

●   ●   ●

---

[5] For example, as a result of its proceedings against Peat and Touche, the Commission has injected itself into the process of drafting accounting firm audit manuals for those firms. Likewise, pursuant to the order entered in the proceeding against Laventhol, that firm was required to secure Commission and court approval to change audit procedures reflected in the firm's manual.

[6] That this approach is "overly crude" has been conceded by no less an authority than an SEC chairman who stated:

I have observed in the past that I think our enforcement weapons may be overly crude, or at least not well tuned to achieve our objective. The use of Rule 2(e) has theoretical attraction. In some cases it has clearly seemed like the appropriate remedy with respect to lawyers whose sins have extended to misrepresentations if not outright lies in their dealings with the Commission itself. But I doubt whether it can ever serve as an appropriate vehicle for enunciating professional guidelines.

Garrett, "New Directions in Professional Responsibility," 20 Bus. Law. 9, 13 (1974).

Conclusion

The Commission's questionable use, and abuse, of Rule 2(e) gives rise to serious considerations of the due process afforded the professional who is the subject of such a proceeding, and the larger question of the proper role of the SEC in disciplining and regulating professionals.

If the Commission continues to misuse Rule 2(e) and usurp power it does not really have, and assuming courts countenance such continued activity, then at a minimum the Commission would do well to shore up those aspects of its Rule 2(e) proceedings which are vulnerable to challenge on due process grounds, not the least of which is its failure to require that a professional be subjected to the severe penalty of suspension or disbarment only on a showing of scienter or some higher standard of culpability. Moreover, proof of such culpability should be by clear and convincing evidence, and based on existing principles and standards and not those which grow out of the proceeding and are given ex post facto application. In no event should sanctions be administered absent a clear finding that the professional is likely to engage in future wrongdoing.

In addition, the Commission should refrain from advancing in Rule 2(e) proceedings new or "exotic" theories of accounting principles or auditing standards which are better and more fairly addressed through the hearing and rule-making processes of the accounting profession. The imposition of such safeguards in Rule 2(e) enforcement proceedings goes no further than that which is expected and required in injunctive enforcement proceedings, where the stakes in winning or losing are no greater.

Moreover, the SEC's continued misuse of Rule 2(e) should not be necessary under any view of need, including the Commission's, if the results of the accounting profession's current efforts at self-regulation prove successful. The self-policing efforts of the professional accounting organizations, such as the AICPA and state societies of CPAs, are under way at an accelerated pace and in many instances have been and will be supplemented by increased regulatory activities of the state boards of accountancy which license CPAs. This pervasive scheme of regulation, if actively implemented, should totally preempt the need for SEC involvement in disciplinary matters and thereby foreclose Commission intrusion into the daily activities of the accounting profession.

In the absence of future restraint by the SEC and increased regulatory efforts by the profession, it can be expected that the present-day misuse of Rule 2(e) will not subside.

[ii]   Differences Between Rule 2(e) Proceedings and Injunctive Actions.   In a situation where an accountant has participated in a violation of Rule 10b-5 of the federal securities laws, the SEC could choose to proceed against the accountant by commencing an injunctive action or a Rule 2(e) proceeding. There are differences between each type of proceeding which may lead to the SEC favoring one approach over the other. The differences are as follows:

Forum.   An injunctive action must be brought in federal district court before a federal trial judge. Rule 2(e) proceedings are brought by the SEC's staff before an administrative law judge who reports his or her findings to the SEC. The SEC decides the case. Rule 2(e) proceedings provide the SEC with a "home court advantage."

Standard of culpability.   In an injunctive proceeding for a violation of Rule 10b-5, the SEC must prove that the accountant acted with "scienter," "mere negligence" is not sufficient wrongdong. In a Rule 2(e) proceeding the SEC need not prove scienter. Disciplinary sanctions have been ordered on the basis of negligent conduct.

Future risk.   In an injunctive action, the district court will not issue a permanent injunction absent a showing that the accountant is likely to engage in future violations or wrongdoing under the federal securities law. There is no such requirement of proof in a Rule 2(e) proceeding.

Scope of relief.   In an injunctive action a court may grant the SEC relief in a form other than injunctive relief. In a Rule 2(e) proceeding, the SEC has the power to impose all types of sanctions. Thus, the relief obtainable under Rule 2(e) may be more far-reaching than the ancillary relief occasionally granted by the courts in injunctive proceedings.

Adverse publicity.   Injunctive actions are public proceedings which frequently draw substantial public attention. The adverse publicity to a professional of being a defendant in a case brought by the SEC can have a substantial impact on the accountant's desire to resist the charges. The SEC has publicized the charges in a Rule 2(e) proceeding before they have been subject to a hearing. All significant Rule 2(e) proceedings routinely culminate in a public statement by the SEC of its findings and conclusions in the case. By "going public" the SEC retains in a Rule 2(e) proceeding all the advantages which adverse publicity brings to bear on a professional accountant.

[3]   Professional Self-Regulation: Enforcement of the Code of Ethics

The accounting profession's efforts at self-regulation include promulgating professional standards of practice, implementation of a program of peer review (an audit of the auditors), and enforcement of the profession's Code of Ethics. Enforcement of the Code of Ethics may be by far the most important method by which the profession assures adherence to high standards of professional practice. The Code of Ethics adopted and enforced by the AICPA is the seminal standard by which an accountant's conduct should be measured. The Rules of Conduct embodied in the Code of Ethics may be grouped into two categories: (1) technical standards and (2) behavorial standards.

[a]   Code of Ethics: Technical Standards.   The Rules of Conduct falling within the category of "technical standards" consist of the standards of professional conduct which a practitioner must meet when performing a professional service. Conduct which fails to meet these professional standards not only violates the Code of Ethics, but may also be the basis for a finding of civil liability to the client or third party user of the professional's service.

Rule 201—General Standards provides that a member accountant of the AICPA:

shall comply with the following general standards as interpreted by bodies designated by Council, and must justify any departures therefrom.

A.   Professional Competence. A member shall undertake only those engagements which he or his firm can reasonably expect to complete with professional competence.

B.   Due professional care. A member shall exercise due professional care in the performance of an engagement.

C.   Planning and supervision. A member shall adequately plan and supervise an engagement.

D.   Sufficient relevant data. A member shall obtain sufficient relevant data to afford a reasonable basis for conclusions or recommendations in relation to an engagement.

E.   Forecasts. A member shall not permit his name to be used in conjunction with any forecast of future transactions in a manner which may lead to the belief that the member vouches for the achievability of the forecast.

By its terms Rule 201 sets out certain standards of conduct which must apply regardless of the nature of the service rendered by the accountant.

Rule 202—Auditing Standards provides that an accountant must comply with GAAS when issuing an audit report. Rule 202 directs that:

> A member shall not permit his name to be associated with financial statements in such a manner as to imply that he is acting as an independent public accountant unless he has complied with the applicable generally accepted auditing standards promulgated by the Institute. Statements on Auditing Standards issued by the Institute's Auditing Standards Executive Committee (Auditing Standards Board) are, for purposes of this rule, considered to be interpretations of the generally accepted auditing standards, and departures from such statements must be justified by those who do not follow them.

Rule 203—Accounting Principles is a companion provision to Rule 202. Rule 203 addresses the circumstances where an accountant renders an audit opinion regarding financial statements. It states:

> A member shall not express an opinion that financial statements are presented in conformity with generally accepted accounting principles if such statements contain any departure from an accounting principle promulgated by the body designated by Council to establish such principles which has a material effect on the statements taken as a whole, unless the member can demonstrate that due to unusual circumstances the financial statements would otherwise have been misleading. In such cases his report must describe the departure, the approximate effects thereof, if practicable, and the reasons why compliance with the principle would result in a misleading statement.

The body designated by the AICPA council to establish GAAP is the Financial Accounting Standards Board.

Rule 204—Other Technical Standards provides that "a member shall comply with other technical standards promulgated by bodies designated by Council to establish such standards, and departures therefrom must be justified by those who do not follow them." The standards of practice which govern Management Advisory Services and Compilation and Review Services must be followed, or departures justified, to avoid violating Rule 204.

[b]   Code of Ethics: Behavioral Standards.   Behavioral standards consist of Rules of Conduct which prohibit certain relationships and types of behavior which are inconsistent with holding one's self out as a professional and which would otherwise undermine the accountant's credibility with those who rely upon his professional services. Included within the behavioral standards are rules of conduct dealing with independence, integrity, and objectivity.

[i] Independence, Integrity, and Objectivity.   *Rule 101—Independence* provides that

> A member or a firm of which he is a partner or shareholder shall not express an opinion on financial statements of an enterprise unless he and his firm are independent with respect to such enterprise.

Rule 102—Integrity and Objectivity directs that

> A member shall not knowingly misrepresent facts, and when engaged in the practice of public accounting, including the rendering of tax and management advisory services, shall not subordinate his judgment to others. In tax practice, a member may resolve doubt in favor of his client as long as there is reasonable support for his position.

Independence has been defined by the profession as the ability to act with integrity and objectivity. The Code of Ethics recognizes that:

> Independence has always been a concept fundamental to the accounting profession, the cornerstone of its philosophical structure. For no matter how competent any CPA may be, his opinion on financial statements will be of little value to those who rely on him—whether they be clients or any of his unseen audience of credit grantors, investors, governmental agencies and the like—unless he maintains his independence.

Independence is the concept which vests an accountant with credibility. For nonclient, third party users of an accountant's professional services, credibility is critical to an independent accountant's purpose. If accountants lose their credibility with third party users of their services, the accountants' role in our society may be destroyed or rendered useless.

Because independence is the bedrock of an accountant's professionalism when he is rendering an opinion on financial statements, the accountant must satisfy two tests of independence: (1) the accountant must be *independent in fact* and (2) the accountant must maintain the *appearance of independence*; that is, the accountant's independence must be perceived by clients and financial statement users.

Independence in fact is difficult to prove for it involves the accountant's mental attitude. Short of an accountant stating that he is not independent there is no way that anyone can peer within an accountant's mind to determine if in fact he is independent.

The appearance of independence, the so-called perceived independence, involves an objective consideration of all the facts relating to an accountant's involvement. Under the perceived independence test certain relationships with the client are deemed to violate an accountant's independence without regard to whether the accountant is in fact independent.

For example, an auditor's direct financial interest in his audit client impairs the appearance of independence. It is possible that the direct financial interest has not *in fact* impaired an accountant's independence in mental attitude. As perceived by financial statement users, however, the accountant's independence is suspect or entirely lacking.

Related to maintaining independence is the contention that an accountant should avoid engaging in nonaudit services in magnitude or by type of service where the accountant's professional "image" as an "auditor" might be impaired. Many within the accounting profession hold to the view that to the extent an accountant performs services that are not substantially related to accounting a risk is created that the public's confidence in the accountant will be diminished. The diminution of public confidence relates to the question of whether the public may retain doubts regarding the accountant's ability to perform professional auditing services. In a nutshell, is there a point where the auditor becomes a "nonauditor, business consultant?"

Situations which give rise to questions regarding an auditor's independence in appearance can be as vast as the universe of perceptions maintained by financial statement users. A perception which has been particularly nettlesome involves the issue of the proper scope of services which an accountant may perform without impairing his independence as an auditor. There are no fast and easy answers in the great debate over the question of whether engaging in certain management advisory services places the accountant in management's role thereby impairing independence. Because there are benefits to the audit process which exist by having the auditor advise management in certain areas, it can be expected that there will be no radical changes forthcoming which limit the scope of services an accountant may offer consistent with his obligation of independence.

Independence often plays a pivotal role in litigation against an accountant involving allegations of fraud. If the accountant's independence has been impaired by virtue of an impermissible relationship with the client, all actions or failure to act by the accountant will be suspect. Lack of independence will color all questions regarding the adequacy of an auditor's examination and the fairness of his disclosure.

With the loss of independence, the accountant loses credibility. In litigation the absence of independence may render an auditor's report incredible in the eyes of the judge or jury.

[ii] Responsibility to Clients: Confidentiality. *Rule 301—Confidential client information* provides that an accountant "shall not disclose any confidential information obtained in the course of a professional engagement except with the consent of the client." This Rule of Conduct acknowledges the importance of maintaining the confidences of a client in order to foster and preserve the free-flow of information necessary to render a professional service or advice.

The ethical obligation of confidentiality is not an evidentiary privilege enforceable in court. Although a few states have created statutory evidentiary privileges creating an accountant-client privilege, the vast majority of states have no such privilege. Moreover, the federal courts do not recognize any accountant-client privilege in matters involving federal laws.

Because an accountant may be called upon to divulge client confidential information in the course of a judicial proceeding, client consent to disclosure should be sought. In the event the client does not consent, the accountant should insist that the party requesting disclosure obtain a court order compelling disclosure.

With respect to instances involving the so-called duty to warn or whistle-blowing, particular caution should be exercised to avoid violating client confidences while at the same type avoiding complicity in a fraud. It is possible to defuse a potentially incinerary whistle-blowing situation by resigning and merely advising the appropriate parties that you are no longer the accountant for your ex-client. You need not say more and you need not reveal confidential client information. (See ¶ 6.03 regarding the special disclosure problems relating to the duty to correct.)

In a whistle-blowing situation where the auditor does not resign, he should keep in mind that Rules of Conduct 202 and 203 which mandate GAAS and GAAP take priority over Rule 301. That is, it is no defense to the failure to comply with GAAS and GAAP that the accountant was duty bound by Rule 301 to maintain client confidentiality.

[iii]   *Restrictions on Certain Business Practices: Fees, Advertising, and Forms of Practice.*   *Rule 502—Advertising and other forms of solicitation* directs that an accountant "shall not seek to obtain clients by advertising or other forms of solicitation in a manner that is false, misleading, or deceptive. Solicitation by the use of coercion, overreaching or harassing conduct is prohibited."

Only false, misleading, or deceptive advertising violates Rule 502. If the accountant's advertisement is factual it should be unassailable.

Solicitation may be factual and yet violate the Code of Ethics if it reaches the point of coercion, overreaching, or harassing conduct. Reasonable minds may differ as to what type of conduct constitutes harassment or "overreaching." Because the standards for solicitation are vague, enforcement of Rule 502 may be predicated primarily on solicitation and advertising which is false and deceptive.

Rule 504—Incompatible occupations provides that

> a member who is engaged in the practice of public accounting shall not concurrently engage in any business or occupation which would create a conflict of interest in rendering professional services.

Rule 505—Forms of practice and name provides:

> A member may practice public accounting, whether as an owner or employee, only in the form of a proprietorship, a partnership or a professional corporation. . .
>
> A member shall not practice under a firm name which includes any fictitious name, indicates specialization or is misleading as to the type of organization (proprietorship, partnership, or corporation). However, names of one or more past partners or shareholders may be included in the firm name of a successor partnership or corporation. Also, a partner surviving the death or withdrawal of all other partners may continue to practice under the partnership name for up to two years after becoming a sole practitioner. . . . .

Rule 302—Contingent fees directs that:

> Professional services shall not be offered or rendered under an arrangement whereby no fee will be charged unless a specified finding or result is attained, or where the fee is otherwise

contingent upon the findings or results of such services. However, a member's fees may vary depending, for example, on the complexity of the service rendered.

Fees are not regarded as being contingent if fixed by courts or other public authorities or, in tax matters, if determined based on the results of judicial proceedings or the findings of governmental agencies.

It can be expected that the prohibition on contingent fees will be scaled-down to allow contingent fees in circumstances where an accountant's independence will not be impaired.

Rule 503—Commission provides that an accountant "shall not pay a commission to obtain a client, nor shall he accept a commission for a referral to a client of products or services of others."

A pernicious practice involves the accountant's receipt of a commission or payment from a third-party vendor for recommending to the client the purchase of the vendor's product or service. To the extent this practice occurs without the client's consent or knowledge, the situation begins to approach the realm of an illegal kickback. Apart from the Code of Ethics, in the absence of client consent, the client should not be put at an economic disadvantage.

[c] Code of Ethics: A Look at the Future. The Code of Ethics of the accounting profession will be scrutinized in the coming years to assure that its prohibitions are (1) consistent with maintaining high standards of professionalism and (2) not inconsistent with fostering competition in the marketplace for professional services. Let us join a discussion between Joe Industry, an accountant in industry, and Pete Practice, an accounting practitioner, as they share their thoughts regarding the future of the Code of Ethics.

MR. INDUSTRY: Pete, why do we need a Code of Ethics—all it does is prevent competition among accountants. In fact, it even prevents accountants from offering services in some situations.

MR. PRACTICE: I know that there are provisions of the Code of Ethics which are anticompetitive—for example, the Code of Ethics at one time prohibited advertising and solicitation. In the "good old days" an accountant could not advertise at all. Needless to say that didn't square with the antitrust laws so the rules were cut back to prohibit only false and deceptive advertising.

MR. INDUSTRY: Well there are other rules in the Code of Ethics which chill competition and even prevent accountants from offering services which are requested by clients. . . .

MR. PRACTICE: Give me an example. . . .

MR. INDUSTRY: O.K. The rule which prohibits contingent fee arrangements is overly broad. . . .

MR. PRACTICE: We can't have auditors working on a contingent fee relationship; it would impair their credibility as independent auditors.

MR. INDUSTRY: I'll buy that, but what if independence is not an issue with respect to the service offered by the accountant. For example, assume an author of a book retains an accountant to protect his interests under a royalty agreement. For the author the best fee agreement with the accountant would be to make the accountant's fee contingent on the results he obtains in this adversary type relationship. The harder the accountant works at protecting the author's rights, the more reward the accountant should receive for his efforts.

MR. PRACTICE: I'll go along with that.

MR. INDUSTRY: I think the rule prohibiting commissions should also be abrogated. . . .

MR. PRACTICE: I'm not so sure. If you have professional accountants involved in "hawking" computer systems and other items where they receive commissions, how will the public perceive accountants. Will our integrity and objectivity as it is perceived by clients and the public be impaired? Unlike "value billing" and "contingent fees," the public might perceive the practice of receiving commissions as being inconsistent with an accountant's "image" as a professional.

MR. INDUSTRY: There's that dirty word—"image." Do you recall back in the 1970s when the SEC suggested that an accountant's performance of MAS services may be incompatible with his "image" as an auditor?

MR. PRACTICE: Yeah, I recall that argument.

MR. INDUSTRY: What was the SEC's point?

MR. PRACTICE: I believe that the SEC's staff was concerned that an auditor may become involved with performing MAS to the point that his skills, competence, and interests are really focused more in the area of consulting work rather than auditing.

MR. INDUSTRY: There may be something to the "image" argument *if* the accountant effectively functions as a full-time consultant and a part-time auditor. For example, when our company hires a law firm to help us in a problem area we want to know if the firm practices in that area. If its a labor law problem we are not going to hire a law firm which practices primarily or exclusively in estate planning. The "image" of a law firm affects our judgment regarding their ability to do the job.

MR. PRACTICE: You may be right. I know of a few accounting firms who derive almost 90 percent of their firm revenues from consulting work and less than 2 percent of their fees from audits. My personal opinion is that these fellows have become successful business consultants but they have made a decision to withdraw from the area of auditing—that's my perception of their "image."

MR. INDUSTRY: We will have to watch for future developments regarding this image issue. There is no question that the accounting profession will be increasing substantially that portion of those services which relate to consulting services.

MR. PRACTICE: Yes—and as accountants increase their nonaudit work, the question of the accountant's skill, competence, and commitment to perform audits will become more important.

MR. INDUSTRY: I think so. In my judgment the Code of Ethics of the accounting profession will have to be changed to respond to the dynamic changes occurring in the practice of public accounting. I believe the Code of Ethics is out of date.

MR. PRACTICE: I agree. If you could change the rules what would you do?

MR. INDUSTRY: I would design a code of ethics which is designed to maintain high standards of professionalism among accountants in both private practice and industry.

MR. PRACTICE: Would you eliminate any rules?

MR. INDUSTRY: Yes. All rules which are anticompetitive or arguably anticompetitive. These are the rules which deal with an accountant's business relationships.

For example, I would completely eliminate the rules which prohibit accountants from assuming certain forms of business practice. I would cut back the scope of the rules prohibiting contingent fees and commissions. Certain financial arrangements should be permissible if they are not inconsistent with the rules on independence, integrity, and objectivity.

MR. PRACTICE: What would you do regarding the rules on independence, integrity, and objectivity?

MR. INDUSTRY: I'd keep them. In fact, they are essential to maintaining professionalism as an accountant in industry or as a public accountant.

MR. PRACTICE: What do you mean by "maintaining professionalism"?

MR. INDUSTRY: That's a shorthand way of describing the process by which accountants maintain their credibility. A "professional" must work hard at obtaining and maintaining the trust and confidence of his clients or employer, his fellow practitioners, and the public.

The mere fact that an accountant has an educational degree and state license to practice does not of itself vest the accountant with credibility. Moreover, once you obtain "credibility"—that is, you have standing in your profession—you have to work hard to maintain it.

One big mistake can irreparably damage your credibility.

MR. PRACTICE: That's true. The public's perception of an accountant's independence, integrity, and objectivity is like a fragile piece of crystal—a thing of beauty which must be handled with great care.

MR. INDUSTRY: It seems to me that the cornerstone of any code of ethics could be reduced to three simple rules of conduct:

1. An accountant shall render all professional services and advice in a competent manner including compliance with all applicable professional standards.

2. An accountant shall act with integrity at all times and shall never knowingly misrepresent facts.

3. An accountant shall never subordinate his judgment to others and shall not express an opinion on financial statements of an enterprise with respect to which he is not independent.

MR. PRACTICE: What about the other rules such as client confidentiality, commissions, contingent fees—what are you going to do with them?

MR. INDUSTRY: I think the other rules flow from the three which I have listed. For example, all contingent fee arrangements would be permitted except to the extent to which they affect an accountant's independence, integrity, or objectivity. The same holds for commissions.

The rule dealing with confidential client communications is an element of integrity. The integrity rule also governs various discreditable acts. For example, the retention of client records is really an act inconsistent with maintaining high standards of professional integrity.

I could go on if you would like.

MR. PRACTICE: No, I see your point. But why limit the rules of conduct to these three simple rules? Why not have more rules to cover these specific situations such as confidentiality or false advertising?

MR. INDUSTRY: Competence, integrity, objectivity, and independence are the essence of being a professional. They go to the heart of obtaining and preserving credibility with clients, employers, and the public. With them you are a professional; without them you are not a professional. All other rules of ethical conduct derive from these concepts.

You can have all sorts of rules of conduct if you would like—but wouldn't you tend to deflect attention from competence, integrity, objectivity, and independence? After all, these are the "cardinal rules," wouldn't you agree?

MR. PRACTICE: Amen!

¶ 9.02   Congressional Hearings

The accounting profession is indirectly regulated by the periodic occurrence of congressional hearings which investigate the effectiveness of the accounting profession and the various methods by which the profession is regulated, including SEC, state boards of accountancy, and self-regulation by the AICPA. In 1977 and 1985 the U.S. House Subcommittee on Oversight and Investigations examined the issue of auditor independence and the impact of management advisory services on an auditor's independence and image.

The AICPA's response to these issues during the 1985 congressional hearings is as follows:

Independence

A discussion of the quality of independent audits would be incomplete without addressing the subject of independence, an attribute of CPAs essential to public reliance on audited financial statements. The concept of auditor independence precludes relationships that would be likely to impair the auditor's integrity or objectivity.

As applied to independent auditors, integrity is an element of character that prevents CPAs from intentionally committing a fault of omission or commission in their work. This does not mean that honest errors or mistakes will never occur.

Objectivity is the ability of CPAs to maintain an impartial attitude on all matters relating to the audit of financial statements. It is the quality of being able to evaluate, express, and use facts without distortion by personal feelings, interests, or biases.

The AICPA's Rules of Conduct dealing with independence are based on the criterion of whether reasonable persons, having knowledge of all the facts and taking into account normal strength of character and behavior, would conclude that a particular relationship would pose unacceptable threats to integrity or objectivity. The rules proscribe two general categories of relationships with audit clients:

1.   Certain financial relationships with clients, such as any form of direct or material indirect financial interests. For example, this prohibits a CPA or any of his partners from owning any stock, no matter how little, in a company they audit or from participating in significant joint closely held investments with an audit client or its officers, directors, or principal stockholders.

2.   Relationships in which a CPA has in effect become a part of management or an employee under management's control.

A CPA having such a relationship with a client is prohibited from expressing an opinion on the client's financial statements. In addition, the rules are far more extensive than any brief summary can indicate. For example, investments by a spouse or dependent person are deemed to impair independence. Also, positions held by close relatives can be deemed to affect independence.

The SEC, through its Financial Reporting Releases, has also promulgated extensive restrictions to assure the independence of auditors. The AICPA has worked closely with the SEC on auditor independence matters for many years.

CPA firms take great care to insure compliance with these independence rules. Detailed prohibitions of such things as accepting gifts or favors from audit clients are generally spelled out in written communications to all personnel, who are warned that violators will be promptly punished. Firms also go to great lengths to obtain assurance that their partners and professional staff are abiding by the prohibitions against financial relationships with clients. The peer review process of the AICPA Division for CPA Firms tests compliance with the rules on auditor independence and when violators are found—there have been some— sees that appropriate action is taken by the firm.

There are, no doubt, violations of the rules on independence that go undetected. But to the best of the AICPA's knowledge, compliance is generally at a very high level.

Performance of Management Advisory Services for Audit Clients

Management advisory services consist of a wide range of advice and technical assistance to clients, including some that are audit clients, to help them improve the use of their capabilities and resources. Concerns that providing MAS to audit clients impairs auditor independence have been raised a number of times in recent years.

Numerous studies have been undertaken because of these concerns. The most recent of these studies were by the Public Oversight

Board of the SEC Practice Section in 1979 and by an independent Commission on Auditor's Responsibilities in 1978. These studies found no evidence that such services had been a cause of an audit failure or had resulted in an impairment of independence and did not recommend that prohibitions be imposed on the performance of MAS for audit clients.

Another recent study focused on the research to date, on liability lawsuits against auditors and on complaints filed with state boards of accountancy. It concluded—

> It is not apparent that a problem of any significance actually exists (K. St. Pierre, "Independence and Auditor's Sanctions," *Journal of Accounting, Auditing, and Finance*, Spring 1984).

That conclusion is further corroborated by the results of peer reviews of firms in the SEC Practice Section. The Public Oversight Board stated in its 1983-84 annual report that, based upon its tests of peer reviews, "these procedures have not surfaced any evidence that suggests . . . that performance of MAS by member firms has diluted the objectivity required in the performance of the audit function."

Those concerned about the effects of MAS on auditor independence often express the fear that audit judgments will be unduly influenced by fees earned from MAS engagements performed for audit clients. Such fees are, in fact, no more of a pressure on audit independence than the audit fee itself. Moreover, there also are strong countervailing forces, including the risk of loss of the right to practice and the exposure to liability lawsuits, that bolster independence. In addition, professional discipline and pride and the fact that a CPA firm's economic well-being depends on its reputation in the community, not on fees from a single client, are also important factors.

Some critics urge that auditors not be permitted to provide MAS services because they believe such a prohibition would enhance the quality of audits. However, the AICPA, as well as those who have intimate knowledge of how audits are carried out, believe that the opposite is true. In MAS engagements, CPAs gain an in-depth knowledge and understanding of important aspects of a business enterprise. Like users of financial statements, auditors need to be knowledgeable about the client's industry, how it will be affected by the economy, the quality of management, the effectiveness of internal systems, and similar matters. The more knowledge the auditor has, the better, because auditors need to be able to judge whether the portrayal of a company's transactions in the financial statements are reasonable in circumstances that are becoming increasingly complex.

Moreover, engaging in MAS work requires CPA firms to develop knowledge and skills in new technologies that are directly applied to enhance the performance of audits. For example, the ability to apply computer software and to deal with complex computer systems has become both a necessity and an effective tool in auditing large companies. It is doubtful that the auditing profession could develop and maintain such skills if it were precluded from providing MAS services.

Some critics argue that auditors are "auditing their own work" if they perform MAS for audit clients and that their independence is therefore impaired. This notion is conceptually flawed in a number of ways.

When CPAs provide MAS they act only as outside advisors. They cannot and do not usurp management's authority. Therefore, management must assume responsibility for evaluating, accepting, and implementing the CPA's advice, and AICPA standards require a clear understanding of this before an MAS engagement is undertaken. No responsible management, given its basic responsibility and intimate knowledge of its business, would let outsiders make its decisions for it.

In any event, in expressing opinions on financial statements, auditors are not opining on the quality of such things as the client's systems, organizational structure, or management practices, which are the types of functions on which MAS advice might be rendered.

The purpose of an audit is to have an outside party review management's representations in the financial statements. Unless auditors have, in fact, become a part of management, they are still outsiders with respect to financial statements even though they have provided MAS services to a client. The MAS services themselves have been rendered in the role of an outsider.

In summary, the AICPA believes that it would be a serious mistake to restrict or prohibit the performance of management advisory services by independent auditors. There is no evidence that MAS has impaired the independence of auditors. Moreover, imposing restrictions would remove an important source of assistance to American business. The objectivity and analytical skills of CPAs and their knowledge of a client's business, organization, and personnel gained through audits make them an ideal source of advice to management in the most cost-effective manner.

The AICPA and CPAs are highly conscious of their responsibility to guard their independence at all costs because impairment would destroy the CPA's role as auditor. The AICPA, its SEC Practice Section, and CPA firms themselves have consistently adopted rules and promoted policies designed to bolster the independence of auditors, including enforceable rules of conduct, creation of audit committees of boards of directors, attendance by auditors at shareholder's meetings, management reporting on reasons for changing auditors, CPA firm reporting to boards of directors on MAS fees from SEC clients, and periodic rotation of partners in charge of SEC audits. This is a clear record of sincere desire and dedication to protect the independence of auditors and indicates that the profession would be in the forefront of restricting management advisory services for audit clients if valid reasons for doing so could be demonstrated.

CHAPTER 10

RACKETEER INFLUENCED AND CORRUPT ORGANIZATIONS: CIVIL LIABILITY

¶ 10.01   Civil RICO

The Court's interpretation of the civil RICO statute *quite simply revolutionizes private litigation*; it validates the federalization of broad areas of state common law of frauds, and it approves the displacement of well-established federal remedial provisions [such as the federal securities laws]. We do not lightly infer a congressional intent to effect such fundamental changes. To infer such intent here would be untenable, for there is no indication that Congress even considered, much less approved, the scheme that the Court today defines [to use RICO against legitimate businessess and business people]. (Dissenting opinion, United States Supreme Court Justice Thurgood Marshall, in *Sedima v. Imrex* (July 1, 1985); emphasis added.)

The private civil action to recover treble damages for violation of the Racketeer Influenced and Corrupt Organizations Act (RICO) has unquestionably "revolutionized" civil litigation involving allegations of business fraud. The expansive application of the civil RICO treble damage provisions to fraudulent conduct previously governed by state common law and the federal securities laws has had a tremendous impact on the course of litigation including:

1.   *All* state fraud actions may now be brought in federal court if the fraud constitutes a "pattern of racketeering activity." For example, traditional state law fraud actions for theft of assets or services, diminution of assets, and injury to reputation may now be brought as a federal civil RICO claim.

2.   A party who could not satisfy the requirement for bringing an action under the antifraud provisions of the federal securities laws (e.g., no reliance; no causation; not a purchaser or seller of a security under Rule 10b-5), may now bring a treble damage RICO action if the alleged fraud involves federal mail fraud which is expansive in its application and which does not impose the same strict legal requirements such as standing, causation, and reliance. For example, a party who *holds* a security which decreases in value because

403

of corporate fraud may now sue under civil RICO even though no Rule 10b-5 action could be brought.

    3.   A party who can properly bring a Rule 10b-5 action will have a significant incentive to attempt to "upgrade" his case to a "pattern of racketeering" under civil RICO. The incentive occurs because in a Rule 10b-5 action a plaintiff is entitled only to compensatory damages for his actual injury. Under civil RICO the plaintiff may recover treble damages (*i.e.*, three times his actual injury) and his attorneys fees.

    Civil RICO has eclipsed the federal securities laws in terms of the breadth of its application and the financial consequences of its application. Civil RICO was enacted by Congress in 1970. In 1985 the United States Supreme Court in *Sedima* v. *Imrex* affirmed civil RICO's expansive application.

    In the intervening 15-year period between RICO's enactment and the Supreme Court's opinion, civil RICO has only begun to emerge as a significant federal cause of action for fraudulent conduct. Ironically, the early years of civil RICO gave rise to few lawsuits despite the breadth of its provisions and the significant financial consequences which attended any violation of civil RICO. With the Supreme Court's decision in *Sedima v. Imrex* civil RICO is now positioned to totally supplant all other legal causes of action, state and federal, which govern fraudulent conduct.

    As the United States Supreme Court noted in *Sedima v. Imrex*, there are two observations which may be made with certainty regarding civil RICO:

    1. Congress intended that "RICO is to be read broadly."

    2. "[I]n its private civil version, RICO is evolving into something quite different from the original conception of its enactors."

    RICO's future application is now in the hands of two groups: plaintiffs who will invoke its provisions and the Congress which enacted it.

[1]   Elements of an Action

In 1970 Congress enacted the Racketeer Influenced Corrupt Organizations Act (RICO). By its terms, RICO prohibits certain types of organized wrongdoing. Violation of RICO can subject the violator to criminal penalties or civil remedies.

[a] Prohibited Activities.   Under RICO a "person" who is affiliated with an "enterprise" which engages in or affects interstate commerce may not participate in the following types of conduct:

(a)   A person who has received any income derived directly or indirectly from a "pattern of racketeering activity" may not use or invest any of that income or its proceeds in the "enterprise";

(b)   A person may not acquire or maintain any interest in or control of an "enterprise" through a "pattern of racketeering activity"; or

(c) A person employed by or associated with an "enterprise" may not conduct or participate indirectly in the conduct of the affairs of the enterprise through a "pattern of racketeering activity."

[b] "Person" Defined.   A "person" is defined to include any individual or entity capable of holding a legal or beneficial interest in property. An accountant or accounting firm clearly comes within the definition of a "person" under RICO.

[c] "Enterprise" Defined.   An "enterprise" includes any individual, partnership, corporation, association, or a group of individuals associated in fact although not a legal entity. An accountant's client would fall within the definition of an enterprise.

[d] "Pattern of Racketeering Activity" Defined.   A "pattern of racketeering activity" is defined as a course of conduct which involves the commission of at least two "acts of racketeering activity" during a 10 year period.

[e] "Racketeering Activity" Defined.   "Racketeering activity" is defined by the RICO statute to include the following acts:

(a) Bribery which is indictable under state felony law;

(b) Extortion which is indictable under state felony law;

(c) Fraud which is indictable under the federal mail fraud statute;

(d) Fraud which is indictable under the federal wire fraud statute; and

(e) Fraud which is actionable under the federal securities laws.

The foregoing violations are often referred to as "predicate acts" or "predicate offenses." For example, if a "person" through an "enterprise" performs two or more acts of mail fraud within a 10 year period of each other, a RICO claim may be brought which is "predicated" upon the two acts of mail fraud which are deemed a "pattern of racketeering activity."

"Racketeering activity" occurs whenever activity exists which would be "indictable" under the various state and federal criminal laws which are specified in RICO. It is important to note that RICO's civil remedies may be applied without regard to whether the "person" committing the "indictable" offense was actually indicted by a federal or state grand jury. That is, it is not a requirement under RICO that the defendant have been tried and found guilty of criminal charges on the underlying "predicate offenses." Proof of the predicate offenses will occur in the course of the RICO case against the defendant.

[i] *Federal Mail Fraud: A Broad Predicate Act.*   Federal mail fraud is an act upon which a RICO claim may be predicated. If a person engages in a pattern of activity which involves two or more violations of the federal mail fraud statute, that person has engaged in a "pattern of racketeering."

The federal mail fraud statute is extremely broad in its prohibitions of schemes to defraud. There are two essential elements to proving a violation of the federal mail fraud statute:

(a)   There must be a "scheme to defraud" and

(b)   There must be some type of use of the U.S. mail to further or facilitate the fraud.

With respect to proving a scheme to defraud, the United States Seventh Circuit court of appeals held in *United States v. Keane* that it "is not necessary for all aspects of an alleged scheme to be illegal in their separate parts, but rather only that the scheme as a whole involved fraudulent conduct."

In *United States v. Keane*, the United States court of appeals stated that the mail fraud statute "includes a broad proscription of behavior for the purpose of protecting society," and that:

> the "law puts it imprimatur on . . . accepted moral standards and condemns conduct which fails to match the" reflection of moral uprightness, of fundamental honesty, fair play and right dealing in the general and business life of members of society.

In the *Keane* case the court upheld the criminal conviction of a Chicago alderman who made "secret profits" on land transactions with the City of Chicago in which the alderman had a conflict of interest. The court stated that Keane had breached a duty to disclose the "true facts," holding:

> The defendant's failure to disclose his interest affirmatively misled his fellow alderman and the alleged scheme was of such a nature that it "depended for [its] success upon concealment and deception and could not conceivably [have been] carried out by the guilty party without covering up the true facts."

In sustaining a mail fraud conviction based on Keane's nondisclosure of material facts the court of appeals held that "it is not necessary that a scheme contemplate the use of the mails as an essential element" or that the "defendant actually mailed any thing himself." Observing that the use of the mails is merely a jurisdictional element, the court held that it was enough that use of the mails during the scheme was "reasonably foreseeable."

In the *Keane* case the court of appeals relied on its prior decision in *United States v. George*. In that criminal action an employee of Zenith was found guilty of mail fraud arising out of his receipt of kickbacks from companies from whom he purchased supplies on behalf of Zenith.

In holding that the Zenith employee had committed fraud by failing to disclose the kickbacks, the court of appeals held that:

> not only did [the employee] secretly earn a profit from his agency, but also he deprived Zenith of material knowledge that [the supplier company] would accept less profit. There was a very real and tangible harm to Zenith in losing the discount or losing the opportunity to bargain with a most relevant fact before it.

The court of appeals held that the employee's "duty was to negotiate the best price possible for Zenith or at least to apprise Zenith that [the supplier] was willing to sell his cabinets for substantially less money."

Attorneys and accountants have long been subject to indictment under the mail fraud statute for nondisclosure of material facts. The auditors in *United States v. Simon* were convicted of mail fraud for failing to disclose unlawful financial dealings and embezzlement by the chief executive officer of the audit client. In *United States v. Bronston*, a partner in a large law firm was convicted of mail fraud for not advising of his simultaneous conflicting representation of a client who was competing against another firm client for a New York City bus stop franchise.

The "proscriptions" of mail fraud are extremely "broad." Moreover, it is not necessary that the defendant actually mailed anything himself. It is sufficient that use of the mails to facilitate the fraud was "reasonably foreseeable."

The potential application of the mail fraud statute to an accountant's professional practice is obvious. If an auditor is associated with a set of circumstances where over two successive years two materially false audit reports on a client have been mailed by a client to its shareholders and creditors, the elements are in place for two mail fraud violations *if* the accountant knowingly participated in the schemes to defraud. If the accountant discharged his duty of good faith and honesty, there is no mail fraud violation.

On the other hand, if the accountant breached his duty of good faith and honesty in both of the audit years, the accountant has committed two mail fraud offenses which may be the "predicate acts" for a claim of civil RICO.

[2]   Civil Remedies for Violation of RICO

A person who is injured in his business or property by a violation of RICO may sue in federal district court those people and organizations who participated in the RICO violation. Among the various civil remedies available (which include divestiture by the defendant of any direct or indirect interest in the "enterprise" as well as restrictions on the "future activities" of the defendant) there are two substantial remedies for aggrieved plaintiffs:

(a)   The plaintiff "shall recover threefold the damages" caused by the RICO violation and

(b)   The plaintiff shall recover the cost of the suit, including reasonable attorney's fees.

The trebling of a plaintiff's damages is not unlike the trebling of damages which occurs in federal antitrust lawsuits. It is a recognition by Congress that the unlawful conduct in question should be deterred and penalized.

¶ 10.02   RICO's Application to Accountants: The Great Debate

The application of RICO to "legitimate" business institutions and enterprises has generated a great deal of debate. Let us join another moment of this "Great Debate" as we sit in on a conversation between three friends—Mr. Arnold Auditor, an accountant; Mr. Charlie Suem, a plaintiff's lawyer; and Mr. Joe Defense, a defendant's attorney.

[1]   Introduction to RICO: Elements

MR. AUDITOR: Charlie, pass me another beer and tell me everything you know about RICO.

MR. SUEM: Rico, is that the guy who plays centerfield for the Bulldogs?

MR. AUDITOR: I'm talking about this federal law which is being used against honest business people and accountants—you know, the one that was designed to stop the Cosa Nostra and racketeers.

MR. DEFENSE: I defend accountants and from my perspective the purpose of RICO has been perverted.

MR. SUEM: C'mon Joe, RICO hasn't been perverted. The courts are applying it exactly the way Congress intended. Before we talk about Congress' purpose, let's be sure that Arnold understands how RICO works.

MR. AUDITOR: All I know is that I can be sued in federal court for triple the amount of damages which a plaintiff claims as injury.

MR. SUEM: That's correct, but before a plaintiff recovers "trebled damages" there are quite a few legal elements which he must prove. If a plaintiff proves these legal elements, Congress has determined that the plaintiff should be awarded an amount of money equal to three times the plaintiff's actual damages.

MR. DEFENSE: Charlie, level with Arnold, you try to make it sound like there are some great obstacles to recovery. . . .

MR. SUEM: Well there are. . . .

MR. AUDITOR: Yeah, I bet, like I signed an audit report on a company which went bad. . . .

MR. SUEM: Don't be so cynical Arnold, its not good for your blood pressure. . . .

An accountant may be sued under RICO only if he has engaged in a pattern of fraudulent criminal activity. An accountant cannot be sued under RICO for negligence. He cannot be sued for liability without fault or strict liability. RICO does not make an accountant a guarantor of his client or an insurer of a plaintiff's business risk.

An accountant violates RICO if he breaches his duty of good faith and honesty. If an accountant engages in a pattern of dishonest activity he may subject himself to liability under RICO.

Is it too much to ask an accountant or any business person for that matter to refrain from participating in a pattern of dishonest, fraudulent conduct?

MR. AUDITOR: Well . . . maybe not. . . .

MR. SUEM:	Keep in mind that RICO was designed to deter and defeat "enterprise criminality" and as a consequence not every claim of fraud will fall within the provisions of RICO.
MR. AUDITOR:	I don't follow . . . what's an "enterprise"?
MR. SUEM:	Under RICO, an "enterprise" would include, for example, an accountant's client—whether the client was a person, a partnership or a corporation—as long as the enterprise engages in interstate commerce or its activities affect interstate commerce. . . .
MR. DEFENSE:	Which includes most entities which do business in the United States. . . .
MR. SUEM:	That's correct, enterprise is broadly defined under RICO.
MR. AUDITOR:	What does RICO prohibit?
MR. SUEM:	RICO prohibits a person—which is defined to include you and your accounting firm—from participating directly or indirectly in the conduct of the affairs of an "enterprise" through a "pattern of racketeering activity."
MR. AUDITOR:	"Pattern of racketeering activity," what's that?
MR. DEFENSE:	It's breaking knees with baseball bats to collect debts!
MR. SUEM:	Under RICO a "pattern of racketeering activity" is defined to be much more than organized "blue collar" crime such as the extortionate debt collecting practices to which Joe refers. RICO prohibits a pattern of organized white collar criminal activity.
MR. AUDITOR:	Such as?
MR. SUEM:	A pattern of two mail fraud schemes which are indictable criminal offenses under the federal mail fraud statute.
MR. AUDITOR:	That's a pattern of racketeering activity?
MR. SUEM:	Yes, as long as the two predicate offenses—the violations of the mail fraud statute—occur within 10 years of each other.
MR. AUDITOR:	Can you paint the big picture for me: how does all this relate to an auditor of a company?
MR. SUEM:	Assume that an auditor has been complicit with the management of a company in a fraud. . . .
MR. AUDITOR:	Why do I have to assume that?
MR. SUEM:	Because if there is no fraud by the auditor there's absolutely no basis to assert a RICO claim. I told you, this is not a negligence statute or a liability without fault statute. This is a fraud statute.
MR. AUDITOR:	OK, ok, so the auditor is fraudulent, where's the *"enterprise criminality."*
MR. SUEM:	The "enterprise criminality" is turning this so-called legitimate business corporation into what's been described by the courts as an "engine of theft" against others through a pattern of racketeering activity.

MR. AUDITOR: Where's the pattern of racketeering activity?

MR. SUEM: If the auditor issued fraudulent audit reports for two successive audit years which were mailed to unsuspecting shareholders, lenders, and bondholders, that's mail fraud.

MR. DEFENSE: And that's a pattern of racketeering! Simple isn't it?

MR. AUDITOR: Simply terrible it is!

[2]   RICO: Congress's Intent

MR. AUDITOR: I thought RICO was designed to eliminate or combat organized crime?

MR. DEFENSE: That's correct, Arnold. Congress wanted to create a powerful legal weapon against organized crime. In fact, it considered outlawing membership in the Cosa Nostra but it was advised that such legislation would be unconstitutional.

MR. AUDITOR: Why?

MR. DEFENSE: You can't criminalize a person's status or associational affiliation.

MR. AUDITOR: What do you mean?

MR. DEFENSE: For example, you can't have a law which makes it unlawful to be a member of a certain accounting association or a member of a certain social club. Even if all the members of the social club engaged in criminal activity the law would unconstitutionally prohibit status— someone within the club might not engage in criminal conduct.

Only conduct can be criminalized, not the status of those who perform the crime.

MR. AUDITOR: If Congress could not criminalize a type of defendant what could it do?

MR. DEFENSE: Congress ended up drafting this statute, which prohibits certain activities which are the type engaged in by organized crime. The problem is that the statute was drafted so broadly it has been misapplied as one Congressman predicted.

MR. AUDITOR: What did he say?

MR. DEFENSE: Congressman Mikva said that:

This bill is for the purpose of controlling organized crime in the United States. . . . [W]here in the bill does one find the definition of organized crime? . . . My objection to this bill in toto is that whatever its motivates to begin with, we will end up with cases involving all kinds of things not intended to be covered, and a potpourri of language by which you can parade all kinds of horrible examples of overreach.

None of his fellow congressmen were listening and *voilá*—we have this powerful statute which is now being applied to businesses and accounting firms which have nothing to do with the organized crime-controlled entities which the statute sought to attack.

MR. SUEM: Whoa! Slow down, Joe. I think you jumped to a conclusion.

MR. DEFENSE: How so?

MR. SUEM: First, Congress's intent was not limited to attacking merely organized crime of the "blue collar" type such as the Cosa Nostra. If you read the legislative hearings behind RICO it's very plain that Congress was concerned about the billions of dollars lost in this country through the actions of white collar criminals. Congress designed RICO to attack organized white collar crime which acted through the medium of so-called legitimate business enterprises.

White collar crime in this country has been estimated by the U.S. Department of Justice to cost all of us $100 billion annually. RICO was designed to attack that portion of this white collar crime which results from the manipulation of institutions or "enterprises" of respectibility by a pattern of fraudulent activity.

MR. AUDITOR: Charlie, how do you define "white collar crime?"

MR. SUEM: I don't, the Justice Department does — it includes "those nonviolent offenses which principally involve elements of deceit, deception, concealment, corruption, misrepresentation and breach of trust."

MR. DEFENSE: Charlie, RICO was designed for the purpose of controlling organized crime.

MR. SUEM: Stop right there! How do you define organized crime?

MR. DEFENSE: Well. . . .

MR. SUEM: Joe, you and I both know that Congress purposefully avoided a definition of organized crime. In fact, when Congressman Mikva asked the rhetorical question which you quoted, Congressman Poff, one of RICO's sponsors replied:

The gentleman inquired rhetorically as to why no effort was made to define organized crime in this bill. It is true that there is no organized crime definition in many parts of the bill. *This is, in part, because it is probably impossible precisely and definitively to define organized crime.* But if it were possible, I ask my friend, would he not be the first to object that in criminal law we establish procedures which would be applicable only to a certain type of defendant? Would he not be the first to object to such a system? [Emphasis added.]

Joe, let's assume that Congress could constitutionally make mere status a crime and that membership in "organized crime" was a criminal violation.

MR. DEFENSE: Ok.

MR. SUEM: How would you define organized crime?

MR. DEFENSE: Well, membership in the Cosa Nostra would be prohibited.

MR. SUEM: What's the Cosa Nostra and how would you prove someone belonged?

MR. DEFENSE: Well . . . I'm not sure what it is exactly. . . .

MR. SUEM: What if a group of senior citizens started a bingo group and called themselves the Cosa Nostra, is that the criminal organization you are after?

MR. DEFENSE: Don't be ridiculous!

MR. SUEM: Doesn't my example prove that merely labeling a group of people "organized crime" proves absolutely nothing! Don't you have to look at the type of conduct you want to outlaw, and proscribe that conduct regardless of who engages in it?

MR. DEFENSE: I don't follow.

MR. SUEM: You believe RICO was intended to go after only organized crime like the Cosa Nostra?

MR. DEFENSE: Yes, that's organized crime.

MR. SUEM: What about organized motorcycle gangs which were not an organized criminal threat at the time RICO was passed in 1970? Would they be organized crime within RICO?

MR. DEFENSE: Sure, in fact the government has used RICO against them.

MR. SUEM: Why do you consider motorcycle gangs to be the subject of RICO when they weren't even a threat in 1970 when Congress passed this Act?

MR. DEFENSE: They engaged in the kinds of organized unlawful conduct RICO was intended to eradicate.

MR. SUEM: You looked at the type of unlawful conduct these organized groups of people perform and you concluded RICO applies, correct?

MR. DEFENSE: Yes.

MR. SUEM: Motorcycle gangs aren't part of the Cosa Nostra, yet you agree RICO applies.

MR. DEFENSE: Yes.

MR. SUEM: What if a group operates a home improvement company which gives them access to homes which they subsequently burglarize, is this a RICO violation?

MR. DEFENSE: Yes. There are plenty of cases which hold that this is a RICO enterprise and a pattern of racketeering.

MR. SUEM: Should it be?

MR. DEFENSE: Of course. These people are organized, they're engaging in criminal activity and they're using a legitimate business enterprise to pull off their scam. No problem, RICO applies.

MR. SUEM: What if one of the homeowners only lost $10,000 which is covered by home insurance?

MR. DEFENSE: RICO still applies; the amount of money is not relevant: what counts is that this homeowner was victimized by an organized group of persons using a legitimate enterprise as their vehicle or "enterprise" for unlawful conduct.

MR. SUEM: Does it matter that the burglars are not members of the Cosa Nostra.

MR. DEFENSE: It's not relevant. This is organized criminal activity under RICO.

MR. SUEM: Let's assume that after our homeowner gets his check from the insurance company for $10,000 he finds out that he has been victimized again—this time he has lost $1 million to a group of people who operated through an otherwise legitimate business company.

MR. DEFENSE: Who are the people—the Cosa Nostra?

MR. SUEM: No, assume the company engages in investments and that the chief executive officer has embezzled money in a Ponzi scheme. He has been assisted by the company's treasurer and the independent auditors who knew of the fraud yet issued clean opinions for two successive audit years. Do we have a RICO violation?

MR. DEFENSE: Yes . . . the courts say so. . . .

MR. SUEM: How is this situation different from the burglary ring which victimized the homeowner?

MR. DEFENSE: Well. . . .

MR. SUEM: Wasn't the homeowner victimized again by an organized group of persons who used a legitimate enterprise for their unlawful pattern of fraud?

MR. DEFENSE: (silence)

MR. SUEM: There is one difference: the home burglary ring only took $10,000 of his money while the chief executive officer with assistance from the treasurer and auditors took $1 million.

Do you believe, Joe, that as a policy matter RICO should be applied to an organized blue collar crime where $10,000 is stolen, but it should not be applied to an organized white collar crime where $1 million is stolen?

MR. DEFENSE: I don't have an opinion as to that!

MR. SUEM: I'll bet the homeowner-victim might have an opinion regarding the greater threat to him and society in those circumstances.

MR. DEFENSE: Accountants and attorneys will never be racketeers no matter how misguided their conduct!

MR. SUEM: Racketeering means many things to many people. Webster's dictionary defines it as a fraudulent scheme, enterprise, or activity. Other commonly understood definitions include a business that obtains money through fraud. RICO defines racketeering the same way.

MR. DEFENSE: I don't care how you define racketeering, its not right to lump accountants and attorneys in with burglars.

MR. SUEM: You're right, in many respects a dishonest accountant or attorney can inflict much more damage than a burglar could ever hope to accomplish in his life time!

MR. DEFENSE: Sez who?

MR. SUEM: So says the United States court of appeals in New York. Judge Friendly said in *United States v. Benjamin*

                In our complex society the accountant's certificate and the lawyer's opinion can be instruments for inflicting pecuniary loss more potent than the chisel or the crowbar. . . . Congress equally could not have intended that men holding themselves out as members of these ancient professions should be able to escape criminal liability on a plea of ignorance when they have shut their eyes to what was plainly to be seen or have represented a knowledge they knew they did not possess. . . .

MR. DEFENSE: Well . . . that case did not involve RICO!

MR. SUEM: That's true, but a few years later the United States court of appeals in New York had this to say about the application of RICO:

                Even if we were free to question the determination of the attorney general, we could not accept the proposition that the Congress did not intend to include corruption, obstruction of justice and perjury within the purview of the statute. While crimes of violence engineered by gangs of thugs are of course repulsive and clearly within the concept of organized criminal activity, the concerted corruption charged here is equally odious. The fact that the alleged perpetrators are presumably respectable and entrusted with responsibility by an electorate or a profession or by stockholders does not suggest, in our view, that they are incapable of engaging in organized criminal activity. We all stand equal before the bar of criminal justice, and the wearing of a white collar, even though it is starched, does not preclude the organized pursuit of unlawful profit.

                In that same opinion the court of appeals observed:

                "Organized criminal activity" is not defined in the statute, however, it is clear that it was not intended that it be given a restrictive interpretation. Congressman Poff described the term as being "broader in scope than the concept of organized crime; it is meant to include any criminal activity collectively undertaken. . . ." 116 Cong. Rec. 35293 (Oct. 7, 1970). Senator Hruska, a co-sponsor of the bill, advised the Senate that the term included all criminal activity that was "not an isolated offense by an isolated offender. . . ." 116 Cong. Rec. 36294 (Oct. 12, 1970).

MR. DEFENSE: It's just not right. Accountants and attorneys should not be treated as "racketeers"—the mere labeling of a person as a "racketeer" is highly prejudicial and inflammatory.

MR. SUEM: There you go again—you're more concerned with the "label" than the conduct. Being labeled a racketeer is only prejudicial when it's true!

MR. DEFENSE: An accountant who engages in a scheme to defraud is not a racketeer.

MR. SUEM: Frankly, I don't care what you call him . . . other than honest. Joe, don't get hung up on labels—look at the conduct—and if the shoe fits the accountant or attorney, he wears it!

[3]   RICO Applies to "Garden Variety Fraud"

MR. DEFENSE: The trouble with RICO is that even if it should apply to some white collar crime, it's being used by plaintiff's lawyers to create a treble-damages federal lawsuit for "garden variety fraud."

MR. SUEM: What is a "garden variety fraud?"

MR. DEFENSE: Let me think. . . . It's a state law claim, the typical fraud claim that arises out of a breach of contract action!

MR. SUEM: Under your definition would this garden variety claim be an indictable federal mail fraud offense?

MR. DEFENSE: It's possible. . . .

MR. SUEM: Under your definition could this "garden variety fraud" involve a scheme to defraud investors who lost $50 million?

MR. DEFENSE: It might. . . .

MR. SUEM: Could you be more specific as to the type of garden variety fraud which is not serious enough to be indictable under the federal mail fraud statute and which does not involve a substantial economic loss.

MR. DEFENSE: Just give me a minute to think, and I'll come up with a definition of garden variety fraud.

MR. SUEM: While you're thinking, let me say that I doubt that the victim of an organized criminal fraud would be willing to accept your opinion that certain *fraud* is garden variety, that's assuming you can think of a good definition of garden variety.

MR. AUDITOR: Joe, while you till the garden for some definition of garden variety fraud, I have a question for Charlie. How does an accountant or businessperson avoid civil RICO claims?

MR. SUEM: Don't participate in organized criminal fraud. Act in good faith and there will be no problem.

MR. DEFENSE: That's a facile explanation! Good faith is a concept which is subject to unpredictable interpretation by the jury!

MR. SUEM: Are you saying that you have trouble recognizing or understanding the difference between honesty and dishonesty?

MR. DEFENSE: Of course not. I know when someone has been dishonest.

MR. SUEM: Good faith is the duty to act honestly. If you are troubled by the fact that you must act in good faith to avoid civil RICO claims, I have some terrible news for you!

MR. DEFENSE: What's that?

MR. SUEM: Good faith is the guiding light by which we gauge whether our actions will subject us to a criminal indictment for fraud! If good faith is such an unpredictable standard perhaps we should do away with all criminal fraud statutes!

MR. DEFENSE: (silence)

[4]   Should There Be Limitations on an Accountant's Liability Under RICO?

MR. AUDITOR: Accountants have become such an easy target for litigation—we must have some protection; can't legislation be passed which limits our liability or gives us a safe harbor when we engage in certain types of work.

MR. DEFENSE: That's what we need Arnold—some help from Congress and state legislatures. We need help from what's been described as "the vagaries of each litigational outcome . . . a situation of litigational roulette." It has been said that accountants are "always subject to the proclivity of triers of fact to give plaintiffs relief at the expense of defendants' 'deep pockets.' "

MR. SUEM: Joe, you don't really mean that, do you? Do you actually believe that our system of justice has been perverted; that it is a situation of "litigational roulette" where common sense and facts are thrown out of the courtroom and replaced by the "proclivity of triers of fact to give plaintiffs relief at the expense of defendants' 'deep pockets.' " Is that what you're saying, Joe?

MR. DEFENSE: Uh . . . well. . . .

MR. SUEM: If it is, that may be the type of argument which Arnold and all accountants want to hear, but it is hardly a fair reflection of what goes on in the trial courts of our country.

MR. AUDITOR: Aren't we "deep pockets" and isn't litigation an expensive game of chance?

MR. SUEM: Absolutely not! Look, it's easy for a corporate lawyer or a discovery lawyer, like Joe here, to tell you what's wrong with the jury trial system. When was the last time you tried a case before the jury, Joe?

MR. DEFENSE: Well . . . its been a few years. . . .

MR. SUEM: I try jury trial cases all the time. And when an office lawyer, like Joe, who advises corporations and doesn't try cases, tells you the jury trial system doesn't work—that's like someone who has never played baseball telling Babe Ruth that he will never hit a home run swinging the bat the way he does!

MR. AUDITOR: Don't all lawyers try cases before juries?

MR. SUEM: Absolutely not and therein lies the fault both for (1) the common misperceptions regarding the jury trial system and (2) the fact that imperfections do exist in the jury trial system because nonjury trial lawyers get involved—they try to pinch hit for Babe Ruth without having played the game before.

MR. DEFENSE: Charlie, accountants' liability cases are too complex for the jury to understand!

MR. SUEM: Nuts, I say! That insults the intelligence of the juries. In fact, I have had juries comprised of people whose knowledge and educational training far exceeds the intelligence of the presiding judge or even some of the lawyers in the case!

    Besides, the jury trial system works if the jury trial lawyers know what they are doing!

MR. AUDITOR: What do you mean, Charlie?

MR. SUEM: I've always felt that being a jury trial lawyer is one of the "skilled" positions in the legal profession. It is up to the jury trial lawyer to take a complex, complicated situation and reduce it down to its "simplest common denominator."

MR. AUDITOR: What's that?

MR. SUEM: That's the point at which the facts of the case are readily understandable to the jury and will compel a jury to decide the case in favor of your client. That's the jury trial lawyer's job. If he fails in his job he shouldn't blame the jury.

    In fact, I'm amused that the greatest criticism of the jury trial system comes from those lawyers who don't try cases before juries—if you haven't played baseball perhaps you should take a few cuts at the plate before you conclude the game's no good!

MR. AUDITOR: Don't you think we should put limitations on litigation, I mean the costs are unbelievable.

MR. SUEM: I agree with you, Arnold.

MR. DEFENSE: The plaintiff's lawyer finally agrees with us, holy cow! We will save money in litigation if we get rid of contingent fee cases and class actions.

MR. SUEM: No! In fact, you will deprive deserving plaintiffs a remedy for their injuries and the costs of litigation in this country will go up, not down!

MR. AUDITOR: How can it go up?

MR. SUEM: Let me demonstrate. You are aware of the *Miller* case which I recently won involving the little girl who was hit by a drunken driver.

MR. AUDITOR: Oh yes, that was a great victory, Charlie. That little girl deserved every penny the jury gave her.

MR. SUEM: I agree. The driver had four previous convictions for drunk driving— he claimed that being the chief executive officer of Atax Inc. drove him to drink. That's not much help for the little girl. She's a quadriplegic for the rest of her life with some brain damage—

MR. AUDITOR: As I recall, she was standing on the corner waiting for her grade school bus and this clown ran up on the curb and hit her. That must have been an easy case for you to recover a verdict.

MR. SUEM: Wrong! The chief executive officer retained his corporate law firm to defend him. They racked up $500,000 in legal defense fees.

MR. AUDITOR: What did you do to cause them to incur such fees!

MR. SUEM: Nothing. I was working on a contingent fee. The little girl's parents had no money to hire a lawyer—they both work at blue collar jobs. Here's the rub, the chief executive officer's defense was (1) take the offensive and (2) ultimately protract the case and try to wear us down.

    As a contingent fee lawyer for a plaintiff your time is money you may or may not receive. A contingent fee lawyer does everything he can to bring a case to trial immediately: it makes no sense for a contingent fee lawyer to drag a case out, clogging up the court system.

    It also makes no sense for a contingent fee lawyer to engage in pointless, irrelevant discovery. I only depose those witnesses and look at those documents which are necessary to prove my case. The motive of a contingent fee lawyer is to spend only that legal time which is absolutely reasonable and necessary.

MR. AUDITOR: Well how did the chief executive officer's firm roll up $500,000 in legal fees?

MR. SUEM: They did it through their discovery tactics. In my judgment they did things which were absolutely unreasonable and unnecessary. They are the ones who abused the broad discovery system which regretably exists in our courts.

MR. AUDITOR: How did they abuse the system?

MR. SUEM: They asked for access to files and documents and took depositions of all types of people where the testimony and documents were not relevant to the case. It was the classic case of lawyer overkill engaged in by a group of "discovery lawyers" who seldom try cases in court.

MR. AUDITOR: How do these lawyers get paid?

MR. SUEM: By the hour, their meters are running all the time—that's the problem, they get paid "win, lose, or draw"—the motive to do *only* that which is reasonable and necessary may be less strong or absolutely missing.

MR. AUDITOR:	Is there a way to control this abuse?
MR. SUEM:	One famous lawyer, who I highly respect, has suggested that perhaps we should follow the British system of justice where the losing side picks up the other side's costs.
MR. DEFENSE:	Arnold, Charlie's a plaintiff's lawyer, he'll never go along with that.
MR. SUEM:	Actually, I'm a jury trial lawyer—not a "discovery lawyer" or a "litigator"—and I would go along with it. It would go a long way to eliminating frivolous lawsuits brought by plaintiffs and it would deter harassing, vexatious discovery tactics by defense lawyers if they are aware that their client will pay three elements of damage if they lose, namely:

1. The underlying judgment against the defendant;
2. The defense lawyer's attorney fees; and
3. The plaintiff's attorney fees which presently are not recoverable under the law.

       Reducing the costs of litigation is not a one way street limited only to regulating the plaintiffs' lawyers. A fair amount of what's wrong can be laid directly at the door of the defense attorney.

MR. DEFENSE:	All right so there are some problems with the judicial system which are caused by the lawyers who run the system—let's get back to RICO. I think its application should be limited only to those circumstances where an accountant has previously been indicted and convicted of mail fraud by the U.S. Department of Justice. The Justice Department has guidelines in applying criminal RICO; they exercise restraint in prosecuting RICO. They limit the use of RICO to serious crimes.
MR. SUEM:	Joe, you know I used to be a federal criminal prosecutor. Sure, RICO is applied sparingly by the Justice Department. All criminal statutes are implemented with a great deal of caution or discretion.

       When the Justice Department uses criminal RICO or any other criminal statute they are seeking to deprive a person of something more important and fundamental than his money. . . .

MR. DEFENSE:	What's more important than money?
MR. SUEM:	How about your "life, liberty and pursuit of happiness"?

       The Justice Department uses RICO and all criminal statutes sparingly. A person's liberty is on the line. In fact, in criminal white collar matters, it is a rare case where the defendant can make the criminal charges go away simply by writing out a check for restitution. Usually, the government seeks incarceration of the wrongdoer. Because of the heavy penalty to be exacted, the government uses RICO sparingly.

       Also, keep in mind that Congress enacted the civil remedies under RICO to enlist the aid of the victims of white collar crime in the efforts to reduce the significant economic losses incurred yearly through corruption, deceit, and fraud.

MR. AUDITOR: How much is that estimated to be?

MR. SUEM: The Justice Department estimates possibly $100 billion per year. There's no way that the Justice Department can wage a war on economic crime by itself. It needs to enlist the aid of the private sector.

Who's the best representative in the private sector to conscript in this "war"?

MR. AUDITOR: The victim.

MR. SUEM: You got it. Congress recognized that absent an economic incentive you're not exactly going to encourage victims to jump into this battle to do what the Justice Department hasn't the resources to perform. Moreover, Congress also recognized that those who participate in organized economic crime need to be deterred.

MR. AUDITOR: What did Congress do to encourage victims to help and to deter the wrongdoers?

MR. SUEM: It enacted the "treble damages" provision.

MR. AUDITOR: Isn't that a radical, unprecedented move?

MR. SUEM: No. It's precisely what was done in the area of antitrust. There Congress determined that certain "anticompetetive conduct" was antithetical to a free and honest economic market. With RICO, Congress has stated that certain "fraudulent conduct" is a threat to a free and honest market.

MR. AUDITOR: How about limiting the liability of accountants. I hear lawyers say that damages have been assessed by juries that are out of proportion to fault, and outrageous in view of the fees earned by accountants.

MR. SUEM: Don't believe everything you hear. Besides, limiting liability to the fees received has absolutely no logical connection to the fault done. Assume you go to a doctor for a chest X-ray and he fails to note an obvious cancerous growth on your lung which was curable but now is terminal. Should your lawsuit for relying on his negligent opinion be limited to the $50 x-ray and $40 office visit?

MR. AUDITOR: No. . . .

MR. SUEM: Why should a person who invests his life savings relying on an auditor's *fraudulent* audit reports over several years be limited to recovering the auditor's fees?

MR. AUDITOR: (silence)

MR. SUEM: Are fraudulent auditors deserving of more favorable treatment than negligent doctors?

MR. AUDITOR: Ok, I get the point. . . . I still think accountants are all too often made the scapegoats for bad business decisions by investors, lenders, and bondholders. Everyone, and I mean everyone—courts, juries, and financial statement users—fails to understand the difference between audit failures and business failures. Investing is a process of placing capital at risk.

Some of these people think auditors are insurers of risk. With RICO they have been given one more arrow in their quiver.

MR. DEFENSE: Arnie, RICO is more like an MX missile in their quiver.

MR. SUEM: I'm not sure that "everyone" is confused between audit failures and business failures. Let me say this: there are probably several audit failures that go undetected and unnoticed each year but no one gets sued.

MR. AUDITOR: Why do you say that?

MR. SUEM: It's the "no harm, no foul rule." An audit can be done in a grossly negligent and reckless manner but if the financial statements are solid—they are materially accurate, there's no fraud—no one will complain.

MR. DEFENSE: How can an accountant be negligent or reckless and the financials still be right?

MR. SUEM: Its easy! Take Hog Co. here in town, biggest meat packer in the country. They have an extremely capable internal accounting department which prepares their financials. When Hog Co. turns over those financials to be audited, those financials are materially accurate statements of financial position and operations! The independent auditor doesn't make them more accurate. He only makes them more "credible."

If the independent auditors are negligent or reckless in their audits, Hog Co.'s financials will still be accurate despite the auditors.

This is an instance where a complete "audit failure" goes undetected and unnoticed because the client presented an accurate bottom line. It's a situation of "no harm, no foul."

It is only when the financials are not materially accurate statements that innocent people who relied on those financials are harmed. That's when people start to scrutinize the role of the auditor. In that respect if there seems to be a high correlation between "business failure" and allegations of "audit failure" it may be due to the fact that auditors *never* get sued by investors where there is an "audit failure" but no corresponding "business failure" or injury to the investor.

MR. AUDITOR: I never looked at it that way. . . . I still think that financial statement users expect too much of auditors. Sometimes they try to shift their risk-taking losses to us! That's not right!

MR. DEFENSE: Well said, Arnie, there are too many frivolous lawsuits against auditors resulting from bad business investments. When are these people ever going to learn that a riskless capital market will destroy economic incentives—in a market without losers there can be no winners!

MR. SUEM: An eloquent statement, Joe, but it needs a post-script: In a market with risks an auditor's importance to nonclient users of financial information derives solely from the fact that the auditor is a credible, nonbiased, independent source of information which is useful in assessing risk and the allocation of limited capital resources within the market. If an auditor loses credibility with financial statement users, the auditor loses everything. With credibility an auditor serves a purpose in the capital market, without credibility he serves no purpose.

MR. AUDITOR: Credibility?

MR. SUEM: Auditors are the first people to tell you that the preparation of accurate financial statements is management's responsibility, right?

MR. AUDITOR: Right.

MR. SUEM: You merely report on them, right?

MR. AUDITOR: Right.

MR. SUEM: Its management's responsibility to make the financials accurate; you make them credible.

MR. AUDITOR: Yes.

MR. SUEM: If you can't make the financials credible, management, investors, lenders, and bondholders will find that they can do without you.

MR. AUDITOR: I see. . . . credibility really is everything when it comes to services which are intended to invite reliance by nonclient users.

MR. SUEM: Absolutely. And the quickest way to lose credibility with the public is to look for gimmicks designed to limit your legal liability. The public will perceive limitations on your liability as limitations on your legal responsibility. You can't have it both ways.

Accountants don't sell a product which is used by a third party, they sell to the public their believability.

MR. AUDITOR: Have we come to the point where accountants are held to strict liability?

MR. SUEM: No. If a manufacturer produces a lawn mower which is defectively designed, the manufacturer is held to strict liability to the users of that lawn mower. There's liability without regard to whether the manufacturer is at fault. The courts have determined that the risks of a defective product should be borne by the manufacturer, not the hapless consumer. The manufacturer knows that people will continue to buy lawn mowers. Thus, the onus is placed on the manufacturer to take the risks with the rewards.

Accountants are not being held for liability without fault. Furthermore, accountants are held liable to *all* users of financial statements only if they engage in *fraud*.

When an auditor issues a negligent or fraudulent audit report, you are talking about an entirely different situation than products liability. This is not assessing liability without fault, it's assessing liability for fault, indeed substantial fault if it's fraudulent.

MR. SUEM: In recent times, the courts have widened the scope of an accountant's liability for negligence. The courts have decided that between the innocent victim and the negligent auditor, the latter should bear the burden of his own wrongdoing. Does that strike you as a crazy proposition?

MR. AUDITOR: (silence)

MR. SUEM: Perhaps there is one other factor which has occurred to the courts which distinguishes accountants' liability from products liability.

MR. AUDITOR: What's that?

MR. SUEM: There will always be an economic market for the sale of lawn mowers unless of course we do away with grass.

There is a limited economic market for the sale of credibility which is all the auditor sells to financial statement consumers. If the auditor can't deliver credibility there will be no demand for the product or the market will seek alternatives.

That leads to an interesting paradox.

MR. AUDITOR: What's that?

MR. SUEM: By regulating the few auditors who are incompetent or dishonest, the courts have protected the accounting profession's position in the marketplace where credibility is a vital commodity.

¶ 10.03   Accountant's Liability: Seminal RICO Decision

In *Schacht v. Brown* the United States Seventh Circuit court of appeals upheld a civil RICO complaint against three separate auditing firms arising out of the bankruptcy of an insurance company. The plaintiff alleged damages of $100,000,000 (*before* RICO-trebling) resulting from the "fraudulent prolongation of [the] corporation's life beyond insolvency" thereby "deepening" the insurance company's insolvency.

Schacht v. Brown
711 F.2d 1343 (1983)

Before CUMMINGS, Chief Judge, WOOD, Circuit Judge, and HOFFMAN, Senior District Judge.

HARLINGTON WOOD, Jr., Circuit Judge.

This is an . . . appeal from the district court's order denying defendants' motion to dismiss the complaint; it was certified to this court for resolution of controlling questions of law. . . . While the district court did not limit its certification to a particular question, it stated that it viewed the "controlling question" to be whether the plaintiff may sue for the type of injury he alleges here under the Racketeer Influenced and Corrupt Organizations Act, 18 U.S.C. §§ 1961–1968 (hereinafter, RICO). In order to reach this jurisdictional issue, however, we find it first necessary to determine the standing of the plaintiff, the Director of Insurance of the State of Illinois (Director), who is the statutory liquidator of Reserve Insurance Company (Reserve), to maintain the action, and to determine the sufficiency of the complaint. We conclude that the Director has standing, that his complaint is sufficient, and that it alleges an injury which may be redressed by a civil action under RICO.

I. Factual Background

Although the alleged events giving rise to this action are complex, they may be outlined briefly for the purposes of this appeal. The main focus of the allegations is that, as a result of the fraudulent actions of the various defendants, Reserve's corporate parent was caused to continue Reserve in business even though the latter was insolvent, and was caused to saddle Reserve with additional liabilities and drive it deeper into insolvency, all of which consequences resulted in damage to Reserve, as well as its policyholders and creditors, exceeding $100,000,000.

The complaint recites that, as of December 31, 1974, Reserve was insolvent as a result of its policy of accepting extraordinarily high-risk insurance business and underreserving and maintaining insufficient surplus for potential claims. In late 1974, the Director alleges, the Illinois Department of Insurance became concerned about the diminution of Reserve's surplus, and initiated negotiations with the officers and directors of Reserve and American Reserve Corporation (ARC), Reserve's corporate parent, to rectify the problem. While these negotiations were proceeding, however, the officers and directors of Reserve and ARC caused their companies to enter into an agreement with defendants Societe Commerciale De Reassurance (SCOR), a deal brokered by SCOR Reinsurance Company (SCOR Re). Under the terms of this agreement, Reserve ceded to SCOR most of its more profitable and least risky business (in return for SCOR's payments of commissions to Reserve), most of which business SCOR in turn secretly retroceded to another ARC subsidiary, Guarantee Reserve Co., Ltd. (GRC). Also, because the capitalization of GRC was insufficient to cover the potential losses involved in this retrocession, the Director alleges, ARC's officers and Directors secretly agreed to guarantee GRC's obligations to SCOR. The purpose of these agreements, the Director charges, was to enable Reserve to report on paper a smaller volume of business and an increase in surplus and thus a lower liability-to-surplus ratio, a fraudulent result which concealed and exacerbated Reserve's actual insolvency.

By concealing Reserve's continued liability for the retroceded business and hence Reserve's continued insolvency, the Director alleges, the defendant directors and officers were able to fraudulently obtain approval of the Illinois Department of Insurance for the cession agreements and were able to reach a consent agreement with the Department in April, 1975 which enabled Reserve to continue operations if certain surplus requirements were met. In addition, the subsequent continuation of these concealments effected through the SCOR agreements enabled Reserve's officers to violate the explicit surplus maintenance requirements of the consent agreement, the Director avers, while the SCOR agreements had the further cumulative effect of draining away from Reserve its more profitable and less risky business and over $3,000,000 in income. If the Department had at any time known of Reserve's actual insolvency, the complaint charges, it would not have permitted Reserve to continue to write insurance and suffer further dissipation of its assets, but would have caused Reserve to stop writing insurance pursuant to Ill.Rev. Stat., ch. 73, § 756.1 (1981). The complaint alleges that defendants SCOR and SCOR Re were aware of the fraudulent purposes (and the further crippling impact upon Reserve) of the underlying agreements which they entered into and brokered. The director further alleges that the defendant accounting firms, Coopers and Lybrand, Alexander Grant and Co., and Arthur Andersen and Co., knew of Reserve's insolvency and of the further impairing effect of the SCOR agreements and Reserve's continued operations, but that, despite this knowledge, each of them prepared unqualified opinion letters as to ARC's consolidated financial statements in 1974, 1975, 1976 and 1977, even though those statements failed to disclose that the SCOR agreement was entered into to conceal Reserve's insolvency, that the SCOR agreement did not remove any substantial risk of loss from Reserve and ARC, that the SCOR arrangement had been used to evade the consent agreement, that Reserve was at all times insolvent, and that the SCOR arrangement resulted in the multiplication of Reserve's high risk business while draining it of its least risky and most profitable business. In short, the Director claims that SCOR, SCOR Re and the accounting firm defendants joined with ARC and Reserve's officers and directors in a multifaceted, fraudulent scheme which kept Reserve operating long past insolvency in a manner which resulted in enormous losses to the latter company.

In 1979, Reserve was finally adjudicated insolvent and the Director was designated as the Liquidator of Reserve pursuant to Ill.Rev.Stat., ch. 73, §§ 799 *et seq.* (1981). Under that statute, the Director is vested with all rights of action belonging to Reserve. Ill.Rev.Stat., ch. 73, § 805 (1981). Pursuant to that mandate, the Director filed this action in district court in 1981, seeking relief for damages sustained by Reserve as a result of the alleged fraudulent scheme under RICO and a variety of Illinois statutory and common law theories. In January, 1982, the district court granted the defendants' motion to dismiss fifteen pendant state law claims, but denied their motion to dismiss Counts II and IV, seeking relief under RICO, and Counts I and III, alleging and seeking relief for damages resulting from a criminal conspiracy under Illinois law.

II.   The Director's Standing: Capacity and Equitable Estoppel

RICO considerations aside, defendants Grant, Coopers and Lybrand, Arthur Andersen, and SCOR and SCOR Re argue that the Director either lacks standing *ab initio* to maintain the present action or is estopped from doing so. Their main argument proceeds in two stages. First, they note, the Director as Liquidator acquires only those rights of action that would accrue to Reserve itself; the Director may not assert the legal claims of Reserve's policyholders or creditors. As the next step, they argue that since the Director admits that Reserve's officers and directors instigated the illegal conduct here, the Director, standing in the shoes of Reserve, is estopped from proceeding against the extra-corporate confederate defendants under our decision in *Cenco, Inc. v. Seidman & Seidman*, 686 F.2d 449 (7th Cir.1982). SCOR and SCOR Re argue additionally that, *Cenco* considerations

aside, prevailing law does not permit an insurance liquidator to pursue on behalf of the corporation he represents claims for losses stemming from the artificially and fraudulently prolonged life of the corporation and its consequent dissipation of assets.

Even accepting the first step of the defendants' argument, *i.e.*, that the Director may prosecute only those legal actions available to the corporate body, we disagree with the defendants' contention that *Cenco* applies to the instant case, or that, even if it does apply, its underlying policy forbids the Director from maintaining the present action on behalf of Reserve. In addition, we reject SCOR and SCOR Re's fallback position that Reserve lacks standing to sue, either derivatively or through a receiver, to recover damages resulting from the fraudulently extended life of the corporation and its concomitant dissipation of assets.

Our reasons for finding *Cenco* inapplicable to the estoppel issue in the present case are twofold. First, the main controverted claim in *Cenco* arose under Illinois common law, and therefore this court's analysis of circumstances under which the knowledge of fraud on the part of the plaintiff's directors be imputed to the plaintiff corporation were merely an attempt to divine how Illinois courts would decide that issue. . . . By contrast, the cause of action here arises under RICO, a federal statute; we therefore write on a clean slate and may bring to bear federal policies in deciding the estoppel question.

Second, even if the estoppel holding in *Cenco* were relevant to a RICO claim, an important prerequisite for its invocation in the present case is lacking. The *Cenco* court limited its estoppel analysis to cases where "the managers are not stealing from the company . . . but instead are turning the company into an engine of theft against outsiders." . . . As the court explained,

> Fraud on behalf of a corporation is not the same theory as fraud against it. Fraud against the corporation usually hurts just the corporation; the stockholders are the principal if not only victims. . . . But the stockholders of a corporation whose officers commit fraud for the benefit of the corporation are beneficiaries of the fraud.

In *Cenco*, this court found that the fraudulent inflation of the corporation's inventories and hence stock prices clearly benefited the corporation to the detriment of outside creditors, stock purchasers and insurers; this fact, in the court's view, made the case ripe for an analysis of whether the directors' knowledge of the fraud should be imputed to the benefited corporation. By contrast, the complaint in the instant case alleges a far-reaching scheme in which, as a consequence of the illegal activities of Reserve's directors and the outside defendants, Reserve was, *inter alia*, fraudulently continued in business past its point of insolvency and systematically looted of its most profitable and least risky business and more than $3,000,000 in income—all actions which aggravated Reserve's insolvency. In no way can these results be described as beneficial to Reserve.[1] *Compare Security America Corp. v. Schacht*, No. 82–C–2132, slip op. at 3, 4 (N.D.Ill. Jan. 31, 1983) ("particular fact pattern" established that plaintiff corporation had been created solely to carry out fraudulent scheme and thus had no other purpose than to be "engine of theft" against outsiders under *Cenco*).

Defendants argue nonetheless that since the alleged fraudulent scheme had the effect of continuing Reserve's active corporate existence past the point of insolvency to the detriment of outside creditors and policyholders, Reserve was *pro tanto* benefited. But the fact that Reserve's existence may have been artificially prolonged pales in comparison with the real damage allegedly inflicted by the diminution of its assets and income. Under such circumstances, the prolonged artificial insolvency of Reserve benefited only Reserve's managers and the other alleged conspirators, not the corporation. *See In re Investor's Funding Corp.*, [1980] Fed.Sec.L.Rep. (CCH) ¶ 97,696 at 98,655 (1980). More colloquially put, if defendants' position were accepted, the possession of such "friends" as Reserve had would certainly obviate the need for enemies. We do not believe that such a Pyrrhic "benefit" to Reserve is sufficient to even trigger the *Cenco* analysis which seeks to determine the propriety of imputing to the corporation the directors' knowledge of fraud.

Even if a *Cenco*-type analysis were applied to the instant case, however, it would not yield the result that defendants urge, *i.e.*, estoppel of the Director based on the imputation to Reserve of the directors' knowledge of fraud. In *Cenco*, we undertook a two-pronged analysis to determine whether such imputation should occur: whether a judgment in favor of the plaintiff corporation would properly compensate the victims of the wrongdoing, and whether such recovery would deter future wrongdoing. *Cenco*, 686 F.2d at 455. We find that, if warranted by the proof at trial, recovery by the Director on behalf of Reserve would do both.

First, any recovery by the Director from the instant suit will inure to Reserve's estate. And under the distribution provisions of the governing liquidation statute, it is the policyholders and creditors who have first claim (after administrative costs and wages owed) to the assets of the estate. Ill.Rev.Stat., ch. 73, § 817 (1981). Thus, the claims of these entirely innocent parties must be satisfied in full before Reserve's shareholders, last in line for recovery, receive anything.

Moreover, there is no indication here that the Director's success entails the likelihood of the kind of "perverse" compensation pattern which we declined to permit in *Cenco*.

---

[1] These defendants argue that, since Reserve was a wholly-owned subsidiary of ARC, the owners of Reserve, i.e. ARC shareholders, automatically benefited from the direct draining of Reserve and the fraudulent prolongation of Reserve's life. This argument founders on both logic and fact. First, it defies common sense to suggest that a parent corporation's shareholders are not injured when their directors fraudulently prop up, drain, and thereby deepen the insolvency of a subsidiary for whose liabilities the shareholders will eventually be liable. The damage resulting to the parent corporation's shareholders is as real as if the management had impaired a valuable working asset or sold it for a meager sum far less than its present value. Second, as a factual matter, the complaint alleges that not all of the proceeds resulting from the crippling of Reserve redounded to the benefit of ARC and ARC's shareholders. According to the allegations, as a result of the SCOR agreements, ARC was secretly exposed to increased liability for GRC's performance; also as part of these agreements, SCOR allegedly received additional payments from ARC in excess of $2,500,000 for its assistance in furthering the scheme.

In *Cenco*, the court was troubled first by the fact that among the shareholders benefiting from a successful recovery were the corrupt officers themselves, *Cenco*, 686 F.2d at 455; here, the defendants do not claim that the wrongdoing officers or directors hold equity positions in Reserve entitling them to recover from the instant suit. We were also troubled in *Cenco* by the prospect of double recovery by the shareholders via the plaintiff corporation in view of the *previous* successful recovery of damages by these same shareholders in a direct suit against the defendants. In this case, by contrast, the other actions noted to this court based on these alleged events have yet to result in any recovery. Of course, if the Director recovers successfully in the instant suit, the defendants in these actions will be able to assert the previous satisfaction of the claims of the shareholders, policyholders, and creditors of Reserve as a bar to subsequent recovery.

Second, from the standpoint of deterrence, this court in *Cenco* based its refusal to permit the plaintiff to recover unimpeded by the directors' knowledge in large part on two circumstances not present here: 1) that the directors, as shareholders, would recover directly from the suit, and 2) that there existed large corporate shareholders in a position to police the plaintiff's corrupt officers, an activity that would be discouraged by allowing the shifting of corruption-caused loss to outside defendants. *Cenco*, 686 F.2d at 456. By contrast, here, as noted earlier, there is no evidence that the wrongdoing officers of Reserve would benefit directly from the instant suit. There is also no evidence here of the existence of large corporate shareholders capable of conducting an independent audit, as in *Cenco*, and whose lack of investigatory zeal would be rewarded by a decision favorable to the Director.

The court in *Cenco* also expressed reluctance to permit even innocent, atomized shareholders to recover damages for wrongdoing in which their officers were implicated, but that concern must be viewed against the background of the recovery of many of those same shareholders in an earlier action, and the fact that, suing directly, the full recovery in the later suit would inure to them. Significantly, due to the operation of the liquidation statute here, Reserve's shareholders are last in line for recovery from Reserve's estate and will receive only a residual recovery from the instant suit, if successful after trial, after all of the policyholders and creditors are compensated in full. Thus, unlike the situation in *Cenco*, permitting recovery in this case would not send unqualified signals to shareholders that they need not be alert to managerial fraud since they may later recover full indemnification for that fraud from third party participants. In sum, we believe not only that *Cenco* is not applicable to the present case, but also that even if it were, application of its compensation and deterrent principles would not inhibit the right of the Director to proceed against the defendants here.

We turn finally to SCOR and SCOR Re's fallback argument that, even if the Director were not barred from proceeding under *Cenco*, the Director still lacks standing to sue on behalf of Reserve. Citing *Bergeson v. Life Insurance Corp. . . . , Kinter v. Connolly . . . , Patterson v. Franklin . . . , Kelly v. Overseas Investors, Inc. . . . ,* and *Cotten v. Republic National Bank . . . ,* these defendants argue that a corporation may never sue to recover damages alleged to have resulted from the artificial prolongation of an insolvent corporation's life. Next, they argue, since Count II and Count IV of the instant complaint assert that "Reserve continued to write insurance" as a result of the underlying mail fraud, and "Reserve's assets were dissipated notwithstanding that Reserve was at all times insolvent," the sole thrust of the Director's complaint is that the damages to Reserve occurred only because Reserve continued to do business past its point of insolvency. Therefore, they conclude, the Director's claim in this case is barred by the general rule prohibiting a corporation from suing for damages caused by the artificial prolongation of its life.

We reject both premises of this argument. First, in the underlying allegations here, the Director charges that the damage to Reserve stemmed not only from the mere extension of the normal business operation of Reserve, but from specific actions crippling Reserve which were taken as an integral part of that extension. *Inter alia*, the Director alleges that with the smoke-screen of the underlying mail fraud, Reserve's directors and other defendants were able to drain Reserve of over $3,000,000 of income, and to drain Reserve of its most profitable and least risky business, thereby deepening Reserve's insolvency. Thus, the "asset dissipation" alleged was not only that which resulted from the normal operation of the business, as in the cases cited by the defendants, but also that which resulted from the bleeding of Reserve which was a part of the underlying scheme to defraud.

Alternatively, to the extent that the cited cases suggest that a corporation may not sue to recover damages resulting from the fraudulent prolongation of its life past insolvency, we decline to speculate that the Illinois courts would accept this restriction on the Director's freedom of action. For each of these cases rests upon a seriously flawed assumption, *i.e.*, that the fraudulent prolongation of a corporation's life beyond insolvency is automatically to be considered a benefit to the corporation's interests. *See, e.g., Bergeson*, 265 F.2d at 232; *Kinter*, 81 A. at 905; *Patterson*, 35 A. at 206. This premise collides with common sense, for the corporate body is ineluctably damaged by the deepening of its insolvency, through increased exposure to creditor liability. See *In Re Investor's Funding Corp.*, [1980] Fed. Sec.L.Rep. (CCH) ¶ 97,696, at 98,655 (S.D.N.Y. 1980). Indeed, in most cases, it would be crucial that the insolvency of the corporation be disclosed, so that shareholders may exercise their right to dissolve the corporation in order to cut their losses. See Ill.Rev.Stat., ch. 32, §§ 157.75, 157.76 (1981). Thus, acceptance of a rule which would bar a corporation from recovering damages due to the hiding of information concerning its insolvency would create perverse incentives for wrong-doing officers and directors to conceal the true financial condition of the corporation from the corporate body as long as possible. We are not prepared to conclude that the Illinois courts would adopt such a regime.

III. The Applicability of RICO

We turn now to defendants' contentions that the injury to Reserve which the Director al-leges is not compensable under RICO. The civil damage provision of RICO, 18 U.S.C. § 1964(c), creates a private right of action with treble damage recovery for "[a]ny person injured in his business or property by reason of a violation of [§ 1962]." Section 1962 enumerates two violations relevant to the instant case: § 1962(a) makes it "unlawful for any person who has received any income derived, directly or indirectly, from a pattern of racketeering activity . . . to use or invest, directly or indirectly, any part of such income, or the proceeds of such income, in acquisition of any interest in, or establishment or operation of, any enterprise" which touches interstate commerce; and § 1962(c) makes it "unlawful for any person employed by or associated with any enterprise [engaged in interstate commerce] to conduct or participate directly or indirectly, in the conduct of such enterprise's affairs through a pattern of racketeering activity. . . . " Finally, RICO § 1961 defines a "pattern of racketeering activity" as at least two occurrences within ten years of any of several predicate offenses, including mail fraud.

In his complaint, the Director alleges that injury to Reserve stemmed from the violation by the defendants of both § 1962(a) and § 1962(c). The underlying "pattern of racketeering activity" alleged consists of the mail fraud which occurred in connection with the mailing of the fraudulent financial statements of Reserve which all defendants knew did not disclose Reserve's insolvency or the purpose and effects of the SCOR deal. Count II of the complaint alleges that the officers and directors, SCOR and SCOR Re used income derived from the pattern of racketeering activity in the operation of their businesses in violation of § 1962(a), and that the same defendants conducted the affairs of ARC, SCOR, and SCOR Re through the underlying pattern of racketeering activity, in violation of § 1962(c). Count IV alleges that the officers and directors and the three defendant accounting firms used income derived from the racketeering activity in the operation of ARC and the accounting firms in violation of § 1962(a), and that the officers and directors and the accounting firms conducted the affairs of ARC and the accounting firms through a pattern of racketeering activity in violation of § 1962(c).

Because each of the described violations amount to alternative characterizations of the same conduct, i.e., the cooperation of the defendants in a scheme which impaired Reserve, we can find that RICO applies if any one of the Director's theories is sufficient to invoke the statute. Indeed, we find, after careful consideration, an adequate description of a compensable civil RICO claim in the portions of Counts II and IV of the complaint which allege injury to Reserve as a result of the defendants' direct or indirect participation in the conduct of ARC's affairs through the alleged mail fraud in such a manner as to artificially prolong Reserve's existence and worsen its insolvency and losses.

The defendants contend that numerous fatal defects inhere in these portions of the Director's complaint. . . . Second, and more generally, they argue that Congress did not intend that the civil provisions of RICO would be applicable to the general universe of business fraud encompassing the acts alleged here.

B. The Application of RICO to Business Fraud

The defendants' main line of attack upon the Director's complaint is that, while it alleges conduct to which RICO might literally apply, Congress did not intend that the statute would reach so far. To allow the Director's complaint to proceed, they argue, would be to unreasonably federalize the common law of "garden variety" business fraud, and eclipse the federal securities laws, providing treble damage actions for all securities-related mail fraud. We agree that the civil sanctions provided under RICO are dramatic, and will have a vast impact upon the federal-state division of substantive responsibility for redressing illegal conduct, but, like most courts who have considered this issue, we believe that such dramatic consequences are necessary incidents of the deliberately broad swath Congress chose to cut in order to reach the evil it sought; we are therefore without authority to restrict the application of the statute.

We begin our analysis with the plain language of the statute, which provides that "any person" may be liable for a violation of § 1962(c). "Person" is defined at § 1961(3) as "any individual or entity capable of holding a legal or beneficial interest in property. . . ." It does not appear that any of the defendants seriously argue that we should impose a further gloss on that definition requiring that the "person" be affiliated with "organized crime." Such an argument would, of course, be unavailing in light of the clear decisions of this and other courts that application of § 1962(c) "is not restricted to members of organized crime." Nonetheless, defendants argue, the use of civil RICO suits against business fraud, such as that alleged here, would duplicate existing state law and federal securities law remedies, would not further the purposes of the Act, and was not within the contemplation of Congress.

The chief problem with this argument is that Congress was well aware of the range of application authorized by RICO's capacious statutory language. But Congress was equally adamant that the fight against organized criminal social exploitation not be impeded by an overly narrow definition of actionable conduct. Congressman Poff, a sponsor of the bill, defended the broad reach of the act by noting,

> The curious objection has been raised to [RICO's provisions] that they are not somehow limited to organized crime—as if organized crime were a precise and operative legal concept, like murder, rape or robbery. Actually, of course, it is a functional concept like white-collar or street crime serving simply as a short-hand method of referring to a large and varying group of individual criminal offenses committed in diverse circumstances.

And as Senator McClellan conceded, "Of course, it is true that Title X will have some application to individuals who are not themselves members of La Cosa Nostra or otherwise engaged in organized crime. However, that is not a reason to cut back its scope. . . ." Later, he noted that "the Senate report does not claim . . . that the listed offenses are committed *primarily* by members of organized crime, only that these offenses are characteristic of organized crime." In short, Congress chose to provide civil remedies for an enormous variety of conduct, balancing the need to redress a broad social ill against the virtues of tight, but possibly overly astringent, legislative draftsmanship. It is not for this court to reassess the balance struck.

That deference to the conscious assessment of Congress should be our guiding principle is made especially clear upon examination of the defendants' specific objection that our reading of RICO will unreasonably eclipse existing federal civil remedies for securities law violations by providing a treble damage action where two acts of mail fraud accompany the disputed sale or purchase of securities. Defendants' contention proves too much, for such a result is to a degree *explicitly* accomplished, even without the simultaneous presence of mail fraud, by the designation in § 1961 of "fraud in the sale of securities" as a predicate offense giving rise to a civil damage action where an enterprise is operated through such fraud; clearly, such an outcome is not the result of a strained interpretation of RICO, but rather is explicitly mandated. Defendants' objection that our interpretation will unreasonably bring into the federal ambit regulation of common law fraud likewise proves too much, for such a realignment of the federal-state role has already been accomplished in the criminal sphere through the existence of the mail fraud statute itself. Moreover, the defendants, in raising the spectre of the opening of the litigation floodgates, overlook the fact that neither common law fraud nor securities law violates will, by themselves, be automatically eligible for redress through a civil RICO action; there is the additional requirement under § 1964(c), discussed *infra*, that an interstate enterprise be conducted "through" a pattern of such activity.

In sum, defendants' profession of alarm at the expansion of federal jurisdiction over business fraud through RICO amounts to nothing less than a dispute with the very design, and not the mere application, of the statute. As the Supreme Court has noted in the criminal context,

> [T]he language of the statute and its legislative history indicate that Congress was well aware that it was entering a new domain of federal involvement through the enactment of this measure. Indeed, the very purpose of the Organized Crime Control Act of 1970 was to enable the Federal Government to address a large and seemingly neglected problem. The view was that existing law, state and federal, was not adequate to address the problem, which was of national dimensions. That Congress included within the definition of racketeering activities a number of state crimes strongly indicates that RICO criminalized conduct that was also criminal under state law, at least when the requisite elements of a RICO offense are present. As the hearings and legislative debates reveal, Congress was well aware of the fear that RICO would "mov[e] large substantive areas formerly totally within the police power of the State into the Federal realm." [citations omitted] . . . In the face of these objections, Congress nonetheless proceeded to enact the measure, knowing that it would alter somewhat the role of the Federal Government in the war against organized crime and that the alteration would entail prosecutions involving acts of racketeering that are also crimes under state law. There is no argument that Congress acted beyond its power in so doing. That being the case, the courts are without authority to restrict the application of the statute.

United States v. Turkette, 452 U.S. at 586, 587, 101 S.Ct. at 2531 (1981).

In view of this legislative history, it is not surprising that most courts in this and other circuits have had little trouble in entertaining RICO civil actions for damages flowing from the operation by otherwise "legitimate" business people of enterprises through a pattern of mail fraud and securities law violations. *See, e.g., Bennett v. Berg*, 685 F.2d 1053 (8th Cir.1982), *pet. for reh. en banc granted*, Sept. 17, 1982 (upholding finding that defendant mortgage lender, insurance company, developer, accountants, attorneys and corporate directors caused compensable RICO damages through operation of retirement community through, *inter alia*, mail fraud).

Another major problem with the sort of judicial pruning of RICO's civil provisions, advocated by defendants, where business fraud is alleged is that there is simply no legitimate principled criterion through which to accomplish this distinction. Presumably, the infiltration of a corporation by an organized crime syndicate and the subsequent commission of fraud which results in the looting of the corporation's assets for the syndicate's benefit would and should form the basis for a legitimate RICO action. But the only way in which to distinguish this case from the commission of "garden variety" fraud by "legitimate" corporate directors and outside corporations and auditors, as here alleged, is the presence of an "organized crime" nexus in the first case. Indeed, most courts [that] have squarely exempted "normal" business or securities fraud-related claims from RICO's coverage have been forced to rely on the already discredited "organized crime" limitations. Obviously, having already rejected

the "organized crime" limitation . . . , this court does not wish that limitation to be revived under the guise of determining the kinds of activity covered by RICO.

In short, while we are mindful of the jurisprudential maxim that statutes are not to be interpreted woodenly and without regard to their aim, we do not see how any legitimate or principled tailoring of RICO could be effected without impairing the broad strategy embodied in the act. If Congress wishes to avoid the inclusion under RICO's umbrella of "garden variety" fraud claims involving the operation of enterprises through mail and securities fraud, it may easily do so through removing mail and securities fraud from the list of predicate acts enumerated in § 1961. That is not, however, a program which may be undertaken by this court.

1.   The *Schacht* decision had to deal with the Seventh Circuit's prior decision in *Cenco v. Seidman & Seidman* where the Court of Appeals held that "fraud on behalf of a corporation is not the same theory as fraud against it." The *Cenco* decision held that there should be no recovery against the auditors by the corporation when the fraud benefits the corporation. The *Schacht* decision held that *Cenco* was a limited decision and that in any event the fraudulent prolongation of a corporation's life beyond insolvency as alleged in *Schacht* is not a *benefit* to the corporation's interests.

2.   The Court of Appeals held that civil RICO applies to "garden variety" fraud claims.

¶ 10.04   Accounting Firm's RICO Complaint Against Its Client

RICO has been used by accounting firms against former clients. The treble damages provisions have been asserted to recover lost fees, expenses, and injury to business reputation. The following case is an example of a RICO complaint by an auditing firm against its ex-client.

Alexander Grant & Co. v. Tiffany Industries, Inc.
742 F.2d 408
(8th Cir.1984)

Before ROSS, JOHN R. GIBSON and BOWMAN, Circuit Judges.

JOHN R. GIBSON, Circuit Judge.

Alexander Grant and Company, a public accounting firm, appeals the dismissal of its complaint brought against its former client,

Tiffany Industries, and certain Tiffany officials and employees under Title IX, the Racketeer Influenced and Corrupt Organizations (RICO) provision of the Organized Crime Control Act of 1970. We reverse and remand for further proceedings.

Grant was retained by Tiffany from 1970 through May, 1978. In 1979, Grant filed an action under RICO's civil remedy provision, 18 U.S.C. § 1964(c), against Tiffany, its president Farrell Kahn, and Kahn's secretary Gail Martin. Grant claimed that it was the target of a pervasive scheme of mail and wire fraud designed by the defendants to obtain a favorable audit for the fiscal year 1977. Tiffany allegedly sought the favorable audit to obtain credit on better terms and to mislead its stockholders and the Securities & Exchange Commission into believing that the company was financially healthy.

The first allegation is that Kahn, in an effort to inflate the value of Tiffany inventory, falsely represented to Grant that Steelabrade Corporation, a supplier of products to Tiffany, held $500,000 worth of Tiffany inventory as of March, 1978. Grant requested confirmation of this claim from Steelabrade president James Murphy. Kahn and Martin, knowing Murphy would not comply, instead requested that he compile a schedule of all purchases of Steelabrade products by Tiffany during 1977. The two then attached a copy of Grant's confirmation request to the schedule and fraudulently inserted language above Murphy's signature stating that "[t]his inventory was at our premises at December 31, 1977, and March 1, 1978." These documents were then mailed to Grant.

Grant's second claim of fraud concerns an alleged sale of $3,500,000 worth of Tiffany products to the government of Nigeria. Grant learned through the course of its audit that a substantial portion of the products sold had not yet been purchased by Tiffany. Grant questioned whether Tiffany could, under these circumstances, record in its financial statements the substantial earnings resulting from this sale. In response, Tiffany personnel stated that the sale should be certified because they had issued purchase orders for the products as of June 30, 1977, and that the products were held by ten suppliers who were simply awaiting further shipping instructions. Grant requested confirmation of this claim from the ten suppliers. Kahn and Martin backdated purchase orders and mailed to Grant forged letters from the suppliers confirming the representations made by Tiffany personnel.

Grant, still apprehensive, sought "reconfirmation" of the same information. Kahn and Martin then pressured six suppliers to sign and mail reconfirmation letters back to Grant.

Grant further asserts that Kahn and Martin typed two letters at Tiffany's St. Louis County offices allegedly from Nigerian bank officials. The two letters, one a forgery and the other "on information and belief" a forgery, represented that the two banks had extended $3,500,000 in loan commitments to the Nigerian government to enable it to purchase the Tiffany products. Grant also claims that Tiffany used false information to persuade four independent public accounting firms to certify the Nigerian sale, thereby pressuring Grant to do the same. These certifications were then mailed to Grant. By April 1978, Grant suspected that it was being defrauded and reported its concerns to the Securities & Exchange Commission as required by SEC regulations.

Grant asserts that it was damaged in three respects as a result of Tiffany's fraudulent representations. First, it claims that it suffered "theft of services," i.e., the fraud required it to spend substantially more time on the Tiffany audit with a commensurate increase in fees, none of which have been paid. Second, it contends that the SEC investigation caused it to spend large amounts for attorneys' fees, document requests, and other expenses. Third, Grant argues that the fraud caused it to suffer damages to its business reputation.

I. Standing

[1] The district court did not hold, nor does Tiffany argue, that Grant has failed to plead facts sufficiently alleging that Tiffany committed a substantive violation of RICO under section 1962(c). Rather, the district court relied on *Cenco* and its holding that the accounting firm in that case suffered only "indirect" injury insufficient to grant it standing under section 1964(c).

We believe that *Cenco* is distinguishable from this case. In *Cenco*, the accounting firm of Seidman & Seidman was a co-defendant with Cenco, Inc., in a class action brought by persons who had purchased Cenco stock at allegedly inflated prices due to the company's fraudulent representations. The co-defendants cross-claimed against each other: Seidman argued that it too had been defrauded by Cenco and sought as damages under RICO indemnification for its liability to the shareholders. In this case, Grant seeks not indemnification but damages for the amount of its lost fees, the amount spent by reason of the SEC investigation, and the amount representing its loss of business reputation. We believe these are direct injuries, distinguishable from a claim for indemnification which, by its very nature, is secondary and indirect.

Second, and more compellingly, we are unpersuaded by the reasoning employed in *Cenco*. Judge Posner, writing for the panel, reasoned that the case was one of first impression and that the "language of section 1964(c) provides no answer * * * and there is no useful legislative history relating to the provision." The opinion thus focused on whether recognizing a cause of action in favor of Seidman would be consistent with the "compensatory and deterrent objectives of RICO" and would comport with its primary purpose of " 'cop[ing] with the infiltration of legitimate businesses.' " The court concluded that the objectives and purpose of RICO would not be served by permitting such actions, and also expressed concern with the volume of treble damage lawsuits an opposite decision might spawn.

We cannot agree that Grant's standing under section 1964(c) is to be determined by means of an appeal to RICO's purpose and objectives. Section 1964(c) provides a civil remedy for "[a]ny person injured in his business or property by reason of a violation of section 1962 * * *." This language is unambiguous and, "in the absence of a 'clearly expressed legislative intent to the contrary, that language must ordinarily be regarded as conclusive.' "

We find no legislative history supporting the direct-indirect dichotomy; indeed, to the extent that the concept of indirect injury is a surrogate for concerns of federal-state relations and crowded court dockets, the legislative history indicates that Congress recognized that these were necessary costs in the fight against organized crime. It is simply

"beyond our authority to restrict the reach of the statute" in this manner.

We also observe that Judge Posner, in the post-*Cenco* decision of *Sutliff, Inc. v. Donovan Cos.*, 727 F.2d 648 (7th Cir.1984), determined the scope of RICO with considerably greater deference to its plain language than he did in *Cenco*. We believe that *Sutliff* robbed *Cenco* of much of the precedential value accorded it by the district court. Insofar as the approaches in the two cases differ, the task of reconciliation is left to the Seventh Circuit.

We conclude that Grant has suffered injury within the meaning of section 1964(c).

II. Racketeering Enterprise Injury

Section 1964(c) provides that a civil remedy is available to persons suffering injury "by reason of a violation of section 1962 * * *." Yet section 1962(c) does not prohibit "racketeering activity;" rather, it makes it unlawful for a person to "conduct or participate * * * in the conduct of [an] enterprise's affairs through a pattern of racketeering activity * * *." Tiffany reasons that the language of these two sections combines to limit civil recovery to persons suffering a "racketeering enterprise injury"—*the conduct of an enterprise through a pattern of racketeering*—and does not create a cause of action for those suffering injury only from the underlying predicate acts. Tiffany asserts that Grant's injuries have resulted solely from the particular acts of mail and wire fraud outlined in the complaint.

We have characterized the attempt to limit the scope of RICO by seizing on the "by reason of" language contained in section 1964(c) as a "reitera[tion] in new guise [of] the argument that no [distinct] 'enterprise' is alleged * * *." As advanced by Tiffany here, a racketeering enterprise injury also appears to bear some resemblance to the commercial or competitive injury concept and to the requirement that RICO is applicable to only those defendants associated with organized crime. We rejected both of these restrictions in *Bennett*. We recognize that a racketeering enterprise injury is a slippery concept whose definition has eluded even those courts professing to recognize it. "Underlying this [racketeering enterprise injury] requirement is the familiar judicial discomfort with the potential breadth of RICO's civil component."

We need not further consider the nature of a racketeering enterprise injury, however, for it is clear that Grant's complaint does not simply allege injury from the underlying predicate acts. It contends that Tiffany was conducted through a pattern of mail and wire fraud that enabled it to remain in business. As a result of this extended life, Grant continued to provide its accounting services to Tiffany for a time greater than it would have had the fraud not occurred. This also increased the harm resulting to Grant's business reputation. We conclude that these allegations sufficiently plead an injury "by reason of" a RICO violation.

The Second Circuit recently held in *Sedima, S.P.R.L. v. Imrex Co.*, 741 F.2d 482 (2d Cir.1984), that the "by reason of" language in section 1964(c) requires that the injury result from mobster activity or the efforts of organized crime. As indicated previously, this requirement is contrary to our holding in *Bennett*. We do view our decision today as consistent with the Second Circuit's decision in *Bankers Trust Co. v. Rhoades*, 741 F.2d 511 (2d Cir.1984). Both require that civil RICO plaintiffs allege something more than injury from the underlying predicate acts. We recognize, however, that the Second Circuit in *Bankers Trust* defines that "something more" in a far narrower fashion. *See also Furman v. Cirrito*, 741 F.2d 524 (2d Cir.1984) (criticizing the requirement of a racketeering enterprise injury imposed by *Sedima* and *Bankers Trust*).

Appellee Kahn asserts in the alternative that no "racketeering enterprise injury" exists because Tiffany never secured the favorable audit from Grant, and therefore its business operations were never enhanced, nor did it receive any financial advantage, from its racketeering activity. We are not persuaded by this argument. As concluded above, Grant's complaint sufficiently alleges that its injury resulted from the operation of Tiffany through a pattern of racketeering activity. Moreover, Kahn's argument would lead to the anomalous result that the racketeering activity must be allowed to proceed to successful completion before civil recovery is permitted. No interpretation of the plain language of RICO's civil provisions supports the position that Grant must silently tolerate the significant costs and risks associated with ongoing fraud before it seeks redress.

¶ 10.05   RICO SURVIVES THE U.S. SUPREME COURT

On July 1, 1985, the United States Supreme Court issued its decision in *Sedima v. Imrex* which affirmed the application of civil RICO to "legitimate" business enterprises and those persons affiliated with such enterprises including directors, officers, and professional accountants. The Supreme Court observed that civil RICO "has become a tool for everyday fraud cases brought against 'respected and legitimate enterprises'." Nonetheless, the Supreme Court held:

> Congress wanted to reach both "legitimate" and "illegitimate" enterprises. The former enjoy neither an inherent incapacity for criminal activity nor immunity from its consequences. The fact that [civil RICO] is used against respected businesses allegedly engaged in a pattern of specifically identified criminal conduct is hardly a sufficient reason for assuming that the provision is being misconstrued.

In upholding the application of civil RICO to "legitimate" enterprises the Supreme Court conceded it had "doubts" as to whether "in its private civil version, RICO is evolving into something quite different from the original conception of its enactors." The Court concluded that "this defect —if defect it is— is inherent in the statute as written, and its correction must lie with Congress."

Justice WHITE delivered the opinion of the Court.

The Racketeer Influenced and Corrupt Organizations Act (RICO), Pub. L. 91–452, Title IX, 84 Stat. 941, as amended, 18 U. S. C. §§ 1961–1968, provides a private civil action to recover treble damages for injury "by reason of a violation of" its substantive provisions. 18 U. S. C. § 1964(c). The initial dormancy of this provision and its recent greatly increased utilization[1] are now familiar history. In response to what it perceived to be misuse of civil RICO by private plaintiffs, the court below construed § 1964(c) to permit private actions only against defendants who had been convicted on criminal charges, and only where there had occurred a "racketeering injury." While we understand the court's concern over the consequences of an unbridled reading of the statute, we reject both of its holdings.

I

RICO takes aim at "racketeering activity," which it defines as any act "chargeable" under several generically described state criminal laws, any act "indictable" under numerous specific federal criminal provisions, including mail and wire fraud, and any other "offense" involving bankruptcy or securities fraud or drug-related activities that is "punishable" under federal law. § 1961(1). Section 1962, entitled "Prohibited Activities," outlaws the use of income derived from a "pattern of racketeering activity" to acquire an interest in or establish an enterprise engaged in or affecting interstate commerce; the acquisition or maintenance of any interest in an enterprise "through" a pattern of racketeering activity; conducting or participating in the conduct of an enterprise through a pattern of racketeering activity; and conspiring to violate any of these provisions.

Congress provided criminal penalties of

imprisonment, fines, and forfeiture for violation of these provisions, § 1963. In addition, it set out a far-reaching civil enforcement scheme, § 1964, including the following provisions for private suits:

> Any person injured in his business or property by reason of a violation of section 1962 of this chapter may sue therefor in any appropriate United States district court and shall recover threefold the damages he sustains and the cost of the suit, including a reasonable attorney's fee. § 1964(c)

In 1979, petitioner Sedima, a Belgian corporation, entered into a joint venture with respondent Imrex Co. to provide electronic components to a Belgian firm. The buyer was to order parts through Sedima; Imrex was to obtain the parts in this country and ship them to Europe. The agreement called for Sedima and Imrex to split the net proceeds. Imrex filled roughly $8,000,000 in orders placed with it through Sedima. Sedima became convinced, however, that Imrex was presenting inflated bills, cheating Sedima out of a portion of its proceeds by collecting for nonexistent expenses.

In 1982, Sedima filed this action in the Federal District Court for the Eastern District of New York. The complaint set out common-law claims of unjust enrichment, conversion, and breach of contract, fiduciary duty, and a constructive trust. In addition, it asserted RICO claims under § 1964(c) against Imrex and two of its officers. Two counts alleged violations of § 1962(c), based on predicate acts of mail and wire fraud. See 18 U. S. C. §§ 1341, 1343, 1961(1)(B). A third count alleged a conspiracy to violate § 1962(c). Claiming injury of at least $175,000, the amount of the alleged overbilling, Sedima sought treble damages and attorney's fees.

The District Court held that for an injury to be "by reason of a violation of section 1962," as required by § 1964(c), it must be somehow different in kind from the direct injury resulting from the predicate acts of racketeering activity. 574 F. Supp. 963 (EDNY 1983). While not choosing a precise formulation, the District Court held that a complaint must allege a "RICO-type injury," which was either some sort of distinct "racketeering injury," or a "competitive injury." It found "no

---

[1] Of 270 district court RICO decisions prior to this year, only 3% (nine cases) were decided throughout the 1970s, 2% were decided in 1980, 7% in 1981, 13% in 1982, 33% in 1983, and 43% in 1984. Report of the Ad Hoc Civil RICO Task Force of the ABA Section of Corporation, Banking and Business Law 55 (1985) (hereinafter ABA Report); see also *id.*, at 53a (table).

allegation here of any injury apart from that which would result directly from the alleged predicate acts of mail fraud and wire fraud," *id.*, at 965, and accordingly dismissed the RICO counts for failure to state a claim.

A divided panel of the Court of Appeals for the Second Circuit affirmed. 741 F. 2d 482 (1984). After a lengthy review of the legislative history, it held that Sedima's complaint was defective in two ways. First, it failed to allege an injury "by reason of a violation of section 1962." In the court's view, this language was a limitation on standing, reflecting Congress' intent to compensate victims of "certain specific kinds of organized criminality," not to provide additional remedies for already compensable injuries. *Id.*, at 494. Analogizing to the Clayton Act, which had been the model for § 1964(c), the court concluded that just as an antitrust plaintiff must allege an "antitrust injury," so a RICO plaintiff must allege a "racketeering injury"—an injury "different in kind from that occurring as a result of the predicate acts themselves, or not simply caused by the predicate acts, but also caused by an activity which RICO was designed to deter." *Id.*, at 496. Sedima had failed to allege such an injury.

The Court of Appeals also found the complaint defective for not alleging that the defendants had already been criminally convicted of the predicate acts of mail and wire fraud, or of a RICO violation. This element of the civil cause of action was inferred from § 1964(c)'s reference to a "violation" of § 1962, the court also observing that its prior conviction requirement would avoid serious constitutional difficulties, the danger of unfair stigmatization, and problems regarding the standard by which the predicate acts were to be proved.

The decision below was one episode in a recent proliferation of civil RICO litigation within the Second Circuit and in other Courts of Appeals. In light of the variety of approaches taken by the lower courts and the importance of the issues, we granted certiorari. 469 U. S. ——(1984). We now reverse.

II

As a preliminary matter, it is worth briefly reviewing the legislative history of the private treble damages action. RICO formed Title IX of the Organized Crime Control Act of 1970, Pub. L. 91–452, 84 Stat. 922. The civil remedies in the bill passed by the Senate, S. 30, were limited to injunctive actions by the United States and became § § 1964(a), (b), and (d). Previous versions of the legislation, however, had provided for a private treble damages action in exactly the terms ultimately adopted in § 1964(c). See S. 1623, 91st Cong., 1st Sess., § 4(a) (1969); S. 2048, S. 2049, 90th Cong., 1st Sess. (1967).

During hearings on S. 30 before the House Judiciary Committee, Representative Steiger proposed the addition of a private treble damages action "similar to the private damage remedy found in the anti-trust laws. . . . [T]hose who have been wronged by organized crime should at least be given access to legal remedy. In addition, the availability of such a remedy would enhance the effectiveness of title IX's prohibitions." Hearings on S. 30, and related proposals, before Subcommittee No. 5 of the House Committee on the Judiciary, 91st Cong., 2d Sess., 520 (1970) (hereinafter House Hearings). The American Bar Association also proposed an amendment "based upon the concept of Section 4 of the Clayton Act." *Id.*, at 543–544, 548, 559; see 116 Cong. Rec. 25190–25191 (1970). See also H. R. 9327, 91st Cong., 1st Sess. (1969) (House counterpart to S. 1623).

Over the dissent of three members, who feared the treble damages provision would be used for malicious harassment of business competitors, the Committee approved the amendment. H. R. Rep. No. 91–1549, pp. 58, 187 (1970). In summarizing the bill on the House floor, its sponsor described the treble damages provision as "another example of the antitrust remedy being adapted for use against organized criminality." 116 Cong. Rec. 35295 (1970). The full House then rejected a proposal to create a complementary treble damages remedy for those injured by being named as defendants in malicious private suits. *Id.*, at 35342. Representative Steiger also offered an amendment that would have allowed private injunctive actions, fixed a statute of limitations, and clarified venue and process requirements. *Id.*, at 35346; see *id.*, at 35226–35227. The proposal was greeted with some hostility because it had not been reviewed in Committee, and Steiger withdrew it without a vote being taken. *Id.*, at 35346–35347. The House then passed the bill, with the treble damages provision in the form recommended by the Committee. *Id.*, at 35363–35364.

The Senate did not seek a conference and adopted the bill as amended in the House. *Id.*, at 36296. The treble damages provision had been drawn to its attention while the legislation was still in the House, and had received the endorsement of Senator McClellan, the sponsor of S. 30, who was of the view that the provision would be "a major new tool in extirpating the baneful influence of organized crime in our economic life." *Id.*, at 25190.

III

The language of RICO gives no obvious indication that a civil action can proceed only after a criminal conviction. The word "conviction" does not appear in any relevant portion of the statute. See §§ 1961, 1962, 1964(c). To the contrary, the predicate acts involve conduct that is "chargeable" or "indictable," and "offense[s]" that are "punishable," under various criminal statutes. § 1961(1). As defined in the statute, racketeering activity consists not of acts for which the defendant has been convicted, but of acts for which he could be. See also S. Rep. No. 91–617, p. 158 (1969): "a racketeering activity . . . must be an act in itself *subject* to criminal sanction" (emphasis added). Thus, a prior conviction requirement cannot be found in the definition of "racketeering activity." Nor can it be found in § 1962, which sets out the statute's substantive provisions. Indeed, if either § 1961 or § 1962 did contain such a requirement, a prior conviction would also be a prerequisite, nonsensically, for a criminal prosecution, or for a civil action by the government to enjoin violations that had not yet occurred.

The Court of Appeals purported to discover its prior conviction requirement in the term "violation" in § 1964(c). 741 F. 2d, at 498–499. However, even if that term were read to refer to a criminal conviction, it would require a conviction under RICO, not of the predicate offenses. That aside, the term "violation" does not imply a criminal conviction.

See *United States v. Ward*, 448, U. S. 242, 249–250 (1980). It refers only to a failure to adhere to legal requirements. This is its indisputable meaning elsewhere in the statute. Section 1962 renders certain conduct "unlawful"; § 1963 and § 1964 impose consequences, criminal and civil, for "violations" of § 1962. We should not lightly infer that Congress intended the term to have wholly different meaning in neighboring subsections.[2]

The legislative history also undercuts the reading of the court below. The clearest current in that history is the reliance on the Clayton Act model, under which private and governmental actions are entirely distinct. *E.g., United States v. Borden Co.*, 347 U. S. 514, 518–519 (1954).[3] The only specific reference in the legislative history to prior convictions of which we are aware is an objection that

---

[2] When Congress intended that the defendant have been previously convicted, it said so. Title 18 U. S. C. A. § 1963(f) (Supp. 1985) states that "[u]pon conviction of a person under this section," his forfeited property shall be seized. Likewise, in Title X of the same legislation Congress explicitly required prior convictions, rather than prior criminal activity, to support enhanced sentences for special offenders. See 18 U. S. C. § 3575(e).

[3] The court below considered it significant that § 1964(c) requires a "violation of section 1962," whereas the Clayton Act speaks of "anything forbidden in the antitrust laws." 741 F. 2d, at 488; see 15 U. S. C. § 15(a). The court viewed this as a deliberate change indicating Congress' desire that the underlying conduct not only be forbidden, but have led to a criminal conviction. There is nothing in the legislative history to support this interpretation, and we cannot view this minor departure in wording, without more, to indicate a fundamental departure in meaning. Representative Steiger, who proposed this wording in the House, nowhere indicated a desire to depart from the antitrust model in this regard. See 116 Cong. Rec. 35227, 35246 (1970). To the contrary, he viewed the treble damages provision as a "parallel private remedy." *Id.*, at 27739 (letter to House Judiciary Committee). Likewise, Senator Hruska's discussion of his identically worded proposal gives no hint of any such intent. See 115 Cong. Rec. 6993 (1969). In any event, the change in language does not support the court's drastic inference. It seems more likely that the language was chosen because it is more succinct than that in the Clayton Act, and is consistent with the neighboring provisions. See §§ 1963(a), 1964(a).

the treble damages provision is too broad precisely because "there need *not* be a conviction under any of these laws for it to be racketeering." 116 Cong. Rec. 35342 (1970) (emphasis added). The history is otherwise silent on this point and contains nothing to contradict the import of the language appearing in the statute. Had Congress intended to impose this novel requirement, there would have been at least some mention of it in the legislative history, even if not in the statute.

The Court of Appeals was of the view that its narrow construction of the statute was essential to avoid intolerable practical consequences.[4] First, without a prior conviction to rely on, the plaintiff would have to prove commission of the predicate acts beyond a reasonable doubt. This would require instructing the jury as to different standards of proof for different aspects of the case. To avoid this awkwardness, the court inferred that the criminality must already be established, so that the civil action could proceed smoothly under the usual preponderance standard.

---

[4] It is worth bearing in mind that the holding of the court below is not without problematic consequences of its own. It arbitrarily restricts the availability of private actions, for lawbreakers are often not apprehended and convicted. Even if a conviction has been obtained, it is unlikely that a private plaintiff will be able to recover for all of the acts constituting an extensive "pattern," or that multiple victims will all be able to obtain redress. This is because criminal convictions are often limited to a small portion of the actual or possible charges. The decision below would also create peculiar incentives for plea-bargaining to non-predicate-act offenses so as to ensure immunity from a later civil suit. If nothing else, a criminal defendant might plead to a tiny fraction of counts, so as to limit future civil liability. In addition, the dependence of potential civil litigants on the initiation and success of a criminal prosecution could lead to unhealthy private pressures on prosecutors and to self-serving trial testimony, or at least accusations thereof. Problems would also arise if some or all of the convictions were reversed on appeal. Finally, the compelled wait for the completion of criminal proceedings would result in pursuit of stale claims, complex statute of limitations problems, or the wasteful splitting of actions, with resultant claim and issue preclusion complications.

We are not at all convinced that the predicate acts must be established beyond a reasonable doubt in a proceeding under § 1964(c). In a number of settings, conduct that can be punished as criminal only upon proof beyond a reasonable doubt will support civil sanctions under a preponderance standard. That the offending conduct is described by reference to criminal statutes does not mean that its occurrence must be established by criminal standards or that the consequences of a finding of liability in a private civil action are identical to the consequences of a criminal conviction. Cf. *United States* v. *Ward, supra*, at 248–251. But we need not decide the standard of proof issue today. For even if the stricter standard is applicable to a portion of the plaintiff's proof, the resulting logistical difficulties, which are accepted in other contexts, would not be so great as to require invention of a requirement that cannot be found in the statute and that Congress, as even the Court of Appeals had to concede, 741 F. 2d, at 501, did not envision.

The court below also feared that any other construction would raise severe constitutional questions, as it "would provide civil remedies for offenses criminal in nature, stigmatize defendants with the appellation 'racketeer,' authorize the award of damages which are clearly punitive, including attorney's fees, and constitute a civil remedy aimed in part to avoid the constitutional protections of the criminal law." *Id.*, at 500, n. 49. We do not view the statute as being so close to the constitutional edge. As noted above, the fact that conduct can result in both criminal liability and treble damages does not mean that there is not a bona fide civil action. The familiar provisions for both criminal liability and treble damages under the antitrust laws indicate as much. Nor are attorney's fees "clearly punitive." Cf. 42 U. S. C. § 1988. As for stigma, a civil RICO proceeding leaves no greater stain than do a number of other civil proceedings. Furthermore, requiring conviction of the predicate acts would not protect against an unfair imposition of the "racketeer" label. If there is a problem with thus stigmatizing a garden variety defrauder by means of a civil action, it is not reduced by making certain that the defendant is guilty of *fraud* beyond a reasonable doubt. Finally, to the extent an action under § 1964(c) might be considered quasi-criminal, requiring protections normally applicable only to criminal proceedings, cf, *One 1958 Plymouth Sedan v. Pennsylvania*, 380 U. S. 693 (1965), the solution is to provide those protections, not to ensure that they were previously afforded by requiring prior convictions.

Finally, we note that a prior conviction requirement would be inconsistent with Congress' underlying policy concerns. Such a rule would severely handicap potential plaintiffs. A guilty party may escape conviction for any number of reasons—not least among them the possibility that the Government itself may choose to pursue only civil remedies. Private attorney general provisions such as § 1964(c) are in part designed to fill prosecutorial gaps. Cf. *Reiter v. Sonotone Corp.*, 442 U. S. 330, 344 (1979). This purpose would be largely defeated, and the need for treble damages as an incentive to litigate unjustified, if private suits could be maintained only against those already brought to justice.

In sum, we can find no support in the statute's history, its language, or considerations of policy for a requirement that a private treble damages action under § 1964(c) can proceed only against a defendant who has already been criminally convicted. To the contrary, every indication is that no such requirement exists. Accordingly, the fact that Imrex and the individual defendants have not been convicted under RICO or the federal mail and wire fraud statutes does not bar Sedima's action.

IV

In considering the Court of Appeals' second prerequisite for a private civil RICO action—"injury . . . caused by an activity which RICO was designed to deter''—we are somewhat hampered by the vagueness of that concept. Apart from reliance on the general purposes of RICO and a reference to "mobsters," the court provided scant indication of what the requirement of racketeering injury means. It emphasized Congress' undeniable desire to strike at organized crime, but acknowledged and did not purport to overrule Second Circuit precedent rejecting a requirement of a organized crime nexus. The court also stopped short of adopting a "competitive injury" requirement; while insisting that the plaintiff show "the kind of economic injury which has an effect on competition," it did not require "actual anticompetitive effect." 741 F. 2d, at 496; see also *id.*, at 495, n. 40.

The court's statement that the plaintiff must seek redress for an injury caused by conduct that RICO was designed to deter is unhelpfully tautological. Nor is clarity furnished by a negative statement of its rule: standing is not provided by the injury resulting from the predicate acts themselves. That statement is itself apparently inaccurate when applied to those predicate acts that unmistakably constitute the kind of conduct Congress sought to deter. See *id.*, at 496, n. 41. The opinion does not explain how to distinguish such crimes from the other predicate acts Congress has lumped together in § 1961(1). The court below is not alone in struggling to define "racketeering injury," and the difficulty of that task itself cautions against imposing such a requirement.

We need not pinpoint the Second Circuit's precise holding, for we perceive no distinct "racketeering injury" requirement. Given that "racketeering activity" consists of no more and no less than commission of a predicate act, § 1961(1), we are initially doubtful about a requirement of a "racketeering injury" separate from the harm from the predicate acts. A reading of the statute belies any such requirement. Section 1964(c) authorizes a private suit by "[a]ny person injured in his business or property by reason of a violation of § 1962." Section 1962 in turn makes it unlawful for "any person"—not just mobsters—to use money derived from a pattern of racketeering activity to invest in an enterprise, to acquire control of an enterprise through a pattern of racketeering activity, or to conduct an enterprise through a pattern of racketeering activity. § § 1962(a)–(c). If the defendant engages in a pattern of racketeering activity in a manner forbidden by these provisions, and the racketeering activities injure the plaintiff in his business or property, the plaintiff has a claim under § 1964(c). There is no room in the statutory language for an additional, amorphous "racketeering injury" requirement.

A violation of § 1962(c), the section on which Sedima relies, requires (1) conduct (2) of an enterprise (3) through a pattern[5] (4) of racketeering activity. The plaintiff must, of course, allege each of these elements to state a claim. Conducting an enterprise that affects interstate commerce is obviously not in itself a violation of § 1962, nor is mere commission of the predicate offenses. In addition, the plaintiff only has standing if, and can only recover to the extent that, he has been injured in his business or property by the conduct

---

[5] As many commentators have pointed out, the definition of a "pattern of racketeering activity" differs from the other provisions in § 1961 in that it states that a pattern *requires* at least two acts of racketeering activity," § 1961(5) (emphasis added), not that it "means" two such acts. The implication is that while two acts are necessary, they may not be sufficient. Indeed, in common parlance two of anything do not generally form a "pattern." The legislative history supports the view that two isolated acts of racketeering activity do not constitute a pattern. As the Senate Report explained: "The target of [RICO] is thus not sporadic activity. The infiltration of legitimate business normally requires more than one 'racketeering activity' and the threat of continuing activity to be effective. It is this factor of *continuity plus relationship* which combines to produce a pattern." S. Rep. No. 91-617, p. 158 (1969) (emphasis added). Similarly, the sponsor of the Senate bill, after quoting this portion of the Report, pointed out to his colleagues that "[t]he term 'pattern' itself requires the showing of a relationship. . . . So, therefore, proof of two acts of racketeering activity, without more, does not establish a pattern. . . ." 116 Cong. Rec. 18940 (1970) (statement of Sen. McClellan). See also *id*., at 35193 (statement of Rep. Poff) (RICO "not aimed at the isolated offender"); House Hearings, at 665. Significantly, in defining "pattern" in a later provision of the same bill, Congress was more enlightening: "criminal conduct forms a pattern if it embraces criminal acts that have the same or similar purposes, results, participants, victims, or methods of commission, or otherwise are interrelated by distinguishing characteristics and are not isolated events." 18 U. S. C. § 3575(e). This language may be useful in interpreting other sections of the Act. Cf. *Iannelli v. United States*, 420 U. S. 770, 789 (1975).

constituting the violation. As the Seventh Circuit has stated, "[a] defendant who violates section 1962 is not liable for treble damages to everyone he might have injured by other conduct, nor is the defendant liable to those who have not been injured."

But the statute requires no more than this. Where the plaintiff alleges each element of the violation, the compensable injury necessarily is the harm caused by predicate acts sufficiently related to constitute a pattern, for the essence of the violation is the commission of those acts in connection with the conduct of an enterprise. Those acts are, when committed in the circumstances delineated in § 1962(c), "an activity which RICO was designed to deter." Any recoverable damages occurring by reason of a violation of § 1962(c) will flow from the commission of the predicate acts.

This less restrictive reading is amply supported by our prior cases and the general principles surrounding this statute. RICO is to be read broadly. This is the lesson not only of Congress' self-consciously expansive language and overall approach, see *United States v. Turkette*, 452 U. S. 576, 586–587 (1981), but also of its express admonition that RICO is to "be liberally construed to effectuate its remedial purposes," Pub. L. 91–452, § 904(a), 84 Stat. 947. The statute's "remedial purposes" are nowhere more evident than in the provision of a private action for those injured by racketeering activity. See also n. 10, *supra*. Far from effectuating these purposes, the narrow readings offered by the dissenters and the court below would in effect eliminate § 1964(c) from the statute.

RICO was an aggressive initiative to supplement old remedies and develop new methods for fighting crime. See generally *Russello v. United States*, 464 U. S. 16, (1983). While few of the legislative statements about novel remedies and attacking crime on all fronts, see *ibid.*, were made with direct reference to § 1964(c), it is in this spirit that all of the Act's provisions should be read. The specific references to § 1964(c) are consistent with this overall approach. Those supporting § 1964(c) hoped it would "enhance the effectiveness of title IX's prohibitions," House Hearings, at 520, and provide "a major new tool," 116 Cong. Rec. 35227 (1970). See also *id.*, at 25190; 115 Cong. Rec. 6993–6994 (1969). Its opponents, also recongizing the provision's scope, complained that it provided too easy a weapon against "innocent businessmen," H. R. Rep. No. 91–1549, p. 187 (1970), and would be prone to abuse, 116 Cong. Rec. 35342 (1970). It is also significant that a previous proposal to add RICO-like provisions to the Sherman Act had come to grief in part precisely because it "could create inappropriate and unnecessary obstacles in the way of . . . a private litigant [who] would have to contend with a body of precedent—appropriate in a purely antitrust context—setting strict requirements on questions such as 'standing to sue' and 'proximate cause.'" 115 Cong. Rec. 6995 (1969) (ABA comments on S. 2048); see also *id.*, at 6993 (S. 1623 proposed as an amendment to title 18 to avoid these problems). In borrowing its "racketeering injury" requirement from antitrust standing principles, the court below created exactly the problems Congress sought to avoid.

Underlying the Court of Appeals' holding was its distress at the "extraordinary, if not outrageous," uses to which civil RICO has been put. 741 F. 2d, at 487. Instead of being used against mobsters and organized criminals, it has become a tool for everyday fraud cases brought against "respected and legitimate 'enterprises.'" *Ibid.* Yet Congress wanted to reach both "legitimate" and "illegitimate" enterprises. *United States v. Turkette, supra.* The former enjoy neither an inherent incapacity for criminal activity nor immunity from its consequences. The fact that § 1964(c) is used against respected businesses allegedly engaged in a pattern of specifically identified criminal conduct is hardly a sufficient reason for assuming that the provision is being misconstrued. Nor does it reveal the "ambiguity" discovered by the court below. "[T]he fact that RICO has been applied in situations not expressly anticipated by Congress does not demonstrate ambiguity. It demonstrates breadth." *Haroco, Inc. v. American National Bank & Trust Co. of Chicago, supra,* at 398.

It is true that private civil actions under the statute are being brought almost solely against such defendants, rather than against the archetypal, intimidating mobster.[6] Yet this defect—if defect it is—is inherent in the statute as written, and its correction must lie with Congress. It is not for the judiciary to eliminate the private action in situations where Congress has provided it simply because plaintiffs are not taking advantage of it in its more difficult applications.

We nonetheless recognize that, in its private civil version, RICO is evolving into something quite different from the original conception of its enactors. See generally ABA Report, at 55–69. Though sharing the doubts of the Court of Appeals about this increasing divergence, we cannot agree with either its diagnosis or its remedy. The "extraordinary" uses to which civil RICO has been put appear to be primarily the result of the breadth of the predicate offenses, in particular the inclusion of wire, mail, and securities fraud, and the failure of Congress and the courts to develop a meaningful concept of "pattern." We do not believe that the amorphous standing requirement imposed by the Second Circuit effectively responds to these problems, or that it is a form of statutory amendment appropriately undertaken by the courts.

V

Sedima may maintain this action if the defendants conducted the enterprise through a pattern of racketeering activity. The questions whether the defendants committed the requisite predicate acts, and whether the commission of those acts fell into a pattern, are not before us. The complaint is not de-

---

[6] The ABA Task Force found that of the 270 known civil RICO cases at the trial court level, 40% involved securities fraud, 37% common-law fraud in a commercial or business setting, and only 9% "allegations of criminal activity of a type generally associated with professional criminals." ABA Report, at 55–56. Another survey of 132 published decisions found that 57 involved securities transactions and 38 commercial and contract disputes, while no other category made it into double figures. American Institute of Certified Public Accountants, The Authority to Bring Private Treble-Damage Suits Under "RICO" Should be Removed 13 (Oct. 10, 1984).

ficient for failure to allege either an injury separate from the financial loss stemming from the alleged acts of mail and wire fraud, or prior convictions of the defendants. The decision below is accordingly reversed, and the case is remanded for further proceedings consistent with this opinion.

It is so ordered.

• • •

Justice MARSHALL, with whom Justice BRENNAN, Justice BLACKMUN, and Justice POWELL join, dissenting.

The Court today recognizes that "in its private civil version, RICO is evolving into something quite different from the original conception of its enactors." The Court, however, expressly validates this result, imputing it to the manner in which the statute was drafted. I fundamentally disagree both with the Court's reading of the statute and with its conclusion. I believe that the statutory language and history disclose a narrower interpretation of the statute that fully effectuates Congress' purposes, and that does not make compensable under civil RICO a host of claims that Congress never intended to bring with RICO's purview.

I

The Court's interpretation of the civil RICO statute quite simply revolutionizes private litigation; it validates the federalization of broad areas of state common law of frauds, and it approves the displacement of well-established federal remedial provisions. We do not lightly infer a congressional intent to effect such fundamental changes. To infer such intent here would be untenable, for there is no indication that Congress even considered, much less approved, the scheme that the Court today defines.

The single most significant reason for the expansive use of civil RICO has been the presence in the statute, as predicate acts, of mail and wire fraud violations. See 18 U. S. C. § 1961(1). Prior to RICO, no federal statute had expressly provided a private damage remedy based upon a violation of the mail or wire fraud statutes, which make it a federal crime to use the mail or wires in furtherance of a scheme to defraud. See 18 U. S. C. § § 1341, 1343. Moreover, the Courts of Appeals consistently had held that no implied federal private causes of action accrue to victims of these federal violations. See, e. g., *Ryan v. Ohio Edison Co.*, 611 F. 2d 1170, 1178–1179 (CA6 1979) (mail fraud); *Napper v. Anderson, Henley, Shields, Bradford & Pritchard*, 500 F. 2d 634, 636 (CA5 1974) (wire fraud), cert. denied, 423 U. S. 837 (1975). The victims normally were restricted to bringing actions in state court under common-law fraud therories.

Under the Court's opinion today, two fraudulent mailings or uses of the wires occurring within ten years of each other might constitute a "pattern of racketeering activity," § 1961(5), leading to civil RICO liability. See § 1964(c). The effects of making a mere two instances of mail or wire fraud potentially actionable under civil RICO are staggering, because in recent years the Court of Appeals have "tolerated an extraordinary expansion of mail and wire fraud statutes to permit federal prosecution for conduct that some had thought was subject only to state criminal and civil law." *United States v. Weiss*, 752 F. 2d 777, 791 (CA2 1985) (Newman, J., dissenting). In bringing criminal actions under those statutes, prosecutors need not show either a substantial connection between the scheme to defraud and the mail and wire fraud statutes, see *Pereira v. United States*, 347 U. S. 1, 8 (1954), or that the fraud involved money or property. Courts have sanctioned prosecutions based on deprivations of such intangible rights as a shareholder's right to "material" information, *United States v. Siegel*, 717 F. 2d 9, 14–16 (CA2 1983); a client's right to the "undivided loyalty" of his attorney, *United States v. Bronston*, 658 F. 2d 920, 927 (CA2 1981), cert. denied, 456 U. S. 915 (1982); an employer's right to the honest and faithful service of his employees, *United States v. Bohonus*, 628 F. 2d 1167, 1172 (CA9), cert. denied, 447 U. S. 928 (1980); and a citizen's right to know the nature of agreements entered into by the leaders of political parties, *United States v. Margiotta*, 688 F. 2d 108, 123–125 (CA2 1982), cert. denied, 461 U. S. 913 (1983).

In the context of civil RICO, however, the restraining influence of prosecutors is completely absent. Unlike the Government, private litigants have no reason to avoid displacing state common-law remedies. Quite to the contrary, such litigants, lured by the prospect of treble damages and attorney's fees, have a strong incentive to invoke RICO's provisions whenever they can allege in good faith two instances of mail or wire fraud. Then the defendant, facing a tremendous financial exposure in addition to the threat of being labelled a "racketeer," will have a strong interest in settling the dispute. See Rakoff, Some Personal Reflections of the *Sedima* Case and on Reforming RICO, in RICO: Civil and Criminal 400 (Law Journal Seminars-Press 1984). The civil RICO provision consequently stretches the mail and wire fraud statutes to their absolute limits and federalizes important areas of civil litigation that until now were solely within the domain of the states.

In addition to altering fundamentally the federal-state balance in civil remedies, the broad reading of the civil RICO provision also displaces important areas of federal law. For example, one predicate offense under RICO is "fraud in the sale of securities." 18 U. S. C. § 1961(1). By alleging two instances of such fraud, a plaintiff might be able to bring a case within the scope of the civil RICO provision. It does not take great legal insight to realize that such a plaintiff would pursue his case under RICO rather than do so solely under the Securities Act of 1933 or the Securities Exchange Act of 1934, which provide both express and implied causes of action for violations of the federal securities laws. Indeed, the federal securities laws contemplate only compensatory damages and ordinarily do not authorize recovery of attorney's fees. By invoking RICO, in contrast, a successful plaintiff will recover both treble damages and attorney's fees.

More importantly, under the Court's interpretation, the civil RICO provision does far more than just increase the available damages. In fact, it virtually eliminates decades of legislative and judicial development of private civil remedies under the federal securities laws. Over the years, courts have paid close attention to matters such as standing, culpability, causation, reliance and materiality, as well as the definitions of "securities" and "fraud." See, *e. g., Blue Chip Stamps v. Manor Drug Stores*, 421 U. S. 723 (1975) (purchaser/seller requirement). All of this law is now an endangered species because plaintiffs can avoid the limitations of the securities laws merely by alleging violations of other predicate acts. For example, even in cases in which the investment instrument is not a "security" covered by the federal securities laws, RICO will provide a treble damage remedy to a plaintiff who can prove the required pattern of mail or wire fraud. Cf. *Crocker National Bank v. Rockwell International Corp.*, 555 F. Supp. 47 (ND Cal. 1982). Before RICO, of course, the plaintiff could not have recovered under federal law for the mail or wire violation.

Similarly, a customer who refrained from selling a security during a period in which its market value was declining could allege that, on two occasions, his broker recommended by telephone, as part of a scheme to defraud, that the customer not sell the security. The customer might thereby prevail under civil RICO even though, as neither a purchaser nor a seller, he would not have had standing to bring an action under the federal securities laws. See also 741 F. 2d 482, 499 (1984) ("two misstatements in a proxy solicitation could subject any director in any national corporation to "racketeering" charges and the threat of treble damages and attorneys' fees").

The effect of civil RICO on federal remedial schemes is not limited to the securities laws. For example, even though commodities fraud is not a predicate offense listed in § 1961, the carefully crafted private damage causes of action under the Commodity Exchange Act may be circumvented in a commodities case through civil RICO actions alleging mail or wire fraud. See, *e. g., Parnes v. Heinold Commodities, Inc.*, 487 F. Supp. 645 (ND Ill. 1980). The list goes on and on.

The dislocations caused by the Court's reading of the civil RICO provision are not just theoretical. In practice, this provision frequently has been invoked against legitimate businesses in ordinary commercial settings.

As the Court recognizes, the ABA Task Force that studied civil RICO found that 40% of the reported cases involved securities fraud, 47% involved common-law fraud in a commercial or business setting. Many a prudent defendant, facing ruinous exposure, will decide to settle even a case with no merit. It is thus not surprising that civil RICO has been used for extortive purposes, giving rise to the very evils that it was designed to combat. Report of the Ad Hoc Civil RICO Task Force of the ABA Section of Corporation, Banking and Business Law 69 (1985) (hereinafter cited as ABA Report).

Only 9% of all civil RICO cases have involved allegations of criminal activity normally associated with professional criminals. The central purpose that Congress sought to promote through civil RICO is now a mere footnote.

In summary, in both theory and practice, civil RICO has brought profound changes to our legal landscape. Undoubtedly, Congress has the power to federalize a great deal of state common law, and there certainly are no relevant constraints on its ability to displace federal law. Those, however, are not the questions that we face in this case. What we have to decide here, instead, is whether Congress in fact intended to produce these far-reaching results.

Established canons of statutory interpretation counsel against the Court's reading of the civil RICO provision. First, we do not impute lightly a congressional intention to upset the federal-state balance in the provision of civil remedies as fundamentally as does this statute under the Court's view. For example, in *Santa Fe Industries v. Green*, 430 U. S. 462 (1977), we stated that "[a]bsent a clear indication of congressional intent, we are reluctant to federalize the substantial portion of the law of corporations that deals with transactions in securities." *Id.*, at 479. Here, with striking nonchalance, the Court does what it declined to do in *Santa Fe Industries*—and much more as well. Second, with respect to effects on the federal securities laws and other federal regulatory statutes, we should be reluctant to displace the well-entrenched federal remedial schemes absent clear direction from Congress. See, *e. g.*, *Train v. Colorado Public Interest Research Group*. 426 U. S. 1, 23–24 (1976); *Radzanower v. Touche Ross & Co.*, 426 U. S. 148, 153 (1976).

In this case, nothing in the language of the statute or the legislative history suggests that Congress intended either the federalization of state common law or the displacement of existing federal remedies. Quite to the contrary, all that the statute and the legislative history reveal as to these matters is what Judge Oakes called a "clanging silence," 741 F. 2d, at 492.

Moreover, if Congress had intended to bring about dramatic changes in the nature of commercial litigation, it would at least have paid more than cursory attention to the civil RICO provision. This provision was added in the House of Representatives after the Senate already had passed its version of the RICO bill; the House itself adopted a civil remedy provision almost as an afterthought; and the Senate thereafter accepted the House's version of the bill without even requesting a Conference. Congress simply does not act in this way when it intends to effect fundamental changes in the structure of federal law.

1.   The Court noted the ABA Civil RICO Task Force report which categorizes as of 1984 the reported civil RICO cases by year of disposition. Surprisingly, only 3% of all civil RICO cases were decided in the first 10 years of the statute.

2.   The Supreme Court rejected the argument that a civil RICO case could only be brought following a criminal conviction of the underlying "predicate acts." The Court observed that such a "rule would severely handicap potential plaintiffs." The Court stated that civil RICO's "private attorney general provisions . . . are in part designed to fill prosecutorial gaps." The Court did not want to defeat this purpose.

3.   The Court also rejected the contention that application of civil RICO to legitimate businesses would "stigmatize defendants with the appellation 'racketeer'." The Court stated that "[a]s for stigma, a civil RICO proceeding leaves no greater stain than do a number of other civil proceedings."

4.   The American Institute of Certified Public Accountants filed an *amicus curiae* brief urging the Supreme Court to restrict the application of Civil RICO to situations where the predicate acts were the subject of a criminal conviction. The AICPA argued that "[a]lmost all private RICO actions have been brought against legitimate business, the intended beneficiary of RICO."

5.   The Supreme Court invited Congress to take corrective measures to reduce the scope of civil RICO. The Court stated:

> The "extraordinary" uses to which civil RICO has been put appear to be primarily the result of the breadth of the predicate offenses, in particular the inclusion of wire, mail, and securities fraud, and the failure of Congress and the courts to develop a meaningful concept of "pattern."

The Supreme Court put the onus on Congress to take another look at civil RICO. Absent congressional action, civil RICO will become *the* litigation tool of the 1980s and 1990s.

TABLE OF CASES

INDEX

449